Praise for Adam Bellow's

IN PRAISE OF NEPOTISM

"A remarkable feat of philosophy and history." —*Chicago Sun-Times*

"Nepotism, like sex, is a powerful human motive that many people are too squeamish to examine. Adam Bellow has made an important contribution to our understanding of the human condition with this sparkling and eye-opening natural history of an underappreciated but eternally fascinating topic."

—Steven Pinker, author of *The Blank Slate* and *How the Mind Works*

"This is no brittle screed . . . but an impressively full-blooded and wide-ranging work of scholarship. . . . [Bellow's] analysis of the complexity and flexibility of nepotism's forms is utterly enthralling and stimulating."

—*Publishers Weekly*

"Will be widely admired, regardless of the author's paternity."

—*Esquire*

"A remarkable accomplishment, the kind of specialized history that makes you see the larger issues and events rather, and sometimes surprisingly, differently. The book is fluid, readable, and fun."

—*The Washington Times*

"Nepotism is widely condemned yet even more highly practiced. Adam Bellow shows why this is so, and he makes a fascinating and well-researched argument that this is not necessarily a bad thing."

—Walter Isaacson, author of *Benjamin Franklin: An American Life* and *Kissinger: A Biography*

"Exemplifies the joy and value of amateur scholarship. . . . Warmly recommended."
—*Library Journal*

"Adam Bellow's provocatively titled book is the first serious look at a subject riddled with hypocrisy."
—*The Globe and Mail* (Toronto)

"Adam Bellow is like the best teacher you ever had. You are awed by his range and erudition, and you are carried along by the page-turning drama he makes of ideas and history. To see nepotism as a natural human impulse, a force in the advancement of civilization, and an enemy and friend of democracy and free markets was all a revelation. And Bellow's description of a benevolent and inclusive nepotism is a strikingly original idea that will make this book a landmark."
—Shelby Steele, author of *The Content of Our Character* and *A Dream Deferred*

ADAM BELLOW

IN PRAISE OF NEPOTISM

Adam Bellow is the former editorial director of the Free Press and is currently an editor-at-large for Doubleday. His articles and reviews have appeared in *Talk*, *National Review*, and *The Atlantic Monthly*, where a section of this book appeared.

ANCHOR BOOKS

A DIVISION OF RANDOM HOUSE, INC.

NEW YORK

IN PRAISE OF NEPOTISM

A HISTORY OF FAMILY ENTERPRISE FROM KING DAVID TO GEORGE W. BUSH

ADAM BELLOW

FIRST ANCHOR BOOKS EDITION, JULY 2004

Published in the United States by Anchor Books, a division of Random House, Inc., New York, and simultaneously in Canada by Random House of Canada Limited, Toronto. Originally published in hardcover in the United States by Doubleday, a division of Random House, Inc., New York, in 2003.

Anchor Books and colophon are registered trademarks of Random House, Inc.

The Library of Congress has cataloged the Doubleday edition as follows:
Bellow, Adam, 1957–
In praise of nepotism : a natural history / Adam Bellow.—1st ed.
p. cm.
1. Family. 2. Nepotism. 3. Patriarchy. I. Title.
HQ503.B415 2003
306.85—dc21
2003043487

Anchor ISBN: 0-385-49389-4

Author photograph © Sigrid Estrada
Book design by Gretchen Achilles

www.anchorbooks.com

Printed in the United States of America
10 9 8 7 6 5 4 3 2 1

FOR ALL MY FATHERS

CONTENTS

INTRODUCTION: *The New Nepotism—and the Old* 1

PART I: NEPOTISM IN HISTORY

1. **WE'RE ALL GOODFELLAS NOW:** *An Introduction to the Nepotistic System* 29
2. **FROM BIOLOGY TO CULTURE:** *A Natural History of Nepotism* 50
3. **CLAN, CASTE, AND TRIBE:** *Nepotism in Non-Western Societies* 79
4. **CLASSICAL NEPOTISM:** *The Hebrews, Greeks, and Romans* 113
5. **THE SON MADE PERFECT:** *Nepotism in the Christian West* 160
6. **THE GOLDEN AGE OF NEPOTISM:** *Borgia, Bonaparte, and Rothschild* 188

PART II: NEPOTISM IN AMERICA

7. **COLONIAL NEPOTISM:** *From Settlement to Revolution* 241
8. **THE CITY OF BROTHERLY LOVE:** *The Nepotism of the Founders* 277
9. **THE NINETEENTH CENTURY:** *Nepotism in the North, West, and South* 315
10. **THE ROOSEVELTS:** *The Middle Class Revolt Against Nepotism* 369
11. **HEIRS APPARENT:** *JFK and the New Meritocratic Nepotism* 418
12. **THE ART OF NEPOTISM** 463

POSTSCRIPT: *American Nepotism Today* 485

ACKNOWLEDGMENTS 509

NOTES 512

INDEX 549

INTRODUCTION

THE NEW NEPOTISM— AND THE OLD

For almost two years leading up to the November 2000 elections, expectations focused on Vice President Albert Gore Jr. and Texas governor George W. Bush. Both were the sons of important political families. Gore's father had been a powerful and respected Democratic senator from Tennessee. Bush was a third-generation Republican: his grandfather had been a senator, his father had been president, and his brother was the governor of Florida. Their rivalry sparked an immediate interest in the "return" of political dynasties.

Gore, an able and hardworking politician, was described as a child of privilege whose public career had begun literally at birth, when Gore Sr. persuaded his local paper to carry the news on its front page. Gore grew up in a Washington hotel, attended the exclusive St. Alban's School, and once sat on the lap of Vice President Richard M. Nixon as he presided over the Senate. After twenty-four years in public life he had compiled an impressive record of government service. Bush too was a talented politician, a two-term governor who had smoothly assumed control of his father's political network. His self-effacing modesty and charm balanced his obvious lack of preparation and contrasted favorably with Gore's formal and wooden demeanor. Yet Bush suffered from the silver-spoon dilemma. Following closely in his father's footsteps without equaling his accomplishments, Bush seemed derivative, uncertain: a bad copy of his father. To many he seemed aptly described by the comment once aimed at Bush Sr. by then–Texas agricultural commissioner Jim Hightower: "He is a man who was born on third base and thinks he hit a triple."

Much of the election year commentary focused on the psychological drama of growing up in a dynastic family. *New York Times* columnist Maureen Dowd called it a "Freudian face-off" between two men named after famous fathers and molded by strong mothers. Neither had evolved a compelling political vision "beyond furthering the interests of the party machine and pleasing their fathers," the *Economist* declared. Both were also described as reluctant heirs who had briefly rebelled against their families' expectations but were finally no match for them. Thus, Gore had opposed the war in Vietnam, but enlisted as a military journalist so as not to harm his father's reelection (the old man was defeated anyway). Later he did a stint in divinity school and toyed with a career as a reporter; but in 1976, with the air of a man embracing the inevitable, he ran for his father's old congressional seat, and went on to become a senator, vice president, and two-time presidential candidate. According to Dowd, he was the model of the Good Son that our society professes to admire.

In contrast to Gore's studied impression of a dutiful heir laying sacrifices on the ancestral hearth, Bush played the role of the Prodigal. An indifferent student, problem drinker, womanizer, possible drug user, a drunken Bush reportedly once challenged his father to go *mano a mano* in the driveway. Bush seemed to be having difficulty shouldering the burdens of the firstborn son in a dynastic family. But he had straightened himself out, come back to Jesus, and returned to claim the presidential mantle from his younger brother Jeb. Moreover, just as Gore was driven partly by the need to redeem his father's frustrated ambitions, Bush too was thought to be performing an act of filial piety, avenging his father's defeat by Bill Clinton and Al Gore in 1992.[1]

Many were offended by the idea that the presidency could be claimed as a birthright, as though it were family property. But others saw in Bush the authenticity Gore lacked, suggesting that the rebellious youth who eventually accepts mature responsibilities is better liked and trusted than the dutiful son who suppresses his true inclinations to please a demanding father. Perhaps that is why, in the end, Bush's silver-spoon upbringing and lax preparation seemed to bother Americans less than Gore's oppressively earnest sobriety.

In effect, then, the 2000 election was a referendum not on the validity of dynastic succession in a democracy but on which kind of successor we prefer. The Prodigal Son had defeated the Dutiful Son. The glad-handing frat boy was marginally preferred to the humorless, brownnosing wonk.

It had become a standing joke during the campaign that Bush mixed up foreign countries and could not remember their leaders' names. No pretense was made that we were electing a genius. Instead, Bush told reporters that he would have a staff of seasoned foreign policy advisers—all associated with his father's administration—not to mention the ex-president himself. In short, Americans were conscious that in casting a vote for George W. Bush they were electing not just a man but a family. Nor did it escape anyone's notice that the outcome was decided by a Supreme Court dominated by Reagan-Bush appointees.

The raw fact of such dynastic advantages was a slap in the face for many Americans. "I emigrated for this?" protested columnist Andrew Sullivan, a naturalized citizen, a few weeks before the election. "The only other countries that have recently passed power from father to son," he observed, "are North Korea, Jordan and Syria." Journalist Lars-Erik Nelson agreed: "Bush's spectacular career rebuts the notion that America has become a meritocracy, in which we are all born equal and then judged upon our intelligence, talent, creativity, or aggressiveness." Meanwhile Hendrik Hertzberg worried in *The New Yorker* about the return of the "hereditary principle."[2]

Hertzberg's fears were apparently justified. No sooner had Bush taken office (after an invocation by the son of Billy Graham) than he began handing out appointments to members of other Republican families. Michael Powell, son of Secretary of State Colin Powell, became chairman of the Federal Communications Commission. Elaine Chao, wife of Sen. Mitch McConnell, became secretary of labor. Chao's chief labor attorney, Eugene Scalia, was the son of Supreme Court Justice Antonin Scalia. Elizabeth Cheney, the vice president's daughter, became a deputy assistant secretary of state; her husband became chief counsel for the Office of Management and Budget. And in a crowning act of nepotistic chutzpah, Bush acceded to Sen. Strom Thurmond's request that he appoint twenty-eight-year-old Strom Thurmond Jr. U.S. attorney for South Carolina. Nor was that all by any means.[3]

According to some observers, Bush had set a standard for official nepotism exceeding that of any other president. Washington UPI correspondent Helen Thomas declared that the Bush administration had become "a family affair, reeking of nepotism." (Nepotism is often said to reek, as though it were a pile of dirty laundry.) "You'd think an administration headed by the son of a former president might be a teensy bit leery of appearing to foster a culture of nepotism," wrote Andrew Sullivan, returning to his antidynastic theme. "I am not saying that Michael Powell is unqualified for his job," he went on. The real question was whether he had gotten his job over the heads of other qualified applicants on the strength of his family ties. Evidently, the answer was yes. Producing a long list of other people who had gotten jobs in Washington through family connections, Sullivan concluded: "All this nepotism is a worrisome sign that America's political class is becoming increasingly insular."[4]

These critics have a point: the American political class is increasingly filled with the offspring of political families. Moreover, observers of both left and right agree that the trend contradicts cherished American principles. But this is a false opposition. Family traditions are very much a part of our national fabric, much more so than most people realize. Their relative eclipse since World War II has been the exception, not the rule, in American history, and their return is an encouraging sign, not a cause for alarm. To the contrary, it is precisely the kind of nepotism of which this country needs, not less, but more.

The 2002 midterm elections were a revealing snapshot of the successor phenomenon in politics. All over the country, the sons and daughters, brothers and sisters, wives and widows of former officials were strongly in evidence. Most prominent was Florida governor Jeb Bush, reelected with a handy lead. In Massachusetts, Mitt Romney (son of former Michigan governor George Romney) also became governor. In New Hampshire, John E. Sununu (son of a former governor and presidential chief of staff) beat sitting governor Jeanne Shaheen for a U.S. Senate seat. In Arkansas, Sen. Tim Hutchinson (whose brother Asa is a former congressman and now runs the Drug Enforcement Administration) lost his seat to state attorney general Mark Pryor, son of former Arkansas governor and senator David Pryor. Mississippi's Chip Pickering won reelection to Congress and avenged the humiliation of his father, former state party chairman Charles W. Pickering, whose nomination to the federal bench had been rejected by Senate Democrats. (Pickering's campaign manager was Henry Barbour, the nephew of former RNC chairman Haley Barbour.) Lucille Roybal-Allard, who occupies the California congressional seat once held by her father, was also reelected. And in North Carolina, political wife Elizabeth Dole won the Senate race against Erskine Bowles, a former Clinton chief of staff (also the son of a local politician). Meanwhile, in the wake of the Democrats' defeat, the position of House minority leader was claimed by Rep. Nancy Pelosi, the daughter of a five-term Maryland congressman and Baltimore mayor, who had risen swiftly in California politics in part through the skillful use of dynastic connections.[5] Pelosi was opposed by Harold Ford Jr., a young black congressman who had succeeded to his father's seat in Tennessee.

Still, not all was rosy for political successors. Despite the efforts of political fairy godfathers Bill Clinton and Ted Kennedy, candidate Andrew Cuomo dropped out of the New York governor's race two days before the primary. Bill Simon Jr. (son of former Treasury secretary William Simon) lost his race for California governor. In Georgia, Republican Max Burns, a college professor, defeated Charles Walker Jr., the son of the president of the state Senate, in the race for Congress. In Louisiana, incumbent senator Mary Landrieu, whose father was mayor of New Orleans, won only 46 percent of the vote, which forced her into a runoff (she later won by a narrow margin). Jean Carnahan, elected to the Senate after her husband's death, in 2000, was turned out of office. Most dispiriting for Democrats, Kathleen Kennedy Townsend lost her bid for election as Maryland's governor. Townsend's race was widely considered a test of the Kennedy name, and coming on the heels of her cousin Mark Kennedy Shriver's primary defeat in a Maryland congressional race, the loss suggested the end of the "Kennedy magic."

On September 11, 2001, Islamic terrorists launched devastating attacks on American soil and George W. Bush embraced the war on terror as the center of his presidency. Americans discerned a new sense of purpose and mission in Bush, and they were also intrigued by the dynastic subtext underlying this turn of events. The fact that Bush's war was in some degree a personal vendetta against Saddam Hussein, the man who had tried to assassinate his father, didn't bother the electorate too much. If anything, the confluence of public and personal motives, seamlessly blending family honor and national interest, seemed to promise that the son would finish the job that his father had started.

"As a democracy the United States ought presumably to be able to dispense with dynastic families." So wrote historian Arthur M. Schlesinger Jr. in 1947. He must be sorry that he ever said this, judging by the number of times the statement has been thrown back in his face. For despite a long-standing conviction that political dynasties are somehow un-American, quite the opposite is true. America has always had its share of political families, and for much of our history most presidents, senators, representatives, governors, and even Supreme Court justices came from the tiny percentage of the population that constituted our country's political class.[6] But while the American elite displays consistent castelike tendencies, it has also remained for the most part open and meritocratic.

The American elite broadened significantly after the Civil War and became broader still after the Depression and World War II, when the dominance of the old WASP Establishment began to decline. The postwar economic boom resulted in a great expansion of the middle class, accompanied by a rights revolution, a burst of unfettered individualism, and a spreading wave of family dissolution. Many new groups entered politics, and for the first time the true diversity of American society was reflected in public affairs. Yet now the pendulum seems to be swinging back in the other direction: dynastic tendencies long associated with the hated WASP elite have reappeared. According to the *Economist,* the Bush-Gore campaign was merely the tip of a "dynastic iceberg" in American politics. New Jersey's Rodney Frelinghuysen, for example, represented the sixth generation of his family to serve in Congress since 1778, and Louisiana congressman Robert Livingston was the descendant of a seventeenth-century political dynasty that used to own most of the Catskills. But the phenomenon was hardly limited to members of the WASP elite: most political successors were from middle class families, many with immigrant or minority roots.[7]

This striking proliferation of family ties was broadly described in the press as a "new nepotism" or (alternatively) a "new dynasticism" in American politics. Some speculated that it was part of a general shift toward specialization and niche occupations in the U.S. economy. There was also the undeniable advantage of bearing an established brand name in a media-driven electoral system, along with easy access to parents' fund-raising and political networks. Whatever the cause, the dramatic surge in family succession signaled a quiet revolution in American politics, as a new generation came forward to claim its inheritance.

Some viewed the new political successors as opportunists trading on their famous names and family connections. But many others embraced the notion that continuing a family tradition has a dignity and value of its own. The same note of ambivalence was sounded in the case of political wives like Lynne Cheney and Elizabeth Dole, who launched independent careers on the back of their husbands' success. Hillary Clinton became the prime example of this two-career-family nepotism, and in November 2000 the Illinois native and longtime Arkansas resident won election to the U.S. Senate from New York, despite charges of carpetbagging and trading on her husband's name.

Far from being an exception, then, the nepotistic Bush administration was firmly in the center of a trend. Nor was the New Nepotism an isolated phenomenon, confined to politics alone. Take business, for example. In May 1998 the *New York Times* profiled a number of business heirs in an article called "Born to Be Boss," including Jane Lauder of Estée Lauder, champagne heiress Caroline Krug, and Maurizio Borletti of Christofle silver. This was followed by a flattering profile of the Ciprianis, a three-generation restaurant empire. An elaborate Father's Day feature, "Bringing a Son Up Right (Right Up to the Top)," celebrated a number of father-son firms like that of Earl Graves and his three sons, publishers of *Black Enterprise* magazine; the Sterns, owners of Hartz Mountain Industries; the Wilpons, owners of the New York Mets; and the New York real estate empires of Rudin and Tisch. In July, Elinor Ruth Tatum formally took over the *Amsterdam News*, New York's leading black newspaper. Founding editor Wilbert Tatum had made his daughter editor in chief even before she graduated from NYU's journalism program. But she had worked at the paper for years, starting as a gofer. "I was the boss's daughter," Tatum said, acknowledging staff perceptions of nepotism, "but I proved myself." The same month the *New York Times Magazine* lavishly profiled Lachlan Murdoch, twenty-six-year-old heir apparent to the $13 billion media conglomerate run by his father—himself a former "boy publisher," who built his father's small-circulation Australian newspaper into a globe-spanning corporate enterprise. Also in 1998, Harold McGraw III became the first family member to head the McGraw-Hill publishing company since 1983, while Ford Motor Company announced that William Ford would take over as CEO—the first family member to run the business in a generation. These and other family appointments (like that of William Wrigley Jr., who took over the family chewing gum business in 1999) were called signs of a "new nepotism" in American business. Rather than simply continuing their fathers' work, moreover, these scions were expected to take their firms in bold, exciting new directions.

The persistence of nepotism in business is perhaps to be expected when we consider that something like 90 percent of all American businesses are still family owned or controlled, including about 40 percent of the Fortune 500. More surprising is the rise of family succession in areas traditionally ruled by merit and achievement, including the arts, entertainment, and sports.

Unlike painters and musicians, many of whom (like J. S. Bach or the American Peale family) spawned large creative clans, most writers have been solitary figures. Playwriting was considered a family craft in ancient Athens, but in the intervening centuries, one is hard-pressed to name more than a handful of examples. By contrast, we are now in the midst of a veritable explosion of literary successors. What's more, this explosion has occurred mainly within the past two decades.*

The music industry is a further case in point. In 1998 Sean Lennon and Jakob Dylan both released CDs (Sean's half brother, Julian, had

*Rather than encumber the text or footnotes with a long list of examples, I would ask readers to consult the Postscript for a comprehensive (though nonexhaustive) survey of successors in American politics, business, and culture.

launched his own musical career in the 1980s). Both the sons of Ringo Starr are drummers, and Zak Starkey now plays for the Who. Enrique Iglesias, son of Julio Iglesias, had put out four CDs by the time he was twenty-four and had sold over 14 million records; his older brother, Julio Jr., is also pursuing a career as a singer.

Hollywood may be the most visible arena of the New Nepotism, if only because we so often can see the results on a forty-foot screen. The men who built the movie industry were nepotists on a grand scale, and some of Hollywood's greatest figures (director William Wyler, producer Irving Thalberg, screenwriter Budd Schulberg) owed their breaks to family ties. Today there is a new generation of actors, writers, producers, and directors whose parents or siblings have helped them get into the business.

Television is another industry where *who* you know apparently means more than *what* you know. A 1993 industry survey found that barriers to entry remained high and that academic degree programs conferred no real advantage. One respondent complained that the hiring of "girlfriends and girlfriends-to-be" by producers had turned the industry into "a nepotistic prostitution ring." Asked about the best way to get ahead in television, one person answered: "Marriage to a film-editor's daughter."[8]

We think of sport as a Darwinian arena where only the fittest survive. Yet family ties increasingly permeate sports and sports-related professions. Kobe Bryant, the son of former NBA player Joe "Jellybean" Bryant, jumped directly from high school to the Los Angeles Lakers in 1996. NFL quarterback Peyton Manning is the son of retired NFL star Archie Manning. Left fielder Barry Bonds is the son of Bobby Bonds and the godson of Willie Mays. Other baseball scions include Pete Rose Jr., Robbie Alomar, Dale Berra, and Moises Alou.

Stock car racing is also becoming a family business. The same goes for hockey, college basketball coaching, sports broadcasting, and the rarified domain of golf course architecture.

No social scientist has studied this phenomenon. But you don't need a degree in sociology to realize that the boom in generational succession is something new in scope and character. The question is, what does it mean? Why is it happening now in the most democratic and individualistic society on earth? Doesn't it fly in the face of our commitment to equal opportunity and merit? Are we creating a new caste hierarchy based on occupation, similar to that of the medieval guilds? More to the point, how will we square our embrace of the New Nepotism with our traditional aversion to the Old?

Things were different in what we think of as the bad old days, before the massive class mixing and upward mobility brought about by World War II, not to mention the civil rights and feminist movements. Back in the 1920s and 1930s, nepotism was everywhere, and far from being controversial, it seemed as natural as breathing—for a certain class of people. A young man of good family who went to Groton or Choate was admitted as a matter of course to Harvard, Princeton, or Yale, after which he joined his father's Wall Street firm and one or more exclusive clubs, where he mingled with other men of his set. If he didn't go to work for his father, he worked for someone else's; and if he married the boss's daughter, he could expect to be put on the fast track to the executive suite.

No one can pick up the phone these days and get their kid a high-paying job, a record deal, or a spot on the national ticket. But more and more, such intervention isn't necessary. Growing up around a business or vocation—learning how it works, getting to know the people in it—creates a powerful advantage that is tantamount to nepotism, and when exercised unworthily it carries a similar stigma.

If all of this can be called nepotism—and it can—it is clearly a new kind of nepotism, a modern or (if you will) postmodern nepotism that adapts an ancient impulse to contemporary cultural conditions. This new, postmodern nepotism works for the most part subtly and invisibly, creating opportunities for those who have connections in a given field, and increasingly excluding those who don't. All that is required to profit from this kind of opportunity is a willingness to take advantage of it. Indeed, the New Nepotism differs from the Old in being not so much a matter of parents hiring or getting jobs for children as of children choosing to follow in their parents' footsteps. To that extent, the successor phenomenon looks less like nepotism on the part of mothers and fathers than it does like opportunism on the part of sons and daughters.

Dictionaries trace the word "nepotism" to the Latin *nepos,* meaning nephew or grandson. But while technically accurate, this etymology is misleadingly narrow. The word actually derives from the Italian *nepote,* which can refer to almost any family member, of any generation, male or female. The term *nepotismo* was coined sometime in the fourteenth or fifteenth century to describe the corrupt practice of appointing papal relatives to office—usually illegitimate sons described as "nephews"—and for a long time this ecclesiastical origin continued to be reflected in dictionaries. (Even today, some dictionaries list the subordinate definition of "nephew" as "illegitimate son of an ecclesiastic.") The modern definition of nepotism is favoritism based on kinship, but over time the word's dictionary meaning and its conventional applications have diverged. Most people today define the term very narrowly to mean not just hiring a relative, but hiring one who is grossly incompetent—though technically one would have to agree that hiring a relative is nepotism whether he or she is qualified or not. But nepotism has also proven to be a highly elastic concept, capable of being applied to a much broader range of relationships than simple consanguinity. Many practices that are in fact nepotistic don't look like nepotism, while practices that seem normal and acceptable to some look like nepotism to others.

To understand the nature of a thing it is best to begin with its critics. Thus, from the workingman's perspective nepotism means hiring or promoting the boss's son-in-law, nephew, or girlfriend over the heads of more qualified candidates. This violates our basic sense of fairness and elicits strong reactions of revulsion and distaste, both for those who practice nepotism and (even more perhaps) for those who profit from it. Yet nepotism is often the rule in family businesses, and it is usually accepted as "the way things are" by everyone involved. Such nepotism appears to be a problem only when the beneficiary is manifestly unqualified.

Economists view nepotism as an obstacle to healthy change in business firms, promoting waste and inefficiency. Yet some acknowledge that nepotism may be a rational practice, since engaging in extensive talent searches is a cost that might well be avoided. Still others argue that hiring family members is the best way to promote important values of trust and solidarity within a business enterprise. And despite official nepotism policies, most large companies prefer to hire the relatives of existing employees, since the proven conduct of a relative is the best guide to the behavior of a prospective worker.

Many Americans see nepotism as a means for the rich to warehouse their unemployable sons while keeping the lower classes in their place. In this view, nepotism appears as part of a strategy of class and elite domination. There is much to be said for this argument. Historically, most elites that have risen through merit of one kind or another normally seek to keep their gains within the family and contrive various ways to pass on property and status to their children. Yet systematic nepotism has been practiced just as widely by the poor and working classes: there are multigenerational families of cops and firemen, and so-called father-son unions still dominate the building trades. In fact, the Old Nepotism has been practiced more or less continuously by both the upper and lower classes as a rational group strategy. It was the middle class that pushed the merit principle, and this is one of the things that makes the New Nepotism such a surprising development: the fact that it is essentially a middle class phenomenon.

In politics, nepotism has appeared in various forms: that of hereditary family rule under a monarchy, the domination of a landed or commercial oligarchy, and (in democratic societies) as a species of corruption linked to patronage. The American Revolutionaries wanted nothing to do with hereditary rule from abroad and feared the dynastic ambition of rich and powerful men in their own country. Early American politics was obsessed with such fears, and the result has been a long struggle to free our political system from its lingering entanglement with the family. The tension between birth and merit was most famously articulated in the debate between John Adams and Thomas Jefferson about the prospects for a "natural aristocracy." Both wished to see the nation governed by an elite of talent rather than birth, but disagreed on whether this could be achieved. Though we seem to have gone pretty far toward realizing Jefferson's dream of a true meritocracy, we have not been able to do away with nepotism and patronage completely. (While some might object that patronage and nepotism are two different things, there is really a good deal of overlap. Nepotism itself is a species of patronage directed at family members. Wherever patronage exists, moreover, nepotism rarely lags behind.)

From the feminist perspective, the word "nepotism" evokes a long list of slights against women stemming from patriarchal dominance. In this view, nepotism is associated with the historical preference for sons over daughters, ranging in form from primogeniture, arranged marriages, and the systematic exclusion of women from the workplace to footbinding and female infanticide. Even after the feminist revolution, nepotism continues to play a role in rearguard efforts to preserve the male monopoly on power. This is evident from the intensity of the feminist campaign against exclusive men's clubs, old boys' networks, and the glass ceiling that blocks the advancement of female executives.

To African Americans, nepotism is tantamount to racism, since favoritism toward whites—whether related to oneself or not—is morally no different from discrimination against blacks. This is why proponents of affirmative action often say that whites hypocritically deny to blacks what they practice themselves as a matter of course. "Nepotism is perhaps the oldest and most subtle form of white affirmative action," explain journalists Deborah Cooksey and Marilyn Easter. Other forms of positive discrimination for whites, according to these authors, include corporate tax breaks, S&L bailouts, redlining, prep school connections, membership in exclusive clubs, and grandfather clauses.[9]

Economist Matthew S. Goldberg suggests that it is not so much a prejudice against blacks as a positive preference for whites that explains most discriminatory behavior: "*Racial nepotism* rather than racial animus is the major motivation for much of the discrimination blacks experience." Derrick Bell elaborated on this notion in *Faces at the Bottom of the Well*: "whites tend to treat one another like family, at least when there's a choice between them and us. So that terms like 'merit' and 'best qualified' are infinitely manipulable if and when whites must explain why they reject blacks to hire 'relatives'—even when the only relationship is that of race." Bell is not really stretching or misusing the term "nepotism" here. His usage is consistent with that of sociologists like Pierre van den Berghe, who has elaborated a scholarly paradigm that defines an ethnic group as "a very large extended family that inbreeds to some extent."[10]

Proponents of economic globalism decry the role of nepotism in fostering bureaucratic corruption and crony capitalism in Africa, Asia, and Latin America; and everyone abhors the resurgent ethnic nationalism that has led to genocidal violence in India, Rwanda, and the Balkans—a violent form of particularism that ultimately springs from the nepotistic preference for one's own cultural, linguistic, or religious group. Even the Dalai Lama comes down on nepotism in *Ethics for the New Millennium,* where he includes the stubborn preference for our own families, communities, and ethnic groups in a list of man-made evils that we must strive to overcome in the twenty-first century. From this angle, nepotism is not just a legal, moral, or political infraction, but a spiritual one as well.

These perspectives reflect the prevailing negative view of the Old Nepotism: it burdened the economy, corrupted government, reduced women and children to chattels, disadvantaged blacks and other minorities, throttled meritocracy, promoted amoral selfishness, and reinforced the American class system. The New Nepotism is clearly different, and it elicits different reactions. For one thing, the American social environment has become more competitive; the playing field is much more level than it was one hundred, fifty, or even twenty years ago, and it is no longer possible for nepotism to be practiced indiscriminately, or in a way that masks incompetence. Time and again we hear that while a famous name may get you in the door, you have to prove your worth or face the consequences.

It is worth dwelling for a moment on the differences between the Old Nepotism and the New. The Old Nepotism involved parents hiring their children outright or pulling strings on their behalf. It was also highly coercive—obedient daughters married according to their parents' wishes, and dutiful sons allowed their fathers to chart their careers and often to select suitable brides for them as well. The New Nepotism operates not (so to speak) from the top down but from the bottom up: it is voluntary, not coercive; it springs from the motives of children, not the interest of parents; it tends to seem natural rather than planned. It reverses the flow of energies in the nepotistic equation, so that instead of parents holding themselves out as examples for their children, today's children validate their parents by following in their footsteps. While not nepotism in the classic sense, it is rightly called nepotism because it involves exploiting the family name, connections, or wealth. The method may be different, but the result is much the same.

Mainly, however, the new nepotism differs in combining the privileges of birth with the iron rule of merit in a way that is much less offensive to democratic sensibilities. This is what explains the astonishing latitude—in effect, the room to fail—that we seem perfectly willing to grant the new successor generation. Americans increasingly feel that there is nothing wrong with hiring a relative, so long as he or she is qualified. We even say that when we hire a relative or pull strings to help relatives who *are* qualified, that is not really nepotism. But this leaves us in the logically inconsistent position of saying that hiring a relative is or is not nepotism depending on the relative's performance.

The reason we have tied ourselves in knots around this question is really quite simple: there is a missing distinction in our lexicon between *good* nepotism and *bad*. Of course, in order to recognize such a distinction we would have to completely revise our view of nepotism as bad by definition. But this should not be difficult, because our negative view of nepotism is not a natural or God-given law, but the result of several centuries of social and cultural history.

Europeans in general have a much more relaxed and balanced view of nepotism. Despite the occasional scandal—such as the forced resignation in 1999 of twenty EU commissioners charged with blatant nepotism—they tend to accept it as part of the fabric of things. In contrast, the extreme antipathy to nepotism is an American phenomenon. Moreover, it is an attitude that America has been busily exporting to the rest of the world (with mixed success) for the last fifty years, along with the whole complex of values and practices associated with modern technocratic liberalism.

The American rejection of nepotism represents the victory of the egalitarian ideals enshrined in the Declaration of Independence, the Constitution, and the Bill of Rights. But this victory may be more apparent than real, since in practice our condemnation of nepotism is highly selective. In effect, we censure nepotism on the one hand and practice it as much as we can on the other. In order to do this, we have to engage in a massive conspiracy not to notice how much nepotism actually goes on in our society. Nepotism happens in plain sight, but it is covered by a thick veil of hypocrisy.

The Old Nepotism was defined as illegitimate and undesirable, a form of social cheating. But it was based on positive impulses—the desire to provide for your children and to pass on a meaningful legacy. There is a natural impulse on the part of parents to pass something on to their children, just as children wish to accept whatever their parents have to give. The sum of these transactions is the way we pass on our cultural traditions and values. For when we talk about nepotism, what we are really talking about is the transmission of property, knowledge, and authority from one generation to the next. Without these links, the human project would be doomed. This is the knowledge that Americans have lost—the knowledge that nepotism, broadly defined, is the bedrock of social existence.

Before we can understand the New Nepotism, we must understand the Old. And since nepotism is nothing if not an aspect of the family, we must begin by recovering the lost understanding of kinship. We view nepotism as the act of an individual who selfishly seeks to confer benefits on a relative. But nepotism in its primary setting is indistinguishable from the obligations of mutual aid and assistance incumbent on kin. It is not really selfish, then, but an expression of altruism, although it is an altruism limited to family members. Because we live in what might be called a "postkinship" society, we have forgotten what we once knew about the intimate connections between kinship and human community.

Nepotism is not a cultural construct but, originally at least, a hardwired biological given—a drive as basic as sex and aggression. Nor is nepotism a human invention, but the essential building block of all societies, human or animal. We will therefore begin by exploring the role of biological nepotism in social cooperation, describe its role in the formation of human families, and consider what distinguishes human from animal nepotism, namely the capacity for extending kinlike altruism and trust to widening circles of people. The means for this extension is the cultural system of kinship. For most of human history, the bonds of kinship were the essential building blocks of all societies, from primitive hunter-gatherer bands to tribal states to multiethnic empires. This is the phase of history that we will call Ancient Nepotism. Most developing societies still rely upon this ancient kin-based system, and many of the problems associated with modernization arise from the clash between tribal nepotism and the bureaucratic structures that have been imposed on it in the postcolonial period.

What makes Western development different has been our ability to balance the demands of kinship with the entrepreneurial spirit, which is rational and individualistic. This entrepreneurial nepotism has its ultimate roots in the civilizations of ancient Israel, Greece, and Rome—the phase of development that we will call Classical Nepotism. In Europe, this complex of practices and attitudes was transformed by Christianity and the rise of capitalism into a dynamic force, which we will call Western Nepotism, that liberated the energies of entrepreneurial families.

All societies are organized at the most basic level around the processes of marriage, reproduction, and inheritance. Every society therefore evolves a nepotistic formula geared to its needs and conditions. America has developed a formula that represents a historical accommodation between our need for biological and social continuity and our liberal ideals. American nepotism is not the nepotism of the feudal aristocracy; still less that of the Greek or Roman oligarchies, the Indian caste, the Chinese clan, the African tribe, or the Australian or Amazonian band. Instead it is a highly flexible adaptation that has evolved to meet the needs of a mobile and pluralistic society.

This modern nepotistic formula arose as the result of a long historical process whose dominant trend has been the breakup of the large extended families typical of agrarian societies and the emergence of the nuclear family as the fundamental unit of industrial civilization. Concurrent with this trend has been the unique American project of creating a true meritocracy, our attempt to fulfill the egalitarian promise that has been at the heart of American politics for over two hundred years. This project has involved a long war between the hereditary principle and the principle of merit.

The American war against nepotism began in the seventeenth century with the abolition of English inheritance practices like entail and primogeniture, whereby the family estate was passed intact to the eldest son. The replacement of this practice with a more egalitarian pattern of partible inheritance swept the country after the American Revolution, largely thanks to Thomas Jefferson, who hoped to break up the great landed estates of the colonial period. The war on nepotism continued in the nineteenth century with laws against polygamy and the marriage of cousins—traditional arrangements associated with Ancient and Classical Nepotism—and the creation of a federal civil service based on merit and efficiency, not family connections. In the twentieth century, the war on nepotism entered its "progressive" phase with strictures on the use of political patronage to benefit kin, culminating with the historic New Deal and civil rights legislation that uprooted the last legal barriers to equal opportunity. Just as the merit system seemed to have triumphed, however, challenges were brought under the same civil rights provisions that targeted antinepotism rules as discriminatory, especially against women.

Today, some of our most divisive arguments revolve around the nepotistic formula: abortion, contraception, divorce, single parenthood, surrogacy, cloning, gay marriage, day care, interracial adoption, fostering, spouse and child abuse, elder care, and the politics of the estate tax all touch on fundamental processes of marriage, reproduction, and inheritance. In addition, issues like immigration, affirmative action, and multiculturalism pit ethnic identity groups against one another, suggesting that even in America the claims of ethnic nepotism have yet to be transcended. We speak the language of individual rights, but our politics is still largely driven by group identification and interests.

The New Nepotism has been treated lightheartedly by most observers, but it is a serious matter because it involves the role and status of elites in a democracy. Elites and upper classes have always been controversial for Americans, and since the Revolution we have viewed them with suspicion. Yet a century of sociology has concluded that elites are a practical necessity for any society. The real question is, What kind of elite will you have: an open, meritocratic elite continually refreshed from the lower strata of society, or a closed and exclusive elite that merely seeks to perpetuate its power and privilege?

The tendency of American life since World War II has been toward increasing individualism, mobility, and the dissipation of family bonds.

The "return" of nepotism therefore seems especially disturbing. The American elite has traditionally been open and meritocratic, and that is why critics like Hendrik Hertzberg and Andrew Sullivan are not wrong to point out the worrisome consequences of reviving the hereditary principle. Several writers have recently noted that after a long period of extreme mobility and social mixing, the United States is undergoing a new process of stratification. Call it what you like—the overclass, the cognitive elite, the meritocracy—the new elite increasingly lives in its own segregated communities, sends its children to the same exclusive schools, marries within its own class, and acts in other ways to pass on its accumulated wealth, position, and privileges. In other words, the meritocracy appears to be in the process of becoming an exclusive, inbred caste.[11]

Such, at any rate, might be the argument of those who deny the legitimacy of the hereditary principle. But this is not my view: rather, I would suggest that the return of the hereditary and dynastic principle in the heart of the American elite represents a valuable corrective to the extreme tendencies of meritocracy itself. As Christopher Lasch has argued, an elite that regards itself as fit to rule by virtue of its "merit" owes no gratitude or deference to anyone. It has no "ethical tie" to the mass of ordinary people and is therefore unresponsive to their needs. We spent two centuries trying to get nepotism out of government, but Lasch's argument suggests that meritocracy unleavened by nepotism lacks a necessary humanizing element.

The ideal situation would be a balance between these two principles, a balance we appear to have struck with our new and distinctively American form of meritocratic nepotism. The New Nepotism is therefore not the return of something tribal and archaic but the transformation of an ancient practice into a new and more acceptable form, one that can satisfy the permanent human impulses involved in nepotism without violating the American social compact. It is an authentic product of the American genius for balancing equality (with its tendency to deny natural differences) and liberty (with its tendency to produce unequal results).

But it is not enough simply to explain the New Nepotism. Since we are not going to get rid of it anytime soon, Americans must come to terms with it, and that means learning to practice it in accordance with the unwritten rules that have made it, on balance, a wholesome and positive force. For if history shows anything, it is that nepotism in itself is neither good nor bad: how it is practiced is what matters. Those who observe these hidden rules are rewarded and praised; those who do not are punished, often savagely. These simple rules will be explained in a concluding chapter, "The Art of Nepotism."

One of the most remarkable facts about nepotism is that no one has written a book on the subject. The first and only work explicitly devoted to nepotism is a seventeenth-century tract called *Il Nipotismo di Roma,* subsequently translated as *The History of the Popes' Nephews.* More than three hundred years old, it is available only on microfilm.

This omission comes as something of a shock. Surely, given the present advanced state of the human sciences, there is no practice or behavior that has not been exhaustively studied, and it is hard to avoid the conclusion that the failure to do so in this case is the result of an ideological blind spot.

My original idea was to write a short, polemical book on the model of William A. Henry's *In Defense of Elitism,* starting from the premise that if nepotism persists to the extent that it does, despite being held in opprobrium, then there must be a pretty good reason. This is not to endorse nepotism—still less other practices, like adultery or murder, that spring from appetitive drives—only to acknowledge its basis in a permanent and unchanging aspect of human reality. I had planned to make the case for nepotism as both natural and necessary, though obviously problematic in a society based on equality and merit. Pretty soon, however, I discovered that my subject was much richer and more complex than I had thought. In order to have anything intelligent to say about nepotism, I had to understand the nature of kinship, and in order to grasp the nature and uses of kinship, I had to know something about human evolution and social development. Since nepotistic patterns have varied widely over time and across human cultures, I had to look at the subject historically and culturally. In addition, the role of nepotism in the fortunes of various individuals and families had to be teased out from biographical accounts. There was no single source I could consult to gain this knowledge. Therefore I had to traverse a wide range of scholarly fields, including evolutionary biology, anthropology, religion, sociology, psychology, political science, history, law, economics, and other disciplines. In the end, I had to *write* the book I needed to *read* in order to write the shorter polemical work I had envisioned.

Having stumbled on this large, untreated subject, I have tried to do it justice, but it is like trying to illuminate a vast underground cavern with a penlight. I make no claim to original scholarship, and the authorities I cite bear no responsibility for my arguments. While I have consulted a wide body of academic work, I have proceeded not in a scholarly manner but in the spirit of inspired nineteenth-century amateurs like Sir Henry Maine and Lewis Henry Morgan. Sailing in uncharted waters, these writers speculated broadly on the relations between kinship and society, blissfully unfettered by disciplinary boundaries and guided only by an unquenchable enthusiasm for their topic. Like them, I have managed to sketch the broad outlines of a neglected subject that others may explore more systematically.

That being the case, I should acknowledge that the book need not be read sequentially or in its entirety. There will doubtless be some readers whose interest in the African tribe, the Confucian clan, or the Indian caste is limited. Not everyone may be equally fascinated by the struggles of the medieval state and church to reduce the power of the tribal kindreds, or by the nurturing role of maternal uncles in feudal society. These readers may feel free to skip ahead to the parts that do interest them.

Over the years that it took me to write it, people have reacted very differently to the idea of a book "in praise of nepotism." Some seemed to think that by seeking to explain and understand the persistence of nepotism and shed light on its constructive contributions, I must therefore be defending great wealth and inherited privilege. Others have shown impatience with my historical approach and have pressed me to say where I "come down." What's my bottom line on nepotism? Am I for it or against it? Thumbs up or thumbs down?

To such readers I would reply that this is a history, not a polemic. As such it is not a contrarian attempt to defend an unpopular practice but a serious effort to shed light on the functional aspects of nepotism. The present chapter (supplemented by the above-mentioned Postscript) has tried to show that we are in the midst of an enormous boom in generational succession, one that seems to contradict our public creed of opportunity and merit. This phenomenon has gone largely unnoticed or has been apprehended in a piecemeal fashion. The few who have commented on it have voiced a near-hysterical alarm that we are returning to a status-based society, complete with a corporate aristocracy and a political House of Lords. No one has been willing to defend this ominous development, and neither will I: readers who may be expecting a reactionary screed arguing that because liberals think nepotism is *bad,* it must therefore be *good,* should seek their entertainment elsewhere. Nor do I plan on making sweeping public policy pronouncements, although I will certainly try to illuminate some of the ways in which nepotism impinges on our current debates. But I have no wish to reduce this complex subject to a political slogan or an argument about "family values." This is a book about the way things are, not the way we might wish them to be. Still less is it a triumphalist narrative intended to prove that the American form of meritocratic nepotism is superior to others. I simply hope to show that American nepotism is a culturally specific adaptation that suits the needs of our open, meritocratic society. If other societies continue to practice a more traditional form of nepotism, this is because their public culture does not require them to do otherwise.

Nevertheless, the book does have an argument, one that I think can be stated in a way that few would reasonably quarrel with. Nepotism is a basic human instinct, like sex and aggression. When Sigmund Freud published his revolutionary theory of human motivation, many people thought he was somehow endorsing the "primitive" impulse to murder your father and sleep with your mother. But what he really meant to do was make us *conscious* of these impulses. For only when we are conscious of our motives do we have the power to act on them responsibly. The same applies to nepotism—another drive that is basic to human survival. Like these other instinctual drives, it is not really a question of whether nepotism is bad or good: nepotism simply *is.* The pertinent question is, How can we practice it so that it does not obstruct our efforts to create a good society? As we will see all too often in subsequent chapters, nepotism unchecked by laws and strong ethical prescriptions does tend to run to extremes. The solution is not to get rid of nepotism—something we neither can nor wish to do—but to apply it constructively. But that is a challenge we will take up at the end of the book.

One might also ask whether I am really the right person to write such a study. After all, I am not a social scientist or historian but an editor of general-interest nonfiction books. But I come by my interest in the subject honestly, since I too am an example of the New Nepotism and am thoroughly familiar with the peculiar strains of twenty-first-century heirship. As some readers may already know, I am the son of a famous writer (novelist Saul Bellow) who has made his career in the publishing business. Though my father had nothing to do with my getting a job, my employers were well aware of the connection, and they undoubtedly assumed not only that I had "the right stuff" to be an editor by virtue of my parentage, but that my name and social background would be useful in my publishing career. So while I can't be called a beneficiary of nepotism in the conventional sense, I did enjoy advantages unavailable to others at the entry level. Nor is it likely that I could have written and published this book without the added value that my name brings to the project.

Moreover, as an example of the social phenomenon that I am describing, my objectivity may reasonably be questioned. Am I seeking to justify the privileges that my name and social access have provided? Am I, by the same token, too reductive in my treatment of great men and their debt to their families—bringing the perspective of a supporting cast member to the task of debunking the cult of genius and the myth of the self-made man? I think it best if I admit these biases up front and try to mitigate their impact in what follows. Readers must judge the outcome for themselves.

Finally, a word is necessary about my use of the word "nepotism." I fully realize that I am using this word very broadly and in a way that makes it seem at times indistinguishable from the normal obligations of kinship. Anthropologists may frown at this elision, and with reason. I am very far from wanting to suggest that what we call nepotism is simply the operation of a normal and natural preference for kin. Nepotism is properly defined as "undue preference for a relative" where fair and open competition should prevail, and we must not lose sight of this important ethical distinction. Later on, when we talk about the "nepotistic" motives and actions of historical or literary figures in societies based on kinship, we do not mean to imply that their actions are illegitimate in the modern sense. Nor do we mean to reduce their motivations to an individual preference for kin as opposed to simply following the rules of a kin-based society.

For most of human history, the very idea of nepotism as we define it today would have been unintelligible, and in some parts of the world it still is. The distinction between kinship and nepotism is a cultural artifact, a product not of nature but of history. The story I am trying to tell is the history of nepotism as an idea, and that is a story that can only be told in light of the long conflict between kinship and the state. Nepotism as we know it is a product of that conflict, or to put it in the form of an equation: kinship plus the state equals nepotism. To that extent, this book is less a history of nepotism than of anti-nepotism, or the attempt to limit and confine our natural preference for people we define as family members to acceptable areas. The growth of the state and a civil society based on laws and contracts has led us to regard the exercise of these preferences as a form of corruption; but we can't seem to get rid of the impulse, and it creeps back in no matter what we do.

People tend to put nepotism in the category of something personal, a selfish breach of ethics that is mildly scandalous but not that shocking in the greater scheme of things. Though we sense that the troubling emergence of occupational castes in the heart of the American elite has something to do with nepotism, it is hard to put our finger on what that is; and this is where our narrow modern definition of nepotism begins to interfere with our perceptions of reality. I will argue that nepotism is both an individual and a collective phenomenon, or to put it another way, that the sum of thousands upon thousands of private decisions based on nepotism adds up to something larger. All these millions of decisions are part of an unconscious social process, repeated many times in history, whereby upwardly mobile groups form self-conscious elites and pass their wealth and status to their children by a variety of nepotistic strategies.

At the same time, nepotism is something we can hardly do without.

For one thing, nepotistic concern for the welfare of children is the engine of the capitalist system: take that away and you destroy the main incentives for innovation and the creation of wealth. For another, meritocracy unleavened by personal ties is inhumane, as ample evidence will show. Finally, on the individual level, nepotism is a profoundly *moral* relationship, one that transmits social and cultural values and forms a healthy bond between the generations.

In short: nepotism works, it feels good, and it is generally the right thing to do. It has its origins in nature, has played a vital role in human social life, and boasts a record of impressive contributions to the progress of civilization. Nor, despite our best efforts over hundreds of years, have we succeeded in stamping it out. And a good thing, too. For if we have not made as much progress as we like to believe in our misguided war on nepotism, we have in some respects already gone too far.

[illegible] of the [illegible] system [illegible] and the [illegible] by [illegible] that [illegible] between [illegible]

The [illegible] works [illegible] the [illegible]

PART I

NEPOTISM IN HISTORY

CHAPTER 1

WE'RE ALL GOODFELLAS NOW

AN INTRODUCTION TO THE NEPOTISTIC SYSTEM

Most Americans have seen Francis Ford Coppola's *Godfather* trilogy, a Hollywood epic that celebrates three generations of an American mafia dynasty. Based on an equally popular novel by Mario Puzo, *The Godfather*'s astonishing success fueled the rise of its director and his stars and spawned a host of imitations, establishing the gangster movie as the definitive American film genre of the late twentieth century. References to *The Godfather* permeate popular culture. Many people know the script almost by heart. Real gangsters are even said to have adopted the rituals and language of the Corleone family—a strange case of life imitating art.

Most influential of all was *The Godfather*'s humanizing vision of the mafia itself. Throughout the 1950s and 1960s, the public perception of the mafia was formed by grainy images of gangsters lying sprawled in pools of blood or twisting their guilt-ridden hands during televised anticrime hearings. Puzo and Coppola took us inside the feared and hated Cosa Nostra to show us the mafia as not only an ethnic phenomenon but also, and more importantly, a family affair.* From the exuberant opening scene—the backyard wedding of Don Corleone's daughter Connie, with its boisterous singing and dancing, its manly hugs and

*Coppola himself has a strong sense of family and evidently believes in working closely with his relatives. See the Postscript for details.

kisses, its copious eating and drinking, and its envelopes stuffed with cash for the new bride and groom—Americans fell in love with the vitality, passion, and loyalty of the tightly knit Corleone clan.

As befits the saga of a dynastic family struggling to survive amid drastically changing conditions, the first *Godfather* movie showed us the passage of authority from one generation to the next. The second combined two narratives: Michael Corleone's attempt to move the family into legitimate enterprise in the 1950s, and his father's earlier rise from penniless orphan to mafia potentate. Thus it is that in *The Godfather Part II* we find the future Don Corleone working in a small family-owned grocery store in New York's Italian immigrant neighborhood, sometime after the turn of the century. The grocer treats him like a son, and it is easy to see why: Vito Corleone (played by Robert DeNiro) is an honest, hardworking young man who is struggling to support a wife and child.

Into the store comes Fanucci, a swaggering neighborhood tough in a white linen suit and wide-brimmed hat. Fanucci belongs to the Mano Nero, the grocer's son explains—the extortionist Black Hand: he shakes down all the local merchants. Fanucci takes the grocer aside. *"Quest' è il mio nepote"* ("This is my nephew") he explains, indicating a slack-jawed young man who stands slouched in the doorway. Apparently the nephew needs a job. Wringing his hands in distress—but what else can he do?—the kindly grocer fires Vito.

In this scene the young immigrant's faith in the American promise of equal opportunity and justice for all is exploded. The truth about the New World is exposed—it is just like the old one. The strong exploit the weak and the authorities do nothing. Vito therefore turns to crime without compunction. He smuggles liquor during Prohibition and quickly branches out into loan-sharking, gambling, extortion, and labor racketeering. In his dealings with the outside world, it's fair to say, he is exceedingly harsh and uncompromising. Yet we sense that he remains a man of honor, because within his family and among those who respect and value his friendship, he upholds the kind of justice that the laws will not enforce.

Despite the reams of criticism attendant on Coppola's films, no one seems to have noticed that Vito Corleone begins his criminal career after being victimized by an outrageous act of nepotism. Americans can sympathize with this: what happens to young Vito is unjust; it offends our deepest instincts about fairness and equality. We hate the bully Fanucci and despise his young lout of a nephew. We think people should be rewarded on their merits and that everyone should make it on their own. But the lesson Vito derives from this experience is not what we expect. Instead of cursing Fanucci's nepotism like any other red-blooded American, he apparently concludes that Fanucci is right: the secret to succeeding in this country is to practice your own brand of nepotism, and thereby beat your rivals at their own game.

If Vito Corleone is the kind of self-made man Americans profess to admire, he has achieved his success by relying first and foremost on his kin. The criminal organization he creates is an extension of his family, and it is run on the same basic terms. To emphasize this theme, *The Godfather* opens on the day of his daughter's wedding, a day on which, by Sicilian tradition, a man must grant whatever favor he is asked. A line has already formed outside his office for this purpose, and it is in these initial encounters in the Don's darkened study that we first measure the importance of "family values" like friendship, honor, and respect to Vito Corleone.

First up is Amerigo Bonasera, a local mortician. The two men's wives are lifelong friends, and Signora Corleone is godmother to their daughter. This unfortunate girl has been beaten and disfigured by two thugs who tried to rape her. The boys have been arrested and found guilty, but one of them is the son of a local politician and the judge has let them off with a suspended sentence. Now the wretched father comes to the Don seeking vengeance. He asks him to kill the young men.

The Don listens to this woeful tale in inscrutable silence. Then, somewhat surprisingly, he rebukes the poor man with a lecture on civic ideals. Bonasera has tried to be a good American, to live according to the law like other citizens. All very well. But now he sees the error of his ways. "You accept judgment from a judge who sells himself like the worst whore in the streets," says Corleone contemptuously. Why should the Don help him now? In the past, when Bonasera needed money, he had borrowed from banks, like a beggar, at ruinous interest. "But if you had come to me," the Don intones, "my purse would have been yours. If you had come to me for justice, those scum who ruined your daughter would be weeping bitter tears this day. If by some misfortune an honest man like yourself made enemies, they would become my enemies . . . and then, believe me, they would fear you."

Bonasera hangs his head and in a strained whisper accepts the Don's offer of friendship. Brushing aside the insulting suggestion of payment, Corleone replies, "Some day, and that day may never come, I will call upon you to do me a service in return. Until that day, consider this justice a gift from my wife, your daughter's godmother." With this, Corleone brings the reluctant Bonasera into his private moral universe and makes him a part of his family. When the mortician kisses his ring and calls him "Godfather," he affirms their new connection in the idiom of kinship.

Corleone is next approached by his godson Johnny Fontane, a popular singer and actor whose career is on the downslide. His marriage is in trouble, his voice is shot, and now a big-time Hollywood producer has refused to give him a part in a film that could put him back on top. Again, surprisingly, the Don berates his godson and harshly mocks his tears. "Godfather, what can I do? Oh, what can I do?" he mimics cruelly. "You can start by acting like a man. *Like a man!*" he shouts, slapping Johnny's face. He particularly upbraids him for neglecting his friendships. "You've been a fine godson, you've given me all the respect. But what of your other old friends? One year you run around with this person, the next year with another person." This is not the way a man behaves. "Friendship is everything," Corleone declares. "Friendship is more than talent. It is more than government. It is almost the equal of family. Never forget that. If you had built up a wall of friendships you wouldn't have to ask me to help." Nevertheless he promises to work out Johnny's problems on condition that he spend more time at home, because "a man who is not a father to his children can never be a real man."

Finally, he must receive Luca Brasi, a hulking strongman whose attachment to the family is legendary. The Don is reluctant to see him. But Brasi didn't expect to be invited, and his gratitude must be acknowledged. Admitted to the darkened inner sanctum, Brasi haltingly reads a brief statement of thanks and expresses his good wishes for the bride and groom: "and may their *first* child be a *masculine* child," he says with comical formality. It is easy to forget from this homely and even endearing performance what Puzo drives home in his novel: Luca Brasi is a dangerous brute who has done many terrible things, including, it is whispered, burning a baby alive. Brasi belongs to a side of the business from which Corleone would like to shield his family. But like so much that is ugly in life, it intrudes unbidden anyway.

Puzo's choice of the term "godfather" to describe Don Corleone is hardly accidental. Rather, it reflects his painstaking research into the cultural traditions of his homeland. Vito Corleone is closely modeled on the traditional mafia capo, a figure who may still be found today throughout the impoverished regions of Sicily and southern Italy. The fact that such men are typically addressed as *padrino*, or godfather, is not a metaphorical conceit but an accurate description of their social role. Moreover, the initial encounters in the Don's darkened study are consciously designed to display the various formal and informal relationships that such a man might use to forge the complex social network that we call a mafia family.

As everyone knows, there are really two Italys: the line between Europe and the Mediterranean runs through the center of the Italian peninsula. Northern Italy is wealthy, modern, secular, and liberal; the south is poor, agrarian, religious, and conservative. The northerner is essentially a European who has embraced the modern capitalist ethic, accepting the rule of law and the authority of the state. The southerner is a Mediterranean whose culture has been shaped by different influences—Greek, Spanish, Saracen, and Norman—and whose outlook belongs to an earlier phase of modernity. Italian culture as a whole is family-centered and traditional, but while even in the modernized north the family remains the basis of the social structure, in the south (according to one authority) "the family *is* the social structure."[1]

For centuries, southern Italy has suffered chronic poverty, violence, neglect, and political uncertainty. Famine, conquest, foreign rule, and exploitation by a rapacious oligarchy have left the region in a notoriously backward condition. As a result, most southerners are insular and suspicious, trusting neither church nor state. They don't accept the government's definition of a crime, and they certainly don't expect the state to maintain law and order or provide other essential services. Instead they rely completely on their relatives.

This is what sociologists call a "low trust" society. In a world where everyone who is not a relative or friend is necessarily an enemy, a man's word and his personal honor are irreplaceable assets that must be vigorously defended. At its most extreme, such radical suspicion of outsiders culminates in what political scientist Edward Banfield has termed "amoral familism." Found for the most part in conditions of extreme privation, amoral familism promotes cooperation within families but undermines cooperation between families; it thereby perpetuates the very culture of poverty that produced it. The mafia family's "outsider" status and its code of *omertà,* or loyalty and silence unto death, are the essence of this familistic culture.

In form, the traditional mafia family is a series of concentric rings clustered around a dense biological core. American families are small—the nuclear unit plus a tight circle of kin—but the Sicilian family is embedded in a much wider network of relatives. These relatives belong to different lineages within a large extended family, or clan. Each lineage has its own head—the senior male member—and the clan as a whole has a *capofamiglia,* who heads the dominant group. The traditional mafia organization is based on the capo's immediate family and draws members from related lineage groups.

The family's rank and power are determined by the violence and cunning of its members, particularly its capo. Unlike bureaucratic organizations, in which authority derives from one's position in the hierarchy, the capo's authority is personal, based on his capacity for "honor"—his ability to dominate others through force of character backed by the credible threat of violence.[2]

Honor is a key concept in Sicilian society, as it is in most peasant societies. Paradoxically, however, honor is not a personal quality but a collective one: it belongs not to the individual but to the family of which he is a part. No one must be allowed to challenge or impugn the family's honor; friends and enemies alike must know that insults will be punished and retribution will be terrible and swift.

As the family's interests expand, its power and influence are extended through a network of friends and associates. The means for this extension is the institution known to anthropology as "fictive kinship." All societies, from the most primitive to the most highly advanced, have developed means of incorporating strangers by according them the status of relatives. Marriage and adoption are the oldest, but fostering, indenture, and apprenticeship are also forms of fictive kinship, as are patronage, blood brotherhood, and ritual or "bond" friendship. All these pseudo-kinship forms are still in use in many African, Asian, and Latin American societies, where they are freighted with important obligations and sustained by public ceremonies, rituals, and oaths. All are employed by the mafia capo to create an artificial family that extends his power deep into the countryside.

The keystone of the structure is the spiritual relation of godparenthood. Godparents in our society are little more than ornamental fixtures, nominally charged with the religious education of the child. But in Italy and other Catholic countries, godparenthood is a sacred bond considered the equivalent of parenthood. A typical Italian child acquires two adult sponsors at baptism, two more at confirmation, and another two at marriage. These adoptive parents are addressed as *comare* and *compare,* literally "co-mother" and "co-father." The bond of *compareggio* not only links the child and his godparents but forges an alliance between their families. The proliferation of such ties means that most Italian villages are basically large clans—a network of related lineage groups linked by webs of marriage, blood, and spiritual kinship.[3]

The obligations of *compari* are indistinguishable from those of close kin. (And not just in Italy: the Russian word for godfather—*kumovstvo*—is synonymous with "nepotism" and denotes protection of a nephew or kinsman.) *Compari* are required to aid one another, lend one another money, never quarrel, and always be kind and helpful. Marriage is forbidden between families linked by *compareggio,* and the relationship can also be inherited. Given the importance of *compareggio* in supplementing kinship ties, it is no surprise that a mafia capo frequently assumes the role of godfather to the children of his relatives, friends, and associates, usually at their request. It is a highly effective means of extending his power and unifying his criminal network. It is therefore more than merely a mark of respect that he is called *padrino* by his followers, who also call one another *compari.*

The mortician Bonasera is linked to Corleone by a tie of *comparaggio.* Yet he does not address the Don in this familial capacity. Instead he approaches him as a businessman, offering to pay for his services. Corleone is affronted by this offer. The Don doesn't want to be *paid,* he wants to be *owed.* What matters to him is creating a moral relationship based on respect for his honor. By establishing an open-ended pledge of mutual assistance, he obliges Bonasera to treat him like a kinsman—someone whose request for aid cannot be denied, no matter what.

As we gather from Corleone's sermon to Johnny Fontane, the family also relies heavily on friendship. Indeed, Sicilians rarely use the word "mafia" at all and refer instead to *gli amici*—"the friends." Italian-American gangsters still use these terms ("a friend of mine" or "a friend of ours") to designate their criminal associates. We think of friendship as strictly an emotional bond, but all friendships involve a mixture of sentiment and utility: true friends delight in being useful to one another. We know there's something fishy about the "friendship" the Don offers Bonasera. For one thing, it is clearly not entered into willingly by Bonasera himself. It is an offer he cannot refuse. Yet at the same time, we recognize the Don's desire to help Bonasera, and we sense that his friendship is real.

This kind of unequal friendship is best described as a species of *patronage.* To Americans, the word "patronage" suggests a political relationship—it conjures images of backroom deals and party hacks dispensing jobs to their supporters. But in peasant societies, patronage is a vital economic and political institution. One of the oldest forms of spontaneous social organization, patronage is found mainly in societies lacking strong centralized institutions and characterized by large-scale inequality. In exchange for protection, political intercession, and other benefits, the patron receives loyalty, labor, political support, and most important, prestige. Since one man's patron is generally another man's client, a chain of such relationships extends from the top to the bottom of society. Political support flows up these chains and benefits flow down. The anthropologist Julian Pitt-Rivers coined the term "lop-sided friendship" to describe this bond between social unequals. To call such an arrangement friendship may seem to stretch the word beyond all recognition; yet friendship was clearly involved. Despite its inequality, sentimental bonds do form between the parties to a patronage relationship. There is also reciprocity and mutual dependence. If the patron does not treat his clients honorably, they will not respect him; if they do not respect him, his authority collapses.

Don Corleone has a well-earned reputation as a man who honors friendship and takes pleasure in doing favors for his friends. Once again, Puzo's depiction is sociologically accurate: the bestowal of gifts and favors is an important part of the capo's activity. Here is how Giuseppe Genco Russo, one of the most powerful Sicilian mafia bosses of the 1940s and 1950s, described himself to an interviewer:

> If I can do a man a favor, no matter who he is, I will; because that's how I'm made. . . . I can't say "no" to anyone. The trouble I'm put to is not so great that I have to refuse people in need. . . . Very often warm-heartedness will win a man gratitude and friendship, and then the time comes to ask for one thing or another. . . . Folks come and ask how they should vote because they feel the need for advice. They want to show that they are grateful to those who have worked for their good.[4]

Russo wasn't doing all this just to be friendly. The ability to deliver votes to his political friends in Palermo and Rome enhanced his prestige and enabled him to obtain benefits for his clients. While it is easy for us to regard such a man as a parasite cynically posing as a public benefactor, the role he plays as a dispenser of gifts and favors is crucial to the moral economy of a peasant society.

The genius of the mafia has been its organizational simplicity, the resilience of its values, and its ability to adapt to a changing environment. These capabilities are clearly related to its familistic character—its roots in a culture of nepotism. The fact that the traditional mafia organization was composed of blood relatives allowed it to perpetuate its values while constantly shifting to exploit new opportunities. To a remarkable extent, the American mafia has maintained these inherited patterns: its history has largely been the story of Italian immigrants struggling to preserve their cultural values in a hostile environment. But the American mafia was never as nepotistic as its Sicilian counterpart, and as its reliance on nepotism declined even further, it became progressively more violent and amoral.

The real-life model for Vito Corleone was probably Carlo Gambino, the last old-fashioned don and in his day the most powerful mob boss in America. The history of the Gambino family says much about the inner rot that has overtaken the American mafia. Ironically, it was undone less by Gambino's vaunting ambition than by his nepotism—his attempt to keep the power in his own family after his death.

Carlo Gambino grew up in Palermo and was inducted into the Honored Society as a teenager under the sponsorship of his mother's Castellano relatives. In 1921 he moved to Brooklyn, where his Castellano cousins got him a job with a trucking firm they owned. His boyhood friend Tommy Lucchese introduced him to the bootleg liquor trade, and he soon landed a place with a coarse Neapolitan gangster named Joe Masseria.

Gambino was one of an estimated 4.7 million Italians who came to America between 1820 and 1930. The newcomers settled in dense urban neighborhoods, reproducing life at home in minute detail, down to the importation of their own familiar foods. The insularity and clannishness of these neighborhoods was primarily due to the fact that they essentially *were* clans: a network of extended-family groups, linked by kinship, marriage, and godparenthood. The typical immigrant spoke no English, seldom left the neighborhood, obtained work through a padrone, or contract labor boss, from his old hometown, and mixed with his relatives and *compari* in private social clubs. The immigrants also preserved their strong family model, with its patriarchal structure and expectation of filial obedience.

Italians were first recruited from street corner gangs as enforcers for Irish and Jewish racketeers. When Prohibition transformed the immigrant ghettos into booming grain alcohol factories, the first criminal families emerged. Conflict raged, until by 1930 a loose Sicilian "union" had been formed, dominated by old-country gangsters known as Mustache Petes. The Mustache Petes had things pretty much locked up in the immigrant neighborhoods, but while they monopolized gambling and labor racketeering and controlled the production of liquor, they could not arrange for its distribution and delegated the task to their juniors, who were more attuned to life outside the ghetto. The scene was therefore set for a revolt against the older generation.

The first stage of this revolt was the so-called Castellamarese War of 1930. Essentially an ethnic civil war between Sicilians and Neapolitans for control of the bootlegging business, the conflict ended when a second-generation gangster named Lucky Luciano betrayed Joe Masseria to his enemies. Masseria's rival, a Sicilian named Salvatore Maranzano, proclaimed himself "boss of bosses" and announced a new order modeled on Caesar's Roman legions. Maranzano's organization, called Cosa Nostra ("our thing"), was divided among five families, each with its own jurisdiction. Maranzano reigned supreme, collecting tribute from all. Meanwhile, recruitment continued to be largely based on kinship, and membership was limited to men of Italian blood.

Maranzano's organization soon fell victim to the same generational tensions that had led to the Castellamarese War, as personified in the relationship between Maranzano and Luciano themselves. Maranzano was an Old World patriarch like Vito Corleone who created a rigid hierarchical organization; the thoroughly Americanized Luciano had no use for Maranzano's old-school notions about honor and respect, and was interested only in money. Maranzano made plans to eliminate his junior partner, but Luciano struck first, killing Maranzano and purging the old guard. Then he announced the elimination of Maranzano's hierarchical organization and the creation of a looser, self-governing syndicate headed by a twelve-man commission.

Luciano's national syndicate governed by a criminal board of directors has often been likened to a modern business corporation, one that filled a demand for illicit goods and services that the aboveground capitalist economy could not lawfully provide. In truth, Luciano's Cosa Nostra was not a modern corporation at all but a *pre*modern corporation, updated with modern methods of accounting and oversight. There was nothing in the way of an actual organization, and the families themselves continued to be based on traditional structures. Thus while many of the values prized by the old mafiosi were rejected by their Americanized sons, the potent legacy of kinship continued to animate Italian-American crime families well into the third and fourth generations.

During the Castellamarese War, Gambino had defected to Maranzano, and after Maranzano's murder he found himself attached to Vince Mangano's family. The Mangano brothers controlled the Brooklyn waterfront, along with Albert Anastasia and his brother Tough Tony, head of the powerful International Longshoremen's Association.

Gambino began his climb to power by creating his own family within the family. To tighten his bonds with the Castellanos he married his cousin Kathryn; he also brought over two of his brothers from Italy and put them to work in his crew. But his rise was blocked by Anastasia, a fearsome gangster who was also the head of Murder Incorporated. When the Mangano brothers were murdered in 1951, Anastasia took control, and his family soon became one of the most powerful in New York. But his violent propensities and disregard for the unwritten rules of the mafia led to his downfall. At the instigation of rival mob boss Vito Genovese, Gambino arranged his murder in the barbershop of the Park Sheraton Hotel and then took over the family, making his brother Paul Gambino and his cousin Paul Castellano *capiregime*. He then had Genovese implicated in a drug deal. Genovese died in prison ten years later.

Gambino by now had three sons and a daughter who became pawns in his dynastic criminal enterprise. Tommy, the oldest, married the daughter of Tommy Lucchese, and became vice president of one of his trucking firms. By 1962, Tommy Gambino owned the six largest trucking companies in the garment district, with a personal fortune of over $100 million. Gambino's other sons went to work for their father in the garment center.

With the death of Tough Tony in 1963, the waterfront reverted to Gambino, along with Tony's son-in-law Young Tony Scotto, a talented labor leader who was soon both a vice president of the ILA and a capo in the Gambino family. Gambino also began to loot Idlewild (now

Kennedy) Airport, obtaining his foothold through his partner and in-law Lucchese. Over four thousand men now worked for Gambino. The illegal businesses he ran took in billions of dollars a year. Yet like Vito Corleone, he remained to all appearances modest and unassuming, a good neighbor and family man.

Gambino now set out to obtain control over the other New York families. He first moved against Joseph Bonanno, whose interests were in gambling and narcotics. A war ensued; Bonanno lost and retired to write his memoirs. When Lucchese died in 1967, Gambino claimed the right to oversee his family. He also exercised considerable influence over the Colombo family, whose boss he had earlier installed. After Joe Colombo's murder in 1971, probably by agents of Gambino, he placed a godson in charge, and a botched drug deal enabled him to remove the acting head of the Genovese family and replace him with his friend Funzi Tieri. After a lifetime of Machiavellian scheming, Gambino had fulfilled his dream of becoming boss of bosses.

Far down the food chain in Gambino's family, an up-and-coming thug named John Gotti was learning his trade in the crew of Carmine "Charlie Wagons" Fatico. Caught hijacking a truck, Gotti and his brothers Gene and Peter were sentenced to two years in the federal prison at Lewisburg. There, in the cell block known as Mafia Row, Gotti received an advanced degree in criminal methods from Carmine Galante, the imprisoned boss of the Bonanno family, and four hundred other wiseguys.

When Gotti was released in 1972 he had a wife and four kids to support. Nepotism might have saved him from a life of crime had he accepted his father-in-law's offer of a job in his construction business. Instead he and his brothers rejoined Fatico's crew. Fatico put Gotti in charge of local gambling operations, and he quickly made his name as a brutal enforcer. When Fatico was indicted for loan-sharking he named Gotti acting boss. He was still not a "made" member of the family, but Gotti got his break when Gambino's nephew Manny was kidnapped and killed by a Hell's Kitchen gang led by James McBratney. Gotti and two other men accosted McBratney in a Staten Island bar and shot him dead.

Gambino was now in failing health, and as death approached in 1976 he began making plans for succession. Underboss Neal Dellacroce was the obvious choice, but Gambino chose his cousin and brother-in-law Big Paul Castellano, with instructions to leave the family to his son Tommy in case of his death or incapacitation. To appease Dellacroce, he awarded him control of all the family's Manhattan rackets. Dellacroce was not satisfied, but as an old-school gangster he believed in respecting the boss. However, many lieutenants and soldiers were offended by Gambino's nepotism and worried that Castellano would also indulge in favoritism toward his sons and Gambino nephews.[5]

Castellano had spent his whole life in the rackets, starting with his father's neighborhood lottery, then working for Mangano, Anastasia, and finally his cousin Carlo. Along the way he tightened his ties with Gambino by marrying one of his sisters-in-law. Paul's closeness to Gambino had given him aristocratic status in the mafia, and unlike the self-made Carlo he projected an air of entitlement that rubbed real gangsters like Dellacroce and Gotti the wrong way. The overweening confidence that came from considering himself Gambino's heir apparent ultimately caused him to lose touch with the violent reality that underlay his power.

As Gambino biographer John H. Davis observes, Castellano's downfall was traceable to his ascension through nepotism rather than merit. "If he had been more street smart, if he had been a genuine Cosa Nostra boss who had fought for his position, not merely inherited it," Davis observes, Castellano would have taken Gotti out before passing him over. Instead he foolishly informed Gotti of his intention to break up his crew. To discuss this insulting demotion, he proposed a meeting at Sparks Steak House on December 16, 1985. Castellano and underboss Tommy Bilotti were gunned down as they got out of their car.

John Gotti was definitely a don for the eighties. With his carefully coifed silver hair, his double-breasted suits and flashing pinkie rings, his broad smile and insouciant jokes for the cameras, Gotti was the perfect mafioso for the dawning amoral celebrity culture. Dubbed the Teflon Don by New York's tabloids, Gotti beat rap after rap with the help of his unctuous lawyers and at least one proven instance of jury tampering. Finally in December 1990 Gotti was indicted on multiple counts of conspiracy to commit murder, along with Tommy Gambino, underboss Frank Locascio, and consigliere Salvatore Gravano. "Sammy the Bull" Gravano had risen from a Bensonhurst street gang at the same time as Gotti. A hardened killer with nineteen murders to his credit, he started as an enforcer in the Gambino construction rackets and had gradually taken them under his personal control. Gotti's indictment put Gravano in danger not only of going to jail but of losing his considerable wealth. His riveting testimony put Gotti behind bars for the rest of his life.[6]

In the mafia, as in the world of legitimate business, the self-made man is more respected than one who inherits his position, and Gotti was more respected by the rank and file than Castellano, the silver spoon mobster. Yet both were missing crucial elements of leadership. While Castellano lacked the qualities of the self-made man that Gambino possessed, Gotti's example suggests that the self-made man is nothing but a thug if he lacks the "civilizing" influence of traditional mafia values. Though Gotti was a true-believing mafioso who declared his ambition to turn the Gambino family into "a real Cosa Nostra," he failed to follow the cardinal rules of discretion and silence. Gotti was heard on tape railing against indiscreet loudmouths who talked into FBI microphones, then proceeded to spill detailed information about his own activities. Not a stupid man, Gotti apparently believed his own press as the untouchable "Teflon Don"—a mistake Gambino would never have made.

Is the mafia really a family in any meaningful sense of the word? Or is it merely a criminal gang dressed up with familial trappings? The answer depends on the family. Most Italian-American crime families were originally partnerships between close relatives that were tightened through marriage and godparenthood. In a seemingly natural and unconscious process, these tight-knit criminal clans, once established, began forging a dense network of marital links. At one point, three of the five heads of New York's crime families had children who were married to one another. The offspring of Carlo Gambino and Tommy Lucchese were married as a step toward Gambino's ultimate domination of the five New York families, and Bill Bonanno married Rosalie Profaci with the blessing, indeed the connivance, of their fathers. Francis Ianni documents the complex weave of marital relationships among the twenty families that make up the Zerilli organization of Detroit and traces their further links through marriage and *compareggio* with other families in Buffalo, New York City, and New Orleans. Far from being accidental, this was very much a systematic process. As Ianni explains, "Of the sixty-odd Mafia bosses identified as participants at the famous Apalachin meeting in November 1957, almost half were related by blood or marriage, and even more if godparenthood is included as a kin relationship." Rather than a nationally directed criminal syndicate, this looks more like an incipient dynastic system of the kind that underlies all oligarchic classes from ancient Rome and Renaissance Florence to nineteenth-century Philadelphia and Boston. As sociologist Digby Baltzell has observed, the values of the Boston and Philadelphia elites were "not too different from those of the Italian-American family portrayed in *The Godfather.*"[7]

The concept of an artificial family sounds strange to American ears, but that is because we have an unusually narrow and restricted view of kinship. Americans think of kinship as a strictly biological relationship; but kinship is a cultural invention, part of the primitive tool kit of human survival, and as such it is highly plastic and adaptable. The Sicilian mafia grew directly out of rural kinship networks as a means of imposing order on a chaotic environment: family status was extended to outsiders through both formal and informal means, and kinlike patterns of behavior were encouraged that knit the enterprise together. Sicilian mafia organizations were rightly called families because the relationships established within them produced kinlike ties of reciprocity and trust.[8]

In contrast to the five families of New York, most other Italian-American crime families remained closely held enterprises managed by actual relatives. These smaller families, about whom we hear very little, have been much more successful as going concerns, and some have made the transition envisioned by Vito Corleone from organized crime to legitimate enterprise. But the biggest and most powerful mafia groups necessarily relied on unrelated persons to the point where few if any were still run by their founders' descendants. The less nepotistic the New York families became, the more they became like any other criminal gang—amoral, violent, and unstable. It was only a matter of time before the rapidly breeding mistrust within the mafia destroyed the kin-based code of *omertà* on which its safety and integrity depended.

The most talked about television series of the last several years has been *The Sopranos,* a shrewd and witty adult drama about a dysfunctional mafia family whose capo suffers from anxiety attacks. *The Sopranos,* along with comic films like *Analyze This,* seemingly marked a new therapeutic phase in the American romance with the mafia: the baby-boomer don in midlife crisis.

If Gotti was a don for the eighties, Tony Soprano was unmistakably a don for the nineties. Soprano is a man of contradictions. He is the heir to a family tradition to which he is fully committed, yet does not wish to pass it on to his children. He wants his son to respect him, but not to be like him. He wants to preserve his daughter's innocence, but he also wants to rub the ugly truth about the source of her security and comfort in her face.

Tony Soprano embodies the heat death of the nepotistic system represented by the mafia: in him we see the decline of the virile nepotism of Vito Corleone to a point where so much energy has leaked out that the system can no longer sustain itself. The sons in *The Sopranos* and *Analyze This* struggle with depression and anxiety brought on, their psychiatrists tell them, by buried rage against their fathers. They keep nice suburban homes, barbecue on weekends, go to soccer games, and worry over when and how—or whether—to tell their kids about their business. No wonder they need Prozac.

One infallible sign that the mafia has been mainstreamed and Americanized is that its specialized vocabulary has seeped into the very foundations of public discourse. The word "mafia" itself, once too explosive to be uttered, has become a common way of describing the ad hoc networks that snake and twist through modern life, from private business to government agencies to college faculties. The glib new mafia-speak reached a journalistic peak in January 2000 when Maureen Dowd penned an extended comparison between candidate Al Gore and Tony Soprano, whom she described as "a thoughtful and increasingly self-aware family man who always does what he has to do." Wondering whether Gore had the stomach to take on a primary challenge from Sen. Bill Bradley, Dowd observed, "If you wanna be boss, you gotta be willing to whack some people." The Bushes were dubbed "the WASP Corleones," and their code of *omertà* is similarly harsh: those who violate it "summer with the fishes."[9]

The saturation of American discourse with this *Godfather*-inspired vocabulary is amusing, but it is a joke only on one level. On another, it reflects the incipient triumph of Don Corleone's social and moral philosophy. In a contemplative mood toward the end of *The Godfather*, the old Don says to Michael, "I don't apologize for the way I lived my life. But I refused to be a fool, dancing on a string held by those big shots." In these comments, the Don's whole worldview is expressed: in this corrupt, dishonorable world, you either pull the strings or play the fool. The only honorable alternative is the one that he has chosen—total independence, based on the loyal support of family and friends.

Mafiosi often claim that they merely satisfy eternal human appetites, and regard their opponents as moralistic hypocrites. As Big Paul Castellano put it to the FBI agents who conducted him to a federal courthouse,

> Hey, I know you disapprove. That's why we're here, after all, isn't it? So the United States government can make the point that *we do not approve of how certain guineas make their living.* Okay. Fair enough. If I was the government I'd put my ass in jail for a thousand years. . . . But not because I'm *wrong.* You see, that's the part I object to—this idea that the law is right and that's the end of the story. Come on. We're not children here. The law is—how should I put it?—a convenience. Or a convenience for some people and an inconvenience for other people.[10]

To a certain extent, we agree. It's true that our public tradition celebrates America as a land of opportunity where all are created equal, where wealth and privilege hold no sway, and where merit is always rewarded. There is plenty of evidence for this view of America as an exceptional nation. But there is also plenty of evidence for the alternative view, namely that the system is corrupt, the game is rigged, and influence trumps merit.

In one episode of *The Sopranos,* Tony's wife, Carmela, tries to get their daughter admitted to Georgetown by pulling strings. "It's all connections now, it's who you know," she complains to her husband. If the rules don't apply to everyone, why follow them? Since the game is fundamentally unfair, she thinks nothing of intervening on her daughter's behalf, though she is careful to do so without her knowledge lest that harm her self-esteem. To the extent that this episode reflects a pervasive attitude toward the institutions of American democracy, it can fairly be said, "We're all goodfellas now." It's a short step from this kind of thinking to the radical familism of a man like Vito Corleone. We may deplore his methods, but we have to respect the old Don for facing this reality squarely and not flinching from its consequences.

The mafia makes a good starting point for a history of nepotism in human affairs. After all, it is the nepotistic organization par excellence—the ultimate family business. The mafia preys on people's needs, exploits their weaknesses, and uses violence, intimidation, and corruption as its tools. Yet its amazing tenacity in the face of all our efforts to destroy it is, if nothing else, a powerful testament to its sheer efficacy as a mode of organization. Hack at its branches as we may, we seem unable to uproot it. This fact alone should make us take respectful notice of its nepotistic character—all the more so as our continuing fascination with the mafia suggests that the nepotistic values it embodies may yet have merit and legitimacy in our eyes.

The Godfather's appeal for American audiences was due in part to the nostalgia of assimilated ethnics for the comforting closeness of the immigrant family and the nepotistic system that sustained it. This system was hardly an Italian invention: it is typical of all societies based on the Old Nepotism, and it was deployed in different ways by different groups as a means of adapting to American life, taking such collective forms as ethnic mutual aid societies, unions, and political machines. The core of that appeal was the dark, commanding figure of the patriarchal father—a dominating figure who will tell you what to do, establish norms for your behavior, and who is capable of harshness and brutality, yet who also will reward your obedience by giving you the whole world and everything in it.

This kind of father no longer exists in America. The authority of fathers has been weakened by a gradual campaign of disenfranchisement that began with the liberal revolutions of the eighteenth century and continued with a protracted political and legal assault that eventually replaced the father's powers with those of the state. Yet now that we have effectively killed off this patriarchal father, we experience a predictable nostalgia for him. This may simply be an expression of the patricidal guilt that Sigmund Freud discerned at the heart of civilized society. But it may also signify our genuine longing for the father and the nepotistic system that produced him.

Moreover, despite the suppositions of eighteenth-century social contract theorists, it is the mafia-style corporate family—not the isolated sovereign individual—that represents the default mode of social organization. Throughout history, men have built upon their families, drawing on their resources of loyalty and trust to advance their collective ambitions. As they rose, they linked themselves by marriage and other fictive kinship ties to other families, creating a web of family interests that in time became a conscious, institutionalized elite. The Roman aristocracy, the ancient Chinese bureaucratic class, and the mercantile and banking clans of Venice, Florence, Amsterdam, and London were all products of this pattern of family enterprise.

In Western societies, the growth of the state and the market have reduced the importance of families and liberated individuals to pursue their own personal ends. But in most other parts of the world, these familistic patterns still predominate. This is notably the case in Arab countries, most of which are ruled today by monarchs or dictators who continue to base their power on their families, clans, or tribes. But even in America, this pattern is more common than we think. American history, and Western history in general, is much involved with the rise and fall of dynastic groups that based their power on the ad hoc webs of kinship that they wove around their families. As the Roman historian

Ronald Syme expressed it, "In all ages, whatever the form and name of government, be it monarchy, republic, or democracy, an oligarchy lurks behind the façade." This is not a conspiracy theory of history but a recognition of the neglected importance of families in public affairs.

The mafia is a deep repository of cultural history and knowledge about the actual foundations of society, and that is why it has become such a powerful symbol of the deep contradiction underlying our national creed. The remainder of this book will seek to shed fresh light on those foundations, beginning with the deeply ingrained habits and impulses that induce us to favor our kin.

CHAPTER 2

FROM BIOLOGY TO CULTURE

A NATURAL HISTORY OF NEPOTISM

You might think it doesn't matter which elephant a hunter kills, especially if the animal is an older female past her breeding years. But the killing of such females, whose long tusks make them an attractive prize for poachers, may be hastening the extinction of these endangered animals. Elephants live in female-centered "families" consisting of a mother, several daughters, and their offspring. (Males go off on their own after they grow up.) When elephant babies are born, their grandmother and aunts inspect them carefully and help them to take their first steps. Because the nursing mother must be constantly foraging to find the two hundred pounds of food she needs each day, these surrogates are vitally important. Sisters, aunts, and cousins all cooperate in looking after the newborn. The family also relies on older females, with their long social memories, to remember the location of good feeding grounds and to distinguish friends from foes. The more time the group can spend foraging and resting instead of defending its territory, the more offspring it can raise. The matriarchs thereby contribute to their daughters' reproductive success, and removing them can seriously harm the group's survival. The same applies to other species like dolphins, whales, and chimpanzees.

Ants are famously cooperative, but ant colonies are ultra-competitive, and when ants from two colonies meet—even when they belong to the same species—they fight each other to the death. Ants from one colony may also kidnap and enslave ants from another. (E. O. Wilson has remarked that if ants possessed nuclear weapons, they would destroy the world in less than eighteen hours.) Yet scientists have recently discovered several enormous Argentine ant colonies that are unusually peaceful and cooperative. One such supercolony stretches all the way from Mexico to San Francisco. Several more exist in Europe, including one that follows the Atlantic and Mediterranean coast from Portugal and Spain through France and Italy, a distance of four thousand miles. Comprising millions of nests and billions of individual ants, it is the world's largest biological society. In their native habitat, these ants are highly aggressive, ripping the limbs off ants from other colonies. But ants from one end of the supercolony may be introduced to nests hundreds of miles away without friction. Scientists explain this by the "genetic bottleneck" caused by migration: descended from a small group of closely related individuals, the ants are essentially a large genetic family.

In the summer of 2002, Americans were saddened by the story of fifty-five pilot whales that had beached themselves on the shores of Cape Cod. Though many were pushed back into the sea, they returned the next day and soon became fatally disoriented. According to scientists, these whales are very social, living in pods that include several generations of relatives. The whales are strongly attached to their kin and refuse to abandon one another. While this kind of intense social bonding may be useful in the open sea, allowing them to defend against predators, support injured or sick relatives, or find and hunt food, it can be very dangerous in the shallow waters off the cape. Despite repeated attempts to save them, the whales eventually died.

These stories illustrate different aspects of the role of nepotism in insect and animal societies. In the first case, human interference threatens to disrupt the delicate cycle of intergenerational dependence in elephant families. In the second, a lack of normal aggression among closely related ants has allowed a foreign species to multiply and spread at a fantastic rate, conquering a vast ecological niche. In the third, a strong tendency to nepotism, splendidly adapted to conditions in one arena, proved fatal in another.

Since the publication in 1975 of E. O. Wilson's groundbreaking

Sociobiology there has been an explosion of interest in the biological basis of cooperation, and a large number of neo-Darwinian books have appeared on the subject. These authors have their differences, but all agree that nepotism is the ultimate source of social behavior in nature. Thus Raghavendra Gadagkar explains: "When animals favor close genetic relatives or distant relatives as recipients of beneficial acts, they are said to be practicing nepotism." Nepotism is the hallmark of what are called "social species," those that display a capacity for cooperation in mating, provisioning, defense, and the rearing of young. "Throughout the animal kingdom," observes biologist Mary Maxwell, "nepotism is the norm for social species. I go further: the practice of nepotism *defines* social species."[1]

But while all these writers acknowledge the importance of nepotism, none of them has focused on it as a phenomenon in its own right, and some of them find it downright embarrassing. Dr. Gadagkar bends over backwards to assure us that his use of the term to account for cooperation in nature implies no endorsement of the practice among humans. Matt Ridley asserts that nepotism is a "dirty word," since every action we consider virtuous reflects the taboo against selfishness; and nepotism—favoring one's offspring—is supremely selfish. On the other hand, Steven Pinker suggests that nepotism may be a victim of cultural prejudice, and Maxwell goes out on a limb to say that it is only a "cultural belief in fair play" that makes nepotism appear to be a shady practice.

All this queasiness springs from an understandable reluctance to make general arguments about human behavior based on analogy to animals. No responsible scientist wants to commit the naturalistic fallacy, deriving the "ought" of human conduct from the "is" of biological nature. But we may also take seriously the suggestions of Pinker and Maxwell that our cultural bias against nepotism may be clouding our view of its character.

Are we nepotists by nature? Is nepotism in our genes? The short answer is yes, and there is plenty of evidence to support the idea. Since humans are the social animal par excellence, it would be more surprising to biologists if humans *didn't* practice nepotism. Yet nepotism in humans is not simple, fixed, or static: unlike animal nepotism, it does not remain operative solely at the biological level but has a second life in culture. This is what makes human nepotism different from that of other social species: the capacity to create kinlike attachments by extending the benefits of altruism to people who are not biological relatives. Thereby nepotism grows and twists like the strands of a tenacious vine through human history.

Of course, the fact that something may be natural doesn't necessarily make it good or right from the perspective of a modern society. On the other hand, if nepotism does have a biological basis we may have to accord it the same grudging respect we grant to other basic instincts, whether we like them or not. Acknowledging its roots in an unchanging aspect of human reality is the first step toward developing a more constructive approach to the problems it causes. But before we can judge whether we have evolved beyond the need for nepotism, we have to understand it as a positive and necessary thing in its original context, before it was transformed into a problem by the progress of civilization.

The purest case of nepotism in nature is that of the cellular slime mold. In these simple compound organisms, which are really colonies of identical cells that reproduce clonally—simply dividing without any sexual mixing of genes—some cells spontaneously form a protective outer husk and stalk, while others become fertile spores that disperse to new habitats. What prompts this altruistic sacrifice on the part of the dead outer cells? Why, if they are all identical, do some commit genetic suicide so that others can go on to reproduce? The question has been harder for scientists to answer than one might think. But the example serves to show that when biologists speak of nepotism they mean something very specific, namely an organism's willingness to forgo reproduction in favor of close biological relatives.[2]

Nepotism is also said to occur among ants, bees, and wasps—the species known as hymenopterans. The selfless behavior of these species and their amazing capacity for cooperation are, of course, proverbial. Worker ants will sacrifice themselves in large numbers to defend the nest; many have evolved a sting and venom apparatus that causes the attacker's viscera to be detached when the victim pulls away. Older workers assume dangerous foraging activities with a life expectancy of only fourteen days from the start of their forays. The nepotism of female worker ants involves forgoing reproduction, and in many species their unfertilized eggs are fed to the queen and the larvae. E. O. Wilson calls the existence of these sterile females "the single most important feature of insect social behavior." Why? Because their sole function is to care for the queen and her offspring, not to mate and reproduce. Their radical altruism tightly integrates the colony and makes possible a much more advanced specialization of labor.[3]

Such altruistic sterility is mainly seen in hymenopterans, but it also appears higher up the evolutionary scale in the naked mole rat, a bizarre-looking underground creature of the Ethiopian desert. Mole rats are the world's most nepotistic mammal, unique for their insectlike reproductive strategy. In a colony of several hundred mole rats, only one female is allowed to reproduce, mating like a hymenopteran queen with two or three males while the others work with amazing efficiency to extend and sweep the burrow's vast network of tunnels, groom one another, forage for food, and start new colonies. No other mammal has a single reproductive queen or displays the same degree of hivelike integration.

Voluntary celibacy also occurs in some bird species, like the green-fronted bee-eater, whose members show an altruistic willingness to act as helpers at the nest. Especially in situations where territory for breeding and expansion is limited, mature birds may stay home and assist their parents in raising more brothers and sisters. The helpers build the nest, feed the mother, incubate the eggs, and guard and feed the chicks. Parents get so used to having these helpers around that a father may actually try to prevent an offspring from going off to breed on its own. Such behavior may also be seen among humans, as in the case of mothers who "cling" or live vicariously through their children, and fathers who dominate their children and refuse to let them make their own decisions.

It is one thing to forgo reproduction in favor of kin. It's quite another to commit suicide on their behalf. That is why one of the most frequently cited examples of nepotism in nature is that of Belding's ground squirrel, which gives out warning calls at the approach of a predator. Researchers found no evidence that warning calls distracted predators or reduced the likelihood of future attacks. Moreover, the altruists were often chased down and killed for their trouble. The study found that squirrels are most likely to give alarm calls when close relatives are present.[4]

The problem with all this evidence of cooperation and self-sacrifice is that it flies in the face of classical Darwinism. According to Robert Wright, Darwin kept the idea of natural selection to himself for nearly a decade because the altruistic behavior of ants and other "ultrasocial" species posed "an insuperable challenge" to his theory. Natural selection is supposed to be a selfish struggle in which only those who succeed in the competition for resources (territory, food, access to mates) get to reproduce. The successfully competing organism is thereby said to maximize its reproductive fitness—its ability to pass on its genes to the next generation. No self-respecting organism should forgo its reproductive opportunities. Furthermore, a species as a whole evolves by weeding or "selecting" out undesirable traits and rewarding those that are adaptive by spreading them throughout the population. If the species cannot get rid of bad, or maladaptive, traits and produce enough fit individuals, it very soon dies out.

But if reproductive fitness is the ultimate goal of natural selection, how could altruistic tendencies survive? How could a warning gene be passed from one generation of squirrels to the next if its bearers are killed and cannot replicate themselves? A truly selfish organism should aim to reproduce at any cost; but if that were the case, natural selection should have long since weeded out any altruistically inclined amoebas, insects, squirrels, birds, or mole rats.

It was not until recent decades that evolutionary biologists resolved the problem of altruism in nature with the idea of kin selection, a special modification of Darwin's theory of natural selection introduced in 1964 by biologist William D. Hamilton. E. O. Wilson based his breakthrough studies on Hamilton's ideas, and Richard Dawkins popularized them in *The Selfish Gene*.

Hamilton solved the mystery of altruism by focusing on the real protagonist of natural selection: not the individual organism, as Darwin assumed, but the genes the organism carries. Genes do not exist in isolation as a form of personal property; they are a common inheritance among the larger group of relatives to which each individual belongs.

Logically, then, if parents have an interest in preserving the offspring that carry their genes, they must also have an interest (though a lesser one) in preserving other relatives who share the same endowment. Each of these individuals is related to the others by some fixed genetic proportion. Parents, children, and full siblings share 50 percent of their genes. Grandparents, uncles and aunts, and nieces and nephews share 25 percent, and cousins share 12.5 percent. Hamilton's Rule predicts that an altruist's investment in her relatives will be repaid if her resulting loss of fitness is offset by a proportionate increase in theirs. By this formula, altruism toward a niece or nephew must be compensated by a fourfold increase in offspring, while in the case of a cousin the number of children produced must be eight.

Just as kin selection is a special form of natural selection, Hamilton coined the phrase "inclusive fitness" to describe a special form of reproductive fitness. Inclusive fitness explains how genes for altruism may not only survive the winnowing of natural selection but spread throughout the population as a whole. Reproductive fitness is measured by the number of an individual's successful offspring; inclusive fitness by the success of a significant number of relatives bearing a proportion of one's genes, which thereby get included in the next generation. Depending on their degree of genetic relatedness, animals that exert themselves to benefit relatives may increase their own fitness by doing so. Selfish genes can thus produce unselfish traits with no net loss of reproductive fitness—even if those actions lead to the altruist's death.

Perhaps the best way to illustrate this idea is to cite the old conundrum often raised in introductory ethics classes. Suppose your brother and a stranger were drowning: which would you save? Though some might briefly hesitate, most will probably admit that they would choose to save their brother. The terms are sometimes changed to alter the stresses involved: your brother or your friend, your mother or your daughter, a fellow countryman or a foreigner. While we place altruism on a moral plane above kinship, the question forces us to engage in calculations that reveal the limits of altruism and the nepotistic underpinnings of many moral choices. Most people will say that they would save their brother for reasons of sentiment, but the underlying impulse to preserve their shared genetic heritage probably has a lot more to do with it. Likewise, most people would save their daughter over their mother on the grounds that the mother has lived her life while the child has hers ahead of her; but it is also the case that a daughter will pass on your genes while an aged mother cannot. These are examples of kin selection—the often unconscious decision to favor relatives in preference to strangers.

On the other hand, some people value their friends above their relatives and might well sacrifice the latter, regarding the chosen bond of friendship as morally superior to the given or unchosen one of kinship. This dramatizes one of the more interesting truths about the processes that drive evolution, namely the increasing role of choice in human affairs. Natural selection is unconscious and involuntary, a simple matter of the interaction between a given set of genes and a changing environment. Sexual selection—the second Darwinian principle—involves a good deal of unconscious compulsion but gives the individual some power of choice in selecting a mate. Kin selection, though compulsory in animals, is almost entirely voluntary among humans—necessarily so, given the difficulty humans sometimes have in knowing who their relatives are. The growing role of choice in the formation of kinship bonds has reached the point where, in America at least, we have come close to overturning the old truth that you can't choose your relatives.

Hamilton's theory of kin selection explains the reproductive altruism of creatures ranging from multicelled organisms to highly individualized predators (lions also display patterns of breeding and cooperation based on kin selection). The absolute altruism of slime mold cells occurs because the cells are identical twins: it makes no difference to the genes which individuals reproduce, since they are all carbon copies of each other. The radical altruism of sterile worker ants is likewise due to their unusually high proportion of shared genes. The peculiarities of the hymenopteran reproductive process produce offspring who are more closely related to their sisters than they are to their parents (they share three-fourths of their genes rather than the usual one half). This means it is more profitable for a worker to invest in raising sisters than to reproduce directly: an ant that trades offspring for sisters gets more inclusive fitness by raising one sister than one offspring. As Gadagkar observes, "she actually has to work less as an altruist than she has to as a selfish individual."[5]

It is equally hard to see the Darwinian rationale for the altruism of Belding's ground squirrel unless one applies Hamilton's Rule, which holds that the evolutionary value of preserving the lives of close relatives may be greater than preserving one's own. The same applies to mole rats: according to Lee Dugatkin they share a "whopping" 81 percent of their genes, even more than ants and bees. Similarly, the altruism of celibate bee-eaters isn't selfless at all from the genetic perspective; in fact it's parasitical. Because helpers almost always (94 percent of the time) choose to assist close relatives, what they lose in fitness by not breeding they gain back by helping their relatives do so. The value of this sacrifice is clear from the result: the average productivity of nests with nepotistic helpers is double that of those without them.

Clearly biological nepotism is a powerful and necessary force in nature, nothing to be trifled with. Without it there would be no basis for cooperation and no possibility of building any kind of society, whether of insects, mammals, or the cells that make up our own bodies. By promoting a genetically selfish form of altruism, biological nepotism provides the glue for these societies. So in a rather surprising and elegant way, the pursuit of individual genetic selfishness gives rise to an altruistic system that benefits the species as a whole.

Are human beings all that different? Humans share many features of their social and reproductive systems with animals, including pair-bonding and parental attachment, territoriality, and (to some extent) incest avoidance. Nepotism is perhaps the strongest proof of our relatedness to other social species. There seems no doubt that human beings were massively selected for nepotism because it was, in simple reproductive terms, a highly adaptive behavior. Nor is there disagreement about the evolutionary value of this trait. Nepotistic species, Sarah Blaffer Hrdy explains, "overcome natural obstacles and adapt to diverse environmental challenges better than those that are not." Anthropologist Helen Fisher concurs: "Nepotism is one of our original family values."[6]

Matt Ridley wisely cautions us against the naïve error of thinking that human society got started through nepotism: "There is no evidence," he writes, "for the inbreeding and vicarious reproduction that is a necessary part of any nepotistic colony."[7] We may as well acknowledge that Ridley is right: while kin selection on its own is powerful enough to hold together small-scale biological communities, outside of a tight circle of genetic relatedness its potency swiftly diminishes. Though high levels of inbreeding are plainly integral to the unity of many human societies, kin selection on its own cannot explain their existence.

But Ridley's narrow view of nepotism as "vicarious reproduction" obscures both the distinction between animal and human nepotism and the important continuities between them. For the impulse we call nepotism cannot really be reduced to kin selection. Biological kin selection is the purest form of nepotism—the kind we share with other social animals—but it is only one component of the nepotistic impulse among humans. That impulse is a compound of two other important principles, namely *coercion* and *reciprocal altruism.*

"Kin selection" has already been defined as an organism's unconscious drive to forgo reproduction when doing so may significantly increase the reproductive fitness of a relative. "Coercion" at the most basic level means simple physical control, as in the case of the green-fronted bee-eater that prevents its young from going off to reproduce. Especially in its earlier phases, human nepotism owes a good deal to simple coercion. (Coercion can also take the form of an ideology that justifies unequal or exploitative relationships.) The term that remains to be explained is "reciprocity."

Reciprocal altruism—defined as beneficial behavior toward others in the expectation of an equal or greater return—is an attempt to influence another's behavior by treating him or her in a benevolent or helpful way. We express the same idea more concretely when we tell our kids that if they want other children to like them, they should try being nice to them first. Though reciprocity has long been a byword in behavioral studies, reciprocal altruism emerged as one of the key elements in human sociability through the pioneering work of biologist George C. Williams, who argued that evolution should favor individuals who maximize friendships and minimize antagonisms. Williams suggested that this tendency was at the root of complex social orders involving the division of labor and systems of abstract exchange.[8]

While reciprocity is not unique to humans, we have developed it much further than other animals. Only the higher mammals (such as dolphins, apes, and elephants) possess this capability, which requires relative longevity, group stability, and sufficient brain capacity to recognize other individuals and keep score of their generous actions. Since the mechanism involved is one of taking turns and trading favors, it also requires a capacity for trust, an adequate memory, and a well-calibrated sense of relative values.

Robert Trivers, who first applied the principles of game theory to human reproductive behavior and the study of cooperation, used the term "reciprocal altruism" to describe the mechanism by which individuals extend trust to nonrelatives. Robert Axelrod later tested this theory with a computer game called Tit for Tat, which reproduced Trivers's "altruistic system" through an expanding web of simulated interactions. As Robert Wright explains, a simple feedback system allowed Tit for Tat to distinguish between cooperating and noncooperating programs: cooperators were rewarded, noncooperators ("cheaters") were shunned. Axelrod found that cooperative behavior "feeds on itself" to produce a growing sphere of trust. Eventually, noncooperative programs are excluded and "social harmony" prevails.

The theory of reciprocal altruism has found strong support in behavioral studies of animals. West Indian guppies will break off in pairs to investigate the approach of a possible predator and return to warn the group. Experiments reveal that this behavior owes more to reciprocal altruism than it does to kin selection: the tiny fish partner up on the basis of simple cues that signal a willingness to cooperate. Much has also been made of the fact that vampire bats will sometimes share food with unrelated individuals, particularly pregnant females unable to hunt for themselves. The beneficiaries later return the favor, and often form a lasting partnership.

If trust breeds trust, however, the opposite is also true: mistrust breeds mistrust. Reciprocal altruism has a darker side, which anthropologist Marshall Sahlins has called "negative reciprocity." As we will see, both aspects are important to the dynamics of kin-based societies.

The social life of primates serves to illustrate how reciprocal altruism functions to enhance and extend the unifying force of kin selection.

Primates live in groups of ten to eighty individuals. The core of the group is composed of females and their offspring, with a dominance hierarchy of males based on physical strength and seniority. Some primate species are monogamous, but as a rule there is no permanent pair-bonding—hence no proper primate families. The fundamental social unit is therefore that of the mother and child. Cooperation is essential to survival—females cooperate in gathering food and protecting the young, while males cooperate for hunting and defense—and primates display strong nepotistic preferences in most cooperative behaviors, including grooming, coalitions, and adoption and surrogate parenting. Grooming is important because apes cannot remove their own parasites. Mothers groom their offspring, who return the favor later on, and adult primates usually continue to choose their kin as grooming partners. Yet apes may also form grooming bonds with unrelated partners, which suggests that the habit of reciprocity learned from their mothers may be extended to nonrelatives. The same is true with respect to alliance formation. Male baboons form coalitions to steal females from dominant males; chimpanzees also gang up to depose alpha males and divide the sexual spoils. Most such coalitions are formed between biological relatives. Yet unrelated primates form alliances as well. Moreover, grooming exchanges between nonrelatives can lead to an alliance later on.[9]

With their widely spaced births, prolonged infant dependency, capacity for attachment, and cooperative bonds with offspring, primate mothers closely resemble those of our own species. This resemblance includes the ability to manipulate the bonds of biological kinship for political advantage. The most famous primate mother in the annals of behavioral science is Flo, the endearing mother chimp studied by Jane Goodall. Flo's maternal attributes—her tenderness and patience—were a strong part of her appeal for viewers of the several *National Geographic* specials in which she played a starring role. Yet these anthropomorphic qualities were only part of the story of her success as a mother: there were also Flo's highly successful dynastic stratagems. Relying heavily on her sons, some of whom had risen to high positions in the dominance hierarchy, as well as several former consorts with whom she shared offspring, Flo carved out a stable, protected sphere in her male-dominated group. She was thus able to provide for herself and her young and protect them from invading outside males and other dangers. Indeed, Flo provides a model of maternal nepotism that would be the envy of any human mother.

According to Sarah Blaffer Hrdy, Flo was an "entrepreneurial dynast" who contrived to pass on her territory and other accumulated benefits to her children. Thus her daughter Fifi continued to use Flo's supportive network even after her mother's death. The guarantee of rich, consistent nourishment and the protection of male kin allowed Fifi to begin breeding at an unusually early age, and she has so far produced seven offspring. Flo's nepotism therefore translated into higher reproductive success for her daughter. Flo's sons Freud and Frodo are also highly successful in the dominance and reproductive sweepstakes. "Thus does Flo's family prosper."[10]

Biological nepotism is of obvious importance in getting primates to the threshold of humanity, but it is only the beginning of the story. While kin selection is undoubtedly the starting point for human nepotism, it is only one component of an impulse that owes at least as much to culture as to nature. Indeed, nepotism can be considered the ultimate basis of culture, since what anthropologists call culture is initially constructed out of the cooperative bonds between close relatives. Culture, in effect, is what people *do* with these natural bonds, using them to create the social instruments they need for their survival.

By combining kin selection with reciprocal altruism and elements of coercion, nepotism evolves well beyond its biological origin to play a crucial role in the formation of human societies. Biological kin selection accounts for the mother-child bond and in large part for the family itself. The infusion of kin selection with reciprocal altruism extends the nepotism of the family to the territorial band—itself largely composed of blood relatives. With the emergence of the incest taboo and the invention of marriage and kinship, the web of nepotistic sentiments extends to unrelated individuals and groups. Thereafter, nepotism flowers into a full-blown array of kinship ties.

Nepotism is nothing if not a product of the family, and the family begins for humans, as for primates, with the bond between mother and child. The importance of this bond for the production of a normal and healthy adult cannot be overstated. At the most basic level, the mother's nepotistic preference for her child is vital to its physical survival; but it is equally important as the source of early training and instruction. Infants learn the basic norms of social interaction from their mothers. Their bond must be secure enough to give the growing child the confidence to explore its environment, yet not so strong that it overwhelms the developing instinct for independence. That is why we criticize inattentive or neglectful mothers, as well as those who dominate or cling.

In *Mother Nature,* Sarah Blaffer Hrdy sets out to determine whether there is really such a thing as a maternal instinct. Without a doubt, she concludes, a great deal of motherhood is based on innate biological cues. Like other primate females, women "in the right frame of mind" find all babies "fascinating and attractive." Hrdy presents evidence that pregnancy, gestation, and childbirth physically alter the female brain, creating new neural pathways and accentuating sensory capacities of smell and hearing that benefit the newborn and facilitate attachment. A cascade of hormones in the final months of pregnancy prepares the new mother to bond with her infant, and in the days just after birth women literally "fall in love" with their babies. Massive doses of estrogen and progesterone sharpen their responsiveness to infant scents and sounds, and the stimulus of breast-feeding intensifies their reaction to these cues. To a very real extent, a mother's body "merges into synchrony with her baby's needs" such that its survival and well-being become her most pressing concern.

Most of the powerful emotions that inform human maternal nepotism date from the early historical period when mothers had to be in constant physical contact with a child just to prevent its being eaten by wild animals. Babies for their part seem to require the assurance of being cared for by committed kin; denied this consistent level of care and attention, the infant may not mature into an adult capable of realizing its full empathic potential.

But while we have tended to idealize mother love as a virtual merging of mother and child, maternal altruism is neither uniform nor totally consistent. For one thing, motherhood is, in biological terms, an expensive proposition: "The mother's gift of life can be measured in calories, minerals, opportunities to invest in other children present and future, charged against her own continued survival in times of famine," Hrdy writes. This means that the same woman may behave very differently toward her children at different times and in different circumstances, ranging from the availability of adequate nourishment to the desirability of the father. Human mothers frequently discriminate between their children—for example, feeding a son while starving a daughter—and usually favor the one with the best chance of going on to reproduce their genes. Mothers may also trade off existing children against future ones by spacing births, abortion, or infanticide.[11]

The intensity of human maternal altruism in most places most of the time is sufficiently explained by the fact that mothers share half of their genes with their offspring; this means that the reproductive interests of mother and child are largely congruent. Abundant proof is found in nature, where the most self-sacrificing mothers—as we would expect, given Hamilton's Rule—are found in the most inbred populations. Yet Robert Trivers has argued (or rather, his theory has been taken to imply) that there is a latent conflict of interest between mothers and children: while the mother's reproductive interest is best served by having another child as soon as possible, the child's is served by forcing her to wait. To this end, children adopt a variety of strategies, such as becoming more demanding (the terrible twos), or regressing, as a means of getting parents to commit more resources and care than they might like. Children want to stay on the breast longer than their mothers want to nurse them (though children also have an interest in the welfare of their siblings, who share half of their genes). Mothers for their part apply a nepotistic calculus to offspring. If her life or reproductive opportunities are threatened by an overly dependent child, a mother may sacrifice it in the interest of other (potential or actual) children.

So it is not maternal nepotism that distinguishes humans from animals. Maternal attachment among humans is no stronger than it is among primates. The real revolution in human affairs was the appearance of paternal nepotism and the consequent emergence of the family—the first distinctly human institution.

Despite the widely held assumption that the monogamous nuclear family is the natural foundation of society, anthropologists know that it first had to be created out of recalcitrant human materials. While the mother-infant bond is natural, most male animals don't stick around too long out of concern for their offspring and mate but go off as soon as possible in search of other females to inseminate. In contrast to the nurturing nepotism of female primates, who concentrate on bringing a few offspring to maturity, males seek to maximize their reproductive fitness by having as many offspring as possible. To that end (like some lions), male primates who enter a new group may kill existing young when they take over the harem. (The loss of their infants induces estrus in female primates, making them available again for reproduction.) Primate fathers do care for and protect their own young, but most have little interest in monogamy. Originally, human males were not that different: fathers had to be recruited to the family, and induced to invest their nepotistic energies in supporting the mother and child.

The human family begins in the conjugal pair bond: the exclusive childbearing and child-rearing alliance formed by a man and a woman. Pair-bonding (as distinct from marriage) is necessary for humans because we are born too soon and mature too slowly. In consequence of man's evolving upright posture, Robin Fox explains, female pelvic size began to shrink just as the human cranium was growing to accommodate a larger brain. This made childbirth much more difficult and dangerous for humans than for other primates. Selection therefore favored mothers who dropped their offspring early, before the head was fully formed. It also meant that human children were born at a point when they should still be in the womb completing their development. While primate young are largely independent after weaning, humans require protracted nurture and protection well into adolescence. Human mothers thus require long-term cooperative relationships with males. This may explain why human females are sexually available at all times and do not undergo visible estrus or fertility cycles like primates and other mammals. However, since permanent sexual availability is as much a threat to social stability as it is an inducement to permanent bonding, another principle of solidarity was called for. That principle is the force of paternal nepotism.

Nature presents a wide spectrum of paternal behaviors, from highly attentive caregivers to careless or infanticidal fathers. Some male primates have at least the potential to be responsive, caring fathers, although a reasonable certainty of paternity is required. Males can obtain this kind of certainty only by staying close to the mother and policing her sexual conduct.

Thus it is largely the Darwinian demand for paternal certainty that drives and reinforces the formation of stable families. A human male could always go in search of a new sexual partner, but if he wished to be sure of reproducing his genes, he had to be on hand to help ensure his child's survival. Therefore evolution must have rewarded males who chose to invest in their offspring rather than those who pursued the more typical primate strategy of having as many as possible. Evolution may also have rewarded females who selected mates with nepotistic tendencies. The result was massive winnowing of human genes for nepotism. This is in accord with Darwin's argument that sexual selection—the largely female power of choosing mates for qualities deemed useful or attractive—exerted as much pressure on human evolution as natural selection.

Male and female strategies of nepotism continue to differ. Maternal nepotism is focused mainly on providing protection and nourishment. Human mothers (like elephants and dolphins) are also more dependent on their relatives. Indeed, much of their social activity is focused on maintaining these relationships, an activity anthropologists call "kin-keeping." In contrast, fathers are more concerned with the survival and continuity of their lineage. For the most part it is fathers who maintain the cults and rituals that pass property, authority, and knowledge between the generations. These and other differences in nepotistic focus and concern have been remarkably consistent throughout history.

Before we pursue the links between biological nepotism and wider forms of kinship, we need a deeper understanding of how nepotism functions as a source of moral and emotional ties within the family. Ultimately this is because we want to know how nepotism feels—and why it feels so good that many people continue to practice it despite the social costs it may incur. Therefore we must excavate the nepostitic sentiments that bind the human family together. Simply put, why do we experience special emotions toward those whom we believe to be blood kin?

Darwinian theory emphasizes the role of kin selection in forming human families and keeping them together. But families are unified by other bonds than reproductive interest. Indeed, it cannot really be said that human beings are conscious of these interests at all, no matter how important they may be at the ultimate level.

In fact, as behavioral researchers have shown, families are bound together by moral sentiments of affection and trust. The trick is to explain where these sentiments come from. While biological kin selection can explain parental attachment and investment in offspring, genetic selfishness alone would not produce a corresponding sense of obligation among children. If classical Darwinian theory is right, our willingness to care for our parents should decline as they grow old and we become more independent; yet veneration of parents and elders is a universal feature of human societies. As Robert Wright puts it, "The stubborn core of familial love persists beyond its evolutionary usefulness." Grandparents do invest resources in our siblings, offspring, and other relatives who share our genes, thus making them more valuable than they appear. But mere genetic selfishness cannot explain how powerful attachments can develop beyond the biological family, as in the case of adoption and friendship.

For Darwin, the basis of sociability was the capacity for sympathy, or fellow feeling. Philosophers from Aristotle to Adam Smith had said much the same thing, but Darwin believed this sentiment had evolutionary roots and was not exclusive to humans. He thought he could identify feelings of friendship and sympathy among primates, and theorized that higher moral capabilities were rooted in natural instincts that long predated humankind.

A good deal of research now appears to support this contention. Our genes have indeed been heavily selected for traits conducive to sympathy, self-control, and a desire for equity, or fairness. These endowments tend to foster individual success and enhance the survival of families and groups. Otherwise, as James Q. Wilson has observed, evolution would have favored different traits, "such as a capacity for ruthless predation, or a preference for immediate gratifications, or a disinclination to share."[12]

For Wilson, we are not born moral animals but creatures with an inborn social reflex that allows us to develop such capacities. The raw materials of the faculty we call conscience are the infant's "prosocial" behaviors—smiling, laughter, frowning, and other responsive and communicative abilities that are clearly innate and not learned. The mechanism underlying moral development is the impulse called "affiliation," namely the infant's instinct for attachment to its mother (or a surrogate). Out of this emerges sociability—"the state in which moral understandings are shaped." The attachment instinct is so strong that it is very difficult to extinguish (not that one would want to!) "even with the use of the most severe punishments." The corresponding "affectional response" in parents is triggered by various signals, or "releasers," one of which is presumed biological kinship.[13]

The moral equipment we require for social life are the capacities for *sympathy* and *guilt.* Both have a genetic basis and are ultimately linked to kin selection. Nature makes us feel empathy toward siblings in distress, and guilt when we neglect them. *Gratitude* is another moral reflex that "can get people to repay favors without giving much thought to the fact that that's what they're doing."[14] Compassion, guilt, and gratitude are nepotistic traits selected by evolution to promote cooperation with close relatives.

If the faculty we call conscience is initially a biological reflex concerned with the welfare of relatives, it is up to our parents and kin to raise this reflex to the level of real moral capability—defined as an ability to tell right from wrong, respect for fairness, self-control, a sense of duty, and a capacity for altruistic attachments beyond the family. The means for this is what we might call an education in reciprocal altruism. As with the game of Tit for Tat, the moral training we acquire in early childhood tells us that cooperation and honesty will be rewarded, while selfishness and deception will be punished. Generosity and gratitude are the sentiments that we apply to cooperators; envy and hate to noncooperators. Together these capacities create a basis for life in society.

Strict Hamiltonians derive these sentiments from reciprocal altruism, not kin selection, and no attempt is being made here to reduce the one to the other: the two things are demonstrably distinct. Nor do I mean to denigrate the importance of ethical instruction, or to suggest that only the products of healthy or intact families can be moral. This is clearly not the case. However, evolutionary theory does suggest that love of kin developed to help us propagate our genes: the reason we have these sentiments at all is that over evolutionary time, love of kin increased our odds of genetic survival. Compassion, guilt, and gratitude may be linked to reciprocity, but since reciprocity requires a strong initial bond of trust to get started, it seems fair to conclude that if it were not for kin selection, reciprocity could not come into play as a factor in human society. Thus the two are inextricably entwined. Even the normally hardheaded Robert Wright waxes lyrical when he writes, "Given the likely links between kin selection and reciprocal altruism, one can view the two phases in evolution as a single creative thrust, in which natural selection crafted an ever-expanding web of affection, obligation and trust out of ruthless genetic self-interest."[15]

We may therefore acknowledge Matt Ridley's argument that nepotism (narrowly construed as biological kin selection) is not the basis of human society, while pointing out that it *is* to some considerable extent the basis of the family and of the moral capabilities that allow us to extend kinlike attachments to strangers. As Mary Maxwell reminds us, "the ability of altruism to be passed on genetically depended in the first instance on its being a practice directed exclusively toward relatives."[16] The family is therefore best understood as a nepotistic crucible, brewing new forms of human connectedness out of the stuff of these primary bonds. The question is how this was done: how did early humans learn to transfer their nepotistic instincts to nonrelatives, forming stable reciprocal bonds in the absence of a system of laws and government? The answer is that it was done through the creation of *new* nepotistic bonds in a cultural system of kinship.

The appearance of the family conferred tremendous advantages on our earliest ancestors. It allowed them to develop a sex-based division of labor, provide more efficiently for the raising of children, and reduce potential conflict over mates. But while the family itself is very ancient, the territorial band is undoubtedly much older and was the earliest form of social organization. Human beings evolved in small subsistence groups and were, in ways that still affect us powerfully today, specifically adapted to the conditions of life in a community of close biological relatives.

The earliest human bands were chimpanzeelike groups centered on a dominant male or males, surrounded by females and offspring, with younger males (cadets) at the periphery. The emergence of the pair bond restructured these bands as loosely ordered compound families, probably a group of brothers and male cousins, each with his own mate and offspring. The first so-called "fraternal interest groups" probably appeared well over a million years ago in the grassy plains of Africa. Lacking formal governance or even the most rudimentary language or culture, these groups continued to be structured hierarchically (like ape societies) by sex, seniority, and strength.

Once formed, however, the family is hardly a static affair. Instead it is intensely dynamic. While powerful forces within the family draw it together, there are others—equally potent—that drive it apart. The centripetal and integrating force is biological nepotism; the centrifugal forces are those associated with sex and aggression. These forces are potentially disruptive since they undermine cooperation and can lead to status conflicts in the family. Therefore they must be either channeled outward or (as Sigmund Freud surmised) psychologically sublimated.

In *Totem and Taboo,* Freud speculated that in the "primal horde," the father ruled as a virtual tyrant, keeping the women for himself and driving off the sons as they matured. Ultimately the sons rebelled, killing and devouring the father. Consumed with guilt, they projected the father as a divine being or spiritual ancestor, whom they appeased with worship and sacrifices. Confronted with the problem of sexual competition, however, the brothers chose to preserve fraternal harmony by denying themselves the father's women. This, according to Freud, was the origin of the earliest human culture, based on ancestor worship, the incest taboo, and a primitive system of kinship. Though Freud's account is ahistorical, his psychological insights into the powerful ambivalence of family relations are worth bearing in mind as we explore the nepotistic dynamics at the core of all human societies.

The solution to the problem of sexual competition among primates is to drive away maturing males, who go off to look for mates in other bands. This is not an option for humans, since survival dictates that the family stick together as long as possible. Left to their own devices, primitive men might well have remained isolated and virtually autonomous, retaining their sons for hunting and defense and keeping their women to themselves. But this could not continue, lest the cohesive benefits of kin selection be canceled out through genetic inbreeding.

The related problems of sexual aggression and inbreeding were eventually solved by two great cultural inventions: the incest taboo, and the corresponding rule of exogamy, or marriage outside the family. The interaction of these rules explains how human beings evolved from the fraternal interest group to the simplest hunter-gatherer societies.[17]

All societies have rules forbidding incest, though how it is defined and who is included in the prohibition may vary from one culture to the next. Some societies, including our own, limit the proscription to the nuclear family and (usually) first cousins. (In-laws are supposed to be off limits but the rule is not always observed.) In other societies, like those of many North American Indians, the incest prohibition includes more distant classificatory relatives, who have the status of blood kin without actually being so. In China it was forbidden to marry anyone with the same surname; since Chinese clans are very large, this rule effectively eliminated hundreds of thousands of people as potential spouses, no matter how remote the presumed biological tie.[18]

The incest taboo probably began with the natural aversion to mating between mother and son—a trait selected by evolution to prevent the sexual competition that would undermine paternal nepotism. The aversion to brother-sister mating is also apparently natural, and is widely observed among primates. At the same time, the mother has an interest in keeping her family close, and evolution therefore programs us to have strong feelings of attraction for our siblings. (Thus when primates become dominant, some males do mate with their sisters.) The likely solution to this problem among early humans was the practice of sister exchange, often accompanied by a pattern of preferential cross-cousin marriage in which the brother's daughter married the sister's son. In this way, Robin Fox speculates, the sublimated fantasy of sibling copulation could be gratified in the next generation.

Thus despite the many problems with Freud's account of the family's origin, his fundamental insight in placing sublimated sexual impulses at the center of the family seems valid. Greek mythology presents the problem in a typically arresting way with the story of Kronos, the creator god who devoured his children so as not to be supplanted by his son Zeus. Kronos still stands as the archetype of the bad father whose nepotistic instincts are so impaired that he cannot let go of his children. Many modern fathers (and mothers too) may recognize themselves in the image of this greedy, selfish tyrant. For in a sense we do wish on some level to ravish and devour our children. We want to keep them to ourselves, and have to be induced by a combination of taboos and incentives to channel those desires into a healthy nepotism, which is to say, a long-term strategy tending to their reproductive benefit. This erotic component of nepotism is very pronounced in the dynastic families that we will look at later on.

Since the hunter-gatherer mode of existence is seasonal, nomadic, and highly labor intensive, it required many square miles of territory to support even a small human group. Accordingly, probably quite soon after the emergence of the conjugal family, the fraternal interest group fissured into a number of nuclear families who fanned out over a large common territory. The size and composition of such bands were a matter of ecology: where there was sufficient natural abundance, extended families stayed together out of preference. In conditions of greater scarcity, nuclear families dispersed, regathering at intervals for feasting and religious rites. At such times, alliances were formed with other families, usually based on the marriage of two or more children.

In such conditions it is very difficult to distinguish what we would call nepotism from the sum of other human interactions. Biological kinship was the first and for a long time the only basis of cooperation, since for all practical purposes no one else really existed. Given the size of most hunter-gatherer territories (about half the size of Long Island for an average group of fifty), early humans probably encountered few people socially who were *not* blood relatives. Members of other bands were rarely seen and certainly could not be trusted: they were natural competitors for scarce and uncertain resources, and a stranger with no established tie to the group was either driven off or killed without compunction.

Consider the situation of primitive man. Naked to the elements, engaged in a daily struggle for survival—who is there to help him but his relatives? A human being is dependent on his relationships with family members from the moment he is born. He needs his mother to nurture and protect him and teach him elementary social skills. He needs his father to instruct him in the arts of survival and initiate him into the ways of men. He needs his brothers to hunt with, and a larger group of relatives to defend his territorial rights against strangers. Ultimately, however, none of these relationships is more important than having a spouse; therefore he seeks to acquire a wife as soon as possible.

In his first experience as a fieldworker, the anthropologist Claude Lévi-Strauss observed an odd phenomenon:

> One of the deepest impressions which I retain from my first experiences in the field was the sight, in a central Brazilian native village, of a young man crouching for hours upon end in the corner of a hut, dismal, ill-cared for, fearfully thin, and seemingly in the most complete state of dejection. I observed him for several days. He rarely went out, except to go hunting by himself, and when the family meals began around the fires, he would as often as not have gone without if a female relative had not occasionally set a little food at his side, which he ate in silence. Intrigued by this strange fate, I finally asked who this person was, thinking that he suffered from some serious illness; my suppositions were laughed at and I was told, "He is a bachelor."[19]

The importance of having a spouse in primitive societies cannot be overstated. Even today in some places it may require the full-time efforts of both partners to fend off starvation. This is why in most tribal societies to be unmarried is a pitiable and even contemptible state. Unmarried men and women are despised and jeered at and considered to be bad people, and at their deaths there are no dignified observances. Often their bodies are simply tossed into the forest and abandoned to wild animals. A man needs a wife because their partnership increases the amount of food they can obtain, and because she gratifies his need for sex. But her value as a productive laborer may be equaled or exceeded by her value as a *reproductive* laborer, because she also provides him with offspring, which have value in themselves.

If having a spouse is desirable, having one with many relatives is more so. Tribal people often say, "We marry in order to have brothers-in-law," a proverb that underscores the importance not only of having many relatives but of acquiring more by marriage. Kin are wealth and power in a primitive society. When a man obtains a wife, he gains not only a domestic labor partner but often, in her father, brothers, and other male kin, hunting and trading partners, ritual friends, and military allies. As Carleton Coon observes, "A man who hunts on his neighbours' territory without permission risks being killed, but if he has a brother-in-law in the next camp he stands a chance of getting permission to hunt there if he needs to . . . and if a man has two or more wives from different bands, so much the better."[20]

The system of alliances created by this pattern of bridal exchange is called a *connubium,* a word that wonderfully expresses the commingling of political, economic, and marital relationships in primitive societies. A *connubium* usually originates with two intermarrying bands but may grow to include several more. The simplest kind of *connubium* is one in which two neighboring groups exchange wives on a reciprocal basis. Usually the groups are distinguished by association with various opposing elements in nature—light and dark, winter and summer, heaven and earth—and are also associated with totemic animals. (The word "totem" is derived from an Algonkian term meaning roughly, "He is my relative.") Thus the Tlingit Indians of the Pacific Northwest are divided into moieties, or marriage groups, called Raven and Wolf. When a Raven woman marries a Wolf man she is lost to her family of origin; in time, however, her daughter will marry a Raven man, thereby compensating the loss and completing the cycle of exchange in the next generation.

Some cultures trace their dualistic social structure to a pair of mythological ancestors, often two brothers, and when new groups join the reproductive system, new ancestors are generally added retroactively. Even today most ethnic groups maintain a fiction of common descent, as do nation-states like Germany, England, and France. The moieties may also share political and religious functions—certain offices may be vested in one or the other, such that cooperation is necessary for the observation of important rituals. After several generations, as the web of kinship ties grows more complex, the *connubium* becomes the boundary of tribal or ethnic identity: the moieties come to be seen as two parts of one people, sharing a common territory, language, and culture. The origins of the tribe in a number of warring bands will be forgotten, though it may be commemorated in symbolic games or traditional athletic rivalries.

Marriage, then, was not primarily an emotional commitment between a man and a woman—although the preferences of children are often respected in even the most primitive societies—but an alliance between kin groups. The bride and groom were simply pawns in a nepotistic social strategy. Daughters and sisters were used as a medium of commercial and diplomatic exchange, while sons were exploited for labor and defense.

These facts remind us that early man did not unduly sentimentalize his bonds with family members. Children were regarded as an asset in the great survival sweepstakes. This attitude of having property in children remains one of the central features of nepotism throughout human history. Well into the nineteenth century, parents virtually owned their children and controlled their lives, dictating where they lived, what they could do, and whom they could marry, and this coercive dimension of nepotism is undoubtedly one of the reasons it has such a bad reputation today. On the other hand, we should beware of assuming that the love of children is somehow a modern invention. Parental exploitation and parental love are not, as we tend to believe, mutually exclusive tendencies, and nepotism frequently combines them.

The invention of marriage is a watershed in the history of nepotism because it represents the extension of kinship beyond the immediate family. When we marry, we accept our spouse's relatives as kin and agree to treat them nepotistically, as though we were "one blood." Not only are we required to extend the incest taboo to our in-laws, all the other reciprocal obligations of close kin apply to both families. Ultimately, of course, this reflects the recognition of our shared genetic interest in the offspring; but kinship status can also be extended unilaterally as a means of incorporating strangers into the group. Our modern habit of referring to new immigrants as "naturalized" attests to the persistence of this tribal way of thinking, where citizenship means adoption into the national family.

Kinship structures every interaction in a tribal society, perhaps most importantly the distribution of food. Such societies have elaborate rules for the sharing of food from a kill, starting with the hunter's closest kin and working outward. Kin are required to share food with one another, and food sharing remains even in modern societies a symbolic marker of kinship. We still say that a devoted mother "takes the food out of her own mouth" to feed her child. The ritual sharing of food among strangers has likewise been a sign of inclusion or adoption by the group. Travelers to remote regions today often find that food is pressed upon them and that they are obliged to eat whatever is served, even if other family members go hungry; the importance of this ritual is hard to grasp unless we understand their urgent need to propitiate powerful strangers. The gift of food is thus self-interested because it carries a moral compulsion. An Eskimo hunter willingly shares his kill with people beyond his family circle, partly because it cannot be preserved and will spoil if not consumed. But making a gift to a stranger is also useful because the rules of reciprocity require him to return the favor in due course. As Robert Brain observes, the safest place for an Eskimo to store his surplus food is in another man's belly.

This brings up another aspect of primitive societies, namely the importance of gifts. Weddings and other social and religious occasions are usually marked by exchanges of gifts, and these exchanges can become very elaborate. Dowries and wedding gifts between the families are common in all societies. In many places gifts are exchanged with visitors on both arrival and departure. The potlatch ceremony practiced by the Indians of the Pacific Northwest involves truly extravagant exchanges in which men vie for social status with expensive feasts and gifts, to the point of economic ruination.[21]

Sociologist Marcel Mauss reflected on the principles of primitive gift exchange in an elegant little book called *The Gift* that is a classic of the field. Mauss distinguished three aspects of what he called the gift economy: the obligation to give, the obligation to receive, and the obligation to repay. We will have occasion to refer to these principles later on in other contexts. (The view that generosity is the proof of a leader's legitimacy continued to inform expectations of European monarchs well into the nineteenth century.) Mauss also noticed that in the gift economy, there is no real distinction between persons and things: the objects exchanged are thought to partake of the giver's own substance. When we offer a gift we give a part of ourselves, and the giver is not whole until that substance is returned.[22]

Many anthropologists have built on Mauss's essay, but all concur that gift exchange embodies the principle of reciprocity that maintains equilibrium within and between human groups. One might say that in the moral economy of kinship, the *gift* represents the positive pole of reciprocity, while the negative pole is represented by the *feud.* Sublimating conflict in gift exchanges like the potlatch keeps primitive society in balance. These transactions also elicit sentiments of generosity and gratitude that help to bind societies together.

The awareness that life is a gift is very apparent to primitive man. Living at the mercy of the elements, he knows that the very sustenance he requires is a gift from the gods or from nature, and he propitiates these spirits by offering gifts in return. His children are a gift, having value in themselves and as a medium of alliance and exchange. He also knows that his own life is a gift from his mother and father. They received it from their parents, and he will pass it in turn to his children, along with all the power, wealth, and knowledge he has managed to accumulate. Such a man holds nothing back, for whatever he withholds is thereby lost: he is what he is able to transmit.

Nepotism in this original, primitive context is fully integrated with the economic, political, and spiritual life of human beings. It is a manifestation of the gift in relations between fathers and sons, mothers and daughters, and siblings and other kin. It would be an error to romanticize this original human condition, but it is vital to our understanding of nepotism as it is practiced today. For nepotism is still concerned with the transmission of a legacy, with human continuity, and it is still the source of moral sentiments that link one generation to the next. Indeed, nepotism at its best may be considered the last bastion of the ancient gift economy. Even in modern societies based on markets, contracts, and individual rights, the spirit of the gift continues to animate the practice of nepotism.

Here the natural history of nepotism ends and its cultural history begins. It is a story that must be told against a background of growing complexity in human affairs, and at this point we take leave of biology and evolutionary explanations for human behavior. Such explanations may be valid for individuals, and we neglect their importance for the persistence of nepotism at our peril; but they are certainly not acceptable as explanations for the behavior of human groups. The argument of this chapter has been that while nepotism in humans clearly has deep biological roots, as it also does in animals and insects, we have elaborated on this basic biological phenomenon in several human-specific ways, including having males invest in offspring, leveraging reciprocal altruism, designating fictive kin, and arranging marriages for strategic purposes. Nepotism as a cultural and historical phenomenon is therefore best understood not merely as an individual transaction motivated by genetic selfishness—which it certainly is at one level—but as part of a collective strategy focused on the maintenance of social continuity through marriage, reproduction, and inheritance.

At the center of this nepotistic system is the reproductive imperative, but the system's larger purposes are cultural: the transmission of property, knowledge, and values from one generation to the next. This nepotistic formula is part of the essential tool kit of human survival, and as such its practice changes with the progress of human societies: birth rates go up or down, family structures expand or contract, and the nature of property changes along with patterns of succession and inheritance. In some non-Western societies, nepotistic formulas that represented successful adaptations at an earlier stage of history have become obstacles to modernization. In the West, nepotism has changed considerably, becoming less collective and more individualistic over time. The end of the story is not in doubt: nepotism must and will continue. But the nature of its present phase has yet to be described or understood.

CHAPTER 3

CLAN, CASTE, AND TRIBE

NEPOTISM IN NON-WESTERN SOCIETIES

According to a recent poll of international businessmen, Brazil ranked among the fifteen most corrupt nations on earth. "As often as they can get away with it," one journalist wrote, Brazilian politicians and officials "use the machinery of state to advance their interests and to help friends and relatives." The king of Brazilian nepotism was a regional court judge who employed a total of sixty-three relatives—including his wife and children, nephews, nieces, cousins, and daughters-in-law. Each month the members of his clan brought home almost $250,000, or about 10 percent of the court's total salary budget.

"When Governor Lininding Pangandaman of the Autonomous Region of Muslim Mindanao calls a staff meeting," wrote John McBeth, reporting from the Philippines, "it is more like a family reunion." Thirteen relatives held key positions in the regional government, including eight of the fifteen cabinet slots. Hundreds of other relatives and friends occupied middle- and lower-level jobs throughout the regional bureaucracy. A political opponent called it "an orgy of nepotism unparalleled in our history." But nepotism, even on this scale, is nothing new in Mindanao. According to one politician, "It is a gauge of your political strength to see how many positions you can get for your close relatives."

The day after his 1993 victory against a conservative incumbent on a strong anticorruption platform, Greek prime minister Andreas Papandreou appointed his wife and other family members to top jobs.

Mrs. Papandreou, a thirty-eight-year-old former flight attendant, became chief policy adviser, Papandreou's son was made deputy foreign minister, his wife's cousin became deputy culture minister, and his personal physician became minister of health. These actions flew directly in the face of Papandreou's campaign promises to rid the government of nepotism.[1]

As ruler of Indonesia for over thirty years, Mohamed Suharto presided over an unprecedented economic boom that was a model of postcolonial development. But by the early 1990s the greed and corruption of the president's family had aroused real international concern. Suharto's six children owned dozens of businesses that enjoyed government-controlled monopolies and preferential trading agreements, were granted billions in unsecured loans from state banks, and acted as paid agents for foreign firms wishing to be steered smoothly through the national bureaucracy. As they said in Indonesia, "The Suhartos have everything, except a sense of shame." The collapse of Indonesian currency in 1997 sent shock waves through the global economy. It also unleashed a flood of finger-wagging editorials in the Western press about the evils of nepotism and crony capitalism in Indonesia, Singapore, Malaysia, and other Asian countries. (The problem is so widespread in the region that it has its own acronym: KKN, short for "collusion, corruption, and nepotism.") Suharto was forced out of office and his children were removed from their many directorships amid calls for the return of their vast illicit fortune, estimated at some $40 billion.

The press reports such stories in an impotent, exasperated tone and uses terms like "blatant," "flagrant," and "rampant" to describe the extent of the problem. Indeed, what seems most striking about the Suhartos and their ilk is their utter lack of shame about their nepotism. Far from being secretive about it, they boast of their nepotistic achievements and are in many cases openly admired for them. We seem to have entered a looking-glass world where our values of efficiency, merit, and fairness are turned upside down. And so we have: for in these societies, nepotism is actually considered a *good* thing, something to be proud of, not a vice to be concealed.

The tolerance of nepotism in many parts of the developing world may be puzzling to outsiders, but it is hardly accidental. Far from being the problem it is here, nepotism in these societies is (or was) an ingenious cultural solution to the social and political problems of an earlier period, and a system of relations based on nepotism has been the basis of society for hundreds and even thousands of years. Modern bureaucracy, in contrast, is a recent phenomenon imported from abroad and often imposed on an unwilling populace. What we are therefore witnessing in these countries is not a deplorable lack of public spirit but a struggle between two starkly incompatible ethical systems. It is the unresolved conflict between these warring systems that produces the type of corruption we call nepotism.

The modern values we embrace are those of technocratic liberalism. The alternative appears in different forms and is variously referred to as familism, tribalism, or ethnic nationalism. All of them fall under the heading of what might be labeled Ancient Nepotism. The era of Ancient Nepotism is a distinct phase of history, lasting some ten thousand years, in which the principles of kinship that evolved in the earliest stages of human existence produced a broad array of social institutions. Here we will consider the main collective manifestations of Ancient Nepotism: the tribe, the clan, and the caste. Each represents a cultural adaptation of nepotism to unique ecological challenges, and each of the great ancient civilizations is based on some or all of these forms. The *tribe* is found throughout the world, but we will view it primarily in the African context. The *clan* is an element of the tribe that reached its highest level of development in China. India is the classic setting for the examination of the *caste* and the complex challenges of ethnic nationalism. All remain deeply in thrall to these archaic institutions and are only now struggling to break free of them, so far with limited success.

AFRICA: THE ETERNITY OF THE TRIBE

Official corruption is not unique to Africa, but nowhere is it seen on the same sweeping scale. In Nigeria alone, corrupt politicians and businessmen have siphoned off an estimated $36 billion in aid and investments—enough to pay off the country's whole foreign debt. But the problem is thoroughly pervasive in African societies: as one sociologist observes, "I have seen hospitals in West Africa where the patients had to pay nurses to bring them a chamber pot."

Though not the worst sort of corruption by any means, nepotism draws particular attention as a symbol of the rot in many African societies. Thus one recent story reported that Air Zimbabwe's general manager had come under criticism for hiring three nephews as senior managers and putting other family members on the payroll. Previous attempts to remove him had been blocked by his patron, the minister of transportation; both men were members of President Robert Mugabe's Zezuru clan. In late 2000, John Agyekum Kufuor was elected president of Ghana on a promise to clean up corruption and nepotism; eighteen months later his brother was the defense minister, his brother-in-law was the senior minister, and his nephews were in other top positions. Zambian president Levy Mwanawasa appointed his brother to a high position in the state's intelligence service. Congolese president Laurent Kabila put his son in charge of the army; the son succeeded his father after his assassination in January 2001. Kenyan president Daniel arap Moi (who finally stepped down in early 2003) preserved his hold on power over many decades partly by ensuring that political supporters were succeeded in elected office by their sons.

Given the extreme pressures of modernization in many African societies, it is not surprising that we so often hear complaints about corruption and nepotism. What we don't often hear is what it is like to be an African official besieged by requests for aid from a large group of kinsmen, fellow villagers, and tribesmen. The number of people who feel entitled to make demands on a midlevel African bureaucrat may run into the thousands. In such conditions "there is much to excuse nepotism," say Ronald Wraith and Edgar Simpkins. Any man who rises to a level of importance is automatically surrounded by relatives and friends who confidently look to him for patronage: "The tradition of centuries leaves them in no doubt that he will provide for them, and that if jobs do not exist they will be created." Such trifling responsibilities would shock and overwhelm a British or American official, but an African takes them for granted: "For why should a man become big and powerful except to look after his relations?"[2]

As Wraith and Simpkins put it, "there is really very little to say [about nepotism], except that public life is riddled with it, and that everybody knows this." Indeed the pervasiveness of nepotistic corruption in Africa is matched only by the peculiar tolerance that seems to go with it. Whatever we may think, another scholar observes, nepotism and graft "are not unmitigated evils, and are in fact largely good and acceptable" as viewed by the populations of many African societies. "Had it been otherwise, these practices would not be as widespread and persistent." According to Stanislav Andreski, "[A] top politician who is not known to have acquired a vast fortune is singled out for praise as some kind of ascetic."[3]

All this suggests that the social values of Ancient Nepotism are very much alive in Africa, where the vast majority of people continue to live completely within the horizon of the family, clan, and tribe. Not only have most African officials been brought up under a vigorous system of extended kinship, their education and training have often been paid for by their families and tribal associations. "If [an official] put his duty to the state above this debt of gratitude," Andreski explains, "they would regard him as a despicable traitor, ostracize him and perhaps demand an immediate repayment in cash of what they have spent on him." Thus with very few exceptions, an African official will give all the appointments he controls to his kinsmen.

It should also be clear that when people speak of nepotism in Africa what they really mean is *tribalism.* To Westerners, the tribe is an object of horror. Recent conflicts in the Balkans and the former Soviet republics were ascribed to a resurgence of tribalism. The Rwandan genocide provided an appalling reminder of the unreasoning hatreds generated by tribal society. Violent separatist movements from Sri Lanka to Canada have been blamed on incipient tribalism. Middle Eastern despotisms are sometimes described as "tribes with flags." Almost the worst thing one can say about a conflict anywhere in the world is that it reflects a reversion to tribalism.

Africans rightly complain that Western images of tribal life reflect the prejudices of the colonial era. From Tarzan the ape-man to movies like *Zulu,* in which screaming hordes of tribesmen overrun the calmly reloading British regulars, our image of the tribe is that of something dark and primitive. Squalid, poor, and ignorant, the tribe as we imagine it subordinates the individual and suffocates his will to self-expression. Needless to say, this image of the tribe is based on ignorance, half-truths, and racial prejudice. We have a very shallow understanding of life in a tribal society. Tribes are not amorphous groups of people milling about in the jungle, dancing and shaking their spears. They are well-defined, self-regulating entities, structured as a series of interlocking kinship groups. The largest unit of tribal society is the *clan.* The clan develops out of the extended-family structure called the *lineage.* The lineage is a collection of *extended families* united by common descent. These corporate entities are cultural inventions—nepotistic adaptations that developed in response to the problems posed by the invention of agriculture about ten thousand years ago.

The discovery of agricultural and pastoral techniques led to the first permanent settlements. It also raised pressing questions that put an immediate strain on the simple organization of the human band. How would the ownership and use of land be regulated? How would group membership be defined and rights to property transmitted? As populations multiplied and spread, how would the group maintain its unity? Early humans had discovered that they could use the bonds of kinship to meet their basic needs for reproduction and survival. Neolithic humans took the use of nepotistic bonds to the next level. By manipulating rules of marriage and descent, they created what anthropologists call corporate descent groups, or lineages.

All of us belong to a descent group of some kind. Even Americans, who have very little consciousness of kinship, have a clearly definable kin group. The size and character of our kindred depends on the *descent rule* we apply. The simplest rule, and the one that we apply, is called *bilateral descent.* A bilateral kin group includes all of an individual's biological relatives: his father and mother, grandparents, great-grandparents, and all of their descendants on both sides. Bilateralism is ideal for small-scale hunter-gatherer societies, where harsh ecological conditions prohibit the formation of large groups (though not all hunter-gatherer societies are bilateral). It is also most appropriate for our own industrialized society, in which the small, highly mobile nuclear family is once again the most adaptive unit. As we have seen, however, kin selection quickly weakens as a cohesive force beyond a circle of close relatives. Each person in a bilateral system occupies the center of his or her own kinship sphere, which does not overlap with anyone else's except for those of full siblings. Therefore, when the population boom brought about by the agricultural revolution created a need to organize growing populations into larger self-governing units, bilateralism gave way to social groupings based on lineal descent.[4]

Lineal systems divide the field of kinship into artificial groups defined by descent from only one parent, the mother or father. In a patrilineal society, a man's father, siblings, and other paternal relatives belong to his primary kin group; his mother and her relatives do not. People still recognize their maternal kin, but for inheritance and other practical purposes these relatives do not really count. The result is a series of large, nonoverlapping corporate groups that have clear boundaries, stable membership, and the potential for organized action. Such lineages are capable of limitless expansion. Lineage organization is also well suited to the control and transmission of property, especially farmland, herds, and the sorts of skills that may be passed down from father to son—economic, priestly, and political. A group of related lineages constitutes a clan, and a "family" of clans make up a tribe. Lineal tribes are typically loose village federations; stateless and egalitarian, they regulate their internal lives according to the nepotistic patterns of the family and clan.[5]

The male or female bias of the lineage is a function of ecology. Patrilineage is typical of pastoral and hunting societies that remain fairly mobile and depend on cooperative labor among fathers, sons, and brothers. Matrilineage is found in small-scale agricultural societies where the most important work is done by women; women also own the lands and other property, which pass to their descendants in the female line.[6] The patrilineal African family typically consists of a patriarchal father living in a walled compound with his wives and children, their families, and other relatives in a group that may total sixty people and span up to four generations. An African village is an assemblage of such compounds, divided into wards inhabited by members of the same lineage. The village may be composed of unrelated lineages, but everyone in it belongs to a household, every household belongs to a lineage, and every lineage belongs to a clan.

The African father presides over the family hearth and the worship of the ancestral spirits. In his pioneering studies of religion, Sir James Frazer suggested that ancestral cults originated in primitive fear of the dead. Early humans assumed that the spirits of dead relatives had the power to help or punish them, depending on how they were treated. The purpose of the sacrificial cult was to placate the spirits' jealousy and anger and enlist their aid by offering gifts of food. These sacrifices may be seen as efforts to manipulate the spirits by ensnaring them in gift relations with the living. By inviting them to share our meal we bring them into our family circle and oblige them to treat us nepotistically. Ancestral cults were practiced in other ancient civilizations and continued to be central to the life of classical Western societies. Unconscious survivals of ancestor worship may even be seen in many modern dynastic families.

The nepotism of the clan is much more coercive than that of the band, and lineal societies have many complex rules and regulations. Clan and lineage membership defines where you may live, since (due to their connection with farmland) many descent groups are also residential units. All property is owned by the clan—individuals are merely its custodians. Religious and political authority is vested in the clan, and it is also a means of recruitment for war. Lineage and clan members are required to help and support one another and are responsible for one another's actions. When one commits a crime, the whole clan shares the cost of compensation; if a clansman is harmed or killed, all his brothers are obliged to seek revenge.

Feuding is the bane of tribal societies, and it forms a large part of their negative image today. The feud embodies the negative aspect of the reciprocal altruism that unites kin-based societies. Yet there is also evidence that in tribal societies—like that of the Nuer, studied by E. E. Evans-Pritchard—the threat of retribution helps maintain internal peace. Transgressors know that retaliation not only will be swift and sure, but may lead to a cycle of violence that can spread to other villages and soon spiral out of control. Even in Western societies, it took centuries for national states to put an end to clan-based feuding and impose the rule of law.

Tribal politics is an extension of relations within the family and clan. The lineage head is an elder chosen for his qualities of leadership and sometimes referred to simply as "he who knows best." Though it may or may not be hereditary, the office carries no coercive power. But this generally isn't necessary in a society where the authority of elders is such that a simple word of correction is enough to return most individuals to the path of expected behavior. These and other self-regulating aspects of tribal societies have led many anthropologists to stress their peaceful and egalitarian character.

The embryonic African state usually develops around the village chieftancy at a point where growing disparities in wealth allow the head of a dominant lineage to assert his authority beyond his kin group. When a chiefdom grows wealthier and more powerful than its neighbors, the loose village confederacy becomes a statelet headed by a king with powers of life and death and a retinue of wives, courtiers, appointed officials, and bodyguards. His circle of supporters, drawn from his own lineage and clan, constitutes the germ of an aristocratic ruling class. Plural marriage enlarges the king's kindred and establishes alliances with other powerful clans. In this way, the monarch becomes the hub of a vast network of nepotism that welds the nation into a giant family, or superclan. The use of polygamous marriage turns nepotism into a legitimating ideology—a paternalistic fiction in which the king is seen as father of the nation.

The European colonial powers adapted this paternalistic ideology to their own purposes. Most successful were the British, who quickly learned that the best way for a tiny administrative elite to dominate a large native society was to govern through existing social structures. Sociologist George Ayittey observes that so long as Europeans accommodated themselves to the kin-based structure of African politics they enjoyed good relations with Africans for four hundred years. After they tried to impose European institutions, carving up African territories at the Berlin Conference of 1880, they were expelled in less than a century.

Western observers often say that the nation-state has failed in Africa: the arbitrary division of the continent by the retreating colonial powers has exploded in a bewildering array of tribal, ethnic, linguistic, and religious identities. The state itself, instead of fairly adjudicating conflicts, has become an instrument for systematic looting and exploitation by the dominant group. The result, all too often, is bureaucratic paralysis, economic breakdown, and social collapse. African leaders such as former Ivory Coast president Félix Houphouët-Boigny often pin the blame on tribalism. But the very leaders who most loudly denounce tribalism often surround themselves with members of their own tribe. Opposition leaders who attack the tribalism of the dominant group are usually no better.[7]

Yet while such nepotism may arouse resentment, it is not seen as morally wrong, because it springs from obligations that most Africans still share. Indeed, Stanislav Andreski notes that there are really two kinds of corruption in developing societies: "solidaristic" graft, which aims at benefiting kin, and "egoistic" graft, which seeks only private enrichment. In Somalia, where urbanization and development have made little impact, graft remains solidaristic—with the result that its proceeds are widely distributed. In the cities of West Africa, teeming with detribalized and rootless individuals, corruption is more egoistic. Such people "tend to have few scruples of any kind, and eagerly and ruthlessly seize every opportunity to make illegal gains while shirking their duties towards their kin."[8]

Westerners seem to expect African societies to make the leap from tribalism to modernity without the intervening phases of feudalism and nationalism. Unlike Europe, however, in Africa national states have been imposed on tribal societies still based on Ancient Nepotism. It is both unrealistic and dangerous to break up these nepotistic solidarities with nothing to put in their place. Yet the tone of much Western reporting on Africa remains profoundly patronizing, and the use of terms like "backward," "benighted," and "intolerant" hints at a deeper psychological aversion to the tribe itself. These loaded terms reflect our view that African nepotism is rooted not simply in greed and ambition—vices we can readily understand—but in tribal loyalties we find alien and threatening. Nepotism to us is one more proof of continuing African darkness.

CHINA: THE GENIUS OF THE CLAN

Historians marvel at the unity, stability, and continuity of Chinese civilization over a period of three thousand years. This remarkable achievement is usually credited to the powerful and distinctive complex of social values at the heart of Chinese culture. Less often mentioned is that culture's foundation in an even older system of extended families, lineages, and clans. Like other ancient civilizations, China emerged out of tribal structures going back beyond the dawn of written history. But China's subsequent development appears to be unique, passing from tribalism to feudalism to an imperial-bureaucratic social order that speeded the adoption of Chinese culture by a dazzling diversity of peoples. Other Asian, African, and Near Eastern societies went through a similar process, but only to the point of feudal monarchies of limited size and duration. What allowed the development of a vast and powerful empire in China was the balance it achieved at an early stage between nepotistic solidarity and bureaucratic rationality. Without an efficient national bureaucracy, the huge terrain of China could never have been unified long enough to achieve the cultural uniformity that bound this huge society together for thousands of years. The ultimate source of that system is the philosophy of Confucius, whose achievement was to translate the values of Ancient Nepotism into a rigorous ethical doctrine that balanced filial piety with principles of merit.

The ultimate origins of Chinese civilization are shrouded in myth, but it undoubtedly evolved from neolithic societies based on the lineage, clan, and tribe. The first Chinese kingdom to leave historical records was created about the middle of the second millennium B.C. by the Shang, a warrior caste that ruled a simple agricultural society characterized by slavery and serfdom. The Shang state was rudimentary, little more than a group of noble families that controlled the military, religious, and political functions of government. Royal power was an extension of the king's patriarchal authority over his clan, disseminated through a vast patronage network forged out of kinship and marriage alliances and unified by the worship of a common mythological ancestor, Shang-Ti. The ability to create and exploit such kinlike bonds for political ends was one of the great strengths of early Chinese civilization. Because these ties were personal, however, the monarch was obliged to spend his time roaming the kingdom paying formal visits to the aristocratic clans through whom he exercised his power. With no fixed capital or national bureaucracy, this tribal state was primitive and weak. But while the Shang were eventually displaced, the nepotistic basis of their social and political order was preserved by subsequent dynasties.

In time the Shang were supplanted by northern invaders called the Chou. The first Chou monarch, Wen the Civilized, was succeeded by his son, who was succeeded by his uncle, the "sagacious" duke of Chou. The duke greatly extended the borders of the kingdom and established its administrative system; he is also credited with founding the characteristic ritual, music, and other arts of Chou civilization. The Chou presided over a vast domain of widely scattered city-states, often separated by natural obstacles and hostile barbarian tribes. Since they could not rule such a kingdom directly, they parceled out their holdings among their relatives, who were allowed a free hand so long as they provided yearly tribute. Like the Shang, therefore, the Chou king governed China as the head of a large extended family.

As the Chou dynasty declined, China entered a long crisis known as the Period of Warring States. Constant warfare brought social and moral chaos in its wake: legitimate rulers were murdered by their ministers, wives were abducted by powerful lords, adultery and incest were reported, corruption and bribery spread, and even relatives could not trust one another. As though to signal the utter collapse of nepotistic bonds, in 593 B.C. the citizens of Sung were besieged for so long that they were reduced to eating their children. (Because they couldn't bear to eat their own, however, they exchanged children with their neighbors before killing them.) Such was the turbulent world in which Confucius was born.

Confucius was not an ivory-tower intellectual but a reformer and activist who developed his ethical philosophy in response to the breakdown and collapse of the clan-based feudal system in his lifetime. Born in 551 B.C. to an impoverished noble family in the eastern state of Lu, he was three when his father died, yet somehow he acquired an education and spent many years as a clerk in the service of local aristocratic families. Like others of his time, Confucius (his proper name is K'ung Ch'iu) had been brought up to revere the great Chou kings, especially the noble duke of Chou, since it was his eldest son, Po Ch'in, who had founded the state of Lu with a grant of six clans from his father. This story underscores the importance of the clan as the basic unit of Chinese society. If you are going to start a colony, the best procedure is to bring along a few hundred families organized in ready-made, self-governing units. That way you can more easily transplant the social order of your homeland to the soil of the new colony.

Confucius saw himself not as a philosophical innovator but as the reviver of an ancient code of ethics propounded by the great Chou monarchs. His specialty as a teacher was the training of young men for official careers through the study of poetry, music, and ritual, but his larger purpose was to restore China to its former glory as an ordered society based on reverence for the family and ancestors. The fame of his teaching soon spread, and he attracted a school of followers, including many sons of noble families.

Confucianism is not a religion but an ethical system based on filial piety: the bond between father and son is the model for all social and political relationships. The master principle of Confucian philosophy, *hsiao,* consists in putting the needs of one's parents first, deferring to their judgment, and observing the prescribed behavioral and ritual proprieties. Confucius cited *hsiao* as the basis of *jen* ("humanity"), the cultivated love of other people that was the Confucian moral ideal. The essence of this teaching was *reciprocity,* or treating others as you would have them treat you.

Confucianism was not a democratic philosophy but an ethos of legitimate authority: sons owed obedience to their fathers, and fathers owed obedience to the king. Only when relations in both family and state were based on righteousness and love could society be ordered as it should. As a good father made good sons, so a good ruler made good subjects. Confucius recognized that the virtues of filial piety and fraternal affection learned in the family were of great importance to good government. Correct behavior beyond the family was merely an extension of filial virtues to society at large. When asked why he was not more active in public affairs, Confucius replied that to be a good son and brother was itself a contribution to good government. One of his most famous sayings, when asked how one might go about reforming the state, was, "Let fathers be fathers, and let sons be sons."

Confucius never held a high official post of any consequence. He lived and died a relatively poor and humble man, a quixotic reformer who never realized his dream of refounding the state on higher nepotistic principles. After his death, his students dispersed, achieving distinction in the service of great families and establishing their own schools. A series of texts were produced, including the *Analects*, or sayings of the master, and the five Confucian classics. Of these, the most important was undoubtedly the work known as the *Classic of Filial Piety*. Using the examples of great kings renowned for their piety and virtue, the book presents the ideal ruler as the father of his people and his subjects as obedient children. The five classics became the basis of all Chinese education, and thereby exercized an enormously stabilizing and unifying effect on Chinese history.

Confucius's vision of the good society as a harmonious family was beautiful but deeply impractical. Confucianism was born in the breakdown of feudal society and represented a reactionary attempt to reestablish its paternalistic order. This was no longer possible, however: China was already very large and needed a stable ruling structure. Under a series of emperors, China was unified politically, administratively, and culturally. The emperors built a network of roads and canals and imposed uniform laws and cultural standards, but their greatest creation was the national bureaucracy. Under the Han dynasty, Confucian scholar-officials instituted a system of schools and rigorous examinations for entry and advancement in the state. Confucianism became the ethos of Chinese bureaucracy and in time the official state cult. The system of imperial rule supported by Confucian bureaucracy and education held China together for the next two thousand years.

Dynasties have come and gone but the family and clan remain the foundation of Chinese society. Though ultimately all Chinese would be incorporated in clans, for a long time they were mainly the province of the upper class. Commoners did not concern themselves with relatives beyond their locality, but members of aristocratic lineages maintained wide kin connections and took great pains to document their genealogies. All clans were ranked, and since access to political office and other privileges was distributed on this basis, the government took the lead in drawing up, authenticating, and publishing official genealogical tables.

Clans of this type do not arise spontaneously but are a conscious creation, requiring extraordinary dedication and sacrifice from one generation to the next. The stimulus for the creation of a clan usually came from men of the scholar-official class, who organized their kin in a "great family" structure in order to further their political ambitions. Just as often, however, poor rural folk would approach an educated relative and solicit his leadership.

The first step in founding a clan was the creation of a register. Then came a written genealogy, the election of officers, the purchase of a common burial ground, and the construction of an ancestral hall. The head of a large clan was a potentate—a godfather figure who had a share in local government and distributed the proceeds to his family and friends. Families who formed themselves into clans not only increased their power and influence but were eligible for grants of special authority, tax exemptions, and access to official positions for their educated members. The clan was a powerful engine of social mobility, a ladder by which men could climb to heaven, drawing their relatives up after them.

Successful Chinese clans were strictly ordered. Contributions were expected from all members, officers were elected in regular meetings, and a rigid code of behavior was enforced. Elaborate genealogies listed the clan's illustrious ancestors and included prefaces on the clan's aristocratic origins, essays expounding on the virtues of family harmony, information on clan ritual, and the rules of the clan. These rules represented Confucianism in action and concerned the proper conduct of parents and children, brothers and sisters, and husbands and wives. They promoted the Confucian virtues of modesty, honesty, caution, and self-restraint. Arrogance, pride, and self-will were condemned, as were drinking, gambling, and recourse to prostitutes. Conspicuous acts of charity and filial piety, gifts of property to the clan, and other meritorious actions were commended; support for widows, orphans, and the elderly, the education of young men, and dowries for poor daughters were often required. Members were enjoined to be careful in their choice of friends, to be charitable and deferential toward neighbors, avoid disputes, obey the law, pay taxes promptly, and bring neither disgrace nor envy on the clan.

As in Africa, the core of the Chinese clan was the ancestral cult. Sacrifices were made to male ancestors in the four preceding generations, and so important was it for a man to have an heir to mourn him that men with extra sons were expected to offer them to their sonless brothers and cousins. For a man to remain a bachelor was considered unfilial, and rules for the selection of spouses and the provision of heirs were of signal importance. The rules also dealt with relations between the clan's branches, the administration of common property, and reward or punishment of clan members. Filial impiety was punishable by flogging. Adultery and physical assault were also grave offenses. Quarreling, dissension, gossip, and wifely interference were strongly discouraged. Punishments ranged from oral censure and fines to corporal punishment, forfeiture of privileges, or expulsion.

In China, where familism has been a way of life for thousands of years, problems associated with nepotism unavoidably arose—most visibly in the arena of imperial succession. Like the tribal kings of Africa, Chinese monarchs forged polygamous alliances that linked the branches of their clan and allied them with other powerful clans throughout China. Given the vastness of the empire, the size of the royal harem was immense (the first Ch'in emperor reportedly had three thousand wives and concubines), and harem politics—driven by the fierce passions of maternal nepotism—was ferociously competitive. Royal favorites had enormous power, and their fathers or brothers were often appointed to high office regardless of qualifications. Senior officials might present an attractive daughter or niece for the emperor's enjoyment, and many favored concubines also promoted their family's interest. When a monarch was succeeded by an infant son, queen mothers and their relatives assumed complete control of the government.

The other problem area was that of the imperial bureaucracy. The creation of a civil service was akin to tossing a live cow into a school of piranhas. The noble families swarmed around it, biting off chunks for themselves and their kinsmen. If not prevented, the noble clans would have turned it into a hereditary fief. Accordingly, the Neo-Confucian officials of the Sung dynasty instituted an even more rigorous system of entry and advancement tests and discouraged favoritism by making sponsors liable for their protégés' performance. Yet various factors conspired to limit the effectiveness of these reforms. For one thing, the emperors continued to use the bureaucracy for patronage: the civil service provided a convenient means of repaying political debts. In addition, senior officials were allowed the privilege of filling a certain number of "protected" slots, and a single official might bring in twenty kinsmen or more. Ultimately, the civil service was coopted by a tight-knit group of clans, whose branches might continue to supply government officials for ten generations or more.

In their efforts to keep the civil service free of nepotism, the emperors were hampered by the very nature of Chinese society. A Chinese official was in a position to greatly benefit his family and was encouraged to do so by immemorial tradition. As the Chinese proverb goes, "When a man becomes an official, his wife, children, dogs, cats, and even chickens fly up to heaven." Since officials were not paid very much, the government frequently turned a blind eye to the practice. Ultimately, however, nepotism came to be perceived as a serious problem, and in a number of cases, examiners who tried to favor their relatives were put to death. Finally the persistence of nepotistic corruption led the emperors to try a novel experiment, turning over many functions of the state to a cadre of eunuchs.

Chinese monarchs had employed eunuchs as far back as the eighth century B.C., but the practice was undoubtedly much older and stemmed from the need for a polygamous king to ensure the paternity of his heirs. Traditional Chinese historians condemn eunuchs as corrupt and power hungry, but most such chronicles were written by members of the Confucian elite, who despised eunuchs as a class. Confucius himself had condemned the use of eunuchs and declared them both ignoble and untrustworthy, since a man who chose to emasculate himself had severed his link with his ancestors. A eunuch was especially shameful since he had no son to perform the customary rites for his soul after death.[9]

The emperors seem to have viewed their palace eunuchs as selflessly loyal, and many were indeed able and devoted retainers who preserved their thrones against organized official factions or the clans of royal consorts. But history also shows that the eunuchs' reputation for honesty, docility, and loyalty was largely unfounded; many used public office to accumulate enormous fortunes; others intrigued to disastrous effect in dynastic politics. Eunuchs were especially adept at manipulating the nepotistic rivalries of the harem. They were also able to dominate the many impressionable child emperors who had been raised by them and trusted them completely.

The experiment with eunuchs sheds revealing light on the long attempt in Western societies to replace the family in public life with an impersonal regime of bureaucratic efficiency. The emperors assumed that a man without sons of his own has no reason for corruption: like a sterile hymenopteran drone, his loyalty would be wholly attached to the sovereign. But even eunuchs have families, and (like the celibate "fathers" of the Catholic Church) many enriched themselves and showered benefits on their relatives. Moreover, as the size and luxury of court life increased, many enterprising families had one of their sons castrated in order to be eligible for palace employment. Ultimately eunuchs became such a destabilizing force that in the end, the cure for nepotism may be said to have been worse than the disease. Nevertheless, the practice was widely imitated in the ancient world, and eunuchs were found in great numbers in the Roman, Byzantine, and Ottoman bureaucracies.

Many of the most successful revolutionaries—like the mythological Moses or the historical Augustus and Napoleon—have been social reactionaries who sought to strengthen or restore the traditional family; in contrast, some of the most conspicuous failures have been social progressives who tried to remake the family in their image. Confucius was the former type: by abstracting the nepotistic principles embodied in the traditions of the well-ordered Chinese family into an all-embracing practical philosophy, he achieved a balance between nepotistic solidarity and bureaucratic rationality that allowed the development of a vast and powerful empire. The communist revolution of Mao Zedong, in contrast, sought to break up the family and replace it with the state. Though successful in the short run, the experiment proved disastrous and, in the long run, unsustainable.

For thousands of years the Chinese state had relied on families and clans to maintain social order, and had supported their authority with laws that enforced filial piety. Starting in 1949, the Chinese communists launched a campaign to reduce the influence of families and break up the authority of clans. This had long been Mao's ambition: as early as 1917 he had written, "To replace the family with the nation—this is audacity." He also spoke of abolishing the gerontocratic clan system and the authority of the "evil clan elders." Many of these reforms were well intentioned: freedom of marriage and divorce liberated Chinese women from the control of their fathers and husbands. Others deprived the clan of its traditional social roles. Clan-based militias were disbanded, and the elders' councils that were the traditional basis of local authority were replaced by revolutionary peasants' councils and women's and youth associations. Clans were also relieved of responsibility for maintaining local schools, repairing roads, and building dams and irrigation systems. Land reforms deprived the clans of property and redistributed it to poorer peasants.

The first generation of communist youth enthusiastically embraced the new regime, and many joined the party with the encouragement of parents who viewed the party apparatus as a new means of upward mobility. But during the Cultural Revolution of the 1960s (representing a struggle between Maoist radicals and "conservatives"), these trends went too far, and a political caste system was created based on each family's historical background, with those who had landowning or capitalist forebears consigned to the bad-class category. This had the effect, among other things, of dividing the interests of parents and children. It became necessary for many children to conceal their family history, and in some cases children denounced their parents as reactionaries in order to establish their revolutionary bona fides. Others used the campaign as an excuse to attack their teachers, local officials, or other authority figures. Many historians now regard the Cultural Revolution as a youth rebellion run amok.

One particularly affecting account of the communist attempt to denature Chinese society is the memoir *Wild Swans* by Jung Chang. In 1949, Jung's mother married Wang Shou-yu, a young communist official who was a paragon of socialist virtue. Wang refused to use his position to help his family. He made his wife—also a communist official—walk on a long journey while he rode in a government car, and demoted her two grades in rank just to forestall accusations of favoritism. He also vetoed his brother's promotion in a state-run tea-marketing business. As Matt Ridley remarks, "Communism would have worked if there were more such men, though it would have been a bleak kind of success in which people could not be nice to their relatives. But most people are not like Wang Shou-yu. Indeed, given their immunity from criticism, Communist officials have consistently proved more corruptible and more nepotistic than democratic ones. Universal benevolence evaporates on the stove of human nature."[10]

Ridley is not the first to notice the paradoxical fact that nepotism flourishes in communist bureaucracies. The Soviet *nomenklatura* was famous for its nepotism: beginning in the 1920s and even earlier, children of party officials were enrolled in special schools, often studied abroad, and enjoyed the best assignments in the country's foreign service. The family of Nicolae Ceauşescu dominated communist Romania for decades until they were ousted in a democratic coup. In North Korea, Kim Il Sung became the envy of communist dictators everywhere when he managed to pass supreme power to his son, Kim Jong Il. Likewise, nepotism is rife within the Chinese Communist Party, and it is one of the issues that sparked the democratic protests at Tiananmen Square in 1989.

Chinese leaders from Mao to Deng Xiaoping have denounced nepotism and promised to end it. Party officials periodically announce programs to curb nepotism, promulgate new rules, and send inspectors around the provinces, but these initiatives do little to dislodge the "red aristocracy" that has taken hold since the first revolutionary generation. Mao himself, the son of a peasant farmer, urged party officials to put the interests of the state above their families. Nevertheless, many top leaders enjoy their positions due to family connections: former president Jiang's uncle was an early communist leader, and Premier Li Peng was the adopted son of Chou En-lai. Deng also did well for his children, and other officials have followed his lead.[11] The result is a new class of "princelings" who are proving a major embarrassment. The party princelings are called *yanei,* meaning children of the local magistrate, a term of resentment that dates from the fourteenth century. By 1991, as many as five thousand *yanei* held prominent posts in the government, the military, or state-owned institutions.

The Western press clearly enjoys these tales of communist bedevilment by the irrepressible spirit of human selfishness, and an unmistakable tone of schadenfreude pervades most coverage of the subject. The reason is not hard to understand. For most of the twentieth century, communists claimed to be creating not just a new society but a new kind of man, free of the vices that private property and individualism had bred in the decadent Western bourgeois. The all too human vice of nepotism allows us to deflate their tiresome sermons, revealing one more way in which the communist project has failed. But it also illustrates an important truth about nepotism: in states with too much power, no less than in states with too little, nepotism has a tendency to run to extremes. If even the Chinese Communists couldn't get rid of it, what realistic hope have we of doing so?

INDIA: THE GORDIAN KNOT OF CASTE

In 333 B.C., after subduing Asia Minor, Alexander the Great passed through Anatolia in what is today northeastern Turkey. In the city of Gordium he was shown an ancient chariot with its yoke lashed to the pole by an intricate knot. According to local tradition, this knot could be untied only by the future conqueror of Asia. Legend has it that Alexander cut through the knot with his sword (though an earlier version has him simply withdrawing the pole). The Gordians were suitably impressed and Alexander continued on his way, bearing the prophecy out with his remarkable victories. Reaching the Indus valley in 326, he defeated the Indian king Porus and founded a city. How much farther he might have gone is a question that has fascinated posterity, but the patience of his soldiers was exhausted and he was obliged to turn back.

The episode of the Gordian knot presents a striking contrast between Western rationalism and Eastern deviousness and inscrutability—and seems to illustrate what happens when the two are brought together. But while Alexander left his mark on Western civilization, his conquest of northern India did not leave much of an impression. That ancient society was a Gordian knot of a different kind—tougher and more resistant than the one that he had sliced through with his sword. Indeed, while India has many times been conquered, it has defeated all attempts at reformation. Even under the hundred-year British Raj, the sword of Western bureaucratic rationalism was chipped and blunted on the Gordian knot of Hindu civilization.

This is hardly surprising in a culture steeped for thousands of years in the institutions of Ancient Nepotism. As in Africa and China, in India civilization emerged out of tribal traditions going back to the Neolithic era. The great national epics—the *Mahabharata* and *Ramayana*—date from the first millennium B.C., when nomadic pastoralism was giving way to a more settled pattern of village-based agricultural life, and they plainly reflect the importance of clan and tribal federations in the struggle for dynastic succession.[12] The tradition of dynastic rule runs so deep in modern India that it has been very hard to shake, and many leading politicians are the scions of great families that have long been influential in their region. Of all these families, none has been more important or representative than the Nehru-Gandhi clan. Jawaharlal Nehru was the first prime minister of independent India, the main author of its constitution, and the architect of an ambitious scheme of modernization that was intended to catapult India out of the agrarian dark ages into the era of industrial democracy. The unintended outcome of this project affords another object lesson in the resilience of Ancient Nepotism.

India, it has been said, is a nation of villages. Each village is a knot of occupational and ritual relationships, held together by the force of Ancient Nepotism: priests, landowners, tenant farmers, artisans, and servants are tightly woven in a web of kinship and kinlike relations based on blood and marriage, clanship, caste, and patronage.

The family is the center of Indian life, and most individuals live and die within its orbit. Intimate and lively, it is a self-contained world, autonomous in some respects but bound to other families in an endless round of celebrations, ceremonial occasions, and elaborate gift exchanges. As in Africa and China, most Indian families are compound groups comprising several generations, all living under one roof. They participate in common religious observances and have a share in the family's property. Since Hindu fathers are enjoined to retire from active life upon the marriage of their eldest son, many families are fratriarchies, ruled not by a domineering father but by an elder brother. Hence they depend even more upon the principles of fraternal harmony emphasized by Hindu culture, for if the brothers fell out, the family could be destroyed by the division of its patrimony. (In the *Mahabharata* two brothers quarrel over their inheritance and are reborn in their next lives as beasts.) Therefore rigid rules of behavior are required. A principle of seniority affirms the authority of the eldest brother, who will inherit the family property and assume the father's role. He is also the first to marry, and his wife has higher status than the wives of his younger brothers. Sexual temptation is prevented by elaborate rules of avoidance between young wives and their male in-laws. But the highest virtue is the reciprocal principle of mutual aid and sharing among brothers and other relatives, in good times and bad.

If harmony between brothers is important, that among women is even more so. The life of a Hindu woman is sharply divided: a brief happy period in her father's house, then the trauma of marriage to a stranger and entry into his household, where she will spend the rest of her life. Yet a woman's bonds with her natal kin remain strong, and the divided loyalties of the family's women are often the main source of trouble. According to Dr. Irawati Karve, the women "were at once the strength and weakness of the house."

> They were the strength because they fought with desperate courage on behalf of their husbands and sons. They were the weakness because in the case of a fight between their husbands and fathers, natural ties might make them side with their fathers. While it was the endeavor of a man to keep his sons

> united, each of the sons' wives wanted her husband to dominate and, failing that, to separate from the joint family with his share of the patrimony.[13]

In this way a multivalent female nepotism—attached in turn to fathers, husbands, and offspring—fuels the engine of both cohesion and conflict within the Hindu family.

Where kin groups function as an economic unit, the selection of a mate is a means of recruiting new workers; hence not only the parents but the whole extended family takes a lively interest in the qualifications of the prospective spouse. Mate selection requires a keen eye for desirable qualities and shrewd bargaining skills. Many myths of traditional societies involve the search for a suitable mate, often pitting qualifications of beauty and attractiveness against those of fortitude, patience, and skill. This might be thought of as the "Can she bake a cherry pie?" aspect of marriage. Arranged marriages have a bad reputation in Western societies, but from the Hindu perspective one must admit they make eminent sense. Nor is the outcome necessarily unhappy. Mohandas K. Gandhi and his wife met for the first time on their wedding day, when they were both thirteen, and remained devoted to each other for the rest of their lives.

When a new wife enters the household she faces immediate tensions. She is bossed around by her mother-in-law, spied on by her husband's younger sisters, and ignored or treated coldly by the males. Many Hindu songs and proverbs reflect pityingly on this torment for young girls. Everything changes when she gives birth to a child and comes into her own as a mother and wife. In later life, especially if she marries the eldest son, she plays a role of real importance in the family, and if her husband dies she can become a female despot, bossing the whole household, including her husband's aged parents.

Such families obviously require an orderly approach to succession, and this is supplied by the Hindu doctrine of *asrama*, or the four stages of life. According to Hindu tradition, a man's life is divided into four parts. In early childhood he is treated with great indulgence and is showered with affection from all sides. At eight he enters the period of celibate study, during which he takes instruction in the sacred texts and learns his father's trade. At twenty he marries and assumes the status of a householder, which lasts until his eldest son reaches the same grade. He then enters the final phase of the cycle, giving himself up to meditation and worship, supported by his children. The most praiseworthy Hindus are those who renounce worldly possessions altogether and withdraw into ascetic contemplation. This arrangement smoothes the transition of authority from one generation to the next. Sons owe their fathers absolute obedience in the first stage of life, but fathers are equally obliged to retire gracefully, thereby avoiding both the evils of gerontocracy and the inevitable revolt of the younger generation. (The Mahabharata War was the outcome of an aged king's refusal to observe these life-cycle conventions.)

Closely connected with *asrama* is the theory of life called "the three debts." According to Hindu tradition, each man is born with three debts he must repay in order to reach heaven: a debt to his ancestors, a debt to the sages, and a debt to the gods. The first he repays by marrying and founding a family. The second is paid through respect for the sages and the study of sacred lore, and the third by daily worship and the performance of sacrifices. Failure to repay these debts forces a man to repeat the whole process until he succeeds: release from the cycle of reincarnation will come, Dr. Karve explains, "only when the terrible creditors are fully satisfied." Since marriage and the begetting of sons are a religious obligation, to remain unmarried or childless is a source of great shame. A bachelor does not enter heaven but becomes a ghost. If a woman dies a spinster, a marriage ceremony might be performed with the corpse and she could then be cremated with the honors due a married woman.

The Hindu joint family is not much different from the compound families of Africa and China. The difference lies in the number of corporate identity groups to which it belongs. Clans were important as mutual aid units in Indian villages but they did not, as in China, develop into independent economic or political actors. Instead, Indian society has traditionally been organized at the level of the caste. While caste exists in other places (in America the system of legally enforced segregation under Jim Crow approximated the workings of a caste), nowhere else has it been institutionalized with so many legal, religious, and political supports. But while much maligned by Westerners, the Hindu caste system is best understood as a creative response to the incredible ethnic, religious, and linguistic diversity of Indian society, integrating its many elements into an occupational hierarchy that both reflects and fosters nepotistic values: a living symbol of the Hindu view of life.[14]

In a section of the Rigveda (the oldest Vedic text) there is a poetic description of the four Hindu castes, or *varnas*, emerging from the body of the god Prajapati. The Brahmins, or priestly caste, emerged from his mouth; the Ksatriyas—the landowning class who supplied the political and military leaders—from his arms; the mercantile Vaisyas from his thighs; and the Sudras, or servant classes, from his feet. The rigid caste hierarchy of Indian society is thus a reflection of its Hindu cosmology. For Hindus, only the spirit is pure; anything to do with the body and its functions ("blood, death, and dirt") is impure. This concern with ritual purity translates into a social order in which occupations dealing with bodily emissions, the care and feeding of the body, or the bodies of the dead are consigned to the lower castes. Caste membership is ascribed by birth, and in keeping with the Hindu doctrine of reincarnation, it is considered a karmic reward for conduct in past lives.

Castes are usually viewed as economic groups based on a common occupation; but with their pattern of in-marriage and self-governing structures, they are more like clans or tribes.[15] What we call castes are compound entities comprised of *jatis*, or birth groups, made up of related families living in the same town or village. Because they must marry outside their local kin group, *jati* members choose wives from families of the same caste in other villages. Their mutual conduct is also imbued with the values of Ancient Nepotism. *Jati* members treat one another like kin and use kinship terms in addressing one another; thus all older men in the *jati* are called Father, Grandfather, or Uncle. A large village may have up to thirty such groups, including landowners, farmers, and priests; artisans like carpenters and blacksmiths; service groups including barbers and washermen; and menials such as sweepers and laborers who dig ditches, remove night soil, and dispose of dead animals. While the lower castes are despised and discriminated against in many ways, the complex web of mutual dependency limits the potential for abuse. Brahmins may be polluted by the touch of a butcher, water carrier, or midwife, but since they are enjoined from performing such tasks themselves, they are dependent on the lower castes to maintain their ritual purity.[16]

If families, clans, and castes are the structural elements of India's complex social system, the cords that bind it all together are the kinlike ties of patronage. In the absence of a cash economy, the artisan and servant castes perform their services for the priestly and landowning castes in exchange for an annual payment in grain. But the patron also performs political and economic favors for his client. The web of intercaste relations based on patronage is called *jajmani.* Once formed, *jajmani* relationships are permanent and can be passed on from father to son. (Thus a carpenter's clients might be divided at his death among his heirs.) Like relationships within the caste itself, *jajmani* relationships are modeled on kinship. While caste distance is maintained, the closeness and trust between the parties is like that between relatives, and kin terms are commonly used.

The patron-client relationship, of course, partakes of primitive gift relations. The whole caste system is pervaded by the spirit of the gift, and Marcel Mauss devoted several pages of his classic treatise to a discussion of the gift economy that has preserved social harmony in India for thousands of years. The Brahmins play a crucial role in the Hindu gift economy, for it is the religious duty of making gifts to the Brahmins that primes the cosmic pump. The Brahmins receive gifts of food from the other castes and make return in the form of religious services. The blessings that flow from these exchanges are thought to have a generative power that unites the whole caste system in the cycle of natural increase.[17]

The British had ruled India as they ruled their other colonies, by coopting the existing social structure. Though they introduced a uniform legal code and banned certain practices (such as the immolation of wives on their husbands' funeral pyre), they made little real attempt to change the cultural traditions of this vast and complicated society. The new government of independent India was not so humble. The founders of modern India were nationalist visionaries who wished to bring the country into the twentieth century as rapidly as possible. The leader of this Westernizing effort was the father of democratic India, Jawaharlal Nehru.

Like many leaders of the founding generation, Nehru was an educated Brahmin more English than Indian in his outlook. The son of a wealthy lawyer and political activist, he went to Harrow and Cambridge and spent two years in London becoming a barrister before returning to India. There he joined the Indian National Congress under the sponsorship of his father, who was one of Gandhi's principal lieutenants. Gandhi made him a leader of nationalist youth, and he ultimately replaced Gandhi as head of the Congress Party in 1942. After independence, Nehru became prime minister and was returned to office repeatedly until his death in 1964.[18]

A secular rationalist and Anglophile like his father, Nehru believed in the need for a Western-style administrative system based on merit and efficiency. He was particularly impressed with the apparent success of communist China and Russia in rapidly modernizing their vast agrarian societies. As a socialist, moreover, Nehru regarded the crosscutting distinctions of religion, caste, and tribe as ideological disguises for "objective" economic class relations. With the spread of socialist enlightenment and the progress of the national idea, these false identities would wither away and a stable two-party system would emerge, embodying the true identity and interests of the Indian majority.

In politics, Nehru stood firm for his principles. Despite Muslim fears of domination by the Hindu majority, he rejected appeals for political representation on religious, linguistic, or tribal grounds. The number of Indian states was arbitrarily reduced, which forced people of different backgrounds into unified administrative districts. Caste and its system of unequal privileges were banned by the new constitution, of which Nehru was the principal architect, along with other "irrational" practices. One of his proudest achievements was the reform of the ancient Hindu civil code that finally enabled widows to enjoy equality with men in matters of inheritance. He also staked out India's position as a leader in the movement of nonaligned nations, which sought neutrality during the Cold War. (His ideological loyalties remained with the Soviet Union, however.)

Indira, Nehru's only child, studied at Oxford and in 1938 joined the National Congress party. (In 1942 she married Feroze Gandhi—no relation to the Mahatma—a lawyer who died in 1960.) When Nehru became prime minister, Indira acted as his official hostess, secretary, and confidante; a growing power behind the scenes, she finally served as Congress Party president. Though plainly grooming her for a public career, Nehru seemed alert to the danger of creating a dynasty, and he made sure that his successor was chosen by free and open methods. Nehru told an interviewer, "I am not capable of ruling from the grave. How terrible it would be if I, after all I have said about the processes of democratic government, were to attempt to handpick a successor." Like it or not, however, it was inevitable that the father of his country would leave a potent legacy for his descendants to exploit.

After Nehru's death, Indira became minister of information in Lal Bahadur Shastri's government. When Shastri died in 1966, party leaders chose Indira to succeed him, expecting her to be a passive figurehead. Instead she engineered a party takeover and made herself undisputed head of the government. As prime minister for the next eleven years, Indira's policies were largely an extension of her father's: populist socialism in economics and nonalignment in the Cold War. But though popular with the masses, she felt threatened and insecure, and these tendencies, combined with her near-mystical belief in the historic mission and importance of her family, produced a marked authoritarian demeanor.

Initially, her elder son, Rajiv, showed no interest in politics. Instead it was Sanjay, the "spoiled and tyrannical" younger child, on whom Indira pinned her hopes. Although he went to the nation's most expensive private schools, he never finished university. Instead he had his mother get him a job at England's Rolls-Royce factory and at twenty-three obtained a government license to create a "people's car." The outcry against Sanjay's license continued for years, but Mrs. Gandhi was so firmly in control that she was able to ignore it.

In 1975, Indira was convicted on charges of electoral fraud; declaring a national emergency, she suspended the constitution, imposed press censorship, and imprisoned her opponents. In the ensuing period of open dictatorship, she pushed through numerous programs intended to benefit the poor and modernize India. Sanjay toured the provinces issuing orders in her name. He was clearly being groomed for succession, but at a vastly accelerated pace. Like his mother, Sanjay was impatient with constitutional process and (like his grandfather) with Indian reality itself. In a move that would have horrified Gandhi, he launched a modernization program consisting of mass vasectomy, bulldozing slums, abolition of dowries, and compulsory schooling. These high-handed policies were interpreted as an attack on the family, the home, and marriage itself, making Sanjay overnight the most hated man in India.

Indira's sweeping defeat in 1977 was blamed on her indulgence of Sanjay. Yet three years later she was reelected at the head of her own party. Sanjay was also elected, and began building his own faction in congress. When Indira made him secretary general, it was a clear sign that she intended him to succeed her.[19] Later that year, however, Sanjay was killed in a plane crash, and Rajiv was now drawn into politics, easily winning his dead brother's seat. Four years later, after his mother was assassinated by Sikh nationalists, the forty-year-old Rajiv was thrust into her place. Rajiv proved a serious and capable leader, committed to modernization and rooting out corruption. But soon the very qualities of outsider and neophyte that had made him seem like a fresh breeze began to make him unpopular. In 1989 he was defeated, and in 1991, Rajiv Gandhi was assassinated by Tamil separatists—like his mother, falling victim to the forces of ethnic particularism that his family had opposed for three generations.

Americans like to believe that people of different ethnic backgrounds should be able to live together amicably in a pluralist society. Yet only in America do ethnic identities melt and merge in a hybrid majority culture. Even in the European democracies, national unity is based on an underlying sense of solidarity and a fiction of kinship that some scholars have called "ethnic nepotism."[20] America, too, owes more to the nepotistic solidarity of its ethnic and immigrant groups than is often acknowledged. The political history of modern India affords a striking example of the challenges posed by ethnic nepotism in a diverse democratic society.

The first and greatest failure of Indian national politics occurred soon after independence. Mainly as a result of Nehru's refusal to accede to the creation of a Muslim political party, agitation and civil violence increased until in 1947 the country had to be partitioned and a Muslim state of Pakistan created. Administrative attempts to reduce the number of linguistic and ethnic states were also fought tooth and nail, resulting—after thirty years of separatist violence—in the actual expansion of such states. Nor has the party system matured into a pure reflection of class and ideological interests. Instead the system is fragmented and the number of parties is growing larger, with demands for representation on ethnic, religious, linguistic, and other grounds.[21]

Nor has caste disappeared as expected. Caste identity remains strong, and marriages are rarely contracted outside the individual's birth group. A powerful illustration came in January 2001, when a massive earthquake in Gujarat killed over twenty thousand people and left a million more injured or homeless. Though caste-based discrimination has been illegal for decades, six different refugee camps were set up, segregated by caste and religion. Relief workers complained that aid supplies went first to the upper castes and did not get distributed equally to the lower castes: an extraordinary testament to the survival of caste in the face of over fifty years of legal and political pressure. Meanwhile, India's strong tradition of extended kinship was helping to absorb the thousands of children who had been orphaned by the quake.[22]

If India's political history provides evidence for the power of ethnic nepotism, the commercial success of Indians abroad gives even more. In the nineteenth century, Indians followed the British flag around the world and established themselves as economic middlemen throughout Asia and East Africa. According to Joel Kotkin, as early as the 1920s Indian family networks had made major inroads in southern China, Burma, Malaysia, and Japan. Today's Indians have created thriving commercial colonies around the world. The Marawaris—a Rajasthani mercantile caste—organize their businesses around the joint family and use it as a base in their travels. The Sindhis, who constitute a million-member diaspora in Asia, Africa, Europe, and North America, are unusually insular, living together in large communal houses. The Jains, a highly ascetic religious sect who specialize in diamonds, have colonies in Tel Aviv, Antwerp, and New York. Sikhs are concentrated in Britain and North America. Muslim Ismailis and Gujarati Hindus are found throughout East Africa and elsewhere in the developing world. Parsis have been the vanguard of Indian capitalism: adherents of a Zoroastrian faith that emphasizes Calvinist virtues of thrift, hard work, and education, they were among the first Indians to send their sons to Britain. Even the most influential of all Indian business empires, that of the Harilelas, remains a family enterprise dependent on a global kinship network.

Author Ved Mehta writes that nepotism has always been practiced in India, "from high to low, from Prime Minister to sweeper. It is sanctified by the caste system and by religion—by karma and dharma (destiny and duty). Indians even make a rational defense of nepotism, and claim that it is legitimate—not corrupt at all." In a country where a want ad for the humblest government clerkship draws thousands of qualified applicants, Mehta observes, "nepotism is as good a method of selection as any."[23]

Still, despite its fractured nature and persistent social cleavages, India is a functioning democracy, and complaints about nepotism are frequently heard, reflecting the ambivalence many Indians feel about the extent to which family ties continue to predominate in public life. This ambivalence is seen in the debate about political corruption, where we find the same tension as in Africa and China between the values of Ancient Nepotism and those of bureaucratic rationalism. As one irate citizen wrote, "high caste officials and their kith and kin . . . indulge so much in greed, corruption and nepotism that today in India nothing moves without a bribe."[24] The problem goes much deeper than politics, however. India's AIDS control program has been faulted for "mismanagement and nepotism." Many state cricket boards in India (and Pakistan) have been accused of nepotism. Even the popular Miss India beauty pageant has been tainted by sordid tales of fixing, nepotism, and the casting couch.

Awareness of the problem has recently led to the emergence of eunuchs as reform candidates in Indian politics. (As in China, eunuchism was practiced by royal families in India for thousands of years.) Thus in the city of Katni, what began as a theatrical rebuke to corrupt politicians became a surprise electoral victory for a eunuch named Kamla Jaan who had been persuaded by leading citizens to run for mayor. Despite the fact that Jaan could neither read nor write, voters fed up with corruption and nepotism apparently liked the idea. News soon spread to neighboring states: five eunuch candidates were elected in Madhya Pradesh and three more in Uttar Pradesh. There was even talk of forming a national eunuch party.[25]

Yet despite these signs of ambivalence, the tradition of family rule continues to shape Indian politics. Thus in February 1998, the *New York Times* celebrated the rebirth of an Indian political dynasty in the person of Sonia Gandhi, Rajiv's Italian-born widow. Though not a candidate for office, Sonia's aggressive campaigning on behalf of the Congress Party had taken the country by storm. Her daughter Priyanka writes her speeches, and the *Times* noted approvingly that in the next generation she is likely to emerge as a political figure in her own right.

The non-Western societies we have examined are in many ways highly diverse, but they do have certain elements in common. Economically, all were based overwhelmingly on agriculture and are now in some stage of transition to industrial capitalism. They are also slowly shifting from a system of clans and kin groups to the greater individualism of the Western industrialized nations. All display strong vestiges of the patron-client relationship and the continued domination of "big men" who control access to resources and power. Nor should we neglect the role of their religious and ethical systems. Hierarchical societies require an ideology that justifies their naked inequalities, and all the great non-Western faiths promote humility, ancestral piety, and the patient acceptance of suffering.

Every society has the need to regulate its essential biological processes; hence all have rules that govern marriage, reproduction, and inheritance. These rules, which are rooted in a system of family relations and rationalized by an accompanying ideology, constitute each society's unique nepotistic formula. In none of the societies we have looked at are such choices left to the individual. Instead they are highly coercive—a system that might be called "total nepotism." This is because in conditions of privation and scarcity, the need for continuity outweighs the right of individuals to self-determination.

The West is very different, and that difference has to do with the liberation of families and individuals from the power of corporate kin groups. This process has its ultimate roots in the complex legacies of Hebrew, Greek, and Roman civilization—the era of Classical Nepotism. The Hebrews tempered patriarchal power and projected a universal Father-god that became the basis of Western monotheism. The Greeks conceived the idea of a state independent of the tribe, in which fathers and sons engaged as citizens on an equal footing. The Romans must be credited with shifting the basis of the family from *status* to *contract*, which is to say from a conception of kinship based on blood to one based on legal convention. As a result, wives and children gained more control over their persons and property, and the family itself came to be viewed as a cultural construct, something that could be made and unmade at will. Later, Christianity was added, remaking the family in its image and further liberalizing Western patriarchalism. As this process continued, the energies and passions of the family were released and channeled outward to become the great engine of Western development.[26]

CHAPTER 4

CLASSICAL NEPOTISM

THE HEBREWS, GREEKS, AND ROMANS

When King David had become an old man, he complained that he could get no warmth. His servants found a beautiful young girl named Abishag to lie with him: the virgin's body warmed the king, but David "knew her not." Seeing his father's decrepitude, his son Adonijah announced, "I will be king," and assembled a royal retinue of chariots and horsemen. Since in many tribal societies the king's potency is linked to his legitimacy, it is no accident that immediately following this exposure of David's decline, Adonijah made his claim. So began the struggle for succession in Israel's first dynastic family.

Adonijah is David's oldest surviving son (three others have already died). His claim is therefore based on the tribal rule of primogeniture, in which the oldest son inherits the estate. But while David has not formally named a successor, he has already promised his favorite wife, Bathsheba, that her son, Solomon, will rule after him. Hearing of Adonijah's announcement, the prophet Nathan goes to see her.

> Now therefore come, let me give you counsel, that you may save your own life and the life of your son Solomon. Go in at once to King David, and say to him, "Did you not, my lord the king, swear to your maidservant, saying, 'Solomon your son shall reign after me, and he shall sit upon my throne'? Why then is Adoni-

> jah king?" Then while you are still speaking with the king, I also will come in after you and confirm your words.

It is a bit surprising to find the prophet Nathan instigating this harem intrigue. Perhaps he thought the youthful Solomon would be more receptive to advice than his confident and headstrong older brother. Whatever the reason, Nathan's plot succeeds. David declares Solomon his heir and has him publicly anointed.

Adonijah rushes to the temple and places his hands on the altar—a traditional place of sanctuary. Solomon sends word that he will be spared if he accepts his brother's rule. Adonijah agrees, then asks Bathsheba to get Solomon to let him marry Abishag. Solomon rebukes his mother angrily, saying, "Ask for him the kingdom also!" Abishag had the status of David's concubine, and to assume his father's wife was tantamount to a claim on the throne. Therefore Solomon has Adonijah killed.

David—in all probability a historical figure—was the founder of the Jewish kingdom and of a dynasty that lasted four hundred years. The last Davidic monarch was led away to Babylonian exile in 586 B.C. Yet David himself was a usurper who needed to legitimize his rule (in part by the propaganda efforts reflected in the book of Samuel), nor had he made provision for an heir, despite the palpable chill of approaching death. Indeed, the very principle of dynastic succession had yet to be established. Authority in Israel during the long period of popular rule by judges had been fluid and personal; no judge's son had ever succeeded his father.[1] With the emergence of the Hebrew monarchy under David's predecessor, Saul, Israel began the long transition from a religious to a political community. This meant leaving behind certain aspects of tribal government, including its primitive egalitarianism. Yet tribal vestiges abound in David's kingdom; nor did the Jews ever really abandon this tribal mentality. While they contributed the crucial idea of monotheism on which the universal empire of the West was built, through thousands of years of Western history they have remained "a people apart."

THE HEBREWS: A PRODIGAL NATION

The tribal character of the Jews and their religion has long been recognized. Yet while enlightened modern Jews take their stand on universalist values and are among the foremost defenders of meritocracy, Jewish nepotism is an unbreakable vessel that has withstood centuries of assault from within and without. Joel Kotkin calls the Jews "the archetypal global tribe" and credits their amazing success and survival through thousands of years of adversity to the habits of communal self-help and reliance on kin that they have preserved from their earliest history. The roots of this adaptive social pattern lie deep in Judaism's tribal past, above all in the foundational myths of the Jewish people found in the Old Testament. There we see not only the basic template of Jewish social relations—a potent formula based almost entirely on kin selection and reciprocal altruism—but also the first systematic expression of the monotheistic idea with its concept of an all-powerful and benevolent creator God or heavenly father. Just as in Africa, China, and India religious traditions developed that rationalized the transmission of property, authority, and status from father to son, so Judaism originates in a sacrificial ancestor cult that projects the values of the father-son relationship in cosmological terms. It is a testament to the power and appeal of the religious ideology of Hebrew nepotism that most Americans still pray to God the father.

The ancient Hebrews were a loosely organized tribe of seminomadic herdsmen who spread throughout the region of Syria and northern Israel during the third millennium B.C. The smallest social unit was the patriarchal household, a nomadic tent community consisting of the sons of one father together with their wives and offspring. Two or three such households made up a clan *(mishpacha),* and an aggregation of clans made up a tribe, though tribal membership was fluid, with clans and families coming and going at will. As a result, tribal leadership was weak, and fathers held complete sway over their households.

The Hebrew Bible chronicles the history of the Jews as they progress from this original condition of nomadic pastoralism to one of settled agriculture after the conquest of Canaan, the emergence of a stratified urban society, and finally exile and diaspora. This process parallels the change in Hebrew social organization, from the semiautonomous clan, or sib (the period of the patriarchs), to the emergence of a warlike tribal federation (Judges), to the landed oligarchy on which the monarchy was based (Kings). Throughout this long succession of events—and well beyond—the nepotistic patterns of the patriarchal phase defined and shaped the historical Jewish experience.

Most tribal peoples trace their origin to a mythological ancestor, but where others are content to leave the details rather vague, Jews insist upon the historicity of their descent from Father Abraham. Jews are therefore strongly predisposed to view themselves as a large biological family. Moreover, there is nothing fated or foregone about the story of Jewish origins told in the Old Testament. The drama of Jewish descent is a tale of nail-biting suspense in which the continuity of Abraham's line is constantly challenged by external temptations and obstacles as well as by subversive forces within his own family. Indeed the story of Abraham's family, and most of the other stories that constitute the Jewish national epic, are nepotistic parables that explore different aspects of Jewish family dynamics. Many of the patterns they depict have become conventions of Western history and literature; their psychological insights into the problems of succession and inheritance have never been surpassed.

The picture of family life presented in the Bible is shockingly frank and contemporary, and it is no accident that Western writers and artists have returned again and again to these stories. Unlike the civilizations of India, Africa, or China, the Bible offers a realistic image of family life that we moderns can fully relate to. The Hebrew family affords no guarantee of harmony, loyalty, or even affection. Instead, from the beginning, the family is presented as a setting of competition, envy, even murder: the source of our greatest passions and the locus of our greatest sins. It is the dynamism of this patriarchal family, full of competitive siblings, jealous wives, and rebellious sons, that drives the action of the story.

God himself is the central character in the Bible, and he is above all a tribal god, a demanding Jewish father, swift to anger, inconsistent, and inscrutable. He is a father to whom we must prove not just our piety and reverence, but our worth, and not once but again and again. Nor is this God an impartial judge; rather he is mercurial and given to favoritism. Thus in the story of Cain and Abel, God accepts Abel's sacrifice but rejects that of his brother. The jealousy and anger this produces leads to Abel's murder. With all creation as their patrimony, they must nonetheless compete for the affections of the father.

God does not create Abraham out of the dust like Adam but chooses him to be the bearer of his covenant, to be handed down in turn to his descendants. The first order of business, then, is to separate Abraham from his family of origin and establish his lineage. Abraham's family came from Haran in northern Mesopotamia. Abraham was the eldest son of Terah; his younger brothers were Nahor and Haran. Haran's daughter married her uncle; their granddaughter Rebekah married Abraham's son Isaac. Abraham himself married his half sister Sarah, Terah's daughter by another wife.

The first thing to be noticed about these marital arrangements is their nepotistic character, verging on what we would consider incest. This pattern of close marriage among patrilineal relatives is an anthropological rarity, but it has been typical of Semitic cultures for thousands of years. Even today in most Arab societies, the strongly preferred spouse is a "parallel" cousin (the father's brother's daughter or the mother's sister's son).[2] One advantage of this practice is economic: it keeps property within the lineage. Another is the strengthening of solidarity by doubling blood and marriage ties within the family. It also strengthens cultural integrity, since women from other groups, with their foreign beliefs and practices, do not have to be assimilated. A tradition of consanguineous marriage among patrilineal relatives produces a tightly braided line of great endurance and resiliency. The flip side of this insular habit is the political weakness that results from the failure to use marriage as a basis of alliance with other groups.

Abraham's father was a maker of idols, and Jewish tradition has it that one day the precocious child took a hammer to the statues in his father's shop. The rift between father and son is a sign that Abraham will not continue Terah's line but will found his own, based on the worship of one God. The need for this break is expressed in God's first words to

Abraham: "Leave your country, your family and your father's house, for the land I will show you." What does Abraham get in exchange for abandoning his father and (presumably) forgoing his inheritance? "I will make you a great nation, I will bless you and make your name so famous that it will be used as a blessing." God appeals to Abraham on *nepotistic* grounds, promising a degree of reproductive success most fathers never dream of.

Right away, however, obstacles arise. For one thing, Abraham is childless. "See, you have given me no descendants; some man of my household will be my heir." To provide him with an heir of his own body, Sarah gives him her handmaid, Hagar, who bears a son called Ishmael. At last, however, when Abraham and Sarah are very old, God gives them a son of their own. This miracle affirms God's power to fulfill the covenant, but it leads to an immediate conflict in Abraham's family. Before, Sarah was content for Abraham to leave his property to Ishmael. Now her nepotistic instincts are aroused, and she demands that he expel Hagar and Ishmael: "this slave-girl's son is not to share the inheritance with my son Isaac." Abraham is reluctant—he has natural feelings for Ishmael—but God tells him to do as she asks: "for it is through Isaac that your name will be carried on."[3] Why is Isaac and not Ishmael the legitimate heir? The reason seems to be that Ishmael is not a full member of Abraham's patriline, descended on both sides from Abraham's father, but the product of an exogamous union with Hagar. Therefore he cannot receive the covenantal blessing.

No sooner has God fulfilled his promise, however, than he threatens to break it, by demanding the sacrifice of Isaac. This demand not only seems savagely inhuman, it strikes at the root of the covenant. How will Abraham become the father of a great nation if he must drive away one son and kill the other? But his faith in God is strong and he agrees without demur. Abraham's surprising readiness to sacrifice Isaac, like his willingness to drive Ishmael and his mother into exile, suggest that he is (in effect) a bad father but a first-rate patriarch, willing to trade off living sons against the promise of uncounted future offspring. Like a hymenopteran queen who may sacrifice some offspring to preserve the hive, Abraham has the long-term nepotistic vision God requires.

It would be a great mistake to underestimate the importance of mothers in the drama of Jewish descent. Though dominated by their husbands, the Hebrew matriarchs continue to assert their procreative power and authority. What's more, their nepotistic scheming—typical of polygamous households—frequently corrects the fathers' errors about which son represents the legitimate line of descent. Ironically, God's purpose works more often through the nepotism of Jewish mothers than Jewish fathers.[4]

According to religious scholar Nancy Jay, the struggle for succession in Abraham's family reflects a latent conflict between the principles of male and female descent. Unlike other patrilineal societies, which view the father as the source of life and the mother as a passive field in which he sows his seed, the Hebrews did not deny the female role in procreation. But the continued recognition of mothers as a source of social legitimacy creates a problem for a patrilineal society by giving them and their families an equal claim over their sons and leaving ambiguous the question of who is the "real" parent. The struggle to resolve this ambiguity reverberates throughout the early narratives, beginning with Abraham's departure from Haran, where the pattern of descent is matrilineal. In order to establish patriliny, Abraham must go to Canaan, far from the "polluting" female principle. However, because of the strong Hebrew preference for marriage within the patriline, his sons and grandsons must continue to take wives from other branches of the family. Hence there is much journeying back and forth between Canaan, the land of the fathers, and Haran, the land of the mothers. This tension first appears in the story of the search for Isaac's wife. Rather than choosing a bride from among the local peoples, Abraham wants Isaac to marry one of his own relatives. But he is so concerned about the corrupting influence of the matrilineal principle that he sends a trusted servant to fetch the bride rather than let Isaac go himself. The servant chooses Rebekah, daughter of Abraham's nephew, who is the son of his brother and his niece. Rebekah's descent in both lines from Abraham's father makes her an ideal bride for Isaac. Nevertheless, she too will assert the matrilineal principle in Isaac's nominally patrilineal household.

Like Abraham, Isaac has two sons. In a reprise of the theme of fraternal conflict, however, only one will inherit the covenant. Esau,

Issac's favorite, is a hairy-chested man, a vital, energetic outdoor type who loves to hunt. Jacob is smooth-skinned, a quiet man and a dweller in tents who is close to his mother. Esau as the eldest is due to receive his father's blessing and the major share of his estate. But Esau, we learn, has angered his parents by marrying a Hittite woman; therefore, because his offspring will not be full patrilineal descendants of Abraham, he cannot be Isaac's heir.[5] In the famous story of the mess of pottage, the cunning Jacob swindles Esau of his birthright. But he must also have the patriarchal blessing, for through it procreative power and legitimacy flow. The Bible relates that when Isaac is old and blind he tells Esau to go and hunt game and prepare it for him so that he might receive his blessing. (Isaac's blindness is symbolic: he cannot see that Esau has disqualified himself by marrying out of the family.) Overhearing this, Rebekah instructs Jacob to kill two kids from the flock; she then prepares the food and dresses Jacob in his brother's clothes, covering his arms and neck with the sheepskins. Jacob serves his father, pretending to be Esau, and receives the firstborn's blessing. When the deception is discovered, Esau swears to kill his brother. Rebekah tells Jacob to flee to Haran, to the home of her brother Laban.

Laban is the male head of a matrilineal household—a powerful mother's brother who (at this point) lacks sons of his own and stands in need of an adoptive heir. His interest in Jacob, therefore, constitutes a challenge to the claim of Jacob's father. During his stay in Laban's house, Jacob falls in love with Rachel, his first cousin. Laban agrees to let him have her in exchange for seven years' indentured labor, but instead of the promised bride, Jacob wakes to find he has been married to Leah, the unattractive elder daughter.[6] He must work another seven years for Rachel, and stays six years after that. Altogether Jacob's wives and concubines bear him eleven sons and a daughter (the result of a nepotistic competition between the sisters to see who can bear the most sons). However, by remaining in Laban's house Jacob is in danger of reverting to matriliny, and he must therefore return to the land of the fathers. After this, no more marriages are made between the branches of Abraham's family: Jacob's sons all marry outsiders, and from these are descended the twelve tribes of Israel.

The story of Jacob and Laban dramatizes the relationship known as the "avunculate." As Robin Fox explains, the natal bond between brother and sister is so strong that it is only overcome with great difficulty. Only the cultural drive to marry out can force the brother to renounce this erotic attachment, but he remains intensely interested in his sister's offspring, who carry his genes. That is why the incest taboo, which divides the natal family, is often accompanied by a system in which the brother's daughter marries the sister's son: "The consummation that is not open to the parents can still be achieved by the children in the next generation." This is also why, even in patrilineal societies, the maternal uncle remains as a shadowy figure, always ready to challenge the father's rights or to provide the kind of nurturing care that some patriarchal fathers do not.[7]

The biblical story of Joseph and his brothers is another object lesson in the difficulties of preserving fraternal solidarity in the patriarchal family. Joseph is Jacob's favorite child: the famous coat of many colors is the mark of this fatherly preference. But Jacob's favoritism destroys the harmony that should prevail among the brothers, who take revenge by selling Joseph into slavery. Later, after Joseph has become a great man in Egypt, the brothers are reunited and all is forgiven—though not before he has humiliated his brothers and made them bow down to him.[8]

If Abraham is the founder of the Hebrew religion, Moses is the founder of the Israelite nation. The story of Moses is that of an abandoned Hebrew infant, raised as an Egyptian prince, who discovers his true origin and chooses to share the sufferings of his brothers. Family reunification is therefore the crux of the story: biology is destiny for Moses. Egypt in the Jewish mind represents not just physical enslavement but the loss of identity, symbolized by the forgetting of kinship. Moses' return to his family is the first symbolic step toward the recovery of identity and freedom for the people as a whole.

While for most readers the dramatic confrontation between Moses and Pharoah is the heart of the Exodus story, the interesting part for our purposes is what happens *after* the Jews escape from Egypt. The first thing Moses does, according to the Bible, is order a census of each tribe, "establishing their kinship by clans and families." The first chapter of Numbers details this process of reconstituting the Jewish social order by recovering the lost knowledge of Hebrew descent. Only the Levites—

Moses' own tribe—are not counted, for they are to have a special role as priests and guardians of the covenant. Supported by taxation of the other tribes, they did no other work. Moses' brother, Aaron, became high priest, an office he passed down to his descendants. Thousands of years later, at the height of the diaspora, priestly candidates still had to prove their descent from Aaron's line. The elevation of the Levites to a Brahminlike elite living parasitically off the other tribes strongly suggests that Moses' political power, like that of other tribal leaders, was primarily based on his kin group.

But simple kinship is not enough to found a people. Moses is known as the great Hebrew lawgiver, and in this capacity he acted (somewhat in the manner of Confucius) to bring the traditions of Hebrew nepotism into line with the ethical impulse of monotheism. The Mosaic code renewed the Jewish emphasis on ethnic and religious separation, family solidarity, mutual aid, and communal self-help, and gave a powerful new impetus to Jewish procreation. The rest of the Hebrew Bible is the story of the long and often unsuccessful struggle to adhere to this exacting code. Indeed, a favorite Old Testament theme is the indulgent love of fathers for their errant or wayward sons, and the prophets often compare Israel to a prodigal child whose father-God is sometimes angry and punitive, but whose love remains constant and unchanging.

Procreation is the principal concern of Israelite religion. "Be fruitful and multiply," God tells Noah and his sons after the flood. This commandment is repeated many times, and its fulfillment is closely connected with proper religious observance: the reward for following God's law is increased progeny, while apostasy and sin result in diminished reproductive success.[9] Jews (like Hindus) had a religious obligation to marry and have children, and many biblical and Talmudic regulations governing sexual behavior were apparently aimed at maximizing chances of conception.[10] The Mosaic code also banned all forms of irregular and nonreproductive sex, punished adultery with death, and reformed Hebrew marriage practices.

One of the more intriguing aspects of the Hebrew marriage pattern was the custom known as levirate marriage, whereby a man was required to marry his dead brother's wife in order to provide him with an heir. The story of Onan, cursed by God for spilling his seed upon the ground, is often taken as a warning against masturbation. While non-procreative sex was indeed condemned by Jewish law, the sin of Onan was not an offense against God but against his dead brother: he refused to father a child who would be his brother's heir and not his own. Though ultimately abandoned by Western societies, this custom continued in practice for thousands of years.

Family harmony is another nepotistic value enshrined in the Mosaic code, beginning with the rule expressed in the fifth commandment, "Honor thy father and mother." Children were required to respect and obey their parents, parents to love and provide for their children. Jewish fathers had complete authority over their offspring, but Moses placed important limits on its exercise, above all removing the traditional power of life and death. If a man has a disobedient son the parents must bring him before the elders, saying, " 'This son of ours is stubborn and rebellious and will not listen to us; he is a wastrel and a drunkard.' Then all his fellow citizens shall stone him to death." The Hebrews obviously considered filial impiety a great and dangerous evil, deserving the ultimate penalty; but they also thought it wrong for a father to administer such punishment himself.[11] This tempering of the father's power over his children is one of the most important features of classical Western nepotism.

But the essence of the Mosaic code is the establishment of reciprocal altruism at the heart of the Jewish social constitution. Injunctions to communal solidarity and mutual aid laid down in Deuteronomy establish the obligation to create a welfare system for poor Israelites. Likewise, fraternal solidarity is emphasized in the many rules pertaining to business: for example, interest may be charged to non-Jews but not to members of the tribe.[12] Excessive punishments are also proscribed, to minimize within-group violence and promote internal harmony.

So closely bound up are the nepotistic injunctions to procreation, endogamy, cultural separation, and in-group altruism with obedience to God that one scholar concludes, "For the Israelites, there was really only one purpose for God—to represent the idea of kinship, ingroup membership, and separateness from others."[13] In the eyes of the prophet Hosea, Jews who worship other gods commit "harlotry"—that is, a sexual offense—and their punishment is that they "shall not increase." Moses metes out death to Jewish sex offenders left and right, and orders the extermination of whole peoples lest their daughters tempt the Jews to intermarry.

Moses passes his authority to Joshua, the head of his elite bodyguard. Though Joshua was not a Levite, the Bible explains that after Moses laid his hands upon him, Joshua was "full of the spirit of wisdom." This episode establishes a pattern of pseudo-nepotistic succession that is the model for the mentor-protégé relationship characteristic of later societies. The transmission of charismatic authority through the laying-on of hands (or receipt of the mantle, as in the story of Elijah and Elisha) has become a convention of Western literature and art.

After the conquest of Canaan, Israel became a loose tribal federation under the informal and egalitarian rule of priests and judges. Periodically a war leader would arise in one tribe or another, but there was still no basis for a unified national government. But with the growing incursions of Philistines pushing inland from the coast, the need for greater unity was felt and the people cried out for a king. The emergence of the monarchy reflects the shift to a new form of social organization. But tensions with the tribal past continue to exert a potent influence.

Saul, anointed by the prophet Samuel, was a Benjaminite warrior chief who gained some early victories over the Philistine army but lacked the temperament and skills to defeat them decisively. He also remains a tribal chief: Saul based his power mainly on his own sib and filled the most important offices with men of his tribe. The Bible presents Saul as deeply flawed—moody and irascible, vain and insecure, ungrateful and capricious. God abandons him almost at once, and Samuel anoints David during his lifetime, thereby letting it be known that the royal line will pass from Benjamin to Judah.

According to one tradition, David enters Saul's service as a harpist and becomes his armor bearer, but after defeating Goliath he rises to become the leader of Saul's army and wins many great victories.[14] When Saul hears David praised above himself, however, he becomes insanely jealous. Saul's jealousy is presented as irrational, but he had reason to fear David since he had quickly acquired a large following and there was no tradition of dynastic succession in Israel. Moreover, David was not just a poor shepherd lad but the son of Jesse, one of the leading men in Judah. In a Machiavellian scheme worthy of Vito Corleone (who advised his son to "keep your friends close, but keep your enemies closer"), Saul marries David to his daughter Michal. This is a perfectly normal way of dealing with a potential dynastic challenger. Napoleon did the same thing when he married the dashing cavalry commander Murat to his greedy and ambitious sister Caroline. Coopting a talented upstart through marriage makes nepotistic sense: their common interest in the offspring binds the rival to the interests of the royal clan. But Saul's purpose is not to strengthen his dynasty by incorporating David into his family but to lull his suspicions before sending him out to be killed by the Philistine enemy.

Saul's attempt to get rid of David is meant to ensure that Jonathan will succeed him and continue his line: his motive is overtly nepotistic. So it is all the more ironic that his failure as a dynast can be traced to his poor conduct as a father. Harsh and overbearing with his son, Saul at one point condemns Jonathan to death for a ritual infraction and reverses himself only when the people protest his injustice. Similarly, his machinations against David force Jonathan to choose between his father and his friend. Jonathan warns David of his danger, and Michal, whom Saul has taken away and given to another man, connives in his escape. The disloyalty of his children is a comment on Saul's fitness as a monarch. The fate of his line is sealed when Jonathan abdicates his claim, declaring to David: "You are the one who is to reign in Israel, and I shall be second to you." When Saul and Jonathan are killed in battle, David defeats a challenge from another of Saul's sons and takes the throne.[15]

David drove the Philistines back to the coast and united the southern tribes in a kingdom of Judah (dominated, of course, by his own kinship group). Later he added the northern tribes of Israel to his rule, moving his capital to Jerusalem, strategically situated between the two regions. He also brought the Ark of the Covenant to Jerusalem in order, as Paul Johnson explains, "to identify the national religion, the entire people, and the crown with himself and his line."[16] David reigned for forty years, consolidating his mini-empire with a national bureaucracy, an elaborate court, and polygamous alliances with other leading clans. Like Saul, he based his power on his own clan and the great men of his tribe, such as his kinsman Joab, leader of David's personal strike force and head of a powerful faction in his own right. But he also created a new feudal order that allowed him to transcend these limitations, with a standing professional army, a priestly and administrative class, and an impregnable capital that was also the center of the national cult. Though tribal leadership could not be inherited, the monarchy was based not on David's clan or tribe but on a feudal order centered on himself. This is the legacy he prepares to pass on to his children.

David is in many ways the archetypal Jewish father: an immensely attractive figure who combined the attributes of warrior, diplomat, poet, priest, and lover. But David also had his failings, and where Saul was dictatorial and punitive, David provides an object lesson in paternal overindulgence. As a result, his house is plagued by incest, rape, and fratricide. Even as he struggles to create a national state above tribal loyalties, a blood feud breaks out in his own family when his daughter Tamar is raped by her half brother Amnon, who is then killed by her full brother Absalom. Fleeing his father's wrath, Absalom returns some years later, only to foment a rebellion; among his other sins he openly sleeps with David's concubines—a gesture straight out of the handbook of primate dominance politics. But the rebellion fails and Absalom is killed. One of the most poignant scenes in the Old Testament is David's cry of grief—"O my son Absalom, my son, my son Absalom! Would I had died instead of you, O Absalom, my son, my son!" These words express a father's helpless love for the unnatural son who seeks his life. But David's failure to punish Amnon for raping Tamar is clearly to blame, along with his unaccountable delay in naming a successor. Adonijah's earlier rebellion may be ascribed to the same paternal failings: the Bible comments that at no time had his father displeased him by asking, "Why have you done thus and so?"

David was a man of towering passions and great sins, but also one of piety and justice. His successors were men of a different character. Solomon was not a warrior but an Oriental despot with a taste for opulent luxuries and over a thousand wives and concubines. (Like many dynastic successors, he also had a grandiose passion for building: instituting an unpopular system of taxation and forced labor, he constructed a magnificent palace and temple.) Solomon's chief wife was Pharaoh's daughter, for whom he built a separate palace so that she might continue her foreign religious practices. What happens next reminds us of the original reason for the rule against exogamy: "When Solomon grew old his wives swayed his heart to other gods; and his heart was not wholly with Yahweh his God as his father David's had been." Therefore God decrees the end of David's kingdom: "Since you behave like this and do not keep my covenant or the laws I laid down for you, I will most surely tear the kingdom away from you and give it to one of your servants." But God adds, "For your father David's sake, however, I will not do this during your lifetime, but will tear it out of your son's hands."

Apparently it would be an injustice to David to punish Solomon directly. Instead, his punishment is visited upon him through his son Rehoboam, a callow and arrogant youth lacking both his father's wisdom and his grandfather's prowess. Rehoboam rejected the pleas of the northern tribes to lighten their burdens of conscription and taxation, and threatened to increase them instead. He thereby provoked a rebellion, splitting the kingdom in two. Though Davidic kings continued to rule in Judah for three hundred years, the disunited kingdom ultimately made an easy prey for the rising imperial powers of Mesopotamia.

We will continue our exploration of Jewish nepotism in a subsequent chapter, when we consider the astonishing success of the Rothschilds in the era of Jewish emancipation. The outsider mentality of the Jewish diaspora was perfectly adapted to the development of an international financial market amid the turbulence of the Napoleonic Wars. Later we will see how strong traditions of familial and ethnic nepotism helped Jews adapt successfully to the more open conditions of American society. This resilient and adaptive Jewish nepotism is based on a formula that integrates the primary elements of sociality in a perfect, self-perpetuating whole: kin selection (in the form of strong injunctions to endogamy), reciprocity (the within-group altruism promoted by the Mosaic legal code), and coercion (in the form of a religious ideology that rationalizes and supports the other elements). This extreme Jewish particularism produced a grandiose religious claim that became the foundation of Western universalism. The Jewish projection of the father as a universal deity clearly had the potential to include all mankind as his children. Yet the Jews never sought to pursue that potential, either by conversion or by conquest. Instead, like their women, they preferred to keep their God to themselves.

GREECE: THE SONS OF THESEUS

In 415 B.C., the Athenians gathered on the hill above the agora to debate the invasion of Sicily. One of the Greek colonies there had appealed to them for help, and this seemed a good pretext for subduing the whole island. The democratic assembly was easily fired with ambition and greed for this new conquest and appointed three commanders, one of whom was Alcibiades, a rising star in Athenian politics who had distinguished himself in several previous campaigns. But his co-commander Nicias, an older man known for his caution and prudence, begged them to reconsider, reminding them of the losses they had sustained in their long war with Sparta and of the devastating plague (probably smallpox) that had left the city reeling and depleted.

Alcibiades then rose to speak. After making a boastful display of his achievements, his many services to Athens, the wealth and greatness of his family, and his fitness to command the expedition, he asserted that the Athenians could not safely cease their drive for acquisition. "We cannot fix the exact point at which our empire shall stop; we have reached a position in which we must not be content with retaining but must scheme to extend it, for if we cease to rule others, we are in danger of being ruled ourselves." Carried away by his ambition and self-confidence, the Athenians voted the funds for an enormous expeditionary force.

This moment must have seemed to Alcibiades the peak of his career. He had already made his mark in politics at a very young age; now he had become the virtual symbol of youth and vitality, the favorite son of Athens, poised to outshine even his late guardian, Pericles, the greatest man in Greece. Instead, within a year he would be languishing in exile, condemned to death by the Athenians and plotting with the Spartans against his native city. The expeditionary force, having met with stiff resistance, would be broken and dispirited, waiting to be ransomed in the filth and disease of a Syracusan quarry. The misadventure drained the treasury, wrecked the fleet, and claimed the lives of ten thousand men—about a quarter of the Athenian population. The ultimate consequence would be the defeat and destruction of Athens herself, the overthrow of her democracy, and the permanent loss of her empire.

Athenian democracy is often called the source of our political ideals and institutions, including the ideas of equality, individual citizenship, and the notion of a public sphere separate from the family. Even at its height, however, Athenian politics was never insulated from its surrounding familial context. Public life continued to reflect the fundamental importance of kinship—particularly the bond between fathers and sons.

Athens was a father-son affair from top to bottom.[17] The city was referred to as "the land of the fathers," its gods were "the gods of the fathers," and its laws were "the laws of the fathers." A man was usually known by his father's name, as in the Homeric epics, where Achilles and Agamemnon are addressed as "son of Peleus" and "son of Atreus." A man without an honored family name was literally nameless, or "anonymous," while a glorious patronymic signified the promise of greater deeds to come. Athens itself was a valued patrimony handed down through generations, and public rhetoric was filled with exhortations not to let it be diminished or destroyed.

Much of this is consistent with the practices of other patriarchal societies. But there was something different about the father-son relationship in Athens: a core of deep ambivalence arising from the tension between the hierarchical relations of fathers and sons in the household and their political equality as citizens. This peculiar tension at the heart of Athenian kinship—a tension between age and youth, hierarchy and equality, patriarchy and fraternity—goes a long way toward explaining the dynamism of Athenian democracy and the vitality and greatness of its culture. Ironically, the same tensions can be blamed for the democracy's collapse and the destruction of its empire.

Originally, the Attic peninsula was home to four tribes, nominally descended from the four sons of the mythical forefather, Ion. Each was a loose confederacy of clans composed of military brotherhoods called phratries; each phratry comprised a number of patrilineally related households inhabiting a deme, or local district. A man was born into his father's clan and tribe and was bound by blood to all the members of his lineage.[18] The legendary hero Theseus was thought to have united the four Ionian tribes and instituted a commonwealth. He was therefore considered the ultimate patron of Athenian democracy; the Athenians called themselves the sons of Theseus.

The ancient constitution of Athens was the familiar tribal model: a king, a council of clan elders, and a popular assembly of independent farmers. After an interlude of rapacious rule by aristocratic clans, a lawmaker arose whose egalitarian reforms set Athens on the path to democracy. Solon canceled all debts and created a democratic Council of Four Hundred, drawn by lot from the four tribes. A social conservative like Moses and Confucius, his legal code was designed to bolster the moral order of the family by spelling out the mutual obligations of fathers and sons. For example, he forbade anyone from speaking in the assembly who had mistreated his parents or squandered his patrimony, on the theory that a man who does not govern his own household can have nothing useful to say about public affairs.

In 509 B.C., the government came into the hands of Cleisthenes, who replaced the four Athenian tribes with ten new ones based on residence, not blood. Thus was born the concept of a state based on territory and individual citizenship rather than on descent and tribal affiliation. The reformed phratry and deme were designed to be mediating institutions between the private and public spheres. Yet membership remained hereditary, and their solidarity was reinforced by participation in a common cult and strong appeals to kinship ethics.

Extended kinship was still important for commercial partnerships, political alliances, and obligations of blood vengeance; most people also continued to marry within a circle of close relatives, especially among the upper classes. But the individual household was the real focus of Athenian life. Each household had its own religious cult, and the family hearth was the center of sacrificial rituals and ceremonies marking marriage, birth, funerals, and other life-cycle events. Despite the individualism on display in Athenian politics, however, there were no modern individuals in Athens. Citizenship came through membership in a household and the quasi-kinship institutions of the phratry, deme, and tribe.

The Greek household was an institution for passing on property, status, and good character from father to son. An Athenian father had the right to reject a child whose paternity he suspected. Otherwise, formal acceptance was declared one week after the child's birth, at which point the father legally renounced his power of life and death. Unlike in modern democracies, it was extremely difficult for foreigners to be naturalized as citizens. As a rule, one had to be born into Athenian society as the offspring of a registered father and mother. Naturalization when it did occur was a form of ritualized adoption by the state.

Every society faces the problem of what to do with its young men between the ages of puberty and majority. The solution in most Western societies was to send them out on military adventures. This was true for the Greeks and Romans, as it was later for the Vikings and the medieval French nobility. At sixteen an Athenian son was inducted into his father's phratry, and at eighteen he became a citizen with full rights in his father's deme. He now could vote in the assembly and freely enter into contracts. He was also eligible for military service, and he typically spent the next ten years or so making a name for himself (or upholding his father's name) in Athens's many wars and naval actions.

Athenians had definite expectations about the relationship between father and son. A son should be obedient and dutiful and strive in every way to please his father. The father was legally obliged to feed, clothe, and educate his son, teach him a trade, and sponsor him for citizenship. A father was also required to leave his property to his sons and could be sued if he mismanaged it. Sons were obliged to feed and clothe their aged parents, and anyone could bring suit against a son who failed to do so. A son inherited not only his father's property (or debts), but his friends and enemies as well. A son was expected, during and after his father's life, to help him fight his battles, continue his alliances and feuds, commemorate his victories, and avenge his defeats. Many a man's political career was founded on his father's reputation, and sons took every occasion to remind the assembly of their family's past services. Conversely, the bad acts of a father or grandfather could haunt their descendants for generations, and the idea of a family curse was repeatedly explored in Athenian drama. All sons were expected to follow in their father's footsteps, whether on the farm, in trade, or in a political or military career. Though it is rare in any age to find many sons who equal or surpass their distinguished fathers, Athens had numerous examples of sons who succeeded in doing so. Filial piety was thus of clear importance in driving sons to personal excellence and acts of public service.

Nevertheless, Athenians walked a narrow line between piety and assertiveness. Given the emphasis on male equality and independence in democratic Athens, a son who was too obedient risked appearing unmanly. Respect for fathers and paternal pride in sons therefore coexisted uneasily with the glorification of youth, combined with latent fears of its assertion and rebelliousness. This tension is reflected in Greek culture from its earliest origins, beginning with the Greek creation myth, where Ouranos, the god of heaven, imprisons his children in the body of their mother, the Earth. Kronos (with his mother's help) castrates his father and throws the severed member into the sea, where the drops of blood engender the Eumenides—the terrible avengers of wrongs against the family and hearth. Due to a prophecy that one of his sons will depose him, Kronos in turn eats his children. But Zeus escapes and, again helped by his mother, overthrows his father and liberates his brothers and sisters. He then marries his sister Hera and becomes king of the gods, ushering in a new fraternal order to replace the patriarchal domination of his father.

Conflict between fathers and sons is hardly unique to fifth-century Athens; every society must cope with this inevitable tension. Such conflicts arise at two points: when the child becomes a man, founding his own household, and when the father becomes an old man, giving way to the next generation. In the first instance the son must displace, or "kill," his father; in the second, the father must allow his own son to take his place. In Athenian society, these conflicts were mediated in a number of ways: through joint participation in ritual, formal segregation by age groups, the creation of surrogate fathers (either teachers or mentor-lovers), the frequent invocation of solidarity and mutual interest between fathers and sons, and the catharsis of tragedy. But in other ways, latent generational conflict was powerfully exacerbated: through the cultural insistence on equality, the Athenian cult of youthful vigor, the promotion of manly competition and aggressiveness, and the comedies in which fathers and sons are shown as being constantly at odds.

Far from mitigating these tensions, the social constitution of democratic Athens seemingly did everything it could to make them worse. Historian Barry Strauss points not only to the ideal of political equality, which set the patriarchal household in opposition to the fraternal and egalitarian spirit of the public sphere, but also to the Athenian pattern of late marriage and delayed inheritance. Young men came of age at eighteen but did not typically inherit their estates until they had established their own households, usually around the age of thirty. This left a gap of a decade or so in which the young man chafed at having to wait for his patrimony while the older man regarded him with increasing unease and ambivalence.

The Greeks, in other words, did not idealize family life as a harmonious utopia. The father was a king in his own household, yet conflict and rebellion against his authority were also seen as natural and necessary. The family was therefore a mechanism for focusing and resolving generational conflicts that the Greeks understood as inevitable. This tension is present in Athenian households, in politics, and in the themes of contemporary drama.

Consider the myth of Theseus, the legendary founder of Athens. Aegeus, king of Athens, impregnates the daughter of the king of Troezen while returning from the oracle at Delphi. Before departing, he leaves a sword and a pair of sandals under a rock. (This, by the way, is a wonderful metaphor for the burdens of heirship in any society. Many a would-be successor has found the achievements of a famous parent lying like a boulder in his path.) On growing up, Theseus passes his father's first test of manhood by lifting the stone and retrieving the sword and sandals. He then sets out for Athens by the dangerous overland route instead of going by sea—determined to prove himself worthy of so great a father by his acts of strength and courage. Word of his exploits precedes him, and Aegeus, who fears the approaching hero as a rival, plots to kill him with a cup of poisoned wine. But when he recognizes the young man's sword as his own, Aegeus knocks the poisoned cup from Theseus' hands and publicly embraces him. At the time, Athens was compelled to send the flower of its youth each year to Crete as sacrificial victims for the Minotaur, a terrible man-eating creature kept in a labyrinth under the palace of King Minos. Theseus volunteers to kill this monster, a feat he accomplishes with the help of Ariadne, the king's daughter. Setting out for home, however, he neglects to hoist the white sail that Aegeus has told him to use as a sign of success. Seeing his son's ship approach with its black sail of mourning, Aegeus leaps from the cliffs to his death, and Theseus succeeds him as king.

This myth came into wide artistic use during the fifth century B.C., at the height of the Athenian democracy. Found in plays by Aeschylus, Euripides, and Sophocles, some of which are lost, it is the story of a bastard son, abandoned at birth, who (like another tragic hero, Oedipus) feels a burning desire to find and prove his worth to his father—while inadvertently causing his death. Why did the story of Theseus appeal so strongly to the Athenian mythmakers? According to Strauss, democracy needed men who were energetic, assertive, and independent; men who were prepared above all to challenge received ideas and traditions. This youthful vigor and assertiveness enabled Athens to become the leading power in Greece, but it inevitably came at the expense of the authority of fathers. Athenian poets and dramatists were not about to promote an openly rebellious son as their hero: that would be going too far. Theseus was a useful symbol of Athenian manhood precisely because he is a model of filial piety who replaces his father without directly competing against him.

By calling themselves the sons of Theseus, the Athenians advertised the cult of youth and the virtues of the self-made man that they exalted and admired. They saw in Theseus an image of themselves as daring innovators, challenging the limits of tradition. But the story also illustrates a problem that will echo throughout Western history: the self-made man finds it difficult both to acknowledge his debt to his father and to yield pride of place to his son. The story of Theseus goes to the fantasy of every man in a democratic society that he is fully self-reliant and beholden or subordinate to no one. Yet it also expresses the son's ambivalence toward the father who stands in his way, and the father's mixed feelings about the son who must someday replace him.

The greatness of Athenian democracy has tended to obscure the fact that it was a relatively brief affair, lasting only about three generations. Its founders were the so-called men of Marathon, the heroic liberators of Greece who defeated the Persian invasion of 490 B.C. and established the preeminence of Athens. Their sons were good inheritors and stewards of their patrimony—statesmen, generals, and businessmen who built an empire and presided over a great enlightenment that turned the city itself into an everlasting tribute to democracy. The greatest member of this generation was Pericles, for thirty years the leading man in Athens.

Pericles was in many ways the ideal political son. His mother was the niece of Cleisthenes, who had founded the democracy, and his father, Xanthippos, not only fought at Marathon but drove the Persians out of Greece for good the next year at Mycale. Pericles had been tutored by the greatest teachers in Greece and distinguished himself with his brilliant and studious mind. His character, moreover, was notably sober and serious.

Pericles launched his career with great circumspection, waiting until his father's death and the inheritance of his estate. He began by sponsoring a new play by Aeschylus, *The Persians,* whose subject was bound to remind the public of his father's heroic exploits. He then spent several years in military service, where he distinguished himself for bravery and was elected general at thirty. The next year he was chosen to conduct a public prosecution that was also an act of filial piety: he led the political attack on Cimon, the leader of the dominant party in Athens.

The democracy of this period was still fairly conservative, limited to men of the propertied classes. Its leader, Cimon, was the son of

Miltiades, the hero of Marathon—a wealthy aristocrat and a political enemy of Pericles' father. Political parties in Athens were really just personal factions surrounding some outstanding figure and were referred to as "those around X" or "the friends of Y." Most such leaders were aristocrats and their factions were composed of their relatives, friends, and dependants. Pericles, whose grand-uncle was the founder of Athenian democracy, continued the family tradition by attaching himself to the radical democrats, who advocated expanding the franchise to include the poorest classes. In taking on Cimon, the leader of the conservatives, Pericles was attacking the most powerful man in Athens, one whose faction united three of the city's greatest families, including his own. This may explain why he performed his task with a restraint bordering on diffidence. But though Cimon survived the attack, Pericles had emerged as a rising star in the opposition. Over the next decade, he continued to distinguish himself through military service and supported the leadership of his party. He did not push himself into the front ranks prematurely but (like a good son) patiently awaited his turn. It came soon enough: his party's leader died unexpectedly and Pericles assumed his mantle. With Cimon now out of the way—he had earlier been tried and imprisoned after a military expedition he advocated went badly awry—Pericles became the undisputed leader of Athenian democracy.

Pericles held no permanent office and enjoyed no formal powers of command. His authority was personal, based on a rare combination of administrative ability, moral vision, rhetorical skill, and force of character. Having helped expand the empire as a soldier, he now turned to the task of preserving it. He put an end to imperial expansion and for the next thirty years pursued a policy of moderation and diplomacy abroad and civic improvement at home. He caused the construction of many great buildings and monuments and fostered the arts and sciences, making Athens the center of the first great Western enlightenment. Above all he dramatically expanded the democracy, allowing members of the lowest class to participate in public life for the first time.

Plato viewed democracy as the rule of a mob, lacking moral courage or consistency and dangerously susceptible to demagogues.[19] We need not agree with this assessment, but Plato's view of the Athenian *demos* as an unruly child does help explain the extraordinary public trust in Pericles, whose authority was very much that of a father. According to Thucydides and other contemporaries, Pericles was the only man in Athens who could sway the riotous popular assembly, pointing out its errors, upbraiding its weaknesses, and on occasion shaming it into submission. Pericles was often represented on the stage as Father Zeus—sometimes to comic effect, but more often with respect for his imposing moral presence, his aristocratic bearing, and his commanding paternal authority.

Pericles was a good father to the public at large, a fact that makes his failure as a father in private life all the more perplexing and ironic. In one of Plato's dialogues, Socrates points to Pericles as the leading example of a father whose sons fell short of his achievement. His ward Alcibiades was casually cruel about it, remarking: "Well, if the two sons of Pericles are simpletons, what of it?" In fact, however, Pericles appears to have badly neglected his sons. Their relations were strained by his early divorce from their mother; they also quarreled over money. When one of them borrowed money from a friend of his under false pretenses, father and son ended up in court. The son even accused Pericles of sleeping with his daughter-in-law.

All this must have been extremely painful and embarrassing for the greatest man in Athens, especially since a man who could not govern his own household was thought unfit for public life. But Pericles had even worse luck with his young wards Alcibiades and Cleinias. Related to Pericles through their mother, the boys were orphaned at an early age, and Pericles was named their guardian. Cleinias posed a problem from the beginning—diagnosed as a "psychotic delinquent" by one historian, nothing more is heard of him. But Alcibiades showed considerable promise. He was precocious, bright, and very independent. Superbly educated by the leading private teachers of his day, he was well trained in the art of public speaking. He was also noted for his beauty and had many ardent admirers, male and female. Even his flaws were charming—Alcibiades spoke with a lisp, but it only enhanced his appeal.

But while he undoubtedly had great abilities, there was also something lawless in his character that frankly alarmed his contemporaries.

For one thing, he had a reputation for insolence and disrespect for age and custom. Like many youthful products of sophistic education, he had a tendency to argue with his elders and liked to tie them up in knots. His erotic indiscretions were the scandal of Athenian society. He also flaunted his pride in his aristocratic family, leading many to suspect him of aspiring to dictatorship. Added to this was his extraordinary wealth—his father had left him so rich that he was able one year to enter seven chariots in the Olympic games, taking three of the top four prizes.

Such a clever, headstrong boy clearly needed the attentions of a father; unfortunately he didn't get them from Pericles. He did fall briefly under the spell of Socrates, who tried to guide him to the higher path of philosophy. Ultimately, however, his disgraceful public record was Exhibit A in the capital case against Socrates, who was tried and executed in 399 B.C. on a charge of corrupting the youth.

Alcibiades rose to prominence as a result of an unprecedented generation gap that opened up in Athenian politics after the death of Pericles in 429. Alcibiades not only exploited this gap, thereby making it worse; he himself became a symbol of the rift. The gap was a product of various forces, but above all it seems to illustrate the pattern we saw in the biblical house of David, in which the virtues of the founding generation, conserved by the dutiful sons of the second, may be squandered by the spoiled and careless members of the third. The youth of Alcibiades' generation were not the men of Marathon, in whose shadow their fathers grew up. The second generation had been stable, solid citizens, but they failed to reproduce these virtues in their sons. The whole atmosphere of Athens at this time was that of a questioning, unruly, and aggressive spirit, marked by a love of novelty and a tolerance for youthful indiscretions. In such a setting, Alcibiades' pranks and misbehaviors were indulged as boyish antics. After Pericles' death he took a leading role in politics and diplomacy though he was only in his twenties. At his age Pericles was still earning his stripes as a soldier and political backbencher. In contrast, Alcibiades rose quickly to preeminence. But lacking his uncle's experience, wisdom, and character, he badly overreached and came to grief.

The simmering tensions of this decade are explored in several plays of Aristophanes, which treat the relationship between Pericles and Alcibiades as symbolic of the topsy-turvy relations between fathers and sons at this time. In *Clouds*, produced a few years after Pericles' death, a wealthy father has lost control over his spendthrift son. The young man has been raised with every advantage; paternal care and affection have been lavished on him. Yet he not only talks back to his father but actually beats him onstage. This unthinkable act is laid to the influence of Socrates, who runs the fashionable academy to which the father has sent him. The play ends with the outraged father putting the Socratic academy to the torch.

The death of Pericles ushered in a generation of young leaders whose rash adventurism contrasted sharply with the caution of the older generation. In the 420s, these tensions erupted into politics. "Young men delivered speeches in the assembly and conducted prosecutions in the courts," Barry Strauss observes, "but nothing bespeaks their influence more than the Sicilian Expedition of 415."[20] When Alcibiades exhorted the Athenians to undertake this rash project, he was inviting them to set aside the successful thirty-year policy of Pericles. This alarmed some older citizens like Nicias, but it clearly appealed to the strain in Athenian culture that encouraged sons to go beyond their fathers. Not surprisingly, the failure of the invasion marked a dramatic turning point in Athenian politics. Athenians had had enough of ambitious young men and returned from the rule of the son to the rule of the father. Calls were heard for the restoration of the *patrios politeia*—the laws and institutions of the fathers—a regime "in which old men ruled and young men remained silent."

The trial of Socrates epitomized this restoration. The official charge against him was impiety, but this was understood to mean undermining the respect of sons for fathers, and there was clearly something to this. It is quite true that Socrates challenged the authority of fathers, teaching his young friends to prize virtue and wisdom over kinship and ancestral ties. On the other hand, he made an effort at his trial to depict himself as a good husband, son, and father—an exemplary family man. Moreover, the writings of his most famous disciple, Plato, appear to acknowledge that while attachment to one's kin is lower than philosophy or virtue, it is necessary for a good society. In the *Republic* the discussants agree that in the ideal society, children would have to be raised by the state so as to undermine the nepotistic preference for one's relatives. Yet this could never work in practice, they admit, since parents would still be able to identify their offspring and would undoubtedly find ways to favor them. Plato's conclusion may be a subtle rebuke to Pericles, whose famous Funeral Oration attempted to shift the primary attachment of Athenians from their families to the city. This noble vision was inspiring but could not really be fulfilled: Strauss notes the failure of Athenian democracy to establish the separation between public and private that we take for granted.

The same lesson is drawn in Sophocles' *Antigone,* the third play in the cycle that begins with the story of Oedipus. In the play, the sons of Oedipus have killed each other in a civil war, and their uncle has assumed the throne of Thebes. Creon—an evident stand-in for Pericles—decrees that the body of the rebel Polynices should be left unburied, as befits the lot of traitors. But divine law holds that a man's relatives must bury him and observe the customary rites. Otherwise they may not join their parents in the underworld—the nepotistic family reunion envisioned by Greek religion. Therefore Antigone (who is betrothed to Creon's son, her cousin Haimon) steals out at night and covers her brother's body with earth. For this infraction, her uncle condemns her to death. When Haimon goes to plead her case, the father lectures him on public ethics:

> *For if I nurse unruliness in those who are kin by birth*
> *Then I shall indeed do so outside of the family.*

Creon's public-spirited rigidity leads to the destruction of his family: Antigone and Haimon kill themselves, and his wife expires in grief before the altars. The public man is left alone with his convictions: cold comfort after the havoc his authoritarian virtue has wrought upon his household. Though Antigone's loyalty to her kin is not nepotism in the modern sense, it constitutes one of the first acknowledgments of the *possibility* of nepotism, defined as the conflict between an individual's kinship obligations and the impersonal rules of the state.

Unlike other patriarchal societies, whose institutions were designed to contain and channel generational tensions, the Greeks did not shy away from the conflict between fathers and sons. Instead, Athenian democracy was based on a formula that combined generational solidarity with competition. This model proved unstable—the tension between the needs of the public sphere and the patriarchal household was too great—and it was left to later epochs to strengthen the state to the point where it could stand without relying on either the fact or metaphor of kinship. But the drama of Athenian nepotism offers a preview of later Western history—a history of sons striving not just to honor their fathers but to surpass them and make their own name. A man like Theseus feels the need to earn his patrimony; he doesn't want to have it handed to him just for being someone's son. He wants to fight for his father's recognition, and fully expects his son to do the same. Such men may well achieve great things, but they are not always inclined to make way for the next generation.

ROME: GREAT CAESAR'S GHOST

On March 15 in 44 B.C., Julius Caesar went to the Senate and was accosted by a group of armed conspirators. Relaxed and confident, the dictator was caught completely off guard by the first blow, which came from behind. The old campaigner turned to grapple with his assailant but was quickly overwhelmed. He struggled briefly, trying to avoid the biting blades that tore at his shoulders, chest, neck, and back—twenty-three stab wounds in all. But when he saw Marcus Brutus pressing forward to stab him and bathe his hands in his blood like the rest, Caesar sank to the floor, drew his cloak over his head, and accepted his fate.

We are accustomed to think of Caesar's death as the work of a handful of idealists, but he was murdered in the full Senate by as many as sixty men. So frenzied was the crowd of togaed senators trying to get at him with their knives that some of them missed the target and injured one another. He was literally hacked to death in a murderous outburst that went well beyond partisan resentment to an expression of genuine hatred. But while the assassins spoke the language of constitutionalism and republican virtue, it was too late to save the republic.

Caesar's death unleashed a struggle for power that resulted in the end of the aristocratic order and the birth of an imperial dynasty.

Nothing is worse than a dynastic family gone bad, and the imperial house of Augustus affords one of the worst examples in history of a family corrupted and destroyed by ambition and power. The lurid exploits of Augustus and his heirs have strongly colored the modern view of hereditary rule and of dynastic families in general. Without apologizing for people who poison their mothers, marry their sisters, toss their catamites from cliffs, and make their horses senators, this adverse view has tended to obscure their many lasting contributions.

Even more has it eclipsed the remarkable achievements of the Roman Republic itself. There have been other oligarchies in history, but none has matched the longevity, stability, and unity of the Roman upper class. In roughly four hundred years, Rome went from a muddy village on the banks of the Tiber to the center of the civilized world. The Romans conquered everything in sight, mastered awesome feats of civil engineering, spread their laws throughout the empire, and bequeathed us a conception of citizenship, public office, and the common good that has shaped our own political traditions. Above all, the Romans left us a legal conception of the family, as well as the distinction between public and private that profoundly influenced the development of the Western family and its relations with the state.

An oligarchy is a hereditary ruling class that deploys a broad array of nepotistic instruments to maintain its dynastic integrity. Oligarchies are therefore a manifestation of nepotism in the political realm. Oligarchies play a major role in Western history and may be thought of as the default mode of government everywhere. As historian Ronald Syme has observed, "In all ages, whatever the form and name of government, be it monarchy, republic, or democracy, an oligarchy lurks behind the façade." Throughout the history of the republic, "about twenty or thirty men, drawn from a dozen dominant families, [held] a monopoly of office and power." The real history of Rome was that of the ambitions, alliances, and feuds between these families.

The Roman Republic may be said to have taken a system of government based on nepotism as far as it could go. Indeed the Romans were very inventive and original in their use of nepotistic strategies. By Caesar's day, this closed, self-propagating caste had grown so tightly knit by centuries of marriage, adoption, inherited friendship, and patronage that it was essentially a large extended family. Ultimately this family could neither contain the tensions produced by the fantastic spoils of empire nor accommodate the talents of its most ambitious sons. The Roman historian Livy maintained that the wealth and power of empire corrupted this ancient and dignified ruling class to the point where it could no longer preserve its own values. Only when it had abandoned its hereditary virtues did this proud, rapacious oligarchy succumb to the domination of one family.

Most people are familiar with the legend of Romulus and Remus, two brothers abandoned at birth and raised by a she-wolf: Romulus killed his brother and became Rome's founder and first king. An alternative myth has the city founded by the Trojan hero Aeneas. In reality, Rome was formed in the eighth century B.C. by a gradual amalgamation of Latin and Sabine farming settlements in the hills above the Tiber. This multiethnic origin would prove immensely consequential. Unlike the Athenians, the Romans founded a universal state that admitted the other Italian tribes and eventually all its subject peoples to full citizenship.

The basic unit of Latin society was the patrilineal clan, or *gens,* a self-governing unit with its own ancestral cult and the usual duties of mutual aid, blood vengeance, and so on. The more successful clans supplied the city's ruling class, who were known as patricians. There was also an urban population of men without a *gens* who received aid and protection from aristocratic patrons in exchange for their support.

The growing settlement soon fell under the domination of Etruscan city-states to the north, who supplied Rome's early kings. The kings reorganized the *gentes* into tribes, one for each of the existing Latin, Sabine, and Etruscan ethnic groups, and divided each tribe into military and administrative units analogous to the Greek phratry and deme.[21] As the population increased, so did the number of tribes. The resulting stable yet flexible system allowed the city to expand and incorporate foreign elements while remaining largely self-governing. These reforms combined the solidarity of tribal nepotism with a legal and political conception of the people and the state: the defining formula of Classical Nepotism.

According to myth, the first Romans had no wives and sought connubial relations with their neighbors. These overtures were refused, presumably because the neighbors didn't welcome the new settlement. Finally the Romans invited the Sabines to a religious feast and carried off their daughters. (This sounds like a classic instance of bride capture, a common practice among Neolithic peoples.) The ensuing war was stopped by the women themselves, now honorably wed to Roman husbands and with children of mixed Latin and Sabine descent. The story calls attention not just to the multiethnic origins of Rome but to the role of maternal nepotism in welding these disparate elements into a single *populus Romanus*.

The last Roman kings were the Tarquins, an Etruscan dynasty painted by historians as greedy, treacherous, and cruel—especially Tarquin the Proud, whose tyrannical appetites provoked an insurrection led by Lucius Junius Brutus. Brutus drove the Tarquins out and founded a republic. When his own sons sought to reinstate the monarchy, he ordered their arrest and execution. This terrible sacrifice was meant to inspire respect for the rule of law in a society of equals, and Brutus became the symbol of that manly egalitarian spirit on which the republic relied. His action illustrates the virtue of the public man who sets his duty to the state above the bonds of blood. But Brutus also set the pattern for the Roman paterfamilias, who exercised absolute power over his household. His story constitutes an unmistakable warning to Roman sons not to let their ambitions exceed the bounds of the republican compact.

The core unit of republican Rome was neither the clan nor the individual but the *familia,* a legal entity including all persons and property belonging to the household. Thus at a very early stage, the Roman family began to separate from the *gens,* allowing the creation of a political society composed of heads of households. The household itself was not, as in other societies, a mystical union based on blood but a legal institution with well-defined roles and relationships.

Patriarchal power was much harsher in Rome than in Athens. The

Roman father was absolute ruler of his household: he controlled all of its property and had the power of life and death over everyone in it. A Roman father didn't "have" a child: he "took" one—literally raising it up off the ground where the midwife had placed it. Consequently, the nepotism of Roman fathers was highly conditional. Fathers loved their sons to the extent that they measured up to expectations, and valued them as bearers of the family's name and hopes. As a result, father-son relationships, especially among the upper class, were often distant and formal. Sons called their father *Domine,* or "Master," and no son could become legally independent or inherit his estate until his father's death. A grown son who remained under his father's authority suffered many small humiliations, including the inability to sign a contract, the need to subsist on an allowance, and the threat (frequently carried out) of disinheritance.

The Roman father ruled his household by *auctoritas,* a quality combining the authority of parent, priest, and judge. This authority was based on a complex of personal virtues, including *fides,* or faith and honor; *pietas,* which meant honoring parents and ancestors; and *virtus,* or masculine vigor.[22] Aeneas, the mythical progenitor of Rome, exemplified these virtues and was often called *pius Aeneas.*

The Romans were not an intellectual people: they learned their civic values by being taught to admire and imitate the famous men of the republic and the deeds of its mythical founders. Brutus was a powerful exemplar of republican virtues. Aeneas was the ideal Roman father, a living link between the generations. (In Virgil's epic, Aeneas escapes the destruction of Troy carrying his father on his shoulders and holding his little son, Ascanius, by the hand.) Horatius prevented an Etruscan army from crossing the Tiber, single-handedly holding the Sublician Bridge—too busy doing his duty to wonder what had become of his companions. Cincinnatus—to whom George Washington was frequently compared—came to Rome's aid in an emergency, reluctantly leaving his plow to assume dictatorial powers, then virtuously returning to his farm. Such stories inspired a spirit of emulation and self-sacrifice and a cultlike devotion to the state. Families competed in their services to the state, and were rewarded with political, religious, or military offices. Generational and sibling tensions were thus effectively submerged in the competition to be first among equals.

Political *auctoritas* was vested in the Senate, a literal convention of "fathers" from whose ranks all public offices were filled. Since officers were elected in the tribal assemblies, popular support was necessary, and candidates had to demonstrate their fitness, based on the degree to which they personally upheld traditional virtues. Consequently, the probity, sobriety, and incorruptibility of republican officials were justly renowned. As Livy put it, the magistrates respected the gods, the fathers respected the magistrates, and the sons respected the fathers. So long as this chain of respect was upheld, the republican state was secure.

The Romans also took steps to keep their sons in line by ensuring that no young or untested man would rise to the state's highest office. A formal schedule of offices was established, with minimum age grades for each. Men climbed the ladder step by step, and it often took several generations for a family to reach the higher levels. The highest office, that of consul, combined the roles of chief executive and military leader. The consulate was an ingenious institution for power sharing and stability in the Roman ruling class. Strict annual rotation allowed for the channeling and sublimation of competition within the oligarchy and prevented any individual or faction from gaining too much power.

This didn't stop ambitious families from forming compacts with one another and jointly aggrandizing these offices for long periods of time. Such compacts were called friendships *(amicitiae)* and were sealed by ties of marriage, adoption, and patronage. Real power was tightly controlled by the small circle of noble families who had succeeded in obtaining and holding the consulate for some period of time, passing it back and forth for a decade or more. A "new man" like Marius or Cicero had to be helped to this position by powerful friends with something to gain by opening the ranks of the oligarchy's inner circle. The nepotistic interest of new men in securing the rights and privileges of nobility for their sons helped keep the oligarchy stable as it gradually (and grudgingly) expanded.

The power of a Roman politician was based on his personal faction, beginning with his relatives and friends. These formed the nepotistic core of any party. Friendship was supremely important to the Romans and formed a bond equivalent to kinship. Adoption was another way of adding to the family's strength.[23] Above all, however, building a large clientele was indispensable to political success. Clienteles were based on patronage, a sacred bond of mutual obligation for the Romans. The title of patron was second in honor only to that of father in republican Rome. Patronage relationships were a form of family property, and a young patrician inherited his father's *clientela* along with his friendships and other assets. A large clientele was a symbol of status and power. As Gaston Boissier explains, "A Claudius or a Cornelius, even before he had taken the trouble to oblige anybody, was sure to find his hall half filled every morning with people whom gratitude attached to his family, and he produced a sensation in the Forum by the number of those who accompanied him the day he went there to plead his first cause."[24] Ambitious men attracted such followings by bribery in the form of public games, free wheat and wine, and payments to voters and jurors. Because all this required considerable wealth, a politician's power usually depended on obtaining the magistracy of a foreign province, which he exploited for personal gain.

In the third and second centuries B.C., Rome fought a series of wars with Carthage for dominance in the western Mediterranean. The duel to the death between these powerful city-states was also a personal feud between two military families, the Barcas and the Scipios.

In 251 B.C., the Carthaginian commander Hamilcar Barca lost Sicily to the Romans; withdrawing to Spain, he made his son Hannibal swear a sacred oath to avenge his defeat. After his father's death, Hannibal assumed command of Carthaginian armies in Spain and gave subordinate commands to his brothers Hasdrubal, Gnaeus, and Mago. After seizing Roman properties in Spain, he lead an army across the Alps, elephants included, and plunged toward Rome, leaving a trail of devastation in his wake.

The Scipios were a distinguished consular family with a long history of military excellence. During the First Punic War, Lucius Cornelius Scipio drove the Carthaginians out of Sardinia and Corsica. Forty years later his son Publius encountered Hannibal as he descended from the Alps, and was disastrously defeated. As Publius lay wounded and surrounded by enemies, his own son rushed to his side and saved his life. The father was defeated again by Hannibal at Trebia, and a few years later he and his brother were killed by Carthaginians in Spain. The younger Scipio struck his first blow against Carthage and the hated Barca family in 208, when he defeated Hasdrubal and Mago and drove the Carthaginians out of Spain. He then invaded North Africa, drawing Hannibal away from Rome. His victory at Zama broke the power of Carthage and opened the way for Roman imperial expansion.

No sphere of activity was more important to the Romans than the conduct of their wars. Judging from this outcome, the Romans could hardly have had any complaints about nepotism in the military.

The struggles within the upper class became more fierce and uncompromising as Rome grew fantastically rich on the spoils of empire. Senators vied for lucrative commands and governorships, and their clienteles expanded to include not just tribes of urban followers but foreign cities, provinces, and kingdoms. The rise of a new class of wealthy merchants and financiers put pressure on the old aristocratic system, while the birth of a mass urban public became a destabilizing factor in politics.

Paralleling these developments were changes in the family itself. The autonomy granted to individual families by the republican social order had already diminished the power of the ancient Roman clans. The unprecedented wealth and affluence of the first century B.C. intensified this trend and produced a growing shift to bilateralism, especially among the upper classes. As a result, Roman women enjoyed increasing status and importance. While fathers still governed by *patria potestas,* wives and children acquired more legal rights. The father lost his power of life and death; divorce became more common and could be initiated by either party; husbands no longer owned their wives' dowries outright; and the institution of the will allowed women to inherit and dispose of their own property.[25] Sons too could now engage in a variety of profitable pursuits and could keep what they earned, including what they inherited from their mothers. The idea of legal rights for women and children, along with the all-important power of testation, would be a major legacy to later Western societies.

During the long period of Rome's rise, the competition for honor between the great families had been the lifeblood of the state. But the stakes were now too high, and competition between the most ambitious families grew increasingly volatile. It was only a matter of time before these unbridled rivalries brought an end to the republic.

Gaius Julius Caesar was the scion of an ancient family that had fallen into eclipse and was revived by the patronage of the dictator Marius, who had married Caesar's aunt. His father died when he was eighteen, and his mother, Aurelia, played a major role in his life. As with many a Roman matron, her advice and influence were highly regarded by her son, especially where it concerned the choice of wives.

Though Roman clans were patriarchal, the importance of Roman matrons cannot be overstated. The Roman nobility was a network of families linked by complex webs of marriage, patronage, and *amicitia*; women were the medium and focus of these shifting alliances, and the major nexus points of the system were controlled by powerful matriarchs who exercised a hidden influence over political events. According to Ronald Syme, such women were not merely pawns of masculine intrigue. "Far from it: the daughters of the great houses commanded political influence in their own right, exercising a power beyond the reach of many a senator." Caesar's mother, Aurelia, was one of these great ladies.[26]

An ambitious, energetic, and remarkably self-possessed young man, Caesar rose through a combination of dynastic marriage, the creation of a large clientele, innate military genius, and incessant political intrigue. He performed well in a succession of offices and acquired a silent partner in the person of Crassus, a wealthy financier who helped him build a large popular following by sponsoring gladiatorial games and other lavish entertainments. Caesar was also a master of the Roman art of patronage. He knew well how to attract, exploit, and reward the most capable men, and he collected numerous protégés, whom he advanced in many ways.

On his first military mission, in 61 B.C., he subdued the western half of Spain and returned home with his eye on the consulate. At this point he allied himself with Pompey, then the greatest soldier in Rome. From his magnificent conquests in the East, Pompey had acquired enormous wealth and counted many kings and satraps in his vast clientele. Backed by Crassus, Caesar stood for consul in 59 B.C., and together with Pompey they formed the First Triumvirate. Between them they divided up the world, with Pompey in the East and Caesar giving himself the rich but still unconquered western province of Gaul. To cement their *amicitia,* Caesar married his daughter Julia to Pompey, though to do so he had to break her engagement to the young Marcus Brutus.

Supposedly Caesar called Brutus "child" as he expired. This was no figure of speech: Brutus was listed among Caesar's heirs and was even rumored to be his illegitimate son. Historians discount this possibility, but Caesar obviously felt a strong fatherly attachment for Brutus and had done much to advance his career.

The breaking of Julia's engagement to Brutus undid the dynastic schemes of Brutus's mother, Servilia, one of the hidden matriarchal powers of Rome. Ronald Syme describes her as a woman "possessed of all the rapacious ambition of the patrician Servilii and ruthless to recapture power for her house."[27] Servilia and Caesar had been lovers, and she maintained close ties to him during his meteoric rise. There was even talk that she had given him her daughter as a mistress. She schemed to link her family with Caesar's through the marriage of Brutus and Julia, but Caesar's deal with Pompey put a crimp in this design. Nor, in all probability, was Brutus himself very pleased. Like any Roman noble, Servilia also had her feuds: she hated Pompey, who had killed her first husband, and she passed this bitter hatred to her sons.

With a string of brilliant victories in Gaul, Caesar soon rivaled Pompey as Rome's greatest general, and he used his new wealth and prestige to enlarge his following. The marriage bond with Pompey had kept friction to a minimum, but Julia's death in childbirth broke this tie. When Crassus was killed at the head of an army in Syria, the rivalry between the two generals broke out in open conflict. In this the prime mover was Servilia's stepbrother Cato, a staunch conservative who hated Caesar and had opposed him from the start of his career.

Brutus greatly admired his distinguished uncle Cato and shared his republican principles. After the end of his engagement to Julia he strengthened this tie by marrying Cato's daughter. When Caesar brought his armies into Italy in 49 B.C., Pompey withdrew to Greece, along with Cato and a group of other prominent Romans. Brutus's defection to the side of his father's killer surprised his contemporaries, none more so than Pompey himself.[28] Nevertheless, Caesar gave orders that he was not to be harmed in the upcoming battle, and if possible should be allowed to escape.

Pompey was defeated and fled to Egypt, where he was killed. Cato committed suicide in the old Roman style. As for Brutus, Caesar graciously welcomed him back to Rome and made him governor of a wealthy province. Later he promoted Brutus and his brother-in-law Cassius to prominent positions, and probably intended them for the consulate. Everyone agrees that Caesar would have made Brutus the first man in Rome and quite likely the heir to the throne. However, the same mixture of family ties and traditions that had led Brutus to join Pompey now drew him into the plot against Caesar.

The leader of a Roman party was not a free agent. He occupied a nexus of personal forces united by kinship, friendship, patronage, and family obligations. This had been the case as long as Rome's governing class remained a small, inbred society of equals. But the fantastic spoils of empire and the extension of citizenship to include most of Italy had unleashed political forces that could no longer be contained by narrow oligarchic factions. Caesar had turned Rome's armies into a huge personal clientele, looting the provinces under his control and using the money to subsidize a massive campaign of electoral bribery. He had concentrated power in his own hands, advanced his supporters to office, and flooded the Senate with new men beholden to his patronage. He posed a danger to the state because he threatened to outgrow the bounds of party; the personal ties of the traditional Roman faction could no longer confine him. Therefore he had to be killed.

Caesar was the apotheosis of Roman military virtue—the greatest general in Rome's history and a man of godlike vision and charisma. It was a powerful patrimony for anyone able to claim it. He had attracted many followers; who would be his heir?

First in line was Antony, a loyal and capable soldier who had served Caesar well for many years and was now the dictator's co-consul. He was also Caesar's cousin. Caesar had shown tremendous confidence in Antony, but he also had grave limitations and flaws—he was licentious, coarse, a gambler, often drunk, and a compulsive womanizer. Caesar was a stickler for the traditional virtues and had a great deal of family pride. It seems unlikely that he would choose such a man to carry on his name. Still, as Caesar's deputy it was natural for Antony to assume the leadership of his party. In the aftermath of the murder he called for calm and moderation. Instead of demanding vengeance he proposed that Brutus and Cassius be temporarily exiled, and he even dined with Brutus cordially that night. The next day, however, he made an emotional speech at Caesar's funeral and displayed his bloody garments to the crowd. An angry mob attacked the homes of the conspirators and they were forced to flee the country. Antony then assumed the leadership of the Senate and immediately raised his brothers to high office. He also took charge of Caesar's personal assets and began making appointments and issuing orders in his name.

Caesar's will was then unsealed and read in public. To Antony's surprise, however, Caesar had named an obscure kinsman as his adopted son and heir. This unknown person was Octavius, later to be known as Augustus. Octavius rose to become the first Roman emperor with little more to trade on than his great-uncle's famous name—a magnificent achievement requiring ruthless determination and consummate political skill. One of the most successful dynasts of all time, his reign of over fifty-six years is still the longest period of personal domination in Western history.

Octavius was born in 63 B.C. to a rich provincial family. His father had married Caesar's niece and rose to the Senate under his patronage. After his father's death, Octavius came under the wing of his great-uncle Julius, who rapidly advanced him, enrolling him as a patrician and getting him appointed at only sixteen to the prestigious board of priests. In 46 the young man rode beside him in the triumphal procession after his victory in North Africa. The next year Octavius campaigned with him in Spain, after which Caesar sent him to Greece to complete his studies. It was there that he had news of Caesar's death. Returning to Italy, he found Antony at the head of Caesar's party and in possession of his assets. He also learned that he had been named Caesar's heir by adoption.

Octavius wisely courted the leading figures of the Caesarean party. He then legally accepted the adoption, assuming the name Gaius Julius Caesar Octavianus, and confronted Antony, demanding the funds to fulfill Caesar's lavish bequests to the Roman populace and army. The older man rudely dismissed him, calling him (accurately enough) a mere boy who owed everything to his name. Octavian thereupon paid the dictator's bequests out of his own pocket and withdrew to central Italy, where he quickly raised an army from the veterans of Caesar's Gallic wars, settled on lands he had given them. This vast clientele owed loyalty not only to Caesar but to Caesar's legitimate heir.

Antony's failure to demand vengeance for Caesar's murder had left Octavian a valuable weapon. It allowed him to show his *pietas* by prosecuting a blood feud against Brutus, whereas Antony, who was ready to compromise with the assassins, could be painted as disloyal to his kinsman and benefactor. Octavian therefore pressed for charges to be brought against Brutus and the other conspirators. He then got the Senate to legitimize his illegal command and marched north to attack Antony, who fled across the Alps to raise more troops from his colleague Marcus Lepidus. Octavian marched on Rome, forced the Senate to declare him consul, then marched north again to confront the combined armies of Antony and Lepidus. But the common soldiers refused to countenance a fight between Caesar's heirs, and after two days of tense negotiations a Second Triumvirate was formed, between Antony, Octavian, and Lepidus. After that they turned their forces against Brutus and the liberators.

According to legend, the night before the battle of Philippi, Caesar's ghost appeared to Brutus, indicting his ingratitude and predicting his imminent doom. Such, at least, was the popular story. In the event, Brutus lost the battle and took his own life, as did the "lean and hungry" Cassius, another ingrate whom Caesar had raised to a high position in the state. Thus was Caesar's ghost avenged. But it did not go quietly or fade into oblivion. The apparition may have faded with the dawn, but Caesar's ghost survived in the form of Octavian and the dynasty he founded in Caesar's name.

Once again the victorious triumvirs divided up the Roman world. Octavian then crushed the power of Lepidus and renewed his pact with Antony, sealing it with a marriage between Antony and Octavian's sister.

Marriages, divorces, and adoptions were the outward signs of alliances or feuds among the Roman upper class. Occasionally, however, passion and ambition were conjoined. Such was the match between Octavian and Livia Drusilla, an aristocratic young woman amply endowed with beauty, powerful family connections, and keen political intelligence. Octavian had first married Antony's stepdaughter, but the marriage was never consummated. Next he wed the tedious Scribonia, cementing a brief alliance with Pompey's son. He then met and fell in love with Livia. Livia was a Claudian and had inherited the famous pride of that ancient clan. Occupying a vital nexus in the Roman power structure, she was one of those matriarchal figures who commanded vast political influence behind the scenes through the manipulation of marriage and kinship connections. Tacitus called Livia a "disaster" as a mother and a "calamity" as a stepmother. Even Tiberius, her son, for whom she relentlessly plotted and schemed, openly disliked her and complained of her interference in public affairs. In *I, Claudius,* Robert Graves offers a fictionalized, heightened, often speculative, but still quite plausible portrait of Livia as a ruthless nepotist who would do anything to advance her designs. At the time of her marriage to Octavian, Livia already had one son and was about to give birth to another. Her husband obligingly stepped aside, and she and Octavian were married at the height of her pregnancy. On the day of the wedding, Scribonia gave birth to a daughter named Julia. According to Suetonius, Octavian "snatched the baby from her mother the moment she was born." The girl would become a much-abused pawn of her father's dynastic ambition.

Meanwhile Antony seriously undermined himself by carrying on a passionate affair with Cleopatra, the Egyptian queen and Caesar's former mistress. When he formally divorced Octavia, the alliance with Octavian collapsed. Declaring a state of emergency, Octavian arranged for all the inhabitants of Italy and the western provinces to swear an oath of personal allegiance, thereby establishing the moral basis for his subsequent imperium. After Antony's forces were defeated at Actium, he and Cleopatra committed suicide, leaving Octavian alone at the summit of power.

Or so it seemed. For while we are accustomed to think of Octavian (soon to rename himself Augustus) as an autocratic ruler unaccountable to anyone, he rose to power as the leader of a party and the front man for an oligarchic circle; nor even at his peak could he entirely escape from its constraints. The members of this circle were Marcus Agrippa, the blunt, plainspoken soldier who had won his greatest victories; Maecenas, the wealthy aesthete, diplomat, and administrative genius who supplied money, advice, and connections; and Livia herself: much more than a wife and adviser, she was the keystone in the arch of his faction. Augustus might resist them individually, but he could not oppose all three.

The old consular families had been decimated by decades of civil war; a master of the nepotistic arts, Augustus strove to attach the survivors to his person, his family, and the new political order. This involved the systematic use of every relative he had in the vigorous creation of a large extended family, strengthened by a combination of marriage within the Julio-Claudian clan itself and marital links to other powerful clans. "The schemes devised by Augustus in the ramification of family alliances were formidable and fantastic. He neglected no relative, however obscure, however distant, no tie whatever of marriage—or of friendship retained after divorce. As time went on, more and more aristocratic families were lured by matrimony into the family and following of the Princeps."[29] This was the core of the new oligarchy, centered on his family, that Augustus built upon the ruins of the old.

Augustus liked to present himself as a traditional Roman magistrate, humble in demeanor, simple and pious in his habits. In reality he was the center of a vast network of patronage entirely dependent on his bounty. On his principal adherents he bestowed nobility through the consulate, social distinction through advantageous marriages, and wealth through provincial possessions. These in turn dispensed patronage to their own clients, thereby spreading the web of personal obligation to the farthest reaches of the empire. In this way Augustus created the first centrally directed administrative system in Rome's history. This vast patronage system deprived the Senate and Roman assembly of practical power and concentrated it in the hands of the emperor and his friends. Real politics was soon replaced by courtiership and maneuvering for influence within the family circle of Augustus.

The revolutionary Augustus was also a social conservative who passed a great deal of family-centered legislation. First, to replenish the ranks of the patriciate and society in general after decades of civil war, he took steps to promote procreation. Under the republic a man had to be a paterfamilias before he could hold the highest offices; Augustus renewed and expanded this rule.[30] Couples with three or more children were greatly favored, and adultery was punishable by death. These edicts, which established the foundations of Classical Nepotism, were intended to restore the moral order of the household and the state after a period of social upheaval.

Augustus could bequeath his name and fortune to whomever he wished, but not his imperium or even the leadership of his party. His *auctoritas* was personal, unique, and nontransferable. Yet he gradually succeeded in creating a new office, the principate, whose powers might be assigned or designated by formal adoption. With that accomplished, he wasted little time in preparing the way for a successor who would also be his personal heir and establish his line.

Augustus's manner of disposing of his relatives was high-handed and peremptory in the extreme. His favorite and first choice as heir apparent was his nephew Marcellus. The young man was married to Augustus's daughter, Julia, and advanced to the consulate at twenty-three—ten years before the minimum age—after which Augustus made known his desire to adopt the young man. But he died within the year, and Julia was wed to Agrippa. This marriage produced three sons and two daughters. Augustus married one of the girls to his grandnephew Germanicus. Octavia's daughters by Antony were also married off, the younger to Livia's son Drusus. After Agrippa's death, Julia was married for a third time, to Livia's son Tiberius; though he was happily married to Agrippa's daughter, Augustus forced him to divorce his pregnant wife. After the death of Marcellus, Augustus adopted his grandsons by Agrippa, Gaius and Lucius, but both died within the space of eighteen months. Augustus then adopted their younger brother Postumus along with his stepson Tiberius, who was required in turn to adopt his own nephew Germanicus. But Germanicus died in Syria, and Augustus—at Livia's insistence—disinherited Postumus on suspicion of gross misconduct and sent him into exile.

Though Augustus relied heavily on Livia's sons, he clearly hoped to be succeeded by a member of his own Julian line. Livia for her part used her influence to undermine his chosen heirs and promote her sons instead. Accordingly, Tiberius held the offices of quaestor, praetor, and consul well before the usual age, and was given numerous military commands. Drusus also held important offices and military postings. After Drusus died in an accident, Livia concentrated her ambition on Tiberius; obstacles to his advancement had a habit of disappearing or dying young. Ultimately, says Tacitus, Tiberius "remained alone of the stepsons, and in him everything tended to center. He was adopted as a son, as a colleague in empire and a partner in the tribunician power, and paraded through all the armies, no longer through his mother's secret intrigues, but at her open suggestion." When Augustus withdrew during his last illness, Livia daily issued encouraging bulletins about his health until one day she announced that he had died. When his will was read in the Senate it was to no one's surprise that he divided his estate between Tiberius and Livia.

This was a tremendous victory for Livia, but she herself had no great joy of it. Tiberius kept her at arm's length, often warned her not to meddle in his affairs, and prevented the Senate from naming her "parent of her country" or granting her any other conspicuous honor. He saw her only once in the three years before she died. He didn't bother to visit her in her final illness, left her body unburied for days, and forbade her posthumous deification, although she had ardently wished it.

Turbulent times, a great name, and a preternatural grasp of Roman politics helped launch Octavian's career. The extraordinary result suggests what Alcibiades might have accomplished had he been born a

Roman. A young man advanced to high office well before the normal age, an opportunist trading on his uncle's reputation, a beneficiary and exploiter of nepotism, Octavian succeeded beyond even his own wildest dreams. In one respect a vindication of nepotism, he showed more mettle than his youth, frail health, and inexperience could possibly foretell. As a nepotist, his own record is ambiguous: he failed to preserve his family from the ravages of power and lost the struggle for succession to his wife. Yet he left an influential image for all time of what a ruthless family dynast can accomplish. Henceforth it would no longer be enough for ambitious men simply to conquer the world as Alexander had done; instead they must establish a universal state and bequeath it to their heirs in perpetuity.

Classical Nepotism eases the subordination of sons characteristic of non-Western societies, to the extent that their rebellious energies are channeled to productive ends. It also introduces the distinction between public and private on which we base our modern political and administrative systems. Such societies are more dynamic than those of Africa, China, or India, but they remain highly patriarchal and prescriptive.

In all nepotistic societies, ancient or classical, the individual as such hardly exists apart from the family and kin group. Children are regarded as property, and parents retain the power to decide where they will live, what they will do, whom they will marry. Private and political authority are rationalized by a paternalistic creed, supported by some form of ancestral religion, and expressed through a system of patronage that unifies society from top to bottom in a chain of obligations modeled on the father-son relationship.

Western Nepotism, though it arises from the same complex of institutions, values, and practices, has been much more individualistic than its Ancient or Classical precursors. It is strongly patriarchal, yet it also places limits on the father's authority, ultimately liberating women and children and allowing them unprecedented freedom.

The European nepotism against which Americans define themselves—class-based, paternalistic, and exclusive—is a product of the first millennium of Western history. Out of the wreckage of the Roman

Empire there emerged a Christian civilization based on the unity of church and state and a new pattern of family life vigorously promoted by both. Historians agree that what makes the West distinctive has been the gradual decline of kinship systems and the emergence of the family and individual as actors in their own right. The vitality and growth of European societies is therefore linked to sweeping changes in the overall pattern of marriage, reproduction, and inheritance. We owe this transformation to the action on society of three great institutions: the church, the state, and the market. The impact of these forces on the unique pattern of European nepotism is the story of the coming of the modern world.

CHAPTER 5

THE SON MADE PERFECT

NEPOTISM IN THE CHRISTIAN WEST

In A.D. 778, after a failed incursion into Muslim Spain, Charlemagne withdrew across the Pyrenees to France. As the tail end of his army filed through the narrow pass at Roncesvalles, a group of Basque marauders fell upon the French rear guard and killed them to a man. Many were crushed by large rocks hurled from the cliffs above. Among the dead was Charlemagne's nephew, Count Roland, and his company of knights.

This obscure eighth-century border skirmish would probably have been forgotten had it not been transformed by an anonymous Christian poet into a seminal work of European literature. In the poem, composed some three hundred years after the event, Charlemagne has been tricked into leaving Spain on the promise that the Saracens will convert to Christianity. Roland volunteers to bring up the rear with his companions, known as the Twelve Peers—the flower of French knighthood. But the Saracens pursue them and attack the outnumbered Franks in a battle that rages for hours. When it becomes clear that they are doomed, the noble Olivier asks Roland to blow his horn and summon help. Roland refuses, since to do so would be a stain on his honor. But after Olivier is mortally wounded, Roland takes pity on his friend: he blows a series of blasts on his horn, bursting his temples with the effort.

Miles ahead, the king hears Roland's horn and hurries back to find the mutilated bodies of his knights amid the plundered baggage carts.

When he comes upon the body of Roland himself, still grasping the mighty sword and horn that Charles had given him, the king dissolves in tears.

"God!" says the King, "Now well may I despair,
I was not here the first assault to share!"
Seeming enraged, his beard the King doth tear.

The other Franks weep too, and according to the poet, twenty thousand soldiers faint from grief. Next, for several stanzas, the king laments his fallen champion:

"Roland, my friend, may God to thee be kind!
Never beheld any man such a knight
So to engage and so to end a fight.
Now my honour is turned into decline!"
Charles swoons again, he cannot stand upright.

This extravagant display goes on for pages, with more crying, lamentation, and tearing of the king's hair and beard. Pulling himself together at last, Charles pursues the pagan host. God makes the sun stand still so he has time to smash his enemy. Another battle follows against an even larger army; Charles defeats the pagan king in single combat, with the aid of the archangel Gabriel.

The *Song of Roland* is one of many chivalric romances, known as *chansons de geste,* that circulated in Europe during the eleventh and twelfth centuries. A surprisingly large number of these poems involve the deeds of Charlemagne and his nephews. In one, Charles knights his nephew Anseis and gives him Spain and Carthage, while he grants large fiefs in Saxony to his nephew Baudouin and also arranges his marriage. In another, Charles sends a nephew to defend the papal city. Charlemagne, it seems, has many nephews, and he considers it his duty *and* his pleasure to act as their patron and sponsor.

These chivalric romances did not arise in a vacuum. According to historians, they reflect the new social reality of feudalism and have as their main theme the ideal relation between vassal and lord. This bond is fully the equal of kinship; hence the constant tension in these poems between a man's obligations to his kin and to his lord. But the poems give special prominence to the bond between uncle and nephew. The uncles in these courtly romances often raise the young hero, give him his first horse and sword, and initiate him into manhood by dubbing him Knight. Historians Marc Bloch and Georges Duby attribute the sudden prominence of uncles in the literature of the eleventh and twelfth centuries to the emergence of patrilineal clans among the feudal nobility. The fact that these are uniformly uncles on the mother's side is also significant. Even in the most rigidly patrilineal societies, men do not relinquish their claim on their nephews and grandsons—the sons of their sisters and daughters. Father-son relations in such societies are often harsh and strained, and the maternal uncle may supply the kind of affection and support that the natural father does not.

But *Roland* is a Christian epic, and its spiritualized portrayal of the nephew-uncle relationship reflects the victory of the church over the older kin-based solidarities out of which the high civilization of Europe emerged. Roland is the quintessential Christian hero; there are overtones of the martyrdom of Christ in his death at the hands of unbelieving Saracens and their allies. His very sword, Durendal, containing holy relics in its hilt, became a potent symbol of militant Christianity at the time of the Crusades. Unlike Beowulf, a pagan hero who strives for glory and renown, Roland gives his life to preserve the Christian West from the encroaching Muslim threat. The poem therefore reflects a significant stage in the transformation of the Germanic warrior ethos by the ideal of Christian knighthood, which fused piety and honor in a higher code of chivalry.

The history of Europe, from one angle, is the story of its evolving kinship structures. Specifically, it is the story of the emergence of the family and individual from an enveloping tribal background. Christianity detached the conjugal family from its extended family network and reincorporated it into an alternative system of spiritual kinship. Feudalism replaced the tribal priest-king and his pagan warrior band with a system of patron-client relations. The resulting civilization of the Christian West is the seedbed of Europe. A coherent society in its own right, it is also a society in transition from the crude and often violent nepotism of the tribe to the more civilized but no less corporate nepotism of the Christian Middle Ages.

THE CHURCH: THE SON MADE PERFECT

From its inception, Christianity has had a complex and ambiguous relationship with the family—starting with the family of Jesus himself. The extent of Jesus' family is a matter of dispute, but from the gospels themselves it seems clear that he was not an only child but part of a large extended family. At first these relatives rejected him, but in the end they seem to have become the core of his following. Ties of kinship also linked many of Jesus' other disciples.[1] The identity of these figures has long been debated, but it is more or less accepted that James, who became the first bishop of Jerusalem, was Jesus' actual brother. After his martyrdom, in A.D. 62, James was succeeded by a cousin of Jesus.

In short, the primitive church was a family business, and the authority of Jesus' relatives and of the apostles directly appointed by him was fully recognized by the earliest Christian communities. The question is how the cult of this obscure Jewish family evolved beyond its narrow tribal origins to encompass the whole Western world.

The universal church grew out of sectarian struggles following the death of Jesus between James, the brother of the charismatic founder, and Paul, the visionary zealot who wanted to bring the message of Christ to all the peoples of the empire. James saw the church as essentially Jewish. To him, Jesus was not a revolutionary who had come to overthrow the law of Moses but a prophet in the Mosaic tradition—in other words, James remained within the horizon of tribal nepotism. But Paul wanted to make Christianity appealing to non-Jews by presenting Jesus as repudiating Jewish law and announcing a new universal religion. This meant emphasizing Jesus' divinity, his status as the son of God, at the expense of his humanity, his status as a Jew. Mary could be useful to the increasingly Hellenized cult as the pure and exalted vessel of the divine Logos. But what about the rest of Jesus' family?

These inconvenient relatives had to be erased if Jesus was to be presented as a unique spiritual being with miraculous powers over life and death. Jesus' human father, Joseph, was therefore relegated to the role of a benevolent stepfather and his siblings redefined as half- or stepbrothers and cousins.

Ultimately, Paul's branch of Christianity won out. Zealots usually do, and it is interesting to reflect that while James's conservatism was likely the result of his loyalty to Jesus and the spirit of his teachings, Paul as an outsider was under no such constraints, and his radicalism was given freer play. Ironically, then, Christianity succeeded as a world religion largely due to the erasure of Jesus' family and its importance to his ministry. The surviving adherents of the Jerusalem church continued to observe Jewish law, magnified the importance of James over Peter and Paul, and rejected the doctrine of the virgin birth. These Jewish Christians were a force in Judea as late as A.D. 160, but they were ignored by traditional Jews and finally outnumbered by the Gentile church founded by Peter and Paul.[2]

Paul's victory over James, it must be said, was abetted by the teachings of Jesus himself, assuming they have come down to us in an accurate form. According to the gospels, Jesus presented himself not merely as God's prophet but as his son. In Matthew 3:17—the scene of Jesus' baptism—God speaks from heaven, acknowledging Jesus as his legitimate offspring in the manner of a Greek or Roman father: "This is my beloved Son, in whom I am well pleased." Jesus refers to God as *abba*, the Aramaic word for "father," and in John 10:30, Jesus asserts his radical doctrine of the unity of Father and Son, saying, "I and the Father are one." In John 14:6 Jesus proclaims, "No man cometh unto the Father but by me," a statement that seems to cast Jesus in the familiar role of a prince who controls access to his father's throne.

All primitive religions try to establish relations of kinship with the gods in hopes that they will treat us nepotistically, and many tribal peoples consider themselves to be descended from divine ancestors. But this was a major innovation in terms of the Jewish tradition, and it had dramatic consequences for the conception of the Jews as a chosen people. The Hebrews had understood themselves as God's elect, but not as his literal children. Rather they were the children of Abraham, and through him the heirs to God's covenant. The sonship of Jesus is a powerful warrant of his authority to set aside the old covenant and, "in the name of the Father," to introduce a new form of observance.

What, then, is the significance of the crucifixion of Jesus? What does it mean that God allows the death of his only son? This is a far cry from the blatant favoritism shown by the Greek and Roman gods toward their human offspring, like that of Zeus for Sarpedon and Hercules. Simply put, the death of Jesus constitutes dramatic proof of God's fatherly care for mankind. By sacrificing his only begotten son, God shows that we are all his children. This unique innovation—the extension of divine nepotism from a favored people to all humanity—is what allowed the Jewish system of monotheistic belief to transcend the tribal boundary and encompass other nations. The idea would be developed by Paul into an even more compelling vision of God's universal love, though necessarily at the expense of the human Jesus and his circle of intimate supporters.

The mystery of the Eucharist also transformed the nature of Jewish sacrificial observance. Previously God had been invited to partake of the sacrifice offered by those who sought his protection and favor. The sharing of food with the gods (called commensality) is an ancient means of establishing reciprocal relationships equivalent to kinship. By inviting them to share our table we not only bring the gods into our family circle but put them in our debt, evoking a sense of gratitude and a corresponding obligation to repay our unsolicited gifts. But the exchange we seek is not an equal one. The gift of divine favor is far more valuable than the burnt sacrifice we offer. Seen from this perspective, sacrificial religion is really an attempt to coerce a more powerful being into a patronage relationship by manipulating the rules of reciprocity.

In the Old Testament, God substitutes a ram for Abraham's son Isaac. In the New Testament, God substitutes his own son for the traditional animal sacrifice. Through the sharing of the eucharistic meal, in which the believer symbolically consumes the body and blood of Christ, the Lamb of God, Christians enter directly into the sonship of Jesus, an idea expressed in Revelation 21:7: "I will be his God and he shall be my son."

Yet Jesus also presents himself as a potentially divisive figure who may separate men from their parents, wives, and children. The most extreme expressions of this attitude appear in the gospel of Matthew, where Jesus declares, "I come not to bring peace but a sword," by which he means that adherence to his teachings will necessarily divide a man from his relatives. "For I am come to set a man at variance with his father, and the daughter against her mother, and the daughter-in-law against her mother-in-law." And again, "He that loveth father or mother more than me is not worthy of me: and he that loveth son or daughter more than me is not worthy of me" (Matthew 10:34–37). These old nepotistic ties mean nothing in the new dispensation of faith, and may even be an obstacle to salvation. In place of these blood relatives, the believer finds new kin in the Christian community. "For whosoever shall do the will of my Father which is in heaven, the same is my brother, and sister, and mother" (Matthew 12:50).

These sentiments reflect the status of the early church as a vulnerable and persecuted sect struggling to define itself in opposition to conventional Judaism. The process of separation from Jewish society obviously required the denigration of existing family ties in favor of the Christian community. The ceremony of baptism symbolized the believer's adoption into a new spiritual family. But as the church grew in strength and numbers, it became as much concerned with preserving Christian families as with breaking up non-Christian ones. The goal now was not merely to detach converts from their ancestral beliefs but to strengthen the faith of those who had acquired it within their own families.

At first the Christian home was not only the setting for religious observances but the archetype of the church itself. Paul called the members of his congregation in Ephesus "members of the household of God." It took many generations for the church to emerge from this familial context as a fully independent institution. Meanwhile, the Christian family was a valuable ally in the struggle against heresy and apostasy, and the church took steps to bolster it. Paul's teachings on the family were especially influential, establishing the practical and moral authority of the father over his wife, children, and servants as well as his duty of spiritual guidance and correction.

Paul's ideal family was expressly patriarchal, but it also involved a unique vision of the reciprocal duties between fathers and their families: the authority of the Christian father was tempered by the law of love and by a concern for the needs and rights of wives and children. Paul's doctrine of marriage therefore promoted the spiritualization of family life in a way that deepened the emotional bonds between husbands and wives, parents and children, and heads of households in the larger congregation.

Conversion to Christianity wreaked havoc on the Greco-Roman family, whose unity was based to a large extent on its ancestral cult. Even more divisive was the disposition of family property by wealthy believers. Originally the church had been without possessions and preached the virtues of poverty. The establishment of churches and other religious communities throughout the empire required vast sums of money, as did the fulfillment of Christ's injunction to succor the poor and aid widows and orphans. It was the Roman upper classes who subsidized this growth, primarily by gifts and bequests that often came at the expense of living heirs.

With the conversion of the emperor Constantine in the fourth century, the growth of the church greatly accelerated. Constantine made Christianity the official cult of the Roman state, decreeing that the church could legally own property and that a dying man could bequeath his estate to the church even without a written testament. This new testatory freedom encouraged many individuals to disinherit their kin in favor of the church, which rapidly built up possessions. Here the Roman institutions of the will and of female inheritance made their singular contribution to the triumph of Christianity. For believers the will was first and foremost a spiritual instrument, designed for the salvation of one's soul. Money and property given to the church were used in part for prayers and good works in the donor's behalf. The more you bequeathed to the church, the more credit you banked in the afterlife. This concern for personal salvation pitted the spiritual interests of parents against the material interests of children, and many heirs complained against the practice. Edward Gibbon later cited the "unfortunate children" of these early Christians "who found themselves beggars because their parents had been saints."

So widespread and zealous was the observance of this spiritual injunction to succor the needy—particularly among women, who have always been the mainstay of clerical fund-raising—that steps had to be taken to curtail it. Some of the early Byzantine emperors, concerned by the rapid erosion of wealth among their aristocratic supporters, passed laws to control the flood of legacies. St. Augustine himself declared that the church could not accept a bequest from a man who had disinherited his own son; instead he encouraged men and women to number Christ among their other heirs and leave the church an equal portion. On the other hand, wealthy widows were still exhorted to leave all they had to the church. "Let your father do what he likes with what is his own," wrote St. Jerome to an aristocratic widow. "You are not his to whom you have been born, but his to whom you have been born again, and who has purchased you at a great price with his own blood."[3]

Nothing could more clearly illustrate the tension between the spiritual nepotism promoted by the church and the biological nepotism of the traditional family. Moreover, even Augustine's policy of moderation protected the interests only of biological children. Collateral heirs were out of luck, since under ecclesiastical law only "heirs of the body" had rights; nor could a man supply his lack of an heir by any of the strategies then prevalent throughout the Mediterranean, including adoption, divorce, or plural marriage. The church steadfastly opposed these ancient practices and ruled that men and women without direct heirs had to leave their estates to the church.

It must be said that in pursuing these policies the church sought mainly to fulfill its obligations to the poor and to support its growing membership. In addition, as has often been observed, the new social values of Christianity resulted in greater freedom and individualism in general as well as increased independence for women. The flip side of these gains in individual freedom, however, was diminished care for children by parents selfishly concerned with their own salvation—not to mention the promotion of filial ingratitude and outright disobedience. These developments produced a tortured and ambiguous pattern of relations within the Christian family that goes a long way toward explaining the dynamism that has characterized Western nepotism for the past two thousand years.

Christianity had made its mark on Roman civilization by the end of the fourth century. However, the capital of the empire was now in the East, and in contrast to its Byzantine counterpart, the Western church was small and weak. It therefore placed a high priority on converting the barbarian tribes, and prominent among the saints of this period were the intrepid men who spread the faith to the Saxon, German, Scandinavian, and Celtic lands. Once the heathens were converted, however, the church's work among them was scarcely begun. Central to the success of its mission were combating heresy, endowing new churches and abbeys, and finding the means to support its many members and dependants. To all these ends, the persistence of traditional patterns of marriage, kinship, and inheritance among the barbarian tribes posed a serious obstacle. Therefore the church pursued a dual policy of strengthening the conjugal family against the kindreds while supporting the individual against the family.

Throughout the first millennium, the church's policies regarding marriage and inheritance were strongly at odds with indigenous practices. Among the Franks and Germans, marriage was informal and was not considered valid until the birth of an heir. No stigma was attached to illegitimacy. Divorce and remarriage were common, as were concubinage and polygamy, adoption, marriage between close kin, and the practice known as levirate marriage, whereby a widow was required to marry her husband's brother in order to keep his property in the family. These practices reflect the continued existence of strong, coherent kin groups who owned property in common and shared mutual obligations of aid, support, and blood vengeance.

The church opposed these practices and sought to stamp them out from the fourth century on. It particularly inveighed against kin marriage and greatly expanded the definition of incest to include not just cousins and nieces but stepkin, relatives by marriage, and spiritual kin. The church's ban on cousin marriage is especially striking since there is absolutely no warrant for it in scripture. Not only that, it was practiced by Constantine himself, who consolidated his dynasty by arranging no fewer than four marriages between his own children and those of his half brothers.

Adoption was another common practice of Eurasian societies

forbidden by the church. In the fifth century, the bishop of Marseilles maintained that since all man's worldly goods came from God, to God they should return. While it was possible to make an exception for one's children, leaving one's goods to an adopted or collateral heir was a form of theft, cheating God of what was rightfully his. On the basis of such reasoning, adoption was outlawed in Europe and virtually disappeared from Western societies for the next fifteen hundred years.[4]

It is certainly remarkable that the church should have instituted a sweeping agenda of social reform that ran directly counter not only to the customs of the converted peoples themselves but to the traditions of Roman society and even to the practices enshrined in holy writ. Nor was this project entirely successful—resistance to these changes was strong, even among the clergy themselves, and many of the heresies combated by the church hinged not just on obscure theological disputes but on attempts to revive indigenous practices of marriage and inheritance. But whatever their intention, the result of these new policies was a massive transfer of wealth from traditional kin groups into the hands of the church. Between the fifth and eighth centuries the church acquired possession of one-third of the arable land in Gaul and over 25 percent in Britain. Policies like these quickly made the church the largest landholder in the world, a status it has maintained to the present day.

By such strategies, the church reduced the power of the kin groups and drained their material wealth. The ban on cousin marriage prevented the clans from reinforcing nepotism with endogamous marriages and loosened the bonds between their branches. The long-term effect was to pry the conjugal family away from its surrounding kinship network. At the same time, by insinuating itself into the family as an heir and setting parents against children, the church compromised the nepotistic links between the generations. It took further steps to weaken the authority of parents by promoting the idea that marriage should be consensual, based on the love and free will of the parties, rather than a contract between their families.

Another important consequence of the emphasis on direct heirs over collaterals and fictive kin was to redefine the family in terms of blood relationships—a radical departure from the practice of other societies. Though the conjugal family is everywhere regarded as fundamental, no other culture defines kinship (and therefore nepotism) as narrowly as we do.

In addition, the church promoted an alternative system of spiritual kinship that further weakened family ties. The primary role of godparents was to oversee the religious education of the child and thus inhibit any tendency to lapse into pagan or heretical beliefs. Godparents represented the interests of the religious community and therefore stood in potential opposition to natural parents. That they were treated on a par with blood relatives is evident from the fact that they were addressed by kinship terms, and that the incest prohibition was extended to them in the eighth century. The narrowing of kinship that resulted was balanced by the creation of an alternative kinship network within the Christian community itself. The church does not so much do away with wider kinship as replace it with a spiritual substitute, sublimating nepotistic impulses in the "family" of Christ.

Emerging from the harsh patriarchal background of Greek and Roman society, the divine family of Catholicism exercised a powerful influence on family patterns throughout the Western world. The role of Jesus as a willing sacrifice became a powerful model for the status of the son in European culture. Likewise the cult of Mary, vigorously promoted by the church, endowed the Christian mother with sacred qualities of purity, mercy, and grace. The father-son-mother relationship in traditional Catholic countries still reflects this dynamic of dutiful obedience to the father and worshipful respect for the mother, whose role as an intercessor tempered the arbitrary exercise of patriarchal power. More than that, the mother's exalted status in the family provided an alternative pole of authority, and the continuing importance of her kin increased their role in the lives of her children. Order was still imposed by a strong authority figure, but this figure could be either male or female. This afforded much more scope to maternal nepotism in later European societies.

But the church alone could do only so much. To accomplish its ambitious social program it needed the legal and institutional support of secular authorities. This role was filled by the second great force in the development of Western kinship, the Carolingian state, which cooperated with the church to narrow and privatize nepotism in Europe.

We too easily accept the modern notion that the achievements of great individuals belong to them alone, without reflecting on the degree to which they represent a collective success, the built-up legacy of many generations. So it has been with Charlemagne, the only ruler in history whose claim to unique eminence has been incorporated in his very name: Charles the Great. Rising from the chaos of the post-Roman world, an era of disintegrating tribal institutions and dynastic strife, the Carolingian empire formed a bridge between the collapse of Rome and the feudal society of the Middle Ages. When the *Song of Roland* was composed, this process was largely complete. But in Charlemagne's time it was still an uncertain prospect. Charlemagne himself, despite being a product of several generations of Christianization among the Frankish nobility, was very much a transitional figure—an odd mixture of tribal chief and Christian king. The state he founded, combining elements of Ancient and Classical Nepotism with the rule of law and the beginnings of a centralized bureaucracy, represents a crucial stage between the tribal chiefdoms of the post-Roman West and the medieval monarchies of Europe.

CHARLEMAGNE: THE FATHER OF EUROPE

How do you make your descendants hereditary rulers of Europe within five generations? Start, like Arnulf of Metz, by being born to a noble family with rich holdings in the heartland of Austrasia, in what is today northeastern France. Acquire the right education, training, and sponsorship. Establish yourself at court through your military and administrative skills. Profit from the turbulence of your times by backing the right horse in a war of dynastic succession and be rewarded with more lands and higher duties. Ally yourself by marriage with other noble families. Feud successfully with rival clans. Pass on your legacy intact, train your heirs to exploit and increase it, and become the bishop of Metz and a saint of the church for good measure. Such was the eventful career of the first Carolingian.

Born about A.D. 580 to a family with vast holdings in the fertile plain between the Meuse and Moselle rivers, Arnulf was taught to read and write by monks, then sent to court to be raised in the king's household. After a period of military service he became a manager of royal domains and linked his interests to those of another young nobleman, Pepin of Landen. Marrying his son to Pepin's daughter, he joined their lands in a rich domain that would become the material base of Carolingian power.

The ultimate origins of the Carolingian empire lie in the migrations of the Franks, a loose confederation of Germanic tribes who settled in what is now Holland and the lower Rhine. The Franks were an informal league of clans governed by a chief, a council of elders, and a democratic assembly. There were no hereditary nobles; the king was an elected leader, combining the functions of warlord, priest, and president. The main form of social organization was the *sippe,* a term that meant both a clan or extended family related by blood and an individual household. Marriage was informal, divorce frequent, and illegitimacy was not stigmatized. Inheritance was equally divided among male and female heirs, and adoption and levirate marriage were also common as a means for keeping property in the family. Meanwhile, in the absence of a state or an organized market, social order was maintained by complex systems of obligatory gift exchange that linked the different clans, extended families, and tribes.[5] Such ties were reinforced by the interweaving of family threads through the tribal war band, or *comitatus.* The *comitatus* was typically led by the son of a tribal chief who attracted followers with the promise of pillage and booty. He retained their loyalty so long as he led them to adventure, helped them earn glory, and rewarded them with gifts and estates. The chaotic era of tribal migrations increasingly brought such men to the fore.

In the fourth and fifth centuries the Franks pushed into northern and central France and carved out a group of petty kingdoms, each dominated by a warlord and his followers. Of these, the most successful was Clovis (466–511), a ruthless warrior chief who founded the line of kings called Merovingians. After defeating the Roman legions, driving out the Germans, and establishing his capital at Paris, Clovis became king of a unified territory that included most of Roman Gaul and southwest Germany. Barbarian that he was, Clovis did not create a new kingdom but simply assumed control of the administrative system that survived from Roman times. But he also showed surprising gifts of statesmanship. He restrained the rapacity of his warriors and promoted harmonious relations with the peoples of the region, who greatly outnumbered his own. He also encouraged intermarriage and invented a national myth of common descent from Trojan heroes, linking Franks and Romans by a kind of retroactive cousinhood.

Of equal importance to the foundations of French nationhood, Clovis accepted conversion to Christianity in 496. That this was little more than a shrewd political move is shown by the fact that he converted to Catholicism rather than the Arianism then dominant among the other German tribes.[6] The choice gave Clovis a grateful ally in the pope and made him the natural ruler, rather than the opponent, of the Romanized Gauls of the south. The Frankish state itself was an extension of the royal house. The kin and retainers of Clovis filled the key military and administrative offices, and the sons of noble families who joined his household at an early age were trained for royal service.[7]

According to tribal custom, Clovis divided his kingdom equally among his four sons, who immediately fell to fighting. The original conquest of Gaul by an army of less than six thousand Franks was far less violent and disruptive than the dynastic wars that followed the conqueror's death. The fratricidal wars of Clovis's dysfunctional dynasty make for gruesome reading, with their various poisonings, stabbings, blindings, and beheadings. Nothing better illustrates the dark side of nepotism than the chronicles of these times, penned in horrific detail by a series of quavering clerics. Only Clotaire, Clovis's youngest son, outlived his brothers and briefly ruled a united Frankish kingdom. Yet he too divided it among his heirs, who then commenced the struggle to reunify it.

From this pattern we may infer that the Merovingians lacked the dynastic vision of an Augustus or (much later) a Napoleon. Their nepotism did not extend to the idea of leaving their sons greater and stronger than themselves; instead they were content to have them prove their strength by fighting it out with their brothers. Rising to the top of the heap in this way allowed them to enact the role of the traditional Germanic warrior chief by awarding generous gifts to their followers. It was essentially a pagan competition for honor. Once the game was won, it remained only to play it out again in the next generation.

By the eighth century, decimated by feuds and diminished by the continual division of their lands, the line was visibly enfeebled. The last Merovingians—known as the do-nothing kings—were puppets of the great northern families who ruled the kingdom through an office known as mayor of the palace.

When Clotaire II reunified the Franks in 613, he made Arnulf bishop of Metz and Pepin mayor. After Arnulf retired to a monastery, he entrusted Pepin with the fortunes of their joint dynastic enterprise. Arnulf spent his last years in the company of lepers and acquired the reputation of a saint.

Pepin's son Grimoald tried to put his own son on the throne, but both were overthrown and killed. Grimoald's nephew Pepin II restored the clan to power and was succeeded by his son Charles, who repelled an army of Saxon invaders, defeated an insurgency of Basques, and formed a close association with Boniface, an English monk who played a major role in converting the Germans to Catholicism. The high point of Charles's career was his defeat of an invading Saracen army at Poitiers in 732, which earned him the sobriquet Martel (the Hammer). This battle made him famous throughout Europe and conferred immense prestige upon his family. Martel was an exceptional ruler who reversed the trend toward political fragmentation throughout the West, enhanced the spread of Christianity, and created the first centralized power since the collapse of the Roman Empire. Yet he continued to govern under the cloak of Merovingian authority. After his death, in 742, his sons Pepin and Carloman became joint mayors of the palace. Five years later Carloman entered a monastery, leaving his brother in charge. Finally, in 748, the last Merovingian was unceremoniously shoved into a cloister and Pepin declared himself king. His son Charles, the future Holy Roman Emperor, was nine.

By this time the fiction of Merovingian rule was very thin. Still, Pepin felt the need to screen his usurpation with rational and symbolic justifications. Propagandists put out tracts arguing that a do-nothing king was not fit to rule in the eyes of God; thus was introduced the notion that virtue or merit in a ruler counted more than hereditary right, and that an unfit king could be deposed. These and other materials (including the *Life of St. Arnulf*, whose tomb was now the center of a cult) were disseminated widely. Casting back to the Old Testament story of David, another usurper whose dynastic coup had been legitimized by the prophet Samuel, Pepin lighted on the idea of having himself crowned by a sacred authority. Boniface accordingly persuaded the pope to allow him to anoint Pepin king. But Pepin wanted this grace to encompass his whole family. The pope therefore came to Gaul in person in 754 to reanoint Pepin and his wife, along with their sons Charles and Carloman. This momentous act was the foundation not only of a line of kings but of a unique compact between church and state that would dominate the history of Europe. Pepin later repaid the favor by creating the Papal States, which founded the temporal power of the pope in Italy.

At his death in 768, Pepin continued the old practice of dividing his estate between his sons. But while Charles was the elder brother, he was technically of illegitimate birth, and for this or other reasons their father had left the larger share to Carloman. The brothers were on the point of open war when Carloman fortuitously died, leaving Charles in sole possession of a united Frankish empire. His two young nephews also mysteriously disappeared, but this was the last alleged act of violence by Charles against a member of his family. Indeed, Charlemagne represents a significant departure from Frankish tradition by building on his relatives instead of killing them off to secure his rule.

The next five decades were years of incessant activity during which Charles greatly expanded the Frankish domains through a series of conquests and strove to unify his empire through sweeping political, legal, and monetary reforms as well as the vigorous promotion of Christianity. The question for our purposes is whether Charles was the last tribal chief or the first Christian king. The answer—not surprisingly—is both. This dualism was expressed in the manner and style of his nepotism, which lay at the heart of his statecraft.

The core of Charles's power remained the fertile Meuse basin in northeastern Francia, where his family had its great holdings. There a group of wealthy families and churchmen formed a kind of personal association in support of the Frankish monarchy. In building his state, Charles preferred to draw upon the thirty-odd families who made up this core of hereditary supporters, and when he established a permanent capital he located it at Aachen, in the midst of his ancestral heartland. For most of his reign, however, Charles lived in the traditional manner of a Frankish noble, traveling with his large household from one estate to the next and supporting himself on their produce. Indeed, wherever he went Charles was surrounded by his family and liked to have them near him at all times; even his bath was a public occasion.

Charles was an exceptionally tall, healthy, and vigorous man who loved to hunt and feast. His court was always bustling and convivial. Though illiterate himself, he was fond of intellectual stimulus, and dinner was often accompanied by recitals of poetry or readings from his favorite book, St. Augustine's *City of God.* Yet despite being a pious Christian who attended mass on most days, he ran his family like a traditional Frankish patriarch. Nowhere was this more evident than in his marital career. Although the church preached monogamy and frowned on divorce, Charlemagne in his time had four wives and many concubines. He divorced and remarried at will, had numerous children, and was equally fond of his legitimate and illegitimate offspring. He trained his sons for positions in his government, married them to the daughters of other great families, and eventually made them subkings of his realm. But he refused to allow his daughters to marry before his death, partly out of inordinate fondness and partly to prevent their being exploited by their husbands. As a result, he had to tolerate their illicit amours and illegitimate children right under his nose—hardly the behavior of a Christian king.

Charlemagne's conception of his kingly role was likewise essentially tribal. Though not elected like the ancient Frankish kings, he continued to convene the assembly before each year's military campaign, using it as an occasion to consult with the leading men of the realm and ratify new laws. A further echo of tribal government is the oath of personal loyalty that each of Charles's subjects had to take. This was insufficient to guarantee the peace and unity of his kingdom, so he created a system of vassalage that propagated such ties throughout society. Men were granted large estates in exchange for fealty to the crown; they gave out lands to subvassals, who in turn created vassals of their own. In this way, Charlemagne created a network of mutual obligation centered on the crown that helped to stabilize Frankish society.

The empire had roughly three hundred administrative divisions, or counties, each headed by a royally appointed count, whose duty was to administer justice, collect taxes, and raise troops, often leading them in battle as well. Charles preferred to appoint men from his own ancestral heartland, but for the most part he had to be satisfied with strangers, whom he bound by grants of land and oaths of fealty. To oversee the counts he created a network of envoys who traveled the realm as inspectors. As a practical matter, however, Charles was rarely able to restrain the excesses of the nobles. Removed from the traditional constraints of tribal leadership, and neither Christianized to any great degree nor instilled with any sense of public ethics, the magnates indulged their acquisitive impulses and private dynastic ambitions.

The sheer size and geographical diversity of the empire required Charles to create a series of subkingdoms, which he entrusted to family members and close allies. Aquitaine and Italy he gave to the care of his sons. Bavaria he gave to his brother-in-law. He also created a group of *marchiones* (marquises) to guard the frontiers of the empire. The border area of Maine he gave to his eldest son, Charles; the Breton march, vulnerable to attack from marauding Northmen, he entrusted to his nephew Roland. The rest were handed out to loyal retainers from the ancestral Meuse region.[8]

In short, Charles—like Clovis, though on a much greater scale—made his royal government an extension of his household. This is perhaps the most remarkable feature of the Carolingian state: a vast empire governed nepotistically by a handful of family members augmented by the use of quasi-kin and patronage relationships. In time, the network of patron-client relationships founded by Charlemagne would evolve into the system of feudal nobility that dominated Europe for the next eight hundred years, until the rise of strong national states in the sixteenth and seventeenth centuries.

In A.D. 800, Charles had himself crowned emperor of Europe by the pope. His ambition to restore the *pax Romana* is clear from his choice of the name Charles Augustus. But Charles was probably aware of how badly his empire compared with that of the Romans. Despite his efforts to create a centralized bureaucracy and judicial system, he could neither collect taxes reliably nor compel the obedience of his own delegates. Even finding enough literate men to staff the royal government was a task beyond the scope of his semibarbarous society. Consequently, after his death in 814, the empire broke up into a group of smaller kingdoms ruled by Charlemagne's descendants. Briefly reunited under his grandson, Charles the Bald, by the end of the tenth century Charles's empire was effectively dissolved.

It is not hard to understand why Charlemagne's empire failed to thrive after his death. Europe was still in a long age of transition; cohesion could no longer be provided by the bonds of tribe and clan, and Charles's suppression of the institutionalized feud deprived Carolingian society of another traditional source of coherence.[9] Yet Charles is justifiably remembered as the greatest of his line, overshadowing both his ancestors and his descendants. Charles combined the military talents of a conqueror with those of a diplomat, statesman, and dynast. Though he remained in many ways a tribal monarch, he was a very different sort of king from Clovis. The product of six generations of Frankish nobility, he was as civilized and polished as a man of his era could be. Even though he was not able to realize his dream of a unified Christian empire, he is rightly considered the father of Europe.

THE FEUDAL REVOLUTION

The counts appointed by Charlemagne and his successors were not hereditary lords but officials who served at the emperor's pleasure. But with the slow disintegration of the empire, these magnates increasingly challenged Carolingian authority. Finally, around the year 1000, the counts threw off the royal yoke, claimed hereditary rights to both land and political power, and made the local inhabitants their vassals.

Under the Carolingians the policy of weakening the kin groups had suited both spiritual and temporal authorities. The empire was a vast umbrella under whose cover church and state combined to pulverize the tribal kindreds. Charlemagne's father had promulgated numerous edicts pertaining to the regulation of family life, including the expansion of incest prohibitions to the seventh degree of consanguinity, affinity, and spiritual kinship. Charlemagne added the confiscation of property for those who disobeyed these regulations and tightened restrictions on marriage and divorce (always excepting his own household).

The state also sought to bring the system of private justice and feuding under control. This process began under Charlemagne, when violent crimes were redefined as offenses against the king's law rather than the victim's family. But the feud would linger for centuries in marginal areas of Europe. Nor was the state in such a rush to eliminate the system of compensatory justice, since one-third of all such monetary settlements were claimed by the king.

By the tenth century, traditional kin ties in many parts of Europe had been significantly weakened. In the vacuum that resulted, men urgently needed the protection of powerful lords, and on this largely voluntary basis the system of feudal relations made rapid progress throughout France and Germany. The feudal lord dispensed justice and controlled the economic lives of his dependants, but he was first and foremost a military leader, and his vassals and subvassals owed him at least forty days a year of service at arms. Great lords could field an army of considerable size, though they required commensurate estates on which to settle such a following. The system as a whole was held together by oaths of personal loyalty and sustained by a chivalric code of honor. It was this knightly code—a Christianized version of the bond between the tribal chieftain and his warriors—that the chivalric romances promoted. Knights who served under an oath of fealty were fiercely loyal to their lord, but the greatest fervor was undoubtedly the result of combining kinship and personal fealty, as in the case of Charlemagne and Roland.[10]

The household, or *familia,* of the feudal lord included his own family and those of his vassals and other dependants, and it was expected that his knights would send their sons to serve in his retinue and in exchange receive their training and equipment. The bond between vassal and lord was fully the equivalent of, and a supplement to, traditional family ties—a continuation of nepotism by artificial means. Evidence may be seen in the fact that feudalism emerged only in areas where the campaign against the kin groups had been thoroughly successful; where kin ties remained strong, feudalism did not appear.

Patrilineal descent groups had largely disappeared during the first millennium. Only royal houses like those of Clovis and Charlemagne were organized as lineages, and for a long time it was difficult for a noble family to have an independent existence apart from the king's household. It was not until the nobles broke away and acquired their own hereditary properties that they began to form linear families. The feudal lords also abandoned the Frankish tradition of partible inheritance and shifted to a system of primogeniture, in which estates were passed intact to the eldest son. Thus Georges Duby describes "a narrowing and tightening of the family around the male line" around the year 1000, and notes the simultaneous emergence of a fierce "dynastic spirit." Other signs of this shift are the naming of sons for patrilineal forebears, the creation of family trees, and the demotion of alliances through women to subordinate status.

The construction of genealogies is a fascinating byway in the history of European nepotism. Bilateral kindreds (like those of our own society) are horizontal, centered on a given generation. What matters is maintaining connections with one's contemporaries, and the memory of previous generations quickly fades. In contrast, lineages are vertical corporate structures whose membership is limited to descendants of an ultimate male ancestor. When the powerful landowning families of Europe asserted their claim to nobility in the tenth and eleventh centuries, genealogies were needed to preserve the legitimate line of descent. These family trees not only reveal a growing sense of family cohesion but also did much to create it, and thereby strongly influenced the behavior of subsequent generations. The obsession with lineage and genealogy, to modern eyes one of the most unattractive aspects of the European class system, is not a vain appurtenance of family pride but a practical tool of dynastic ambition.

The rise of noble lineages caused a profound change in the pattern of upper class nepotism. This change was evident in the new relationships that emerged between fathers and sons, fathers and daughters, husbands and wives, and between brothers in aristocratic families. For one thing, it required a new emphasis on legitimate birth. Illegitimate sons, once regarded as full members of the family, must be excluded. Thus was born the brooding figure of the bastard who stalks or skulks through European literature. The bastard may be considered the modern self-made man in embryo. Keenly conscious of his own worth in contrast to the presumed decadence of the legitimate heirs, the bastard gets no help from anyone and has to make it on his own. Representing a challenge to the established order, he is both a destroyer of families and the bearer of the principle of merit.[11]

But the feudal system also engendered tension and conflict within the family. Since only one son could inherit the estate, the old tribal rule of fraternal equality was replaced by a principle of seniority. The eldest son had higher status than his brothers and they were required to defer to him as they would to their father. To add to the system's indignities, only the legitimate heir could marry and have children; his younger brothers, so long as they remained attached to the estate, were forced to live as bachelors. The result was what can only be described as an oversupply of sons among the feudal nobility. Given the high rate of infant mortality, families had to be large, and some nobles had as many as a dozen sons and daughters. With a sufficient dowry, daughters could be married off or placed in convents; but what to do with the young men who had no scope for their ambitions and had to be kept in a state of permanent celibacy?

Those with the aptitude were designated for a clerical career. When a noble entered the church a large gift of land was required, like a dowry, to defray the costs of his upkeep. Indeed, the transaction was very much the equivalent of marriage or adoption, though the family did not thereby lose a son so much as it gained a powerful "daughter"—the church. The other means of relieving the pressure from surplus heirs was to send the young men abroad as knights-errant. Typically they gathered in small companies around the son of a local lord. Reproducing the social relationship between their fathers, the youthful leader provided the members of his *familia* with arms, guided them toward adventure and reward, and (once settled himself) often helped to secure them a wife, preferably a rich heiress or wealthy widow, of whom there were many in medieval Europe. (Those who wished to marry had to seek their brides in foreign parts, since the families of their own district had long since formed a large extended cousinhood.) Much of their time was spent riding from one tournament to another competing for prizes and glory, and they either succeeded in landing a bride or got themselves killed in the fighting—which suited their fathers just fine. You couldn't keep them around the house in any case, since having had a taste of freedom they were even more unruly than before and posed a danger to the neighborhood. "Such was the aristocratic youth of France in the twelfth century," Duby tartly observes: "a mob of young men let loose, in search of glory, profit and female prey."[12] Ultimately this oversupply of young knights had to be channeled into the series of foreign wars known as the Crusades.

As in other patrilineal societies, maternal uncles played a major role in the feudal nobility. Young men who entered holy orders often did so under the sponsorship of a powerful mother's brother—a bishop or abbot—who did his best to advance their interests in the church. But for those who sought their fortune in the lists, the maternal uncle played an equally important role, since it was through him that the young man earned his knighthood and often also found a wife.

We now can see how closely the *Song of Roland* conforms to the social facts of the period in which it was written. The hero is raised by his maternal uncle from the age of eight, along with other members of the royal household. Charles knights him and presents him with Durendal, the legendary sword with which he conquers many nations on his uncle's behalf. The battle horn with which he calls for help—too late to save himself or his companions—is also a gift from his uncle. In addition, Charles arranges his betrothal to the lovely Aude, another ward of his household. Charles's reliance on Roland is greater than his reliance on his own son, and their bond of affection is stronger. When Charles must tell Aude the sad news of Roland's death, he can do no better than offer to replace him with Louis, "who will inherit my estate." But there is no claim that this is an equal recompense, and the girl rejects his offer, going off to die of grief like a proper romantic heroine.

The corollary of all this aid and support of the nephew is the uncle's reliance on his protégé. As William O. Farnsworth observes, "It would seem that the choicest plums of the diplomatic service fall into the mouth of the nephew, that the most desirable offices in general come to him." Such favor has a price, however. To be worthy of this honor, the nephew must incur greater risks than other men: "there are instances where he is sent on the most dangerous missions, in which death is almost certain; and such instances give the poet an opportunity for enlarging upon the distress and despair of the uncle at the necessity which compels him thus to expose the life of his favorite."[13] This is what occurs in the *Song of Roland,* where Charles must assign Roland the dangerous task of bringing up the rear in order to avoid a charge of favoritism.

Nor is this the only sign of the continuing importance of kinship in feudal society. Despite the bond of feudal loyalty between Roland and Charles, and the romantic friendship with Olivier, the continuing vitality of tribal kinship lingers just below the poem's surface. Take Roland's seeming arrogance and pride: Olivier rebukes him for refusing to summon help, but Roland's action is dictated not by pride in his own strength but by the fear of bringing shame upon his kin. Roland's pride and honor are not individual attributes, but collective ones, which is another way of saying that he belongs not to himself but to his kindred.[14]

The *Song of Roland* represents a midpoint in the evolution of European societies away from the tribal nepotism of *Beowulf,* an essentially pagan poem of the eighth century, and toward the rule of law and Christian fellowship—the triumph of church and state over the old tribal system. To that extent, the poem accurately reflects the transitional nature of the Carolingian monarchy itself. Not until later, in the courtly romances of King Arthur and his knights, written at the height of the feudal system, do we encounter the full-blown chivalric ideal. Here at last, in the familiar tales and legends of Camelot, Christian and feudal values come to the fore while kinship recedes into the background. Readers may recall that as a boy, Arthur is raised by Sir Ector. Yet while Arthur's foster brother Kay holds the office of seneschal and is a member of the Round Table, he is a marginal figure who lacks important knightly virtues. Arthur does have a favored nephew in Gawain, but his great champion is Lancelot, a man with no relation to his family. The ideal Christian knight, Lancelot upholds the virtues of piety and chastity, pledging his service to the queen, who may be likened to the

Madonna in a secular cult of the Virgin. In place of obligations of blood vengeance and family honor, the Arthurian romances emphasize love and the spirit of adventure. The courtly virtues—good manners, courtesy, and above all the protection of women—are more important than the martial oaths of Beowulf and the feudal vows of Roland.

Yet what becomes of Arthur's dream? Lancelot succumbs to his lust for Guinevere and sleeps with the wife of his best friend and liege. The Round Table dissolves in fratricidal war. Arthur is killed by his nemesis, Mordred, who is not just his bastard son but the fruit of an incestuous union with his half sister Morgause. Mordred is therefore Arthur's nephew *and* his son, and his appearance represents the resurgence of an ancient feud between the families of Arthur and Gerlois, duke of Cornwall, who was killed by Arthur's father.

On one level, the Arthurian romances reflect the triumph of Christianity and feudalism over the outright paganism of *Beowulf* and the lingering tribal nepotism of *Roland*. The cultural distance from Beowulf to Arthur is a literary measure of this victory. Yet a dark current runs through these romances that seems to express real skepticism about the irrepressible natural element in man, including the solidarity of kinship and the spirit of the feud.

The great kindreds that covered northern Europe between the fall of Rome and the rise of feudalism were loosely organized, self-governing tribal associations based on kin selection and reciprocity in the form of tribal councils, the composition of feuds by a system of *wergild*, and the norms of gift exchange. But with the rise of church and state, there began the great narrowing of kinship characteristic of later Western history. These agencies conspired to pulverize the tribal kin groups and wrest control of the essential processes of marriage, reproduction, and inheritance. As Western fathers lost their ancient prerogatives, they were forced to act less as judges and masters and behave more as benevolent patrons. Yet patriarchal nepotism in Western societies remained extremely harsh. Wives were chattels of their husbands, sons were favored over daughters, and firstborn sons were favored over younger ones. Concern about continuing the line turned the drama of succession into a major source of tension and conflict. Moreover, the father's perpetual doubt about the paternity of his sons required the heir to "prove" his legitimacy again and again by deeds and other signs.

So long as European societies remained primarily agricultural, both economic and political power were monopolized by the great landowning families. The result was a mafia-style system of militarized kin groups supported by their clients and dependents. The first national states emerged from the struggles of these dynastic coalitions. Eventually, royal lineages arose that claimed hereditary rulership; but these early monarchies were weak and insecure. Even strong rulers like Henry VIII and Elizabeth I had to proceed carefully, lest they provoke an insurrection of powerful nobles.

A solution was found in an alliance between the weak national states and the rising commercial elites who financed the monarchs' wars against the nobles in exchange for protectionist trade policies. This alliance was the origin of the European bourgeoisie, which became the standard-bearer of capitalism, merit, and efficiency. The ability to raise a standing army gave the kings a crucial edge over the rural magnates, who could not afford to campaign on an extended basis. Those not crushed outright could be seduced by grants of economic monopoly and other privileges within the gift of the crown. Thus Elizabeth I showered the powerful Percy clan of northern England with favors—"leasing them crown property on favorable terms, bequeathing to them the estates of traitors or estates in conquered lands, and conferring upon them annuities, fee farms, and trading privileges."[15] The Percys soon found themselves utterly dependent on the crown, and like other noble families were forced to decamp from their estates and come to court, the better to protect their vital interests. Such royal patronage could also be used to discipline the nobles. When Elizabeth moved to crush her former favorite, the Earl of Essex, she began by canceling his monopoly on the importation of sweet wine. Unable to secure credit from banks, he had to dismiss his large retinue and retire from court.

Capitalism is supposed to be the great engine of individual liberation from the confines of the family. Yet family interests continued to predominate in economic life. Crafts and trades were passed from father to son or via quasi-nepotistic master-apprentice relationships. Most commercial partnerships were formed between close relatives and tightened by the marriage of children. (Marco Polo went to China with his father and uncle, who were partners in this sort of family venture.) Guilds and early corporations were formed by groups of mercantile or artisanal families who inhabited the same streets or districts, intermarried closely, and established castelike occupational monopolies. Indeed, wherever possible the business was kept in one family. The Bachs, for example, were a particularly tight-knit clan whose many branches intermarried closely and relied on local governments to protect their monopoly on the provision of musical services. The first commercial banks were created by entrepreneurial families like the Fuggers and the Medici, whose family network became the basis for the Florentine state. Likewise, the first joint stock companies were formed by close circles of investors whose ties were reinforced by blood and marriage. Nor was such familism confined to the capitalist end of the spectrum: early labor confraternities were also familistic, with young apprentices and journeymen often living in group homes under the watchful eyes of a surrogate "mother" and "father."

Far from disappearing with the decline of tribe and clan, the nepotistic impulse was transformed with the passage of time from a collective phenomenon into a private pursuit. Once the preserve of noble families, moreover, with the passage of time nepotism became increasingly available to men of the middle class intent on raising their families to a higher level. Thus as the age of the feudal lords began to wane, that of the great dynastic upstarts was just beginning. Never before or since has nepotism been practiced with the same unbridled zest, scope, openness, or flair. It was an era of great familial entrepreneurs whose over-the-top nepotism was frequently the key to their success, and often their downfall as well. The risks were great, but so were the rewards—power, wealth, position, and the founding of a line that would immortalize one's name.

CHAPTER 6

THE GOLDEN AGE OF NEPOTISM

BORGIA, BONAPARTE, AND ROTHSCHILD

Everyone knows the story of *Romeo and Juliet*: a tale of "star-crossed lovers" thwarted by the hatred of their families. We don't know what the quarrel is about, but we know it must be foolish and irrational because no one can remember how it started. Their enmity has simply become a matter of habit, passed down from one generation to the next. Shakespeare himself leaves little doubt where he stands on the matter. The fathers of Romeo and Juliet—the heads of their respective clans—are doddering old fools who stagger out of bed in their nightshirts, calling for broadswords they can barely lift: better to call for a crutch, Lady Montague remarks. Scarcely better are the arrogant young nephews and cousins who make up their retinues. The prince has passed an edict against dueling, but the partisans fight anyway, since for them family honor is a cause above the law.

Shakespeare's play reflects a striking transformation of attitudes. Apparently the feud has gone from a compelling moral obligation, as in earlier works like *Beowulf* and *Roland,* to being an obstacle to personal fulfillment. Moreover, the lovers rebel not just against the hatred of their families but against their whole authority in matters of love and marriage. Juliet's father views her as an instrument in his dynastic plans. He has arranged an excellent match for her—the prospective groom is noble, rich, and handsome. To ask for love and the consideration of being wooed strikes him as the whining of a spoiled, ungrateful child. Yet Capulet's blindness to his daughter's needs and wishes makes us see him not as a loving parent concerned with her well-being, which he is, but as a heartless tyrant who deserves the awful punishment to come.

The deaths of Romeo and Juliet accomplish what their love could not, uniting their two families in grief. The prince drives home the heavy-handed moral: "See what a scourge is laid upon your hate." Generations of choked-up theatergoers have seconded this verdict. Shakespeare's contemporaries probably saw it differently; for them the claims of family and clan were still a powerful factor in everyday life. But for us the lesson is obvious: family pride and honor are stupid and stubborn emotions that should never be allowed to interfere with individual happiness.

Today, the victory of the romantic individualism prefigured in Shakespeare's plays is so complete as to make their dramatic circumstances all but incomprehensible. The practices they hinge on—family feuds, arranged marriages, blood vengeance—have long been consigned to the historical trash heap, and we must make an effort to reconstruct the context in which they made sense. (*Hamlet,* for instance, turns on the conflict between a son's private conscience and his nepotistic duty of revenge.) Yet we would be wrong to conclude that the burgeoning individualism so prevalent in Renaissance literature in any way diminished the importance of families. If anything, the bonds of the nuclear family grew tighter as the power of the kindreds declined. Moreover, men who rose to positions of prominence did so almost exclusively through nepotism—drawing on the loyalty, strength, and support of their kin. Entrepreneurial families were the real engine of European dynamism, and they operated for the most part in seamless cooperation, with little thought of personal "liberation."

The period between the sixteenth and nineteenth centuries in Europe was a golden age for nepotism, in which the constraints of feudal society had been largely removed while the legal and bureaucratic rules of the modern state had yet to be imposed. Europe was therefore an open field for dynastic ambition, and nepotism had free reign in every quarter. This chapter considers three outstanding families that rose to the heights of the European nobility through a combination of extraordinary ability and the disciplined practice of nepotism. Each also illustrates one of the three main avenues of upward mobility open to aspiring families in this period: the church, the army, and the market. Though there are many other families we might have chosen, these are by far the most notorious, and their stories tell us much about the importance of nepotism in the creation of modern Europe.

A PERFECT BASTARD: THE RISE AND FALL OF CESARE BORGIA

Cesare Borgia has cut a strange and compelling figure in European history. Lithe, athletic, menacing, coming and going at odd hours, dressed in a close-fitting black velvet suit, and often masked to disguise the ravages of syphilis, he was the consummate ambitious bastard son, providing the model for countless Italianate villains in Jacobean and Elizabethan drama. Certainly Machiavelli's approving judgment of Cesare as the perfect opportunist has not helped his reputation. The sour Florentine praised Cesare as the ideal amoral ruler in his cynical handbook, *The Prince.* Seemingly everywhere at once, possessing demonic energy and an inhuman ability to control his thoughts and feelings, he was accused of every conceivable crime, from poisoning and incest to sorcery. His career stands as one of the blackest indictments not only of the Renaissance papacy but of nepotism itself.

Few families in history are more reviled or controversial than the Borgias: so hated were they that successive popes refused to occupy their splendid Vatican apartments, which stood neglected for hundreds of years. Though some credit Cesare's father, Pope Alexander VI, with greater piety and vision than his contemporaries did, there is no getting around the magnitude of his vices. He was greedy, cynical, ambitious, and shamelessly carnal. As cardinal he amassed an enormous fortune, built an ostentatious palace, and obtained indulgences that allowed his illegitimate offspring to hold sacred office and inherit lands and titles. As pope he not only made his sons and nephews cardinals but engaged in an all-out civil war with the Roman nobility, seizing at least fifty-nine estates in the surrounding countryside and handing them out to his kin. His daughter Lucrezia has been (wrongly) characterized as the greatest poisoner since Livia. The careers of Alexander VI and his children, both real and imagined, have made the name Borgia a byword for treachery, duplicity, and nepotism.

But controversy follows success, not failure, and any fair assessment of the Borgias must begin by acknowledging that they were indeed a remarkable family. Building on the utterly fortuitous election of one of their family as pope, the Borgias gained a foothold in the church and established themselves at the highest levels of the European nobility. They soon produced a second pope, and over the next two and a half centuries, eleven more cardinals (including a saint), as well as numerous princes and dukes in Italy, Spain, France, and the New World. They were charming, gay, theatrical, intelligent, and passionate. But they were most remarkable for their uncanny ability to pursue a strategy beneficial both to the church and to their own dynastic ends.

The Renaissance papacy is one of the greatest monuments to nepotism in Western history. Indeed, the word *nepotismo* was originally coined to describe the corrupt practice of appointing papal relatives to office. But the papacy is not only the source of the word "nepotism" but of the very idea that using official position to benefit one's relatives is wrong. Institutionalized nepotism had characterized every previous human society; never before had it been defined as an ethical failing.

It is revealing that nepotism first emerges as a problem in this setting. Nepotism goes from being simply the way things are done to an intractable problem *only* in the context of a large-scale bureaucratic institution. We might say that nepotism becomes a problem at precisely the point when the modern distinction between public and private begins to emerge.

To modern eyes the most shocking aspect of papal nepotism is the simple fact that priests could openly have children. From its beginnings, however, the church bore an ambiguous relation to the family. The church was conceived as an artificial lineage in which authority was transmitted from father to father through the medium of the eternal son. To the extent that its members were celibate, this priestly hierarchy resembled the great eunuch bureaucracies of China, Rome, and

Byzantium. But this ideal was generally honored more in the breach than in the observance, and originally priests were permitted to marry and have children. Even after celibacy became official church policy in the eleventh century, many priests continued to have families: not for nothing was clerical marriage one of the main demands of the Protestant reformers.[1] Nor did the denial of the flesh extend to the bonds and obligations of kinship. Priests were allowed to bequeath their estates to their children, and ecclesiastical offices and income from tithes were often treated as a component of family wealth. Whole dynasties were founded on such revenues. Many noble families also founded religious institutions and monopolized their leadership for decades. Even where a founding family did not hold such offices directly, they often retained control of them and used them as sources of patronage.

In its first millennium, the church was not a strongly centralized institution and the pope mainly functioned as a mediator of political and ecclesiastical disputes. Given the violent temper of the times, it was necessary to play one faction off against another. A new pope could govern successfully only if he came from an important Roman family and was able to install his own supporters in the curia (the papal bureaucracy). The politics of religious succession therefore went hand in hand with bloody dynastic feuds, and matters of theology and church policy often took a backseat to these struggles. Such interference increased dramatically after the eighth century, when the Donation of Pepin created the first papal state in central Italy. Suddenly the papacy became a feudal power with its own estates and income. As a result, competition for the office sharply increased. Brawls and riots accompanied papal elections, and force or bribery decided them. The average papal tenure dwindled to less than a year and in some cases only a few weeks.

Papal nepotism dramatically expanded as the growth of church control over central and southern Italy involved it in the challenges of secular administration. New popes inherited a faction-ridden curia and a College of Cardinals that was often hostile and obstructive, and the promotion of kinsmen and others directly dependent on the pope's patronage might be the only way to ensure loyal and trustworthy colleagues.

For a long time the papacy was merely a pawn in the struggles of great Roman families. But in the twelfth and thirteenth centuries, the office became an avenue for entry into the Italian nobility, hence an attractive prize for families from other parts of Italy, whose enormous gains in this period enabled their survival well into modern times. The history of the papacy in this era is little more than a record of their struggles. Thus for a period of time, the office passed back and forth between the Conti and Savelli families.[2] Likewise, the Orsini rose to prominence in the thirteenth century after defeating their main rivals, the Colonnas. Four of the family became cardinals, and one became Pope Nicholas III. Dante consigned him to hell for his nepotism. Nevertheless the Orsini became pillars of the church, supplying a long line of soldiers, statesmen, and prelates.

The Avignon papacy—a period of French domination known as the Great Schism—was marked by especially heavy reliance on kin, beginning with Clement V, who appointed seven nephews to the College of Cardinals.[3] The schism ended with the election of Martin V, the only member of the Colonna family to become pope.

Alonso de Borja was born in Catalonia in 1377, the year of the Western Schism. A brilliant student, he advanced rapidly in the church and entered the service of King Alfonso of Aragon. Borja was both an exceptionally talented diplomat and a devoted servant of the church, with an uncanny ability to serve both masters with equal aplomb, and do well for himself in the bargain. In 1420, when the French yielded the papacy to Italian control, Martin V asked Borja to persuade the self-styled Spanish pope to capitulate as well. In doing so he acted both in the interest of a unified church and of his master, Alfonso, who had his eye on the kingdom of Naples. Borja was rewarded with the bishopric of Valencia, a post that would remain in his family for generations. He capped his diplomatic career by persuading the pope to accept an Aragonese dynasty in Naples, while persuading Alfonso to recognize the pope's traditional suzerainty. His efforts on behalf of both won him a cardinal's hat.

The emergence of the papacy as a secular power required a new cadre of men with greater administrative and diplomatic skills, and in this period the church became a ladder of ascent for lowborn men of proven talent. It also attracted the attention of great families who hoped to use it to advance their private ends. As a result, the College of Cardinals became very worldly, filled with princelings, foreign potentates, ambitious younger sons, and papal relatives. Most were rich, and many had illegitimate offspring. In contrast, Borja's reputation was one of piety, sobriety, and modesty. He did, however, build up his private household with members of his family and other Catalans who would later become the core of his papal court.

Every high church official had an extended household, known as his *familia,* which (in addition to kinsmen) included secretaries, servants, clerics who worked in his department, and the various artists, scholars, and craftsman in his employ. The pope's *familia* ranked highest, but every cardinal, chaplain, or other high curial had his followers, to whom he dispensed whatever patronage he could. Cardinals had particularly large followings: the *familia* of Cardinal d'Este in 1493 included 136 relatives, familiars, and servants. A cardinal therefore had need of considerable resources, including bishoprics, parish churches, abbeys, canonicates, prebends, and other income-bearing offices. Having the foresight to belong to the right *familia* was crucial to advancement in the church, and many a man of humble birth was raised to wealth and status by his service to a noble bishop or cardinal. As the papacy grew stronger at the cardinals' expense, the papal *familia* became the real center of power. The scope of papal nepotism also increased, and by the late fifteenth century the trend toward dynasticism was apparent as each pope not only relied upon his relatives in office but sought to secure their position after his death.

Borja's election in 1455 was the result of a deadlock between the Colonna and Orsini factions. Aging, ill, and nondescript, Alonso seemed unlikely to live long or cause much trouble. But as Calixtus III he showed surprising vigor, strengthening the papacy and promoting a crusade against the Turks. Three of his nephews received commissions in the papal navy as well as strategic castles in the Romagna—the rural stronghold of the Orsini, the Colonnas, and other great families. He made his nephew Pedro Luis captain general and prefect of Rome (an office the Orsini considered their family property), and is thought to have intended him for the throne of Naples. Most hateful of all to the Romans, Calixtus flooded the curia with Spaniards. Though their numbers and rapacity were greatly complained of, these were the only men he could trust in the faction-ridden atmosphere of Italian politics. Nor did he devote much time or energy to enriching his kin: his gifts were sparing, and the benefices he handed out were all in his own Spanish diocese. However, he decided that for the good of the papacy the Roman barons must be tamed, and he encouraged Pedro Luis to crush the Orsini and confiscate their lands. Pedro made himself so hated in his uncle's service that on Calixtus's death, in 1458, armed gangs roamed the city looking for him. The other Catalans were violently hounded from Rome.

All except Pedro's brother, twenty-five-year-old Cardinal Rodrigo Borgia. Like other papal nephews, Rodrigo had been "heaped" (as historians like to put it) with lucrative incomes and offices, including the important post of papal vice chancellor. He was an affable young man, hard not to like, charming, adept, and persuasive. He was also a spirited bon vivant who held a notable attraction for the ladies. But even those who criticized his lavish tastes and sybaritic lifestyle had to admit that he was a highly capable administrator and a gifted diplomat, much in favor with the princes and statesmen of Europe. He also showed considerable bureaucratic skill: he retained the post of vice chancellor for the next thirty-five years and was confirmed in it by five successive popes.

Borgia clearly did not scruple to profit from his position, and he used his long tenure to amass a huge personal fortune. He achieved this wealth through frank abuse of his position—from the acquisition of lucrative incomes and offices to the sale of benefices and indulgences. Criticized for selling a pardon to a man who had killed his own daughter, he reportedly said, "It is not God's wish that a sinner should die, but that he should live—and pay." Borgia held at least five Spanish bishoprics and controlled numerous churches, monasteries, and abbeys. Nor did he neglect to acquire key fortresses in the cities that controlled the northern and southern routes to Rome. Although his eventual election as pope required that he divest himself of these possessions, he spent the rest of his papacy working to recover them through grants to family members—a major aim of Borgia dynasticism.

Borgia survived his uncle's death by swinging the next papal election to Cardinal Piccolomini (Pius II). Fully one-sixth of Pius's appointments were given to relatives, one of whom became (for a few days) Pius III; others married into the noble houses of Italy. His favoritism to his fellow Sienese was so extreme that according to one historian, its scope and character "virtually require an extension of the concept of nepotism."[4] Pius was succeeded by another friend of Borgia's, Cardinal Barbo (Paul II), the nephew of Eugenius IV, and in 1471, Borgia intervened again, to aid the election of Francesco della Rovere as Sixtus IV. An austere Franciscan monk who rose to become head of his order, he was also one of the few Renaissance cardinals who came from humble origins. Yet this pious and ascetic man made six of his nephews cardinals. To enrich them, Sixtus reportedly pried the precious stones out of the papal miter itself. At his death, riots broke out against his nephews and their palaces were sacked. There followed Innocent VIII, rumored to have sired twelve illegitimate children. "Justly may Rome call this man Father," one contemporary quipped.

With Innocent's death, in 1492, the papacy was again thrown open to politicking. Borgia was said to have bought the office outright, and it is certain that he lobbied for it heavily. Meanwhile the king of France had contributed two hundred thousand ducats to buy the election for Cardinal Giuliano della Rovere, who regarded the papal throne as his virtual birthright. Another rival was Ascanio Sforza, backed by his powerful clan, the rulers of Milan. Borgia paid him an enormous bribe and promised to make him vice chancellor. With that, Borgia became Pope Alexander VI, and della Rovere went into exile. Within a year, Borgia had made cardinals of his son Cesare and nephew Juan. He then crafted a series of dynastic alliances, using his children as pawns.

Borgia had nine illegitimate children by at least three different women. Two of his daughters married Roman nobles, and their brother was betrothed to a cousin of King Ferdinand and became duke of Gandia; when he died, Borgia transferred his title (and his fiancée) to his fourteen-year-old half brother, Juan, the eldest of four children by Vanozza Catanei: the other three were Cesare, Lucrezia, and Joffre.[5] Lucrezia was wed to Giovanni Sforza, while Joffre married Sancia, the princess of Naples. Thus within a year, Borgia had linked his family to the ruling houses of Naples, Spain, and Milan.

Borgia now renewed his uncle's feud with the Orsini by interdicting their purchase of some strategic Tuscan castles. This move blew up in Borgia's face when the exiled Cardinal della Rovere persuaded Charles VIII to invade Italy and depose him for simony (the sale of church offices). As French armies descended toward Rome, the Orsini, the Colonnas, and other noble families threw in their lot with the invaders. Through diplomacy, deceit, and the use of his awesome spiritual powers, Alexander survived the attack. But he plainly concluded, like his uncle, that the great Roman clans had to be crushed. His chosen instrument was Juan, the duke of Gandia, whom he intended to settle on lands seized from the Orsini. In preparation for this, Alexander excommunicated the whole Orsini clan and arrested their leader. (Virginio Orsini died in prison, a purported victim of Borgia poisoning.) He then made Juan governor of the territory that included their estates, and also made him papal captain general.

No one seems to have thought much of Juan other than his father—and even he had doubts. Juan had virtually no military experience, so Alexander teamed him up with Guidobaldo da Montefeltro, the duke of Urbino. Unfortunately, though he came from a great military family, the young duke had scarcely more experience than Juan, and the campaign was an unmitigated disaster. Next, seizing an opportunity to salvage Juan's reputation, Alexander sent him to help throw the French out of Ostia. Finally, in a secret proceeding, the pope combined three rich Neapolitan cities into a duchy that he gave to Juan—a first step toward elevating him to the throne of Naples. This outright theft of church property evoked little protest from the College of Cardinals, which was dominated by Alexander's relatives. But Juan was already unpopular with the Roman nobility, and the gift of these cities—among the papacy's most precious jewels—enraged them.

On a balmy night in 1497, Gandia attended an elegant dinner party given by his mother at her villa in a suburb of Rome. His brother Cesare and cousin Juan, both cardinals, were present. Later the three headed back to the Vatican on their mules, but Gandia split off at the Sant'Angelo bridge. The next day, investigators dredged up his body from the filth and sewage of the Tiber. His throat was cut and he had nine other stab wounds in his chest and legs. The pope's sobs were so loud they could be heard outside the Vatican. He locked himself in his room and fasted for three days.

Robbery was ruled out, since Gandia was still dressed in his finery, which included a purse with thirty ducats and a pair of silver spurs. But other motives weren't lacking. Some blamed the Orsini, who may have sought revenge for the death of their leader in prison. Others thought the Duke of Urbino or Cardinal Sforza might be involved. There were also a good many dishonored husbands who might have wished Gandia dead, including his own brother, Joffre. Rumors of jealousy and incest in the pope's close-knit family swirled around the city. But the one name no one mentioned was Cesare's, though their bitter dynastic rivalry was well known. Destined for the church since birth, endowed with wealthy benefices, and a cardinal at eighteen, Cesare was deeply dissatisfied with his ecclesiastical calling. After Gandia's disastrous military showing, Cesare must have hoped that his brother would be packed off to Spain. Instead, their father had contrived to make his favorite son the ruler of a state carved out of papal lands in Naples. Whether or not Cesare killed his brother will never be known, but everyone clearly thought he was capable of it, and the murder does seem to have served his purposes admirably. With Gandia out of the way, he promptly resigned his cardinal's hat and assumed his brother's role as captain general, becoming virtual ruler of Rome.

Handsome, vain, and arrogant, Cesare was clearly stamped by destiny as a man of remarkable energy and talent, even genius. He was also a young man in a hurry: his father was nearly seventy and Cesare knew that time was short. Therefore events unfolded swiftly. First, Alexander abandoned the Spanish-Milanese-Neapolitan axis that he had carefully constructed by the marriages of his other children and allied himself with France, throwing Italian and international politics into confusion. Among other things, this meant that Lucrezia's second marriage (to Alfonso, heir to the throne of Naples) had to be undone. Lucrezia was deeply in love with her husband. No matter: Cesare had him strangled in the pope's own Vatican apartments, despite the protective efforts of Lucrezia and Alfonso's sister Sancia, who was married to Joffre. The sudden reversal of a long-standing policy of alignment with Spain in order to obtain a French ally for Cesare certainly looks like a subordination of church interests to those of the Borgia family. Thus it seemed to many that the restless young man of twenty-four had come to dominate the experienced papal monarch of seventy. More probably, however, Cesare and Alexander were partners in an ambitious joint endeavor: the strategy conceived by Alexander, the execution (and timetable) Cesare's.

The Papal States were in the hands of vicars—secular princes whose families ruled hereditarily, but owed fealty (and tribute) to the church. In practice, however, it had been difficult for popes to assert their authority, and the current rulers were little better than usurpers. Thus while Cesare clearly intended to turn the Romagna into a Borgia fief, his campaigns in central Italy served the interests of the church, and Alexander thought nothing of backing him with all the power at his command.

In 1500, Cesare married a French princess and became duke of Valence. His wife soon bore him a daughter, but Cesare had already marched south with Louis XII to help the French king take Milan, after which he granted Cesare the use of his army. Meanwhile, Alexander issued a bull dispossessing the papal vicars and turned Cesare loose. The year before, Alexander had crushed the Gaetani, imprisoned their head (who soon died), and installed the nineteen-year-old Lucrezia as governor. Now it was the turn of the Sforzas: Cesare forced the surrender of Imola and Forlì and is thought to have raped the beautiful duchess Caterina Sforza. Next came the Colonnas, whose lands were seized by Alexander. He also appointed a flood of relatives to the cardinalate and sold red hats to raise money for Cesare. Rumor had it that he had taken to poisoning elderly cardinals in order to free up their posts.

Cesare now launched a second round of conquests. Once established as duke of Romagna, Cesare set about creating a protective ring of smaller allied states. Two Borgia grandchildren were invested with dukedoms carved out of confiscated lands, and Cesare betrothed his infant daughter to the heir of the duchy of Mantua and married Lucrezia to the son of the duke of Ferrara. In 1502, Cesare conquered the last della Rovere stronghold. But it was his lightning campaign against Urbino that really made his reputation. He certainly dazzled Machiavelli, who wrote to his Florentine masters: "This Lord is truly splendid and magnificent, and in war there is no enterprise so great that it does not appear small to him; in the pursuit of glory and lands he never rests nor recognizes fatigue or danger." Machiavelli was particularly impressed by Cesare's luck, leading him to formulate his famous maxim that fortune (like a woman) favors bold, audacious action.

The Borgias were now at their zenith: anything seemed possible. Alexander toyed with the idea of establishing a monarchy and making Cesare king, though a simpler expedient, given their control over the College of Cardinals, was having Cesare succeed him as pope. Then in August 1503 both men suddenly fell ill, and it was said that they had inadvertently poisoned themselves by drinking from cups intended for their enemies. The seventy-two-year-old Alexander died. Cesare survived, but as Machiavelli later wrote, his own illness at the time of his father's death was the one contingency that he had not anticipated.

The situation at Alexander's death was volatile and complex. The Spanish cardinals struggled to control the next election, French and Spanish armies loomed, the Colonnas and the Orsini gathered strength, and Cardinal della Rovere returned from exile. Cesare's position was briefly strengthened by the election as pope of Cardinal Piccolomini, who ordered the cities of the Romagna to maintain their allegiance to Cesare. But he died a few days later, and Cesare had little choice but to treat with della Rovere, obtaining a worthless promise of continuance in office in exchange for his support with the Spanish cardinals. With that, Giuliano della Rovere was elected Julius II.

It is a tribute to Alexander's personal authority that Cesare was able to exercise this much influence after his death. Nevertheless, the resolute spirit that had marked him during his conquests now seemed to desert him. Friends and visitors (including a disappointed Machiavelli) found him "fretful and irresolute." When Julius demanded that he relinquish his strongholds, Cesare refused and was arrested; it took five months to negotiate their surrender. After this he fled to Naples, then to France, where a few years later he died fighting in the service of his brother-in-law the king of Navarre.

It now seemed as if everything the Borgias struggled to achieve had been destroyed. The noble Roman clans revived, the defeated vicars returned to their cities, the Borgia fiefdoms were revoked. Yet while Alexander VI may have lowered the prestige of the pope as a spiritual leader, he left the papacy itself immensely stronger. The key to judging his success, observes historian Michael Mallett, lies in a proper understanding of his purposes: to advance his family *and* leave behind a unified, well-governed papal state that could be a powerful force in Italian politics. So entwined were these two goals that "it might well be argued that the ultimate Borgia aim was permanent Borgia control of a strong Papacy."[6] And while Cesare met an inglorious end, other branches of the family lived on. The counts of Busset and Chalus are direct descendants of his daughter. Lucrezia's children were cardinals and dukes of Ferrara and Urbino. Joffre's descendants inherited his title and married into the Neapolitan nobility. The Italian Borgias ultimately died out, but the dukes of Gandia continued the Spanish line well into the eighteenth century. A great-grandson, Francis de Borja, helped establish the Society of Jesus in Spain and became the third head of the Jesuit order. He was canonized in 1671.

In his play *Lucrezia Borgia,* Victor Hugo has her say: "Great crimes are in our blood." The Borgia family's reputation was as bad as it could possibly be; yet many admired their audacity and envied their success. Few families would equal or even attempt such heights of ambition, and if nothing else it reflects their supreme confidence that they could accomplish (that is, get away with) anything, so long as they stuck together. Indeed, their resemblance to a modern mafia family is hard to miss. The family's extreme closeness, its total self-reliance, and its utter amorality in dealing with outsiders are all of a piece with this pattern. No breach within the family—not even the murders of Gandia and Lucrezia's beloved Alfonso—could be allowed to harm its unity.

From one perspective, the Borgias offer one more version of an old generational saga. Alonso, the sober, conservative founder who rose through skill and merit to the papacy; Alexander, talented *and* lucky, carefully building on his uncle's patrimony over the next fifty years; Cesare, who had talent but ran out of luck and fell like Icarus, unable to survive without his father's patronage. Yet Cesare's revolt against his father's careful plans suggests that in the modern era, even the most powerful and farsighted dynast cannot assume the meek submission of his heirs. Indeed, the more spirited they are, the more likely they are to carve their own destiny. In this and other ways the Borgias embody the new culture of Renaissance individualism that increasingly encouraged sons to take their fate into their own hands. We apply the term "Renaissance man" to someone who fulfills the courtly ideal of a well-rounded individual, but the true Renaissance man was more like Cesare—an amoral opportunist, ruthlessly bending the world to his will. Renaissance Italy was full of such men: younger sons who displaced their older brothers; wicked uncles like Ludovico Sforza who dispossessed their nephews. But on the whole, successful families supported their members and worked cooperatively to accomplish their goals. Even Cesare, the model for the modern prince and sovereign individual, relied completely on his family. Yet he is also the new prototype for the son in Western culture—a son who impatiently seizes his patrimony and makes of it precisely what he chooses.

BONAPARTE: THE INGRATITUDE OF THE SELF-MADE MAN

Looking back on his remarkable career from his final exile on St. Helena, Napoleon would credit very few with having aided his success. Only his mother would be unstintingly praised, for having raised him in the tradition of Corsican independence and for holding the family together through their long ordeal of poverty: "All that I am, all that I have been, I owe to the habits of work I received in my childhood and the good principles given to me by my excellent mother." Apart from the saintly Letizia, he acknowledged no one else. Instead he expressed some vague ideas about "destiny."

This romantic myth has been largely accepted. Napoleon is seen as the emblematic self-made man, rising through a perfect conjunction of merit and opportunity to become the conqueror of Europe and the emperor of France. His Achilles' heel is thought to be his weakness for his relatives. (Even Adolf Hitler blamed Napoleon's fall on his penchant for placing his brothers and sisters in positions of authority.) Napoleon himself frequently complained about his family and remarked that they had done him more harm than he had done them good. In a limited sense, this may be true. But it is also quite misleading. For despite the cult of genius that he fostered, and whose symbol he became, Napoleon did not come out of nowhere. He was the product of a highly nepotistic ethnic culture that placed loyalty to family firmly above individual interests. Nor did he drag his brothers up the ladder of success like so much baggage: they formed the very rungs on which he climbed. But the biggest omission by far concerns the role of a man who was already dead: Napoleon's father.

Carlo Buonaparte has come down to us as a spendthrift, gambler, and provincial bon vivant, a schemer and dabbler who never amounted to anything. One historian describes him as a Mediterranean Micawber, always in the direst straits, yet cheerfully confident that something would "turn up." Napoleon himself spoke of his father's death as a liberating stroke of good fortune and was even heard to wonder about his paternity, on the conjecture that a feckless rake like Carlo could not have been the source of his own transcendent abilities. But Carlo deserved much better of his son—and of posterity in general. While Napoleon would mock his social climbing, his deathbed conversion, and his attachment to the dying institutions of the Ancien Régime, he was an artful and assiduous nepotist who literally wore himself to death in an effort to establish his children in the ranks of the French aristocracy.

It has often been observed that Corsica is one of those backward regions—like the mountainous interiors of Spain and Scotland or the Balkan peninsula—where the nepotistic solidarity of the clan remained strong and intact long after church and state had eroded its grip on the rest of Europe. What seems not to have been noticed is the fact that some of the most successful families in history came from such areas.[7] The Borgias and the Bonapartes both emerged from nepotistic hinterlands where the state was weak or nonexistent and the clan and feud prevailed. Napoleon's mother came from a particularly fierce mountain clan, and he later remarked that his grandmother could always count on the aid of two or three hundred armed kinsmen in any dispute. "This clannishness, this almost primitive sense of kinship, was something which Napoleon never outgrew," Theo Aronson writes. "It caused him to elevate his relations to positions far beyond their capabilities, and contributed, in no small measure, to his downfall."[8]

Napoleon was pleased to have people think that he came from humble origins. The self-made man must not only rise by unaided merit, he must rise from depths of obscurity that make his merit shine more brightly. Yet the family's extreme poverty is a myth largely invented by the Bonapartes themselves. In fact the family was fairly well-to-do, as such things were measured in Corsica: the Buonapartes claimed to be a branch of an aristocratic Tuscan family and owned a good deal of property, including a town house in the city of Ajaccio.

Tall and handsome, Carlo Buonaparte was intelligent, well-read, and surprisingly cultured. At eighteen, he married Letizia Ramolino, the daughter of another leading family and a famous local beauty. Letizia gave him thirteen children, eight of whom survived, and in all that he later did, Carlo acted not from personal ambition but with the aim of advancing his family. Money was important, but Carlo understood that money (in the form of salaries, commissions, and other emoluments) derived from one's position in the great social pyramid of the Ancien Régime. His career was typical of that of many eighteenth-century men who expended every ounce of ingenuity and effort toward the goal of gaining access for their children to the system of European nobility.

Like many young men of his day, Carlo's imagination had been fired by the republican and nationalist ideals espoused by Rousseau and other critics of the aristocratic system. He therefore attached himself to Pascal Paoli, who was then leading a nationalist revolt against French domination of Corsica. But Paoli was defeated and Carlo adroitly switched sides. The French were granting patents of nobility to qualifying Corsican families and had set aside a number of prestigious scholarships for the children of indigent nobles. If Carlo could prove his aristocratic origins, his children would be eligible to compete for these upper-class affirmative action slots. The Tuscan Buonapartes had never accepted the rude Corsican clan as a branch of their family, but Carlo's father had managed to gain acknowledgment from a member who was a canon of the faculty at Pisa. Carlo therefore went to Pisa, widely known as a diploma mill, where he acquired a law degree and received from his Italian "cousin" a certificate permitting him to use the title "noble Florentine patrician." This was the golden key that would unlock a better future for his family.

Carlo returned to Corsica and opened a small practice, setting his sights on the newly created post of *assesseur,* or associate judge, which carried a sizable income. To obtain this prize, however, influence was necessary, and Carlo and Letizia worked as a team to secure the support of the comte de Marbeuf, the French military commander on the island. Marbeuf became a frequent guest at Carlo's house and enjoyed his famed hospitality, but his visits were more notable for his growing attentions to Letizia. Several witnesses claimed that Marbeuf became her lover, and that at least two of her children were his. Most historians are reluctant to credit these assertions; even those who regard Carlo as the worst sort of opportunist hesitate to suggest that he pimped his wife to an aging French aristocrat. Yet he plainly encouraged the relationship, which continued for twelve years, including long periods when he was absent and the count was virtually a resident in their house.

With Marbeuf's patronage, Carlo obtained the coveted post. Then his patent of nobility was approved and he was elected to the Corsican assembly.[9] When Marbeuf settled a property suit in Carlo's favor, the Buonapartes were at last able to assume the status of nobles. Marbeuf was also enlisted in the all-important cause of advancing the children. Carlo's eldest son, Joseph, Letizia's half brother Joseph Fesch, and a cousin were all started on ecclesiastical careers under the sponsorship of Marbeuf's nephew, the bishop of Autun. Marbeuf also arranged the nine-year-old Napoleon's acceptance to the military school at Brienne. Although Carlo was exactly the sort of poor noble for whom these scholarships were intended, competition was stiff and Marbeuf had to write twice to the minister of war before receiving a favorable reply. Finally, Marbeuf agreed to be godfather to Carlo's infant son Louis: nothing better indicates how high Carlo now stood in the island's social hierarchy, thanks to Marbeuf's patronage.

He now embarked upon an even more ambitious effort, aggressively expanding the family's financial interests by the acquisition of more property, and launching an ultimately doomed attempt to improve a marshy tract on which he planned to grow mulberries for the French luxury market. These projects involved a tortuous pursuit through Corsican courts and French ministries, where again Marbeuf was helpful.

In 1779, Carlo traveled to Versailles on a dual mission for the Corsican assembly and Marbeuf. The journey represented the crowning reward of a decade of effort. Napoleon and Joseph went with him as far as Autun, where Joseph was to begin his ecclesiastical career and Napoleon would study French. Carlo's business kept him in lodgings near Versailles for over four months and involved a complex round of interviews, receptions, consultations, and finally a royal presentation. In April he personally supervised Napoleon's entry at school before returning to Corsica, where he set about improving the Casa Buonaparte with marble mantelpieces, crimson wall hangings, large crystal mirrors, and damask-covered furniture. In 1782, he took Letizia on a costly tour of aristocratic French resorts and arranged for Elisa's admission to St.-Cyr, an elegant school for young ladies founded by Madame de Maintenon. No one knows how Carlo managed to procure this enormous privilege for his daughter, yet somehow he accomplished it.[10]

Napoleon spent five years at Brienne. As a poor boy and the only Corsican, he had a hard time with the other students, but he did credit the school with giving him a sound military education as well as an introduction to French culture.

Few careers illustrate so well the power of the rationalist outlook in opening a path through social barriers. Since childhood, Napoleon had shown an aptitude for mathematics, performing feats of addition and subtraction for the delighted nuns at school. It was this aptitude that won him a place in the royal artillery, an elite unit reserved not for those of high birth but for the ablest students, often boys of humble origin.

In 1783, Napoleon was hoping for early promotion to the École Royale Militaire. But only two boys were promoted that year, and Napoleon was passed over. Meanwhile, Joseph, who had spent four years preparing for the priesthood, announced that he now wished to join the army. A long-standing suit to recover an old family property was losing ground, and Carlo's mulberry project also ran into trouble. Worst of all, the recently widowed Marbeuf had married a pretty young French girl who within a year gave him an heir.

In June 1784, Carlo launched another of his whirlwind trips to France, though he was seriously ill. This time he brought seven-year-old Elisa and another little cousin, stopping at Autun to collect nine-year-old Lucien, whom he hoped to get accepted at Brienne. We must imagine his tender care of these young children on an arduous journey through France by boat and stagecoach. Carlo also hoped to consult the queen's physician about his malady, but he was dying of the same disease that later killed Napoleon, caused by much the same temper and lifestyle. "Over-anxious, over-zealous, over-active, constantly on the move, financially and socially insecure, alternating between need and luxury, skimping and squandering, feasting and starving, he was a natural subject for an ulcer of the stomach, which in the absence of adequate treatment turned to cancer and killed him young."[11] This touching portrait of a nepotistic father who literally wears himself to death for the sake of his children is worthy of Dickens or Balzac.

At Brienne, Carlo and Napoleon discussed Joseph's future. The fourteen-year-old boy displayed a precocious grasp of the issues involved, and it was already clear how much Carlo relied on his son. Leaving Lucien in his care, Carlo hurried on to Paris, where he deposited the girls at St.-Cyr, then appeared at Versailles, where he sought a waiver of the age limits for Lucien's entry to Brienne, early promotion for Napoleon, and admission for Joseph to the artillery or engineers. He then returned to Corsica to pursue the ineffectual diet of soft pears and mineral baths prescribed by the queen's physician.

In October, thanks to his father's efforts, Napoleon was promoted to the École Royale. This was a real aristocratic setting, where the students were required to wear expensive uniforms and were waited on by servants hand and foot. Napoleon's later utterances heaped scorn on the old aristocracy as decadent "imbeciles" and "hereditary asses." These sentiments reflect his impressions of the young nobles he met at school and fit in well with his call for an aristocracy of merit rather than birth. The mathematics exam given to artillery candidates usually required two years of preparation; Napoleon passed it in one.

For Carlo, the latter part of 1784 was taken up with desperate legal maneuvering in the matter of some land on which he hoped to plant an olive grove. In early 1785, once again in ill health, he planned another trip, to place Joseph at Brienne and secure his other interests. A storm at sea and other strains of eighteenth-century travel took their toll, and his health deteriorated rapidly. Referred to the medical experts in Montpellier, Carlo, along with Joseph, was taken in by some Corsican friends. But by this time he was dying, and in his final days, between fits of vomiting and delirium, this worldly philosophical agnostic experienced a profound religious conversion, which Napoleon would later mock: "he had no sooner seen the coffin open than he was seized with a passion for priests; there were not enough for him in all Montpellier." Pitiably, he cried out again and again for Napoleon to come and defend him. After he died, an autopsy revealed one or two large stomach tumors.

Napoleon declined to visit the school's resident priest, explaining that he felt no need of consolation. At the funeral a witness observed that while Joseph wept copiously, the younger boy shed but a single tear.

Carlo died as he had lived, in a chaos of bills, correspondence, and lawsuits. The family's property did not produce much income, and Napoleon (now posted at Valence in the Rhône valley) was the only breadwinner. Elisa was secured at St.-Cyr, but Joseph had abandoned the church for the army, and Lucien now wished to quit the army for either the church or a literary career. Louis was approaching school age, Jérôme was still an infant, and the two younger girls, Caroline and Pauline, would be dependents for some time and could not be married without dowries.

Napoleon wasted no time in asserting his authority. His first act was to decree that Joseph was unsuited to a military career and should study law instead. Meanwhile he brought Louis to live with him in the barracks, where he became the ambivalent object of Napoleon's new and rather brusque paternal feelings. Over the next four years Napoleon made frequent visits home and actually spent more time there than in camp. Letizia devoted herself to her family, washing, cooking, and caring for Carlo's bedridden uncle, a miserly peasant who ruled the roost from a straw mattress stuffed with gold coins.

"For the whole of his life," writes R. F. Delderfield, "Napoleon Buonaparte was acutely conscious of family responsibilities and never, for one instant, did he attempt to shift these responsibilities on to other shoulders, or allow brothers and sisters to stand on their own feet."[12] Note how easily a sense of responsibility slides into an attitude of domination. Napoleon was fond of his siblings, but he was also somewhat distant and imperious, and his patronizing air of knowing best could be infuriating. But while he was more or less firmly in charge from this point, he was never in complete control. The siblings had ideas of their own and they often sided with one of their number against him, especially in matters of love.

Napoleon's career as a nepotist has four main phases. The first, or "peasant," phase reflects the traditional methods of survival passed down through Corsican culture. It required unity, clear patriarchal authority, and unquestioned cooperation. The "bourgeois" phase involved a new set of strategies designed to aid the family in its rise, primarily marriage for economic ends and the search for a series of patrons. The "aristocratic" phase deployed techniques designed to secure the family's new position, including marriage for social ends and the exercise of patronage. To this point, Napoleon's nepotism had been an asset in his rise. But in the final, "imperial" phase it went over the top, going in the process from an asset to an extreme liability.

It is impossible to make sense of Napoleon's story without discussing the French Revolution, a great disruption in the order of society that was the making of him and countless other opportunists. But the revolution was more than a political rebellion: it was also a reaction against the patriarchal model of authority on which the Ancien Régime was based. The monarchies of Europe still rested on the paternalistic ideology of Classical Nepotism. The revolutionaries not only beheaded the king but tried to do away with the idea of a national father, replacing him with a band of republican brothers. Nor was that all: they wanted liberty and equality to rule in the family as they ruled in the state. The Jacobins banned primogeniture, legalized divorce, instituted compulsory public education, granted inheritance rights to illegitimate children, and took other steps that limited the power of French fathers.

These measures—the first of many subsequent attempts to "rationalize" the family—reached their peak under Robespierre, when the state actually tried to replace the family as the focus of French loyalties.[13]

This radical project was short-lived. The vaunted ideal of fraternity proved to be a weak substitute for traditional paternalism, and under the Directory, the revolution recoiled from its extreme rejection of paternal authority and took cautious steps toward rehabilitating fathers as a means of restoring order in French society. For one thing, it had not escaped attention that the leading regicides—including Robespierre and St.-Just—had been bachelors, and among other provisions the constitution of 1795 required that all members of the national assembly be married or widowed. The family was reaffirmed as the bedrock of society, and the importance of paternal authority, tempered by republican ideals, was rediscovered. Thus was born the "good," liberal-paternalist father whom we will meet again in eighteenth-century America.

Napoleon seemed to be an authentic representative of youthful ambition and energy freed from the dead hand of patriarchal domination. He was a younger son who rose through merit to the leadership, first, of his fatherless family, then of his fatherless country. Yet he himself would turn out to be an extreme paternalistic reactionary: the Napoleonic Code completed the restoration of fatherly power that had cautiously begun under the Directory. This was clearly necessary to pull the country back from the brink of a radical experiment for which Western societies would not be ready for at least another century. For France, like most of Europe at this time, was strongly marked by vestiges of feudalism and the ancient gift economy, persisting for centuries alongside the developing institutions of the market and the state. Gifts were not only exchanged between equals but were given to the king and his ministers, as well as to priests, judges, lawyers, and other officials with little sense of impropriety. This legacy is reflected even today in French vernacular expressions like "One favor begets another" and "A thing well given is never lost."[14]

When the revolution broke out in 1789 the Bonapartes were wild with enthusiasm. The brothers tried to foment a rebellion in Corsica, but after Lucien gave a fiery speech attacking Paoli (who had returned to the island), he had the whole family expelled. Thus it was that in July 1793, the bedraggled Bonapartes arrived at the French port of Toulon, where they remained for six months, fruitlessly appealing to the revolutionary government to increase their small refugee stipend. By chance Napoleon encountered a fellow Corsican named Salicetti, who got him a post with a local artillery unit. Salicetti also obtained an appointment for Joseph as a *commissaire* and one for Lucien as a military storekeeper. Like his father, Napoleon would benefit from the ethnic solidarity of Corsicans in France.

Advantageous marriages were the next order of business. Joseph's marriage to a well-off bourgeoise named Julie Clary added greatly to the family's resources at this time. A marriage was also contemplated between Napoleon and Julie's pretty sister Désirée, but her father declared that one Corsican in the family was enough. Meanwhile, Lucien impulsively married Christine Boyer, a sweet-natured but illiterate peasant girl whom Napoleon thought completely unsuitable. He was outraged by Lucien's insistence on putting his own happiness ahead of the family's needs, and swore that he would never speak to his brother again until he divorced her. But Lucien was the only Bonaparte who could never be commanded by Napoleon, and Letizia (as always) sided with Lucien, who was the son most like his father.

When the citizens of Toulon rose in revolt against the Terror, Letizia and her children fled to Marseilles, reduced to begging on the road. Obtaining two unfurnished rooms, she had to queue for food at the local soup kitchen. But just when things were at their worst, Napoleon's star began to rise. It was during the siege of Toulon that Napoleon first distinguished himself, with a boldly executed plan that forced the British navy to abandon the port. This brought him to the attention of Augustin Robespierre, placed in charge of France's southern defenses by his brother, who recommended Napoleon to the first citizen as an officer of "transcendent merit." He thus exchanged the ethnic patronage of Salicetti for that of the most powerful man in France. But as the Terror gave way to Thermidorean reaction, the association with the Robespierres became dangerous. After the fall and execution of Robespierre, Napoleon was briefly arrested. Salicetti obtained his release.

Then on October 5, 1795, in the incident known as "the whiff of grapeshot," Napoleon saved the government by dispersing an angry mob with cannon fire. The same day, through the intervention of a grateful new patron, Paul Barras—a member of the five-man Directory—Napoleon was made general of division, and three weeks later, general of the army of the interior. Suddenly Napoleon was a national hero, the most popular soldier in France. He immediately obtained sixty thousand francs for his mother and sisters, a consular appointment for Joseph, a lieutenancy for Louis, and the Commissary of War for Lucien.

At this point Napoleon met and fell in love with Josephine de Beauharnais, a Creole beauty widowed in the Terror. Currently the mistress of Barras, her Parisian salon had become a real center of influence. Barras, who was beginning to feel apprehensive about his ambitious young protégé, had also tired of Josephine's expensive tastes. He therefore let Napoleon take her off his hands in exchange for command of the army of Italy. The family was horrified and tried to break it up, but only incurred their brother's wrath. To the end, however, Letizia regarded Josephine as an interloper who had tried to steal Napoleon from his family.

Napoleon now marched off to conduct the astonishing forty-three-day Italian campaign—neither the first nor last proof of his genius. With the conquest of Italy, he assumed an air of destiny that strongly impressed those around him. Yet even as he immersed himself in the task of restructuring a conquered nation, he had time for careful thought about his family. Like all aspiring families, the Bonapartes made sure to place a member in each of the major professions. Thus Joseph would be posted as a diplomat to Parma, Lucien would enter politics, and Louis would remain in the army. Jérôme would go to school in Paris. Elisa married a fellow Corsican named Bacciochi, and Pauline married Victor-Emmanuel Leclerc, a leading general in the Italian campaign.

Napoleon's star had risen so high and so fast that the Directors were eager to get rid of him; they therefore approved his audacious proposal for an invasion of Egypt, cutting off English trade with the East. But the campaign was a series of disasters, and in the end Napoleon abandoned his army, hoping to return home ahead of the news of his Egyptian debacle.

We now come to the moment in Napoleon's career that more than any other has been enshrined in heroic mythology. On November 9, 1799, the Abbé Sieyès, a member of the ruling Directory, convened the upper house of the assembly on the pretext of a Jacobin plot. At his suggestion, the senators voted to meet the next day in the palace at St.-Cloud for greater safety. Sieyès also moved to put General Bonaparte in charge of French troops around Paris. When the senators met the next day, the dissolution of the Directory was announced and a new constitution was called for. A rancorous debate ensued. Some demanded proofs of the conspiracy; others called for the election of a new Directory. At this point, Napoleon, waiting in the wings to be summoned as the protector of French liberty, lost patience and burst in on the proceedings. Instead of a stirring speech persuading the senators that only a Roman-style consulate could save France, he delivered an incoherent tirade and was angrily shouted down. He then charged into the assembly's lower house, which was meeting outside in the glass-enclosed *orangerie,* accompanied by four grenadiers. The sight of soldiers sparked a riot. Napoleon was dragged to safety by General Lefebvre amid cries of "Death to dictators!"

All might have been lost but for the intervention of Napoleon's brother, who was chairing the assembly. Lucien Bonaparte banged his gavel but could not establish order. When someone moved that Napoleon be outlawed, Lucien tore off his official sash and flung it to the ground. Then he stalked out of the building and into the courtyard where Napeoleon, pale and shaken, was still recovering from his assault. A veteran street-corner speaker, Lucien mounted a horse and announced that an attempt had been made to assassinate Napoleon by agents in the pay of England. He drew his sword, pointed at his brother's heart, and vowed to run him through if he should ever harm the liberties of France. *"Vive la république! Aux armes!"* the soldiers shouted. Generals Murat and Leclerc led a bayonet charge into the building, causing the terrified deputies to jump out the windows. Within minutes the hall was clear and the government had fallen. Later,

Lucien convened a small group of delegates who dissolved the assemblies and created a new consulate headed by Bonaparte, Sieyès, and the former director Pierre-Roger Ducos. By November 14, Bonaparte had shouldered them aside and established his rule as first consul.

The events of 18 Brumaire strikingly reveal Napoleon's habit of reliance on his relatives: the whole thing was a family affair from first to last. While Napoleon was off campaigning in Italy and Egypt, Lucien and Joseph were elected to the assembly as Corsican delegates. A clever businessman, Joseph had enriched himself through financial speculation and made numerous influential friends. Lucien rose through sheer energy and talent to become president of the assembly, though he was only twenty-four (he lied about his age). The directors Sieyès and Ducos both owed their appointments to him; together they planned the coup and formed an influential clique that included Foreign Minister Talleyrand, Admiral Bruix, Police Chief Fouché, and other key figures. Sieyès would have preferred another general, one more likely to step aside when the job was done, but Lucien's insistence prevailed. It was Lucien who took the offer to his brother and held a series of meetings at his home to hammer out the plan. He also converted at least fifty other delegates to the cause. Joseph used his influence to build support among the Parisian elite and made sure that his brother-in-law, war minister Bernadotte, was safely out of town (Joseph took him to lunch in the country). Napoleon's wife, Josephine, softened up her old friends, the directors Barras and Gohier. Leclerc and Murat were not only staunch military companions, one was already Napoleon's brother-in-law and the other soon would be.

With the success of 18 Brumaire, the family fortunes took another sharp turn for the better. Joseph became a member of the new legislative assembly, Lucien became interior minister, and Louis was made a colonel of dragoons. Caroline was married to Murat, and Pauline's husband, Leclerc, became a divisional commander in Italy.[15]

At the same time, Napoleon's nepotism passed from its bourgeois careerist phase to the level of a dynastic enterprise. But as he assumed the dictatorship of France, he also became a dictator to his family. Not one of them was allowed to make a personal decision without his consent. He was painfully self-conscious about their behavior and always felt that it reflected on him personally. Many of his problems with the family could be ascribed to this tyrannical impatience with their needs and limitations—though he could also be protective, and surprisingly indulgent of their faults.

The keystone of his plan was to create a unified Bonaparte-Beauharnais clan. This is a common practice of dynastic family founders: braiding together two families—planting their roots in one pot, as it were—produces a sturdy double lineage of a kind that we earlier called a connubium, one that recapitulates the primitive exchange of women between tribal marriage groups. Many of the families we have examined (like the Julio-Claudian line of Augustus and Livia) and those we will consider later on (like the Randolphs of Virginia and the Cabot-Lodges of Massachusetts) were similarly formed. But the creation of an artificial clan requires considerable human skills of tact, finesse, and judgment, and while Napoleon was an excellent general, he was by all accounts a dreadful matchmaker. At first he planned on marrying his siblings Jérôme and Caroline to Josephine's children, Hortense and Eugène, but the spoiled young Bonapartes refused: they disliked their stepsiblings intensely, no doubt because the Beauharnais children were in fact modest, well-behaved, and attractive young people of whom Napoleon was genuinely fond. The union of Caroline and Murat—the one ambitious and unscrupulous, the other vain and empty-headed—would prove especially disastrous to his interests. But his attempts to meddle in Lucien's marital affairs blew up in his face altogether. When Lucien's first wife died in 1801, Napoleon hoped to match him with the widowed queen mother of Etruria. Instead, Lucien married the estranged wife of a Parisian banker who was pregnant with his child. Enraged, Napoleon exiled Lucien, who took refuge in the Papal States. There he would remain, living comfortably off his enormous wealth, defying his brother and rebuffing attempts at reconciliation.

Napoleon was not yet emperor, but the question of succession was already on everyone's mind. Josephine had not conceived and there were rumors that Napoleon was impotent. Afraid for her position, Josephine offered to marry Hortense to Louis, making their firstborn son Napoleon's heir. Napoleon expressed his satisfaction with the scheme: "I brought up Louis and look upon him as a son. Your daughter is what you cherish most on earth. Their children will be ours. We will adopt them, and this adoption will console us for not having any of our own." Hortense was appalled at the notion of a *mariage de convenance* with this introverted, gloomy-looking stranger. But Josephine plied her with tears. "You know, my darling, that all the Bonapartes hate me. They want to separate me from your stepfather. They want him to divorce me. And you, only you, can save me. The day you become Madame Louis, they will no longer dare to do anything against me." This nakedly selfish appeal did the trick. But the marriage was unhappy from the start, and while it produced several children, it was not long in coming apart.

All the Bonapartes were difficult, but the youngest were the worst. Pauline had blossomed from a giddy, overindulged schoolgirl into a full-blown voluptuary. But her ambitions fell short of political intrigue, and she remained loyal to the end. The same cannot be said for Caroline, who incessantly plotted to put her husband in line for the throne. Jérôme, the youngest, was a midshipman in the navy, where Napoleon had sent him as a punishment for dueling. "I send you Citizen Jérôme Buonaparte to serve his apprenticeship in the navy," he wrote to Admiral Ganteaume. "You know that he needs to be treated strictly and to make up for lost time." (The admiral was too prudent to take these instructions seriously.) After a while, Jérôme was given his own vessel, and for a year or so he sailed around the Caribbean. Putting in at Norfolk, Virginia, he cut a brilliant figure in provincial society; he also wooed and precipitously wed a beautiful Baltimore heiress. Napoleon was beside himself and demanded he divorce her at once. Jérôme gave in, abandoning the pregnant girl. She later gave birth to a son, the founder of a line of American Bonapartes.

In 1804 Napoleon declared himself emperor, and titles were distributed to the whole family, except Lucien, who refused to pay the price of divorcing his wife. He also promoted fourteen close military associates to the rank of marshal and created a magnificent court to rival that of any ruler in history. Anyone and everyone who had helped him in his rise was now rewarded. The web of Napoleon's patronage extended far and wide, creating the core of a new elite that would dominate France long after his own fall from power.

The next few years saw a succession of extraordinary victories that laid Europe at Napoleon's feet. In their wake, his nepotistic enterprise reached new heights. Joseph and Julie became king and queen of Naples. Elisa and Bacciochi were given the Italian principalities of Lucca and Piombino. Murat was made grand duke of Berg and Cleves. Louis was made king of Holland. Jérôme married a German princess, and a kingdom of Westphalia was created for him. Pauline was granted the tiny principality of Guastalla (she declined to rule it, however, and Napoleon "bought" it back from her for 6 million francs).

Up to now, the Bonapartes had been entirely dependent on their brother. How they might have managed on their own we will never know, for while he gave them wings, he never let them fly. As a result, the hidden strains within the family emerged to bedevil his plans. When Hortense gave birth to a son, Napoleon Charles, Napoleon wanted to adopt the child and make him king of Italy, but Louis would not allow his son to have a higher rank than his. Despite this disagreement, Napoleon made Louis king of Holland, but his attempt to win the nobles over by restoring their lands and titles provoked an angry threat of removal, followed by a ceaseless stream of carping correspondence. Next, having engineered the abdication of the king of Spain, Napoleon had difficulty persuading any member of his family to rule it. Lucien would not divorce his wife to buy a crown. Joseph also turned him down. Louis had been Napoleon's puppet long enough and he too refused. Enraged, Napoleon simply ordered Joseph to quit Naples and accept the throne of Spain, installing the Murats in his place. No sooner was the succession announced than the country exploded in civil war.

Napoleon Charles died in 1807, dashing hopes for a Beauharnais heir. Hortense earned her mother a temporary reprieve when she gave birth to Louis Napoleon (who would one day rule France as Napoleon III). At last, however, Napoleon divorced Josephine, and the family began to debate her successor. Letizia tried to persuade him to marry Lucien's daughter Charlotte, then fourteen. In this way she hoped to reconcile the brothers and put a second Bonaparte on the throne. But the girl proved as headstrong as her father, and in the end he married the Austrian princess Marie Louise. It was not her dowry that attracted him—she was utterly impoverished—but her lineage, which linked her with every ruling house in Europe. In 1811 she gave birth to a son, Napoleon Francis Charles Joseph, whom Napoleon swiftly crowned as king of Rome.

But just as he seemed to have secured his rule at last, Napoleon's dynastic scheme began to unravel. Jérôme had found the pressures of governing a patchwork kingdom ravaged by fighting, crushed by debts and taxation, and bled white by forcible levies too much for his meager abilities. Louis, floundering in Holland, chose to abdicate in favor of his son—an act Napoleon denounced as outright treachery. Napoleon tried to persuade Lucien to return to Paris, but he declined. Livid with his whole rebellious clan, Napoleon exclaimed, "I do not believe any man in the world is more unfortunate in his family than I."

The turning point was 1812, the year of the disastrous Russian campaign. Jérôme, given command of a cavalry corps, disobeyed orders and went home in a huff after being severely reprimanded. Murat, sensing the imminent collapse of the empire, rushed back to Naples to protect his precarious throne. Joseph unwisely offered Wellington a pitched battle in Spain, which he lost, whereupon he fled the country. Meanwhile, Caroline and Murat concluded an agreement with the British and Austrians, making her the only Bonaparte to turn against her brother.

In April 1814 Napoleon acknowledged defeat. Even in his deed of abdication he remembered his family, stipulating that each should receive a sizable stipend while he went into exile as sovereign of the tiny island kingdom of Elba. There he was joined by Pauline and Letizia, who like the wily old peasant she was had been hoarding up money for years—money that would aid his return to power ten months later. Joseph repaired to Lausanne, where he maintained correspondence with Bonapartists across Europe, and Lucien was finally reunited with the family in Rome and even patched up his quarrel with Napoleon. Caroline wrote to Letizia disavowing Murat's treachery and claiming she could not "command her husband." The stern old lady replied, "It was only over your dead body that your husband should have been able to pierce your brother, your benefactor, and your master."

The Bourbon restoration was an unqualified failure, and with dissatisfaction spreading across France and northern Italy, Napoleon led a bold escape from Elba, landing at Cannes with eleven hundred men and swiftly taking Grenoble and Lyon. Entering Paris in March 1815, he was greeted by a massive outpouring of approval. The family rallied to his cause: Joseph resumed his seat in the House of Peers and Lucien entered the Chamber of Deputies. The brothers worked together to consolidate the Bonapartist faction in both houses. In June a combined Anglo-Prussian army advanced from the north, followed by the massed armies of Austria, Russia, and Sweden. Napoleon whipped up an army and charged toward Brussels. Meanwhile, Lucien and Joseph worked feverishly to turn the tide of anti-Bonaparte sentiment in the Chamber of Deputies. At last, however, after Napoleon's defeat at Waterloo, Joseph drafted a statement of abdication, naming as successor the four-year-old king of Rome, now in the hands of his Austrian grandfather. Then Napoleon fled Paris, taking leave of his mother and brothers for the last time. After a brief period as a fugitive he surrendered and was exiled to the island of St. Helena, where he died five years later.

Although the empire had collapsed, their thrones had reverted to their previous owners, and they were barred for life from France, the surviving Bonapartes were all wealthy and titled aristocrats. Joseph settled in New Jersey, where he remained for many years a rich, respected private citizen. Offered the crown of Mexico a few years after Napoleon's death, he politely declined. Both his daughters married their cousins, the sons of Lucien and Louis. Letizia and Lucien received protection from the pope and went to Rome along with Louis, Elisa, and Pauline. Caroline fled to Vienna, where she died, never to be forgiven for her treachery. Jérôme retired to Austria, living off the generous subsidies provided by his father-in-law, the king of Bavaria. Of the original family, only he survived to play a part in the restoration of the empire in 1848 by Louis Napoleon, the third son of Louis and Hortense.

Carlo Buonaparte's reputation has not prospered. His own family dismissed him as an improvident bumbler and spendthrift who left them in the lurch by dying young. "So Carlo went down to posterity," writes

Dorothy Carrington, "extravagant, feckless, weak, vain, muddle-headed, irresolute, irresponsible (the adjectives are lifted from history books), an altogether foolish and worthless person." Yet, she concludes, he left the family in a much better state than he found it, with fertile lands, a fine house, a noble lineage, and a privileged education for his children. "If ever a man deserved to have such a son as Napoleon, it was he."[16]

He certainly did not deserve a monumental ingrate. Napoleon was generous to those who had helped him or his family during their years of struggle. Yet regarding his debt to his father, the one man to whom he owed the most, Napoleon remained strangely silent. Not one word of gratitude to Carlo seems to have escaped his lips in all that is recorded of his thoughts.

In his last exile on St. Helena, brooding on his past mistakes, he clear-sightedly assessed his family's weaknesses and regretted having made his brothers and sisters kings and queens. Most historians concur in this assessment. But the fault was only partly in the Bonapartes. It was mainly in their brother, who by bullying, flattering, cajoling, commanding, and bribing tried to weld them overnight into an unprecedented dynastic system linking all the thrones of Europe under his supreme authority—a dynasty to end all dynasties. This grandiose scheme—and not the limitations of his kin—would be his ultimate undoing. Though they were certainly corrupted by the wealth and power he heaped on them, most would have liked nothing more than to be free of his hectoring influence. Nor should their contribution to his success be underestimated. Though most historians have echoed Napoleon's harsh judgment of his relatives, they were instrumental in his rise, played an active role in his political and military plans, stood by him in his exile, and worked hard for his restoration.

Indeed, taken individually, the Bonapartes were much more capable than most historians give them credit for. Joseph took his duties as king of Naples seriously and could have made an enlightened and popular monarch, but he was never allowed sufficient independence. Lucien, clearly the most gifted of the Bonapartes, masterminded his brother's rise to power and could have become a very able statesman had Napoleon's dictatorial interference not led to a decade-long rift. Only Elisa shows what might have been accomplished by the others had

Napoleon left them alone. She proved such a capable ruler of her small Italian principalities that he later gave her Tuscany as well.

While these nepotistic assignments have been universally criticized, they were clearly integral to Napoleon's strategy. He needed to consolidate his lightning victories with immediate political changes, and he put in these positions people whom he felt he could trust and rely on. Under the circumstances, competence was not his first concern. Loyalty was the key, since he could supply enough competent guidance for all of them. Therefore no one but his own relatives would do, since only they were willing to be hectored, bossed around, and manipulated by their tyrannical benefactor. If they were contentious and quarrelsome, he was overbearing and tyrannical. In any case he never allowed them real autonomy. Nor was he ever deceived about their flaws and limitations: indeed he put them in place precisely because they were inexperienced, dependent on his support, and easily controlled. Yet he always expected too much of them, and they disappointed him again and again. Nor is it surprising that his despotic brand of nepotism earned no thanks: such high-handed and conditional gifts inspire no gratitude.

Thus despite the universal judgment of historians, Napoleon didn't fall because he practiced nepotism; he fell because he practiced it *badly*.

The French Revolution inaugurates a period in which rapid and unceasing social change would be the norm. No longer would life continue in its course undisturbed from one generation to the next, and this meant that fathers would increasingly be left behind, with less and less of value to bequeath. Henceforth self-made men would come to dominate Western societies, and father-son relations would be detached from the old system of Classical Nepotism. Napoleon's ingratitude therefore has a larger significance: it reflects the great disruption that marked the end of the feudal era and the advent of the modern age.

ROTHSCHILD: THE ULTIMATE FAMILY BUSINESS

Mayer Amschel Rothschild and his sons were the inventors of international high finance. They created the modern international bond market and dominated it almost completely, with a brother running a bank in each capital, acting in perfect coordination through a communications network that was the fastest in the world. In time they became even more powerful than the kings they bankrolled. Much of the credit for the century of relative peace in Europe between 1815 and 1914 must go to their family bank, which regarded war and revolution as bad for business.

The perennial question about the Rothschilds is, how did they do it? The answer is, through nepotism, and a carefully conceived dynastic plan. They succeeded in surviving the vicissitudes of fortune by a combination of unusual talent (business ability ran in the family) and the observation of a few simple rules laid down by the family's founder. Women and sons-in-law were excluded from the business; cousins married cousins so as to avoid dissipating the family capital; correspondence was conducted in the private language of the ghetto, known as *Judendeutsch*. Above all, every son was expected to do his part while maintaining the family's unity. These rules were drawn from over three thousand years of Jewish history.

Although the Rothschilds were ultimately a product of the ancient Hebrew nepotism described in a previous chapter, in a more immediate sense they reflected the nepotistic traditions of the ghetto that were formed in the thousand-year Jewish diaspora.

Many Jews had remained in Palestine until A.D. 70, when the Romans finally crushed Jewish sovereignty and destroyed the Second Temple. But by the end of the first millennium, Jewish colonies could be found from Spain to China. Most diaspora communities were founded by a few Jewish families and remained small and exceedingly insular: cousin marriages were common, and uncle-niece marriage was idealized in such authoritative texts as the Talmud and the *Shulkhan Arukh*. This was especially the case in priestly lineages. The family-based Sephardic trading networks that flourished in the sixteenth to eighteenth centuries were also strengthened by consanguineous marriages. During the Middle Ages, Jews were confined to certain occupations and were forced to live in ghettoes. Yet for centuries, while the Christian and Islamic worlds were at war with each other, Jews, with their far-flung kinship networks, functioned as economic middlemen and diplomats. There also arose a group of "court Jews," who played the role of tax collectors, financiers, and bankers to Christian princes. These figures were usually also the leaders of the Jewish community and were indispensable in obtaining patronage for their brethren.[17]

The diaspora gave a strong impetus to Jewish nepotism. High standards of within-group altruism were strongly reinforced by the isolation of Jewish communities and the requirement that they take care of their own. Jewish merchants and craftsmen also formed protective trade associations from a very early period. Meanwhile, Jewish social and reproductive strategies fostered a pattern of high-investment parenting, reflected in widely spaced births, a tendency to late (usually arranged) marriages, a strong emphasis on education, and a preference for males.[18] According to one study of Ashkenazi Jews, parents—especially mothers—had an "unremitting solicitude" for their children and engaged in "boundless suffering and sacrifice." The corollary to such high levels of parental investment is an intense demand for adequate repayment. Hence the stereotype of the oversolicitous Jewish mother and overbearing Jewish father have their roots in long-standing social norms. The intensity of these relationships, combining feelings of love and aggression, selfishness and generosity, gratitude and guilt, have made the Jewish family a powerful engine of personality formation down to the present day, as reflected in many works of Jewish fiction.

By the mid–eighteenth century, large Jewish communities thrived all over Europe; one of the largest and most ancient was in Frankfurt. The home of Goethe and the center of the German Enlightenment, Frankfurt was also one of the most anti-Semitic cities in Europe. While social and economic restrictions had been significantly eased elsewhere, in Frankfurt Jews were still confined to the Judengasse, a long, curving, narrow street—less than ten feet wide in places—with a cemetery at one end and a tall gate at the other. The gates of the ghetto were guarded during the day and locked at night. Three thousand Jews were crowded into this lightless, airless, reeking, and unsanitary warren.

The Jews of Frankfurt were limited to certain occupations; they were also subject to harassment and punitive taxation, and a complex legal code regulated their lives in minutest detail. To keep the number of Jewish families below five hundred, only twelve Jewish marriages were allowed every year; nonetheless the population of the Frankfurt ghetto had doubled in the previous two hundred years, and houses intended for one family had been subdivided many times, to accommodate four or five. Yet despite its privation and squalor, the life of the ghetto was also deeply intellectual and spiritual. There were three rabbinical seminaries in Frankfurt, and it was a great center of Jewish learning. This persecuted community was a dynamo of cooped-up energy, talent, and ambition, attributes powerfully concentrated in the person of Mayer Amschel Rothschild.

The individual entrepreneur is the legendary hero of the capitalist revolution, but early capitalism was invariably *family* capitalism. From craft brotherhoods and guilds to joint stock companies and early corporations, kinship ties pervaded the growing capitalist economy. Early capitalist devices like the partnership agreements called *commende* were developed by Italian merchant families in Genoa and Venice, and medieval merchant associations based in family networks enforced their own legal codes to regulate international markets. Banking—the practice of lending capital at interest—was almost of necessity a family business. International financial transactions were highly uncertain, and trust between partners was essential; in the end, there was no substitute for doing business with one's relatives. Ambitious bankers like the Medici of Florence and the Fuggers of Augsburg, who dominated European finance in the fifteenth and sixteenth centuries, sent their brothers, sons, and nephews to open branches in far-off centers of trade. The Rothschilds would do the same.

Much has been made of the Protestant ethic in the rise of capitalism, but the Jewish business ethic transmitted by Rothschild to his sons was just as potent. Confined to the ghettoes of Europe, Jews were largely bypassed by the first phase of the capitalist revolution. Nor had they been able to join the new middle class that arose in this period, along with the ideology of individual rights and rule of law that favored the growth of commercial society. Jewish entrepreneurs like the

Rothschilds therefore brought to their activities an outsider mentality that enhanced their flexibility and frequently gave them an edge over gentile competitors. The question was whether they could maintain that edge once they had lost their status as outsiders and become successful and assimilated members of society. The fact that they retained it as long as they did is a testament to the character and vision of the family's founder.

Mayer Amschel Rothschild was born in 1744 in Frankfurt's Judengasse, the son, grandson, and great-grandson of Jewish moneychangers. This was one of the few occupations open to Jews, and it was especially common in Frankfurt. The ancient city stood at the confluence of several major trade routes, and foreign merchants flocked to its great biannual fairs. Germany was then divided into dozens of tiny principalities, each with its own system of coinage, and a traveler might have to change money several times in the course of a day. Constant fluctuations in exchange rates allowed a well-informed broker to amass a tidy profit, and with their extensive webs of family and communal connections, Jews were in an excellent position to determine the relative value of different currencies. They also dealt in letters of credit, bills of exchange, and other devices that permitted international transactions without the actual shipment of gold or silver.

After his parents' death from smallpox, family connections landed the twelve-year-old Rothschild an apprenticeship at the Jewish banking firm of Wolf Jakob Oppenheim. The Oppenheims were a family of court Jews who had started in the Frankfurt ghetto and branched out all over Germany. Court Jews were especially common in Germany, where most petty principalities lacked the resources to support a proper bureaucracy; Jewish agents used their financial networks to finance their patrons' wars and subsidize their courts. They also tended to intermarry, making the tiny and exclusive world of eighteenth-century Jewish finance very much a family affair.

Since early childhood, Mayer Amschel had a keen eye for rare and antique coins, and by the time he was eighteen he had developed considerable expertise. In 1763 Rothschild returned to Frankfurt and set himself up as a dealer in rare coins in the crowded family house where his brothers also lived and had their businesses. His break came when one of his clients introduced him to crown prince Wilhelm of Hanau. Prince Wilhelm's immense capital would in time become the basis not only of the Rothschild bank in Frankfurt but of their international banking operations as well. For the present, however, Rothschild merely sold him a few coins and rare medallions. This business kept up, and by 1769 he was emboldened to ask for the honor of calling himself Wilhelm's crown agent. It was an empty title, but it cost neither of them anything and it allowed Rothschild to use the prince's name to enhance his prestige. Currying favor with princely houses or governments capable of large-scale transactions is good business, and Mayer Amschel's descendants would follow his example.

Rothschild now married Gutel Schnapper, the daughter of another well-off merchant and court factor, through whom he gained entry into the exclusive familial world of Jewish finance. Gutel would bear him sixteen or seventeen children, ten of whom survived, and as head of a large family, Mayer Amschel pursued his opportunities with renewed vigor. He traveled a good deal between Frankfurt and neighboring cities and started a catalogue business in rare coins, buying and selling whole collections for his clients. He took the long view in his business affairs, preferring high turnover to maximizing profits. He often undersold his competitors, making less money on each transaction but generating trust and developing strong relationships. These business practices would also become family traditions.

Mayer Amschel soon branched out into commodities and started a private banking business. He also kept abreast of European affairs, displaying that keen awareness of the impact of political events on the business environment that would distinguish all the Rothschilds. In 1780 Rothschild became one of the preferred bankers for the Thurn und Taxis family, hereditary postmasters of the Holy Roman Empire. Meanwhile his business with the court of Prince Wilhelm continued to grow. Rothschild had been cultivating a relationship with a young official there named Buderus, and in 1783 Buderus obtained for him a pass to come and go from the ghetto at will. Rothschild's sons would likewise befriend talented and ambitious men in the non-Jewish world, often helping them rise to positions of prominence. This habit allowed the

Rothschilds to survive the revolutions that wracked France and Germany throughout the nineteenth century.

In 1785 Prince Wilhelm succeeded his father as landgrave of Hesse and thereby became the richest man in Europe. At Buderus's suggestion, Wilhelm agreed to give Rothschild a small percentage of his banking business. Meanwhile, Rothschild's wholesale operations flourished, boosted by the rise in prices caused by the French Revolution, and he brought two of his sons into the trade. In 1792, French armies invaded Germany and plunged the continent into war. Europe's misery was Rothschild's opportunity: he snagged a contract to supply the Austrian army and had to bring in two partners (one of them a cousin) to manage the enormous volume of business.

Meanwhile Rothschild strengthened his links with other Jewish banking families. In 1795 he married his eldest daughter to the son of a wealthy Frankfurt court agent, and the next year his eldest son, Amschel, married the daughter of another. When Buderus was given responsibility for overseeing all of his master's foreign investments, he allowed Rothschild to negotiate one of Wilhelm's loans to the city of Frankfurt. By squeezing out his competitors in the usual way—charging less and paying more—he quickly became Wilhelm's main international banker. Yet unlike Carlo Buonaparte, who exulted in the envy of his neighbors as a sign that he was rising in the world, Rothschild took pains to conceal the extent of his wealth. He plowed all the money he earned back into his business and maintained an extremely modest style of life.

This did not mean he was stingy, however. He chaired the Jewish welfare board and often passed out coins to beggars. As one contemporary recalled, "If one saw a row of beggars in the street looking pleased and comforted, one knew that the old Rothschild had just passed through."[19] This was another family tradition: the synagogues of Europe grew fat on Rothschild largesse, and the early settlement of Palestine was largely financed by Mayer Amschel's descendant Edmond.

Rothschild attended synagogue daily and often entertained distinguished scholars in his home. Yet he also knew that the world outside was changing, and not only was he tolerant of the more liberal strains of Judaism emerging at this time, he had his sons tutored by a leading Reform intellectual. Rothschild himself might remain, like Moses, within the limited horizons of the ghetto, but as his agents in the new, postrevolutionary world, his sons could not.

As the family's business grew, more family members became involved in it. Rothschild's daughter kept the books until an employee was caught stealing; then a professional bookkeeper was hired. But Rothschild relied mainly on his three oldest sons, Amschel, Nathan, and Salomon. It was Nathan who handled the firm's textile trade with England, and the volume soon became so great that it was decided to cut out the middlemen and open an office in Manchester. Thus in 1798, Nathan, who spoke not a word of English, went to London, taking with him half the assets of the firm. This was an indication of the trust Rothschild reposed in his son. On the other hand, Nathan was required to write his father detailed letters every day and in return received a constant stream of advice and instructions.

Years later, Nathan told the story of his departure for England as though it had been his idea. Actually, as biographer Amos Elon observes, the decision "was a strategy carefully thought out by Rothschild himself," one that "ripened to maturity" in discussion with his sons.[20] Nathan was also able to take advantage of the family's connections with the well-organized Jewish community of London. Rothschild had arranged for him to be apprenticed in the firm of their English banker, Levi Barent Cohen; shortly thereafter, Nathan established himself as a textile agent in Manchester, then booming as a result of increased demand from the continental wars. Once established, Nathan showed the same energy, imagination, and zeal as Mayer Amschel, although his father continually upbraided him for his sloppy record keeping. From buying finished wares Nathan branched into manufacturing, as well as dealing in commodities like sugar, coffee, and wine. Within five years he had tripled his money, moved his operations to London, and married one of Levi Cohen's daughters, thereby establishing himself in the front ranks of the small Anglo-Jewish elite.

Hannah Levi came with a large dowry, but her social value was inestimably greater. Her father was not only the richest Jew in England, he was also, as Elon explains, "the hub of a kinship network that linked the Goldsmids, Mocattas, Montefiores and other important Jewish financiers in the City."[21] This is the tight-knit social world of English Ashkenazi Jews that Chaim Bermant has called the Cousinhood: "a compact union of exclusive brethren with blood and money flowing in a small circle which opened up from time to time and then snapped shut again."[22] More than a collection of relatives, the Cousinhood functioned as an organic unit, assuming responsibility for poorer coreligionists in England and abroad and lobbying for increased Jewish rights.

In 1800, Rothschild and Amschel were appointed imperial crown agents by the Austrian emperor Franz II. They received similar appointments from the prince of Thurn und Taxis and several other principalities. In 1806, having failed to come to terms with Napoleon, the landgrave Wilhelm was forced to flee, hiding as much of his vast fortune as he could. He took with him his eldest son, his financial manager Buderus, and his precious account books. Living in exile, the landgrave became almost completely dependent upon Rothschild to manage his affairs. Rothschild proved his loyalty and discretion in this dangerous business, keeping two sets of books to deceive the French investigators.

In November 1806, Napoleon announced a ban on trade with England. This was a godsend to the Rothschilds. Nathan shipped illegal goods to Dutch and German ports, where his brothers were on hand to forward them to Frankfurt. The sons corresponded frequently with their father, sharing political as well as economic news and using the *Judendeutsch* of the Frankfurt ghetto as a private code. Old Rothschild coordinated the whole effort from his headquarters in the Judengasse. All this was a dress rehearsal for the mature international business to come.

When the landgrave moved to Prague, Amschel became his main intermediary with the imperial court in Vienna. Kalmann (Carl) and Jacob (James) were his go-betweens with Buderus, now also a silent partner in Rothschild's bank. Suspected of helping Wilhelm finance an uprising in Westphalia, the Rothschilds were briefly arrested. As a result, Rothschild determined never again to be dependent on a single sovereign client. Instead he dispatched his sons to different parts of Europe and created a real international bank.

In 1809, Buderus persuaded Wilhelm to make Nathan the manager of his sizable English assets, enticing him with a commission rate substantially lower than that of his traditional agents. Within a year, Nathan had invested over half a million pounds of Wilhelm's money in English stocks, under his own name. Needless to say, the acquisition of such assets greatly enhanced his credit rating. The landgrave's money allowed him to seem much richer than he really was, and he used these funds to make short-term loans and speculate in bullion, which was then in short supply.

As Rothschild advanced in years his pace never slackened: still the single-minded concentration on business and profit. He was noticeably more cautious than his sons, and there is some evidence that Nathan, like many business heirs, moved too quickly for his father's taste. But a new note of sentimentality entered many of his letters to his sons, interspersed with his usual terse injunctions, and he appears to have mellowed somewhat. Moreover, it was already clear that Rothschild could no longer direct the family's complex and increasingly dispersed affairs by himself.

This is the point at which many successful family businesses go wrong. The transition from a patriarchy to a fraternal federation is always difficult to manage. But Mayer Amschel had been unusually successful, not only at molding his sons in his image without compromising their instinct for independence, but at impressing upon them the importance of brotherly harmony. This is precisely the combination of insularity and openness that Joel Kotkin and others have identified as the quality that allowed Jewish entrepreneurs to conserve their familistic business culture while adapting to exploit new opportunities.

Not that it all ran smoothly all the time. Nathan, the second son, was clearly the dominant member of the family until the youngest, James, came into his own. He was a driver, a risk taker, and an ill-tempered bully. As the family's agent in London, the strongest of Europe's financial citadels, he often called the shots for his brothers on the continent. Salomon, who was at times driven to tears by the peremptory tone of his brother's letters, called him the "commanding general," with his brothers as his marshals, executing his schemes in the other capitals. Indeed, they were known as the *Finanzbonaparten*—an ironic appellation, considering their contribution to the defeat of the real Bonaparte.[23]

In 1810 Rothschild and his sons signed an "irrevocable" partnership agreement. The sons were granted independent authority to negotiate and sign contracts on the firm's behalf, and shares were allotted according to age and experience. In recognition of the father's "tireless activity" in creating the business and his care for "the worldly happiness of his children," he was given the decisive vote as chief of the family enterprise. Shares could only be inherited by the brothers' male offspring: wives and daughters would neither inherit nor have a right to examine the company's books. Sons-in-law would also be excluded. Litigation against the firm by any of the partners was sharply discouraged by injunctions and penalties. These provisions were intended to promote unity among the brothers and prevent the dispersion of capital.

On September 16, 1812—Yom Kippur—Rothschild collapsed on his way home from the synagogue. Dying, he called for his lawyer and made revisions to his will. The document underscores his obsessive concern not only with the welfare of his sons but with their unity after his death. He had long been aware of the vicissitudes of Jewish family fortunes, once telling Amschel that they never lasted more than two generations; but he said, "keep your brothers together and you will become the richest men in Germany." In his will he urged his sons to behave "with mutual love and friendship" and stipulated darkly: "Any undutiful child that disobeys this my fatherly will or disturbs my [other] sons" will inherit nothing more than the required minimum according to law. From this would be deducted all that their father had spent on them during their lifetimes.

Rothschild may not have instilled his primitive Jewish piety in his children, but he did impress on them his powerful insistence on family unity. "All the brothers shall stand together in everything," he had declared; "all shall be responsible for the actions of each one." Though they often quarreled in later years, this code continued to be observed long after they had scattered across Europe and started their own successful houses. Amschel became head of the Frankfurt bank. Salomon and Karl opened offices in Vienna and Naples, respectively, in the 1820s. But their businesses remained linked. Each owned shares in the others' companies, and their balance sheets were all consolidated at the end of the year.

In 1817 the brothers were ennobled by the Austrian emperor, and would soon become barons. By 1830 they were among the richest men in Europe and lived in extravagant wealth at the top of society. For a time, they controlled absolutely the world markets in government bonds, gold, and other precious metals. They invested heavily in the new technology of the Industrial Revolution, including railroads, steel, and mining. But their primary product was money. They literally constituted a sixth great European power, the one that none of the others could afford to do without. In 1825, Nathan bailed out the Bank of England. In 1831, James bailed out the Bank of France. When Metternich had a problem propping up the Habsburg dynasty, he turned to Salomon to underwrite his schemes.

Up to this point, only kings and princes had had this kind of money and power. That the Rothschilds were able to attain it at all is a testament to the opening of society after the French Revolution. Great wealth produces great envy, and the fact that the Rothschilds were Jewish produced a great deal of ill will. Some of this can be ascribed to anti-Semitism, yet much of what their critics said was true. Like a mafia family, they played by their own rules: they maintained secret intelligence networks, bribed officials, manipulated the exchanges, cut prices to drive out competitors, and generally played hardball in every way.

Having profited from war and confusion, the Rothschilds decided that they preferred peace and stability. Accordingly the brothers became bankers to the Holy Alliance formed by Russia, Prussia, Austria, and England, and supported the Bourbon restoration in France and Italy. This placed the Rothschilds squarely on the side of the reactionary powers of the day. On the other hand, Nathan frequently made loans to liberal governments in Spain, Brazil, and elsewhere. But on the whole, the brothers favored governments that were stable, operated under the rule of law, and granted their citizens rights and freedoms. They did little if any business in backward, absolutist, anti-Semitic Russia. Their greatest successes came in England, the most financially and socially liberal European nation.

By the 1820s, each of the brothers had his own company: Nathan in

London, James in Paris, Salomon in Vienna, Karl in Naples, and Amschel, the oldest and the only one to have no children, in Frankfurt. Though nominally independent, the five houses functioned like the arms of an international bank. Capital was often pooled and directed toward specific enterprises, or to bail a brother out of a scrape, as Nathan saved James during the Revolution of 1830 in France. "In effect," writes Niall Ferguson, "the brothers were establishing that system of international monetary cooperation which would later be performed routinely by central banks, and on which the gold standard came to depend."[24] Having invented modern finance, the Rothschilds went on to dominate it for most of the nineteenth century. It took the rest of the world until around 1880, with the rise of joint-stock banks and "commercial," or deposit, banks, to give them any real competition.

The family's fortune was cemented by Nathan, who seemed never to make a false move. At first, he had most of the money, took most of the risk, and reaped most of the profits, but in time the Paris and Vienna houses drew even with him. The brothers met in Frankfurt in 1836 to draw up a new agreement, but before it could be hammered out Nathan died from an attack of septicemia. His will mirrored his father's: keep the property intact and preserve family unity. If the heirs were to sue, one third of his estate—the biggest in British history to that point—would go to charity.[25]

James, the youngest brother, took over as head of the family. He had settled in Paris and had acquired a bit more polish and sophistication than the others, though he too had a notorious temper. He was an intimate of Balzac, who immortalized him in *Cousin Bette*, and of the poet Heine, who wrote, "Money is the new God and Rothschild is his prophet."

Like other successful business dynasties, the Rothschilds developed an efficient apprenticeship program. Rothschild boys received a modern education, heavy on math, though not too much lest they discover other interests. They started in the firm at the age of twenty or twenty-one, and served time in their uncles' countinghouses. Of the twelve sons in the third generation, five proved as competent as their fathers.

The third generation lost the Jewish accents and ghetto outlook of their fathers. Raised as little princes, they picked up the hobbies (and the vices) of aristocrats. Lionel got himself elected to the House of

Commons, but had to wait eleven years before he could take his seat because he refused to take the oath "upon the true faith of a Christian." But while their cultural assimilation was quite thorough, they clung to their religion, which Ferguson calls "the only barrier between the Rothschilds and the European social elite that the Rothschilds wanted to preserve."[26] Indeed, it amounted to a kind of snobbery. Nothing illustrates this better than the case of Hannah Mayer Rothschild, Nathan's daughter, who shortly after his death renounced Judaism and married a Christian. James was livid that she would abandon "the religion which, thank God, made us so great." Her mother refused ever to speak to her.

The uncles pressured their sons and nephews to continue the endogamous marriage pattern. Both James and Carl married their nieces, and nearly two-thirds of Mayer's grandchildren married one another. Often these were arranged marriages, but the partners seemed to get on fairly well. In many cases, as biographer Frederic Morton observes, the women were as talented as the men, but had to content themselves with behind-the-scenes roles.

By the 1830s, the Rothschilds were at their zenith. In England and France and (as restrictions eased on Jewish property ownership) Italy and Germany, they built immense palaces and country estates, where they planted luxurious gardens and gave dazzling parties. During this period, the family's empire expanded into the world trade in oil and nonferrous metals. But government finance, in nearly every state in Europe, remained the foundation of their business.

The family's attention was soon diverted by the revolutionary crisis of 1848. They clearly saw it coming, but when the crisis came they were holding a lot of bad paper. Salomon had overextended himself in lending to Metternich, and James and Nathan made similar mistakes in the French bond market. The family suffered appalling losses and James saved himself only by threatening to go out of business. He held so many bonds and railroad shares that his fall would have threatened the entire French financial structure.

The brothers now found their oligopolistic position seriously threatened by a new generation of joint-stock and commercial banks. The first and most serious challenge came in France from the Crédit Mobilier.

Organized in 1856 by one of James's former assistants and backed by Napoleon III, it attracted deposits from all over France. Soon it began to compete with the Rothschild bank in issuing state bonds in Italy and Austria and threatened to drive them out of the Austrian railroad business.

That year, Salomon, Amschel, and Carl all died, leaving the third generation and their uncle James to deal with the challenge. Anselm led the formation of an Austrian joint-stock bank, the Credit Anstalt, which wrested back control of the Austrian railroad business. Driven out of Austria, the Crédit Mobilier withdrew to France, where Rothschild machinations drove its stock into the ground. But other banks emerged to take business away from the Rothschilds in England and France, as well as in the German states. Still, in 1875, when Disraeli's government needed 4 million pounds to buy the Suez Canal, he turned to Lionel Rothschild, who wrote him a check, patriotically charging him only 3 percent interest.

As the third generation gave way to the fourth, wide disparities in ability were apparent. In England, Nathaniel became the first Jewish peer of the realm. The ablest member of his generation, he headed the family enterprise. In Vienna, Anselm chose his youngest son, Albert, to run the bank. In France, Alphonse's son Edouard led the family into the oil business and is most notable for his support of early Jewish settlement of Palestine, bringing in colonies of Russian Jews and backing Chaim Weizmann with millions while his British cousins arranged for the Balfour Declaration. Edouard managed the finances of the French house competently but conservatively, protecting what he had rather than deploying it aggressively in the manner of Nathan or James. Adolph folded the Naples branch in 1861 when Garibaldi unified Italy. His sons Mayer and Wilhelm took over the Frankfurt office at the death of the childless Amschel, and between them fathered ten girls. With no sons to inherit, the house came to an end with Wilhelm's death in 1909.

Despite their strenuous efforts to avert it, the world the Rothschilds knew came crashing down in the Great War. Frantic diplomacy by the English and Austrian houses could not prevent the war, perhaps because the European powers no longer needed to borrow from the Rothschilds to raise great armies. When Natty, Alfred, and Leo all died, in 1917, death taxes relieved the family of a good part of its patrimony. In the 1920s and 1930s, they were still strong enough to fend off a hostile takeover of the Vienna bank by manipulating European currency rates. Baron Louis actually bailed out the Austrian government during the Depression, but the Credit Anstalt went belly-up a year later. When the Nazis invaded Austria and France, the Rothschilds were compelled to flee Europe. Vast amounts of precious antiques and artwork ended up in the possession of Hermann Goering. After the war, taxation again depleted the coffers of the British house.

As late as the 1960s, de Rothschild Frères was still the biggest private bank in France, but it is dwarfed by the immense public banks, which have a strength no individual can match. The democratization of finance, the embourgeoisement of the proletariat, spelled the end of Rothschild financial hegemony, and it must have been clear to the family at least from the end of the nineteenth century that this was the way of the world. Unlike the Borgias and the Bonapartes, however, the Rothschilds are still here, still rich, and still admired for their nepotistic exploits.

The Rothschilds had an uncanny knack for knowing how to take advantage of a crisis. This ability, as we have suggested, derived from their outsider status, and it may be stated as a general principle in business that the successful entrepreneur has a slightly paranoid outlook. The question is whether this habit of mind can be transmitted from father to son, and son to grandson. As a rule the answer is no, unless you deny yourself and your family the fruits of your labor, and this the Rothschilds did to some extent by keeping a tight grip on their offspring. Daughters were married to cousins, and sons were sent away to apprentice with their uncles; their education was limited to the necessary minimum, and distractions from business were discouraged, along with any outside interests and hobbies other than the upper class pursuits that went along with their newly achieved status.

Mayer Amschel was the author of all this. His descendants continued in his ways in most respects, and by adhering to his vision they not only prospered but managed (for a time) to cheat the old rule of dynastic decline. Yet while they preserved their nepotistic family culture and their commitment to Jewish philanthropy, they lost their status as outsiders, hence their agility as businessmen.

At the outset, the Rothschilds were something of an anachronism. Yet they established a model for all successful entrepreneurial ventures, and the international financial market that would eventually displace them grew directly out of their family network. They also represent a harbinger of the tremendous change to come in the environment for nepotism in Western societies. For in the modern era, the great engine of middle class mobility would no longer be the church or the army, but the market and (increasingly) the state.

The classical dynast had little to work with other than the nepotistic bonds of kinship itself. His basic tools were marriage and adoption, friendship, patronage, the possession of landed property, and the quasi-religious authority deriving from his status as head of a clan. The early modern dynast had more scope for his ambitions. The emergence of new public institutions offered new paths to upward mobility. The only question was how to exploit them. When people today observe that nepotism is practiced "shamelessly," they are unwittingly evoking a time when there was no firm ethical distinction between private and public affairs. Offices were vested in landed estates and passed down from father to son. It was a very long time from the appearance of such institutions to the point where anyone could be remotely embarrassed by a charge of nepotism.

European history is thus a protracted dialogue between the forces of nepotistic solidarity and the growing emphasis on individualism, merit, and efficiency. Social institutions no sooner arise than they are invaded and subverted by the stratagems of ambitious family founders. Efforts to block these encroachments simply pose a challenge to dynastic ingenuity. At the same time, nepotism itself goes through a change—its scope narrows, yet as opportunities for individuals expand, it also becomes less coercive, more dependent upon sentimental ties, and finally more a matter of volition than necessity. This process has been going on in the West for nearly a thousand years, and the open and egalitarian society of twenty-first-century America represents its culmination—or perhaps its leading edge, since the Western war on nepotism continues to this day. We therefore turn to the story of nepotism in America, where the market and the state achieved their fullest expression, and where the middle class finally came into its own, free of the constraints of class and inherited privilege.

PART II

NEPOTISM IN AMERICA

CHAPTER 7

COLONIAL NEPOTISM

FROM SETTLEMENT TO REVOLUTION

Nathaniel Hawthorne wrote "My Kinsman, Major Molineux" in 1832, but it is set a century earlier, in a period, the author tells us, notable for the growing hostility of Americans toward their crown-appointed governors. In the story, a young man named Robin steps off the ferry late one night at the outskirts of a large New England town. It is the country lad's first visit to such a sizable settlement and he is not sure where to go. Yet his stride betrays his confidence, for he is searching for his kinsman Major Molineux, a man of some importance in these parts.

Robin encounters several townsmen in the darkened streets who wave away his inquiries with varying degrees of irritation and hostility. He is mystified by their attitude but ascribes it to simple bad manners. At the same time, he perceives some strange activity to be afoot in the slumbering town. Accosting a man coming out of his house, he is taken aback by his face, which is painted in a frightful devil's mask, half black, half red. "Watch here an hour, and Major Molineux will pass by," the stranger says mysteriously, and roughly pushes past. Robin sits down on the steps of a moonlit church, where he is joined by a kindly gentleman who asks him his business. Robin explains that he is the son of a country farmer whose cousin has achieved wealth and position. Being childless, he has offered to make Robin his heir. He relates his perplexing encounters and adds that he has been told to wait here until his kinsman passes by.

Soon they hear a distant murmur. Then the sound of shouts and marching feet. A motley procession comes into view, lit by torches and led on horseback by the man with the painted face. Finally a cart appears bearing a solitary figure—a distinguished-looking man in a torn uniform who has been cruelly tarred and feathered. Features distorted with terror, the poor man looks about distractedly, seeking a friendly face. Then his eyes meet Robin's, and they recoil with a shock of mutual recognition: "They stared at each other in silence, and Robin's knees shook, and his hair bristled, with a mixture of pity and terror."

At the sight of this improbable tableau, a ripple of laughter spreads through the crowd. The laughter rises to a shout, and Robin finds himself unwillingly caught up in it. "The contagion was spreading among the multitude, when, all at once, it seized upon Robin, and he sent forth a shout of laughter that echoed through the street—every man shook his sides, every man emptied his lungs, but Robin's shout was the loudest there." This savage burst of laughter comes as a visceral protest against the inequalities of the old aristocratic social order. It expresses all the loathing and contempt that Americans feel toward those who think themselves superior merely because they have inherited wealth and connections. Though this laughter is partly aimed at Robin himself, he cannot help joining in—and indeed, it is one of the essential characteristics of the democratic man that he be able to laugh at himself. In a democracy, no man's dignity is inviolate, and anyone's pretensions may be mocked.

Greatly sobered, Robin asks his companion to direct him to the ferry whence he came. But his new friend will not hear of it. "Some few days hence, if you wish it, I will speed you on your journey. Or, if you prefer to remain with us, perhaps, as you are a shrewd youth, you may rise in the world without the help of your kinsman, Major Molineux."

It is America's great claim to be a society open to talents. Poverty is no bar to those who are willing to make the necessary sacrifices, and any little boy can grow up to be president. We are a nation of self-made men. So we have believed, and so we have told ourselves, for centuries. The natural counterpart to this attitude of rugged individualism is the extreme contempt in which nepotism is held.

Yet from the global perspective, as we have seen, the American attitude toward nepotism is the exception, not the rule. Everywhere else in the world, people tolerate, expect, and even encourage it.

Where did this unique antipathy to nepotism come from? This is not a simple question, and to answer it, we must begin with the earliest phases of settlement in order to show how the seeds of the modern meritocratic form of American nepotism developed out of the underlying family cultures of the colonies themselves.

It is a commonplace to say that colonial America was an extension of English society, but seventeenth-century England was still a collection of regional cultures, and each of the main areas of colonial settlement reflected these cultural differences. In *Albion's Seed*, David Hackett Fischer describes not one but four migrations from the British Isles between 1629 and 1775. Each originated in a different part of England and imported its own traditions and lifeways, including food, clothing, architecture, speech, and religious and political beliefs. First and briefest was the Puritan migration; originating in the densely inhabited counties of East Anglia, it lasted from 1629 to the outbreak of the English Civil War, in 1640. The so-called Cavalier migration (1640–75) brought a second stream of settlers to Virginia and Maryland, mainly refugees from the defeated Royalist counties of the south. The Friends' Migration (1675–1715) was a movement of persecuted Quakers from the North Midlands to the Delaware valley. The fourth migration, of Scots-Irish border folk (1717–75), coming at a time when most of the good farmland in the Atlantic colonies was already taken, pushed south and west from Pennsylvania and Virginia into the American backcountry. In each of these regions a distinctive local culture emerged, characterized by a nepotistic formula that reflected, and perpetuated, its own unique patterns of marriage, reproduction and child rearing, and inheritance. Each region also embodied a somewhat different conception of personal and political liberty: equality in New England, sovereign individualism in Virginia, reciprocal altruism in Pennsylvania, and "natural liberty" in the southern highlands.

In the first phase of settlement, these libertarian traditions reinforced the general drive for independence from Britain. Later their differences would produce an intractable conflict that could be resolved only by the Civil War. Though we will keep these distinctions in view, in much of what follows we will focus on New England, since that region is the crucible not only of the peculiar American form of meritocratic nepotism but of the intense hostility to unearned position and privilege that goes with it.

AUTUMN OF THE PATRIARCHS: THE NEPOTISM OF THE PURITAN COMMONWEALTH

Puritanism originated in the sixteenth century as a movement to separate God's elect—those predestined for salvation—from the sinful mass of mankind. The elect were a minority, but it was possible to tell who they were because they lived in strict conformity with God's laws. The Puritans thought they knew what God demanded of men in every situation and not only strove to conform to these exacting standards but wanted to make everyone else do so as well. These efforts were notoriously unpopular, and as a persecuted sect for most of their history, Puritans had to stick together for security and to propagate the faith. They frequently compared themselves to the ancient Hebrews, beset with dangers and temptations on every hand. But having failed to impose their vision of a godly society on England, they decided to go to the New World and establish one there. The Puritan view of English society as irredeemably corrupt, and especially their perception of the king as a bad political father, would be a powerful influence on the thinking of the American Revolutionaries.

Beginning in the 1620s the Puritans founded colonies at Plymouth and Boston under the charter of the Massachusetts Bay Company. The original Mayflower Compact established a godly commonwealth and limited the privileges of citizenship to a handful of Puritan families; later this was broadened to include all church members, but it was never extended beyond that. Thus, while Puritans were always a minority in Massachusetts Bay, they controlled the colony's government during the first forty years of its history.

The Puritans came for the most part not as individuals or even as families but as whole congregations. Many were related to one another before they left England, and the familistic pattern known as "chain migration" played a major role in the peopling of British North America. This was true of all the American colonies, but New England was distinguished from the start by what Fischer terms "an exceptionally high level of family integration." This tightly nepotistic character had much to do with the region's astonishing growth and success.

The Puritans quickly branched out to form a chain of self-governing settlements, each one surrounded by farms and centered on a church. Early New England was not a unified state but a community of federated townships, marked by what Digby Baltzell calls "hierarchical communalism"—combining a belief in man's equality before God with an equally strong belief in the need for communal control.

The responsibilities of Puritan ministers far exceeded those of spiritual guidance and included the oversight of public works and public order generally. Most of them came from the Puritan heartland of East Anglia; many had known one another before emigrating, and their families frequently intermarried, forming extensive kinship networks. There were originally at least four such genealogical nodes, or "connections," of Puritan ministers, and these quickly grew together into a large ministerial cousinage. (The center of this group was the Cotton-Mather clan, whose founding mother, Sarah Story—married in turn to John Cotton and Richard Mather—may be considered "the genealogical center of New England's elite.")[1] Though preachers could not hold public office, this tight ministerial caste ultimately joined with the small circle of aristocratic, magisterial, and mercantile families to become a tightly inbred social and political elite. The continual rise of such elites, their perpetuation through a variety of nepotistic strategies, and their eventual decline and replacement by new groups has been a consistent pattern in American history, and is continuing even today.

The Puritans established a theocratic government based on the tenets of biblical law. They saw themselves as the heirs to the Hebrew covenant and tried to re-create the patriarchal and family-based religion of Abraham. In accepting this covenant, the Christian believer accepted the obligation to sanctify his entire household. Church and state were seen as an extension of the family, and all the fundamental precepts of Puritan government were derived from the fifth commandment: "Honor thy father and mother."

For Puritans, the most important relation established by God was that between parents and children. This was the only natural form of governance; all others, including marriage, were voluntary and based on a covenant. The Puritan family was large, averaging eight to ten children, and formed a self-sufficient economic unit. Fischer observes that Puritan families were both larger and more intensely nuclear than any others in the Western world. This was the result of a nepotistic formula that combined religious injunctions to fertility with high levels of parental investment under a regime of strong community control.[2]

The Puritan family was the center of economic and religious life, of training and instruction for children, and of social welfare and correction. It was strongly patriarchal, and the father's authority over wife and children was nearly absolute. The Puritan family has a reputation for being harshly oppressive, and Puritan child rearing was indeed focused on discipline and breaking the childish will to independence. Yet this does not mean that Puritan parents were unconcerned about their children: to the contrary, they felt a burning passion for their welfare, and Puritan society was surprisingly child-centered.[3]

A father's obligations to his children were many—first and foremost looking after their spiritual welfare. In fact, by their own account, Puritans had come to America in the first place for the *sake* of their children. As Increase Mather preached in 1679, "It was for your sakes especially, that your Fathers ventured their lives upon the rude waves of the vast Ocean."[4] A Puritan father was required not only to provide for his children when young but to ensure their independence by bringing them up "in some honest lawful calling, labor or employment." Girls were put to work in the household to prepare them to be wives and mothers; they might also be sent to learn housekeeping with other families. In families with several sons, one usually inherited the father's farm or trade while the others were set to different occupations. Often this meant boarding out with other families. The typical Puritan household therefore included the nuclear family along with servants and apprentices, who were considered family members under the father's paternal authority. The sharing of children among neighboring households strengthened the bonds of community.

Fathers were also obliged to find their children a suitable spouse. As with the choice of occupation, children could not be trusted to make these decisions themselves, and a father's obligations were not fulfilled until his children were properly settled. Fathers were especially concerned that their daughters be well taken care of. Yet children's wishes were often respected, since those wedded against their will could not fulfill God's commandment to be a loving spouse, and it was understood that forced matches rarely worked out. That being the case, it is perhaps not surprising that most children showed themselves submissive and dutiful, refusing only those suitors whom they felt they could not love.

Enormous emphasis was placed on education. A Massachusetts law required all masters of households to teach their children and apprentices to read, that they might have direct access to the word of God. Puritans took this duty very seriously, for it was their belief that children did not belong to their parents but to God, who merely loaned them. Failure to provide such instruction was not just a defect of fatherly duty but a crime against the state, which depended on maintaining a continuous supply of believers. The Puritans founded more colleges than any other colony and bequeathed their emphasis on learning to subsequent generations.

Education was the cure for ignorance, but discipline and punishment were necessary to reform the child's self-will and natural bent toward evil. Puritan doctrine held that children were not born pure and innocent but as fallen beings who came into the world needing strong moral correction. Puritan fathers could therefore be stern and strict, administering harsh punishments in fulfillment of their mandate. "Better whipt than damn'd" was Cotton Mather's way of putting it.

The state relied heavily on Puritan households to maintain social order, and many lawbreakers were remanded to their families for correction and punishment. The state was equally concerned with maintaining the wider kin connections that sustained a good society. Puritans had a very broad conception of kinship and made little distinction between kin by blood and kin by marriage, fondly addressing as brothers, sisters, parents, and cousins those with whom they were connected by the remotest of ties. Nor did a widower lose his connection with the family of his first wife after her death; some men even solicited their blessings and guidance when they sought a new bride. Even more remarkable, the second wife also considered herself related to her predecessor's kin. This practice was based on a literal reading of the scriptural text that man and wife became "one flesh." Since death and remarriage were frequent, the web of fictive kinship soon grew thickly in the colony.[5]

God enjoined men to love one another as brothers, but he allowed them to show partiality for those he had placed in relations of kinship. This applied as well to business dealings, and a Puritan merchant could show his Christian love for his kin by conducting his business through them. John Hull, the leading Boston merchant of his day, did a large volume of business with his uncle in London, and continued this connection with his cousins after his uncle's death. Though his business was not limited to relatives, Morgan observes, "he undeniably favored them and put up with treatment he would never have stood from a stranger." His son-in-law, the Boston merchant Samuel Sewall, inherited these connections.

The Puritan commonwealth was a bold utopian experiment, but by the end of the seventeenth century it was already apparent that the state's institutions could not be maintained. Some ministers pointed to wars with the Indians and other problems as signs of God's negative judgment. Many fell prey to fears of witchcraft and demonic possession, giving rise to the infamous Salem witch trials of 1692. Edmund S. Morgan's explanation is simpler: a failure to replenish the ranks of the elect led to demographic decline. Ironically, the ultimate cause of this failure was the Puritans' own weakness for their children: nepotism triumphed over piety—or more precisely, piety came to be equated with nepotism—and the Puritan commonwealth took on the attributes of a closed and shrinking caste.

As the colony prospered and grew, so did the numbers of ungodly men and women. Though the Puritans controlled the state, they were increasingly in the minority, and they were greatly concerned about the effect this would have on their children. Surrounded as they were by bad example and temptation, concerns naturally arose about the future of the commonwealth. Increasingly, ministers devoted their attentions not to converting the mass of ungodly men outside the church but to saving the children of men who were already members. Eleazer Mather wrote, "The holy Ghost gives counsel not to forsake our Fathers friend, much less *your Fathers God.*" William Stoughton declared that on the last day, God would judge us by consulting not the Book of Life but books of genealogy. "There shall then be brought forth a *Register of the Genealogies of New-Englands sons and daughters.* How shall we many of us hold up our faces then, when there shall be a solemn rehearsal of our descent as well as of our degeneracies?" Others threatened that children who did not convert would be cruelly separated from their parents in the afterlife. Morgan concludes, "The church was thus turned into an exclusive society for the saints and their children. Instead of an agency for bringing Christ to fallen man it became the means of perpetuating the gospel among a hereditary religious aristocracy."[6]

Try as they might, however, the Puritans could not bequeath their religious fervor to their children. Grace, Morgan notes, was not hereditary. Morgan's epitaph for the Puritan commonwealth is that it succumbed to the sin of idolatry: "they had allowed their children to usurp a higher place than God in their affections." Thus, while the nepotistic integrity of the Puritan commonwealth had much to do with its initial success, the nepotistic preference for their offspring caused its downfall.[7] This pattern of elite formation, nepotistic tightening and closure, and withdrawal into castelike isolation would be repeated many times in American history.

The rapid proliferation of towns all over New England owed much to the Puritan system of inheritance—a key aspect of the nepotistic formula. The Puritans had long disliked the English system of primogeniture, designed to preserve the estate, and preferred the alternative recommended in the book of Deuteronomy, whereby the children all received an equal share. This egalitarian pattern eventually became the legal norm in every American state. But its result over time is to diminish the size of family estates, thereby forcing younger sons in later generations to seek their fortunes elsewhere. According to Philip Greven's study of seventeenth-century Andover, Massachusetts, the families established by the first generation of immigrants were strongly patriarchal—much more so than they would have been in England. Sons were retained for labor, and daughters for exchange with neighboring families. As a result, young men remained dependent on their fathers well into adulthood, and many did not establish their own households until their early thirties. These patterns strengthened patriarchal power and produced a large, well-integrated kin group. By the third generation, however, arable land was growing scarce and inherited parcels were smaller. Emigration became more attractive as new territories opened up in western Massachusetts and Connecticut, and by the end of the seventeenth century successful families often had several branches, living in widely scattered regions. The marriage of cousins (in defiance of Puritan strictures) linked these families in large informal clans often comprising ten to twenty households extending across several townships; these clans in turn formed connubial connections with other clans to create large, regional kinship networks.

By the fourth generation, the original estates had been partitioned so many times that a return to primogeniture was seen. The eldest son increasingly inherited the farm, which required fathers to apprentice their other sons in trades, educate them for clerical or legal careers, or settle them on farms elsewhere. Only the wealthiest families remained tightly integrated under strong patriarchal authority. The result was a much more independent-minded generation than the previous three—a fact Greven believes has an important bearing on the increasing drive for political independence from Britain. Young men of the revolutionary generation had come to take for granted that independence should follow maturity.[8]

This recurrent pattern of settlement, expansion, and resettlement would be the heartbeat of American demography. The tightening and loosening of nepotistic bonds to facilitate the opening and exploitation of new territories amply illustrates the flexible and adaptive character of kinship, and in New England it led in a remarkably short time to the creation of a distinctive cultural region that would dominate American society well into the nineteenth century. This thriving enterprise ultimately stretched across the northern tier of the continent in a wide arc that historians call "greater New England."

The traditional New England Yankee was self-reliant, thrifty, inventive, and enterprising. He was fiercely independent and egalitarian, yet insisted on moral conformity and looked to the state to enforce moral laws, and his idea of liberty-as-order was not so much individual as collective or communal. These attitudes, which virtually defined American capitalism and strongly influenced our earliest notions of democracy, were theological in origin. In *The Protestant Ethic,* Max Weber argued that the social ideology of "ascetic Protestantism" drove men to achieve wealth as proof of election. This complex theological attitude (strongly supported by Puritan family culture) may underlie the modern conviction that while inherited wealth and position are illegitimate in themselves, they may be earned after the fact by an heir who works harder and shows more diligence than others. Many a modern business scion has felt compelled to prove his merit by coming in early, leaving late, and in other ways redeeming his advantages. So did the descendants of the Puritan elite become a class of powerfully driven businessmen, philanthropists, and civic founders.

The apotheosis of this outlook may be seen in the Adamses, the "royal family" of Boston. Though not particularly pious, the Adamses embodied the rigid theocratic spirit of the Puritan ministers from whom they were descended on both sides. Principled, industrious, learned, frugal, untiring in their devotion to the public good, as demanding of themselves as they were of others, for three generations they perversely opposed the interests of Boston's mercantile elite, losing elections they might have won, because they would rather be right than popular. The Adamses, like New England itself, were a conscious creation, the result of a tremendous concentration of corporate will and effort; the dominant mode of that project was familism exalted to the level of a divine mission. Even the Revolution was a family business: John followed the lead of his cousin Sam, and the two of them teamed up with the equally radical Lees of Virginia in an alliance that would help to move the colonies toward war.

THE OLD OLIGARCHS: NEPOTISM IN COLONIAL VIRGINIA

In 1663, Sir William Berkeley published a pamphlet addressed to the younger sons of England's noble families, promoting emigration to

Virginia: "A small sum of money will enable a younger brother to erect a flourishing family in a new world; and add more strength, wealth and honor to his native country, than thousands did before, that dyed forgotten and unrewarded in an unjust war." Berkeley knew whereof he spoke. He himself was the younger son of an ancient Saxon family that traced its lineage before the Norman Conquest. Arriving in 1641 with a royal commission as governor, he had taken the disorderly colony in hand and transformed it from a rude frontier outpost into a thriving plantation society closely modeled on Stuart England. The Cavalier migration overseen and directed by Berkeley (so called because it consisted largely of emigrants from areas that had supported the Royalist cause in England's Civil War) was so successful that it quickly produced one of the most distinctive and durable elites in American history. This elite differed dramatically from that of colonial New England, but it made an equally important contribution both to the movement for independence from Britain and to the shaping of American history for the next three hundred years. If anything, moreover, it was even more nepotistic in character.

Virginia was initially settled in the late 1500s under the sponsorship of tobacco speculator Walter Raleigh, but the founders of the colony's "first families" came in a concentrated burst during Berkeley's tenure as governor, mostly during the 1640s and 1650s. Like the Puritans, many were refugees from political and religious oppression: defeated in the Civil War, the leading royalist families were dispossessed and their Anglican faith outlawed. Others were younger sons of ancient families (like Berkeley) who sought to establish cadet branches in the New World.

Historians agree that Virginia's distinctive regional culture was forever marked by a "younger son syndrome," developing a culture that was rigidly hierarchical, nostalgic, xenophobic, and obsessed with family honor. A reactionary project from the start, it was the purest extension of the Classical Western kinship ethos to be found on American soil. The Cavaliers wanted no part of the dawning commercial society and its contractual and bureaucratic system. Turning its back on this burgeoning middle class world based on capital and contracts, the colony was a monument to a premodern social order based on land and the ownership of large estates. In time, this would bring them into a fateful confrontation with the North, which had already begun to evolve the more fluid and dynamic kinship system appropriate to an industrial society.

The Virginia family founders did not fight their way up from the bottom of colonial society: they came in at the top and they stayed there, indulging a passion for acquisition unparalleled in American history. Robert Carter, agent for the multimillion-acre Fairfax Proprietary, acquired so much land himself that he became known as King Carter. William Byrd, "the prince of speculators," left his son over twenty-three thousand acres, which he and his heirs enlarged enormously. William Randolph came to Virginia in 1674 and settled in Turkey Island, where he married Mary Isham and became a friend and neighbor of the first Thomas Jefferson. Their mutual descendant would be the third president of the United States.[9]

One of the greatest Virginia families were the Lees. The younger son of an old Shropshire family—another Saxon house of ancient lineage—Col. Richard Lee came to Virginia in 1640 and spent many years in Berkeley's service, becoming the colony's attorney general and secretary of state. By the 1660s he owned seven plantations and hundreds of slaves. Lee married Anne Constable, who like other great Virginia matriarchs passed on the pride of her aristocratic class to her children. The grandsons of this couple were the founders of the family's three branches. Their numerous progeny would include four governors, two signers of the Declaration, a revolutionary general, four Confederate generals, a Union admiral, assorted diplomats, nine members of Congress, and one president (Zachary Taylor).[10]

The majority of such immigrants came from the loyalist counties of the south and west of England. They intermarried extensively on both sides of the Atlantic and in a very short time they became united in a cousinage so dense that one historian has compared them to "a tangle of fishooks." As with the Puritan elite of Massachusetts, these nepotistic connections were centered on groups of families with common origins in England. The so-called Kent connection consisted of the Filmer, Horsmanden, Byrd, Beverley, Culpeper, and Carter families; their genealogical matriarch was Mary Horsmanden Filmer Byrd, to whom almost everyone in the Virginia elite was somehow related. The Northampton connection centered on the Ishams and included the Washingtons, Spencers, Randolphs, Jeffersons, Blands, Beverlys, Bollings, Eppses, and Hacketts. These were not unified clans with the hierarchical structure and direction that implies, but informal communities based on kinship and unified by nepotistic preferences in marriage, business, and politics.

At the center of this web stood William Berkeley. Like the founder of the Chinese state of Lu, praised by Confucius for his sagacity, Berkeley understood the importance of families in establishing a stable social order. Many emigrants came with his active encouragement from Berkeley's home county in England. Berkeley himself married Frances Culpeper—a distant cousin of Pennsylvania founder William Penn—and created his own cousinage connecting the Ludwells, Pages, and Carys, but he was also related to the Washingtons of Northampton and the Filmers of Kent. "Many of these ties were cemented by cousin marriages," writes Fischer, "which were carefully planned to create a web of kinship as dense as that of the Roman patriciate. It is difficult to think of any ruling elite that has been more closely interrelated since the Ptolemies." This tight-knit character of Virginia society was attested by John Randolph, who once advised a boatload of new immigrants against offending any person of note in the colony: "For... either by blood or marriage, we are almost all related, or so connected in our interests, that whoever of a Stranger presumes to offend any one of us will infallibly find an enemy of the whole, nor, right or wrong, do we ever forsake him, till by one means or another his ruin is accomplished."[11]

This inbred elite assumed the leadership of Virginia from an early point and never relinquished it. Planters dominated the twelve-man Royal Council that controlled the distribution of offices and served as the colony's upper legislative chamber and high court. Members of this ruling elite monopolized the colony's offices for over a century.[12] The council also controlled the distribution of land, and needless to say, they awarded most of the largest grants to themselves and their relatives. They also dominated and controlled the rest of Virginia society in their capacity as landlords and patrons.

Virginia's society was polarized and hierarchical, with a wealthy elite at the top, supported by a class of lesser gentry; a large number of tenant farmers, servants, and slaves at the bottom; and a small group of freehold farmers in between. This social structure was a product of the plantation system: Virginia's major cash crop was tobacco, and many of the peculiarities of Virginia's social structure derive from this brute economic fact. To begin with, the pattern of settlement was not, as in New England, a highly centralized one of small towns surrounded by modest farms, but a dispersed one of large estates fronting on Virginia's many rivers, served by small market villages like those of the south and west of England. Indeed, visitors to the colony often remarked on its resemblance to these traditional manorial communities. Rural districts generally comprised some ten or twenty households close enough to be considered neighbors but far enough apart to foster a sense of sovereign independence, which was jealously protected. Each Virginia farmer was considered a gentleman of independent means, and from this independence flowed his dignity and the honor of his family, both of which he was entitled to defend with savage violence. Duels and feuds were common in Virginia, and remained so in the South for many years.

Primogeniture was observed from the beginning and grew stricter as time passed, especially among the upper class; but due to the enormous size of most initial land grants, twice as large as those in other colonies, even the families of lesser gentry and middling farmers remained united, and extensive kin-based neighborhoods developed. In time, a pattern of close marriage turned these districts into insular cousinhoods like those of the British aristocracy. Their members worked, socialized, and worshiped together, and nepotistic business practices turned the local cousinage into an informal credit and loan association. This web of small transactions based on oral contracts among neighbors, kin, and friends was sustained and regulated not by banks and legal codes but by the ethos of the traditional gift economy.

As in any system based on primogeniture, lineage consciousness was high—as reflected in the proliferation of IIs, IIIs, and IVs among the Tidewater aristocracy—and adultery and illegitimacy were harshly stigmatized. Unlike New England, where the marriage of cousins was frowned upon, in Virginia the practice was frequent. Southern households were also larger and less nuclear than among the Puritans, due to the pattern of extended-family settlement and the high mortality levels that routinely cut marriages short and orphaned large numbers of children. A typical Virginia household included numerous uncles, aunts, and half siblings or stepsiblings as well as more distant relatives; a plantation owner's household also included tutors, craftsmen, tenants and their families, visitors, servants, and slaves.

Where Puritan children were enjoined to be submissive and meek, yet were bred to an egalitarian culture, upper class Virginians were encouraged to be proud, strong-willed, and independent, yet were bred to a hierarchical society sanctioned by an aristocratic worldview. This rigid hierarchy was softened by the reciprocal duties of patronage and unified by a complex code of etiquette that many people had to learn from books. The young George Washington copied out one of these guides by hand in order to master the elaborate marks of deference that would aid him in his climb through Virginia society. Yet far from the restless striving inculcated by Puritan pedagogy, Virginians encouraged in their children a Stoic sensibility that encouraged them to greet whatever came with "courage, honesty, dignity and grace." The sometimes contradictory combination of intense family pride and stoic self-mastery became, in Fischer's words, "a coiled spring at the core of Virginia's culture, and a source of its great achievements during the eighteenth century."[13]

The key principle of Southern society was the concept of honor. The obsession with honor is an attribute of all familistic societies, and is essentially hierarchical. Gentlemen had more honor than yeomen farmers, who in turn had more honor than servants; slaves had none. In Virginia, the honor of the ruling class required the subjection of everyone else in a rigid social hierarchy enforced by violence and threats against inferiors. Though rooted in the same English traditions as the Puritan ideal of ordered liberty, this Southern, "hegemonic" view of liberty as defined by one's dominion over others was very different, and produced a quite different result.

The demand for cheap labor to tend the vast tobacco fields led to the importation of large numbers of indentured servants and slaves, and this of course was the great defining feature of Southern society. Indenture and slavery are alien institutions today, but in the seventeenth and eighteenth centuries they were considered normal aspects of a social order based on paternal authority. Right up to the Revolution, most Americans subscribed to the notion of society as a great family, with the king at its head. Though as Englishmen they were proud of their constitutional liberties and fierce spirit of independence, Americans continued to recognize the legitimacy of a society ordered by ranks and degrees. The patriarchal family remained the basis of colonial society, and its naked inequalities could still be rationalized by an ideology of paternalism. At the time of the Revolution more than half of all Americans were probably bound in some form of legal dependency to a social or political father, including wives and children, apprentices, servants, and slaves.

In the eighteenth-century household, husbands and fathers reigned supreme. Women had no independent rights or identity. They had the legal status of children and were often treated and addressed as such. Children themselves were raised to strict obedience and subdued by a combination of harsh punishments and the threat (frequently carried out) of disinheritance. As a result, the emotional bonds between fathers and sons could be fraught with resentment and fear. Children soon passed from the patriarchal authority of a father to that of a master. Domestic service, as in England, was a ubiquitous experience, and many Americans spent a good part of their early lives as servants in the home of a kinsman or stranger. But the practice of indenture rendered service in America a harsher and more lasting condition. About half of all colonial immigrants came over as indentured servants. (In Virginia, the proportion was much higher and mainly consisted of single men, many of them young boys kidnapped for deportation.) An indentured servant was generally someone who had been imported at the expense of his employer and had bound himself to work off that investment. In England, indenture usually lasted no more than a year and servants could change masters if they were unhappy. In America, the expense of immigration rendered the period of service much longer, from five to ten years. Servants were regarded as personal property and could be bought and sold, traded, rented, bequeathed, or seized for nonpayment of debts, and runaways were punished severely. The relationship between master and servant was supposed to be infused with paternalistic sentiments, but it was rarely so in practice, and many indentured servants were treated little better than slaves.

Apprenticeship, though equally binding, was much less harsh and usually briefer. Nor did it reflect a lack of care on his father's part for a young boy to be bound out for several years as an apprentice. Quite the opposite: to apprentice your son in a good trade was the defining preoccupation of colonial nepotism. Apprenticeship was the common way of learning a trade for sons who did not inherit land, and for many it was the sole path to upward mobility. Most fathers were eager to get their sons started in good careers and vied to place them advantageously. The relationship between master and apprentice was meant to approximate that of a father and son, and it often became such in fact. A man without an heir—or who cherished greater ambitions for his own son—would often marry his daughter to an apprentice.

The extreme manifestation of colonial paternalism was the relationship between master and slave. Many families in New York or Boston kept a few slaves as domestic servants and regarded them as members of the household, but Southern slavery was on a larger scale and its paternalistic fiction was both thinner and more necessary. Apologists portrayed the slaves as naïve, childlike creatures incapable of self-control and in need of paternal authority. Older slaves were often called Aunt or Uncle by members of the white family. Most modern commentators have sought to demystify these conventions of plantation paternalism as a crude ideological justification. According to Pierre van den Berghe, however, the view of the plantation as "a kind of big unhappy family" was no myth, since many masters in fact bred with their slaves. (The sexuality of Southern males in general, Fischer observes, tended to be "predatory.") The offspring of these unions were not acknowledged as legitimate children but were generally accorded favored treatment, sometimes lived in the master's house, and were often freed on the death of their father. But the practice had a highly dysfunctional effect on the slave population itself. For women, the path to assimilation for themselves or their children was open through concubinage. Males, in contrast, were sexually disenfranchised and were often unable to maintain families or stable bonds with females. This differential impact on the reproductive success of black men and women resulted in deeply ingrained conflicts of interest that in turn undermined cohesion and solidarity—all by unconscious design.[14]

Such were the main legal and contractual extensions of classical Western patriarchalism in colonial America. They represent the degree to which the structure of relations within the family could be projected into a complex hierarchy rationalized by nepotistic values. Just as important, however, were the informal ties of patronage that helped to knit this hierarchical society together.

Since the fourteenth century, English kings had used patronage to create their own bases of local support to rival those of the great feudal lords. The idea was to link the rural networks of English society to crown and court by coopting local notables. (The rhetoric of patronage combined the Senecan language of benefits with religious metaphors that likened the good patron to an angelic intercessor, or saint. Requests for aid were frank and unembarrassed, with flattering appeals to the magnificence of the patron and obsequious promises of loyalty and gratitude.) Colonial society was likewise held together by the reciprocal exchange of favors, gifts, and services between men of different rank. Though many were irked by the distribution of colonial offices to incompetent royal favorites, patronage was vital to advancement, and all the most ambitious and successful Americans made skillful use of it. Most Americans avidly sought to attract a patron, and once established, to become patrons themselves. It was considered a great credit to rescue a bright lad from obscurity, and would-be patrons were always on the lookout for such promising young men. Even the austere John Adams saw no shame in seeking such assistance: to get ahead as a lawyer, he wrote, one needed "the Friendship and Patronage of the great Masters in the Profession."

One of the most spectacular examples of a career based on patronage was that of John Hancock, the first signer of the Declaration of Independence and longtime Massachusetts governor. Hancock was the son and grandson of Congregational ministers and it was assumed that he would follow in their footsteps. But on his father's death his childless uncle Thomas, the richest merchant in Boston, adopted the seven-year-old John and raised him in his luxurious mansion on Beacon Hill. Thomas put his nephew through Harvard, which he attended with John Adams, and groomed him to take over his business. Before long, Thomas made him a partner, and with his uncle's death the following year he became one of the richest young men in America. Hancock used his uncle's wealth to create numerous friends and dependents. He set up four of his clerks in business and stood godfather to their children. He contributed to public causes, delivered food and fuel to Boston's poor, rebuilt whole neighborhoods devastated by fire, supported widows and orphans and put many through school, personally maintained the Boston Common, and bought the city's first fire engine. "Hancock patronized everyone," writes Gordon Wood. "He made work for people. He erected homes that he did not need. He built ships that he sold at a loss. He sponsored any and every young man who importuned him. He opened trade shops and staffed them. He purchased a concert hall for public use. He entertained lavishly and habitually treated the Boston populace to wine." Adams estimated that no fewer than a thousand families depended on Hancock for their daily bread. All of this ensured his popularity and served to protect him from the rising populist ire stirred up by firebrands like Samuel and John Adams. It also allowed him to form what Gordon Wood calls "one of the most elaborate networks of political dependency in eighteenth-century America."[15]

Though these paternalistic norms and institutions were ubiquitous, they were most deeply entrenched in Virginia, where they survived for many years. Though indentured servitude was soon abolished, along with primogeniture and other aristocratic devices, slavery remained in force until the Civil War. As Fischer makes clear, however, the Virginia slave system was not an accidental by-product of the plantation economy, nor could it be jettisoned without destroying the aristocratic culture it supported. Instead it was part of a conscious strategy of Berkeley and the Cavaliers to re-create the conditions that had sustained the British aristocracy. Slavery and indenture were necessary to fulfill the dynastic ambitions of Virginia's leading gentlemen, which is another way of saying that Virginia's hierarchical society was a by-product of the nepotistic drive to establish one's family in a permanent ruling elite. Virginia was thus a monument to Classical Western Nepotism on the eve of its extinction.

There was, furthermore, a good deal of latent conflict in relations between fathers and sons, as we would expect in any system based on primogeniture. Aging fathers often kept a younger son at home—a "Benjamin"—to run their plantations and handle other business. Like nepotistic helpers at the nest prevented by their parents from going off to start their own families, these sons were kept in a condition of permanent adolescence by a dominating patriarch. Some men were nearly crushed beneath this weight: William Byrd II was so haunted by his father's memory that he ordered his corpse to be dug up so that he could look in his face. Other sons rebelled, if ineffectually. Though Robert Wormley Carter was forty years old and a married man, his father kept him at home on a small allowance. "The two men quarreled endlessly," writes Fischer. "So heated did these quarrels become that the father began to fear for his life."[16] Conflicts also arose between brothers: after inheriting the majority of his father's estate, Philip Lee refused to pay out his father's bequests to his siblings, and made his youngest brother eat and work with the slaves.[17]

These generational tensions were reflected in Virginia's political system—a gerontocracy dominated by the twelve-man Royal Council, composed of the wealthiest planters. The House of Burgesses, a forum for the colony's second sons, rarely challenged its authority. For years it had been dominated by scions of the great Tidewater families, who felt close ties to England. Ultimately, however, the movement for revolt against British authority was led in the House of Burgesses by a fiery cabal of young men including Patrick Henry, Thomas Jefferson, and Richard and Francis Lee, who formed a radical alliance with the Adamses of Boston.

Yet as reactionary and backward-looking as it was, the achievements of this nepotistic oligarchy are not to be discounted. In figures like Washington, Jefferson, John and Edmund Randolph, James Madison, James Monroe, and the redoubtable Lees it produced some of the greatest patriots in American history—men of exceptional character and ability whose virtues equaled those of any aristocratic ruling class in history. Virginians led the way in the Revolution, shaped the country's constitutional and legal traditions, and supplied four of its first five presidents. But their Cavalier utopia was doomed. Unlike the Puritans, who developed a flexible and highly adaptive nepotistic system that allowed them to exploit new opportunities, tightening and loosening family bonds as need arose, Tidewater society was based on a rigid and inflexible patriarchal nepotism whose contradictions in the end were unsustainable.

THE CRADLE OF RECIPROCITY: BEN FRANKLIN COMES TO PHILADELPHIA

In October 1723, a young apprentice named Ben Franklin ran away from his indentures in his brother's printing shop in Boston and made his way to Philadelphia. Arriving early one Sunday morning after several days of arduous travel, friendless, hungry, and practically penniless, he followed his nose to a baker's shop, where he found that a few pence would buy three times the amount of bread as in Boston. Stuffing his pockets with rolls, he followed a crowd of well-dressed and orderly folk into a Quaker meetinghouse. "I sat down among them, and, after looking round awhile and hearing nothing said, being very drowsy thro' labor and want of rest the preceding night, I fell fast asleep, and continued so till the meeting broke up, when one was kind enough to rouse me." Refreshed from his nap, Franklin proceeded down the street in search of an affordable inn. Encountering a young man in Quaker dress, he asked for direction. "We were then near the sign of the Three Mariners. 'Here,' says he, 'is one place that entertains strangers, but it is not a reputable house; if thee wilt walk with me, I'll show thee a better.' "

Franklin was one of many refugees from political, religious, or familial oppression who found shelter and support in Philadelphia. There the milder tenets of Quakerism had given rise to a regional culture that was much more tolerant than either Massachusetts or Virginia: a culture based from top to bottom on the principle of reciprocal altruism embodied in the Golden Rule. This tradition of "reciprocal liberty," Fischer argues, is the Quaker counterpart to the ordered egalitarian liberty of the Puritans and the elitist, hegemonic liberty of the Anglican Cavaliers. While the Virginians would be defeated in the Civil War, the Quakers' active principle of reciprocal liberty would end up completely transforming American social relations, making it possible to include more and more people of differing backgrounds and beliefs in a multiethnic national community.

The Friends' migration began around 1675 and picked up considerable speed in 1682 with the arrival of William Penn, the royal proprietor of the Delaware valley. Like earlier migrations, this one was also a movement of families from a concentrated area of England. Though Quaker theology tended to blur the distinction between kin and community, they were initially a set of kin-based congregations like the Puritans, and they maintained a high degree of nepotistic exclusivity.

The distinguishing feature of Quaker belief was its rejection of the Puritan doctrines of predestination, election, and irresistible grace. Quakers believed not in a jealously exclusive tribal deity or a divinely ordained father-king but in a democratic God of love and light who offered salvation not just to a chosen few but to all mankind. The "inner light" in every man and woman was the path to salvation, but it was up to everyone to follow it individually. Grace could not be forced on anyone. Nor were Quaker communities hierarchical like those of Puritans and Anglicans, but were organized as a series of consensual meetings whereby the community regulated its affairs. Quakers were also distinguished for their egalitarian sentiments—they addressed everybody as Friend—and by their acceptance of religious and ethnic diversity. Unlike the insular Puritans and the xenophobic Cavaliers, Quakers welcomed strangers and dissenters of all kinds, and Pennsylvania quickly became known as a haven for persecuted minorities.

While the English Quakers welcomed these groups, they nonetheless formed a close, inbred elite that dominated the region's politics for over seventy years and firmly imprinted their values on its culture. Like the Puritan and Anglican elites, this Quaker elite was a congeries of family connections formed in England and carried over to the New World. The Quaker connections that dominated rural Pennsylvania, west Jersey, and Delaware were linked by marriage with the core connection, centered in Philadelphia around the family of William Penn himself. But it was also a more open elite than the others, freely admitting new blood, so long as (like Franklin) they married into the core connection.

The Quakers spoke of the Society of Friends in all earnestness as a family and considered themselves members of God's household. Even in their own extended families, distinctions were erased between relatives by blood and marriage: in-laws were addressed simply as Father, Brother, or Sister. Quaker families were also less hierarchical: they regarded the family as a community of equals united not by fear of a dominating patriarch but by relations of love and mutual concern. Marriage was supposed to be for love and must be acceptable not just to the families in question but to the congregation and community at large, and marriage to outsiders could be punished with disinheritance. As a result, many Quakers married late or not at all. But the distinctive Quaker idea of sexual equality ("In souls there is no sex") led to many anomalies, including the prevalence of female preachers. This emphasis on sexual equality extended to a more general bilateralism in Quaker kinship practices.

Child-rearing habits also deviated from those of other colonies. Fischer notes an intense concern for children's welfare not seen anywhere else in the Western world, a difference that ultimately sprang from the Quaker rejection of original sin. Penn himself wrote extensively on the subject and appealed to Quaker parents to reason with their children, using physical punishment only as a last resort; he also warned them not to show partiality but to love and care equally for all, lest favoritism breed envy and resentment. Quaker children were treated very indulgently by their parents and were not sent out to other families, like Puritans. As a result, they were unusually independent and were frequently seen to contradict their elders, to the point of preaching to them on matters of spiritual conduct. This liberty was shocking to outsiders. On the other hand, the larger community took a close interest in the welfare and behavior of children, and correction when it came was often imposed by the group. Quaker children were therefore socialized from an early age to subordinate their wills to the community and adhere to its exacting moral standards. Such people grew up to be modest, industrious, charitable, cautious, and prudent. They were also very enterprising. Quakers were successful bankers, tradesmen, and industrialists, and the Delaware valley would rival New England as America's industrial heartland.

Penn's settlement policies were consciously intended to create a society of independent farmers with no extremes of wealth or poverty. Landholding patterns were much more egalitarian than those of other regions, as were Quaker inheritance patterns. Most Quakers—Penn especially—scorned hereditary orders and all outward show of rank. The only aristocracy he accepted was one of virtue and merit. Quaker politics also differed from other regions, primarily in being more tolerant of dissent. Thus political parties emerged in Pennsylvania long before they were countenanced anywhere else. But government overall was minimalist, with frequent elections, low taxes, and no legally established militia.

Penn's voluminous social and political writings largely boil down to the idea of reciprocal altruism founded on the Golden Rule: do unto others as you would have others do unto you. This modest precept led to radical positions, including a proclivity for pacifism and the earliest stand against slavery in the American colonies. It also permitted people to live together without sharing the same social or religious ideas. The first law passed by the Pennsylvania assembly guaranteed freedom of conscience for all Christian believers and enacted penalties for those who would interfere with that freedom. In addition, the fundamental law of Pennsylvania guaranteed secular rights to life, liberty, and property, representative government, taxation by consent, and trial by jury. The guiding principle of these laws was that all rights demanded for oneself must be extended to others.

The reciprocal principle at the heart of Quaker society and culture would not only become the eventual basis of the pluralistic American creed, it would ultimately develop into a new and more expansive definition of kinship itself. "The Quakers had nothing like the Puritans' Hebraic idea of a chosen people, nor anything comparable to the Anglican gentry's fierce pride of rank and nationhood," Fischer writes. "They looked upon all humanity as their kin."[18] This altruistic definition of kinship, which appears to be a radical departure from or denial of nepotism, is really an *extension* of nepotism from the family and congregation to humanity at large. Reciprocal altruism must be learned and practiced in the family before it can be extended to strangers.

Philadelphia was much more democratic than the other colonies. Not for nothing was it called the City of Brotherly Love. Yet it must also be said that the worldly impulse of Quaker nepotism was not very active or intense. In comparing the elites of Boston and Philadelphia, Digby Baltzell finds that while the upper class of Philadelphia was more tolerant and open than other regional elites, it also tended to be passive and complacent. Most entries for Philadelphia's leading citizens in the *Dictionary of National Biography* are brief, listing the schools they attended, the firms they worked in, and the social clubs they joined. In contrast, the sons of Puritan Boston were intensely active, and their entries typically go on and on, with numerous institutional affiliations, board chairmanships, and philanthropic or cultural activities. For Baltzell, this difference explains the greater success and longevity of the Boston elite as a whole. The Bostonians not only procreated more successfully, they also produced a greater share of "exceptional" men. Thus it is no great surprise to find that most of the civic and charitable institutions of Quaker Philadelphia were founded by that transplanted Puritan, Ben Franklin.

Plainly it is no accident that Franklin, a friendless interloper who wandered off the street into a Quaker meetinghouse and promptly fell asleep, was treated with such courtesy and tolerance. In a Puritan church, a snoring stranger would have been rudely awakened and sent packing, perhaps even clapped in the stocks. Though bred in the Puritan virtues, Franklin found a home among the Quakers and easily adapted to their ways. More open than Boston to foreign ideas, Philadelphia also became the point of entry for the doctrines of the European Enlightenment, hence the center of the tiny American scientific community. Franklin was thus doubly fortunate in his choice, since it was not as a printer but as a scientist that he would rise to international prominence.

More than any American of his age, it is Franklin we revere as the proponent and exemplar of the self-made man, mainly because of his influential writings on the virtues of discipline, frugality, and self-reliance. "A man who makes boast of his ancestors doth but advertise his own insignificance," Franklin wrote. Elsewhere he observed, "Let our fathers and grandfathers be valued for *their* goodness, ourselves for our own." Yet Franklin was very much a man of his time—a patriarch and patron to his kin both near and far. Indeed he was one of the greatest nepotists of the revolutionary era.

Ben Franklin was the fifteenth of seventeen children born to Josiah Franklin, a soap and candle maker who emigrated to Boston in 1685. At the age of ten he was apprenticed in his father's shop, cutting wicks and pouring molds. He hated this work and wanted to go to sea, but his father wouldn't hear of it. Finally Josiah yielded to his son's bookish inclinations and apprenticed him to his half brother James, a master printer nine years his senior. Ben learned the trade quickly and soon became highly proficient. He also gained his first exposure to the world of books and ideas. But he did not get along with James, who is presented in Franklin's memoirs as an envious, small-minded bully who often beat his younger brother. Finally, the seventeen-year-old Ben ran off to Philadelphia. Franklin's career thus began with a rebellion against his father and brother and a violation of his contract of indenture—a preview of the wholesale disruption of paternalistic ties that would soon sweep the American colonies.[19] After a series of adventures, warmly chronicled in his *Autobiography*, Franklin married Deborah Read and set himself up as a printer, publishing his own newspaper, the *Pennsylvania Gazette*, and *Poor Richard's Almanack*—modeled on his brother James's *Poor Robin.* A clever and hardworking businessman, he soon paid off his debts and expanded into stationery and dry goods, including the soap manufactured by his brother John and the salves and ointments prepared by his mother-in-law. By the 1740s he had become the largest paper dealer in the English-speaking world.

If Franklin was a rebel against tyrannical family government, he was a representative man of his times. But in the absence of a developed market economy an ambitious man still needed the help of wealthy and powerful patrons, and Franklin's rise was due as much to his cunning manipulation of friendship and patronage as to his honesty, integrity, and industry. Thus he went out of his way to befriend the leading citizens of the day, James Logan and William Allen, both of whom were intimately connected to the Penn faction. After becoming clerk of the Pennsylvania assembly in 1736 through their good offices, he became a major figure in politics, and in 1737, again through the manipulation of these patronage connections, Franklin became postmaster of Philadelphia. The office was installed right in his shop, and with free access to the mails, his paper's circulation jumped. He also obtained government printing contracts for Pennsylvania, New Jersey, and Delaware. In 1739 his career as an inventor took off with the development of the Franklin stove, which was sold throughout New England by his brothers John and Peter. (Jefferson bought one for Monticello.) He also founded a political club, which was attended by an influential cross section of Philadelphia society and brought even more business his way. At forty-two, having grown prosperous enough to quit business and aspire to the condition of a gentleman, Franklin closed his shop and began a new career as a man of science and political activist. In the latter pursuit he conducted himself in a patrician manner, later declaring that in fourteen elections he had never appeared as a candidate: "I never did, directly or indirectly, solicit any man's vote." He did, however, actively solicit the job of colonial postmaster general, which he obtained in 1753 through friends in London—an appointment that allowed him to inaugurate his career as a family patron.

The great regret of Franklin's life was the couple's dearth of offspring. He and Deborah had only one surviving son, William, and a daughter, Sally. The smallness of his family no doubt inclined Franklin to elect himself a surrogate parent and guardian to many young relatives and friends throughout his long life.

Despite his homilies on the virtues of industry and self-reliance, Franklin was very much an eighteenth-century man, hence utterly shameless and unconscious in his nepotism. He appointed his son, William, to take his place in the Philadelphia post office, then made him comptroller of the whole colonial system. He then enrolled him as a law student in London and accompanied him there in 1757. (William later obtained a royal appointment as governor of New Jersey—in hope, it was said, of winning his father to the loyalist side.) In their absence, the

Philadelphia office was given to the husband of Deborah's niece, who badly mismanaged it. Franklin then gave it to his brother Peter. When Peter died he continued his widow in the job, making her the first woman to hold public office in America. The Boston post office went to Franklin's brother John, and when he died it went to one of his stepchildren—to the displeasure of his sister Jane, who wanted it for her son Benny. He later compensated Benny with the postmastership of New Haven. He also made the son of a friend postmaster in Charleston, and another friend comptroller in New York.[20]

Several children of his sister Ann had moved to London before the Revolution, and were stranded by the outbreak of hostilities. One of these became a protégé of Franklin's. He paid for his schooling, made him his secretary, and had him appointed America's commercial agent in France during the Revolution. A brother and sister of his wife also lived for a time in Franklin's house, and he managed to get the brother a government job. His youngest sister, Jane, had a large family, in all of whom Franklin took an interest. One of her children he established in the soap business, another he took on as an apprentice and set up as a printer, and for a third he obtained a government office.

When the English removed Franklin as postmaster general, in 1774, he asked William to resign his post as well. The son refused. Franklin bitterly resented his disloyalty, and transferred his interest and affection to William's illegitimate son, Temple. He placed him in a good English school, then took him to France in 1776, where he became Franklin's secretary, arousing criticism from his fellow commissioners. Later he tried without success to have Temple appointed secretary of the Paris Peace Commission, and in 1787 he again tried to use his influence to get Temple appointed secretary of the Federal Convention. He then applied directly to Washington for a position in the new federal government, and "seriously resented" the president's failure to accommodate him. However, he did manage to leave Temple well endowed with property and made him his literary executor.

Franklin's daughter, Sally, was a pretty, headstrong girl in whom he labored unsuccessfully to instill habits of thrift and sobriety. When she married Richard Bache, he set the young man up in business, then made him deputy postmaster general and let them live in his Philadelphia house rent free. Toward the end of his life, the widowed Franklin moved in with his daughter's family, doting upon his many grandchildren. He took a particular interest in his namesake, Benjamin Franklin Bache, sending him to school in Geneva and trying (again without success) to get Washington to grant the young man some public office. As one biographer observes, "It was the common feeling of the time that Franklin had used civil office to serve his family more than to serve the public, and so there was sufficient prejudice to make exclusion of his relatives almost a policy with the new government."[21] The young man conceived an understandable dislike for Washington and became a leading opposition journalist. Later presidents would not make the mistake of refusing patronage to members of the press.

While Franklin's persistence on behalf of his relatives had become an embarrassment to his friends, he himself appeared insensitive to the change in their attitudes. This was undoubtedly because Franklin, the oldest of the Revolutionaries, despite his constant exhortations to virtue and his bias in favor of merit over birth, remained a product of the old régime. His example shows how almost overnight the transformation of attitudes wrought by the Revolution turned the practice of family patronage into an odious proclivity for nepotism.

A FAMILY QUARREL: THE WAR ON NEPOTISM BEGINS

If America was a copy of English society, it was a weak and incomplete one, lacking the established structures and social adhesives of the mother country. In Virginia and New Hampshire, where tight-knit oligarchies dominated, politics was relatively stable. Maryland was also controlled by its so-called "Fifty Families." Everywhere else, colonial politics was a fierce clash of family interests. Local offices were monopolized by individual families, and in many colonies family names were used to designate political factions: De Lanceys in New York, Ogdens in New Jersey, Wentworths in New Hampshire. In North Carolina the dominant faction was a group of Cape Fear clans so closely interrelated by blood and marriage that their enemies called them simply "the Family."[22] The Revolution began a long process of disentangling the family from American politics. But the revolt against family rule was neither as swift nor, ultimately, as successful as we tend to assume.

In the mid–eighteenth century a series of demographic, economic, and social changes swiftly widened the gulf between the New World and the Old. Immigration increased dramatically after 1740 and colonial population exploded, more than doubling every twenty years. The British defeat of France in 1763 (in what is usually called the French and Indian War) opened up a half billion acres in the interior, and a flood of new settlers streamed through the Ohio valley, up the Connecticut River, and down the Mississippi. A speculative fever gripped Americans, and many bought and sold several farms in succession as they moved on to greener pastures. With each move, family ties grew more attenuated and the nuclear family itself became increasingly isolated. Fortunes were made overnight, social trust declined, and economic relationships shifted from their traditional basis in patronage to one of impersonal contracts. Many of those who rose to the top of society were completely lacking in polish and manners; touchiness and envy were inflamed, and the social order as a whole seemed no longer divinely ordained but man-made, a human creation. Frontier politics became increasingly fractious, while servants and other subordinates felt freer than in the past and more inclined to insist upon equality with masters. Primogeniture was attacked as a device for the perpetuation of aristocratic privilege. Wives sought the right to divorce, while sons and daughters asserted rights of self-determination. Few fathers dared to exercise the kind of absolute authority they had claimed in the past.

Greatly contributing to the dissolution of hierarchical bonds was the progress of the "enlightened paternalism" promoted by the spread of republican ideas. The greatest influence on the thinking of the American founders had been the writings of John Locke. His liberal constitutional ideas are expressed in *Two Treatises of Government*, but his equally liberal views on child rearing were, if anything, even more influential. In *Thoughts on Education* Locke emphasized a due regard for the independence of children, the importance of their moral education, and the need to rely on love and respect rather than force and fear. Children (like subjects) had rights as well as duties. Bonds of blood were not enough to earn their obedience—parents were obliged to raise and educate them properly. Corporal punishment was out, appeals to reason and affection were in. Enlightened parents were often confused as to how they should implement these precepts, and colonial society was full of perplexed and demoralized fathers who (like the Athenians of old) felt abused by their unruly sons. Already by midcentury, American children were renowned for their resistance to authority.

As the colonies prospered and grew, a series of crises—the Stamp Act of 1765, the Boston Massacre of 1770, the Tea Act of 1773—put a serious strain on the instinctual loyalty to crown and Parliament felt by most Americans, and by April 1775 many were ready for revolution. Ties of kinship closely linked the colonies to England, which Americans still thought of in literal and figurative terms as the mother country. But as the century progressed, Americans began to demand recognition of their growing maturity. "At times," Gordon Wood observes, "the polemics between whigs and tories appeared to be little more than a quarrel over the proper method of child-rearing."[23] Indeed, it is striking how pervasive this familial imagery is in the rhetoric of the American Revolution. John Adams compared England to Lady Macbeth, an unnatural mother who knew "How tender 't was to love the babe that milked her, but yet who could even while 't was smiling in her face, Have plucked the nipple from the boneless gums and dashed the brains out."[24] In *Common Sense,* Tom Paine resoundingly refuted the objections that had been raised against revolution, including the appeal to family loyalty. "Even brutes do not devour their young, nor savages make war upon their families." After hearing of the events at Lexington on April 19, 1775, Paine wrote, "I rejected the hardened, sullen tempered Pharaoh of England for ever; and disdain the wretch, that with the pretended title of FATHER OF HIS PEOPLE, can unfeelingly hear of their slaughter."

In this environment, the appeals of British authorities to the traditional parent-child relationship only worked to undermine their demands for compliance. Paternalism had been rendered useless as a defense of monarchical authority and now served instead to justify the colonists' rebellion. At the same time, the language of contractual rights and obligations came increasingly to the fore—a reflection of the growth of a modern commercial society on both sides of the Atlantic.

The family relationship between England and her colonies was seen to be consensual, a covenant or contract whose terms were protection on the one hand and allegiance on the other. If one party violated these terms, the other was free to withdraw.

The Revolutionaries bitterly attacked the institutions of monarchical society, particularly hereditary privilege and the patronage abuses that had filled up colonial offices with corrupt and incompetent sycophants. Men like Thomas Jefferson, Patrick Henry, and Richard Henry Lee angrily resented the tight circle of Tidewater planters who monopolized high office in Virginia. Boston radicals John and Samuel Adams and James Otis were incensed by the place-seeking and nepotism of Massachusetts governor Thomas Hutchinson and his relatives.[25] In place of this vile system of patronage, with its fawning insincerity and falseness, Adams and his fellow republicans sought to promote a new order of things in which virtue and merit would rule. Their conviction of the goodness and benevolence of man led them to think that this remarkable transformation would come about naturally once the main obstacles had been removed.

This radical project reflected not just the new republican ideas but the Revolutionaries' own social experience. As Gordon Wood points out, many of them had been the first in their family to attend college. Thomas Jefferson, Samuel and John Adams, James Otis, John Jay, James Madison, and other leaders of this generation were men with the talent and ambition to play a leading role in society, yet lacked important family connections. To such as these, the idea of establishing achievement rather than heredity as the standard of worth was extremely appealing. Samuel Adams, the most radical of the Revolutionaries, "despised everything that had to do with genealogy and refused to have anything to do with patronage in any form, even among his own family."[26] John Adams, son of a successful but uncultivated farmer, was powerfully motivated by resentment of the Boston upper crust and expressed his hatred of "all the great Notions of high Family that you find in Winslows, Hutchinsons, Quincys, Saltonstals, Chandlers, Leonards," et al., for "tis vain and mean to esteem oneself for his Ancestors Merit."[27]

With the outbreak of hostilities, most of the leading loyalist families were forced to emigrate. The displacement of colonial elites disrupted the chains of patronage and influence that held colonial America together. Practically the whole Hudson valley aristocracy departed, causing the collapse of the intimate structures of New York society. The same was true for Pennsylvania. The Massachusetts act of banishment in 1778 named forty-six Boston merchants and their families. Some of these left members behind to safeguard the family interests, and in some cases their kin-based networks were able to survive the disruption of exile and war. Mostly, however, their departures opened the way for new families to take their place. Thus in Boston, the Revolution allowed a number of ambitious mercantile families to establish themselves—families that in the century to come would found an even richer and more powerful aristocracy.

The 1780s were a time of dangerous uncertainty as the former colonies sought to reorganize themselves while hammering out the basis for a new national government. In the atmosphere of inflamed republican sensitivity, fears of a new monarchy and aristocracy immediately set in. Many Europeans had expected the victorious Washington to make himself king, and when he retired from public life after the war, presenting Congress with his sword, Americans were heartened by his display of republican virtue. When he agreed to join a private society of former army officers with hereditary membership, it was seen as a move to establish a military aristocracy, and the outcry was so intense that he withdrew. Yet his prestige remained immense, and it was only the fact that he had no children and could not establish a dynasty that made it possible for him to become the country's first president. Indeed, Washington's childlessness persuaded the public to accept the broad grant of executive powers in the new Constitution itself.

In their new laws and constitutions, the former colonies made a concerted attack on the patrimonialism of the old régime. New Hampshire's constitution declared, "no office or place whatsoever in government, shall be hereditary." All of the states abolished primogeniture and entail—legal devices that tended, in the words of a North Carolina statute, "only to raise the wealth and importance of particular families and individuals" in a manner contrary to that "equality of property which is of the spirit and principle of a genuine republic." New inheritance laws stipulated the equal rights of heirs, including wives and daughters, and divorce laws, hitherto limited to New England, were passed in all the states except South Carolina. In addition, societies for the abolition of indentured servitude sprang up, and in a very short time the hateful institution disappeared.

These were the first salvos in a long American war against nepotism in its classical Western form. But it is also the source of a profoundly idealistic view of America as the bearer of a universalist alternative to nepotism. The founders expressed a republican horror of partiality and selfish interest and promoted a new gentlemanly ideal of cosmopolitan humanity. Local and private attachments were held to be the preoccupation of inferior and narrow-minded persons. Tribal, familial, and even national loyalties reflected a lack of enlightened gentility. The evangelical mission of the new country was to unite the world in one great human family.[28]

Nevertheless, the revolt against patriarchy in politics did not involve a complete rejection of the patriarchal family; nor did it cancel out family pride. Even the most radical patriots considered the family the key to the moral and political health of a nation. As Adams told one of his sons in 1799, "There can never be any regular government of a nation without a marked subordination of mother and children to the father."[29]

Nor did the Revolution succeed in implementing universal benevolence and brotherhood. Hawthorne's "Major Molineux" is hardly the last word on patronage and nepotism. Kinship and family patronage continued to play an active role in economic, social, and political life for generations to come. Even the Minutemen of New England were united "less by chains of command than by familial loyalties," Wood writes. (Over a quarter of the Lexington militiamen mustered to fight by Capt. John Parker in April 1775 were related to him in some way.) Family succession to office also continued to be the norm, and enterprising men still looked confidently to their kinsmen and superiors for patronage. Yet so averse were the liberty-loving Americans to any hint of dependency that the euphemistic term "friendship" was generally used to describe these unequal relationships. This hypocritical demand for the concealment of behavior that violates our egalitarian creed is a consistent theme in the history of American nepotism.

The familistic language used on both sides of the revolutionary conflict suggests that at its root, the break with the mother country was a consequence of Britain's failure to admit the American colonists to the status of maturity as equals. In effect, it was a failure of nepotistic household management. The Americans argued with their adversaries as members of one patriarchal family, suggesting that they were seeking not a radical break with Britain but the ascription of a different family status. The British, however, persisted in viewing them as disobedient and ungrateful children. America was therefore born in a furious assertion of self-will against a tyrannical father. Out of this family quarrel came an affirmation of political brotherhood and a lasting suspicion of all hereditary instruments, including (in the extreme case) the inheritance of any property or estate whatsoever. The deep-dyed American prejudice against nepotism obviously has its roots in the republican idealism of the founders. But while that initial idealism was soon to be replaced by the hard-edged realism of Jacksonian democracy, we continue to view the phenomenon through their somewhat impractical eyes.

CHAPTER 8

THE CITY OF BROTHERLY LOVE

THE NEPOTISM OF THE FOUNDERS

The American founders have been viewed as moral and intellectual giants, men who not only led a revolution but established a new nation on a lasting and durable basis. Even today they remain to a large extent disembodied and imposing figures, far above the pettiness, corruption, and venality that has so frequently been seen in their successors. Nevertheless, though they were certainly an extraordinary generation, they were also human beings—fathers and husbands, nephews and uncles, sons and brothers—who struggled with their nepotistic impulses. Most of them succeeded. Some of them failed; and at least one of them failed spectacularly.

The early administrations of Washington, Adams, and Jefferson were years in which the national government was taking shape; partisan sentiments were still largely inchoate and policies to guide appointment to office were completely unformed. As a result, family succession and nepotism were widespread in the new republic, and a public official's relatives thought nothing of approaching him for help. The period between 1789 and the rise of the first modern parties in the late 1820s was one of rule by gentlemen and the leading families of the Revolution. The period did see the beginnings of a shift from family factions to organized national parties; but the leaders of the early republic continued to rely on family-based regional networks. Even as more abstract ideological distinctions began to emerge, these familistic underpinnings continued to be important to the life of American parties.

The classical republicanism to which our first three presidents subscribed assumed the need for a disinterested elite. Faction and party were manifestations of self-interest in politics and therefore great evils; government should be in the hands of leisured gentlemen who would serve not out of selfish interest but from a sense of public duty. Thus Franklin had urged that in order to attract the best men, public officials should not be paid. John Adams replied that for any man—even Washington—to serve without pay was to affect a superiority that he and many others found intolerable: "the people should have too high a sense of their own dignity ever to suffer any man to serve them for nothing."[1]

The Revolutionaries had embarked on the most radical project in history: the wholesale uprooting of all the institutions and conventions of monarchical society, especially any kind of inherited privilege. A wave of egalitarian passion swept through the former colonies and in an amazingly short time wiped out the habit of deference to social superiors. In the vacuum that resulted, the nation was rapidly falling apart as the old ties of kinship and patronage were disrupted, with nothing to put in their place. Vastly accelerating this process were the forces of increased immigration, internal movement, and rapid commercial expansion. The loss of kin and patronage connections created a pervasive climate of mistrust. It also unleashed a fierce competition for marks of honor and preeminence, as well as an inflamed sensitivity to perceived slights and insults. This touchiness and passion for distinction—the desire to be first among equals—was really a result of removing the king from the social equation. Politically, America was becoming a fatherless society. While this liberated the ambitions of the sons, it also threatened a rising tide of competition and conflict.

This outburst of ambition should be encouraged, the founders thought, but it must also be contained. Americans needed some means to regulate the new fraternal competition in place of the old hierarchical bonds. That something turned out to be *party*. As younger men like Hamilton and Madison understood, there would only be one Washington; therefore they proposed the creation of a new political system that could do without a father. In his famous contributions to the *Federalist*,

Madison argued that since men were not and never would be angels, the only protection against the dangers of faction was to construct a system of checks and balances that would harness the many conflicts inherent in democratic life as an engine of prosperity and freedom.

The triumph of self-interest in American politics gave rise to a new class of professional politicians and to a view of government itself as an unending clash of private interests. The reintroduction of selfishness would also make it difficult to prevent the return of patronage and nepotism. Indeed, once the old social system had been uprooted, with all its nepotistic ligaments, these ties had to be re-created through the medium of commerce and politics. A long struggle would therefore be waged not only to establish a viable party system but to harness and adapt these private impulses to constructive public ends. The founders themselves acted out the ensuing personal and psychological conflicts on the national stage, and it is to this intimate family drama among the founding "brothers" that we now turn our attention. It all began in Philadelphia—the City of Brotherly Love.

GEORGE WASHINGTON: STEPFATHER OF HIS COUNTRY

The revolutionary generation has often been described as a "band of brothers." Washington himself used the term many times to describe the officers of the Continental Army. This notion was not original with Washington, of course: it appears in Shakespeare's *Henry V*, and it was already a commonplace in American debates before the war.[2] But this notion of fraternity was more than just a metaphor. The eighteenth-century revolt against social and political patriarchy was an international movement that went far beyond the events of 1776; it was an aspect of the bourgeois revolution that heralded the emergence of a vibrant commercial society on the ashes of the Ancien Régime. In this time of sweeping change, a stable figure of authority was needed. Washington functioned as this transitional figure for Americans who needed to be weaned from a long-standing habit of childlike political dependency. He showed by his restrained and dignified example what a president should be and reconciled Americans to the idea of a strong executive at a time of nervous fears about the return of monarchical power.

A figure of immense prestige at home and abroad, Washington came to be called the father of his country within his own lifetime. The question is, what kind of father was he? For Americans didn't view Washington as a father in quite the same way that, as colonists, they had viewed the English king. Though his authority was certainly paternal, it was muted and restrained, not overbearing and imperious. His dramatic resignation as commander in chief, and his later resignation after two terms as president, were powerful symbolic gestures that set a high standard for political virtue in the young republic. They also demonstrated the role of a good republican father—one who sets high expectations for his sons, yet steps aside to let them run their own affairs.

How did Washington become this unique and indispensable figure in American life? How did he learn to project the enlightened paternalism that made so many young men want to emulate and please him? The answer lies not just in his mature constitutional thought but in his family background and upbringing. For it was here that he received his formative training, first as a fatherless young man dependent on the patronage of his elder brothers, then as a patron in his own right to a large extended family of nephews, cousins, stepchildren, and unrelated protégés. A closer look at these relationships suggests that despite the persistent appeals to political fatherhood, it was not really as a father but as a benevolent stepfather and uncle that Washington's influence was felt.

The Washingtons were part of the Cavalier exodus that came to Virginia in the 1640s and 1650s, establishing themselves through acquisition and marriage as minor members of the landed elite and holding positions in the House of Burgesses and the colonial militia. Augustine Washington, an active speculator in land who greatly increased the family's holdings, had three children by his first wife—Lawrence, Augustine, and Jane—and five children by his second, Mary Ball. The eldest of these was George Washington.

Dying unexpectedly in 1744, Augustine Washington left his oldest son his main estate at Hunting Creek (later called Mount Vernon), settled his younger son at Bridges Creek, and left his widow a small plantation called Ferry Farm, which she held in trust for George. This left eleven-year-old George in an anomalous position as the head of his own sibling group and a junior to his elder half brothers. Growing up among this "band of brothers," he learned early on to balance authority with deference—to be at the same time patron and protégé, ruler and ruled.

Ferry Farm was neither large nor fertile, and George was faced with the prospect of becoming a second-class Virginia planter, unlike his brothers, who had enough property to maintain a more baronial existence. He had been disadvantaged not only materially but intellectually as well. His brothers had been educated in England; George received a home schooling in rural Virginia. If he wished to escape the mediocre fate that his father's untimely death had prepared for him, he would have to rely on himself and whatever patronage he could obtain from his kin and connections.

His brothers married local heiresses and established their own households in the neighborhood, and George grew up in an extended family environment, traveling from one to another. George briefly took up residence with his brother Augustine (also called Austin), but it was Lawrence to whom he looked as a surrogate father, and at sixteen he moved in with Lawrence permanently. Lawrence had married Anne Fairfax, the eldest daughter of his neighbor, Col. William Fairfax. The families had long-standing ties back in England, and in Virginia they had adjoining properties and George often hunted in the countryside with the Fairfax men.[3] In addition to providing George with another surrogate household, Colonel Fairfax brought him to the attention of Lord Thomas Fairfax, the colonel's cousin and the owner of a vast unsettled territory in Virginia's Northern Neck. Having learned to use his father's old surveying tools, George attached himself to an expedition sent by Fairfax to survey his lands on the southern Potomac. Next, largely through Lawrence's influence, he succeeded in becoming surveyor of Culpeper County. This profession not only allowed him to participate in his brother's many speculations but to finance his own small purchases as well.

Lawrence's death in 1752 was a painful loss of a second father to the twenty-year-old George, who nonetheless managed to profit from it. Lawrence had been adjutant of the colony and George, extremely anxious to succeed to the office despite his lack of military experience, applied to Governor Dinwiddie. Through pressure from family friends, George succeeded in becoming one of four regional adjutants. When the French sent troops into Ohio, Major Washington volunteered for the dangerous task of carrying a message to the French demanding their withdrawal. His thorough report to Dinwiddie (and the further intercession of friends) led to a commission as lieutenant colonel.

Although Dinwiddie's fatherly feelings for the young man were clear, George had a very high opinion of his own worth and the two eventually fell out. No matter: he soon acquired a new patron in Gen. William Braddock, who had come to take command of British forces in North America during the French and Indian War. Braddock attached the young colonial officer to his staff and promised to help him obtain a royal commission. Unfortunately, Braddock was killed by the French, thus ending George's hopes of a brilliant career in the British army. But he acquitted himself well in the war and Dinwiddie made him commander of the Virginia regiment. His duties soon brought him into contact with Governor Shirley of Massachusetts, from whom George had hopes of further patronage. But the governor disappointed him by returning suddenly to England.

It is worth pondering the effect on young George of these early frustrations. "Time after time," one historian writes, "young Washington would make demands upon royally appointed father figures with disillusioning results."[4] Dinwiddie (mainly through his reluctance to pay colonial officers as much as their British counterparts) lost Washington's "confidence and respect." Braddock died in battle. Shirley left the country. These deaths and departures—like those of his father and brother—cheated young George of the recognition he felt he deserved. Like many younger sons of the lesser gentry, Washington had an inflated sense of self-worth and a festering resentment of the artificial barriers that seemed to block his rise.

When the war ended, Washington retired from military life and (at twenty-seven) entered the House of Burgesses, like both his older brothers. Once again, the aid and influence of Colonel Fairfax was indispensable, and Washington's marriage to a wealthy widow, Martha Dandridge Custis, established him securely in the front ranks of the Virginia aristocracy. Unfortunately, however, the couple could not have children. Instead, Washington turned his paternal attentions to John and Patsy Custis, and it was in this capacity of an adoptive parent that Washington rehearsed his great political role as father of his country.

Washington showed particular concern for Jacky Custis. The boy was affable and bright but also spoiled and somewhat lazy. After sending him to school, Washington corresponded with his teacher, fretting about his "indolence" and expressing an anxiety to make him "fit for... useful purposes." Jacky was not a brilliant student but he did his best to please his reserved and exacting stepfather, testifying on many occasions to the sincere regard and gratitude he felt for him.[5] He served Washington as an aide-de-camp during the war, and there is little doubt that had he lived, this beloved stepson would have played some role in national affairs. But the young man died of smallpox just as the war was ending.

Patsy Custis died unmarried in her teens, but Jacky had four children, in whom Washington took a keen interest. When Jacky's widow married a Virginia gentleman named David Stuart, George and Martha brought the two younger children to live at Mount Vernon. Washington often consulted Dr. Stuart in regard to their education and welfare. As president, he also appointed Stuart to the commission charged with laying out the new federal city, giving rise to whispers of nepotism. In addition, Washington had an abundance of nephews, nieces, and stepkin—all told, some fifty younger relatives under various family names—in whom he invested a great deal of time and effort. His nephew George Augustine served as an aide at Valley Forge and later married Martha's niece in a match arranged by Washington himself. Bushrod Washington, a Richmond lawyer who managed many of his uncle's affairs, inherited Mount Vernon. George also saw to the education and expenses of George Steptoe and Lawrence Washington, the sons of his deceased brother Sam, as he did with the fatherless children of his sister Betty Lewis, one of whom he employed as a secretary when he assumed the presidency. Despite his weighty preoccupations, Washington kept up a steady stream of correspondence with these young relatives, typically signing himself "your warm friend and affectionate uncle."

Martha's granddaughter Nelly married one of Washington's nephews, further strengthening the tie between their families. But the uncertain career of Nelly's brother, George Washington Parke Custis, would occupy his mind for many years. Great hopes were focused on young Custis, and his persistent mediocrity was a painful disappointment to his family. Though never formally adopted, he was Washington's acknowledged foster child and a long-standing object of nepotistic concern.

Washington showed a keen interest in maintaining his reputation for republican virtue; Brutus had sacrificed his sons to preserve the republic, and Washington strove to emulate this model. His letter of July 27, 1789, to Bushrod Washington is frequently cited as proof: "You cannot doubt my wishes to see you appointed to any office of honor or emolument in the new government," Washington wrote in response to his nephew's request for a judicial appointment, "but however deserving you may be of the one you have suggested . . . the eyes of Argus are upon me, and no slip will pass unnoticed that can be improved into a supposed partiality for friends or relatives."[6] Yet while Washington often protested that he would not use his influence on Custis's behalf, he later admitted that where he and nephew Lawrence Lewis were concerned, "Friendship have got the better of my Scruples."[7]

At fifteen Custis was enrolled at Princeton, but he was not much given to study. In 1798 the boy was transferred to St. John's College in Annapolis, but his performance was no better. When it appeared there might be war with France in 1799, Washington had Custis commissioned as a cornet of horse. (Despite his youth and inexperience, Custis was nominated by then president Adams and confirmed by a unanimous vote of the Senate.) Washington had him assigned to serve directly under Maj. Lawrence Lewis and outfitted the boy in full cavalry regalia, including saddle, spurs, a silver-handled sword and pistols, and a well-tailored uniform. Three months later, he wrote to the secretary of war to request a promotion.

> If ample fortune, good Education, more than common abilities, and good disposition, free from Vice of any kind, give him a title, in the 19th year of his age, his pretensions thereto (though not to the injury of another) are good. But it is not my desire to

> ask this as a favour. I never have, and never shall, solicit any thing for myself, or connexions.[8]

Washington's extreme sensitivity to any hint of impropriety leads him to make this disingenuous disclaimer. But the father of his country had made his wishes clear, and they were unhesitatingly obeyed. In the event, war against France was averted, frustrating Washington's hopes yet again. The old general died the same year.

It seems likely that had he showed the least spark of ambition or talent, Washington Custis would have been advanced to some position of real consequence. As it is, he inherited the Custis estate at Arlington and lived privately on his considerable wealth, pursuing his literary and artistic interests. He also gained fame as a speaker and appeared at political events as a stand-in for Washington, attending every presidential inauguration until his death in 1857. He married Mary Lee Fitzhugh of the Virginia Lees, and his daughter married a cousin on her mother's side, a promising young lieutenant named Robert E. Lee.

Though an ardent republican, Washington's habitual way of thinking about politics continued to reflect eighteenth-century assumptions, and his concerns about the future were often expressed in familial terms. The national disorder he witnessed under the Articles of Confederation put him in mind of the situation of his own family, "early deprived of a father." He further expressed apprehension that the new country, suddenly acquiring its liberty, would "like a young heir, come a little prematurely to a large inheritance . . . wanton and run riot until we have brought our reputation to the brink of ruin."[9] Washington carried this familial conception of politics into his role as the nation's first president. He envisioned himself very much as a national father, though one who must remain aloof and impartial from the wrangles of his sons.

Try as he might, however, Washington was not able to do so; his own principles inclined him to favor one "son" over others, splitting his cabinet and giving rise to the first opposition party in American history. So long as he lived, his immense personal authority imposed some restraint on the sons. After his death, the band of brothers quickly dissolved in fratricidal feuds. Ultimately, this conflict would be channeled and routinized in a system of dynamic opposition—in effect, a permanent civil feud—between contending national parties. Washington himself would have been horrified by this outcome, but it was the direct result of his own failure to sustain a familial notion of politics.

Before assuming office, Washington declared: "so far as I know my own heart, I would not be in the remotest degree influenced, in making nominations, by motives arising from the ties of amity or blood."[10] Yet he was quite willing to patronize other young men for the sake of such connections. In a letter to Thomas Nelson Jr.—the son of a former Virginia governor—the new president wrote: "The sincere regard I had for your very worthy, deceased father, induces me to offer you a place in my family."

It is no accident that Washington referred to his administrative staff as his family. The same term was applied to his close circle of military aides during the war. Though the expression was largely conventional, Washington undoubtedly saw himself as standing in loco parentis to the young men of his staff—sometimes writing to their fathers with avuncular pride to praise their courage and good deeds. Nor had he gone far outside his own social milieu in filling it. Nearly without exception, they came from the best American families, and over a third were Virginians with close ties to Washington's own. Many would play important roles in American life, and nearly all had strong feelings of filial attachment to Washington. They were a gallant group of boys, wild with patriotic fervor and admiration for their chief. Eager for glory, they went dashing around the battlefield with the general's dispatches, careless of risk and proud to have their horses shot from under them. They slept together like a pack of bloodhounds on the floor of whatever command post Washington was using and cheerfully braved the hardships of the war. Despite—or perhaps because of—his reserved and formal bearing, Washington had a way of bringing out the best in these young men, and they not only vied for his approval but fiercely defended his honor. John Laurens was particularly devoted to Washington and fought a duel with Charles Lee, who had disparaged him.

The most famous of these protégés—the closest thing to a real son and political heir Washington ever had—was Alexander Hamilton, whose energy and courage had been drawn to his attention after the battles of Trenton and Princeton. Hamilton, unlike most of Washington's other aides, had no family or birthright. He was the bastard son of an estranged and improvident father, born on the Caribbean island of Nevis and orphaned by the death of his mother. Apprenticed as a clerk to one Nicholas Cruger, a merchant of St. Croix, Hamilton rose swiftly through a combination of merit and enlightened patronage. Through his diligence and gifts, the young man came under the wing of the Reverend Hugh Knox, who in a joint project with Cruger sent him to New Jersey armed with introductions to Elias Boudinot and William Livingston. (The former was to become president of the Continental Congress, the latter the first governor of independent New Jersey.) Under their sponsorship, Hamilton was educated first in Elizabethtown and then at King's College (later Columbia) in New York. He played an active role during the defense of the city and was recommended for a commission by Livingston's son-in-law John Jay.

Hamilton's enemies would call him the American Bonaparte, and while the arc of his career was very different, the comparison is not that far afield—especially as viewed by contemporaries. Both were foreign-born citizens of their adoptive countries who came from small neglected islands to the south. Both started out as artillerymen; Hamilton achieved his first distinction as commander of the battery on Harlem Heights. Both had a firm conviction of their own genius and recognized no man as their superior. Both also used the turbulence of their times to climb rapidly from rung to rung—and from patron to patron—to the top of their societies, building a personal clique as they went. Unlike Napoleon, however, Hamilton had no family to build on, and his career makes even clearer the relative weakness and insecurity of the self-made man in a society based on patronage and nepotism. As a fatherless man and a foreigner, Hamilton lacked a ready-made web of family connections, and he was forced to rely on the ad hoc networks he constructed out of marriage ties and personal relationships. Most of his lifelong associates were men he met at college or on Washington's staff, and to his credit they were all intensely loyal. Hamilton had a gift for forming friendships that mingled affection and interest. This enforced reliance on networking and personal alliances also explains his success as the architect of the Federalist Party.

Washington came to depend heavily on the precocious Hamilton. The relationship was openly paternal, with Washington fondly calling him "my boy." It was a uniquely symbiotic bond, an almost perfect match between a fatherless son and a sonless father. But after four years of loyal service, Hamilton exchanged his place in Washington's artificial family for the more substantial one of Gen. Philip Schuyler, a wealthy New York businessman and politician whose daughter he had married. The Schuylers were linked by marriage to other Hudson valley clans, including the Livingstons, Van Rensselaers, and Jays, and Hamilton used these connections to make a place for himself in the front rank of New York politics, beginning in 1783 when he assumed Schuyler's vacated congressional seat.[11] In his budding legal practice he represented many of Schuyler's friends among the city's leading merchants while participating at a high level in the constitutional debates that formed the new national government—a debate in which his vision of a strong and energetic executive prevailed. In the ensuing ratification struggles, his father-in-law's connections were indispensable in marshaling public opinion against Governor Clinton and his friends, who preferred a weak federal government, the better to preserve their awesome powers of patronage. (Indeed, with 15,000 jobs at their disposal, the Clintons may be said to have created America's first patronage machine.)[12] In the end, of course, the Constitution passed, and in 1789 Washington and John Adams were chosen as the nation's first president and vice president.

Though Hamilton and Washington had fallen out during the war, their partnership was renewed when Washington enlisted Hamilton as Treasury secretary. Hamilton was the first cabinet officer appointed and the longest to serve, lasting almost the whole of both terms. During this time he completely dominated both domestic and foreign policy. So powerful did Hamilton's influence become that many felt Washington was simply a figurehead. This was not the case, however. Washington agreed with Hamilton's emphasis on creating a strong national government, but the issue was intensely controversial and he could not be seen to favor one side over the other. Thus, Hamilton took the heat as Washington's surrogate while Washington played the imposing man of marble.

Washington's cabinet was a model of geographic and political balance. His only partisan criterion had been to appoint no committed antifederalists. Hamilton (New York) had been the strongest proponent of federalism. Secretary of War Henry Knox (Massachusetts) was Hamilton's friend and ally. Secretary of State Thomas Jefferson (Virginia) had initially been a strong opponent of the Constitution but was reconciled on the promise that individual liberties would be protected by a bill of rights to be drafted by his friend James Madison. Edmund Randolph, also of Virginia—a cousin and ally of Jefferson's—was appointed attorney general.

From the outset, Washington's government was divided by the tension between Hamilton and Jefferson. Unlike Hamilton, who envisioned a great national state on the English model, Jefferson wished to preserve the small scale and agrarian base of classical republics like Athens and Rome. If Hamilton stood for commerce and industry, a strong central government, an aristocratic constitution, and a close relationship with England, Jefferson stood for agrarianism, a weak executive, radical democracy, and a fraternal alliance with France. Two more diametrically opposed visions of the American future could scarcely be found, and it is astonishing that Washington appointed them both to his cabinet. If anything, however, it was a testament to his faith in his own authority and to his familial conception of government. Washington had set himself the impossible task of remaining neutral in the struggles of his cabinet. He hoped to create an inclusive national government in which the contending regional and intellectual strains of American politics would be reconciled under his benign paternal leadership. This hope was doomed to disappointment. Competition and rivalry began immediately to strain the fabric of Washington's administrative family and ultimately ruptured it, in the process giving rise to America's first political parties.

Hamilton saw it as his duty not only to develop the nation's economic base but to preserve the constitution he had fought to frame and ratify. This meant uniting the federalist forces and attaching them securely to the new government by chains of interest and dependency. Artfully exploiting the eight-hundred-odd appointments under the Treasury's control, Hamilton built up support for the federalist cause throughout the former colonies, skillfully weaving a network of adherents out of his wartime associates, business connections, and friends, as well as those whom he was able to oblige by personal favors. He also created a potent propaganda wing, founding federalist newspapers in Boston, Philadelphia, and New York. In this way, Hamilton created the basis for local political organizations that could influence public opinion and elect federalist candidates to office.

Though Jefferson had been uncomfortable with some of Hamilton's early measures, he applauded his success in restoring the country's foreign credit and funding its massive debt. But he feared the creation of a monarchical power at the center of American life. A strong and wealthy government would become a fount of patronage that would corrupt the yeoman virtue on which liberty depended. The definitive break occurred with Hamilton's report to Congress of December 14, 1790, advocating the creation of a national bank. Since no such authority was enumerated in the Constitution, Hamilton relied on a doctrine of implied executive powers. The issue split the cabinet down the middle. When Washington assented to Hamilton's doctrine and signed the bill, he violated the Solomonic neutrality on which the harmony of his administration was based. But it was Hamilton's interference in foreign affairs—the area of Jefferson's responsibility—that set off their backstairs feud in earnest.

The great issue of the day was American neutrality in the conflict between England and France. Jefferson had long been a Francophile: like other Americans, he had hailed the French Revolution of 1789, but was weakened and increasingly isolated as it took a frightening turn toward violent anarchy. Hamilton favored a commercial alliance with England and called for abrogating the existing treaty with France on the grounds that it had been made with the previous government. Their vigorous debates over the status of the French treaty became the focal point for opposing congressional factions.

In 1791, Jefferson initiated a secret campaign against Hamilton on multiple fronts. Jefferson first sought to place his own men in Hamilton's department, but Hamilton blocked these maneuvers. Jefferson then asked Washington to transfer the post office from Hamilton's department to his own. Washington ignored this proposal. Yet he allowed Jefferson's State Department to continue its control of the mint despite Hamilton's plausible arguments that it properly belonged to the Treasury. The brothers might squabble and compete, but Washington would not allow them to put their hands in each other's pockets. Meanwhile, fretting over Hamilton's success at establishing a network of federalist newspapers, Jefferson took the unprecedented step of hiring a fiery republican newspaperman, Philip Freneau, as a clerk in his office. This post was merely a cover for his activities as an opposition journalist. Washington deeply resented Freneau's attacks but made no move to dismiss the offending employee. Meanwhile, Jefferson maintained an airy posture of detachment, affecting to have no control over the man.

When Freneau's newspaper ceased publication in late 1792, Jefferson's war against Hamilton entered a third and more direct phase. Through his lieutenants in the House, he initiated a series of resolutions against Hamilton in an attempt to force him out of the cabinet. (The resolutions were utterly frivolous and were soundly defeated.) He also proposed that the functions of the Treasury itself should be divided and assigned to different departments—a naked attempt to destroy Hamilton's base—and directly lobbied Washington in letters and private conversation, accusing Hamilton of aiming to establish a monarchy.

Despite the mounting antagonism between his two closest advisers, Washington remained aloof from their dispute—until it became public. Then he wrote to both in conciliatory tones, pleading that they compose their differences in a spirit of fraternal unity lest the delicate "machine of government" be pulled apart. Each man, replying to Washington's appeals, expressed his hardened opposition to the other. Washington, ever the patient father, persisted in his efforts, laboring to keep Jefferson in the government despite his repeated threats to resign. In the end, however, the pressures of incipient partisanship could not be contained within Washington's political family. On April 19, 1793, Washington issued his proclamation of neutrality—a defeat for Jefferson in his own field of foreign affairs. On July 31 Jefferson handed in his resignation and spent the next three years preparing to run for president at the head of the Republican Party.

JOHN ADAMS: REPUBLICAN DYNAST

Washington handed over the reins of government in 1797 to John Adams after a fractious campaign in which one of the more sensitive issues was that of dynastic ambition. Adams had a son and so might seek to found a dynasty, his enemies declared, while his opponent, Jefferson, had none. Adams was elected by a narrow margin and Jefferson became vice president. But the issue of dynastic ambition was a persistent and, as it happens, well-founded concern. It was the supreme irony of Adams's career that this hater of inherited privilege, this ardent proponent of an aristocracy of merit and careers open to talent, became the founder of the first and greatest American political dynasty.

John Adams's contributions to the creation of the American republic—moving the nation to revolt, helping to draft its Constitution, preserving it by skillful diplomacy, and leading it as president—are unrivaled by any individual of his generation. Yet what is even more remarkable, his descendants were equally talented. This sustained outburst of energy and brilliance in Adams's family over four generations, following four previous generations of bucolic mediocrity, has aroused much speculation. The dynasty's founder seems to have sprung like Athena from the head of Zeus, a total anomaly in terms of his family's history.

The Adamses themselves would ascribe John's phenomenal rise to a confluence of favorable bloodlines—his mother was a Boylston and his grandmother was a descendant of John Alden. We would probably be more inclined to explain it as an instance of pure meritocracy: a case of a man rising to the top through talent and industry. But while his genius is undeniable, genius without opportunity means nothing. Despite the impression that Adams came blazing out of nowhere like a comet, his ascent was really owed to a unique conjunction of forces, including his father's social ambition, the emergence of a new class of professional politicians, and the revolutionary turbulence of his times.

The mysterious spark of ambition in Adams's father was the ultimate cause of his family's rise. As Gore Vidal observes, in marrying Susanna Boylston, Adams's father—a moderately prosperous Massachusetts farmer—had committed *hypergamy,* "that obligatory act of all families destined to distinguish themselves."[13] As the oldest son, moreover, only John received a Harvard education—the golden passkey to the small, restricted society of colonial Boston. Adams may have wished to be regarded as a self-made man, but his debt to his family is clear. Not only did he owe his place at Harvard to his Boylston descent, his father "sacrificed heavily" to send him there. This is not to argue that Adams's success can be reduced to family influence; only that, whatever his personal qualities, the autonomy of the self-made man tends to be exaggerated, both by himself and later generations.

Adams's father expected him to become a clergyman and provincial village leader—a modest step above his own condition. But the self-willed Adams chose his own path and, after a brief period as a schoolteacher, entered legal practice. From the outset, Adams was keenly conscious of the difference between his status and his abilities. At Harvard, where he stood fourteenth in a class of twenty-four according to the practice of ranking students by social degrees, he stood in the top three academically. As a lawyer, he had constantly before him the example of royally appointed officers who owed their positions to patronage; the colonies were a notorious patronage dump, and the prevalence of negligent and incompetent officials was a sore point for many Americans. Hence, along with a burning conviction of his own ability, Adams felt a powerful resentment of aristocratic prejudice and artificial barriers to merit.

This was a conviction that he passed on to his sons, along with a number of other durable patterns, of which the most conspicuous was an extreme reluctance to put himself forward for office. "The office seeks the man" would be an Adams family motto for the next three generations. He also inherited the severe moralism of his Puritan forebears, and like all the Adamses to come he had a hard time squaring his ambition with his conscience. In him we see a secularized version of the theological doctrine of election—an outlook that expects rewards to flow from merit and resents all those whose privileges are not redeemed by proofs of their virtue and worth.

Yet even this dour critic of family privilege and nepotism understood the value of family connections: his marriage to Abigail Smith in 1764 was not only a love match between two spirited intellectual equals, it linked him to one of the most prominent families in Massachusetts. Abigail's father was a leading minister in Weymouth, and her mother (who thought the match unsuitable) was the daughter of John Quincy, speaker of the Massachusetts House and a descendant of a founder of the colony. As Vidal observes, in marrying above his station, like his father, Adams had committed "the obligatory act of hypergamy and his children were now related to *everyone* in Massachusetts."[14] The effect on his legal career was later remarked by his son John Quincy Adams in a biography of his father: "By this marriage, Mr. Adams became allied with a numerous connection of families, among the most respectable for their weight and influence in the province, and it was immediately perceptible in the considerable increase in his professional practice."[15] Soon his practice was the largest in the colony.

During these early years, spent in continual travel to provincial towns in search of cases, the penurious Adams maintained a steady correspondence with his wife, to whom he had entrusted the education of their sons, John Quincy, Charles, and Thomas. Despairing of his own success, he abjured her to make them self-reliant and exhorted her to mold their youthful characters for liberty and virtue. Following his cousin Samuel Adams into politics in the 1760s, Adams devoted increasing time and effort to the revolutionary cause—to the detriment, as he was keenly aware, of his family's fortunes.

> I believe my children will think I might as well have thought and labored a little, night and day, for their benefit. But I will not bear the reproaches of my children. I will tell them that I studied and labored to procure a free constitution of government for them to solace themselves under, and if they do not prefer this to ample fortune, to ease and elegance, they are not my children, and I care not what becomes of them. They shall

> live upon thin diet, wear mean clothes, and work hard with cheerful hearts and free spirits, or they may be the children of the earth, or of no one, for me.[16]

Adams here declares his independence not just from his political father, King George, but from his children as well. His dedication is entirely to the happiness of his country; he owes nothing more than this to his descendants. This determined subjection of private interest to the public good would be a powerful family legacy. His sons' adherence to this code, he had no doubt, would raise them to the leadership of their country. If they failed, it would be their own fault.[17]

Adams's constant harping on this theme sometimes seems a complicated way of rationalizing his own deep-seated familistic impulses. From the beginning, Adams evinced the peculiar confusion between his country and his family that has afflicted public men in modern times. Early in his career he wrote, "What is the end and purpose of my studies, journeys, labors? . . . Am I planning the illustration of my family or the welfare of my country?" Adams posits this as an either-or proposition, but the real answer was yes to both questions. It is important to an understanding of Adams's originality to grasp the way in which he sublimated nepotistic urges in a sense of republican duty.

Biographers have not neglected the contribution of Abigail Adams to the success of her husband and son. Without her at home to mind the farm and raise the children, Adams could not have played so prominent a role in the country's founding drama, and she participated through him in the great events of the day. She fully endorsed Adams's project of raising a brood of young statesmen and heroes, and strove to prepare them for the burdens of leadership that she and John believed would be the family vocation. So well had John Quincy advanced that in 1778, when Adams went to France as a diplomat, he took the eleven-year-old boy as his secretary. Thus began the career of a future American diplomat, secretary of state, and president; it also established a pattern of familial apprenticeship that later generations would repeat.

John Quincy remained in Europe for several years and was educated at private schools in France and Holland. In 1783 the fourteen-year-old boy went to Russia as secretary to the American legate, Francis

Dana, and in 1784 and 1785 he was secretary to the American peace delegations in the Hague and Paris. After the war, the father went to England as American ambassador, taking John Quincy as his secretary. After this thorough seasoning in world affairs the young man went to Harvard where he completed the classical course in eighteen months. He then took to the law like his father and opened a practice in Boston, but there was little to do there and he mainly diverted himself by writing a series of pseudonymous articles defending Washington's policy of neutrality. The articles continued his father's public arguments on the same theme and were noticed appreciatively by Washington. Their precocious brilliance led some to speculate that their author was Adams himself.

In 1794, Washington appointed the twenty-seven-year-old John Quincy ambassador to Holland. In a letter to Abigail, the proud father once more expressed his tendency to identify the public interest with that of his own family: "All my hopes are in him, both for my family and my country." Still, Washington had his work cut out convincing both father and son of the appointment's propriety. John Quincy's reluctance clearly stemmed from a well-founded suspicion that his father had arranged the appointment. (The son confided to his diary: "I have indeed long known that my father is far more ambitious for my advancement . . . than I ever have been or shall be.") As for the father, Washington wrote to him in reassuring tones: "I shall be much mistaken if, in as short a period as can well be expected, he is not found at the head of the diplomatic corps."[18] Adams had the pleasure of presiding over the unanimous Senate vote confirming his son's appointment, and John Quincy went to Holland, bringing along his brother Thomas as secretary.

By 1796 Adams had spent eight years languishing as vice president. On his accession to the presidency, his pent-up ambition and pride were released. This role was his, Adams believed, by virtue of merit alone, and he determined to be uninfluenced by base motives of partisanship. He therefore decided to keep Washington's cabinet and the majority of other officers appointed by his predecessor. This principled refusal to engage in partisan behavior—another Adams family legacy—would prove his undoing as president.

Like Washington and Jefferson, Adams thought that government should be administered by the best men available. Unlike them, however, he did not think that fitness and social status could be separated. Of decisive significance was the training received in the family, since, as Adams wrote, "in all countries it has been observed that vices as well as virtues very often run down in families from age to age."[19] Adams also supported the idea of lifetime tenure and even thought that certain offices might be hereditary.

While in office, Adams largely resisted the temptation to nepotism—indeed he appears to have felt none. There was, however, an immediate question of what to do about his son who was already in government service. The father's inclination was to continue John Quincy's appointment, but he was conscious of the delicacy of doing so. John Quincy opposed the idea, writing to his mother that he had no wish to be viewed as a man who owed his position to family influence. Like his father, he wished to be rewarded on his merits; he also wanted those merits to be rewarded spontaneously, without his having to lobby for it. Both of them wished to be "elected" in the higher sense. The father turned to Washington for counsel, and in a kind and courtly letter the young man's patron overrode his reservations:

> If my wishes would be of any avail they should go to you in a strong hope that you will not withhold merited promotion from Mr. John Adams because he is your son. For without intending to compliment the father or mother or to censure any others, I give it as my decided opinion that Mr. Adams is the most valuable public character we have abroad—and that he will prove himself to be the ablest of all our Diplomatic Corps.[20]

Note that Washington feels compelled to praise John Quincy as not just deserving of promotion but as the most able American diplomat, period. Only this egregious assessment, persuading Adams that he will actually harm the country by his over-delicate reluctance, can reconcile him to the prospect of advancing his son. This elaborate minuet was necessary to ease Adams's conscience, allowing him to translate his paternal inclination into a patriotic duty without feeling he was being hypocritical. Adams made his son ambassador to Prussia, writing to the reluctant John Quincy, with an audible huff, "Merit in my family deserves as much of its Country as in another." Thus Washington intervened a second time in John Quincy's career, performing a role that the father was too principled to fill. He also established a pattern of indirect or surrogate nepotism that later politicians would imitate by employing or advancing one another's children, wives, and other kin.

Abigail did not share her husband's squeamishness about nepotism; to the contrary, she plainly considered it her duty not just to oversee her children's education and marriages but to press the family's interests with the president. In this, she is the forerunner of all dynastic mothers in the tradition of republican familism. When John Quincy married Louisa Johnson, the daughter of the American consul in London, Abigail added the bride's family to what biographer Paul Nagel calls her "expanding maternal empire." When Louisa's father went bankrupt, Adams made him director of stamps. A bankrupt nephew, William Cranch, likewise turned to her for help and was made an assistant judge in the District of Columbia. (Cranch turned out to be an eminent jurist, ending up as chief judge of the U.S. Circuit Court.) Her brother-in-law Richard Cranch was also made postmaster in Adams's hometown of Quincy. But the most flagrant case of nepotism in Adams's administration was undoubtedly that of his son-in-law, William Stephens Smith.

Col. Smith had been an aide-de-camp to Washington and seemed to have a fine career ahead of him. After the war he was sent to London as Adams's secretary. There he met and courted Adams's daughter Abigail, called Nabby by her family. The mother was thoroughly charmed, and the couple married in 1786. (Later, Nabby's brother Charles married Stephens's sister Sally.) After the birth of a son, Smith brought his small family back to New York, where he engaged in dubious land speculations. When Adams became vice president, Smith asked him to have Washington make him ambassador to London. Adams was "appalled" but Abigail was clearly annoyed by Washington's slowness to help his erstwhile protégé. Washington did get Smith a series of appointments, most likely at Adams's urging. When Adams became president he made

Smith colonel of a regiment, but the young man continued to petition his father-in-law for promotion.

Adams had by now decided that his son-in-law was a profligate cur whose shady speculations only managed to lose money for his relatives. He and Abigail pressed Nabby to leave her husband and rejoin the family circle. Nonetheless in 1798, when Washington was asked to come out of retirement and raise an army against France, the two worked hand in glove to promote his interests. Washington proposed Smith for the office of adjutant general; Adams submitted the nomination over two other men who had precedence. One of his own cabinet officers, Secretary of State Timothy Pickering, went in person to the Senate to derail the nomination. Smith was the only candidate rejected, and Adams was deeply chagrined.[21] Shortly afterward, Smith was again proposed for an appointment in the provisional army. This time the Senate confirmed it. Yet Smith continued to cause trouble for Adams by meddling in army affairs.

Prior to leaving office, Adams contrived to make Smith a customs agent for New York. But in 1805 Adams would be embarrassed by his son-in-law's involvement in a disreputable scheme to liberate Venezuela from Spain. A filibustering vessel was illegally launched from New York under the command of a comrade of Smith's; also on board was Smith's oldest son, Billy. The ship was intercepted by the Spanish and the ex-president's grandson narrowly escaped hanging. As a result, Colonel Smith was removed from his post and thrown in jail. When he died in 1816 his debts amounted to a staggering $200,000. Adams later wrote that Smith "did more injury to me in my administration than any other man."[22] This is surely a gross overstatement, however: his worst enemy as president was undoubtedly himself.

From the outset, Adams regarded Hamilton as the man most likely to challenge him for the Federalist nomination in 1800. At the very least, he would need Hamilton's support to defeat Jefferson. Yet Adams seemingly did everything he could to undermine himself, commencing a struggle with Hamilton that would destroy his reelection campaign and send him home after a single term into a long and embittered retirement. The vicious personal attacks they exchanged split the Federalists and threw the election to Jefferson. The humiliated Adams went into retirement blaming Hamilton for his defeat and for the rest of his life continued to speak of him as an inhuman monster. Before resigning office, Adams recalled his son from Berlin, presumably to spare him the embarrassment of being dismissed by Jefferson. John Quincy returned to Massachusetts, where in 1802 he was elected to the state legislature and went from there to the U.S. Senate. The father's eclipse was paralleled by the rise of the son, and the old man lived to see him elected president in 1824.

The brilliance of this dynasty has tended to obscure the many sacrifices required of its members. But the nepotism of the Adams family was peculiarly inward and self-devouring, almost cannibalistic, and for every success there were two or three failures that no one talked about.

Despite Adams's insistence that his sons should become independent as soon as possible, he paid them a quarterly allowance to keep them near at hand and under parental control. Clearly he had no intention of allowing them to chart their own destinies. Though John Quincy glumly accepted his fate, the Adams family was an intense pressure cooker from which his younger brothers longed to escape. But this was not to be.

Charles Adams attended Harvard, where he acquired a reputation for licentiousness. Concerned for his stability, his parents brought him to New York, where they could keep an eye on him. He took to the law and in 1795 he married his sister-in-law Sally Smith and had two children. But the signs of his unhappiness were clear and his brief, unhappy career is a tale of swift decline. By 1800 he had drunk himself to death. Biographer Paul Nagel concludes that "the price of being an Adams" was too high: Charles's rebellion "turned a promising legal career into rubble in less than a decade." In the process, he had made himself the symbol of all those weaknesses the family most feared. The result was complete disavowal. As Charles lay dying, his father the president refused to see him. Comparing himself to King David, he wrote that at least the rebellious Absalom had "some ambition and some enterprise." "Mine is a mere rake, buck, blood, and beast... I renounce him."[23] He was denied burial in the family crypt, and the Adamses never spoke of him again.

Thomas Boylston Adams, the youngest of the family, fared somewhat better. Graduating from Harvard in 1790, he was admitted to the Massachusetts bar. According to Nagel, "his search for identity also became a painful tale of struggle against parental domination." He briefly escaped by accepting John Quincy's invitation of a diplomatic post in Holland, then followed his brother to Berlin. After his father's election as president, he was offered the post of private secretary, but Thomas chose to practice law in Philadelphia, writing, "whatever pain it may cost me I must necessarily isolate myself from my family."[24] After Adams's retirement, Thomas's dependence on his family increased and his self-esteem plummeted. At last he returned to Massachusetts. In 1805 his father and brother arranged his election to the state legislature, but he withdrew within a year due to some unpublished scandal—probably drunkenness. He subsided into quiet self-loathing and ended up as judge of a state court.

In his long retirement John Adams had ample time to reflect on his children's unhappiness; yet he reached a surprising conclusion. One day his ten-year-old grandson, Charles Francis Adams, went upstairs as usual to read to him and recorded these notes in his diary:

> He laments the fate which has thrown so much gloom over our house, [but] something was necessary to check our pride and we have suffered bitterly. We should have been crushed, had the Sons all been distinguished, but now while the World respects us, it at the same [time] pities our misfortune and this pity destroys the envy which would other-wise arise.

Amazingly, Adams rationalized the failure of his younger sons in light of their brother's success: their destruction was a necessary sop to public envy. They thus fulfilled their duty to the family, and Adams could justify their sacrifice in the greater nepotistic scheme. ("The failed sons were fodder for pursuing wolves," observes historian David F. Musto, "allowing John Quincy to escape.")[25] John Quincy himself was the most reluctant and ambivalent heir in American history. Nevertheless, the demon of family pride was strong in him: he passed the Adams legacy on to his own sons, and it was potent enough to mold a generation after that.

THOMAS JEFFERSON: AMERICAN MENTOR

In the family romance of the American founding, Jefferson was an in-between figure. A half generation older than Young Turks like Hamilton and Madison, he was a half generation younger than the patriarchs Washington and Adams. In 1789, when they assumed office, Washington and Adams were respectively fifty-seven and fifty-four; among the younger leaders, Madison was thirty-eight, Hamilton thirty-four, and his chief spokesmen in the Senate and House, Rufus King and Fisher Ames, were in their early thirties. Jefferson was forty-six. He had been among the youngest of the revolutionary leaders in 1776, drafting the Declaration at the age of thirty-three. Now, as a seasoned paterfamilias in his own right, he was an accessible elder brother to the rising generation.

This status was reflected in his attitudes. He looked up to and revered Washington, but did not stand in awe of him; he respected Adams greatly but did not hesitate to oppose him; likewise he played the role of mentor and adviser to his juniors but did not feel entitled to their deference. In his relations with his colleagues he consistently sought harmony and cooperation. He was adept at seeing both sides of every question. He acknowledged the validity of competing interests but appealed to reason and friendship in finding grounds for compromise. He was in many ways the model of a democratic leader in the new fraternal mold.

Yet Jefferson was also—perhaps most famously—a man of contradictions. He mocked the aristocratic pretensions of his mother's family but instructed his London agent to buy title to the Jefferson coat of arms, which he used to adorn Monticello. He was morally opposed to slavery, yet continued to own slaves and had a Negro concubine. Considered the most idealistic of the founders, this otherworldly man who preferred farming and philosophy to politics was fully capable of engaging in deception, character assassination, and backstairs machinations. A public supporter of the Constitution and a strong national government, he privately encouraged his surrogates to oppose both. A man who abhorred party and faction, he built the first opposition party in American history, and as president introduced the partisan practice of removing ideological opponents from office. Not surprisingly, these contradictions were reflected in his attitude toward nepotism. Publicly Jefferson condemned nepotism and slighted his own relatives as president; yet he went out of his way to do favors for his friends and *their* families, and he pressed the interests of his favorite protégé beyond all reason or discretion.

Jefferson was another founding father who married well and so gained entry to the colonial elite. In this, he imitated his father and several generations of Jefferson men. The first Thomas Jefferson married a Branch, from one of the colony's first families, but the family's most important connection was with the Randolphs. The families had been neighbors, friends, and relatives since their founders came to Virginia in the seventeenth century. Peter Jefferson continued this tradition when he wedded Jane Randolph, daughter of the richest planter in Virginia and the cousin of his neighbor, friend, and partner William Randolph. When William died he made the unusual request that Peter move into his house and raise his children. Peter's son Thomas, the future president, was two. Twelve years later Peter died, leaving Thomas, at fourteen, the nominal head of a large compound family. He immediately assumed his father's responsibilities, including his offices of justice of the peace and parish vestryman, which appear to have been hereditary. Fortunately the family was well provided: the girls all had dowries, and Jefferson's personal inheritance amounted to over five thousand acres and thirty slaves. He later wrote that from an early age he had been thrown entirely upon his own resources, but this, as one biographer dryly observes, "was untrue both in substance and detail." His father had not only left him well off but insisted on providing him with the best education colonial Virginia could afford.

Jefferson read law under the eminent George Wythe and won election to the House of Burgesses, where many friends and kinsmen also sat. He then married an attractive widow named Martha Wayles Skelton, more than doubling the size of his estate. The couple had six children, only two of whom survived. The eldest, Martha Washington Jefferson, attended her father at the Continental Congress and accompanied him to France. After her mother's death, in 1782, she became the female head of his household, and when he became president she played the role of official hostess; her husband (and cousin), Thomas Mann Randolph Jr., served in Congress and was later governor of Virginia. Polly Jefferson was born in 1778. Her marriage to her cousin John Wayles Eppes strengthened the ties between her parents' families. Her husband also went to Congress. The combined economic and social strength of the Randolph-Wayles-Jefferson clan represented a substantial power in Virginia.

Jefferson's only son died in 1777 after seventeen days of life, and it may well be true that, lacking a male heir, he was not prone to dynastic ambition. Nevertheless, like other rich men of his station, he was the head of a large plantation family that included not only relatives but workmen, slaves, and various youthful protégés. The lack of a son undoubtedly inspired his activities as a mentor to numerous young men, beginning with those of his own family. His sister Jane had married his good friend Dabney Carr; after Carr's untimely death he brought her to Monticello and became her children's guardian, taking a particular interest in the brightest of them, Peter Carr. Edmund Randolph, a younger cousin on his mother's side, also became a disciple; later they would serve together in Washington's cabinet. But his intimate circle also included many unrelated men, such as James Monroe, a former legal student of Jefferson who became his unofficial spokesman in the constitutional debates.

Jefferson was famously convivial and his comfortable and well-appointed house in Paris, when he lived there as American ambassador, attracted a series of well-born young men who flocked to Europe in those years. To all, Jefferson gave help, advice, instruction, and encouragement. Two became his sons-in-law. Another was the son of a friend from Congress, to whom Jefferson wrote: "Whenever you choose to send him, I am here, and if you think proper to accept my services towards him, they shall be bestowed with the same zeal as if he were my own son."[26] Another young man on whom Jefferson made a lasting impression was John Quincy Adams. During his years abroad Jefferson became quite friendly with the Adamses; he and Abigail corresponded intimately for years. (At one point she jokingly proposed an exchange of children, remarking, "I am for strengthening [our] federal union.") John Quincy spent a great deal of time in Jefferson's company, and years later Adams wrote to Jefferson to share his pride in John Quincy's rise: "I call him our John because, when you were in the cul-de-sac at Paris, he appeared to me to be almost as much your boy as mine."

Of all these protégés, however, Jefferson's undoubted favorite was William Short, the scion of a wealthy Virginia family and a cousin of his good friend Thomas Bolling Robertson. Their relationship was close from the beginning. In 1779, when the younger man was twenty, Jefferson wrote, "Short has put himself under my guidance... he is to me as an adopted son." Under his sponsorship Short was elected to the House of Burgesses in 1783 and became a member of the Executive Council. In 1784 Jefferson had him sent to Congress. Short was also a friend of James Monroe and at Jefferson's urging both bought land near Monticello. In 1785, when he went to Paris as ambassador, Jefferson took Short along as his secretary and sent him on a tour of the continent to complete his education.[27] When the delegation's official secretary returned to the States, Jefferson put Short in his place.

In 1789, Jefferson agreed to become secretary of state. This raised the question of who would get his post in France. Short wanted the job, and Jefferson, according to Nathan Schachner, "exerted all his influence in favor of his 'son.'" His efforts failed, however: "Washington and Congress did not view this inexperienced and untried young man with the fond eyes of a Jefferson."[28] Thus began a long history of frustrated attempts to advance Short's diplomatic career.

Even while Jefferson was in Washington's cabinet he had been indirectly involved in the development of an organized "republican" opposition. The election of 1792 brought considerable gains for the republicans, and in the midterm elections of 1794 they achieved a majority in the House.

Jefferson was able to mount a credible challenge to Adams in 1796 and succeeded in becoming vice president.

The federalists were often accused of harboring aristocratic sentiments; and they were in fact a party based on local commercial elites whom Hamilton had tied to the national government by chains of economic interest and patronage. Regional groups like the so-called Essex Junto of Massachusetts—a nexus of mercantile clans united by business, political, and family interests—were viewed with justified suspicion, and the federalists were indeed a narrow party largely defined by ties of kinship and affinity.[29] The republicans are generally seen as broadening popular participation in politics, but the Republican Party was also based largely on family factions, and its leadership came from the same elite stratum. Virginia men composed the antifederalist core and the party drew its greatest strength from the Tidewater families with whom Jefferson was connected by long-standing personal ties. In Pennsylvania, an important base of strength would be the family and friends of Benjamin Franklin, whom the federalists had slighted for patronage.

The party struggle in New York was particularly important, since it was the base of Hamilton's power in national affairs. Hamilton's problems there had begun while he was still in Washington's cabinet, and reflected the continuing importance of family ties in both local and national politics. In the ratification debates of 1788, he had enjoyed the support of the powerful Livingston family against the antifederalist Clintons and their allies. In 1789 Hamilton engineered his father-in-law's election to the Senate, but in the contest for the junior seat he made the mistake of sidelining a Livingston in-law in favor of his ally Rufus King. When Schuyler came up for a second term, the little-known Aaron Burr, supported by the Livingstons and Clintons, was elected in his place.

Burr was a new type in American politics. A brilliant organizer, moving freely between the various family factions but belonging to none of them, he was the first professional politician in American history. Jefferson distrusted Burr but recognized the need for his support; accordingly he offered Burr the vice presidential nomination. In the election of 1800, Hamilton was completely outfoxed by Burr; Washington's death in 1798 had deprived him of his most powerful patron, and his political humiliation was completed in 1801 when his brother-in-law Steven van Rensselaer failed to become governor in a contest with George Clinton. His bitter rivalry with Burr culminated in 1804 in a duel on the heights of New Jersey that brought an end to the career of the American Bonaparte.

Jefferson, meanwhile, came to the presidency in 1801 determined to undo all that the federalists had done. It was to be a second revolution.

Adams had been successfully turned by Jefferson into a symbol of aristocracy and monarchy, and in fact he was much more conservative than Jefferson and more inclined to respect the hereditary principle in government. According to historian Sidney Aronson, the Adams administration exceeded both Washington's and Jefferson's in the prevalence of family ties: over a third of his appointees were related to other members.[30] Evidently, while nepotism was repugnant to the aristocratic Washington and Jefferson, it was quite tolerable to the middle class Adams, the only founder who accepted the idea of inevitable social inequality.

In his inaugural address, Jefferson struck a familial note, famously declaring, "We are all Republicans, we are all Federalists." His approach to government was "tactful but firm" in the words of one historian, "as though he was the amiable *paterfamilias* of a united clan."[31] Nevertheless he adhered to a strict partisan standard in appointments, though after installing his lieutenants in the cabinet he left them to run their departments without interference. He worked mainly through Treasury secretary Albert Gallatin in legislative matters but maintained close connections with many congressional figures in what one historian calls "the extended Republican family."

Jefferson's appointment philosophy was more egalitarian than Adams's, and he is generally seen as the first and greatest exponent of meritocracy. He made it clear that he was strongly opposed to nepotism, on the grounds that the public would never believe that a president's relative was qualified. Nevertheless, Jefferson knew that this position would be unpopular with his own family and could even be regarded as unreasonable. When his kinsman George Jefferson declined to pursue an office for which his friends had recommended him, Jefferson wrote him a letter of thanks. "It is true that this places the relations of the President in a worse situation than if he were a stranger," Jefferson added, "but the public good . . . requires this sacrifice."[32]

Jefferson agreed with Adams on the desirability of a society governed by the best and most qualified men. He also agreed that the people at large were not a likely source of leadership, since the accident of birth had deprived them of the means of education. Jefferson therefore proposed a complex system that would identify the best and brightest from among the common people—"raked from the rubbish annually"—and train them to exercise the responsibilities of government. But no such class of educated commoners existed or would exist for many generations, and in the meantime, Jefferson insisted on appointing only men who had attended college. Thus, despite his emphasis on equal opportunity and merit, Jefferson was forced to rely on members of the upper class. Nor did he think it contradictory to weigh a man's family background in assessing his qualifications. Like Washington and Adams, he thought that men acquired habits of virtue or vice within their families, and that a great deal could be told about a man by asking who his father was.

While nominally less nepotistic than that of the federalists, Jefferson's administration also rested on familial supports. His cousin, the brilliant but erratic John Randolph, became Jefferson's floor leader in the House: he headed the crucial Ways and Means Committee and became chairman of so many others that he could scarcely attend all their meetings. Randolph's uncle Thomas Tucker Tudor, member of a prominent South Carolina political dynasty, succeeded Gallatin as Treasury secretary, a post he held until his death in 1828. Overall, however, where Adams's administration was characterized by several powerful connections—including that of Adams himself, that of the Greenleaf family, and the groups around Elias Boudinot, John Marshall, and Oliver Wolcott—Jefferson's had fewer such links. Those that did exist included the kin-based clusters around Jefferson, Aaron Burr, and Robert Livingston.

These nepotistic clusters constitute the "deep grammar" of early American government.[33]

No problem in domestic affairs took more of Jefferson's time or caused him more trouble than that of patronage. The "gift of office," he wrote, was the "dreadful burden" that oppresses every chief executive. His use of it was sparing but effective. Though it is generally assumed that he removed only a few men from office, of the 316 appointments he controlled, only a third were still held by Federalists two years into Jefferson's first term. Jefferson was wary of patronage for its potential to divide his supporters, but he understood its utility as a means of cementing his party. He was therefore quite willing to use it as a reward for political loyalty.

Jefferson particularly owed his election to the timely intervention of two families: the Muhlenbergs of Pennsylvania and the Livingstons of New York. Founders of the American Lutheran Church, the Muhlenbergs were an ecclesiastical dynasty who also became the leaders of the large German population that had settled in the Delaware valley. Adams himself blamed his defeat on Peter and Frederick Muhlenberg—"those two Germans"—who had swung the German vote to the republicans. Both were rewarded with patronage. (Peter became a U.S. senator but resigned to assume the lucrative post of revenue supervisor for his state; Frederick was made receiver general of the Pennsylvania land office.) Jefferson also rewarded the Livingstons for their aid in deciding the postelection outcome. When the general election produced a tie between Jefferson and Burr, it was thrown into the House of Representatives. Edward Livingston, a New Yorker who had been expected to support Burr, threw his influence behind Jefferson. Three Livingston men and four Livingston in-laws received federal, state, and local appointments.[34]

Although Jefferson's conduct in regard to his relatives was more stringent than Adams's, he was remarkably indulgent of other people's requests for family patronage. Thus the navy went to Robert Smith, brother of the republican party leader in Maryland. Nor did he draw the line at creating an incipient Burr dynasty in the newly acquired Louisiana Territory: not only did Burr's uncle become a judge, his father-in-law became governor, his brother-in-law become territorial secretary, and his stepson became judge of the principal court in New Orleans. Neither was personal friendship a bar to advancement in Jefferson's mind. To the contrary, as secretary of state, Jefferson had ardently wished he might oblige the many friends who applied to him for places. When he later appointed Thomas Bolling Robertson to a post in New Orleans, he hesitated not because of their close friendship but because he thought the salary too low. Jefferson also reinstated his friend Joseph Whipple as collector of Portsmouth and gave jobs to his friends John Page and Philip Reibelt.[35]

Jefferson's administration has the distinction, as compared with those of Washington and Adams, of having the fewest number of nepotistic ties. But the ensuing stable years of republican government resulted in a growing number of long-lived ministerial families. Elias Boudinot's successor at the mint left his position to his son-in-law, while the family of Joseph Nourse inhabited the Treasury from Washington to Andrew Jackson—it was one of Jackson's wittier campaign promises to "clean out the Noursery."[36] Another official family, long associated with the Nourses, were the sons of Robert Brent, a prominent republican. These patterns were also common among customs collectors and district attorneys.

If history has not heard of William Short, it is not for want of trying on Jefferson's part. As soon as he assumed his duties as secretary of state, he had proposed Short as his replacement in Paris, but Hamilton's friend Gouverneur Morris got the job. Short's reaction was explosive, and Nathan Schachner writes that an anxious Jefferson "sought to soothe his angry 'son.' "[37] Short kept up a stream of angry letters, to which Jefferson responded with rather weak and ineffectual assurances. He did persuade Washington to make Short chargé d'affaires in Paris pending Morris's arrival, but Short continued to prod his embarrassed mentor for a full ministerial brief. Jefferson pleaded for patience: "To overdo a thing with him [Washington] is to undo it. I am steering the best I can for you." Finally, in 1792, Short was appointed minister to Holland, in which post he continued after his mentor's resignation; indeed, Hamilton trusted him as the government's chief financial agent abroad. Eventually he returned to the United States, and in 1809, at the end of his second term, Jefferson tried to make him minister to Russia. Short sailed to France, there to await word of his confirmation. Jefferson's nomination of Short was his last official communication with the Senate. That body, however, rejected the nomination, not for lack of qualifications—Short was considered one of the abler American diplomats of this period—but because it was thought unnecessary to establish such a mission in that country.

Jefferson's administration ended on a nepotistic note that not only belied his aversion to favoritism but revealed how tenacious was the view of public office as a form of family property. His boyhood friend John Page had been made commissioner of loans for Virginia, but was now mortally ill. Jefferson therefore made what Schachner calls the "astonishing" proposal that the office be transferred to Page's son, "with an understanding," as Jefferson put it, "that it should afterwards continue with him for the *benefit of the family.*" Page was deeply grateful, but the son raised unexpected difficulties. Another friend, Thomas Taylor, proposed that the office be assigned to him so that he might funnel the income to Page's family. But Taylor was a federalist and could not be appointed by Jefferson. Instead, Jefferson fixed on the young Benjamin Harrison, a sound republican, who would hold the office in name while Taylor did the work. But an opposition newspaper published a report of the arrangement, and the Senate declined to confirm it despite Jefferson's private appeals to a number of senators. Even so he continued to press Page's interest, going so far as to ask his successor, James Madison, to resubmit the nomination. But Madison, despite their friendship, "prudently declined to commence his administration with such a shady transaction."[38]

It is sometimes said in mitigation of the founders' hypocritical acceptance of slavery that they were men of their times, and could therefore oppose the institution on moral grounds without feeling any particular urgency about ending it. The same applies to their hypocrisy surrounding the issue of nepotism. While they recognized the impropriety of family appointments, they could be remarkably inconsistent on this score.

The founding period was one in which the American attitude toward nepotism took shape as something deeply confused and conflicted. The figures we have examined reflect some fundamental aspects of that conflict. George Washington effected the transition from patriarchal domination to enlightened paternalism in American political culture. He intuitively grasped the need for a strong central government that would act as an impartial referee in national affairs, and was himself a conscious model for this kind of benign paternal leadership. But he remained (like Franklin) very much a man of the eighteenth century and could not easily change his modes of thought and action: time and again, his nepotistic instincts got the better of him. Nor could Americans in general do without a political father, and for a long time, particularly at moments of national crisis, they chose to invest a leader with supreme paternal authority. Indeed, the greatest leaders in American history have been those who not only guided the country through periods of painful transition but offered new models of fatherhood for a rapidly changing society.

The case of Hamilton suggests the opportunities and dangers of a society in which men would no longer strive for favors from above but openly compete with one another for wealth and power. Not for nothing did Hamilton terrify his revolutionary brothers Adams and Jefferson: he was the harbinger of a future in which the liberated ambition and energy of upwardly mobile men would continually remake and overturn the social order. Though compared in his lifetime to Bonaparte, he also had something in common with that other bastard upstart, Cesare Borgia. Both were social outsiders without established families, dependent on a powerful sponsor, and very much in a hurry. Bold and brilliant strategists and energetic improvisers, they flourished so long as their powerful patrons remained to protect them, and in both cases the untimely death of their "father" led to the swift collapse of their careers.

More than any other founder, John Adams struggled with the tension between public duty and family ambition. The Adams family as a whole wonderfully illustrates the ambivalence surrounding nepotism in American politics. Only by sublimating their intense family pride in a puritanical notion of merit could the Adamses square their bottomless ambition with their stern egalitarian creed. Later generations would be tortured by this conflict, but it is really from the Adamses that we inherit the idea of a public service dynasty. Where other societies keep their aristocrats segregated in vestigial institutions like the House of Lords, many of ours have become national leaders at the head of great progressive movements. Political dynasticism has thereby been rendered largely inoffensive in America. The Roosevelts achieved this feat in the first half of the twentieth century, and the Kennedys and Bushes continued the tradition in the second.

Thomas Jefferson embodied both the new fraternal style of political leadership and the tradition of genteel hypocrisy that has allowed nepotism to flourish in America while being denounced at every turn. It was entirely consistent with his character to have acted in a partisan and nepotistic spirit while insisting to the world—and to himself—that he was far above such pettiness. This tradition of high-minded hypocrisy is only one of Jefferson's gifts to posterity. The other is his invention of the surrogate role of the mentor. Mentoring—a popular modern buzzword—is nothing other than a refraction of the father's classical role as a master and teacher. Now that most fathers no longer teach their sons a trade, the scope of paternal nepotism has greatly diminished. As a result, modern sons and daughters now need more fathers than ever. We call these social fathers mentors and we praise their contribution to the lives of young people seeking guidance and instruction.

From one point of view, the replacement of biological fathers with mentors seems to represent a transcendence of biology and a victory over the family. It may also reflect the transformation of nepotism in America into an abstract capability for altruism, defined as a capacity for kinlike attachment to strangers. But have we really liberated the nepotistic impulse from its biological constraints, or are we simply trying to find new objects for our frustrated nepotistic urges? Either way, the mentor relation is in the end a weak substitute for the full-blooded patronage of a father, brother, or uncle.

By looking closely at their family relationships we can see how fallible and human the American founders really were. It is almost always through such ties that public men betray their principles. Yet we should properly be grateful that our founders were so flawed and inconsistent.

Adams's humanizing nepotism is his saving grace, as is Jefferson's hypocrisy. For there is finally nothing more inhuman—even monstrous—than a public man who has extinguished all family feeling.

In the following chapters we will continue our exploration of American nepotism through a biographical focus on some of our greatest presidents, since it is these who often symbolize the deeper changes in family culture that accompanied the country's transformation from a homogeneous agrarian republic to a multiethnic industrial democracy.

CHAPTER 9

THE NINETEENTH CENTURY

NEPOTISM IN THE NORTH, WEST, AND SOUTH

"We are the heirs of all time, and with all nations we divide our inheritance. On this Western Hemisphere, all tribes and peoples are forming into one federated whole." So wrote Herman Melville, the literary prophet of a polyglot American future, as symbolized by the multiethnic crew of the *Pequod* under the rule of its tyrannical patriarch. This polyglot America did not emerge overnight, however. Rather it was the outcome of a struggle between the various regional cultures, culminating in a great Civil War.

After briefly unifying during the War of Independence, the three main regional cultures returned to their habits of squabbling and mutual suspicion. Meanwhile, a fourth migration, of Scots Irish border folk, streamed into the American backcountry, bringing with them their own lifeways and traditions. In the early nineteenth century, each of these regions expanded via massive internal migrations. The area known as greater New England comprised the northern tier of the continent; a Delaware valley exodus spread through the Midwest; settlers from Virginia moved south and west down the Atlantic coast and along the Gulf of Mexico; and settlers from the Appalachian highlands occupied the upper South and old Southwest. So disunited were these regions that some observers believed the new nation must soon fall apart.

The Constitution reflected a compromise between the three main cultural regions; the fourth—the southern and western backcountry—was left out of the constitutional compromise and continued to resist the authority of the national government. Under President Adams, New Englanders came to dominate the federal government and took steps to create a strong national state with broad powers of taxation, regulation, and defense. But the unpopular Adams sparked a realignment that united the South, West, and mid-Atlantic states under the Jeffersonian republicans. This regional coalition dominated American politics for the next quarter century, a period in which the South and the West were greatly enlarged by the Louisiana Purchase and the creation of new states. But while New Englanders frequently found themselves at odds with other regions, New England's peculiar brand of dynamic family-based capitalism turned it into the country's industrial heartland and financial and cultural capital, with a disproportionate power over the rest of the country.

In this chapter we will take a closer look at the federalist elite of Boston, otherwise known as the brahmins; the Jacksonian coalition that rose to challenge its ascendancy in the 1820s and 1830s; and the defeat of Southern nationalism in the Civil War, out of which emerged for the first time a unified national society.

NEPOTISM AND THE BRAHMIN ARISTOCRACY

In 1810, a well-to-do Boston merchant named Francis Cabot Lowell went to England, leaving his business affairs in the hands of his partner and brother-in-law Patrick Tracy Jackson. While there, he toured the cotton mills of Birmingham and Manchester, then the center of the global textile trade. Although it was illegal to export the patented British technology, Lowell inspected the complex spinning and weaving machines so closely that on his return he was able to duplicate and even improve their design. This act of intellectual piracy launched the Industrial Revolution in America. Lowell founded the Boston Manufacturing Company along with Jackson and their friends Nathan Appleton and Abbott Lawrence, who together became known as the Boston Associates. By the time of Lowell's death, a few years later, the company's

Waltham mill was already producing forty miles of cloth a day and paying dividends of 20 percent.

New commercial elites arose in all the seaboard cities in the decades after the Revolution, but few achieved the status of a permanent upper class, and none enjoyed greater success or longevity than the group of about forty closely interrelated families known as the Boston brahmins. In the pursuit of their expanding textile business, the brahmins would develop Boston's physical infrastructure, create a network of financial and cultural institutions, dominate regional politics, and devise a dynastic program that raised their children to the ranks of an American aristocracy. Nothing like this collective achievement had been seen before, and it has never been repeated. Nor should it surprise us that it was largely owed to the disciplined pattern of nepotism practiced by several generations of highly motivated and creative family entrepreneurs.

The rise of the brahmins began in the 1780s, when an ambitious group of Essex County merchants moved to Boston, where they occupied the vacuum left by the loyalist exiles. The move to Boston marked these family founders for distinction, as did their powerful coherence as a group, weaving a dense net of marital, economic, and political ties in the pursuit of their mutual interests. Their success was based on a unique combination of elements derived from the Puritanism of the colony's founders, including a powerful work ethic, an unwavering sense of vocation, a drive to accumulate wealth, and an impulse to swathe their success in the cloak of public virtue and benevolence. Equally important was the nepotistic formula of marriage, reproduction, and inheritance that developed in colonial New England, since this governed the transmission of status and property and shaped the decisions of family heads.

The Boston elite at the end of the eighteenth century included the descendants of Puritan ministerial families (Endicotts, Winthrops, and Saltonstalls), representatives of old mercantile clans (Amorys, Quincys, and Otises), and new men who had made their fortunes in trade, piracy, or speculation during the Revolutionary War (Danas, Lowells, Higginsons, Jacksons, and Lees). The great mercantile firms were family enterprises based on networks of personal contacts. Perkins and Co. represented a cluster of intermarried Forbeses, Cushings, and Sturgises. Other mercantile connections included the Higginsons and Lees of Salem and the Tracys, Jacksons, Lowells, and Cabots of Newbury. The latter connection was at the core of the new industrial elite and would play the major role in its development. At its center were the Lowells, descendants of an English merchant-trader who had settled in Newbury in 1639.

Family founder John Lowell was born in 1743, entered Harvard at thirteen, and after graduating in 1760 turned away from his father's religious vocation to pursue a legal career. He fought in the revolutionary war, represented Boston in Congress, and later became chief justice of the First District Court. Lowell helped to found several major Boston institutions and served on numerous boards and councils, including the Harvard Corporation. He married three women in turn from leading Essex County families, and his sons were the founders of the family's three branches. The eldest, John the Rebel, was a federalist firebrand. The youngest, Charles, a minister, founded America's first literary dynasty. But it was Francis Cabot Lowell, the middle son, who founded the New England textile industry and secured his family's place in the emerging upper class. Their marriages and those of their children rapidly proliferated ties among the Essex County families.

The Cabots—Boston's other acknowledged first family—were descended from three brothers who arrived in Salem around 1700, made advantageous marriages, and soon became both numerous and rich. John, the youngest, thrived in business and became a leading merchant. Four of his thirteen children married Higginsons. (There were also multiple marriages with the Dodges, Lees, and Jacksons.) George Cabot, known as the "federalist sage" of Boston, was born in Salem of a Higginson mother and went to Harvard about the same time as John Lowell. He married his double first cousin, Elizabeth Higginson, made a fortune during the war in privateering, and became a U.S. senator in 1791. His granddaughter married a wealthy merchant named Lodge; their son Henry Cabot Lodge founded one of America's most distinguished political dynasties.

If Francis Cabot Lowell established the New England textile industry by an act of intellectual piracy, his actions were consistent with the buccaneering spirit of his forebears. Most of the great Boston merchants had made their fortunes during the Revolution, or even earlier, as privateers—a fancy word for legalized pirates—and their general business conduct exemplified family capitalism in its rawest and most elemental form. The Jacksons and Lees, for example, "duped buyers, bribed officials, sold spoiled goods, traded with the enemy in wartime, and spread false rumors that enabled them to sell high or buy low."[1]

The natural counterpart to this rapacious exploitation of outsiders was their open and vigorous nepotism. The Boston merchants actively recruited sons and nephews and put them to work in every aspect of their enterprise. Serving their apprenticeships at sea or in the countinghouse, they acquired the skills and knowledge necessary to enter business with their relatives or start their own firms. Mercantile capitalism was decidedly meritocratic, but while many a humble seaman rose from fo'cs'le to quarterdeck, sometimes marrying the boss's daughter and becoming his heir, preference was given to kindred. This remained true despite the fact that not all relatives gave a satisfactory account of themselves.[2]

As with landed estates, the Puritan abandonment of primogeniture tended to dissipate capital, and ambitious merchants could broaden their business or raise money for expansion only through partnership. Such partnerships were usually entered with kin and often tightened through marriage. Business partners, whether related or not, often married one another's sisters, and their descendants might continue to intermarry for several generations. Reducing the number of heirs through the marriage of cousins concentrates the family's capital and passes more of it on intact. The practice of sibling exchange—in which two or more children of one family marry children from another—is an even more efficient means of achieving this end. Such practices enabled the merchant families of Salem and Newbury to parlay their accumulated capital into enormous trading fortunes.[3]

The Boston merchants financed and led the Revolution because British policies were bad for trade; the same men supported the conservative policies of the federalists because they were good for trade. Working in close cooperation with Hamilton, a scion of the New York financial elite, the Essex County merchants became the center of New England federalism and acted as an informal party directorate known as the Essex Junto, a tightly intermarried group of families that supplied the political leadership of Massachusetts for many years. Their ethos was highly elitist, and they viewed populist democrats like Jefferson and Jackson as dangerous radicals. "The sea is no wet-nurse to democracy," wrote Samuel Eliot Morison. "Instant and unquestioning obedience to the master is the rule of the sea; and your typical sea-captain would make it the rule of the land if he could." As Thomas Wentworth Higginson attested, "The habits of the quarterdeck . . . went all through the Federalist party of Massachusetts."[4] Melville's indomitable Captain Ahab is the virtual embodiment of this type.

The term "Boston brahmins" was coined by Oliver Wendell Holmes, himself a member of this class, who delivered a paean to family tradition in his celebrated memoir, *The Autocrat of the Breakfast Table:* "No, my friends, I go (always other things being equal) for the man who inherits family traditions and the cumulative humanities of at least four or five generations." Not for nothing was the image of the caste invoked by Holmes. The brahmins exhibited many features of a closed status group, including social exclusivity, ancestral pride, occupational monopolies, and a pattern of endogamous marriage. It is doubtful that another case exists in which nepotism was extended so successfully through a complex web of marital, economic, and institutional ties, rising from the level of the family to encompass a whole class of people. Nepotism allowed the brahmins to make the transition from commercial to industrial capitalism, control the regional economy, and dominate its political and cultural life for over a century.

The brahmins did not become a true upper class overnight, however; the move to Boston was only the first stage in a great dynastic drama. The family founders made their fortunes in shipping and trade and established themselves in the new economic elite. But in the first decades of the nineteenth century a series of shocks, including Jefferson's embargo against Britain, the collapse of the Federalist Party, and an economic crisis after the War of 1812, faced the merchants with the prospect of extinction. It was the energy and resourcefulness of the second generation, leading the shift from commerce to industry, that permitted their survival as a group.

Most of the original Boston Associates were Essex Junto men: Lowells, Cabots, Jacksons, Lees, Higginsons, Amorys, Russells, Gorhams, Tyngs, and Duttons. But there were also a number of new men whose admittance to the enclave showed (however briefly and selectively) its meritocratic bias and its openness to talent. Unlike Lowell and Jackson,

Harvard graduates with inherited wealth and connections, Nathan Appleton and Abbott Lawrence were former plowboys who never attended college and rose through ambition and acumen to the directorship of several major companies. It was some time before the old Puritan-merchant elite fully accepted these men, and for a while they were snubbed as upstarts. Eventually, however, the older families invested in the new textile companies and their children assumed an active role in their direction; Appletons and Lawrences intermarried with the gentry, and they began to appear on the boards of prestigious social and cultural institutions. These men and their families formed the inner circle of the Boston Manufacturing Company, and a series of marriages between their children strengthened their bonds. Throughout the nineteenth century, members of the extended Lowell kinship network or their associates acted almost exclusively as the company's directors and managers.

A series of new mills went up in the 1820s and 1830s, organized on a basis of coordinated interests rather than as competing firms. In addition, a network of roads, canals, and railroads was constructed to ship in raw materials and ship out finished goods. A huge amount of capital was needed for these enterprises. Accordingly, a large number of financial, charitable, and cultural institutions were created that served the dual purpose of pooling and channeling capital for investment and preserving family wealth.

The primary instruments for the creation of these institutions were the testamentary trust and the charitable endowment. Under the first, family capital could be handed over to a trustee while its income was divided among the heirs; the second left the family's principal in the care of a trustee or corporate body with its income earmarked for a variety of social welfare purposes. These novel instruments produced the *effect* of primogeniture—conserving family wealth—with no unequal treatment of the heirs.

As historian Naomi Lamoreaux explains, the New England banking industry was organized by and for prominent merchants as an extension of their family enterprises. These early banks were simply "the financial arms of kinship groups," intended to raise investment capital for their members.[5] John Lowell founded the First National Bank of Boston in partnership with his cousins Thomas Russell and Stephen Higginson. The charter subscribers to the Suffolk Bank included Nathan Appleton,

Patrick Tracy Jackson, and Amos and Abbott Lawrence. Acting as a regional clearinghouse, the Suffolk Bank provided a much-needed degree of stability and regulation for the banking industry as a whole. It also allowed the partners to increase their working capital in the form of substantial loans to the textile interests heavily represented among its founders and directors, often with no collateral other than the signature of the company's chief officer and two reputable guarantors. Though such practices would be illegal today, they should not be dismissed as abuses. Rather they are a sign of the very different function banks performed in nineteenth-century New England—less like modern commercial banks than investment pools created to finance family enterprises in which outsiders could participate through the purchase of stock.

Scholars have traditionally viewed kin-based business networks as an impediment to modernization, but the New England example shows that incorporating such networks in a set of interlocking financial institutions can offset the risks of capitalizing large-scale industrial enterprises. The capital thus accumulated was used to build new mills, expand the network of canals and locks along the Merrimack, and finance the development of New England's railway and communications infrastructure. Without such institutions, New England's industrial development would have been severely slowed and the regional economy would never have achieved its remarkable vitality.

The brahmins also founded a number of social, educational, and cultural institutions. The first wave included the Harvard Medical School (1782), the Boston Dispensary (1795), the Athenaeum (1807), the McLean Asylum (1811), the Massachusetts General Hospital (1821), and many others. Traditionally these philanthropic activities are viewed as reflections of brahmin noblesse oblige, but they also served dynastic ends. These institutions, based on charitable endowments, assumed many of the social welfare obligations formerly borne by wealthy families.[6] Moreover, since even the most successful business could not support all of the family's sons, training some to staff and run these institutions lightened the burdens on capital. Accordingly, over the third and fourth generations, the proportion of brahmin sons involved in business declined, while increasing numbers sought careers in law, medicine, the church, education, and the arts. Far from weakening their families, these institutional affiliations broadened the base for brahmin influence over society as a whole.

By the middle of the nineteenth century the Brahmins had created an extensive network of institutions that relieved them of the need to provide social services, supplied useful careers for their sons, and made large blocks of capital available. Once established, however, these institutions began to exert their own priorities. New criteria of merit and efficiency were asserted to ensure that their funds were not abused for private ends. Meritocratic pressure was also applied to recruit the most capable men. This had the beneficial effect of shifting professional training in medicine, law, education, and other fields from a basis of informal apprenticeship to one of formal and accredited instruction. Merit and efficiency flourished in the compost of nepotism.

A key institution in the consolidation of the Boston elite was Harvard University: as Betty G. Farrell puts it, "the great families built Harvard, so to speak, while building themselves."[7] The Harvard Corporation, a board of seven wealthy men who closely supervised the college's finances and hiring policies, was composed of elite representatives. The sons of brahmins went to Harvard, and its presidents and faculty were often gentlemen recruited from their ranks, like Henry Adams. Needless to say, nepotism was commonplace. For example, William James was examined for his medical degree by Dr. Oliver Wendell Holmes, an old family friend. James was not certain he could qualify, having been abroad for most of the required three years of study. According to biographer R. W. B. Lewis, "the doctor asked the candidate a single question, and when William answered correctly, Holmes . . . said: 'That's enough! If you know *that,* you must know everything. Now tell me—how is your dear old father?' "[8]

None of this was considered the least bit irregular. Harvard dynasties were common: more than fifty Cabots went to Harvard, and Eliots and Lowells held leadership positions almost continuously for two hundred years. Like other brahmin institutions, Harvard also sheltered members who had suffered financial reverses. (After the failure of their enterprises, Stephen Higginson and Jonathan Jackson were given posts as treasurers.) Yet Harvard was also an engine of upward mobility for middle class men like Edward Everett, Henry Wadsworth Longfellow, and Andrews Norton.

Elite sponsorship of cultural institutions like the Museum of Fine Arts and the Boston Symphony Orchestra helped consolidate the brahmins' role as arbiters of taste. The founding of these and other institutions, including the Athenaeum, the Lowell Institute, the *North American Review,* and the Massachusetts Historical Society, ensured Boston's cultural dominance and made it the Athens of nineteenth-century America. It also helped legitimize the brahmins' claim to the leadership of society as a whole.

The complex of brahmin-founded, -financed, and -led institutions produced a number of family dynasties in medicine, law, and the church. The Harvard Law School fostered a group of legal dynasties, including branches of the Lowells, Danas, and Paines. Patrician John Warren founded the Massachusetts Medical Society in 1781 and Harvard Medical School in 1782; Massachusetts General Hospital was also founded by Warren and his son, along with James Jackson, brother of P. T. Jackson. Thereafter, Warrens, Jacksons, and Shattucks dominated medicine in Boston. The Unitarian Church afforded another venue for the sons of the elite, becoming (along with Harvard) the main vehicle for the dissemination of upper class values and ideas.

The physical topography of Boston itself owes much to a series of massive landfill and construction projects intended to accommodate its rapid growth during the nineteenth century. These brahmin-financed and -directed efforts transformed it from a provincial town into a modern city by expanding streets and wharves and public markets, improving lighting and sanitation, and building parks and bridges. In the process, the brahmins bought up huge tracts in Beacon Hill and Back Bay, which became elite residential enclaves, with new (mainly Irish) immigrants concentrating in the city's North End. The sons and daughters of these enclaves—raised in the same neighborhoods, educated in the same schools, marrying into one another's families, doing business with one another, working in the same institutions, socializing in the same exclusive clubs—grew increasingly aware of themselves as a distinctive and well-defined class. Great care was also taken by the brahmins in arranging their children's marriages. Cousin marriages and links between the partners in the textile and mercantile firms were common at first, though after a few generations the families' wealth and status allowed their children more freedom of choice. But while the sons and daughters of securely founded families could be given greater latitude, their choices were powerfully shaped by their social environment.

Too much cannot be made of the closeness and intimacy of the brahmin elite. This is best apprehended through the testimony of their wives and daughters, whose diaries and daybooks afford an inside view of this privileged society. Judging from their entries, the lives of brahmin women were an endless round of visits, teas, and dinner parties. This constant socializing had a purpose beyond entertaining the young ladies of Boston. Anthropologists call this function "kinkeeping," and it is what women do in all kin-based societies, from the Zulus to Jane Austen's provincial English gentry. Genealogical relationships atrophy and disappear if they are not kept up, and it was the task of the family's women to maintain them. It was women who spun the delicate tissue of brahmin society, keeping track of family affairs, guiding and arranging elite marriages, and maintaining the network of ties through which Boston's commercial, institutional, and political affairs were given informal direction.

The brahmin kinship networks, like those of the Roman aristocracy, grew increasingly dense and entwined. Yet while these networks overlapped and their boundaries were often vague, distinct clusters remained, and some were more successful than others. In this connection it is useful to compare the dynastic strategies of the original Boston Associates: the Lowells, the Appletons and Lawrences, and the Jacksons each represent a nexus of families who intermarried and shared business and institutional interests over several generations. To the extent that their marriage and occupational patterns differed, so too did their material outcomes.

Farrell characterizes these strategies as "tight" or "open" kinship networks. A good example of the former is the Lowells. A dense pattern of first-cousin marriages within a small circle of Lowells, Cabots, Amorys, and Gardners reflected the twin obsessions of the family's founders: the drive to accumulate wealth and to preserve the family's social exclusivity. But the resulting "tight" network was not so tight that it shunned alliances with other families, and in every generation sons and nephews enhanced the family's business interests and played a leading role in civic and cultural affairs, while sons-in-law were recruited from other successful families. While a great deal of pressure was brought to bear on Lowell sons and daughters to conform to the family's needs, this ramifying network meant that sons were not completely at the mercy of their fathers but could make use of their connections with a wide group of uncles, cousins, and in-laws. This enabled the Lowells to preserve their position in commerce and manufacturing while branching into other areas. As a result, Lowells and their relatives continued to hold prominent positions in business, politics, and culture well after the Depression and World War II.[9]

The "open" kinship network exemplified by the Appleton and Lawrence families is more typical of self-made men without deep roots in the establishment. William and Amos Lawrence each had seven or eight children, whose many marriages linked them to other leading families. Unlike the Lowells, however, the Lawrences also married outside their immediate circle with those who had taken the lead in other branches of commerce and industry. A similar pattern marked the Appletons, who established strong links with the core brahmin families while forging ties with those involved in newer concerns. This strategy allowed them to maintain their connections with the established elite while taking advantage of the increasingly diversified economy of nineteenth-century New England.

It was possible to go too far in either direction, of course. Too wide a set of marriages could disperse the kinship network, while a family could restrict its marriages too tightly, turning a strategy aimed at enhancing solidarity into a habit of crippling insularity. The former was the fate of the family of Patrick Tracy Jackson, Lowell's original partner. Lowell and Jackson had started out on much the same footing. Both were the sons of long-established Essex County families; their fathers shared political and business interests, and Lowell's marriage to Jackson's sister in 1798 cemented this link. After Lowell's death, in 1817, Jackson assumed the direction of the business. His successor was not his own son, however, but his partner's nephew and son-in-law John Amory Lowell. Jackson's brothers, meanwhile, did not go into business with him like the brothers of most other brahmin founders but entered careers in medicine and law. Family diversification has its place, but in this case the lack of nephews and cousins as heirs and partners in the second generation undermined the family's position in Boston's emerging elite. Two generations later, Lowell's descendants would be millionaires many times over. The net worth of Jackson's grandchildren quickly diminished, and by the end of the century they had dropped out of the elite altogether.

These patterns aren't consciously planned so far as we know, but they clearly don't happen by accident. Each dynastic family chooses its own way of regulating both its marriage practices and its occupational traditions. Successful brahmin families would gradually adapt their marital patterns to reflect their changing circumstances, while for others a pattern of close marriage that had been a source of strength later became a source of weakness. Though it is hard to say why such patterns change, the fact that they often do is clear testimony to the difference between families that know how to adapt to changing circumstances and those that do not.

The snobbish and exclusive brahmin elite has furnished the leading example of what one historian calls "a staid aristocracy in decline." This was perhaps inevitable as the center of industrial and commercial life passed in the mid–nineteenth century to vibrant immigrant cities like New York and Chicago. Yet the nepotistic strategy they devised to preserve their families' wealth and status has itself been seen as a major contributing cause. Rather than allowing their fortunes to pass directly to their heirs, the brahmin founders established custodial trusts that removed the family wealth from their control. The brahmins thereby short-circuited their sons' entrepreneurial talents and hindered them from exploiting new opportunities, setting them up to be displaced by the new professional-managerial class that emerged after the Civil War. Meanwhile the brahmins created a world of their own from which they ventured forth with increasing reluctance. Trading power and leadership for the preservation of their status and security, they became increasingly inward-looking and succumbed to the temptations of caste. But while the high-water mark of brahmin dominance seems to have passed after 1860, it may be a mistake to conclude that their actual power declined. As Farrell shows through careful reconstruction of the brahmin kinship networks, they or their surrogates remained very much in control of Boston's new industrial and financial institutions. Moreover, the interlocking directorates that linked these institutions were heavily drawn from brahmin kinship networks.[10]

In the end, the brahmins did decline, displaced in politics by the Irish machine and by the new industrial and financial centers of New York and Chicago. Yet the lingering impression of inbred snobbery and elitism associated with the brahmins should not obscure the remarkable feat they accomplished, namely the creation of an aristocratic establishment in the midst of a new democratic world. Whatever we may think of it today, this collective achievement must be considered one of the greatest monuments to nepotism in American history.

ANDREW JACKSON: FRONTIER FAMILIST

James Monroe's retirement from the presidency in 1823 marked the end of America's founding political era. Franklin, Washington, and Hamilton were dead. Adams and Jefferson would die, by a famous coincidence, on July 4, 1826. The question of who would succeed Monroe therefore concealed a larger issue: who was the legitimate heir of the founding fathers? Five candidates quickly emerged: William H. Crawford, John C. Calhoun (who accepted the vice presidential nomination instead), John Quincy Adams, Henry Clay, and Andrew Jackson. Of these, the leading candidate was Adams, the brilliant secretary of state who had secured possession of Louisiana and Florida and drafted the Monroe Doctrine. He already had the greatest résumé in American history, and his name and family background made him a living link to the founders. Merit and heredity thus conspired to strengthen Adams's claim.

But he was strongly challenged by Andrew Jackson, a self-made man of the western frontier. Though he had been too young to fight, Jackson had witnessed the Revolution and carried a scar on his face from the sword of a British officer. His exploits in the War of 1812 and the Indian wars had made him a national hero. Jackson revered the founders and considered the current government corrupt. Twenty-three years of Republican incumbency had produced an entrenched office-holding class that looked—and was—increasingly hereditary. The election of 1824 was thus a symbolic contest between a self-made man and the son of a former president—a referendum on the nature and sources of merit.

Jackson won the popular vote, but without a clear Electoral College majority, the contest was thrown to the House. Crawford suffered a stroke, and Clay pledged his support to Adams in exchange for an appointment as secretary of state. Denouncing this "corrupt bargain," Jackson decamped to Tennessee and immediately commenced his next campaign. With the help of an able New York machine politician named Martin Van Buren, Jackson lent his name to the creation of the first modern political party, uniting Northern workers, Southern planters, and Western farmers against the hated New England elite. Four years later, after one of the bitterest campaigns in U.S. history, he rode to overwhelming victory.

Monroe had presided over an "Era of Good Feelings" noted for reduced partisan conflict. In reality, it was an era of painful transition from the elite patrimonial politics of the early republic to the mass politics of the industrial age. Both earlier parties had collapsed after 1815, and politics became a naked competition between regional and personal cliques. Meanwhile the 1820s saw a series of shocks, panics, and threatened rebellions, and a great westward movement that emptied whole towns in the East and caused hundreds of new settlements to spring up in the hinterlands. Eleven new states were formed between the Revolution and 1830, and the spread of universal male suffrage created a vast new voting public. As the western sections grew, the dominance of wealthy planters, bankers, and industrialists increasingly irritated the fiercely independent frontiersmen. Jackson was the hero of these independent spirits, and under his leadership a great revolt occurred against the power of entrenched family interests. But while Jacksonians inveighed against nepotism as an instrument of elite domination, they busily contrived to turn the presidential power of patronage into the poor man's equivalent.

Few careers have been as inspiring to Americans as that of Andrew Jackson. His admirers worshiped him as a self-made hero who had risen from the soil, like Cincinnatus, to preserve the founders' precious gift of liberty. Yet he was also plainly driven by ambition, greed, a desire for personal glory, and a bottomless hunger for land. Jackson has been seen in many guises: as the Great Westerner, as a frontier capitalist and greedy speculator, as a populist antecedent of Franklin D. Roosevelt, and as a Jeffersonian reformer. Michael Rogin has applied a Marxist-

Freudian lens that sees him as driven by "infantile rage." While all these views contribute something, that of David Hackett Fischer solves a number of apparent mysteries about Jackson by viewing him against the background of the great Scots Irish migration from which he emerged.

The Scots Irish were the last of the four English migrations that arrived between 1629 and 1800. Originating in northern Ireland, the Scottish lowlands, and the English border country, the majority were landless farmers or wage laborers, crushed for generations by the oppressive rule of robber clans and landlords. The Scots Irish entered the country mainly through Boston and Philadelphia and settled in western Massachusetts, Pennsylvania, and the hinterlands of Virginia, Maryland, the Carolinas, and upper Georgia. Though the states offered easy terms to settlers, incessant Indian attacks, hunger, disease, war, domestic violence, family feuds, and the depredations of bandits and "regulators" made life as dangerous and uncertain in the New World as it was in the Old.

Fischer makes a great point of the chronic insecurity of the English border country and its uniquely dysfunctional culture. In this long-contested terrain between England and Scotland, the fundamental fact of life was poverty. Mortality was high, literacy low, and drunkenness, illegitimacy, and violence endemic. Whole families made a living out of stealing sheep and cattle. Clan membership or the payment of protection—known as blackmail—were the only source of safety. The resulting climate of fear and mistrust was reflected in a habitual suspicion of institutions and resistance to authority. It also produced great strength of character and will, qualities conducive to leadership and a warrior ethic. Every boy was raised to be highly aggressive, to display fierce family pride, and to avenge insults with death. Feuds and blood money were the usual way of settling disputes—legacies that persisted in Appalachia and the Ozarks for centuries. (The most famous is the feud between the Hatfields and the McCoys.)[11] Another holdover was the abduction of brides by rival clans. Such practices were aspects of a traditional kin-based society in which trust is restricted to relatives. The migration itself was a movement of clans, in which a few related families would open up an area and send for their relatives. The result was a series of rural enclaves inhabited by different kinship groups.[12]

Jackson's legend stressed his roots among the people and his character as a self-made man. In fact, like most of the leaders produced by this migration, he descended from landed gentry and spent his whole life in a struggle to reattain that status. Jackson's grandfather was a wealthy merchant in northern Ireland. His father led a party of immigrants to America in 1765, then followed his wife's four sisters and their families to Carolina. There Jackson was born in 1767, the youngest of three brothers, two months after his father's death in a farm accident. The elder Jackson left his widow two hundred acres, but Jackson's mother abandoned the farm and moved in with one of her sisters.

Jackson was described in his youth—much like the young Napoleon, whom he greatly admired—as constantly fighting and challenging other boys. He was suspicious, argumentative, and prone to hold a grudge. He was also characterized by a strong sense of justice, an instinct for loyalty, and a natural air of command.[13] These and other traits, Fischer argues, can be traced to his cultural background. Backcountry nepotism differed strongly from that of other regions. Unlike the Puritans, who aimed to break the will of unruly young boys, Scots Irish child-rearing practices were positively "will enhancing," their primary purpose being to foster "fierce pride, stubborn independence and a warrior's courage." Competitive games and contests of strength were encouraged, and young boys were given their first small tools and weapons at an early age. The effect was to produce what Fischer calls "a society of autonomous individuals who were unable to endure external control and incapable of restraining their rage against anyone who stood in their way."[14]

Like many frontier mothers, Mrs. Jackson was a repository of inherited folk wisdom. Jackson grew up on tales of Robin Hood and William Wallace, and he later insisted that his wards read the histories of the Scottish border captains on whom he had modeled himself. One contemporary recalled Aunt Betty Jackson as a "Spartan mother" who taught her son that a man must never cry and must always solve his problems personally. Her last words, often quoted by Jackson himself, were: "Never tell a lie, nor take what is not your own, nor sue anybody for slander or assault and battery. *Always settle them cases yourself.*"

When the Revolution came, the backcountry was deeply divided, fracturing the tenuous frontier society along clan and family lines. Jackson's brothers died, as did his mother, leaving him an orphan at fifteen.

Jackson later often said he had no living blood relations in America. But this was not the case: his mother's Crawford relatives took him in and helped him in various ways—even setting him up in business as a saddler. (The business failed.) Moreover, he had inherited land from his father and had a substantial legacy from his grandfather. Determined to lead a gentleman's life, however, he sold his farm and went to Charleston, where he gambled away all his money. Jackson thus began his career in fine American form, by squandering his inheritance. Even so, one of his Crawford uncles paid for him to study law in North Carolina, after which he decided to follow his friend James McNairy over the mountains to Nashville. In doing so he left behind his past, conveniently also forgetting his debt to his mother's kin. He never mentioned the Crawfords again, and seems to have forgotten they existed.

Nashville was a raw frontier settlement founded in 1779 by a pair of Scots Irish entrepreneurs named Robertson and Donelson. McNairy had obtained an appointment in Nashville as chief judge and offered Jackson a job as a prosecutor. There was not much call for legal niceties in the backwoods, but he quickly earned a reputation as a strong and fearless man who would bring any wrongdoer to justice.

As a man who had progressively been stripped of kin connections by the migrations of his father and grandfather, the deaths of his parents and siblings, and his own removal west, Jackson needed to rebuild his social network. His first step was to attach himself to the Donelsons. John Donelson had been killed a short time earlier, and when Jackson was not out riding the circuit, sleeping in the woods with hand on rifle, he lodged with his widow, who took in boarders to protect her home from Indian attack. Donelson had been one of the area's largest landowners; his sons were connected to the powerful Blount faction that dominated Tennessee politics. Jackson was regarded as an up-and-coming lawyer and militiaman who had stepped in after Donelson's death to be his wife's protector. Thanks to the Donelsons' patronage, he picked up clients among their friends and took his first steps in business and politics under their sponsorship.

Rachel Donelson was then living at her mother's house, and Jackson fell in love with her. Though she was married at the time, her husband's violent temper apparently drove her to leave him. Jackson ran him out of town, and after hearing that the Virginia legislature had granted him a divorce, Jackson and Rachel were married. Later it turned out that she had *not* been divorced as she thought, and they married again once her divorce became official. But Rachel's "adultery" later became a major campaign issue, and Jackson fought several duels and killed at least one man to defend her honor.[15]

Jackson rose quickly through his connections with the Donelsons and Governor Blount, who made him attorney general for the Cumberland district in 1790. In 1796 he was elected to the state's constitutional convention. He went to Washington as Tennessee's first congressman, served in the Senate, then returned to be a judge of the superior court. He soon became a rich proprietor, with a plantation and a hundred slaves. As such he stood with Tennessee founders like Blount, the Robertsons, and the Donelsons in opposing the great national families of the federalist elite.

The War of 1812 was the making of Jackson as a national figure. The battle of New Orleans was a smashing victory in which a handful of Americans were killed, compared to over two thousand British—though as it happened, American peace commissioners had already concluded a treaty and the war was officially over. Jackson's imposition of martial law in New Orleans was likewise controversial. But the public approved of his actions, whether he had authority for them or not.[16]

Rachel was unable to have children, and the couple compensated by surrounding themselves with wards and protégés. One—the son of Rachel's brother Severn—was legally adopted: the couple named him Andrew Jackson Jr. Another nephew, Andrew Jackson Donelson, became their ward, as did grandnephew Andrew Jackson Hutchings, the son of Jackson's partner John Hutchings, who was also John Donelson's grandson. The proliferation of little Andrew Jacksons shows his concern to pass his name to future generations: he plainly saw himself as the founder of a clan. A web of marriages between these wards and their Donelson cousins tightened the links between the clan's branches and joined it to other prominent families. Jackson also acquired as wards the daughters of land magnate W. T. Lewis, who later married close associates of Jackson. In addition, there were the five grandsons of Thomas Butler who fought in Jackson's campaigns, and two of whom married

Rachel's nieces. Clearly Jackson, the posthumous son, had a compulsion to surround himself with fatherless young men. Sadly, however, none of them amounted to much. The only one with any promise was Andrew Jackson Donelson, who became Jackson's ward in 1805. Placed at West Point, he graduated second in his class and served for two years as Jackson's aide-de-camp. He later accompanied Jackson to Washington and served as his secretary, while his wife played the role of official hostess after Rachel Jackson's death.

From an early stage, Jackson also began to collect the group of friends and associates who would aid him in his rise, building an artificial clan united by business and political interest, marriage, adoption, and friendship. Jackson's Tennessee lieutenants were, like himself, aggressive and acquisitive businessmen and frontier politicians. Most were of Celtic origin, twice or thrice displaced by their family's migrations. Yet they carried their Scots Irish heritage with its retrograde concept of honor and other legacies, including respect for the clan leader, or thane. In the border country, leaders were chosen for their courage, strength, and cunning—qualities established on the battlefield or in a contest with a challenger. Jackson was becoming a tribal chief like Shakespeare's Macbeth, the thane of Cawdor. His own conception of the clan was that of a chivalrous Christian brotherhood like the fellowship of the Round Table or the companions of Roland. He lived, writes one historian, "as though he were a knight-errant, surrounded always by forces of evil conspiring to unseat him and corrupt his world."[17] His moral universe was likewise Manichaean, divided into enemies and friends. Friends were to be aided, trusted, and indulged; enemies could be deceived, bullied, and manipulated.

The central figure in Jackson's circle was John Overton, a frontier lawyer, speculator, and slave dealer; the men were lifelong friends and business partners. In 1814 Overton proposed that Jackson run for governor, and in 1821 he got the state legislature to endorse Jackson as a presidential candidate. He also formed a group called the Nashville Committee, which in 1823 got him elected to the U.S. Senate. In Jackson's political family, Overton played the role of consigliere. Jackson's military second was John Coffee, who had married Rachel's niece. Coffee held the rank of brigadier general, and his courage and battlefield skills were a match for Jackson's own. Indeed, Jackson owed his two greatest victories, at New Orleans and Horseshoe Bend, to Coffee's timely intervention. Coffee's training as a surveyor enabled him to spy out the best tracts of land for himself and his friends, and Jackson had him appointed to numerous treaty and boundary commissions. He looked after Jackson's business interests, and his daughter married Andrew Jackson Hutchings. William B. Lewis was a rich Virginian who married one of Jackson's wards. Lewis played a key role in the Nashville Committee and helped orchestrate replies to Jackson's critics. In the White House, his task was to turn away office seekers—an unpleasant assignment that nonetheless afforded him considerable power. Other members of the clan included William Carroll, George Washington Campbell, Felix Grundy, John Henry Eaton, and Hugh Lawson White. Two younger protégés were James K. Polk—a future president, known as Young Hickory—and Sam Houston, founder of the republic of Texas.

Without these loyal lieutenants, Jackson never could have attained the heights of national power. Their loyalty, however, relied much more on local interests and personal respect for Jackson's leadership than ideological purity. In order to become president, Jackson had to ally himself with a man whom most of his friends disliked and mistrusted. His willingness to do so marks the beginning of Jackson's shift from traditional clan head to party leader.

Martin Van Buren was, like Jackson, a Jeffersonian who rose from humble origins. He was also an organizational genius who had built the patronage machine known as the Albany Regency into the dominant force in New York politics. After Jackson's defeat in 1824, Van Buren set out to reconstruct the Jeffersonian New York–Virginia axis that had dominated national politics for twenty years. He reached out to South Carolina's John C. Calhoun and brought his own Albany Regency and a group known as the Richmond Junto into alliance with Jackson's Nashville Committee to form the Democratic Party. The Democrats created a network of Jackson Committees in every state and county, organized a series of conventions, held numerous picnics and rallies, and disseminated anti-Adams propaganda through a chain of opposition newspapers.

Adams's presidency had been a failure from the outset. Faced with a republican majority in Congress, he continued to press for a vigorous Hamiltonian program of national development, ensuring that he would accomplish none of his goals. Moreover, his failure to use patronage to strengthen his position led directly to his downfall. The stubborn refusal to use his power either to remove ideological opponents or reward his political friends assured that, like his father's, his would be a one-term incumbency.[18]

The election of 1828 was a reprise of the earlier confrontation between a self-made man and a scion of the federalist elite. But where in 1824 it had arguably been to Adams's advantage to be the son of a former president, it now became a liability. Adams was portrayed as hopelessly out of touch, a man who had never worked an honest day in his life and who despised the common people. His family was mockingly referred to as "the House of Braintree" and his father as "King John the First." Jackson, in contrast, was a rugged frontiersman, "not dandled into consequence by lying in the cradle of state, but inured from infancy to the storms and tempests of life."[19] But the attack on patronage and nepotism was the real centerpiece of Jackson's campaign. Public office, he declared, was not "a species of property," and he promised to "clean out the Noursery," a reference to the family of Joseph Nourse, which had been entrenched in the Treasury Department since Washington. Jackson swept the country, taking every region but New England.

Jackson was more right than wrong in his indictment of the government as a nepotistic elite. It was a legitimate issue, and Adams was its living embodiment: he never could have become president if he hadn't been a president's son. A poor politician, he hated to campaign, couldn't admit even to himself that he wanted to be president, and refused to sully his hands with the business of patronage. His stand against nepotism was really part of a greater Puritan fastidiousness that rendered him unfit for party leadership. It did, however, fit him admirably for the moral leadership he showed in later years, when he stood in Congress thundering against slavery.[20]

The election precipitated an unprecedented invasion of office seekers from every corner of the country. The demand for jobs went down to the level of gardeners, messengers, and janitors. Previous presidents abhorred the idea of removing a man for his political beliefs. But Jackson had a mandate for reform and he made clear that he intended sweeping changes. His main targets were the "rats" from the Treasury and other departments who could be charged with corruption or theft. He also made good on his promise to end the practice of inherited office: "One dismissed employee of the Custom House in Boston went 'in a transport of grief' to [cabinet secretary] Ingham with a plea to be informed of the cause of his dismissal, only to be told that offices were not hereditary." On the other hand, Jackson did not apply his new principle evenly. He may have rooted out the Nourses, but he left the Pattersons in control of the mint, a position they had held for thirty years.[21]

Despite his veneration of the founders, Jackson's appointment philosophy was completely at odds with theirs. To begin with, Jackson challenged the idea that higher education must be a prerequisite for office: any man of normal competence could serve. He also disagreed that too much rotation was disruptive, and after three months in office Jackson announced a four-year rule for federal appointments. Adams had explicitly rejected rotation, lest it render government "a perpetual and unremitting scramble for office."[22] Jackson vigorously rebutted this view:

> Now, every man who has been in office a few years, believes he has a life estate in it, a vested right, and if it has been held twenty years or upwards, not only a vested right, but that it ought to descend to his children, and if no children then next of kin. This is not the principles of our government. It is rotation of office that will perpetuate our liberty.[23]

With that, Jackson ended the concept of life tenure in office. Nevertheless, Adams was right. The principle of partisan replacement did lead to a "perpetual scramble for office" and gave birth to what became known as the spoils system—so christened by one of Van Buren's lieutenants, who declared on the Senate floor, "to the victor belong the spoils."

The election of 1828 took place against a background of tremendous changes wrought by what historians call the "market revolution." Factories displaced craftsmen and skilled laborers, giving rise to a new class of urban workers. A transportation boom facilitated commerce and internal migration. In the South, the opening of new territories produced a surge in large-scale cotton and grain production that wiped out subsistence agriculture in many areas. The rise of a market economy challenged traditional arrangements based on paternalism, including the master-apprentice system, cottage industry, and family welfare. Increased mobility and social dislocation undermined the dominance of established families and disrupted kinship networks. The extended family declined and the nuclear family itself became less hierarchical, more of an egalitarian partnership between husband and wife. Women and children also began to acquire legal rights, and a specialized body of family law began to emerge, weakening the power of fathers and husbands. Divorce became more common and custody disputes began to be decided on the basis of the "best interests of the child." Adoption was legalized and the inheritance rights of single mothers and illegitimate children were recognized. Laws were also passed to create separate female estates. Children themselves gradually ceased to be viewed as property and were seen as having value in themselves. Especially among the middle and upper classes, birthrates fell and investment in individual children increased.

As the family withdrew from work and politics, it came to be idealized as a refuge from the outside world. The idea of separate male and female spheres emerged: fathers worked outside the home, while mothers assumed the responsibilities of child rearing and character formation. Family ties were based less on patriarchal authority and more on affection and sentiment. Such was Jackson's vision of the family he created around Rachel at his Tennessee plantation, called the Hermitage—the very name suggestive of the new idealized vision of home as a haven from the storms outside.

These and other changes in the structure of family life led many to predict the dissolution of the family itself. Prison officials and proponents of public schooling like Horace Mann warned that taking fathers out of the home would breed delinquency and contribute to crime and mental illness. As Michael Rogin notes, however, this was all part and parcel of the great democratic experiment. In America, the pressure on sons to rise above their fathers' station caused anxiety not felt by those born into traditional societies, where status was hereditary. In a country where such barriers were absent, Alexis de Tocqueville remarked, men had no one to blame for their failure but themselves.

The challenges to Classical Nepotism in economic and family life were mirrored in the rise of party politics. The new party structures began the separation of political power from family control and social status. They took the nominating process away from the old family-based political cliques and gave it to a series of state committees and conventions. They also instituted the practice of campaigning for office, ending the older genteel system in which the people were asked to choose between candidates selected by an elite caucus. After Jackson's election this party apparatus continued to function, raising money, distributing speeches and letters from party leaders, and supporting local political organizations by dispensing patronage to the faithful.

In the northern states this brought to prominence a host of "anonymous" men—mostly lawyers. Important as party now was, however, family influence was not banished. In the South and West especially, party organization continued to be based on local juntos and family factions.[24] Further, while Jackson presided over the creation of a party system that sought to separate family interest from political office, he continued to characterize his own authority in familistic terms.

The limitations of this approach were exposed in the scandal known as the Eaton Affair. John Henry Eaton had served under Jackson in the War of 1812 and married one of his wards before becoming (with Jackson's help) a U.S. senator. During the 1828 campaign Eaton wrote many of Jackson's letters, speeches, and pamphlets, and Jackson named him secretary of war. After the death of his first wife, Eaton married Peggy Timberlake, the daughter of a Washington tavern keeper whose reputation was not of the best. The other cabinet wives refused to receive her, and their husbands went along. Jackson was outraged and demanded that his "family" close ranks. The defense of Peggy's honor became an obsession, and Jackson pursued it with such vigor and obstinacy that it split his official family in two.

This episode has given historians much difficulty, and it was equally mystifying to Jackson's contemporaries. Most historians note the parallel between Jackson's impassioned defense of Peggy Eaton and that of his recently deceased wife. The parallel is obvious, but in Fischer's view the episode is best explained by Jackson's clan-based, "border chieftain" outlook. To Jackson, Eaton was "more than a son." The younger man had even fought a duel to defend Rachel's honor. When he married Peggy Timberlake, she too became a member of the clan. A stain on Peggy's honor was therefore a reflection on Jackson himself. Those who accepted her, like Polk and Van Buren, remained within the fold; those like Andrew Jackson Donelson and his wife who viewed her as a dangerous manipulator were sent packing. Meanwhile Van Buren worked subtly to paint Calhoun—his main rival for the presidential succession—as the real author of the attack. In the end, Jackson demanded the resignation of the entire cabinet—an unprecedented act that served to enlarge the power of the presidency itself. It also secured Van Buren's place in Jackson's affections and left him the acknowledged heir apparent. Van Buren became vice president in 1832 and succeeded Jackson as president in 1836.

From its beginnings, American politics has been animated by two principles of equal legitimacy: concern for merit and efficiency on the one hand, and the need to cultivate friendship and personal loyalty on the other. John Quincy Adams tried to rule based on the criterion of merit alone without acknowledging the human dimension of politics. His cabinet was full of disloyal officers, but because they were good at their jobs he left them alone; as a result he came to grief. On the other hand, Ulysses S. Grant, whose two terms mark the lowest point of corruption and nepotism in U.S. history, allowed his political friends to run wild, and his administration was paralyzed by scandal.[25] The greatest presidents have been those—like Jackson, Lincoln, and the two Roosevelts—who combined a genuine respect for merit with a genius for manipulating patronage to knit together complex coalitions and alliances.

The founders' rejection of nepotism had been largely intellectual. Opposed to it in principle, they often indulged it in practice. Jackson's appointment philosophy completed the separation of family from office begun by Washington, Adams, and Jefferson. At least, it was his stated principle that he would take "but one of a family at a time." He explicitly set out to end inheritance of office and nepotism, and made ideological purity a legitimate criterion of both appointment and removal. On the other hand, he saw no reason why his friends should be excluded. "If my personal friends are qualified and patriotic, why should I not be permitted to bestow a few offices on them?"[26] (This statement may be considered the source of the hypocritical distinction between nepotism and other kinds of favoritism.) What's more, Jackson never abandoned his familial notion of politics. In his farewell address, the old man warned that with the passing of the fathers, the only hope for future harmony lay in the "fraternal attachment which the citizens of the several States bear to one another as members of one political family." The alternative, he somberly pronounced, was "Civil warr."

THE BROTHERS' WAR: LINCOLN AND THE TRANSFORMATION OF KINSHIP

Denton Offut's store was the center of village life in New Salem, affording a clever and ambitious young man like Abe Lincoln an opportunity to get to know every voter in the neighborhood. With his ready wit and inexhaustible fund of jokes and stories, he quickly became very popular. He also developed the reputation for integrity and fair dealing that would serve him well in later life, and it was here that he became known as Honest Abe.

New Salem was a typical Illinois frontier town, settled by groups of families that had drifted north from Virginia, Kentucky, and Tennessee, intermarrying as they went. John Clary had married Rhoda Armstrong and settled with his in-laws at a place called Clary's Grove. His brother maintained a store at New Salem, and his nephew Jack Armstrong became the leader of a local gang. The Clary's Grove boys were the terror of the neighborhood, and a storekeeper who failed to pay them tribute in the form of free drinks would have his place of business wrecked.

Offut often boasted of his young clerk's formidable strength, and Bill Clary bet him $10 that his nephew could beat him. The whole countryside turned out to watch the fight. Some say Lincoln bested Armstrong, others that they fought to a draw. According to one witness, "after struggling for a long time without either one prevailing, Lincoln said, 'Jack, let's quit. I can't throw you—you can't throw me.'" The fight ended in friendship, and Lincoln not only earned the gang's respect but became their informal leader: a second in their fights, a peacemaker in their feuds, and an undisputed judge in their contests. For years they were his devoted followers and later his stalwart partisans and vote getters.[27]

In the Western heroic tradition, the youthful leader often establishes his authority by besting the strongest young tough in the neighborhood. King Arthur beats the undefeated Lancelot, and Robin Hood knocks Little John off a bridge with a blow from his staff. The difference is that Lincoln was a democratic leader, not a king or bandit prince. And in Lincoln's view, the essence of democracy was friendship. Lincoln's whole career is a study in the uses of friendship in a democratic society and its limitations in the face of a great national crisis. Friendship was instrumental in his rise, in his approach to party politics, and in his use of political patronage.

Lincoln has been viewed from many angles, but never in terms of his importance to the history of nepotism. Earlier we specified that nepotism combines three essential ingredients: kin selection, coercion, and reciprocal altruism. In the smallest societies, composed entirely of relatives, kin selection suffices to create a basis for cooperation and trust. As societies grow larger, reciprocity and coercion play a larger role. In large-scale, multiethnic societies like ours, kin selection diminishes sharply in favor of reciprocity (in the form of a legal code) and coercion (in the form of a national ideology backed by the power of the state). If we imagine nepotism as a continuum, with kin selection at one end and reciprocal altruism at the other, we can describe American history as a shift from left to right. America goes from being an agrarian society, based on kinship and patronage, to a commercial and industrial society of isolated individuals, united by a national idea and governed by the norms of reciprocal altruism. The Civil War was the turning point in this process, and Lincoln was both its agent and its symbol. As a result of his leadership our national identity became less a matter of blood and more a matter of affiliation and belief. The key to this revolution was Lincoln's liberation of reciprocity as a constructive and positive force in American life.

Lincoln's gift for friendship was nourished by three sources: his early reading, the cultural traditions of his heritage, and the raw egalitarian democracy of the frontier. He used this gift for friendship in his rise and applied it in an ever-widening circle to the problems of party unity, political patronage, and national identity.

The image of the barefoot country boy who rose to be president through merit and hard work was crucial to Lincoln's political success.

Summing up the democratic spirit of his age, he once said, "I don't know who my grandfather was, and I am much more concerned to know what his grandson will be." The corollary to this myth is the denigration and erasure of his family. In the biography of Lincoln written by his partner, William Herndon, Lincoln's family were described accurately enough as "poor whites" who drifted west like human flotsam seeking better opportunities. But he greatly exaggerated their poverty, obscurity, and misery in an effort to show that his hero deserved more credit than other self-made men—not because he had risen so high, but from such a low place. "Lincoln rose," wrote Herndon, "from a lower depth than any of them—from a stagnant, putrid pool."

Lincoln was indeed a self-made man, authentic as they come. Yet it is not true that he rose from depths of miserable obscurity and owed nothing at all to his family. The social distance Lincoln traveled was not as great as most people believe. Lincoln's father may have sunk below the level of his birth, but the family itself was long established and had claims to gentry status—claims of which the future president was hardly unaware. Nor was he indifferent to his ancestry.

Samuel Lincoln came to Massachusetts in 1637, where he prospered. His grandson Mordecai moved to New Jersey, married Hannah Salter, of a prominent Quaker family, and later became a Pennsylvania landowner; he served as justice of the peace and his sons were elected to the assembly. His grandson John moved to Virginia, and John's grandson Abraham went to Kentucky on the advice of his kinsman Daniel Boone. After John was killed by Indians, his estate of nearly six thousand acres passed to his eldest son, Mordecai Lincoln. His brothers Jacob and Josiah thrived, but Thomas Lincoln, the president's father, did not. He apprenticed himself to a carpenter, married his niece, Nancy Hanks, and moved to Kentucky, where he purchased a small farm. This farm failed, as did a second. He then acquired a third at Knob Creek, where he managed for a while to make a go of it. There the couple's children Sarah and Abraham were born.

Little is known of Lincoln's mother aside from the fact that she was sensitive, good-natured, and deeply religious. Lincoln idealized her memory—"All that I am or hope to be I owe to my angel mother." But Lincoln probably wasn't thinking of her influence in *material,* but in *spiritual* terms. Herndon later reported a conversation in which Lincoln extolled the virtues of illegitimate children and revealed that he himself was the descendant of an illegitimate union between Nancy Hanks's mother and a rich Virginia planter. "From 'this broad-minded unknown Virginian,'" writes biographer David Donald, "Lincoln believed he had inherited the traits that distinguished him from the other members of his family."

Thomas Lincoln's reputation is no better than that of Carlo Buonaparte. He has come down to us as an illiterate vagrant who spent his life buying farms on credit, watching them fail, and moving on to greener pastures. While his older brothers became rich and influential, Thomas never learned to read, and like many a frontiersman he preferred hunting, fishing, and odd jobs of carpentry to the tedium of farmwork. But while it may be true that Thomas Lincoln was a failure who speedily sank to the bottom of the social scale, the fault was only partly in himself. His lot was that of a younger son who had to make it on his own in a turbulent era. Added to this was a string of bad luck and poor judgments. Nor is it true that he lacked ambition. His many migrations and the acquisition of one farm after another are signs of energy and purpose.[28] He was unlucky in his purchases, however. The deeds to two of his farms proved defective, and after some contention involving the third he decided to try his luck elsewhere. Selling his property at a loss, he moved to Indiana, settling in a town called Pigeon's Creek. Bad luck struck again when Nancy Lincoln died, and Thomas returned to Kentucky. He came back with Sarah Johnston, a widow with three children of her own. Sarah brought some order to the squalid frontier cabin, and though illiterate herself, she insisted that Abe learn to read.

Tom Lincoln has been described as a brute who treated his son like a servant, beating him and dragging him away from his books by the ear to do his chores. In fact, he was neither a harsh disciplinarian nor opposed to his son's education. Lincoln went to school when there was one for him to go to; usually there wasn't. Otherwise he read voraciously, whenever he got a chance. Moreover, the beatings his father inflicted were mainly due to Lincoln's laziness. Often when plowing a field he would pause at the end of a furrow to read, in order (he said) to let the horses breathe.

Lincoln's early reading was confined to the Bible, Aesop's *Fables*, *The Pilgrim's Progress*, Grimshaw's *History of the United States*, Parson

Weems's biography of Washington, and *Robinson Crusoe.* Aesop's *Fables* often deal with the consequences of selfish or shortsighted actions. Characters in Aesop generally get what they deserve for violating basic rules of reciprocity like fairness, generosity, and gratitude or by falling prey to envy, greed, and spite. "Honesty is the best policy," "Persuasion is better than force," "There are two sides to every question," "Two wrongs don't make a right," "Revenge is a two-edged sword," "Turnabout is fair play," "When you betray a friend you harm yourself." One of Lincoln's favorites was the story of the bundle of sticks. One day a father summoned his three quarrelsome sons, showed them a bundle of sticks, and told them to break it. Each one tried, but none could do it. The father then untied the bundle and broke them one by one. You see, he told them, how easy it is to break the sticks when they are not united. Let this be a lesson to you: union gives strength.

A similar lesson is found in the rejection of retributive justice by Jesus and Paul. For the harsh Old Testament tradition that demanded an eye for an eye, Jesus substituted the gentle admonitions "Love thy neighbor as thyself" and "Turn the other cheek." "Do not repay evil for evil," counsels Paul. Lincoln was not a churchgoing Christian and was later suspected of atheism. He drew from Christianity mainly its ethical doctrine of justice and mercy, and he made it his rule throughout life.

Lincoln's Quaker heritage may also have inclined him to this principle. The Quaker tradition of reciprocal liberty is based on the Golden Rule—do unto others as you would have others do unto you. This recognition of moral equality is also the basis of friendship. Not for nothing did the Quakers call themselves the Society of Friends. In Pennsylvania, rights of political representation and religious toleration went beyond those in any of the other British colonies. Laws against search and seizure and unjust taxation, the protection of property, and the right to a jury trial were other manifestations of the reciprocal principle. This practical application of the Golden Rule also led Quakers to develop a powerful antislavery consensus.

The lessons of reciprocity that Lincoln absorbed from the Bible and Aesop harmonized with the democratic and egalitarian spirit of the frontier. Frontier life as Lincoln knew it was crude and unpretentious. Large families were crowded together in one-room cabins, sanitation was nonexistent, privacy unthinkable. Everyone drank heavily, and fights and feuds were common. A society of such rude, unfettered individualists could never be based on consensus but only on a shared respect for fairness and equality.

Lincoln's grasp of reciprocity and its role in the creation of trust may be seen above all in his genius for friendship. Lincoln made friends with astonishing ease and was most alive in company with others. He went to all the local gatherings—corn shuckings, logrollings, barn raisings, wool shearings, hog killings, quilting bees—and invariably gathered a crowd, holding them rapt with his humorous tales. Often he would put down axe or hoe and mount a stump to make a speech, and the other men would gather round to listen, laughing so hard their bellies ached. These speeches often drew upon the parables and fables he derived from the Bible and Aesop. But sociability alone was not enough, and in this raw frontier society Lincoln's great stature (he was six feet four) and physical strength proved valuable assets. His size and strength earned respect and grudging tolerance for his pronounced peculiarities.

Thomas Lincoln's ill repute—like that of Napoleon's father—seems to have begun with Abe himself. There was little similarity between them, and perhaps we shouldn't wonder that Abe ascribed his very different inclinations to the shadowy legacy of his dead mother. Thomas for his part was clearly ambivalent regarding his son's intellectual interests, and unlike more socially ambitious fathers whose nepotism took the form of a heavy investment in their sons' education, Thomas showed no interest in seeing Abe rise above his own station and tried to keep him on the farm as long as possible. But in 1830, having attained his majority, Abe struck out on his own, and when Denton Offut offered him a job in New Salem, he eagerly accepted.

While Lincoln's family can hardly be described as "a putrid, stagnant pool," he knew he could expect no help from them. His greatest asset was his character: everybody liked and wished him well. Lincoln was rich in social gifts, and this was all the capital he needed for a start in frontier politics. In 1831, he joined the militia to fight in the Black Hawk War and was elected captain by his fellows (the unit was mainly comprised of his friends from the Clary's Grove gang). The next year, he decided to run for state assembly. Most Westerners were followers of Jackson, but Lincoln's hero was Henry Clay, the great Whig orator and statesman. Lincoln ran on a Whig-inspired platform of internal improvements, support for education, and a national tariff. He also called for legal restraints against usury, reflecting his concern to limit the exploitation of one man by another. Though he won every vote but three in New Salem, he was virtually unknown outside the district and was soundly defeated.

Where did this spark of political ambition come from? While some have ascribed it to the influence on frontier youths of Andrew Jackson, Lincoln may also have been motivated by a knowledge of family history. Despite his father's slide into obscurity, his great-uncles were successful planters, military officers, and public officeholders. Isaac Lincoln owned forty-one slaves, and Uncle Mordecai, a Kentucky landowner with six thousand acres, had served as county sheriff and justice of the peace. Lincoln saw a good deal of Uncle Mord, and the image of this successful and powerful man, so unlike his father, must have given him a larger view of his own prospects. Indeed, Lincoln undoubtedly knew of at least seven male relatives who had recently held public office in Kentucky, Illinois, and Indiana.[29] Thus, in choosing to pursue a genteel career in law or politics, he was not so much rising above his father's station as pursuing an established family tradition. Though he avoided any mention of these "wealthy and popular" connections in his various campaigns, according to one historian this family background "could only have been a source of pride and strength."[30]

Lincoln was viewed in his own lifetime as a person who had made it on merit and virtue alone, without the help of family or kin. A great deal is invested in this view, as it is in the idea that he was always, in a sense, what he was destined to become. Our purpose here is not to debunk that idealized image, but simply to show that Lincoln understood as well as anyone else the importance of a family tradition and the value of familial connections. Lincoln had as much social ambition as the next man—maybe more—and his rise in frontier politics was marked as much by the skillful manipulation of patronage and marital connections as it was by his undoubted personal qualities of diligence, intelligence, and character.

Lincoln's defeat in 1832 had left him at loose ends and he therefore accepted an offer to go into business with a storekeeper named Berry.

Partnership is another relation governed by reciprocity, and throughout his life Lincoln instinctively sought to form partnerships as he also formed friendships. The store went belly-up within the year and Berry died, leaving a mountain of debt. Twenty-eight years later, Lincoln described his predicament in a brief autobiography. "He was now without means and out of business," he wrote of himself, "but was anxious to remain with his friends who had treated him with so much generosity." Lincoln's faith in his friends was well founded. County surveyor John Calhoun made Lincoln his assistant and later had him appointed deputy surveyor. In 1833 his friends obtained for him the postmastership at New Salem. He also took to frequenting the courts and began his lifelong study of the law.

In 1834 Lincoln was elected to the Illinois legislature, joining the nine-man Whig delegation from Sangamon County whose leader was John Todd Stuart, a major figure in the political clique known as the Springfield Junto, centered on the powerful Edwards family. Lincoln served four terms and made numerous friends, including Cyrus Edwards, brother of the late senator and governor Ninian Edwards, and Ninian Wirt Edwards, the governor's son, who would later become Lincoln's brother-in-law. The high point of his legislative career was the removal of the state capital from Vandalia to Springfield, a controversial issue that Lincoln managed so well that several men from other districts supported him despite their constituents' interests. As one former member recalled, "We defended our vote before our constituents by saying that necessity would ultimately force the seat of government to a central position; but in reality, we gave the vote to Lincoln because we liked him, because we wanted to oblige our friend, and because we recognized him as our leader."[31] At a celebratory dinner given by Stuart, Lincoln toasted "All our friends—They are too numerous to be now named individually, while there is no one of them who is not too dear to be forgotten or neglected." Nor did he: when Lincoln became president only three other members of the old Sangamon delegation were still active. All received lucrative patronage appointments.[32]

In 1837, Lincoln moved to Springfield and entered legal practice with his friend and mentor Stuart. Famously, he rode into town on a borrowed horse and stopped by the store of Joshua Speed to inquire about a bed. Speed immediately befriended him and invited him to share his room, rent free. Their closeness lasted for the rest of Lincoln's life. Speed's brother later became Lincoln's attorney general.

Lincoln's sense of family vocation may also explain his pursuit of potential brides above his station. In his Vandalia years he had courted several girls of better breeding than himself. Now he found himself included in the circle of the gubernatorial Edwards family. Ninian Edwards had married Elizabeth Todd, of a good Kentucky family, and her sisters married other leading citizens. When Lincoln wooed and married Mary Todd—Edwards's sister-in-law and a cousin of John Todd Stuart—he acquired a family connection to the junto. Mary's friends thought Lincoln her social inferior, but Edwards and Stuart supported the match, saying somewhat mysteriously that it was "for policy."

When Stuart went to Congress in 1839, Lincoln accepted an offer of partnership from Stephen T. Logan, the leading lawyer in the state. The partnership dissolved in 1844 when Logan took his son into the practice, and Lincoln set up his own practice with William Herndon, who had read law in Logan's office. "Many found the new partnership puzzling," David Donald writes. His reasons may have been political—Lincoln had set his sights on higher office, and Billy Herndon (son of a state senator) was the leader of a group of young Whigs whose support he would need. But he was also plainly tired of being a protégé and wanted to take his turn at being a patron. Though Billy was his junior, Lincoln observed his rule of reciprocity and split the profits fifty-fifty.[33]

Reciprocity was not just the basis of friendship and partnership: it could also be used to heal party strife, which Lincoln saw as a kind of civil war. The spirit of reciprocity marked Lincoln's whole approach to party politics, as shown by his role in bringing order to the nominating procedures of the Illinois Whigs. The same emphasis would characterize his approach to building the Republican Party, and his later use of patronage as president.

When Stuart announced in 1843 that he would resign after two terms in Congress, an intense rivalry ensued among Whig regulars. Lincoln had already deferred his aspirations for four years to accommodate his friend and partner Stuart. Now he was faced with two new rivals, John Hardin and Edward Baker, able politicians who were also good friends. (Indeed, he had named his second son Edward Baker Lincoln.) Lincoln had long argued that to be a real national force, the Whigs must practice organized party politics instead of the elite-dominated personal politics still prevalent on the frontier. He also pressed for the expansion of reciprocity within the party itself. Thus at the Illinois Whig convention that endorsed Hardin's candidacy, Lincoln put forth a resolution committing the party to the principle of rotation in office and the holding of regular nominating conventions. In making the case for conventions, Lincoln had to counter a strong streak of antiparty sentiment among Illinois Whigs, and he resorted to the Aesopian fables derived from his earliest reading.

> That "union is strength" is a truth that has been known, illustrated and declared, in various ways and forms in all the ages of the world. That great fabulist and philosopher, Aesop, illustrated it by his fable of the bundle of sticks, and he whose wisdom surpasses that of all philosophers, has declared that "a house divided against itself cannot stand."[34]

To resolve the impasse, Lincoln now proposed a private deal with his two rivals whereby each would take a turn in Congress. Hardin would serve first, then Baker, then Lincoln. The first two elections (in 1843 and 1845) went as planned, but when Hardin decided to run for a second term, Lincoln wrote him a long letter reminding him of their agreement and stressing the Aesopian idea that "turnabout is fair play." Hardin rejected this appeal and Lincoln was obliged to outflank him, lining up endorsements throughout the district and getting the party to reaffirm his principle of institutional reciprocity. The whole campaign hinged on this issue, with Lincoln saying that all he wanted was "a fair shake." Lincoln claimed no superiority over Hardin but rested his entire case on the idea of rotation in office. Party newspapers agreed, editorializing that "turnabout is fair play" and that it was "Abraham's turn." Finally Hardin withdrew, leaving Lincoln free to claim the nomination.

Though Lincoln was as ambitious as the next man, he was prepared to wait his turn, defer to his friends, and show good faith by going last. This program is the essence of reciprocity. It also explains why Lincoln was so angered by Hardin's failure to respect their agreement: If reciprocity is broken, the spirit of friendship collapses. As in the computer game of Tit for Tat, negative reciprocity takes over and propagates distrust instead of harmony.

Elected to Congress in 1847, Lincoln joined the Whigs under the leadership of Webster, Clay, and Adams. In 1848 he was instrumental in obtaining the endorsement of Illinois Whigs for Zachary Taylor and worked tirelessly on his behalf. After the election, Lincoln tried to obtain a cabinet post for Edward Baker and an appointment as land office commissioner for himself, to no avail. Annoyed by this poor requital of his services, he went back to legal practice and spent the next five years in deeper cultivation of his intellect. Above all he had time to contemplate the question of slavery, which had become the central problem of American politics. In the early 1850s a series of compromises had dampened sectional hostilities over slavery and its extension to the western states. Nevertheless, throughout this period a growing sectional consciousness emerged. While the North had been transformed into a thriving industrial and commercial society by massive streams of European immigration, the South had remained largely agrarian and its population much more stable and homogeneous. Finally the Kansas-Nebraska Act of 1854 split Whigs and Democrats into sectional wings, and a meeting of free-soil elements in Ripon, Wisconsin, announced the formation of a new Republican Party. In 1858, at a party convention in Springfield, Lincoln stated the case with brutal clarity: the American house was fatally divided. The "house divided" speech made Lincoln a national figure and launched his presidential bid in 1860. But it was also the last time an American politician could appeal to the idea of the nation as a family. When the Civil War began, a deeply divided country could still be addressed as a household. By the end, though it was united as never before, this metaphor no longer applied.

Presidents from Washington to Jackson had spoken of America as an extended political family. Though this was always understood to be a fiction on one level, it was rooted in a system of social relations that seamlessly extended the authority of the patriarchal household to society at large. By Lincoln's time, however, that fiction had worn very thin. Lincoln's call for family harmony was a last-ditch appeal to this once-persuasive metaphor, and its failure suggests that the Civil War resulted partly from a breakdown in the household vision of American politics.

As David Hackett Fischer points out, every president up to 1856 had been the product of a single cultural region. But as America industrialized, becoming both more mobile and more ethnically diverse, the basis of political unity shifted from family to party and from kinship to ideology. Beginning with James Buchanan, a series of "omnibus" presidents of mixed regional descent appealed to an increasingly diversified electorate. Lincoln, with his Puritan-Quaker ancestry and Western roots, embodied the three regional cultures in the emerging Republican coalition. Though he set little store by his Puritan ancestry, he did retain its legacies of legalism, conscience, and the plain style in speech and dress. The Quaker tradition of reciprocal liberty was also fundamental to his outlook.

As late as 1859 Lincoln disclaimed any aspiration to the presidency. But as the Democrats fragmented and his reputation grew, his friends began to think he could be nominated. After his Cooper Union speech won the hearts of New York Republicans in February 1860, presidential hopefuls Salmon P. Chase and Simon Cameron floated his name as a potential running mate, and he received the endorsement of the Illinois Republicans. Now Lincoln's lifelong cultivation of friendship paid off. The core of his faction were old Illinois cronies like Joseph Medill, Richard Yates, Orville Browning, David Davis, Joshua Speed, Billy Herndon, Stephen Logan, and John Todd Stuart. To these were added friends from Congress and national party figures like Leonard Swett of Maine and Samuel Parks of Vermont. Together these friends set out to make him president. Norman Judd arranged for the convention to be held in Chicago, giving Lincoln a home court advantage, and separated the New York and Pennsylvania delegations so they couldn't confer during votes. Parks and Swett secured their home state delegations, and Logan and Browning lined up other constituencies. Despite explicit instructions to make no binding deals, Lincoln's friends were liberal with promises of patronage. Davis won the Indiana delegation on this basis, and Medill clinched the last four crucial votes by telling the head of the Ohio delegation, "Chase can have anything he wants."

Lincoln's election brought immediate results: South Carolina seceded, followed by six other slaveholding states. By the date of his inauguration, on March 4, 1861, Jefferson Davis had already announced the Confederacy. Lincoln's inaugural address warned the seceded states to return or face the consequences. Yet he ended on an elegiac note: "I am loath to close. We are not enemies, but friends. We must not be enemies." This plaintive appeal to friendship was unavailing. The cycle of mistrust—of negative reciprocity—had spiraled out of control: the South was lost to the violent logic of the feud.

It has often been said that the worst thing about civil war is that it divides families and pits brother against brother.[35] The American Civil War was indeed a great disruption in the structure of society, ripping apart the fragile fabric that had held the country together for nearly a century. This rupture did not occur all at once, however, nor did it happen uniformly. North and South did not split evenly along the Mason-Dixon Line. In many places, sympathies varied county by county and town by town. Even in the Deep South states of Florida, Georgia, and Texas, pockets of Union sentiment remained throughout the war. Nor was the North monolithic: Pennsylvania, New Jersey, and New York all had large Southern-born minorities. Pro-Southern sentiment was also strong among Boston textile manufacturers (the so-called Cotton Whigs) and New York bankers. Some proposed that if the Union dissolved, New York should follow suit and declare itself an open port.

Southern nationalism was a powerful force, deeply rooted in kinship and culture. The relative homogeneity of Southern populations, the extended kinship ties typical of an agrarian society, and a deeply ingrained tradition of local sovereignty all enhanced the region's unity. The South had also preserved its military ethos, with its ubiquitous militias, its military academies, and its clan-based code of masculine honor. The North, in contrast, had been rapidly industrialized, flooded with new immigrants, and galvanized by a revolution in transportation and commerce. Though large and potentially powerful, it was riven by class and regional interests, divided political loyalties, and a powerful nativist movement. The differences between North and South were so deep that many in

America and Europe had come to believe that the South was well on its way to becoming an independent nation.

Southern culture was profoundly conservative, and historians have long emphasized the role of kinship in preserving its continuity. Frank L. Owsley believed that Southerners were "a genuine folk long before the Civil War," and explained that the source of this unique solidarity was "the closely knit family with its ramified and widespreading kinship ties."[36] The spirit of Southern nationalism itself was rooted in this nepotistic ethos. According to Daniel Crofts, most Southerners lived in static rural communities "defined by kinship, habits of mutuality, and an intricate network of patron-client relationships."[37] People in these districts voted as a group and took their lead from local oligarchies. Such ties naturally extended to a broader solidarity with the cause of Southern nationhood. Notwithstanding evidence of intense class conflict within this Southern society, freehold farmers who had no stake in slavery themselves eagerly enlisted to defend the South against what they perceived as a challenge to their cultural existence. As one Southern unionist observed: "Sympathy with friends and kindred became the bond that united the South. Tens of thousands of men who had no heart for secession, did have heart for their neighbors and kindred. This almost universal fellowship and sympathy drew men together in behalf of a cause which one-half of them had disapproved." Those who tried to swim against this current were treated harshly.[38]

If the Civil War was an ideological matter to Lincoln and the slaveholders, for many others on both sides it was just as much a matter of loyalty to family and kin. Indeed the failure of symbolic nepotism at the national level corresponded with an intensification of blood-based nepotism at the sectional level, and this aspect of the crisis has been generally neglected. Nowhere was this more evident than in recruitment drives held across the South in which wives and mothers exhorted their men to preserve Southern honor and defend hearth and home against Yankee aggression. Lincoln's election and the threat of force had deeply stirred these kin-based loyalties: it was a challenge to Southern nepotism, bringing it into play as an active political principle. (We should also recall that most military units were raised locally and were largely composed of relatives, neighbors, and friends.) Yet such nepotism had its limitations: the same protective impulse that had led men to march off to war later led them to abandon the cause and desert from the army in droves. When Southern women, tired of coping on their own, demanded their return, many soldiers dropped their rifles and went home.

By April 1861 the seven slave states had seceded, but the eight states of the upper South were hanging in the balance. If they could be kept in the Union, all might not be lost. Yielding to the radicals, Lincoln called for the raising of seventy-five thousand troops. This had the effect of galvanizing prosecession sentiment throughout the upper South. Fraternal metaphors flew thick and fast. Gov. Beriah Magoffin announced that Kentucky would "furnish no troops for the wicked purpose of subduing her sister Southern states." Tennessee's governor also refused to comply, but promised "fifty thousand if necessary for the defense of our rights and those of our Southern brothers." In Virginia and North Carolina as well, it was felt that "the South must go with the South . . . Blood is thicker than water." Virginia seceded two days later, followed by Arkansas, North Carolina, and Tennessee. This left Maryland, Delaware, Missouri, and Kentucky. Maryland was only kept in by a threat of invasion. Delaware was likewise retained largely by force. Missouri's governor tried to convene a rebel government but his efforts were crushed.

That left Kentucky—in Lincoln's view, the key to the whole struggle. Kentucky was evenly split, and here the phrase "the Brothers' War" was no mere metaphor: "domestic ties were rent asunder, brother against brother, father against son, the whole social structure crumbling in the vast upheaval." The state's three great political families—the Clays, Crittendens, and Breckinridges—were "torn down the middle."[39] The Bluegrass region around Lexington was also home to Mary Lincoln's family, many of whom were slaveholders. Thus as the American household divided, Lincoln's family split as well. Mary's oldest brother and half sister were unionists, and Lincoln made her cousin postmaster of Lexington. But her youngest brother, George, and three half brothers joined the Confederate Army, and her three half sisters were the wives of Confederate officers. Lincoln offered a commission to her brother-in-law Ben Hardin Helm, but after painful deliberation he refused, and later died at Chickamauga. On the day he received the news, Lincoln told Judge Davis, "I feel as David of old did when he was told of the death of Absalom." When Mary's brother was killed at Shiloh, Lincoln was compared by Southern journalists to Cain.

Many thought Lincoln had bungled by calling for troops. Certainly Southern unionists blamed him for making their position untenable. But Lincoln saw that reciprocity had failed: fraternal appeals must be suspended and the right of coercion invoked to save the Union. At this moment, Lincoln may be said to have abandoned the fraternal approach that marked his earlier career and assumed the role of patriarch: a stern father who refuses to share authority and calls implacably for filial sacrifice. In the process he made the presidency more powerful than it had ever been before. As the war progressed, this new patriarchal quality in Lincoln asserted itself more and more.

Even before leaving Springfield, Lincoln was besieged with office seekers: "they descended on him in such numbers that Springfield's hotels and boardinghouses were crammed and the overflow put up in sleeping-cars."[40] At one point, having contracted a slight case of smallpox, he said to his secretary: "Tell all the office seekers to come at once for now I have something I can give to all of them."

Lincoln's first task was to assemble a cabinet that was sectionally and ideologically balanced and would repay his political debts. In this, he was handicapped by the promises made on his behalf by his friends at the Chicago convention. Yet instinctively he knew how to proceed, writing to William Seward: "In regard to the patronage, sought with so much eagerness and jealousy, I have prescribed for myself the maxim 'Justice for all.'"[41] This Aesopian rule of reciprocity would stand him in good stead.

His first appointment went to Seward: the New York governor became secretary of state. Another disappointed candidate, Pennsylvania senator Simon Cameron, became secretary of war. These men were opposed by Gov. Salmon P. Chase of Ohio, who became secretary of the Treasury, and Montgomery Blair, who became postmaster general. Caleb B. Smith of Indiana, a Cameron man who had pledged his state to Lincoln, was rewarded with Interior. Gideon Welles of Connecticut became secretary of the navy. Edward Bates of Missouri, a Blair ally, was named attorney general.

No less than members of Congress, the cabinet members bickered and maneuvered to obtain jobs for friends and relatives. Nepotism was routine. Seward made his son assistant secretary of state and gave jobs to his campaign biographer and publisher. A second son was made an army paymaster, a third became a brigadier general, and a nephew was made consul general at Shanghai. Cameron dismissed most of the War Department staff to make room for his dependents. Nor were other cabinet officers remiss in rewarding their favorites.[42]

The customs collectorships were among the most lucrative jobs in any administration, and the port of New York was the biggest. Approached by a worried delegation of New York Republicans friendly to Chase, Lincoln assured them that neither side would eat up everything. Citing his Aesopian creed of reciprocity, he advised them, "Make out a list of places and men you want, and I will endeavor to apply the rule of give and take." Lincoln's friend Edward D. Baker had gone west to found the California Republican Party, then moved to Oregon, where he performed the same service and was elected senator. Baker made it clear that he expected to have the power of dispensing patronage in California. But a delegation of California Republicans urgently petitioned against it, and a furious struggle ensued. Lincoln divided the spoils, granting some to one faction and some to the other—but making sure that Baker's son-in-law got the San Francisco mint.

Given the obvious need to keep foreign governments from aiding the rebels, one is struck by the cavalier manner in which Lincoln allowed diplomatic and consular posts to be handed out as spoils. Very few of these appointments were made on the basis of merit, the happiest exception being the posting of Charles Francis Adams to London. The other major diplomatic posts were used by Seward to repay campaign debts. The minor postings went to relatives and friends of party notables, and the secondary appointments were distributed ad lib to sons and nephews.[43] Lincoln also took special care to provide for the families of Republican newspapermen. The *Philadelphia North American* received a large government advertising contract and its Washington correspondent was named minister to Portugal, while the editor's four sons were given military and civil appointments. The publisher of the *Philadelphia Evening Bulletin* received advertising contracts and was made a navy agent, and the editor's seventy-three-year-old father became a superintendent of warehouses.

The brightest constellation in the new Republican firmament were the Blairs, a political dynasty whose longevity and influence rivaled that of the Adamses. Francis Preston Blair had been a fiery Kentucky editorialist who was tapped by Andrew Jackson to start a party newspaper in Washington. As a leading member of Jackson's kitchen cabinet, he greatly expanded his publishing enterprises, and obtained a lucrative government printing contract. The stately mansion across from the White House bought by Blair in 1863 still bears his name. The family always acted with unity to advance their political and personal interests and those of their friends, especially where patronage was concerned. As Harry J. Carman observes, "One hardly ever spoke of this Blair or that Blair; usually they were referred to as 'the Blairs.' "[44]

Blair had two sons and a daughter. Montgomery Blair, with Jackson's aid, went to West Point and served in the Seminole War before studying law under Thomas Hart Benton. A brilliant lawyer, he defended Dred Scott in the famous Supreme Court case and married the daughter of Levi Woodbury, a former congressman, cabinet officer, and Supreme Court justice. Frank Blair Jr. also studied law, and served briefly as attorney general of the New Mexico territory before becoming a Missouri congressman. The Blairs had been staunch Democrats, but as the split between North and South deepened, they skillfully adapted and played a major role in the creation of the Republican Party. Frank Sr. presided over the Pittsburgh convention of 1856 and was one of Lincoln's key supporters at the Chicago convention of 1860. Frank Jr. single-handedly kept Missouri in the Union, raising seven regiments and putting down a secessionist insurrection. As a result, the Blairs enjoyed considerable influence with Lincoln. Montgomery became postmaster general, whereupon he got his brother promoted to brigadier general and helped his brother-in-law become assistant secretary of the Navy, as well as using his powers of patronage to repay various family debts. Meanwhile, Elizabeth Blair had married Samuel Phillips Lee, a distinguished naval officer and relative of Robert E. Lee who might well have joined the Confederacy but for the influence of his wife and in-laws. (Lee ended up commanding the Union blockade for over two years.) Frank Sr. also acted for Lincoln as an emissary to Robert E. Lee, offering him the command of Union armies, and it was to old Blair that Lee uttered his famous remonstrance on the supremacy of kinship over patriotism.[45]

When not indulging the nepotistic impulses of his colleagues, Lincoln was not above a little of his own. In addition to appointing his wife's relative Edward Wallace to the Philadelphia Naval Office, he named another Wallace an army paymaster, and made her cousin John Todd a brigadier general. The Philadelphia collector's post went to J. W. Pomeroy, whose main virtue was to be related by marriage to Mrs. Lincoln. Meanwhile Lincoln arranged for his own son Robert Todd Lincoln to attend Harvard Law School and then to be a captain in the adjutant general's department. Later he was attached to the staff of General Grant. Lincoln also took care to place his many friends in good positions.[46] Nor was Lincoln's administration an exception in the number of government contracts handed out to friends, contributors, and local partisans. According to Carman, "Lincoln . . . seems not to have been averse to turning a little of the spoils into special channels. He was pleased when his friends received contracts 'on fair and just claims to the Government and to themselves.' "[47] Indeed, the origins of the Blair-Fremont feud that disrupted Missouri politics throughout the war had its roots in the rivalry between their friends over government contracts.

Surely we would expect the Union Army to be nearly sacrosanct. Yet even here politics was uppermost. The number of political debts repaid with staff commissions is astonishing to modern sensibilities. The Union Army's officer corps was an infamous patronage dump, and it would be amazing if the practice did not seriously damage the war effort—except that in all probability, the same thing was practiced in the South. Thus, Fitzhugh, Custis, and Rooney Lee all became Confederate generals.

The upshot of all this is clear: Lincoln's first administration was a mess—the result of a veritable feeding frenzy over federal, state, and local appointments. Personalism and expediency, not merit, dominated the majority of decisions. Clearly Lincoln, a man of principle if ever there was one, did not allow this to blind him to more pragmatic considerations. Or rather, he was conscious of an equally compelling principle—that of loyalty to friends and party faithful. His actions demonstrate his understanding that the inner life of politics is an aspect of the gift economy, involving the continual exchange of favors and requital of debts. Hence, in making appointments, Lincoln carefully consulted with the senators and congressmen of the states and districts concerned, with the governors of those states, and with cabinet officers regarding jobs in their states or even the appointment of men from their states to jobs in other departments. This was the way to knit the new party together in a web of reciprocal altruism. Thus he wrote to Connecticut senator James Dixon: "The bearer of this, Mr. Bronson Murray, now resident in the fourth district of Connecticut, wishes to be collector for that district. He is my acquaintance and friend of some years' standing, whom I would like to oblige, but I should not like to appoint him against the wish of yourself and other Union friends there."[48]

While Lincoln may have had the power to command, he wished to govern in a Solomonic fashion. Hence he was constrained to ask for favors in the specialized vocabulary of patronage that goes back to Stuart England and beyond, saying that such-and-such an office was "not in my gift" or "in the gift" of so-and-so. Lincoln bent over backwards to give people the idea that the distribution of jobs was being done not by personal fiat but as part of a friendly commerce in favors. Patronage could knit the party together only if men at every level were empowered to dispense their own appointments, earning the gratitude of their adherents in turn and thereby tightening the web of party unity.

Nonetheless, the overwhelming pressure to effect a given outcome sometimes led him to adopt a peremptory tone. Pressed particularly hard by an importunate office seeker, Lincoln wrote to James Pollock in something less than courtly fashion: "You must make a job for the bearer of this, make a job of it with the collector and have it done. You *can* do it for me and you *must.*" A revealing bit of correspondence is the following letter from Lincoln to Francis S. Corkran, newly appointed Baltimore naval officer, who had ignored Lincoln's request that he give the job of deputy to a certain F. S. Evans. Clearly annoyed by Corkran's failure to comply, Lincoln wrote in stilted tones:

> I am quite sure you are not aware how much I am disobliged by the refusal to give Mr. F. S. Evans a place in the Custom-House.

> I had no thought that the men to whom I had given the higher offices would be so ready to disoblige me. I still wish you would give Mr. Evans the place of Deputy Naval Officer.

When Corkran persisted in his refusal, Lincoln wrote to Secretary Chase: "I have been greatly—I may say grievously—disappointed and disobliged by Mr. Corkran's refusal to make Mr. Evans deputy naval officer, as I requested him to do. A point must be strained to give Mr. Evans a situation."[49]

If it had not been a time of crisis, Lincoln would undoubtedly have maintained a higher standard in appointments. However, if it bothered him at all—and there is no real indication that it did—he was probably able to rationalize the riot of nepotism and favoritism in his administration not simply on grounds of expediency but as being consistent with his principle of reciprocity, which he plainly saw as the key to his role as a party-builder. Shared ideals were crucial to the integrity of Lincoln's government, but the humanizing bonds of reciprocity must also be employed to knit the government together. Nor was this the end of Lincoln's use of reciprocity. He not only employed it to unite the Republican Party but sought to extend it as the basis of a new approach to coalition politics. Ultimately this led to a radical redefinition of American citizenship itself.

The 1840s and 1850s had been marked by a dramatic surge in immigration. Where only about 250,000 immigrants had entered the country between 1800 and 1830, in the 1840s and 1850s ten times that number arrived, most of them German and Irish. In response, a strong nativist movement arose that greatly accelerated the breakdown of established political parties. In his youth, Lincoln had encountered many immigrants—there was a large German population around Springfield—and he instinctively abhorred ethnic prejudice, which he saw as incompatible with the axiom of equality at the heart of the American creed. Coupled with this was his awareness of the voting power the new immigrants possessed, and he was determined to bring them into the Republican Party. All that was lacking was a governing philosophy that could effect their seamless inclusion into American society.[50]

Lincoln had long been concerned with the problem of national unity. In 1838, well before the beginnings of the ultimate secession crisis, he had addressed the problem in his first Lyceum speech. There he observed that for the past sixty years, sentiments of national unity had ultimately derived from the remembered experiences of the Revolution, passed down in American families. "The consequence was, that of those scenes [of Revolutionary struggle], in the form of a husband, a father, a son or a brother, a living history was to be found in every family.... But those histories are gone. They can be read no more forever." Lincoln thus concluded that where *passion*—in the form of the remembered wounds of battles fought and won—had once served to hold the republic together, that role would henceforth have to be supplied by *reason,* in the form of reverence for the laws and the Constitution.

Speaking in Chicago twenty years later on July 4, 1858, Lincoln observed that the true challenge to national unity derived from the fact that half the country's population was now made up of European immigrants and their descendants—"German, Irish, French and Scandinavian."

> If they look back through this history to trace their connection with those days by blood, they find they have none, they cannot carry themselves back into that glorious epoch and make themselves feel that they are part of us, but when they look back through that old Declaration of Independence they find that these old men say that "We hold these truths to be self evident, that all men are created equal," and then they feel that the moral sentiment taught in that day evidences their relation to those men, that it is the father of all moral principle in them, and that they have a right to claim it as though they were blood of the blood and flesh of the flesh of the men who wrote that Declaration, and so they are.[51]

Lincoln's statement sweepingly redefines American citizenship as a matter not of blood or descent but of "fidelity to our country and its institutions." This may seem to do away with kinship altogether, but Lincoln's speech is better understood as *universalizing* kinship by redefining it as a moral and intellectual commitment to the founding premise of American democracy: "All men are created equal." Once we accepted this premise, it followed that men would recognize their kinship and treat one another as brothers.

This expanded view of the American community went well beyond that of earlier presidents. Even Jackson, the great democrat, had limited his expansive view of the national family to those of English or Scots Irish descent. Jacksonian democracy unified the diverse regional cultures of the English diaspora in a broader Anglo-American ethnicity. Lincoln extended this definition even further to include all those of European descent, regardless of national origin—as long as they were white. Indeed, Lincoln is for all intents and purposes the inventor of "whiteness" as an ethnic category. To that extent, his universalist creed is simply more high-minded hypocrisy about nepotism. It denies the authority of kinship, but it is based on the suppression of the classical kinship ethos, as epitomized in his defeat of Southern nationalism. Nor (despite his genuine abhorrence of nativism and racial prejudice) did his new definition of kinship include blacks, Hispanics, Indians, or Asians.[52]

Lincoln also did his part to advance the nineteenth-century war on nepotism—primarily by signing the Morrill Act, which made monogamy the law of the land. This provision was a blow against the Mormons, a persecuted sect who had gone west seeking freedom to observe their peculiar beliefs. But the growing campaign to impose Victorian family norms on the culturally diverse American populace could not abide this nonconformity.

The American West is often characterized as a setting of extreme individualism where traditional ties and attachments were broken up and old communal identities shattered. The rapid spread of permissive divorce laws throughout the West supports this view; so many people sought to take advantage of them that many western states became known as divorce mills. Yet paradoxically, the West was equally hospitable to nepotistic impulses of the most archaic kind. Throughout the nineteenth century a steady stream of emigrants trickled west, but after the passage of the Homestead Act in 1862, the stream became a flood, and hundreds of new settlements dotted the midwestern plains.[53] Much of this occurred in the familiar chain-migration pattern, with individuals and families blazing a trail and sending for their relatives. Many families banded together to form emigrant associations, pooling capital and knowledge in a way that greatly reduced the risks of relocation, and the journey west was often eased by lengthy stops along the way with relatives who had migrated earlier. The same patterns applied to Europeans, with waves of chain migration resulting in the transplantation of whole districts to the American Midwest. The result was a series of immigrant enclaves that maintained their foreign cultural traditions for several generations.[54]

The ability to maintain a state of near-total isolation made the West particularly attractive to dissenting religious groups and utopian communities. Over the centuries, America has been home to many such experiments. Most have disappeared, and the main factor in determining their longevity has been their attitude toward sex and reproduction. The more nepotistic the group—the more focused on the creation of large, stable, intact families—the longer it survived. Harmonists and Shakers, who practiced celibacy and relied on conversion to replenish their ranks, soon died out. Conversely, those that practiced open or group marriage, like the Oneida community founded in New York by Joseph Noyes, sooner or later ran afoul of the nepotistic instinct. (Utopians often underestimate the power of parent-child attachment.) In contrast, the Amish, Amanas, and Hutterites, who established closed monogamous communities, still survive today.[55]

Of all these groups, by far the most successful were the Mormons—today the fifth-largest religious group in the United States, with over 9 million members worldwide. The Mormons were founded in 1830 by Joseph Smith, who claimed to have received a divine revelation in upstate New York. Smith's project of creating a "new Israel" included the revival of ancient social practices described in the Old Testament. His sect attracted many converts, but persecution forced them to move westward in a series of migrations to Ohio, Missouri, and Illinois. There Smith received a further revelation directing him to institute polygamous marriage. After Smith was lynched by an angry mob in 1844, his disciple Brigham Young brought the Mormons on their "exodus" to Utah and established the independent state of Deseret in 1849.[56]

Mormon polygamy has often been viewed as a form of patriarchal domination motivated by sexual selfishness, but according to historians it is better understood as a highly successful group survival strategy.[57] From the outset, persecution caused the Mormons to rely upon their family and kin. The adoption of polygamy not only produced a bumper crop of children but extended the web of kinship throughout Mormon society. The resulting networks were very large: at his death, for example, the Mormon patriarch Benjamin Johnson was related by blood or marriage to more than eight hundred people. Mormons considered polygamy to be "the very quintessence of their faith." On the other hand, they were very free in granting divorces to both men and women, an equal cause of anti-Mormon hostility. When the U.S. government recognized the Utah Territory in 1850, bringing the Mormons back under federal law, a long-running struggle ensued to reform their marriage practices.

The murderous hostility toward polygamy is perplexing, but according to sociobiologists it all comes down to nepotism. Since all men seek to maximize their reproductive fitness, it is in the interest of each man to have as many offspring as he can. This is why in societies that still allow polygamy, the practice is found mainly among high status males.[58] The nineteenth-century war against polygamy was therefore fueled by nepotistic envy on the part of other males. But it was also part of a broader campaign to regularize American social relations in light of the new, bourgeois morality that emerged with the industrial age. Polygamy was viewed as a threat to the sanctity of the monogamous family by the same Puritan-Quaker crusaders who pushed temperance, abolition, and feminism. Indeed, in 1856 the Republican Party officially denounced polygamy and slavery as the "Twin Relics of Barbarism."

The 1862 Morrill Anti-Bigamy Act, signed into law by Abraham Lincoln, was not enforced, due to the Civil War. As Lincoln observed with characteristic sagacity to a Mormon representative, "You tell Brigham Young if he will leave me alone, I'll leave him alone." Mormon requests to be admitted to the Union after the war were rejected, and further antipolygamy statutes were enacted in 1882 and 1884; but Mormons refused to recognize them. Meanwhile, confounding the expectations of those who viewed polygamy as inherently antifemale, Mormon women organized to protest the measures, and in 1870 Utah became the second territory in the nation to grant women the vote, decades before most eastern states.[59]

If polygamy was viewed as a legacy of barbarism, so was the marriage of cousins. Kansas passed the first law prohibiting consanguineal marriage in 1861, and the movement quickly spread to other states. According to Martin Ottenheimer these laws had little to do with any actual biological risks; instead their passage was driven by fears of racial degeneration, informed by crude Darwinian notions about the effects of inbreeding on "fitness."[60] Such notions dovetailed neatly with the vitalist ideas espoused by late Victorians like Lewis Henry Morgan, the founder of American anthropology. Morgan, who had made a lifelong study of marriage and kinship among the Indians of upstate New York, devised a grandiose evolutionary scheme whereby man was said to have progressed from savagery to barbarism to civilization.[61] Since marriage practices had ostensibly evolved along the same spectrum, from "primitive" endogamy to "civilized" exogamy, cousin marriage was an aspect of the middle stage of barbarism—the stage embodied by the Indians. Thus Morgan's friend and colleague Joshua H. McIlvaine observed that the "degradation and inferiority" of American Indians were the result of "intercourse among cousins."[62]

Europeans were thought to have evolved beyond this primitive stage; but (as the example of the Mormons showed) the process was not irreversible, and intellectuals like Morgan constantly worried about the potential for backsliding and decline.[63] The American West was thus perceived as a setting for both moral regeneration and potential regression to savagery, and it is hardly accidental that the civilized struggle against the "barbarous" practices of polygamy and cousin marriage took its most violent turn in the Indian wars of this period. While the usual explanation for these wars is the settlers' need for land, they may also be seen as part of a larger conflict between the system of tribal nepotism represented by the Indians (and Mormons) and the monogamous nuclear family that arose with the industrial age.[64]

Surviving American Indians continue to preserve their tribal cultures, though in greatly reduced circumstances. These tribal cultures are virtually inseparable from patterns of kinship associated with Ancient Nepotism. Like Mormons and Hutterites, the Indians' attachment to their premodern lifeways is tolerated by mainstream society largely on religious grounds. Though charges of nepotism are sometimes raised by those who seek a change in tribal government, such notions are fundamentally foreign to Indian culture. The modern Sioux consider nepotism a white man's concept that doesn't apply to a society in which everyone is related by blood, marriage, or fictive kinship ties.[65]

These are important qualifications to the notion that the West was a setting of extreme individualism. Indeed, the untamed western territory routinely called forth latent familistic tendencies. Not only did trailblazing pioneers rely on their extended families for daily survival, many outlaw gangs were also family based. The first train robbery in U.S. history was carried out in 1866 by the four Reno brothers; but the James-Younger gang that terrorized Missouri in the 1860s and 1870s is the leading example. Frank and Jesse James rode with their cousins, the four Younger brothers, and at least three other relatives. The four notorious Dalton boys were cousins of the James and Younger brothers and grew up on tales of their outlaw exploits.[66] The James gang also served as a training ground for other bandits. Bill McCarty robbed his first train with the Jameses and later started his own gang with his two younger brothers. Butch Cassidy apprenticed with the McCartys, and his Hole-in-the-Wall gang included the three Logan brothers. The Bonneys, Clantons, Cooks, and Doolins are other notable examples.

Given what we know about the familistic nature of organized crime, this is less surprising than the fact that law enforcement in the West was frequently also a family business. Wyatt Earp and his deputy brothers were far from exceptional. Especially in New Mexico and Arizona—enormous territories that could not be policed by one man—marshals and sheriffs frequently deputized family members. (The Daltons started out as marshals before turning to horse theft and train robbery.) Though controversial in some quarters, the practice was defended on the grounds that relatives would work for less and were more trustworthy than strangers, and many marshalcies became family affairs. This was especially true in Hispanic districts, where according to one historian, the local marshals practiced blatant nepotism.[67]

Even as the new national culture took shape and social relations were regularized under Victorian family norms, the West provided a haven from the efforts of middle class moralists to bring American domestic relations into conformity with the needs of the industrial age. The West stands outside the sphere of middle class domesticity, a refuge for both utopian experiment and reactionary withdrawal, and it is here that in the next century the ethos of American kinship would finally transcend the bonds of blood and become an elective affinity.

If Lincoln stands for anything it is the triumph of friendship over kinship as the principal American bond. His contribution as a statesman was to liberate the reciprocal altruism latent in the radical doctrine of equality enshrined in the Declaration of Independence. Rededicated to its founding propositions—a set of philosophical ideals rather than an ethnocultural tradition—America was well on its way to becoming a universal nation, one that anyone could join simply by espousing its basic beliefs. Yet Lincoln's idea of national kinship was limited to whites of European (or, at a stretch, Russian) background.

Why did he not extend reciprocal altruism to blacks and other racial "inferiors"? If asked, he would probably have said that no reciprocity is possible without moral and intellectual equality. But while Indians, Hispanics, blacks, and Asians were not comprehended in Lincoln's expanded definition of kinship, in time his new conception would extend to them as well. Indeed, since politics from this point on increasingly involved the forging of ethnic coalitions, national parties would henceforth be based on a formula that combined reliance on ethnic nepotism with appeals to ideological principle.

CHAPTER 10

THE ROOSEVELTS

THE MIDDLE CLASS REVOLT AGAINST NEPOTISM

The long struggle against corruption and patronage that was to be the centerpiece of the Progressive Era can be viewed as the political phase of the war on nepotism that began with the Revolution and even earlier. This war had commenced with eighteenth-century reforms that reduced the patriarchal power of fathers, primarily by democratizing inheritance and institutionalizing divorce. In the nineteenth century, the war continued on two fronts: a movement to regularize marital practices by banning such practices as polygamy and cousin marriage, and an attempt to purge the party system of its familistic elements. This effort peaked under the New Deal, which saw the passage of antinepotism laws and their widespread adoption in both public and private institutions.

Yet throughout this period, nepotism flourished at two levels: a national WASP establishment was formed out of the regional Republican elites, united by business and marital ties, while at the working class level, ethnic nepotism built the urban machines, the labor movement, and the immigrant economies. At both levels, nepotism was the preferred mode of procedure. As in Europe, it was the middle class that pushed the merit principle. This middle class revolt against upper class privilege and working class ethnic nepotism was a Roosevelt family enterprise. Though different in many ways—Teddy led the nation as a Republican, Franklin as a Democrat—the two had many similarities. Both fought the party bosses while attacking the plutocrats in their own class. Yet both were astute politicians who privately came to terms with both the bosses *and* the plutocrats, while publicly denouncing them. Together they presided over the broadening of American democracy and the inclusion of the immigrant masses in the emerging middle class. Teddy Roosevelt inaugurated this family enterprise; his cousin Franklin saw it to completion.

TEDDY ROOSEVELT GROWS UP

In July 1881, President James A. Garfield was shot to death by Charles Guiteau, a man described as "a disappointed office seeker." Guiteau is often called a madman, and he was, but he was not without rational motives. At that time the spoils system established by Jackson was in full flower, and twenty years of Republican incumbency had turned the party of Lincoln into a nepotistic sinkhole. Public outcry against the corrupt administration of President Grant had started a small but vocal reform movement, and now the party was divided between pro-patronage "Stalwarts" under the leadership of Senator Roscoe Conkling of New York, and anti-patronage reformers. The Stalwarts had grown rich under Grant and had suffered under Rutherford B. Hayes. In 1880 they wanted to nominate Grant for a third term, but he was too tainted by scandal, and the reform-minded Garfield was chosen instead, with Chester A. Arthur—a spoilsman—as vice president. Guiteau was an obscure party hanger-on from Illinois who had campaigned for Garfield and felt he was owed a reward. Thus when he fired his revolver, he was not just avenging a personal slight but engaging in partisan politics. Shouting that he was a Stalwart, he declared, "Arthur is president now!"

Garfield died, and Arthur took his place. Yet Garfield's murder had the opposite effect of that intended by Guiteau: it galvanized the anti-patronage movement and whipped up enough public support to pass the Pendleton Act of 1883, creating a national merit system and establishing the first legal restrictions on nepotism in American history.[1]

Twenty-two-year-old Theodore Roosevelt read about the murder while vacationing in Europe. Like all Americans, he was shocked and appalled at the way the perpetual scramble for office drove men mad and turned them into homicidal maniacs. But he had special reason for alarm, for to Teddy the battle with the spoilsmen was not just a public concern; it was also a family feud. This feud had begun in 1876, when his father, Theodore Roosevelt Sr., had personally attacked Senator Conkling at the national Republican convention. The next year Conkling returned the favor when he blocked Roosevelt's appointment as collector of the New York Customs House.

Though it is hard to imagine Teddy Roosevelt being overshadowed by anyone, he was very much in awe of his father, and for very good reason: Theodore Roosevelt Sr. was one of the most admired men of his age. Unlike his own father, the hard-driving C. V. S. Roosevelt, Theodore Sr. was an indifferent businessman but an ardent and active philanthropist who had founded numerous charitable and civic institutions, including the Children's Aid Society, the Metropolitan Museum of Art, and the Museum of Natural History. But his pet cause was the Newsboys' Lodging House. Newsboys in those days were homeless orphans—as many as twenty thousand stray boys roamed the streets—and the fatherly Roosevelt spent many hours talking to the boys and finding homes and jobs for them. He was just the sort of benevolent older businessman who so often appears in Horatio Alger novels to give the deserving young bootblack a hand out of poverty. As one friend recalled, "He literally 'went about doing good.'"[2]

In 1876, Roosevelt became involved in the National Reform League along with prominent friends like Henry Adams, Frederick Law Olmstead, Peter Cooper, Henry Cabot Lodge, William Graham Sumner, and William Cullen Bryant. These men believed that politics had become a quagmire of corruption because fastidious patricians like themselves had abdicated their duty as citizens. Roosevelt became their standard-bearer: his attack on Conkling had made him a national figure, and the high-profile New York collectorship would have put him in line for a cabinet position and possibly elected office.

The New York Customs House has been called "the ultimate political plum," and by 1876 it had become a potent symbol of all that was rotten in American politics. Two-thirds of the nation's import duties were collected there, and it was staffed to the gills with political hacks who used their position to extort enormous fees and bribes, kicking back a fixed percentage to the party. Collector Arthur, though not personally corrupt, was a thoroughgoing spoilsman who strongly believed in using patronage to maintain party unity. When President Hayes named Roosevelt to replace him, hoping to force his resignation, the Senate Commerce Committee (chaired by Conkling) objected; when Hayes resubmitted the nomination, Conkling delivered a ninety-minute speech on the Senate floor declaring Roosevelt his personal enemy, and the appointment was rejected. The nominee himself had rather dreaded the prospect and in a private letter to his son he professed his relief. Yet Conkling's very public triumph over the patrician Roosevelt was undoubtedly a painful humiliation for both father and son.

When Roosevelt unexpectedly died of stomach cancer two months later, he was eulogized from every pulpit in the city. Newspapers dubbed him "Greatheart" and lamented his untimely passing. Newsboys thronged the street outside his house and over two thousand mourners crammed inside the Fifth Avenue church. Teddy, then a nineteen-year-old Harvard freshman, stood very much in his dead father's shadow. All his life he had compared himself to his father and found himself wanting. Now he despaired of fulfilling his legacy.

Teddy Roosevelt is generally acknowledged to be one of our greatest presidents, yet few are cognizant of the extent to which he got his start through family connections and was driven throughout his career by familial motives. Indeed, he appears to have been a good candidate for the new science of Freudian psychoanalysis: his whole life may be seen as a crusade to avenge his father's death and affirm his patrician ideals. By an incredible effort of will, this weak, asthmatic, nearsighted boy turned himself into a vigorous paladin of reform—a Christian knight who rides out bravely to battle the dragon. But Teddy's dragon had two heads: corrupt party bosses like Roscoe Conkling and corrupting robber barons like Jay Gould and Cornelius Vanderbilt. Teddy would devote the first half of his career to fighting the machines and the second half to fighting the trusts. Both were major battles in the American war against nepotism.

The scandals of the Gilded Age were not simply a product of individual greed and corruption; they were the result of immense changes taking place throughout American society. After the Civil War, the American economy exploded. The number of industrial enterprises increased by almost 80 percent, demand for coal and iron boomed, and railroads built with enormous grants of land and public subsidies linked major cities in a modern transportation network. Enormous sums of capital flowed into commercial and industrial enterprises, and the corporation became the keystone of American business. Since corporate charters were still granted by political bodies, public and private interests were inextricably entwined. And at the intersection of business and politics stood the bosses and fixers who controlled the local partisan machines. State and city governments across the country were turned over to "political brigands," and corruption was both brazen and widespread.[3]

The nineteenth century was a golden age for nepotism. Most business was family business, and politics was still in the early phases of a struggle to disentangle itself from family interests. Admission to West Point continued to be obtainable through bribes and political influence, and the armed forces contained any number of soft jobs that politicians handed out to the sons of their friends and contributors. The navy in particular was filled with scions of great families, many of whom had intermarried: Prebles, Rodgers, Mackenzies, Decaturs, and Perrys.[4] But nepotism was not just an individual phenomenon; it was also a collective endeavor—part of a highly successful group strategy that was active at two social levels.

The postwar boom produced a class of nouveaux riches whose nepotistic instincts caused them to seek admission for their sons to the exclusive institutions of the old-line aristocracy. While the old upper classes deplored the vulgar and rapacious robber barons, they needed the infusion of capital to maintain their privileged status. Accordingly there arose for the first time a truly national upper class that integrated the established Boston brahmin, New York Knickerbocker, and Main Line Philadelphia aristocracies with a new crop of bankers, lawyers, financiers, and industrialists. Its forming grounds were elite boarding schools like Andover, Groton, and Choate that served to socialize young neophytes and infuse them with upper class values. Guaranteed admission to Ivy League colleges, they entered their fathers' Wall Street firms, intermarried with other good families, and joined the interlocking directorate of corporate boards and trusteeships that controlled American business behind the scenes. By 1900 this WASP elite was at its peak, dominating not only business and politics, but culture as well.[5]

Meanwhile, immigration reached new heights as masses of Germans, Irish, and Scandinavians were joined by Italians and large numbers of eastern Europeans—Poles, Slavs, Russians, Jews, and Magyars. The immigrants flooded into American cities, where they supplied the cheap labor that fueled the industrial boom. Excluded from most mainstream institutions, the immigrants created their own. The American Catholic Church, the urban machine, and the early labor movement were creations of the immigrant communities. All are collective expressions of Classical Western Nepotism.

Rarely if ever do the boss and the political machine receive any kind of defense. But while we are undoubtedly well rid of them, they were an organic and necessary aspect of their time, and their ill repute is partly an artifact of Progressive propaganda. Although the case for machine politics used to be made in its day very frankly, that case has been largely forgotten. But it is worth recalling here, because it is closely connected with the traditional view of party politics as based on an ethic of friendship. This in turn was an extension of the nepotistic ties that bound traditional communities together.

The urban political machine was an invention of the Irish, who began to emigrate to this country in the 1840s and 1850s. Crowded together in squalid neighborhoods and consigned to low-paying jobs as manual laborers, the Irish applied their considerable human and organizational skills to the challenge of providing basic services. By the Civil War they had already created the two institutions that would form their lasting legacy: the American Catholic Church and the political machine. The church provided educational and welfare services, while the machine enabled the immigrants to obtain control of urban police and fire departments, many of which are still heavily staffed by their descendants.

The heart of the machine was the saloon—the traditional forum and gathering place for Irish workingmen—and saloon keepers frequently doubled as political organizers. Big Jim Pendergast started out as a saloon keeper and Democratic precinct captain in Kansas City's First District. The father of Joseph P. Kennedy was a saloon keeper and ward captain in East Boston. Though graft, corruption, violence, and fraud were staple tools of the machines, they were not lawless collections of bandits but disciplined organizations built on personal loyalty to the organization and its leaders. "Reciprocal loyalty was the key," writes Thomas Sowell. "The highly controlled hierarchy of machine politics meant that each individual had to wait his turn for advancement—a pattern common in Ireland, where waiting patiently (and unmarried) to inherit the family farm was the custom." Machine politicians underwent a long period of testing and apprenticeship, but once they reached the top they could expect to stay in power for a long time, "often for life."[6]

The Irish maintained their monopoly over the church for many years, although in time, Italians, Germans, Poles, and other Catholics created parish institutions of their own. They likewise maintained their hold on the machines long after waves of postwar immigration had built up other large foreign minorities. Irish control of political machines in Boston, New York, Buffalo, Chicago, San Francisco, and Kansas City was at its height in the 1880s and 1890s, when many urban wards had already turned Italian and Jewish. Only the introduction of civil service exams—a great cause of reformers like Roosevelt—allowed Jews to begin replacing the Irish in municipal jobs in Boston and New York. A similar pattern was evident in the church, where American-born Italians often saw newly arrived Irish priests promoted over their heads.

The machines were not only products of ethnic nepotism; they were pervaded by personal nepotism as well. This is only natural, for wherever there is favoritism, nepotism rarely lags behind. Pittsburgh's boss Chris Magee had over sixty relatives who made up the core of his machine. Magee "received a start in politics from an uncle, used a nephew to watch the councils, employed a brother to secure franchises for his street railway interests, and finally wrecked his machine in a quarrel with two cousins." Edward Butler of St. Louis raised his three sons on politics and brought them all into his organization: one of them served for eight years as city attorney and was elected twice to Congress. There were also the three Vare brothers of Philadelphia, Boston's Martin Lomasney—who ruled with the help of his brother and cousin—and the Pendergast brothers of Kansas City, founders of the Missouri Democratic machine whose favorite son was one of America's most admired presidents, Harry S Truman.[7]

The classic statement of the case for patronage appears in *Plunkitt of Tammany Hall,* an indispensable little book containing the wit and wisdom of Tammany sachem George Washington Plunkitt as expressed in a series of freewheeling interviews with a reporter from the New York *Evening Post.* Like other politicians of his day (the book was published in 1905), Plunkitt viewed the party as a human institution, held together not by ideology or abstract ideals but by reciprocal obligations and favors. Plunkitt brazenly defended patronage as the backbone of government: "Men ain't in politics for nothin'," he pronounced. "They want to get somethin' out of it." He was very indignant about civil service reform, called it "the greatest fraud of the age" (it was frequently derided by spoilsmen as "snivel service"), and speculated that the horrors of competitive exams had turned more than one patriotic young man into an anarchist. "Isn't it enough to make a man sour on his country when he wants to serve it and won't be allowed unless he answers a lot of fool questions about the number of cubic inches of water in the Atlantic and the quality of sand in the Sahara desert?"

Plunkitt is perhaps best known today for his defense of "honest graft." In Philadelphia, Plunkitt related, a city superintendent had ripped the zinc roof off the almshouse and sold it for scrap. "That was carryin' things to excess," Plunkitt said. "Of course, if [he] had the political pull and the roof was much worn, he might get the city authorities to put on a new one and get the contract for it himself, and buy the old roof at a bargain—but that's honest graft. It's goin' about the thing like a gentleman." There were plenty of chances for a man to make money in politics without breaking the law, and Plunkitt was proud of his alacrity in seizing them: "I seen my opportunities and I took 'em."

Plunkitt also boasted of his prowess in holding on to his district, which he ascribed to his intimate knowledge of the residents and the services he rendered them.

> What tells in holdin' your district is to go right down among the poor families and help them in the different ways they need help.... If a family is burned out I don't ask whether they are Republicans or Democrats... I just get quarters for them, buy clothes for them... and fix them up till they get things runnin' again.... Who can tell how many votes these fires bring me?[8]

The eminent practicality of machine politics was acknowledged by none other than Jane Addams, the founder of Chicago's Hull House and a leading nineteenth-century reformer. In an article called "Why the Ward Boss Rules," Addams observed that in politics, "the successful candidate must be a good man according to the standards of his constituents." The prevailing ethic in most big-city immigrant neighborhoods was *friendship,* and the ward boss embodied this ethic: he found jobs for constituents, paid rent for the indigent widow, intervened with the cops or magistrate, gave presents at weddings and christenings, bought tickets at charity auctions, provided flowers and funeral carriages. "What headway can the notion of civic purity, of honesty of administration, make against this big manifestation of human friendliness, this stalking survival of village kindness?" In contrast, the "goodness" of civic reformers who prate and lecture about purity and virtue "is not dramatic; it is not even concrete and human."[9]

Properly understood, therefore, the urban machine was not (or not merely) a corrupt conspiracy of venal men but a highly successful nepotistic adaptation, a modern manifestation of the tribal gift economy. In the absence of a welfare state, the machines provided services the immigrants could not obtain elsewhere. In exchange, they were glad to give their votes to whatever candidate the bosses chose to nominate. Nor was the reform movement as altruistic and public-spirited as it seems. While nepotism continued to be active among the upper and lower classes, the war against institutionalized nepotism was for the most part a middle class project. As in Europe, so in America, the rising middle classes had long struggled to clear a path between the Scylla of aristocratic privilege and the Charybdis of communal solidarity. The middle class led the way in the creation of independent institutions that afforded a means of mobility for those whose wealth was not tied up in land: the church, the state, the market, and the military. In their struggle to gain access to these institutions, the middle classes championed the principles of merit and bureaucratic efficiency. Once established, however, they typically resorted to the same old nepotistic strategies in an effort to consolidate their gains and pass them on to their children. This process illustrates what sociologist Robert Michaels calls "the iron law of oligarchy."

In its long march through the institutions, the middle class was often abetted by aristocratic reformers who for one reason or another found it expedient to undermine the dominance of their own class. This curious phenomenon is best understood as part of a struggle within the upper class itself between the tendencies of caste and aristocracy. According to Digby Baltzell, all social elites tend to become castelike in their attitudes and behavior. The Roman Republic collapsed because its ruling class could not absorb the wealthy merchants who had risen with the empire. The French Revolution occurred because the French aristocracy imitated the Romans, trading the leadership of their society for the protection of their privileges and refusing to admit new men to their ranks. In contrast, the British aristocracy survived because it opened itself to the rising middle class at key points in its history. American elites display both tendencies, often simultaneously. Upwardly mobile groups establish themselves and then form barriers to those who would follow. Nepotism has been a crucial element both in the effort to preserve a closed elite and in the struggles of new groups to compete with or gain entry to it. But while the struggle between new blood and old has often been fierce, our national elite has over time become consistently more open, and this has been the secret of America's stability and strength.

Thus if the American reform movement was in some respects a class war—an alliance of white-collar professionals and patrician reformers who wished to keep the ethnics in their place—it was also a war within the upper class itself. Teddy's father and his friends were as appalled by the rapacious vulgarity of the plutocratic upstarts in their own class as they were by the rising power of the unwashed immigrant masses. Teddy's role as he conceived it—in a family tradition that he inherited from his father and bequeathed to his cousin Franklin—was that of a patrician reformer who strove to keep the American elite aristocratic in the highest sense, and prevent it from degenerating into an exclusive and moribund caste.

The Roosevelts were a tight-knit and fanatically loyal tribe brought up to observe an exacting code of honor and duty by an imposing but kindhearted father. Though bright and energetic, little Teddy was a weak, asthmatic child who gave the family much heartache. At last his father told him that he must "make his own body" or he would never lead a normal, healthy life. Teddy literally rebuilt himself—often rowing twenty-five miles a day—developing such powerful chest muscles that years later when he was shot by an assailant while making a speech, he ignored the bullet and continued talking until he had finished.

Teddy was deeply depressed by his father's death and though he tried manfully to fill his shoes, he obsessively accused himself of unworthiness. But the event had also left him very rich, and at Harvard he was suddenly embraced by the exclusive inner circle of young men with names like Cabot, Saltonstall, and Quincy. (It was through his friend Richard Saltonstall that Teddy met his first wife, Alice Lee.)[10] Many of these friends would later view him as "a traitor to his caste"—a man who "should have been on the side of capital."

After graduation, Teddy turned for guidance to his uncle Robert Barnwell, a successful lawyer and politician, a reform leader active in the fight against Tammany Hall, and—as sportsman, author, and adventurer—a colorful and inspiring figure in his own right. (He was also a philanderer and bigamist who maintained a second family in a house around the corner.) Teddy read law in Barnwell's office and enjoyed his uncle's support when he decided to enter politics. This was greeted with criticism from friends and relatives, who thought his father would not have approved. Yet Teddy pressed ahead, clearly indicating that he would not allow his personal ambition to be stifled by filial piety.

Unlike his father, whose approach to public life had been decidedly patrician, Teddy plunged into the rough-and-tumble of party politics. He was determined to prove his worth by working his way up. Yet like most great opportunists, he was also a beneficiary of forces beyond his control: his candidacy was backed by a Republican politico who wanted to wrest control of the district from a rival, and Teddy was put up purely on the strength of his father's name. He also received support from his father's old friends in the Silk Stocking District: Willie Astor, Elihu Root, William Evarts, J. P. Morgan, and several others vouched in a public letter for his honesty and integrity.

Teddy's youth did not go unnoticed by his opponent, who mocked him as a rich boy trying to climb his father's coattails. The same charge would later be leveled at FDR, and with about as much justification. Yet in the end Teddy's birthright was more of a help than a hindrance. As the *New York Post* declared, "Mr. Roosevelt has hereditary claims to the confidence and hopefulness of the voters of this city, for his father was in his day one of the most useful and public-spirited men in the community." One can hardly imagine such a statement being made today. Yet the press, the party, and the public were all prepared to take Teddy on credit. He would prove himself a worthy successor to his father or withdraw to private life like other Roosevelts. Either way, he could do little harm and much good.

Teddy was elected easily and at twenty-three became the youngest member of the legislature. Barnwell called in favors to procure choice committee assignments, and the hyperactive, nearsighted young man with the million-dollar chip on his shoulder soon became the standard-bearer of reform in state politics. He was initially treated with contempt by party regulars, and the Speaker of the House refused to recognize him. But Roosevelt was not to be ignored, and in the end he earned the respect of his colleagues and was returned for a second and third term. In 1883 he helped pass the first state civil service law, and later extended it to the cities, mandating competitive exams in police and fire departments and other agencies.

In everything he did, Teddy was supremely conscious of his father's example: "I honestly mean to act up here [Albany] on all questions as nearly as possible as I think Father would have done if he had lived," he wrote. He further pledged that he would adhere to the gentleman's code of never placing party above principle. Gradually, he gave up looking after his father's old causes; yet he still managed to feel that he was continuing Theodore's work.[11]

Teddy's growing realism about politics appears in his decision to support the party's nominee in 1884. James G. Blaine was considered hopelessly corrupt at the Chicago convention, and Teddy worked hard for his defeat. When Blaine obtained the nomination, most of the older reform leaders bolted to the Mugwump candidacy of Democrat Grover Cleveland. Instead, Teddy took a deliberate step away from his father's example by choosing to stay in the party, an action that brought howls of execration from his allies. "Theodore, beware of ambition!" warned the *Boston Daily Globe,* as though speaking in his dead father's voice. Friends wrote angry letters; former classmates cut him in the street. Yet Teddy instinctively knew that to leave the party in a huff would doom him to political oblivion.

Earlier that year, a double tragedy had devastated Teddy when, by an awful coincidence, his wife and mother died on the same day. Teddy reacted by throwing himself into his work, submitting dozens of bills and becoming known as the Cyclone Assemblyman. When he went to Chicago he was already an object of intense curiosity and interest. The *Chicago Times* called him "the most remarkable young politician of the day" and added that he had made his mark despite his privileged background. With tongue only partly in cheek, the paper observed, "The advantage of being a self-made man was denied him. An unkind fortune hampered him with an old and wealthy family."[12] Yet immediately afterward, Teddy withdrew from public life and headed west, where for the next three years he hunted, ranched, explored, and wrote numerous books.

Most biographers ascribe this precipitous act to the deferred emotional crisis brought on by the deaths in his family. But it seems equally possible that the struggle between ambition and filial piety, brought to a head by his decision to place party over principle, precipitated a crisis of identity that forced him (briefly) from the public stage. Teddy needed time to complete his self-development and remake himself in a new image. For this purpose, the West was the ideal environment. Like other Eastern families, the Roosevelts regarded the West as a naturally healthful environment and sent their children there to reap its benefits. The West was firmly fixed in Teddy's mind as an arena in which he would encounter the kind of intense physical challenges that had helped him overcome his childhood weaknesses. It also symbolized the rugged individualism that, like many Victorians, he thought vital to the future of democracy, and of civilization itself.

Teddy's writings in this period contributed much to the romantic image of the cowboy. In a steady stream of articles, letters, and books he described the independent, hard-bitten men of the frontier as "frank, bold, and self-reliant." Coupled with this keen admiration was a powerful need to prove himself to these rugged individuals, who looked decidedly askance at the effete dude with his buckskin shirt, Tiffany-handled Bowie knife, and thick spectacles. Yet Teddy plunged into the ardors of the range with characteristic vigor, spending hour after hour in the saddle, enduring freezing cold and blistering heat, and surviving on water and biscuits with never a word of complaint. Teddy's asthma had always improved on his brief spells away from home, and it seems plausible to think that despite his intense attachment to his family, he felt suffocated by its closeness and exceedingly high expectations. So it is no surprise that Teddy's western sojourn, marking the longest period of separation from his family, completed his journey toward physical and emotional health.

During this period Teddy disavowed any interest in politics. But he kept up with his political friends, especially Henry Cabot Lodge, who had been his instructor at Harvard. Together they had led the fight against Blaine at Chicago, and both had chosen to remain in the party while their older colleagues bolted. Lodge was the scion of a distinguished brahmin family and his support for Blaine cost him as dearly with proper Boston as Teddy's had with Knickerbocker New York. Lodge had also been a friend of Teddy's father, and the association deepened Teddy's feelings for his mentor. The attachment was mutual: according to Stephen Hess, more than anyone else, it was Lodge who would mastermind Teddy's rise to the presidency.[13]

In the race for New York mayor in 1886, Democrat Abram Hewitt was being challenged by Henry George, a radical social philosopher. Neither would be a friend to New York's Republicans. Teddy was approached by representatives of state boss Thomas Platt and persuaded to throw his hat into the ring. Although the "Cowboy Candidate" ran a vigorous campaign, he finished last. Nevertheless Teddy managed to generate a tremendous amount of enthusiasm and proved his viability as a political candidate.

Thomas Nast's cartoon portrayals of a corpulent, gross-fingered William Tweed have fixed the image of the political boss as a grasping, coarse, obnoxious figure. The quite different reality is best conveyed by the thin, baldheaded, sober, and ascetic Thomas Platt. Platt had risen from the back room of a drugstore in Owego, New York, to become a powerful force in state politics. A protégé of Conkling's, he occupied a series of party positions and eventually became a congressman and senator. In 1881—in a replay of the struggle over Roosevelt's failed nomination—Conkling and Platt resigned their Senate seats in protest against Garfield's appointment of a reformer to the Customs House. Their purpose had been to shame the president into withdrawing his appointment, but Garfield's death derailed their scheme. Conkling's career abruptly ended and he retired to legal practice. Platt took over the faltering Republican machine and methodically rebuilt it, becoming known as the "Easy Boss" of New York State.

Roosevelt's relationship with Platt bears more reflection than it usually receives, since it was mainly due to his support that Teddy became first governor of New York and then vice president. Twenty years Teddy's senior, Platt was closely associated with Conkling, his father's old nemesis. Moreover, he was the heir and conservator of established practices against which Teddy would lead an attack that was also a generational revolt within the party.

After his defeat in 1886, Teddy again withdrew from politics. He married his childhood playmate Edith Carow and began to fill his spacious home at Sagamore Hill with a large clan of boisterous children. Ted Jr. was born in 1887, followed rapidly by Kermit, Ethel, Archibald, and Quentin. There was also Alice Roosevelt, the child of his first marriage, known to the family as Sister. Teddy acted like an overgrown scoutmaster to this troop—a stout, bespectacled Peter Pan. Deeply involved with his children, he also wrote them marvelous letters, which were published as a best-selling book after he died.

Though Teddy had achieved his own identity, he continued to depend upon his family, especially the women. This warm bath of female support included his wife, his sisters, and his daughter, all of whom were his devoted lifelong partisans. His sister Corinne turned his house into a shrine after his death and wrote an adoring memoir. But he was especially close to his sister Bamie. Indeed, David McCullough's description of their relationship offers a striking portrayal of vicarious sibling nepotism. Bamie had always played a maternal role in Teddy's life, and this aspect of their relationship deepened after the deaths of his first wife and his mother. Theodore "gave focus to her life; he was her consuming interest, her favorite subject, her primary means of self-fulfillment."[14] When Teddy went west, she became a foster mother to baby Alice; after her brother Elliott's death she took a maternal interest in his eight-year-old daughter, Eleanor, the future wife of Franklin Roosevelt, and she also took charge of the children of her cousin James Roosevelt after the death of his wife. She was the very model of the Victorian spinster who lives through her nieces and nephews, investing her nepotistic energies in them like a sterile worker bee.[15]

It was Bamie who encouraged Teddy's ambition, and she went out of her way to encourage his friendship with Lodge. In 1887 he stumped for Benjamin Harrison, and with Harrison's victory he set his sights on the position of U.S. Civil Service commissioner. Wire-pulling by Lodge managed to land him this low-status assignment: few people wanted the job. Yet Teddy clearly saw its possibilities: it was the first of many "bully pulpits."

Assuming his father's mantle as the wellborn opponent of patronage, graft, and corruption, Teddy launched a noisy campaign against the spoilsmen in both parties. His exposure of corruption in the Baltimore post office caused the dismissal of twenty-five Harrison appointees and seriously embarrassed the president. He also clashed with Thomas Platt when he launched an investigation at the New York Customs House. Yet he was kept on to the end, and it was a testament to his efficacy in the job that in 1892 his appointment was renewed by incoming Democrat Grover Cleveland.

In his role as a paladin of civil service reform, Teddy must have felt that he had finally fulfilled his father's promise. Corinne called him "the spirit of my father reincarnate." But he needed new dragons to slay, and when the newly elected reform mayor of New York offered him a job on the city's police commission, he leaped at the opportunity. The New York City Police Department had deteriorated to one of the lowest points in its history.[16] Platt tried to block Teddy's appointment but was unable to do so, and Teddy brought his moralistic crusade to police headquarters, where his theatrical exploits soon became a staple of the tabloid press. He toured the slums with Jacob Riis, and the conditions he saw there fueled his indignation over the economic exploitation of immigrants and the callousness of "the wealthy criminal class." But he finally went too far in his obsession with enforcing the law against the sale of liquor on Sunday. This bluenosed campaign alienated working class ethnics, and it was suddenly time to move on.

Once again he turned to his friend (now Senator) Lodge, who tried to get him made assistant secretary of state in the McKinley administration. When that failed, Lodge and his friends set their sights on the Navy Department. But Platt's agreement was required, and the Easy Boss opposed him. To obtain his support, Teddy did something his father would certainly not have approved. Platt was seeking election to the Senate against Joseph Choate, a reformer and a personal friend of Roosevelt's. Roosevelt refused to support Choate, and this act of calculated betrayal won Platt's endorsement. National party chairman Mark Hanna reluctantly gave his approval, and the Senate confirmed Teddy's appointment as assistant navy secretary—a position that would be a Roosevelt sinecure for several generations.[17]

When the battleship *Maine* was mysteriously sunk in Havana harbor in February 1898, war fever broke out in the country. Teddy became an ardent hawk, lobbying ceaselessly for war, partly on the grounds that America had to grow up and face its responsibilities abroad. At last McKinley yielded and called for a declaration of war.

On one level, Teddy's war fever was a reflection of the late-Victorian obsession with war and military glory. The Anglo-American upper classes shared a dislike of grubby-minded materialism, a fear of racial decline, and a romanticized view of war as the ultimate test of masculine virtue. The upper class penchant for blood sports was an aspect of this masculine cult. As an ardent nationalist, Teddy also believed that war would be good for America, granting it renewed purpose and unifying its disparate elements. Teddy not only imbibed this cult of democratic manliness himself, he impressed it very strongly on his sons. But Teddy had more personal reasons for his jingoistic fervor. Instead of doing his patriotic duty in the Civil War, his father (like other rich young men) had hired an anonymous surrogate to go in his place. He later regretted the lapse, and biographers agree that it was a lasting source of shame to his son. It might therefore be said that the Spanish-American War was fought partly in order to prove Teddy Roosevelt's manhood.

When war broke out, Teddy left his post at the Navy Department and with his friend Leonard Wood formed the First U.S. Volunteer Cavalry Unit—a gentlemen's outfit known to history as the Rough Riders. The reckless charge up San Juan Hill (if indeed this fabled incident occurred as he described it) would be the spark that reignited his career. To Teddy, it was the vindication of a lifelong goal to leave behind "an honorable name." Should he accomplish nothing else, he wrote, that day's lighthearted butchery would serve his descendants "as an apology for my having existed."

While Teddy was battling the spoilsmen and charging—or pretending to charge—up San Juan Hill, Thomas Platt had been rebuilding the New York Republican machine, and by 1898 he had achieved near-absolute control of nominations, party funds, and patronage. On Teddy's return from Cuba, he was immediately approached by an emissary from Senator Platt who asked him whether, if elected governor on a Republican ticket, he would "make war on the machine." Teddy said that he would consult Platt on appointments but would finally have to act as his conscience dictated. Platt may not have liked this, but he had no real alternative, since the Republicans stood little chance of winning without Roosevelt.

Teddy immediately launched his campaign, touring the state by train with a group of Rough Riders and verbally reenacting the famous charge a dozen times a day. His victory is usually ascribed to his effectiveness as a campaigner, but the backstage machinations of Platt and his lieutenants should not be underestimated. Platt manipulated government printing contracts to keep Republican newspapers in line, and when money was needed to get out the vote, Platt raised a huge slush fund from Roosevelt's Wall Street friends, beginning with J. P. Morgan. Since votes could then be purchased for $5 each, this puts Teddy's narrow margin of seventeen thousand in a somewhat equivocal light. According to Harold Gosnell, "Platt had grounds for boasting that he had 'saved Roosevelt.'"[18] Plainly he intended to collect on Teddy's debt.

Platt's main interests in the state were the control of the legislature and the distribution of spoils. The party boss was used to making these decisions unilaterally and passing them up to the governor. But on the very first occasion when Platt made such a proposal, Roosevelt demurred and named his own man instead. Throughout the two years of his tenure, he and Platt had many such run-ins, but Teddy always managed things so as not to embarrass or antagonize the older man. This masterful handling of Platt contrasts sharply with their earlier relationship, which was much more adversarial. The great intervening event, of course, was the Spanish-American War. Up to that point, Teddy's public role had been a faithful reenactment of his father's. In effect, he had to complete his father's career before he could begin his own. Having healed his psychic wound at San Juan Hill, Teddy finally emerged as an actor in his own right. In coming to terms with the machine, Teddy showed that he was secure and confident enough to deal with the devil as his father would never have done.

And come to terms with it he did. For while he did what he thought right in matters of major importance, he left the day-to-day administration of the state to Platt. Nor was his elaborate show of respect for Platt an insincere pose. As he wrote to Lodge in 1899, "I do not believe it very likely that he will come to a definite break with me, because I like him personally, I always tell him the truth, and I genuinely endeavor to help him, if I can, with proper regard for the interest of the State and party." Moreover, many of Platt's associates were, in Roosevelt's estimate, men of high integrity.[19]

Yet while Roosevelt kept his promise not to disturb the machine that had got him elected, he used his bully pulpit to oppose the corporate interests that had corrupted the legislature. He thus inaugurated the second phase of his career—his war against the trusts. Teddy proposed strict controls on utility and transportation companies, higher corporate taxes, stronger liability laws, and public disclosure of corporate earnings. He also supported legislation to ease the burdens of the working class and pressed for a tax on inheritance. After a particularly grievous set-to that adversely affected the state's insurance industry—a major party contributor—Platt hatched a scheme to get rid of him by kicking him upstairs. The incumbent vice president had recently died, and Platt proposed Teddy for the position. The would-be matchmaker had to overcome stiff resistance on all sides: McKinley wanted another running mate, national party chairman Mark Hanna opposed it, and Roosevelt himself preferred to stay in a real political office.[20] Yet Platt prevailed, and in 1900 Teddy was elected with McKinley. Justly proud of his achievement, Platt came to Washington on inauguration day "to see Theodore take the veil." Six months later, McKinley was assassinated and Roosevelt unexpectedly became president.

The sense of Roosevelt's career as a family enterprise did not diminish in the White House. Like other chief executives, Teddy appointed his friends to cabinet posts and other jobs. Many he had inherited from his father: Charles J. Bonaparte became attorney general, and John Hay was retained as secretary of state. Hay was succeeded by Theodore's friend Elihu Root, and when Root resigned he gave the job to his old classmate Robert Bacon. William Howard Taft became secretary of war, and Leonard Wood became a brigadier general. Lodge was too much the patrician to accept an appointment from a friend, but remained (along with Bamie) Teddy's unofficial consigliere. Meanwhile the Roosevelts moved into the White House, where their effervescent family life preoccupied the national press for the next eight years. The nation was utterly charmed by images of Teddy playing baseball on the lawn or leading troops of delighted schoolchildren on a romp through the stately rooms of the executive mansion. His friends considered him little more than an overgrown child. Yet this most youthful of all presidents also served as a model for the new middle class American father: at once a moral and professional exemplar, and an accessible, bighearted playmate.

More than any other president, Teddy Roosevelt fulfilled Hamilton's famous prescription for "energy in the executive." As the cornerstone of his domestic Square Deal program he curbed the power of the trusts and strengthened the security of working people. He first turned on J. P. Morgan, an old friend of his father who had supported his first political campaigns. The battle went all the way to the Supreme Court, which backed the government's charges of restraint of trade by Morgan's billion-dollar Northern Securities Company, and he brought similar suits against American Tobacco, Standard Oil, DuPont, the New Haven Railroad, and forty other trusts. Asserting America's status as a world power, he expanded the navy, globalized American trade, passed sweeping conservation laws, and built the Panama Canal. Ironically, this militant imperialist won the Nobel Peace Prize.

Much debate has centered on whether Teddy was a radical bent on uprooting the capitalist order or a conservative intent on saving it. The answer appears to be both. Teddy came to office at a time of massive upheaval in American life, when the emergence of a labor movement in the North and a populist movement in the South threatened an outbreak of class warfare. When he assumed the presidency he was clearly a moderate reformer, but in his second term he moved sharply to the left, leading industrialist Henry Clay Frick to complain that the "sonofabitch" wouldn't "stay bought." But Teddy was determined that America would not suffer the fate of ancient republics, with the poor dispossessing the rich or the rich exploiting the poor. His solution was the creation of a middle class society, and he became the effectual leader of a middle class revolt against the plutocrats. He vocally attacked the "wealthy criminal class" and pushed for legislation that would broaden the scope of government oversight, protect the rights of working people, and heavily tax corporate and high-end individual incomes.

The centerpiece of this program was his campaign against hereditary wealth. Teddy's proposed income and inheritance taxes were to be steeply graded—a direct blow against the nepotistic interests of the wealthiest Americans—and his constant hammering on the corruption of inherited wealth and privilege permanently changed the public's views on this great question. Teddy believed that the selfish pursuit of wealth and inherited ease were a grave threat to national health. Americans must strive to earn their places in society and at all costs not be weakened by the power and prosperity their fathers had bequeathed them. Teddy's tax proposals were therefore on one level a reflection of his interest in eugenics. Nevertheless, his middle class bias was clear from the stipulation that he would apply the income tax progressively, "and with such heaviness to big inheritances as to completely block the transmission of enormous fortunes to the young Rockefellers, Vanderbilts, Astors and Morgans."[21]

Teddy's receipt of Booker T. Washington in the White House and his appointment of Jewish dry goods magnate Oscar Straus to a cabinet position were a deliberate rebuke to upper class racism and anti-Semitism. He welcomed the new immigrants but he also required them to leave their old loyalties at the door and become true-blue, 100 percent Americans. He denounced the idea of "hyphenated" Americans and also firmly rejected the view of Great Britain as America's mother country. Instead he insisted upon America's being recognized as a mature nation in its own right. It is as though he did not wish either his country or himself to be thought of as somebody's son. Biographer Henry Pringle is not alone in seeing in him the expansive new "American ego" that emerged in the 1890s, and it may truly be said that along with Teddy himself, America had finally grown up. Yet in the midst of his greatest triumphs, Teddy's sense of his father's spirit was stronger than ever. By sheer coincidence, the first night Teddy spent in the White House was his father's birthday. Teddy had hung a large portrait of his father behind his desk at Sagamore Hill so that the pale blue eyes could be always upon him. Now he remarked to his sisters, "I feel as if my father's hand were on my shoulder."

In the history of American nepotism, Teddy Roosevelt was a figure of great practical and symbolic significance. He presents the classic instance of a highly meritorious person who succeeded brilliantly by making the most of his inherited advantages. He was a dutiful heir and successor who was also, in an important sense, self-made. Like Theseus, the emblematic hero of democratic Athens, he was a pious son who superceded his father and profited from his death, but did not kill him; a rebellious son who sublimated his revolt by acting it out in a spirit of filial piety. He therefore represents a turning point at which the nepotistic drive becomes internalized. No longer a pressure exerted by fathers on sons, it becomes for the most part a psychological pressure exerted on sons by themselves.

Teddy Roosevelt's career suggests a striking parallel with that of another great democrat, Pericles. Both were the sons of distinguished public men who continued their fathers' feuds, combining the vindication of family honor with an equally powerful sense of public duty. Both were rich patricians who betrayed their narrow class interest in order to lead a democratic revolt against the plutocrats. Both were also good political sons who played a series of minor roles while awaiting their turn for party leadership. Moreover, both presided over a period of tremendous expansion as their vibrant commercial societies crossed the threshold from republic to empire, and both articulated a powerful new vision of national purpose and identity. As if that were not enough, both were obsessed with expanding their country's naval power, and consciously offered a model of virtue and good citizenship for the rising middle class. Finally, both were succeeded not by their own sons but by gifted opportunists who appropriated their mantle. Pericles had Alcibiades; Teddy had Franklin D. Roosevelt.

THE BOSS'S NEPHEW: FDR AND THE NEW DEAL FAMILY ROMANCE

In 1937, at the height of the Depression, Ferdinand Lundberg published a detailed exposé of the American business elite. His argument was simple: "The United States is owned and dominated today by a hierarchy of its sixty richest families, buttressed by no more than ninety families of lesser wealth." Among the most egregious abuses committed by these families was their open and lavish nepotism. "Scratch any big corporation executive and the chances are even that you will find an in-law of the wealthiest families," Lundberg wrote. Instead of being harmed by the Depression, moreover, this class had actually grown richer, its power and wealth consolidated by a series of dynastic marriages. The Rockefellers alone had intermarried with half of the country's sixty richest families. Lundberg concluded: "Modern capitalism has become, like feudalism before it, a family affair."[22]

One legacy of the Depression has been a deep-seated populist prejudice against the Protestant establishment. We get our modern stereotype of the boss's lazy son-in-law or nephew from the annals of WASP business culture: the world of white shoe legal and financial firms, insurance companies, and first wave industries like textiles, steel, and railroads. Franklin D. Roosevelt is today considered one of this country's greatest presidents, a fearless and inspiring leader in two great national crises and the only one elected to four terms. Few recall that at the outset he was considered an opportunistic lightweight—the very model of the incompetent nephew who rises not through merit but through family connections. Yet it is hardly accidental that in the greatest crisis since the Civil War, a nation of farmers and immigrants put their trust in the cousin and nephew of Theodore Roosevelt.

Franklin Roosevelt was born in 1882, the year his cousin Teddy (they were actually fifth cousins) went to Albany. Although the family's Oyster Bay and Hyde Park branches had long been associated with different political parties, they also felt a close affinity. Teddy's brother Elliott was not only the father of Eleanor Roosevelt but the godfather of her cousin (and future husband) Franklin. Nor were intrafamily marriages unheard of: Franklin's father, James Roosevelt, originally wanted to marry his cousin Bamie, but married the beautiful and imperious Sara Delano instead. But James died young, and Franklin grew up at the center of a doting matriarchal household. The fatherless boy clearly needed a male role model, and who better than cousin Theodore? In 1897, Teddy gave a speech at Groton in which he admonished the boys that they were "not entitled to an ounce of privilege" and warned, "Much has been given to you, therefore we have a right to expect much from you." Sitting in the audience, fifteen-year-old Franklin was elated. His mother did not share his enthusiasm.

According to Geoffrey C. Ward, Franklin's distant connection with Theodore was a source of both pride and frustration. "At Groton and at Harvard he had been known always as a Roosevelt, but could never claim to be one of *the* Roosevelts."[23] Teddy himself was fond of Franklin, but the rest of the family disdained him as a superficial young man dominated by his mother. At Harvard he was passed over for the Porcellian Club, unlike Teddy and his sons, and this painful rejection has been considered the source of his surprisingly sharp animus against his own class.

Franklin deeply admired his famous older cousin and all but forced himself upon him as a protégé. He crossed party lines to vote for Teddy in 1904, and in 1905 he stunned his mother when he announced his engagement to his cousin Eleanor. The president gave her away at the wedding, and joked, "Well, Franklin, there's nothing like keeping the name in the family." While no one doubts Franklin's affection for Eleanor, the match was plainly opportunistic. "His love for Eleanor was real," writes Ward, "but her closeness to the immediate family of the man he admired most on earth must have been an important part of her dowry."[24]

If Teddy's start in politics was nepotistic, Franklin's was even more so. Like Teddy he attended Columbia Law School, but had no interest in the law. His first job at Carter, Ledyard & Milburn was arranged by his mother. Bored with legal practice, Franklin boasted to his fellow clerks that his career would be exactly like Teddy's. He would join the New York legislature, become assistant secretary of the navy, governor of New York, and finally president. The most remarkable thing about this prediction—apart from its insufferable arrogance—is its amazing accuracy. The fact that every word of it came true suggests that despite his amiability, Franklin's life was very much a matter of design.

By 1908 Teddy was out of office and had gone back to hunting and exploring, while the next generation of Roosevelts crowded the wings. His own son Ted Jr., his nephew Theodore Douglas Robinson, and Corinne's son-in-law Joseph Wright Alsop all had political ambitions. Franklin could have run in either party, but Ted Jr. and his cousins were already avowed Republicans. Moreover, the Democrats had lately enjoyed a string of victories fueled by the middle class ethnic revolt sparked by Teddy himself. All things considered, it made more sense to follow his father's tradition as a reformist Cleveland Democrat.

In 1910, Franklin eagerly accepted the suggestion of Democratic politico John Mack that he run for state Senate in Dutchess County, where he enjoyed a home advantage. The upstate Democrats were weak and the reformists had little to lose in fielding FDR, whose utter lack of qualifications made it clear that for them, all that counted was his name. He was running in a Republican stronghold against a popular incumbent who dismissed him as a "rich young man" and called his candidacy a joke. Yet fortune favored the young upstart. The Republicans were split on reform, and the Democrats, whose stronghold was the cities with their ethnic wards, put on their most aggressive upstate campaign in years. FDR spoke in pleasing generalities of better, cleaner government, gleefully ripped the "boss-ridden" Republican Party, and avoided taking a fixed, concrete, or quotable position on any major issue. It also didn't hurt to be a Roosevelt: "The young candidate didn't bother to correct any mistaken impressions that he was a son or nephew of the Roosevelt President."[25] In the end, he won a narrow but significant victory and became (like Teddy) the leader of a small group of reform-minded "insurgents" in Albany.

Franklin's record in the legislature is mainly one of reformist posturing. He had virtually no program, having assumed the Progressive mantle with little thought as to how it should be applied. The press gave his anti-Tammany speeches wide play, but this did not help him build a power base in upstate New York, or even in his own district, based on patronage.[26] Facing reelection in 1912, he allowed himself to be pushed by Louis Howe into becoming a vocal advocate of agricultural reform. Howe was a respected Albany newspaperman who would act as Franklin's political mentor and strategist for the next thirty years. (As early as 1912, Howe began addressing him in letters as "Beloved and Revered Future President.") FDR's relationship with Howe is one of the great symbioses of modern politics, with FDR playing the charming and affable front man while Howe, the backroom tactician, "concentrated on the secret maneuver, the manipulation of the press, the organization of personal loyalties and patronage hunger."[27] FDR stumped hard for reelection in 1912, and when he suddenly fell ill, Howe finished his campaign. The total reelection costs were over $3,000, half of which came from relatives and friends. But his huge margin was probably due to the effect of Wilson's coattails and to the fact that cousin Teddy was running in the same election on the Progressive Bull Moose ticket. The three-way race split the Republicans and handed Woodrow Wilson the presidency.

Franklin's reelection had left him in office but surrounded by political enemies. Fortunately his endorsement of Wilson paid off, and in 1913 (as predicted) he became assistant secretary of the navy and immediately set out to steer patronage to his anti-Tammany allies, putting Howe on the federal payroll as a special assistant. Howe handled FDR's political affairs and cultivated the impression that his office was the place to apply for New York independents seeking jobs and influence. He was particularly successful at ingratiating his boss with the new assistant postmaster general, and gradually managed to gain indirect control of New York postal appointments.

Franklin, like his cousin, was a "big navy" man and an ardent proponent of military expansion; the cautious Wilson, the isolationist secretary of state William Jennings Bryan, and Navy secretary Josephus Daniels opposed this aggressive approach. When (after the sinking of the *Lusitania*) Wilson changed course and ordered a large naval buildup, FDR plunged into the work. A fortunate by-product of these efforts was the creation of close relationships with various shipping magnates and labor leaders. In 1920, FDR was named as a running mate by presidential candidate James M. Cox, who needed his reformist profile to mitigate the (accurate) impression that he was the choice of the urban bosses. FDR had few real options. The New York insurgents had collapsed, and Howe's post office patronage was not enough to build a real upstate political machine. His acceptance therefore marked a stage in FDR's increasing realism: if he wished to have a future in politics, like Teddy he would have to come to terms with the machine.

Franklin owed this nomination to the machinations of his old sponsor John Mack and other friends. But undoubtedly his greatest debt was to the Roosevelt family name. What Stephen Hess calls "FDR's jump from second-echelon bureaucrat to presidential running-mate" was mainly the product of his coattail connection with Teddy. The elder Roosevelt's death the year before had put the nation in a sentimental mood. As Franklin toured the country, people called to him, "I voted for your father!"[28]

The 1920 election split the Roosevelts in two. While Franklin campaigned as the heir of Woodrow Wilson, the Oyster Bay Roosevelts viewed him as an upstart cynically exploiting his connection to the late president. Teddy's sister Corinne became the first woman to address a national convention when she seconded the Republican nomination of Leonard Wood for vice president. Alice Roosevelt and her husband, Congressman Nick Longworth, badmouthed Franklin in Washington, and Ted Jr. followed him around the country disavowing him as a "maverick" who did not have the family "brand."

The Democrats lost the election, inaugurating a twelve-year Republican ascendancy. FDR accepted a generous appointment as vice president of a Maryland bonding house headed by patrician yachtsman Van Lear Black, bringing Howe along as his assistant.[29] Then, in 1921, he was stricken with polio and began a lifelong battle to recover the use of his limbs. Black insisted he remain on the payroll, however, and Franklin's ties with labor leaders resulted in the placement of numerous bonds with the company. Howe also called in Franklin's chips with naval contractors. Meanwhile, Roosevelt gave jobs to the sons of Tammany leaders and Brooklyn politicians. Their office volume doubled in five years.

Like Teddy's, Franklin's character was deepened by his struggle for health—meeting a physical challenge brought out the best in all the Roosevelts. His mother wanted him to give up politics, but Howe and Eleanor kept his ambition alive. ("By God, Franklin will be president, legs or no legs!" Howe declared.) Howe trained Eleanor to play a more active role in her husband's career and she now became Franklin's legs and often his voice as well. In the process, she fulfilled the ideal union of the family's two branches. Eleanor was the true heir of the Oyster Bay Roosevelts, and the merging of their identities brought the genteel philanthropic and reforming spirit of her grandfather into play as a component of Franklin's appeal.

Many biographers have noted Franklin's transformation from superficial youth to mature statesman. But his superficiality had always been a pose to some extent. People who grow up in the shadow of a famous person sometimes conceal their ambition under a pretense of modesty and diffidence, keeping expectations low so if their bid for glory fails, they may not have that far to fall. This is how FDR appears to have proceeded. He came across as a pleasant young man with no particular drive or ambition, and took everyone in, including (it appears) his own mother. The only ones let into the secret were Eleanor and Howe, who never underestimated his ambition and devoted their lives to fulfilling it.

In 1924, Ted Jr. ran for governor of New York against popular Democratic incumbent Alfred E. Smith. Filling in for Franklin, Eleanor seconded Smith's nomination at the state convention and followed Ted around the state in a special car with a steaming teapot on the roof to remind the voters of his unfortunate involvement with the Teapot Dome scandal during a stint at the Navy Department. Ted's defeat sealed his fate and cleared the way for Franklin, who began his comeback the same year by rising dramatically, with braces on his legs, to nominate Smith for president at the Democratic national convention.[30] Four years later, FDR renominated Smith and obtained his endorsement as a candidate for governor. Smith lost, but FDR won, and four years later (again as predicted) became the Democratic presidential nominee.

Since 1900, a number of important changes had conspired to make the Democrats the new majority party. The most significant were large-scale immigration and the rise of an organized labor movement. Both were indispensable to FDR's creation of the New Deal coalition. In addition, the stock market crash and the Depression discredited the Republican incumbents and put the Democrats over the top. These developments have been amply described, but rarely have their nepotistic aspects been explored. The following account attempts to show not only the neglected role of ethnic nepotism in creating the urban machines and the labor movement, but how the failure of ethnic nepotism in the face of a great national crisis led to the transcendence of these parochial loyalties and the forging of a new majority party.

Twenty million immigrants entered the country between the Civil War and the Immigration Acts of 1921 and 1924, when Congress closed the "golden door." Most of these spent two or three generations in low-status jobs before moving up to join the middle class. But different groups progressed at different rates, depending on their nepotistic unity. We are sometimes led to think that the majority of immigrants arrived alone and penniless, pulling themselves up by their bootstraps. While that was true enough in many cases, the majority were able to depend upon a well-developed network of support established by those who had come earlier. Immigrants arriving in the late nineteenth and early twentieth centuries did not confront a howling wilderness like the colonists in Massachusetts Bay. Instead, they were greeted at the docks by family members, friends, or representatives of local fraternal associations. Many had jobs waiting for them when they arrived. The result was a pattern of dense residential enclaves and corresponding economic niches. Scholars often speak of these developments in an abstract way, as though these ethnic communities grew by themselves, like mushrooms in the soil of urban ghettos. In fact, their growth reflects the aggregation of many thousands of individual decisions based on nepotism.

Ethnic nepotism was also seen in the emergence of a complete set of parallel institutions created by and for the immigrants. These began with simple burial and loan associations and rapidly grew to include newspapers, schools, banks, orphanages, old age homes and hospitals, churches, insurance companies, and a staggering array of commercial enterprises. Whole ethnic subeconomies emerged, providing goods and services not otherwise available.

The Irish, who began arriving in the 1840s and 1850s, had applied their organizational genius to the creation of the American Catholic Church and the urban machines, and also formed a large number of mutual aid and voluntary associations. These institutions were needed to compensate for certain weaknesses: their Catholic faith made them unwelcome in Protestant America and their relative lack of skills and education consigned them to manual labor for two or three generations. Italians—mostly unskilled workers from the south—also progressed fairly slowly. Like the Irish, they tended to congregate in urban neighborhoods, where they re-created the conditions of home in minutest detail; but while they too created mutual aid societies, powerful local attachments led to an extreme proliferation of small agencies that undermined cooperative efforts. The Germans, who possessed greater skills as artisans and farmers and were aided by strong mutual aid societies created by earlier immigrants, established themselves in the middle class much more quickly. Jews too, though subject to the same prejudice and exclusion as the Irish, possessed sophisticated skills, and their strong emphasis on education and communal self-help enabled many to escape the urban ghettos in the second generation. Jews and Germans were also able to establish national communal institutions, while other groups remained divided by locality or region.

The Jews present perhaps the best example of a group that developed a successful niche strategy through a pattern of organized nepotism. Small communities of Sephardic Jews had settled in this country in the eighteenth century, but the first large wave of Jewish immigrants were Germans who arrived in the 1840s and 1850s. Most were educated men, and many dispersed across the country as itinerant peddlers and storekeepers. The three Seligman brothers—often called the American Rothschilds—started out as peddlers in rural Pennsylvania; they soon branched out to other regions, created a chain of department stores, and brought more relatives over to work for them. The Lehmans likewise started with a peddler's cart in Mobile, Alabama, which they built into a wealthy cotton brokerage. The Guggenheims, who amassed more money than the Rockefellers, also built a dry goods empire. These and other families became the founders of the Jewish banking and investment firms of J. & W. Seligman, Lehman Brothers, Kuhn, Loeb, and Goldman, Sachs, and like the far-flung networks of medieval Jewish merchants, they were linked by a dense web of intermarriage. Stephen Birmingham observes that in the first two generations, many Jewish founding fathers married close relatives. Solomon Loeb and Abraham Kuhn married each other's sisters. Two Sachs sons married two Goldman daughters. Uncle-niece marriages also occurred, though they had to be performed in Europe because the practice had been banned in the United States.[31]

But it was mass Russian and east European immigration beginning in the 1880s—totaling about 2 million in under twenty years—that made Jews numerous enough to create their own ethnic niches. Russian Jews flocked to the booming garment industry. Clustered in dense neighborhoods at the edge of the factory district, their clannishness and concentration made possible, indeed required, the creation of an ethnic economy: Jewish factory owners employed Jewish workers to create goods sold by Jewish merchants to Jewish customers. This economic strategy kept competition with other groups to a minimum and allowed Jews to concentrate resources on themselves, reinforced by the powerful injunctions to communal charity and self-help that permeated diaspora culture. Jews also invested heavily in education and showed an unusual determination to hold on to their children: for several generations, the taboo against out-marriage remained strongly in force.

Students of immigrant adjustment often speak of a process of "ethnic succession," wherein one group gives way to another as they move up the social and economic ladder. This phenomenon is seen in every arena, from housing, work, and politics to sports and entertainment. Thus in the labor movement, successive waves of immigrants were pitted against established groups as strikebreakers and were gradually assimilated, only to be challenged in turn by new groups. Boxing was for a long time an Irish sport, passed through a brief Jewish phase, became largely Italian, and ended up black and Latino. The same pattern appeared in organized crime, and was also seen in politics: though the Irish were the first to crack the WASP political monopoly, by the Civil War the Germans had already infiltrated the urban machines of Milwaukee and Cincinnati. After World War I, Slavic and Jewish immigrants also sought careers in urban politics. Italians were relative latecomers, but in the 1940s they seized Tammany from the Irish.

In the cutthroat competition between ethnic groups, nepotism—as seen in patterns of high parental investment in offspring, cooperation among siblings, a willingness to support aged parents, and habits of mutual support among other relatives—often made a crucial difference. Most European immigrants brought with them a strong legacy of peasant familism, though in many cases these legacies were dormant and revived only under the pressures of immigrant life. Moreover, the competitive advantage of each group was strongly affected by its nepotistic formula. Ethnic nepotism differed as a function of age at marriage, family size, investment in education, and the transmission of values and skills. Eventually these traditions flowed together in the American melting pot and dissolved into a uniform pattern of kinship. But in the intensely competitive phase of adjustment and settlement, these nepotistic legacies determined the speed of middle class assimilation.[32]

All these currents came together in the creation of the labor movement, the greatest single legacy of the mass European migrations. We are taught to view this movement as a struggle between economic classes, but it was primarily an ethnic phenomenon. Most unions arose among workers in a given ethnic niche who banded together for mutual aid and protection. Nepotism at both the group and family level therefore played a vital (if largely unheralded) role in the rise of American labor.

The earliest unions were formed by skilled miners, mechanics, and factory workers from England and the British Isles. As non-English-speaking immigrants arrived in greater numbers, they were excluded from these unions and had to form their own. Highly skilled German and Scandinavian workers who came over in the 1840s and 1850s gave a big boost to the American labor movement. But unity among workers was still a long way off due to linguistic and cultural barriers. The various German unions maintained a central body to represent their interests. The same separatist tendency was evident in the creation of the United Hebrew Trades and the Italian Chamber of Labor. Ethnic competition within the trades was keen and often violent: "An endless catalog could be drawn up of conflict between Cornish and Irish hard-rock miners, Yankee and French Canadian textile workers, Irish and English anthracite miners, white and black locomotive firemen, Italian and native laborers, and so on." Yet these ethnic solidarities were crucial to the strength of labor unions, especially when it came to the discipline required for strikes and collective bargaining. A particularly interesting case were the Molly Maguires, who terrorized the anthracite coal fields of Pennsylvania in the 1860s and 1870s. According to historian Kevin Kenny, this organization, formed by immigrants from a depressed rural section of northwestern Ireland, carried out a campaign of assassination and violence to protest their exclusion from apprenticeship programs dominated by English and Welsh miners.[33]

Labor leaders have grown wise in the invention of rules and procedures to keep the benefits of membership in the family, and the privilege was often enshrined in their charters and bylaws. The apprentice system was a favorite means of controlling access and was frequently manipulated for nepotistic ends and to keep wages high by limiting new members. The stonecutters' constitution provided that any local could set the number of apprentices in the yards under its jurisdiction, with stonecutters' sons enjoying preference. The carpenters' union of Tacoma, Washington, made a similar provision, and the lathers of Cleveland, Ohio, declared that "no apprentice shall be admitted to work in any shop unless he is a son of a member of this union in good standing." This nepotistic pattern continued for decades in the building trades, which are still known as "father-son unions."[34]

The problem for more ambitious organizers was to take advantage of these tribal solidarities while avoiding their divisive potential. Most large-scale unions emerged slowly as federations of ethnic locals united by a common occupation and little else. The American Federation of Labor, led by Samuel Gompers, focused on economic issues to the exclusion of political ones precisely to avoid these crosscutting antagonisms. Though Gompers's creed of "pure and simple unionism" held that unions "should open their portals to all wage workers irrespective of creed, color, nationality, sex or politics," it was a long time before this ideal was put in practice. Moreover, Gompers's sense of solidarity was limited to English, German, and Scandinavian workers.[35]

Thus for all the rhetoric about the brotherhood of workers, it was really the brotherhood of workers related to *them* that mattered most. This familistic limit on the fraternal spirit of labor was most evident in the case of blacks, who were excluded by nearly all union charters. (The main exceptions were Gompers's AFL; the syndicalist Industrial Workers of the World, also known as the Wobblies; and John L. Lewis's United Mine Workers, which welcomed Italians, Slavs, Asians, and blacks.) In the labor market, blacks have consistently fared worse than other groups. Abandoned by federal troops in 1877, southern blacks were subjected to a harsh régime of segregation and quickly became second-class citizens. Though a great northward migration began during World War I, when jobs opened up in the booming war industries, terrible race riots in East St. Louis and Chicago helped widen the gap with the unions. Blacks did manage to establish a foothold in the railroad industry, but these unions were particularly racist. The first black union, the Brotherhood of Sleeping Car Porters, was organized by A. Phillip Randolph in the 1920s. Black hotel workers also organized successfully. In the end, however, blacks were pushed out of many economic niches by more aggressive (and more nepotistic) groups.

Antiblack prejudice severely retarded the development of labor federations. The prevailing sentiment was expressed with singular directness by a member of a southern machinists' union who said: "I will never sit in the local of the I.B.E.W. or any other organization and refer to the Negro as a brother."[36] Such evidence clearly attests to a lack of class consciousness on the part of American workers. Not until the Great Depression would the failure of ethnic economies and ethnic political leadership persuade workers of different backgrounds to view themselves as having common interests.[37]

Nepotism in union leadership has been a persistent and sometimes scandalous problem. But this is a product of the nature and dynamics of union organizing itself. Rank-and-file members always preferred a leader of their own nationality, and labor leaders typically viewed their constituents as a personal clientele: "the emergence of a foreign-born leader on the executive board of an established union frequently reflected a pact in which he brought his countrymen into the union in exchange for a post for himself," wrote one observer.[38] The union official labored to obtain benefits for his followers and thereby secure his position. In this respect he was not that different from the political precinct captain or ward boss.

In short, nepotism was born with the labor movement and continues to permeate it from top to bottom. Notable labor dynasties have included the Reuther brothers of the UAW, John L. Lewis and his family in the United Mine Workers, and William L. Hutcheson, who ruled the carpenters' union for thirty-seven years and was succeeded by his son. Most famous, of course, has been the succession of James Hoffa Jr. to the leadership of the International Brotherhood of Teamsters.[39] This kind of thing requires no justification in the eyes of union members themselves, who seem quite prepared to put up with it. The reason is not hard to understand: while nepotism is thought of as a practice of the rich, institutionalized nepotism represents in many cases the workingman's only chance to do for his son what the rich man does for his as a matter of course.

Immigrants and workers, many of them Catholics, naturally gravitated to the Democratic Party in preference to the WASP-dominated GOP. But what put the Democrats over the top in 1932 were the crash and the ensuing Depression.

In any history of nepotism in America, the Great Depression merits more than a few paragraphs. For while the Depression is usually viewed as an economic and political crisis, it was experienced in a very direct and personal way as a challenge to American families.

The first wave of the crisis saw the collapse of the ethnic economies. According to historian Lizabeth Cohen, hundreds of ethnic savings banks, insurance companies, and building and loan associations were wiped out, real estate plummeted, neighborhood stores went out of business, and church-based charity and welfare institutions were quickly overwhelmed. The fraternal insurance and loan associations that had been the anchor of ethnic life in the 1920s failed as more and more people proved unable to keep up their payments. It was a humiliating blow to ethnic pride at a time when most communities still insisted on taking care of their own. The Depression also heightened class tensions within groups, as paternalistic employers withdrew their support and businessmen discontinued their contributions to local welfare associations. These changes caused a widespread crisis of ethnic identification and communal leadership that ultimately produced a more unified working class consciousness—though in the short term the labor movement also lost strength, declining from 5 million in 1920 to about 3 million in 1933.

The Depression wreaked havoc on traditional families, many of which were at the same time pulling together and falling apart. Most men over forty found themselves unemployable, and women and children took their place in the labor market. The result was an inversion of family roles, while constant worry over money increased friction between husbands and wives and parents and children. Many fathers could not cope with the loss of authority, becoming angry, depressed, or abusive. Wives and children meanwhile gained a new sense of independent worth. Mothers asserted their newfound authority, and some couples reported sexual problems.

The collapse of patriarchal authority in the family, the workplace, and the ethnic community at large led to a profound generational crisis. "Many young people who were used to contributing a fair share of their income now found they had to turn over everything," Cohen writes. "Clothes and recreation, to say nothing of schooling and marriages, had to be put off." Not all children were willing to make such sacrifices, preferring to strike out on their own. Overall, however, the Depression temporarily halted and reversed the loosening of family bonds that had begun with the Industrial Revolution. Thoroughly assimilated first- and second-generation Americans found themselves forced to stay home (often to work in the family business) rather than pursue their own ambitions. An entire generation of upwardly mobile young Jews was "lost" in this way. Yet at the same time, Jewish family and communal traditions helped them weather the crisis more successfully than others.[40]

As if to illustrate these deep reserves of nepotistic strength, while other economic sectors were reeling, the Hollywood film industry, pioneered by a group of hard-driving Jewish entrepreneurs in the 1920s and 1930s, thrived and grew. Warner Bros. was founded in 1919 by the four sons of a German Jewish immigrant. Adolph Zukor and William Fox built Paramount and Fox Entertainment, Carl Laemmle founded Universal, and Louis B. Mayer and Samuel Goldwyn created MGM—all with the help of their relatives. While all these founding fathers were united in their drive to put their ethnic pasts behind them, they relied on Jewish networks to raise capital and showed intense family loyalty.[41] As the studios grew, so did the presence of kin, and the habit of nepotism became a standing joke.[42] But the Depression raised Hollywood nepotism to new heights: "Before long, everyone began to hear stories of some idiot nephew assigned screenwriting credit for a movie whose title he couldn't pronounce, of an ungainly daughter miraculously transformed into a glamorous starlet, or of a deadbeat brother-in-law hired to direct because his family got tired of lending him money."[43]

The greatest Hollywood paternalist was "Uncle" Carl Laemmle, known for his habit of hiring anyone and everyone who needed a job. He sponsored dozens of young immigrants from his hometown in Austria and put them to work on the lot. Laemmle's nepotism was both the making and unmaking of his studio. (One of his most talented protégés was producer Irving Thalberg, the son of a Long Island neighbor who was a friend of his wife's.) After building Universal into a successful business, Laemmle handed the studio over to his son on the boy's twenty-first birthday in 1929. But instead of the single-reel westerns and family comedies on which his father built the company, Junior veered into more upscale, big-budget projects. His first effort, *All Quiet on the Western Front,* was a huge success, winning the Oscar for best picture in 1930. Junior also pioneered the modern horror genre with Bela Lugosi's *Dracula* and Boris Karloff's *Frankenstein.* But as the studio suffered a series of setbacks early in the Depression, Junior refused to trim his sails. As a result, Laemmle was ultimately forced to remove his son and sell the studio.

Junior's failure to adapt to the Depression was perhaps understandable, though it also reflects a pattern in many family businesses in which a younger generation, raised in privileged circumstances, loses touch with the father's unerring "street" sensibility. Yet the films he did make are a lasting legacy to American cinema, and had it not been for the Depression his vision might well have been vindicated.

Thus, while nepotism may have built the ethnic machines and the labor movement, it largely failed in the Depression, as did those other vestiges of a kin-based social order, economic and political paternalism. Nepotism alone would not be enough to get the nation through the economic crisis. FDR therefore presided over a vast expansion of government power, ushering in a new era in which the state became a surrogate parent, employer, and patron. Like Lincoln, he employed a universalist ideology to transcend ethnic and regional differences, while using patronage to tie these groups securely to his party.

Walter Lippmann had called FDR an opportunist without fixed views or real convictions, but it was precisely this opportunism that would make him such an effective coalition leader during a period of national crisis. He ran in 1932 on a platform of studied vagueness, touting a policy of fiscal conservatism and being careful not to make too many promises. But it would have been hard for any Democrat to lose that year, and FDR's coalition (not finally cemented until 1936) united the many enemies of the WASP establishment: western farmers, southern populists, northern workers, blacks, Jews, Italians, and other marginal or disadvantaged groups. The diverse cultural values of this broad coalition could not all be reflected in government, but FDR contrived to turn this weakness into a strength, focusing on economic and social reforms and announcing that the New Deal was to be a series of "pragmatic experiments."

Not since 1860 had a president brought a new party to office in the midst of a national crisis. And like Lincoln (and Jackson) before him, FDR used patronage to establish his government and unite his diverse coalition. His establishment of sixty-five new federal agencies has been called "one of the most spectacular resurgences of the spoils system in American history," creating a hundred thousand new jobs, listed in a directory known as the Plum Book.[44] Under the tutelage of Howe, FDR had become one of the greatest masters of patronage in American history. For example, according to White House aide James L. Rowe, the creation of the Federal Trade Commission was partly a means for FDR to repay his political debt to Sen. Kenneth McKellar, who filled it with "layers and layers of Tennessee lawyers." Likewise the Justice Department was "overwhelmed by Montana lawyers." Decades later, John F. Kennedy's antipoverty program served much the same purpose.[45]

Roosevelt is usually painted as the enemy of bossism and political machines. The bosses were indeed united in opposing his candidacy, though when it became clear that he would win the nomination, several of them switched sides. Far from being punished, they were welcomed into the fold and duly received their share of patronage. In return, the machines proved their importance in the implementation of FDR's program. They helped secure the vice presidential nomination of Henry Wallace in 1940, and the machine-controlled congressional delegations from New York, Chicago, and New Jersey afforded strong support for FDR's foreign and domestic policies. FDR's much-publicized war against Tammany's Boss Curry was aimed not at destroying the machine's power but at putting it in friendly hands. When Mike Kennedy became Tammany leader in 1942, Roosevelt came through with federal patronage to bolster his leadership.

The New Deal was thus a vast patronage network that enabled the new president to reach directly down into the urban neighborhoods and attach the voters to his party. Jews, for example, many of whom had been galvanized by landlord-tenant disputes in the early thirties, were brought into Democratic politics through neighborhood political clubs, and it was through these familial channels that Jews became a force in national politics.[46] The party had moved closer to Jewish interests in the twenties with its support for organized labor and open immigration. FDR cemented Jewish loyalty with his zealous advocacy of social insurance and public welfare programs. He gave Felix Frankfurter, Henry Morgenthau, and Bernard Baruch high positions in his administration, and appointed hundreds of other Jews to civil service positions. Blacks also benefited from New Deal patronage. Under FDR an unprecedented number of blacks received federal appointments—although because segregation was still the rule in government agencies, they received less than other groups.

The process of ethnic succession was also at work in the cities, as seen in the administration of Fiorello La Guardia. La Guardia, a liberal Republican, had been born in New York City the same year as FDR, spent his youth in Arizona, lived in Europe, and spoke half a dozen languages. Half Italian and half Jewish, a practicing Episcopalian who married first a Catholic, then a Lutheran, he was the perfect representative of the new American pluralism. His election as mayor of New York in 1933 was a resounding victory for Italians, Jews, and blacks over the Irish monopoly. La Guardia dramatically increased the presence of these groups in appointive positions and broadened the merit system. As a result, the proportion of blacks, Jews, and Italians in city jobs increased, while that of Irish fell.

With the passage of the 1935 Wagner Act, which guaranteed the right to collective bargaining, the labor movement revived and at the same time ended its decades-long avoidance of political alignment. It now became a permanent element in the Democratic coalition, contributing heavily to FDR's campaigns. Roosevelt also continued Teddy's crusade against inherited wealth, enacting a whopping 70 percent estate tax and a gift tax of over 50 percent. "The transmission from generation to generation of vast fortunes by will, inheritance, or gift," he pronounced, "is not consistent with the ideals and sentiments of the American people."[47] But the centerpiece of the New Deal was, of course, the establishment of the American welfare state, whose cornerstone was the Social Security Act of 1935.

Though workers' compensation and limited retirement supports had been enacted in the 1920s, they did not go nearly far enough. Study of the problem had intensified with the onset of the Depression, but it was a spontaneous movement of retired and elderly persons that made it a pressing political issue. (The emergence of the elderly as an active, independent constituency was the fortuitous result of weakened family ties and improved health conditions.) The Social Security Act was a sweeping piece of legislation that guaranteed welfare and unemployment benefits, aid to dependent children, old-age pensions, disability insurance, maternity care, public health work, and vocational rehabilitation. While most of these programs were administered by the states, social security funds were to be administered directly by the government. Nothing indicates more clearly the trend toward the increasing dependency of individuals on the state.

In this respect, the New Deal merely capped a process of growing state involvement in family life that had begun in the late nineteenth century with the rise of compulsory public education and other child welfare legislation. According to demographer Norman Ryder, mass education was the primary agent in reducing reliance on kin and undermining the authority of fathers: "Boys who go to school distinguish between what they learn there and what their fathers can teach them." For Ryder, education subverts the family and encroaches on the sphere of its traditional liberties, in order to prepare the young for their role as citizens and workers in an industrial society. Social historian John Caldwell concurs in this emphasis on public education, citing it as the main agent in the decline of the autonomous family. What's more, the rise of compulsory schooling correlates closely with the mysterious decline in nineteenth-century birthrates, beginning in New England, where public schooling was first introduced in the 1850s, spreading to other states throughout the century. According to Allan Carlson, the Social Security Act represented another "aggressive seizure of family functions." By redistributing income from current workers to current retirees, the government "socialized" the insurance value of children and effectively cut the economic bonds between the generations.[48] The long-term result has been to reduce the dependence of old people on their children, with a corresponding change in attitude on the part of the children themselves, who feel less and less responsible for their parents' support.

Yet while the New Deal has been viewed by many critics as intending these effects, its underlying impulse was conservative. Carlson observes that the Social Security Act was crafted largely by a group of social theorists called "maternalists," who believed that mothers belonged in the home and opposed creating incentives for them to enter the labor market. For these "radical" New Dealers, the basic social unit was the father-headed family, and they defined an adequate living as a "family wage"—enough to enable a man to support a wife and children. According to Carlson, feminist historians who see the New Deal as a reactionary attempt to strengthen the patriarchal family are perfectly right. Hence the otherwise perplexing refusal to fund day care centers, the endorsement (by Labor secretary Frances Perkins and Eleanor Roosevelt) of unequal pay for women, the disincentives to female employment built into AFDC, and the encouragement of home industry and self-sufficient families.[49] Even the antinepotism statutes passed in this period were motivated by family-centered thinking. Thus while conservatives often view the New Deal as an attack on the family, in fact it was launched and directed by people who were trying to *strengthen* the traditional father-centered household. Their efforts, though well-meaning, had the opposite effect.

As the 1932 elections approached, a national scandal erupted when Rep. J. R. Mitchell of Tennessee introduced a bill outlawing the appointment of relatives to congressional staff positions. In recent years, several states had introduced such regulations. Mississippi passed an antinepotism bill in 1926, and similar laws were introduced by Idaho (1929) and Utah (1931), followed by Iowa, Oklahoma, Texas, and Nevada. But Congress was a law unto itself, and delegates from all these states had put numerous relatives on the payroll.

The first attempt to introduce such a bill in Congress was made in

1930 by Ulysses S. Stone of Oklahoma. "I couldn't reconcile a member waxing eloquent over the grafting 'interests' when I knew he had a wife on the pay-roll at $3,900 who came to the office only once a month and then only to draw her pay," he told Washington journalist Raymond Clapper. The bill never got out of committee—not surprising, since the committee's chairman had a son on the federal payroll. In 1932 Rep. Grant E. Mouser of Ohio tried to add an amendment to a general economy bill that would have prevented members of Congress from employing family members who did not actually perform the services for which they were paid. The amendment was voted down two-to-one without a roll call.

In 1932 Representative Mitchell called for an investigation of the problem: "A full, truthful and unbiased record should be made available of the innermost workings of this hideous monster nepotism." Though he met with stiff resistance, his campaign aroused strong public interest and soon the press was clamoring for details. Mitchell's investigation revealed that 133 congressmen and at least thirty-seven senators had given jobs to relatives. A typical editorial cartoon showed a long line of congressional relatives collecting cash at the Capitol Hill pay window, with the caption "Who said Congress hasn't done anything to end unemployment?" Public feeling ran high and a number of congressmen and senators lost their seats. One of these was Iowa's Sen. Smith W. Brookhart, a dyed-in-the-wool populist who had risen from log cabin origins. "He fought the poor man's battles," Clapper wrote, "his farmer constituents worshipped him as a god." Yet in the 1932 campaign his opponent toured the state reading from a list of Brookhart's boodling relatives, including two sons, two daughters, and two brothers. This was too much for the voters, and after forty years he was unceremoniously turned out of office.

It was bad enough that members of Congress employed family members; worse was the fact that many were no-show, or ghost, employees, who came in only once a month to pick up their check. Some didn't even do that. The daughter-in-law of Ohio senator Simeon D. Fess was listed as assistant clerk of the Senate Library Committee, which he chaired. Her address was given as the Carleton Hotel, which is where the senator lived. Actually she resided with her husband in Toledo, where her government paycheck of $2,200 a year was thoughtfully mailed to her.

The greatest nepotist of all was Reed Smoot of Utah, a veteran of thirty years in the Senate, generally considered one of the nation's greatest public servants. His dedication was exemplary. During the year and a half that the Hawley-Smoot tariff bill was under consideration, the senator never missed a meeting of the Finance Committee and took part in the debate over every one of its thousands of schedules. Yet at the same time he used the government as "a feather bed for a nepotic army, for worthy young Mormon students, his henchmen, friends, and vigilantes." Smoot had built up a truly impressive patronage network: "Smoot men were found on every rung of the official hierarchy . . . all the way from the Supreme Court of the United States down to the rubbers in the marble bath of the Senate Office Building. At one time in the Seventy-Second Congress, three generations of the Smoot family were on the pay-roll, including a grandson who was a Senate page." As Clapper relates, "There was nation-wide amazement when there was assembled for the first time a list of Senator Smoot's major patronage achievements." He carried a son and two daughters-in-law as paid clerks in his office and placed dozens of young Utah men and women in jobs all over Washington. Many had obtained professional degrees with Smoot's help and then returned to Utah: "More than half the lawyers in Salt Lake City were educated in Washington while holding patronage jobs in the government."[50]

Mitchell's antinepotism bill—the first in U.S. history—banned the hiring of relatives up to the third degree of consanguinity (aunt and uncle, or nephew and niece) and also prohibited members of Congress from engaging in the time-honored practice of hiring one another's kin.[51] There was no provision for removing those already in federal jobs; the bill merely specified that when the civil service dismissed employees, it should first dismiss those whose spouses were also employed by the government. The law can therefore be construed as intended not to outlaw family employment per se but to ensure a fair distribution of jobs among families. In any event, the antinepotism law was short-lived: Congress repealed it five years later.

In contrast to this orgy of congressional nepotism, FDR was "relatively scrupulous" when it came to his own family. Blithely citing "family tradition," he appointed Henry Latrobe Roosevelt assistant naval secretary, the fifth family member to hold the job. Eleanor's uncle David Gray became ambassador to Ireland, Warren Delano Robbins went to Canada, Preston Delano became comptroller of the currency, and Nicholas Roosevelt became deputy director of the Office of War Information. Several had been in government service before, and all were apparently well qualified. In addition, FDR's son Jimmy was made his private secretary at $10,000 a year, over Eleanor's objections: "Why should I be deprived of my eldest son's help and of the pleasure of having him with me just because I am the President?" Jimmy had been active in Massachusetts politics, where he formed an alliance with political boss James Michael Curley and was reported to be eyeing a run for governor in 1936. But poor health deferred his hopes for a political career until after his father's death.[52]

Franklin and Teddy each had four sons and a daughter, and it is interesting to compare how they turned out. Teddy's sons were raised to be sportsmen, adventurers, and soldiers. He constantly drilled into them his creed of military glory, and they often reenacted his famous charge up San Juan Hill, using his hat and sword as props. They all felt the need to live up to their father's example, and when they got their chance in World War I they served with conspicuous bravery. As Quentin (the youngest) put it: "It's rather up to us to practice what Father preaches." Alas, the invasion of Europe was very different from the "splendid little war" at San Juan Hill. The Roosevelts gaily charged straight into the maw of modern mechanized warfare. Archie was severely maimed; Ted was gassed and wounded; Quentin was shot down and killed. Teddy hung the twisted axle of his plane in the trophy room at Sagamore Hill, right next to his old hat and sword.

Ironically, none of Teddy's surviving sons seemed able to become his political heir. Ted Jr. was elected to the New York assembly in 1919, running against an opponent who cruelly jibed, "My hat's in the ring too— and it isn't my father's." Defeated by Al Smith for New York governor, he was appointed by President Harding assistant secretary of the navy, where he got mixed up in Teapot Dome. When World War II broke out he petitioned to be reinstated in command of his old infantry unit and was promoted to brigadier general. Ted and his son Quentin II fought together in North Africa and at D-day. Ted was in the first transport to hit Omaha Beach and showed incredible bravery as he walked up and down for hours with his cane, directing and encouraging the men.

If Teddy tended to be overinvolved with his sons, Eleanor and Franklin were notoriously *under*involved. Franklin's preoccupation with politics, his fight with polio, and his four terms in office left little time for fatherhood. Eleanor for her part had modern ideas about parenting and was reluctant to be seen as an overbearing mother. As a result, the boys were brought up in a spirit of benign neglect. This pattern did not change when Franklin became president. "The Roosevelt boys deeply resented having to make appointments to see their presidential father," reports Stephen Hess. This may explain the constant stream of bad behavior and embarrassing publicity: "There were innumerable speeding tickets, traffic accidents, divorces, and smashed photographers' cameras." Nor did they show much discretion in their business affairs. Anna and Elliott both accepted lucrative jobs with William Randolph Hearst, their father's bitterest critic. Jimmy, just out of college, took a sinecure in the insurance business, knowing full well that he was being paid for the use of his name. Later he established his own firm and was frequently accused of trading on his father's connections. The children's marital troubles were also food for scandal. Between the five of them, there were fifteen marriages and ten divorces. All the first marriages were with members of elite families, capped by that of Frank Jr. to Ethel Du Pont. However, the boys performed quite well in World War II, and if they did not quite come up to the mark set by Theodore's sons, they served with admirable courage.

Three of Franklin's sons went into politics. In 1949, Frank Jr. ran for Congress from New York's Twentieth District—the liberal Upper West Side—and was elected easily. He so resembled his father in his features, speech, and gestures that some critics claimed he had studied recordings of his father's voice. He served for three terms. Meanwhile, in 1950 Jimmy challenged Earl Warren for governor of California and lost by a million votes. Four years later he won election to a safe Democratic congressional seat in a poor district of Los Angeles (he served for five terms). The same year, Frank Jr. launched his bid to follow his father and great-uncle as governor of New York, but the party turned to Averell Harriman instead. In 1960 he came to the aid of John F. Kennedy in the West Virginia primary by impugning Hubert Humphrey's war record. (Critics called it "a new low in dirty politics.") JFK appointed him secretary of commerce, and President Johnson named him the first chairman of the EEOC. In 1965, Jimmy lost a race for mayor of Los Angeles and took his mother's old job at the UN. The same year, Elliott ran for mayor of Miami Beach on the slogan "A man with a name Miami Beach can be proud of." Not surprisingly in a heavily Jewish district filled with people who felt they owed their social security payments to his father, Elliott won. It was the highest office he ever achieved.

As Stephen Hess observes, the Roosevelts can be considered a political illustration of the adage "Shirtsleeves to shirtsleeves in three generations." Their example shows that American political dynasties rarely prosper on the national level and are more typically a state or local phenomenon. Americans seem to feel that there ought not to be such dynasties, and they have dealt out many more rebukes than rewards to ambitious presidential offspring. Yet Hess also points out that, judged by any other standards than those of their father and great-uncle, Franklin's boys would be considered quite successful. After all, Teddy and Franklin Roosevelt were a tough act to follow, and their sons' careers betray the crushing effects of growing up too close to such an outsized personality. It may well have been easier for Franklin to become Teddy's heir than for the sons of either man to follow their fathers. For while a son usually feels obliged to make himself in his father's image, as Teddy had done, a more distant relative like Franklin clearly felt no such pressure. It was enough for him to appropriate Teddy's name and political program without feeling that he had to measure up to Teddy's standards in every respect.

In this regard, FDR seems very like another self-anointed political heir, the adopted son of Pericles. Like Franklin, Alcibiades was a handsome, rich, and spoiled young man whose greatest asset was his powerful seductive charm. His restless ambition was recognized early by friends and enemies alike, and everyone agreed he had the talent to do anything he wished. But he was also considered suspiciously unprincipled, a glib opportunist with dictatorial ambitions who understood very well how to ingratiate himself with the crowd and manipulate its passions. Like Franklin, he edged aside the natural sons of Pericles and claimed the great man's mantle.

FDR did not, like Alcibiades, destroy the democracy his uncle built, and in some ways he continued his mentor's political impulse and mission. (His campaigns for steeper income and inheritance taxes, for example, were continuations of Teddy's war against elite nepotism.) He presided over a great expansion of the democratic franchise, took on the economic trusts, and vastly enlarged the powers of the presidency. In addition, his creation of the welfare state and support for the labor movement replaced the machines as social welfare providers and fatally undermined them as a political force. A brilliant politician and party builder who forged a new majority coalition out of diverse ethnic blocs and interest groups, he laid the basis for a powerful interventionist state that ultimately undermined these groups and dissolved the American populace into a middle class society of atomized individuals. Instead of relying on intermediaries, the modern state forges direct ties with every citizen, becoming blind to cultural and ethnic differences: a benevolent superpatron presided over by an affable, smiling, but ultimately detached corporate father. Franklin Roosevelt was the first of these blandly detached father-executives, of a kind that would become all too common in the postwar world, and as such an ideal figurehead for the new paternalistic welfare state: an impersonal bureaucratic simulacrum that distributes largesse for which no one is properly grateful.

Franklin and Eleanor Roosevelt may thus be considered harbingers of the modern two-career family, whose children—emancipated alike from nepotistic domination and concern—grow up without their parents' stable presence in the home. The dispiriting results are plain to see: the sons of FDR inherited his charm and social ease but were distressingly casual about living up to their parents' expectations or ideals and accepted various jobs, commissions, and favors as their birthright. Franklin himself was the model of the new American father who has allowed the state to take his place in the lives of his children: a fond but largely passive absentee who watched with seeming equanimity as they floundered through a series of bad marriages and failed business ventures. A gifted opportunist and improviser, FDR had invented himself out of whole cloth and apparently expected his sons to do the same. One gets the sense that had he lived, he wouldn't have lifted a finger to help them. The sons he got are just the kind you would expect: spoiled opportunists who didn't hesitate to sell their family name to the highest bidder. Perhaps if he had been more involved with his sons, a bit more nepotistic—more like Teddy—they might have turned out better.

CHAPTER 11

HEIRS APPARENT

JFK AND THE NEW MERITOCRATIC NEPOTISM

In November 1960, John F. Kennedy became the youngest elected president in American history, declaring in his inaugural address, "The torch has been passed to a new generation." The theme of youth was especially timely. The postwar baby boom had reached its peak. Millions of young couples fled the cities for the suburbs, leaving the ethnic ghettos behind along with their extended kinship networks. Families also became smaller: the average number of children per family shrank, while the old three-generational household gave way to one composed of only two. John F. Kennedy was the natural leader of this emerging "postethnic" society. But while his own small family seemed to embody the postwar trends of nuclearity, mobility, and shrinking family size, the presence of the large Kennedy clan in the background provided a reassuring reminder of the immigrant past, as well as an image of the status to which most middle class Americans aspired.

If the 1960 election was the signal for a generational transfer of power, it was a transition marked not by violent overthrow but filial respect: the president's cabinet choices were all senior figures from the top levels of the business, legal, academic, and political establishments.[1] At the same time, however, Kennedy floated the idea of making his younger brother Bobby attorney general. The appointment of a family member to the cabinet was viewed as unacceptable nepotism by many in both parties. Some cited his lack of qualifications: only thirty-five years old, Bobby had never argued a case in court or run a large organization. Others maintained that the president's relative could not perform his duties impartially. Still others rested their opposition on Bobby's personal deficiencies. Constitutional scholar Alexander M. Bickel wrote that Bobby had shown excessive zeal in his war against the mafia. The *New York Times* agreed: "Bobby is marked in particular degree with that streak of ambition and ruthlessness which is a characteristic of the clan."[2]

It was exactly the kind of controversy Kennedy didn't need and shouldn't have courted—one that thrust his family's exclusivity and clannishness squarely before the national eye and raised the specter of dynastic ambition. But Bobby had not been his brother's first choice, or even his second.[3] It was the president's father who had insisted on making Bobby attorney general. Nor was he impressed by cries of nepotism. "Nepotism, my foot!" Joe Kennedy growled. "Why should anybody think that Bobby needs a job?"[4]

Jack's habit of deferring to his father ill befitted a president, yet he feared to oppose him directly. He first asked Sen. George Smathers to take the matter up with Joe. When that failed, he sent Democratic fixer Clark Clifford to talk his father out of it. Clifford was firmly rebuffed.

If Jack required persuasion, Bobby needed even more. He had already rejected a proposal to appoint him to Jack's vacated Senate seat. Bobby abhorred the idea of family patronage and clearly preferred to make it on his own, perhaps as a lawyer or teacher. The debate went on for weeks. Finally, Bobby called his brother and turned him down. But Jack overrode his objections, telling him that he needed someone he could trust, someone "who in difficult times, will tell me the absolute truth." As always, Bobby's struggle to break free and define his own course ended in resigned acceptance. It was his fate to serve the family and its interests.

Newsweek called the appointment "a travesty of justice," the *Atlantic* "a slap in the face to all law-abiding citizens," the *Nation* "the greatest example of nepotism this land has ever seen." Even the Kennedys' friends were dismayed.[5] Yet in the end Bobby converted his critics, winning praise as his brother's "best appointment." He also played a leading role in JFK's administration, leading him firmly in the direction of a positive approach to civil rights, advising him closely during the Cuban missile crisis, and steering him through numerous other difficulties. The Kennedy presidency was in many ways a partnership between two brothers whose relationship has been called symbiotic.

The brothers' willingness to go it alone in the teeth of opposition from all sides was a testament to that symbiotic bond. But above all, it was a tribute to the power of Joseph P. Kennedy's will and dynastic ambition. Having established himself as a titan of business and finance, he set out to make his sons congressmen, senators, and presidents. Astonishingly, he succeeded: none of his sons rebelled against his use of them as pawns in his dynastic scheme, and America was utterly seduced by the youthful and attractive Kennedy clan. What the public only dimly perceived through the smoke screen of publicity he masterfully orchestrated was that the family was organized according to the old rules of Classical Nepotism. While most immigrant families were loosening their bonds, liberating themselves from the constraints of depression and war, the Kennedys maintained the collective discipline and loyalty that had characterized Irish families in a previous era.

The rise of the Kennedy family coincides with other important developments in American life, including the birth of the postwar meritocracy and the egalitarian revolution of the civil rights, feminist, and gay rights movements—movements that opened the door to the final, legalistic phase of the American war on nepotism. The family's trajectory therefore affords an excellent lens through which to view the transformations that fundamentally altered the practice of nepotism in the second half of the twentieth century. Though not products of meritocracy themselves, the Kennedys came to embody its values of intelligence and efficiency and became not only the keepers of the New Deal flame but the standard-bearers for the liberalism of the Cold War era. JFK was also the first celebrity president, and his election inaugurated not just a revolution of youth but the birth of a media culture in which a family name once again became a valuable commodity. The Kennedys led the way in this change, taking us (in effect) from premodern to postmodern nepotism in the short space of three generations.

Unattractive as he was in some respects, Joe Kennedy must be given his due as the greatest American nepotist of the twentieth century. His familism was a gravitational field so strong that none of his sons could break free of it. If one were to choose a figure out of myth to illustrate that overpowering impulse, it would be Kronos, the Greek creator god who devoured his own children. Joe Kennedy's dynastic enterprise illuminates the darker side of nepotism: the fruit of an erotic drive so strong that it destroys the thing it loves.

KRONOS OF BOSTON: THE RISE OF JOE KENNEDY

Joe Kennedy is often called a classic self-made man, and in many respects this is true. Yet like many self-made men, he also took considerable pains to obscure his debt to his family and in-laws. Given the myth he later spun around himself, it is easy to forget that he was not a poor man's son or a penniless immigrant but a third-generation American, the Harvard-educated scion of an influential Irish Catholic family.

According to Thomas O'Connor, many of Boston's Irish politicians were men whose fathers had died young. Assuming responsibility for a large immigrant family, they became patrons to their siblings and later extended that role to the community at large as politicians and ward bosses.[6] Joe's father, Patrick Joseph Kennedy, had been born in Boston in 1858 and lost his own father to cholera before his first birthday. Ambitious and resourceful, he worked his way up from the docks to become a saloon owner and political manager in Boston's East End. There he ran what biographer Richard Whalen calls "a pocket-sized welfare state," providing food, fuel, jobs, and short-term loans to his constituents. A clever businessman, he established an ethnic bank, the Columbia Trust, and became a liquor importer and wholesaler. Kennedy went to the assembly five times and became a state senator in 1892. At the height of his power, he sat on Boston's five-man Board of Strategy, which met in the proverbial smoke-filled room to pick the Democratic slate for each election.

Another member of this board was John Francis Fitzgerald, an outsized political figure and gifted orator known as Honey Fitz. Originally intended for the medical profession, he went to Boston Latin and spent a year at Harvard Medical School before his father's death forced him to quit. Determined to keep his family together, Fitzgerald apprenticed himself to the neighborhood boss, who helped him begin his climb up the political ladder. A born showman who toured Boston's wards singing "Sweet Adeline" at the top of his lungs, he rose to dominate Boston's ethnically mixed North End, and in 1894 was elected to Congress. His grandson would launch his drive for the presidency from the same district in 1946.[7]

In 1905, Fitzgerald became mayor of Boston and packed the city's payroll with relatives, friends, and supporters. He was said to have appointed more bartenders to public jobs than any mayor in history. Like other urban bosses, he relied heavily on his family: Fitzgerald had six brothers who were the core of his machine, his brain trust, and closest advisers; journalists called them "the royal family."[8] A probe of his abuses resulted in a series of scandals that drove him from office, but he was back to serve a second term in 1910.

Joe Kennedy also went to Boston Latin, where he mingled with the scions of the Back Bay elite. His father then enrolled him at Harvard, determined to gain acceptance for his son in the ranks of the Protestant establishment.[9] Joe laid siege to Harvard, going out of his way to befriend the leading members of his class and hoping for membership in the exclusive Porcellian Club. But he was never accepted by the sons of the brahmin elite. Nor should he have expected to be, given their increasingly withdrawn and castelike character in the face of a growing challenge from the rising ethnic communities. Surprised and deeply pained by his rejection, he fell back upon the atavistic familism of all dynastic founders. "Never again would he experience loyalty to any institution, any place or any organization," writes Doris Goodwin.[10]

Like the fictional Don Corleone, Joe's idea of family was both broadly inclusive and sharply exclusive. To relatives and friends he could be warm, affectionate, and loyal; with outsiders he was utterly unscrupulous. In this he resembled no one so much as the piratical sea captains who had founded the great brahmin families. The world of capitalist enterprise was still largely unregulated, and a preternaturally self-confident young man like Joseph Kennedy could slash and burn his way through it at will.

After Harvard, P.J. got Joe a job at the family bank. He learned the business quickly and then obtained (through Mayor Fitzgerald) an appointment as a state bank examiner. In 1913 he used this experience to save Columbia Trust from a hostile takeover. In gratitude, his father stepped down from his position and helped Joe become, at twenty-five, the youngest bank president in the country. From then on, Joe took center stage in the family enterprise while his proud father watched from the wings. He thus learned from his father to view life as a partnership between generations—a gift relation governed by the laws of reciprocity.

In no statement I have seen did Joseph Kennedy announce his intention to found a dynasty. Yet he proceeded in almost every respect as though he had a conscious plan. Nor was this something he could have learned from his father. Indeed it is characteristic of most dynastic founders to depart from their family histories. No one teaches these methods and skills. Dynastic strategies are simply *there,* part of the unconscious heritage of all human beings, waiting to be rediscovered in each generation.

The first step in the creation of a dynasty was obtaining a suitable bride, and Joe had set his sights on Rose Fitzgerald, the belle of Irish Boston. Joe and Rose had met as children and briefly dated during high school. Mayor Fitzgerald had other plans for his lovely, high-spirited daughter and he sent her to Brussels for a year to break it up, but the romance picked up again on her return. Now Joe was in a position to overcome the father's objections, and the engagement was shortly announced. Nine months after the wedding, Rose gave birth to a son, Joseph P. Kennedy Jr. Honey Fitz stood in front of the house and announced to the world that a future president had just been born. He was off by only one.

Kennedy's dynastic enterprise necessarily involved an energetic breeding program; like all patriarchal founders he aimed to produce a large family, and his high reproductive ambition required that Rose be kept constantly pregnant. Joe Jr. was born in 1915, followed two years later by John, and seven more in quick succession. Joe and Rose had agreed early on to keep their children close and hold them aloft in a protected, privileged sphere. Others might join their circle, but the family's gaze would always be turned powerfully inward. Frequent moves reinforced this sense of privileged detachment. As a result, the children became natives of the Kennedy family first, before any city or country.

Joe regarded World War I as a tragic, irrational folly; his attitude recalls that of Vito Corleone toward World War II—a far-off conflict between strangers that had nothing to do with his family. Yet he sized it up correctly as a magnificent business opportunity. Industry was booming and Kennedy seized the chance to become assistant manager of the Bethlehem shipyards at Fore River, Massachusetts. But Joe was already thinking ahead to the slump that would follow in peacetime, and he supposedly turned an energetic sales call on stockbroker Galen Stone into an offer of a job in Stone's office. Joe soon amassed considerable wealth, much of it based on inside information, stock pooling, and other practices now deemed illegal. In this and other phases of his career, he revealed his piratical instincts. He played by his own rules and did not linger but got in, made his pile, and got out.

Historians focus mainly on the rivalry and antagonism between Joe and his father-in-law, neglecting the many ways in which they cooperated in a joint dynastic enterprise. Fitzgerald family patronage of Kennedy took many forms, beginning with the bank examiner's job and including an unsuccessful attempt to get him appointed director of the federal Farm Loan Board. According to Ronald Kessler, the job at the Fore River shipyard was arranged by Fitzgerald to help his son-in-law avoid the draft. The job with Galen Stone was probably also arranged by Fitz, who passed on useful inside tips and introduced him to influential friends like Bernard Baruch. In return, Joe took charge of the Kennedy-Fitzgerald clan's growing financial interests.[11] Joe also became deeply involved in financing and managing his father-in-law's campaigns, and was schooled by him in the brazen techniques of big-city political corruption.

With the passage of Prohibition in 1919, Joe used his father's connections to become an importer of whiskey from England and Canada. Distribution was handled by gangsters, including Frank Costello and Al Capone. Though he kept these unsavory partners at arm's length, his mob ties would prove useful when he needed the support of union voters to elect his son in 1960. He had also begun to attract the circle of loyal retainers, later called the Irish mafia, who would follow him throughout his career, and who would serve his sons with equal dedication.[12]

It is no coincidence that the Kennedys rose at the same time as the great mafia families, and in limited partnership with them. The Kennedys were a corporate family in many ways like the fictional Corleones: a highly disciplined organization built of relatives, friends, and associates, knit together by nepotism and quasi-nepotistic ties. Though Kennedy himself stayed out of direct involvement with the rackets, much of his wealth was illicitly acquired and carefully hidden. He could not have risen so quickly if he had not been willing to operate outside the rules.

In 1928 Kennedy bought a studio and went to California, where he oversaw the production of dozens of low-budget films. Kennedy hated Jews in general but was impressed by the familial and ethnic solidarity of the Jewish movie moguls. It was in Hollywood that he mastered the art of publicity, and he soon collected a circle of writers and journalists, like Arthur Krock of the *New York Times,* who wrote favorable stories at his behest and became the chroniclers of the Kennedy myth. These connections were of crucial importance in Joe's creation of the family "brand."

Nepotism as we know it is a product of the patriarchal family, and Kennedy was a patriarch in the classical mold. He had a clear idea of what he wanted his sons to be like, and they turned out very much as he intended. The model of the vigorous Christian gentleman embodied by Theodore Roosevelt was the natural ideal of a gate-crashing upstart like Kennedy, and he sent his sons to be formed in this mold at the best New England schools. He also imitated the WASP elite by establishing a complex trust that would preserve the family wealth for generations.[13] Henceforth moneymaking would be the province of sons-in-law and other ancillaries. (JFK was not only the youngest elected president, he was also the richest.) But Joe did not want his sons to become spoiled inheritors like the young brahmins he had come to despise at Harvard. Insisting on success both in the classroom and on the playing field, he set exceedingly high standards and would not tolerate complaining or laziness. He candidly assessed each child's strengths and weaknesses, like any other investment, and sought the maximum return. He also instilled a strong sense of corporate identity: the children learned to take responsibility for one another, the older ones setting an example for the younger ones to follow.

In all dynastic families the mother plays a crucial role, for it is she who reinforces the patriarchal program with its message of obedience and loyalty. Throughout these early years, Rose (like Abigail Adams) was in charge of the children. She oversaw their schooling, monitored their social lives, drilled them in their catechism, doled out their allowances, and administered correction as required with a wooden hanger. She also helped to mold them for a future of citizenship and public service, quizzing them on current events in preparation for the dinner table debates Joe liked to stage. As a friend observed, "She's the one who put the family spirit in them." Moreover, any sign of sensitivity or weakness was ruthlessly crushed by both parents. As Joe put it, "Kennedys don't cry."

Despite his frequent absences, Joe was intensely involved with his children, closely following their progress and (like John Adams) writing them daily letters of exhortation and advice: a marvelous mixture of fatherly criticism, high expectations, and warmly supportive encouragement. In psychological terms, his approach to fatherhood was blissfully pre-Freudian. Like an Old Testament patriarch he was implacably demanding, yet he could also be affectionate and generous. He loved his daughters tenderly, and he let his sons know that he was their number one fan and supporter. In return, they worshiped their powerful father and strove to please him, hanging on every word he said. Friends observed that the children tolerated Rose, but Joe was the center of their universe: "Daddy was it." That was fine with Joe, who wanted to be both mother and father to his children. Yet far from crushing them beneath his expectations, Joe produced a brood of remarkably strong and resilient offspring, filled with confidence—indeed if anything, too much confidence. Joe purchased for his sons the kind of radical autonomy that seemed to make anything possible.[14]

Joe Jr. was the eldest and the son most like his father. Tall, handsome, and athletic, he was clearly his father's favorite and the family's heir apparent. He acted as a surrogate father to the younger children and was generally patient and protective. But he had a short temper, was thin-skinned and argumentative, and quick to resort to his fists. No high flyer academically, he made up in grinding effort what he lacked in natural gifts. His brother Jack, though weak from birth and plagued by mysterious illnesses, seemed to take things easier and was adept at sliding by on minimal effort. He was brighter than Joe and had to work less hard for his achievements. Joe took this as a challenge to his dominance and evened things up by brute force. He teased and taunted Jack until the younger boy lashed out, then wrestled him to the ground.[15] Neither parent interfered in these fights, believing it was good for Jack to be toughened up by his virile older brother. Joe Sr. declared that he didn't mind if they fought one another at home, so long as they fought together against outsiders. And fight they must: he entered them in swimming and sailing contests and relentlessly drilled into them that winning was the only thing that mattered. "Coming in second was just no good," Eunice Kennedy recalled. "The important thing was to win—don't come in second or third—that doesn't count—but win, win, win."[16]

But while Kennedy insisted on winning, he didn't insist on winning fairly. After Joe Jr. lost a sailboat race the father "lashed out bitterly," according to William Renehan. To make amends, Joe bought him a new mainsail, and the son started winning again. "Later, Joe Jr. discovered that the new mainsail ran nine inches too high, giving him an unfair advantage against other boats." This episode typifies Kennedy's approach to nepotism, as it does to everything else. He was a classic social cheater—what economists call a "free rider"—who cynically took advantage of other people's willingness to play by the rules, a willingness that he regarded as naïve.[17]

THE FALL OF ICARUS: THE KENNEDYS AT WAR

Because his sons eclipsed him, it is easy to forget how politically ambitious Joe Kennedy was and how seriously he was once taken as a national figure, even a possible president. Yet while his tactical instincts were unerring, his moral compass, conditioned by his narrow-minded familism, was spectacularly wrong at every turn.

Kennedy had been badly frightened by the Depression and feared a socialist upheaval. He thus threw in with Roosevelt, who by 1930 was building a new Democratic coalition. His greatest service was the delivery of eighty-six delegates under the control of William Randolph Hearst at the deadlocked 1932 convention.

FDR owed Kennedy, and Kennedy meant to collect. When his suit for the Treasury Department was rebuffed, he cunningly shifted his attentions to the president's son. Prohibition was on the verge of repeal, and Kennedy sought distribution agreements for various premium whiskeys. With Jimmy Roosevelt's help he obtained them, as well as the shady medicinal licenses under which they were imported. FDR could not have looked with equanimity on this relationship, yet—typically passive where his children were concerned—did nothing to discourage it. Instead he made Kennedy head of the newly established Securities and Exchange Commission, "setting a thief to catch a thief." Next he was appointed chairman of the U.S. Maritime Commission. But Joe had set his sights on London and brazenly lobbied FDR through Jimmy, who was by now under obligation to Joe in a number of ways.[18] When Jimmy became his father's White House secretary, Joe promised to support him in a run for governor of Massachusetts. Shortly thereafter he was named ambassador to England.

FDR apparently thought it would be a great joke to send this son of Irish immigrants to the Court of St. James's. But the president also understood Joe's ambition to establish his family among the WASP elite, and cunningly used it to get rid of him. Arriving in London in 1938, Joe quickly made himself objectionable by his strident isolationism, his critical remarks about FDR, and his evident sympathy for Hitler. However, he did succeed in getting his children into the limelight. The young Kennedys mixed easily with the English upper crust, were presented at court, and met the pope on a visit to Rome. So many stories were published about them that journalists complained about the ambassador's "overphotographed" children.

Part of his sons' education was their exposure to the larger world, and Joe made sure that they acquired an early familiarity with global issues. Joe Jr. spent the summer as his father's secretary and in 1939 made a European tour, sending back a stream of letters that slavishly mirrored his father's opinions. (Jack made a similar tour later the same year.) Old Joe was a great believer in the printed word, observing to Joe Jr. that nothing conferred prestige like authoring a book.[19] He hired a speechwriter to get Joe's letters into shape, but after the Nazi invasion of Poland his fascist sympathies rendered them unpublishable.

With the outbreak of war, Joe sent his wife and children home. Joe Jr. entered Harvard Law School, where he managed to hold his own only through constant tutoring. Jack was also at Harvard finishing his undergraduate studies and contemplating his thesis on England's disastrous policy of appeasement. The thesis received high praise from his advisers, and Arthur Krock suggested it be published under the title *Why England Slept.* Benefiting from the outbreak of hostilities in Europe, it became a surprise best-seller. Rumors persist that the book was ghostwritten by Krock, and that Joe Sr. bought thousands of copies. We may never know the truth, but it is indisputable that Jack received a great deal of help from his father. His view of the subject was essentially the same as Joe's, and his conclusion was lifted wholesale from one of Joe's letters. It was also Joe who persuaded Henry R. Luce to write an introduction, which earned it respectful attention. And Jack himself remarked that the book was "going like hotcakes—Dad's seeing to that."[20] Meanwhile, spurred to maintain his title as heir apparent, Joe Jr. ran in 1940 as a Massachusetts delegate for Democratic presidential challenger James Farley, easily winning the small local race with help from Grandpa Fitz. Joe was already telling people he expected to be president one day.

As German armies rolled across Europe and bombs fell on London, Ambassador Kennedy set his face ever more firmly against American involvement. His main interest was in preserving the capitalist system on which his family's future depended. FDR began to go around him, and their relationship quickly deteriorated. When Kennedy threatened to defect to Wendell Willkie in 1940, FDR recalled him for a private interview. Kennedy should have been inured to Roosevelt's charm, but he fell for it hook, line, and sinker. He endorsed Roosevelt's unprecedented third-term candidacy and assured the country that FDR had no intention of involving them in war. As he had often done before, he couched his amoral pragmatism in nepotistic terms: "After all, I have a great stake in this country," he declared. "My wife and I have given nine hostages to fortune. Our children and your children are more important than anything else in the world."[21]

Joe later claimed that FDR had promised to back his presidential bid in 1944 and also to back Joe Jr. for Massachusetts governor. Both were extremely unlikely, but Joe's raging dynastic ambition made him peculiarly susceptible to flattery. In effect, he was hoist on his own nepotistic petard. Kennedy had at length found himself in the position of many ambitious family founders. The predatory instincts that had made him successful in business rendered him unpalatable to the social and political elite. Unable to enter the promised land himself, he transferred his aspirations to his sons.

Despite their father's efforts to avert it, the inevitability of war was now apparent. Equally apparent, the war would become an arena for his sons to play out the strong competitive urge that Joe had instilled in them. While their sibling rivalry started out in a jocular vein, it soon grew deadly serious. In the end, only one would survive.

In early 1941, Joe Jr. entered naval flight training school. His instructors thought him an overly self-conscious pilot whose head was "too much in the cockpit," concentrating on his dials and readouts instead of trusting the plane and his instincts. Such hesitation and self-doubt are not uncommon in the sons of overbearing fathers, though they are often concealed with reckless bravado: call it the Icarus syndrome. Jack decided to join the army so as to avoid competing directly with his brother.[22] But he failed the medical exam (his ailments included a bad back, asthma, ulcers, and VD). Joe's friend Alan Kirk helped Jack get around the naval health inspection and assigned him to the Office of Naval Intelligence with the rank of ensign, surpassing his older brother in another of what Joe Jr. thought of as Jack's easy, unearned victories.[23]

Even after Pearl Harbor, Joe and Jack had much ado to get themselves into the action and rightly suspected their father of pulling strings to keep them out of it. Joe was assigned to ferry bombers from California to the East Coast. Jack had opted for the dangerous job of a torpedo boat captain, but his commanding officer selected him to remain in the

States as a training instructor. Jack went over his head, courtesy of Grandpa Fitz, to Senator Walsh of Massachusetts, chairman of the Naval Affairs Committee. Shortly afterward he shipped out for the Pacific.

Joe Jr. struck subordinates as a martinet and perfectionist with a stuck-up Harvard attitude. Jack was easygoing and approachable, a natural leader with a knack for inspiring loyalty. When he became a PT commander, he was promoted to lieutenant. Joe wasn't satisfied until he had achieved the same rank as his brother.

On July 19, 1943, *PT 109* was cut in two by a Japanese destroyer. Though he may have been negligent in allowing this to happen, Lieutenant Kennedy acted heroically in getting the survivors to safety. After Jack was rescued, the family held a celebration where he was toasted as a hero. Later, one guest heard Joe Jr. "sobbing in his room."[24] Meanwhile Joe Sr. lobbied Navy secretary James Forrestal to get Jack the Congressional Medal of Honor. Instead he received the Navy and Marine Corps Medal and became a magnet for admiring crowds back home. John Hersey wrote up the story for *Life,* and Joe persuaded *Reader's Digest* to condense the article. He later had a hundred thousand reprints distributed to support Jack's first congressional campaign.

Desperate to outdo his younger brother, Joe Jr. seized the opportunity to fly antisubmarine patrols in the North Atlantic from a base on the English coast. (While there he presided at the wedding of his sister Kathleen to Billy Hartington, the scion of a noble English family.)[25] In August 1944, Joe volunteered for Operation Anvil, in which a stripped-down Liberator aircraft would be filled with high explosives and flown across the channel. Before his departure he told a friend: "If I don't come back, tell my dad that I love him very much." Ten minutes before the scheduled jump time, Joe's aircraft exploded.

News of the tragedy reached the Kennedys two days later at the family's home in Hyannis on Cape Cod. Joe came out on the porch and announced, "Your brother Joe has been lost." He also told them to participate in the sailboat races already arranged for that afternoon, and to win them in Joe's honor. Even his son's death could serve as fuel for his dynastic plan to breed a family of winners.

THE FAMILY MACHINE

World War II reunified the country after decades of class warfare. The struggle with Hitler did much to advance the new national identity formed in the melting-pot years of the twenties and thirties. It also brought a new generation to power, and Joe Kennedy was determined that his son would be its leader.

The shift of paternal attention from Joe to Jack was "like a physical event," according to Arthur Krock. In the past, Joe Jr. had stood between Jack and his father, playing the dutiful heir apparent while Jack dallied as the prodigal. Now he felt "terribly exposed and vulnerable" in the face of Joe Sr.'s ambitions. He also felt Oedipal guilt about surviving his brother, combined with a despair of ever beating him now that he was dead. Yet Jack seemed genuinely eager to launch his own career. The competition with Joe had virtually defined his existence; now that he was free of it, he responded with a vigor that surprised even his cynical father.

JFK's rise from Congress to the presidency in a mere fourteen years was a result of his ability to exploit several significant trends. Of these perhaps the most important was the immigrant revolution. "During the years of the Kennedy family's rise in America," writes Doris Goodwin, "35 million immigrants had entered the United States." These people had struggled to make it out of their ethnic ghettos and into the expanding middle class. The postethnic masses longed to elect one of their own, a leader they could identify with, and the Kennedys appeared to fit the bill. Indeed, much more than Jack himself, it was the Kennedy family that fascinated Americans: "For every story that was written about Senator Kennedy in the 1950s," Goodwin notes, "there were twice as many about the Kennedy family." Their tight structure and esprit de corps "seemed strangely and appealingly anachronistic in the modern world." But JFK was elected not simply because he was the son of Irish immigrants but because he was an authentic American aristocrat. Unlike his parents, he was fully assimilated into the WASP-dominated regional culture; in the words of Massachusetts Gov. Paul Dever, he was "the first Irish brahmin." This aristocratic ethos was reflected in the family's habit of referring to politics as "public service," and it was one measure of Joe's achievement in telescoping two or three generations of familistic striving into one.

In 1945, Joe's advisers targeted Boston's Eleventh District, a mixed bag of working class ethnic neighborhoods that was in many ways a microcosm of the emerging national electorate. When Jack announced his candidacy, Joe established the Joseph P. Kennedy Jr. Foundation, named Jack president, and began "furiously pumping money into Catholic institutions in Jack's adopted district."[26] To run the campaign, Joe drafted his cousin Joe Kane, an old political hand who came up with the slogan "The New Generation Offers a Leader." Speeches were produced by a team of professional writers, neighborhoods were saturated with posters and leaflets, newspapers were blitzed with campaign ads, and a smoothly efficient organization scheduled dozens of events each day and followed up with hundreds of handwritten thank-you notes. Joe worked the phones to ensure favorable press coverage, while the candidate's sisters rang doorbells, hosted teas, and handed out brochures, and Bobby played softball with neighboorhood kids. Nigel Hamilton observes that Joe underestimated his son's political gifts, spending hundreds of thousands of dollars to buy an election that (in Kane's estimation) could have been bought for much less. But Joe was leaving nothing to chance.[27]

Jack finished the primary with 40 percent of the vote and went on to beat the Republican challenger. He was vague on the issues, campaigning on his World War II heroics and sticking to liberal nostrums like jobs, housing, and social security. But his personal magnetism combined with his celebrity status overcame misgivings about his youth and privileged background. Above all it was clear that Jack's appeal to women—an increasingly powerful bloc in postwar politics—would be a significant factor in his rise.

With Jack in Congress, Bobby returned to Harvard. As the third son of an intensely hierarchical family, he received much less attention from his father. Joe may also have perceived him as more Rose's child, sharing her religious piety as well as her dogmatic tendencies. Bobby, who neither smoked nor drank, was always the most moralistic of the Kennedys. A C student who entered Harvard in 1944 through his father's intervention, he fought his way onto the football team, working his way up through sheer force of will from seventh squad to varsity and playing part of one game with a broken leg. He was not popular as his brothers had been, but the few friends he did make, like teammate Ken O'Donnell, would be permanent additions to the family machine.

After Harvard, Bobby entered the University of Virginia Law School and in 1950 married Ethel Skakel, daughter of a wealthy Catholic businessman. The Kennedys were fervent anticommunists, and Bobby was drawn to the domestic crusade headed by J. Edgar Hoover and Sen. Joseph McCarthy. McCarthy had befriended Jack when the two Irish Catholics went to Washington in 1946, and he soon worked his way into the Kennedy circle. When Bobby's first child, Kathleen, was born, McCarthy became her godfather. It therefore seemed natural to ask McCarthy to arrange a position for Bobby at the Department of Justice.

Jack and Bobby had drawn closer in recent years, but their famed symbiosis did not begin to form until Jack ran for the Senate in 1952. It was a race of great symbolic importance, for Jack was challenging the popular Republican incumbent, Henry Cabot Lodge Jr. The first Henry Cabot Lodge had served in the Senate for thirty years and dealt a crushing defeat to Honey Fitz in 1916. The 1952 race, pitting the scions of Boston's leading WASP and Irish families, was thus not only a grudge match for the Kennedys but the culmination of a long-standing ethnic and class war within the state.

Jack might not have run if not for his father's encouragement: "When you've beaten him, you've beaten the best," he said, as though Lodge were an opposing quarterback. Joe must be credited with remarkable prescience, since Lodge was considered unbeatable. But it soon became apparent that the father's domineering style and micromanagement would be a detrimental influence on the campaign. Jack was unwilling to stand up to him, and Ken O'Donnell told Bobby he was needed. Bobby whipped the campaign into shape, building a disciplined organization that took Jack from a weak second place to a seventy-thousand-vote victory over a popular incumbent in the teeth of a national GOP landslide. In the process, he raised the family machine to a new level as a permanent force in state politics. He also forged the three-way partnership that would take them to the White House: Jack the affable front man, Joe providing money and influence behind the scenes, and Bobby running the organization with total dedication and ruthlessness.

Once again, Jack's campaign appealed strongly to female voters, who now outnumbered men in Massachusetts. "What is there about Jack Kennedy that makes every Catholic girl in Boston between eighteen and twenty-eight think it's a holy crusade to get him elected?" asked one bemused observer. Laurence Leamer suggests that Jack appealed not to their heads but to their hearts, or (in nepotistic terms) their reproductive fantasies: "Jack was a dream lover to the young girls who waved their handkerchiefs and God's glory of a son to their mothers." Jack was able to draw on a veritable army of female volunteers, and his mother and sisters staged numerous tea parties all over the state, bringing out thousands of women who would normally never think of attending a political rally.[28]

With Jack in the Senate, Bobby went to work for McCarthy. Meanwhile, a round of marriages launched a new stage in Joe's dynastic program—although as one of the sisters remarked, the bond between the siblings was so close that it had seemed as though no one outside the family could interest them. In this respect the Kennedys resembled other dynastic families, like the Borgias and the Bonapartes, whose closeness was such that they were accused of carrying on incestuous affairs. (The Rothschilds loved one another so much that they married their own nieces.) Jack's former girlfriend Inga Arvad later remarked that there was something incestuous about the whole family. But in a modern society the erotic pull of nepotism must be balanced, as in the hunter-gatherer band, by the centrifugal force of exogamy. Thus in 1953, Eunice married R. Sargent Shriver, the son of an old and wealthy Maryland Catholic family. Shriver had already joined the Kennedy organization as the manager of Chicago's Merchandise Mart, Joe's biggest real estate investment, and he soon became "a trusted cog" in the family machine. Remarking on Shriver's "Kennedyesque" qualities, Murray Kempton chalked it up to "the tendency of sisters in large families to marry young men who remind them of their brothers."[29] The same could be said of Stephen Smith, another son-in-law tasked with chores beneath the dignity of the sons. After marrying Jean Kennedy, Smith went to work for Joe, becoming the family's political manager and bagman. Meanwhile, Jack married Jacqueline Bouvier, a well-bred debutante who added a touch of class to the rude Kennedy clan, and Patricia married Peter Lawford, an English actor who introduced the Kennedys to the lifestyle of the Hollywood Rat Pack.[30] All these spouses and their children were absorbed into the Kennedy family, which now became officially a clan.

McCarthy's fall in 1954 did not leave the Kennedys unscathed. Bobby remained loyal to his patron even after he was censured by the Senate, while Jack weaseled out of taking a position one way or the other, a fact that would not be forgotten by party liberals. McCarthy's committee was taken over by Sen. John McClellan, who promoted Bobby to chief counsel, and it was here that he began his career as an investigative bulldog. Bobby's successful prosecution of Teamster president Dave Beck—and his feud with Beck's successor Jimmy Hoffa—were great publicity for Jack. But they were also very risky, as their father knew only too well. Joe tried to muzzle Bobby, and even got William O. Douglas to ask him to lay off, but he refused. Though it is hard to believe that Bobby had direct knowledge of his father's links to the mafia, it is possible to see his crusade as partly motivated by a desire to purge the family's tainted past. Whatever the cause, he was the only son with the guts to stand up to Joe, and his father respected him for it.[31]

In 1956 Joe strongly opposed Jack and Bobby's plan to get Jack on the national ticket as Adlai Stevenson's running mate. Joe was sure that Stevenson would lose and that Jack's Catholic roots would be blamed. The boys decided to try to win the nomination anyway while Joe was out of the country.[32] The Kennedys worked the convention in their usual way: Eunice lobbied the Mississippi delegation, Bobby literally dragged House majority leader John McCormack to the platform to second Jack's nomination, Sargent Shriver was tasked to deliver his home state of Maryland, and Peter Lawford won over the chairman of the Nevada delegation. In the end, the nomination went to Estes Kefauver. Stevenson lost as predicted, but Jack was now a rising star in national politics.

In 1958, JFK was reelected in the greatest landslide Massachusetts had ever seen. The same year he became chair of the Senate Labor Subcommittee, charged with developing legislation to implement the findings of McClellan's investigations into organized labor. Appearing together at the hearings, Jack and Bobby developed a remarkably effective good cop/bad cop routine: whenever Bobby's questioning got too tough, Jack would appear as if by magic, ask a few lighthearted questions, then withdraw.

Jack had effectively been running for president since 1956, touring the country in a family-owned plane while Joe orchestrated what Richard Whalen calls "a publicity buildup unprecedented in U.S political history." Joe told a friend, "We're going to sell Jack like soap flakes," and boasted that he was already a bigger draw than Cary Grant. Joe's comment was facetious, but it marks a real turning point in American politics: the packaging of candidates like commercial products. The Kennedy brand would be as successful in its way as Coke or Disney. Kennedy spent an estimated $1.5 million on Jack's prenomination campaign (he boasted that for $75,000 he had put Jack on the cover of *Time*). But his most helpful contribution was undoubtedly withdrawing from the public eye, for as both of them knew, the controversial father was Jack's greatest liability.

In August 1959 Bobby quit the McClellan Committee and took over his brother's campaign. Bobby didn't have the looks or charm of his older brothers, and he instinctively took a backseat to Jack, doing the dirty jobs that every candidate needs done. His Manichaean outlook has often been noted: he divided the world into black hats and white hats, good guys and bad guys. This outlook was not just moralistic but, in its essence, nepotistic: the good guys were for Jack and the Kennedys, the bad guys were against them. With none of the competition and conflict that defined Jack's relationship with Joe Jr., Bobby and Jack explored the opposite pole of synchrony and merging, and it has often been suggested that Bobby's aggressive drive was liberated by his identification with Jack. Yet Bobby also took the lead in shaping Jack's moral conscience in this period, staking out strong positions on corruption, the mafia, and civil rights that were far more aggressive than Jack would have taken on his own. Thus it was not always clear which of the brothers was dominant.

In 1960, major factions of the party were opposed to Jack, including unions, blacks, Jews, party regulars, and liberals, who recalled Joe's fascist sympathies and the family's links to McCarthy. Joe brought the machines on board with contributions to powerful bosses like Charles Buckley of the Bronx and Chicago's Mayor Richard Daley. The Teamsters were purportedly sewn up with help from the racketeers who controlled them.[33] For the rest it was decided to appeal directly to the voters in a series of primary races. Once again, the family strategy worked like a charm, with Jack the smiling front man, Bobby the knuckle-breaking manager, and Joe orchestrating publicity and back-room deals. In Wisconsin, the Kennedy machine completely outclassed Hubert Humphrey's low-budget campaign. But the crucial race would be in West Virginia, a depressed rural state with few Catholics, where Humphrey was expected to run strong.

It is generally agreed that the Kennedys stole the West Virginia primary, but most accounts provide a backhanded tribute to the power of the Kennedy machine. The family worked the state relentlessly: "Up and down the roads roved Kennedy names," wrote Theodore White, "brothers and sisters all available for speeches and appearances." One of their cleverest moves was to press Franklin D. Roosevelt Jr. into service: his father was a god in West Virginia and Frank's endorsement swayed a good many voters. Above all there was money: Joe Kennedy mounted "a massive vote-buying operation... the likes of which West Virginia had never seen before."[34] But as Richard Whalen argues, the amount of money spent was less significant than the *way* it was spent. In West Virginia, and later in the national election, Bobby led a revolution that would permanently change the way political campaigns were conducted. It was a revolution "not of substance, but of technique," in which polling, analysis, and above all, television and other mass media were used to overwhelm opponents. It was also a generational revolt in which a new breed of young communications and media specialists displaced the ethnic bosses. By taking the nominating process away from the old ward and county organizations in favor of the primary system, the Kennedy machine pioneered the era of modern mass politics.

In the face of this onslaught, Humphrey fell back on the demagogic charge of nepotism: "I don't have any daddy who can pay the bills for me," he said bitterly. "I can't afford to run around this state with a little black bag and a checkbook." Others echoed this theme in the national press, claiming that Jack was a nonentity controlled by his father. Jack brilliantly deflected these attacks with self-deprecating humor. At a fund-raising dinner he pretended to read a cable from his father: "Dear Jack: Don't buy one vote more than necessary. I'll be damned if I'll pay for a landslide." Joe was furious, but unlike his father, Jack had the ability to laugh at himself that is essential to democratic leadership. He also had the gift of spontaneity—another aristocratic luxury that served him well in politics.

Jack's 61 percent plurality in West Virginia proved he could beat the Catholic curse and paved the way for his nomination victory over Lyndon Johnson at the Los Angeles convention. The Texas senator had criticized Kennedy's notorious absenteeism and hit hard on the rich-boy theme: "I haven't had anything given to me. Whatever I have and whatever I hope to get will be because of whatever energy and talents I have."[35] Johnson also recalled Joe's fascist sympathies and intimated that Jack's frequent illnesses made him unfit for the presidency. The Kennedys—especially Bobby—did not forgive these slights, but they were pragmatic enough to realize that with LBJ on the ticket they would sweep the South and beat Nixon in November. According to Richard Whalen, it was Joe who made the call on Jack's behalf.

Though Joe was still undisputed head of the family, observers noted Jack's newfound authority in dealing with his father: Joe made suggestions, but Jack called the shots. This seems less a matter of tactical withdrawal by Joe than of genuine growth on Jack's part, and the basically supportive nature of their bond. "The great thing about Dad," Jack said at one point, "is his optimism and his enthusiasm and how he's always for you."[36] It is sometimes suggested that the Kennedy boys obeyed their father because they feared him. But fear was only one component of a deeper and stronger emotion. The boys not only respected and looked up to their father, they loved him and felt profound gratitude for his unwavering support.

JFK beat Nixon by just over a hundred thousand votes, the narrowest margin in history. Joe's contributions to Mayors Richard Daley of Chicago and Robert Wagner of New York, among others, paid off handsomely. (The election was followed by very plausible allegations of fraud.)[37] More important for the future, however, was Jack's mastery of television, heralding the coming triumph of style over substance in American politics.

In 1959, Bobby published a book about his war with the mafia called *The Enemy Within*. After the election, Jack presented him with a leather-bound edition inscribed, "To the brother within." The symbiosis was complete.

THE BEST AND THE BRIGHTEST: THE KENNEDYS AND MERITOCRACY

While JFK was rising to national office on a geyser of family money, Harvard president James B. Conant was launching the greatest experiment in meritocracy the world had ever seen. Ironically, the man who would come to embody the new meritocratic spirit in government was a legacy admission to Harvard and a product of old-fashioned nepotism.

The revolt against the old-line WASP elite had begun in the 1930s, and Conant was one of its great visionaries. Inspired by new developments in the field of educational testing, Conant conceived a radical scheme to replace the hereditary WASP elite with a new one of trained professionals selected by objective tests of knowledge and intelligence. This new elite would be the embodiment of the "natural aristocracy" envisioned by Jefferson and Adams. In 1933, as president of Harvard, he introduced the notion of a four-year academic scholarship that would enable boys of modest means to attend college without the customary social stigma, and he asked Henry Chauncey of the Harvard psychology department to develop a test that would identify the best candidates from all over the country. Ten scholarship students were admitted to the Harvard class of 1938, and ten more were admitted each year for the rest of that decade. (Joe Kennedy Jr. also started his Harvard career in 1934, his brother John two years later.) In 1937 Conant persuaded several other Ivy League colleges to follow suit, and after the war he oversaw the creation of the Educational Testing Service, headed by Chauncey, which developed the Scholastic Aptitude Test.[38] Convinced that educational testing would make American society both more open and more efficient, neither man imagined that they were in fact creating what Nicholas Lemann calls "a new kind of class system even more powerful than the old one."[39]

It was John F. Kennedy who made meritocracy fashionable, with his notion of attracting "the best and the brightest" into government service. (The outstanding example was Defense secretary Robert McNamara, a former RAND whiz kid and head of Ford Motor Company.) It was also the most ethnically and regionally diverse elite ever assembled: according to Digby Baltzell, the Kennedys laid the foundations of "a truly representative establishment" that blended the old-stock and new-stock elites of postwar American society. On close inspection, however, the Kennedy elite was a composite of three concentric rings: the family machine, members of the old WASP upper class, and products of the new meritocracy.

Michael Beran explains that in the first half of the twentieth century, the moribund WASP elite produced an unexpected flowering of talent. Thoroughly imbued with the patrician spirit of their class, they had been attracted to FDR and advanced by his patronage. These were the architects and administrators of the modern welfare state, and they remained in authority through several successive regimes; "they tended to perpetuate themselves," Beran writes, "through a skillful practice of the arts of nepotism and favoritism (the 'old boy network')." Beran calls these men "Stimsonians," after Col. Henry Stimson, whose long and distinguished official career "coincided with the golden age of patrician governance." They were also the shapers and custodians of a new, enlightened liberalism appropriate to the paternalistic ethos of the modern welfare state.[40] Though Kennedy's elite defined itself as youthful and meritocratic, the Stimsonians belonged to the older WASP aristocratic class to which the Kennedys aspired and in whose style and values they had been carefully bred. One of these was Harvard dean McGeorge Bundy, who set up a shadow state department in the White House National Security Office. (Bundy and his father had both worked for Stimson; his brother William went to Defense as a deputy assistant secretary.) Dean Rusk, secretary of state, was another. So were Averell Harriman, Douglas Dillon, Chester Bowles, Joseph Alsop, Adlai

Stevenson, J. Kenneth Galbraith, and other stars of JFK's administration. These men—members of what might be called the "meristocracy"—were glittering adjuncts to the inner circle of Kennedy loyalists.

This inner circle included press secretary Pierre Salinger, speechwriters Ted Sorenson and Richard Goodwin, special assistant Arthur Schlesinger Jr., whose role was that of unofficial court historian, and political operatives Larry O'Brien (congressional liaison) and Ken O'Donnell (appointments secretary), who soon became known as the Irish mafia.[41] According to James Hilty, Kennedy's administration "functioned as an extension of the Kennedy family political organization and shared its objective: securing and maintaining power." Yet at the same time, it lived up to its meritocratic claim. JFK's assistants were not toadies and flatterers but an exceptionally talented and able group of men, selected as much for their independent judgment as their understanding of Jack's style and idiom.

The Kennedy machine landed like a flying saucer atop the federal pyramid and sank its tentacles deep into the machinery of government. As a result, unlike other chief executives, Kennedy hit the ground running, sending one hundred messages to Congress in as many days. Esprit de corps was high. Not since Washington had a presidential administration been so often described as a "band of brothers." Jack's patented charm and the glittering style of the White House under Jackie's direction became the focus of a personality cult whose avowed purpose was to "get the country moving" after eight years of Ike's avuncular stewardship. According to Garry Wills, Jack brought his father's piratical instincts into government, galvanizing the somnolent bureaucracy with lightning raids, getting things done in his own way and on his own schedule. Kennedy, "by his personalization of the authority of the President, simply drew up the United States government—or as much of it as could be lifted—into the encapsulated world of charmed Kennedy power" created by Joe.[42]

It is not entirely clear why Joe felt so strongly that Bobby must be attorney general, but he had evidently nurtured the idea for some time. Indeed, for Joe Kennedy the line between helping his sons and refusing to let go of them was never sharply drawn. Meanwhile the debate about Bobby's appointment brought to light the confusion of attitudes surrounding nepotism. Was it nepotism for a president to appoint his brother to the cabinet, or not? Clearly it was, but in the end, the issue hinged on Bobby's character, not his qualifications, which suggested that Americans were bothered less by family patronage than certain intellectuals thought they should be. Political philosopher Michael Walzer later parsed the Kennedy appointment in his book *Spheres of Justice*: "When President John F. Kennedy appointed his brother attorney general, it was without doubt an example of nepotism, but not of the sort that we need be concerned to ban. Robert F. Kennedy was qualified enough, and his closeness to his brother would probably help him in the work he had to do." Walzer's pragmatic view that nepotism may be acceptable and even desirable in certain circumstances contradicts Jefferson's argument that the public will never believe a minister's relative is qualified, and it is one sign of the emergence of a new, meritocratic nepotism in American life.[43]

At Justice, Bobby surrounded himself with what Victor Navasky called "honorary Kennedys"—friends and retainers recruited from the larger entourage assembled over the years by his father and brothers. The Kennedys' ability to inspire the kind of loyalty required to make talented men work long hours for little pay, sacrificing their own ambitions and even their marriages to win recognition and praise from their idols, suggests how close beneath the surface of meritocracy lurks the monarchical impulse. Men are not typically inspired by abstract ideals but by the praise and recognition of superiors. So vital to their retainers was the myth of Kennedy superiority that some of them went to extraordinary lengths to cover up their flaws and systematically deceived themselves and others about them long after they were dead.

Bobby worked hard to shift the Justice Department's focus from Hoover's anticommunist crusade to civil rights, and became deeply involved in the effort to secure equal protection of the law for black Americans. He also carried his personal feuds into the job, beginning with Jimmy Hoffa, against whom he brought an elaborate but unsustainable conflict-of-interest charge. In addition, he continued his private war against the mafia, much to the displeasure of Chicago mobster Sam Giancana and associates, who had made contributions to Jack's campaign and expected to be left alone. But the sensational testimony of former mafia soldier Joseph Valachi in 1963 exposed the inner workings of an organized criminal empire that had already achieved the status of a major corporate enterprise and was well on its way to becoming an inbred caste—an ethnic criminal version of the brahmin elite. Under Bobby's tenure the number of organized crime prosecutions increased exponentially and numerous new statutes were passed.

All of this was Bobby's day job. Added to his exacting duties as attorney general were his equally demanding activities as the president's closest adviser, lightning rod, informal patronage director, international emissary, personal spy, and protector. Bobby was first drawn into the sphere of foreign affairs by the fiasco of the Bay of Pigs on April 19, 1961, just a few months into Jack's administration. JFK had authorized the invasion of Cuba by a group of CIA-trained exiles hoping to spark a rebellion against Castro. Hamstrung by bad planning, poor intelligence, and the withdrawal of crucial air support by Kennedy, the landing was a failure. Castro milked it for maximum effect, publicly calling JFK a coward. That was too much for Bobby, who seemed to feel that Castro had humiliated his brother and vowed to get even with him. Indeed, no episode better illustrates the nepotistic core of Bobby's drive. Many have observed that Bobby regarded the Cuban dictator as a personal enemy and pursued his destruction as part of a family feud (the fact that Castro also had a brother who was his junior partner in dictatorship no doubt intensified this feeling). Nor was that all: Bobby inserted himself deeply into American defense and security affairs, attending Security Council meetings and chairing the Special Group for Counterinsurgency though he was not technically a member. According to one staffer, Bobby was "arrogant, he knew it all. . . . He sat there, tie down, chewing gum, his feet up on the desk. His threats were transparent. It was, 'If you don't do it, I'll tell my big brother on you.' "[44]

In December 1961, Joe Kennedy suffered a stroke that left him confined to a wheelchair, unable to speak. The experience was torture for a man used to giving orders all his life: he raged at everyone and hit out at his sons with his cane when they tried to assist him. Though Joe had made an elaborate show of keeping his distance from the White House, a direct line to his father had been installed on the president's desk and the two men talked a dozen times a day. The sudden loss of the patriarch was undoubtedly a disconcerting development. For the first time, the boys were truly on their own. This may have enabled them to complete their slow movement away from his reactionary views; but it also removed whatever restraint he might have exercised. After all, the brothers and their father had been three parts of one political personality.

With his wide-ranging portfolio, Bobby occupied a unique position in Washington. The independence afforded by his father's wealth and his brother's patronage gave him the luxury of being uncompromising, of being willing to make enemies. The radical freedom purchased for his sons by Joseph Kennedy thus allowed them to become powerful and inspiring agents of change; but it had also made them unsettling to many, and downright dangerous to some. Now, with the father's disappearance, Richard Mahoney observes, "Bobby's contempt for his enemies was . . . unleavened by any sense of limits or by the remotest calculation of their destructive power."[45]

On November 22, 1963, John F. Kennedy was shot to death in Dallas. The president's brother acted quickly, seizing his secret NSC files and the logbooks that recorded the comings and goings of Jack's many mistresses. Bobby also found time to make inquiries as to who was behind the crime; he clearly had his own suspicions, ranging from the CIA, the abandoned Cuban exiles, and Castro himself to the mob and Jimmy Hoffa. All were enemies that Bobby had made on his brother's behalf, and several biographers speculate that in the midst of his grief, Bobby may have accused himself of being indirectly responsible for Jack's death. If so, it was a replay of Jack's reaction to the death of Joe Jr. Moreover, Bobby had to wrestle with the same burden of Oedipal guilt: how to get out from under this dead brother while carrying on in his place.

HEIRS APPARENT: BOB AND TEDDY RUN THE BALL

In 1946, Jack captured the family's hierarchical outlook when he explained that he was running for office to fill his dead brother's shoes. "And if anything happens to me, Bobby will take over, and if anything happens to him, it will be Teddy." After Jack's death there was speculation that Ted would be the family's next presidential candidate. But the Kennedy's rule of primogeniture—so at odds with the principle of meritocracy—decreed that Bobby must become the heir apparent.

Bobby bore a complex legacy. Previously he had resolved his sibling rivalry by merging with his brother under the protection of a powerful father. Now for the first time he was really alone, and he experienced a period of depression and despair before emerging as an individual in his own right. To many he seemed a broken man, walking around Georgetown at odd hours in his brother's old clothes. The turning point appeared to come when Jackie gave him a copy of Edith Hamilton's *The Greek Way*. Bobby's immersion in Greek tragedy deepened his understanding of the permanent and immutable aspects of the human condition. It also introduced the idea of a family curse, or divine punishment for hubris. Above all it taught him to appreciate the inevitable conflict, so present to the Greek mind, between the claims of the family and those of the polis, or state.

A few months after Johnson took office, Bobby resigned as attorney general and began to consider his options, but there was never any doubt that he would pursue a political career. It was his duty to the family and the fulfillment of his own ambitious drive. But his career would traverse a different landscape than his brother's. A revolution was occurring in American society, and it was Bobby's fate to meet this wave, riding its crest to greatness and destruction. His legacy would be a new and more activist liberalism, born of Catholic moralism, personal ambition, and intense family pride.

The causes that divided the nation in the years after JFK's death were civil rights and Vietnam, struggles that unfolded against a background of deeper changes in American life. Rising prosperity, the spread of universal education, and the growth of mass media eased class divisions and fostered a largely unchallenged liberal consensus. Political loyalties shifted from an older set of institutions based on local and family ties (unions and urban machines) to the national parties. At the same time, white flight and the beginnings of industrial decline in northern cities created a large black underclass increasingly dependent on welfare and seething with militant energies. By 1964 the civil rights movement was peaking, the antiwar and black power movements were stirring, and the beginnings of a feminist movement were in evidence. Bobby was the natural heir to his brother's idealism and the perfect figurehead for the youth revolt that Jack had unwittingly started. Moreover, in the new, media-dominated mass politics, he had a tremendous advantage over other politicians, who were still for the most part local figures. But he knew that he had to work quickly, deploying his brother's potent symbolism without appearing to exploit it for personal ends.

In January 1964 Bobby began the crucial task of defining—and claiming—his brother's legacy. In a speech to students at a Japanese university he described JFK as "the leader of young people everywhere," who had fought for peace and justice and against "hunger, disease and poverty around the world. You and I as young people have a special responsibility to carry on this fight!" JFK in fact showed little interest in domestic affairs and had rejected proposals for ambitious social programs. But after three generations of naked ambition it had fallen to Bobby to devise a higher purpose for the family, one that could transform its losses into sacrifices on the altar of public service. It was Bobby who invented the Kennedy legacy, completing the cycle of growth from the raw familism of his father and grandfather and the amoral pragmatism of his older brother to the aristocratic altruism inherited by the present generation.

Bobby weighed a run for Massachusetts governor but decided against it. (If consulted, Joe would have agreed that it was better to diversify the family's geographic roots, as the Bushes have done.) Instead he tried to force himself onto the national ticket as Johnson's running mate in 1964. Johnson wanted no Kennedys upstaging him in his own government. Yet he also feared a challenge from the dead man's heir apparent, so he encouraged Bobby to run for Senate in New York against Republican incumbent Kenneth Keating. The state's liberal elite shunned him, but he positioned himself as an exponent of radically expanding the welfare state, and won with a strong plurality. In this election Bobby showed the Kennedy magic, defined as an ability to unify a disparate electorate, with particular strength among blacks, Puerto Ricans, and working class ethnics. Still, he had campaigned largely on his brother's coattails, constantly invoking his name; the crowds that turned out to cheer him were really for Jack, not for him. The hunger of these crowds for physical contact with Bobby was rather frightening. He would come back with his arms scratched and bleeding from the throngs of people reaching out to touch him.

Meanwhile, Ted's star had also risen. Joe Sr. made a point of treating his sons equally, and with Jack's election in 1960 and Bobby's cabinet appointment, it was time to secure Ted's future: "Whatever he wants, I'm going to see he gets it." What Teddy wanted was Jack's old job as Massachusetts senator. The older brothers were not keen on the idea, but Joe summed things up in his usual way. "I spent a lot of money for that Senate seat," he supposedly said. "It belongs in the family."

Ted was always considered the least gifted of the brothers, hence most in need of his father's assistance. Growing up completely sheltered from the world, doted on by a mother and five sisters, he was a happy and outgoing child with a strong desire to please. He was popular at school and even showed a flair for debate. But in many ways he remained a child long after the age when his brothers had grown up and shown their mettle. Nor did the occasional correction he received from his father and brothers do much good. In the words of Inga Arvad: "The old man would push Joe, Joe would push Jack, Jack would push Bobby, Bobby would push Teddy, and Teddy would fall on his ass."

Ted worked hard in Jack's congressional races and at twenty-six was placed in charge of his Senate reelection campaign under the tutelage of Irish mafia figures Larry O'Brien and Ken O'Donnell. Bobby called him "the best natural politician in the family," and if he resembled anyone it was Honey Fitz, with his large frame, hearty laugh, and exuberant gestures. Of all the sons he was the closest to his roots in the Irish clan politics of Boston. In 1959 he graduated law school and went to work in Jack's presidential campaign, then served as a floor leader at the Los Angeles convention. After the election he strongly considered moving west, but Joe talked him out of it: "You've got a base here, family, friends. Why go off someplace and prove yourself for nothing?"[46] Ted accepted a post as an assistant district attorney in Suffolk County, Massachusetts, before running for Jack's old Senate seat in 1962.

Ted had the good fortune to be running that year in a dynastic free-for-all. State attorney general Edward J. McCormack was the nephew of House Speaker John McCormack; the Republican candidate was George Lodge, the son of Henry Cabot Lodge, whom Jack had beaten in 1952; and independent H. Stuart Hughes, a Harvard history professor, was the son of Chief Justice Charles Evans Hughes. The family machine went into action, fielding an army of volunteers and investing heavily in advertising and publicity. Jack let it be known that his brother would control the state's federal patronage whether he was elected or not. Sensing defeat, McCormack attacked him harshly, declaring that if his name weren't Kennedy, his candidacy would be a joke. But the over-the-top attack only generated sympathy, especially among female voters. Ted crushed McCormack in the primary and went on to defeat Lodge in November.[47]

Ted's candidacy had been greeted in the national press with cries of "dynastic ambition." Many wondered where he got the nerve to start at the top as a senator instead of going into Congress like his brother. The *New York Times* was far from pleased: "the Kennedys have applied the principle of the best man available for the job to almost everyone but themselves. . . . They have invoked the new pragmatism, but cannot see that, where the family was concerned, they applied the old nepotism."[48]

Ted was elected to the Senate in 1962, and Bobby joined him there in 1964—the first time in over a century that two brothers had served in the Senate together. But while Bobby was careful not to upstage his younger brother, the elder was clearly the star; for as everyone knew, Bobby's election was not an end in itself but the first act in a much larger drama. Like Jack, he was too restless for the Senate. Nor did he aspire to the mundane tasks of party management in a divided and byzantine state like New York. From the first he had his eye on the presidency, and though he brushed aside charges of political nepotism and carpetbagging, he could not have denied that his ultimate aim was a dynastic restoration.

In pursuit of this audacious goal, Bobby had to contend with Johnson's surprising liberalism and his announced intention of fulfilling JFK's supposed dream of a Great Society. Indeed, the struggle for Jack's political mantle was very like that between Antony (the party leader) and Octavian (the family heir) after the murder of Julius Caesar. Bobby had long considered Johnson a racial conservative, but in his first few months Johnson nimbly positioned himself as the heir to JFK's social idealism, launching an ambitious legislative program whose crowning achievement was the Civil Rights Act, which Bobby himself had drafted. Bobby was forced to manufacture differences with Johnson, criticizing him for not expanding the welfare state quickly enough and calling his antipoverty program "a drop in the bucket."

Bobby toured the slums of Latin America, called attention to the sufferings of American Indians, and offered outspoken support for the United Farmworkers, led by Cesar Chavez. He advocated federal aid for the Mississippi Delta and created an innovative and widely copied urban renewal program for New York's Bedford-Stuyvesant neighborhood. In 1965 he walked the streets of Watts after a devastating riot. He also widened his circle of contacts to include representatives of the emerging New Left—something his brother would never have done. Yet even as the movement heated up and his eager young aides pressed him to take a hard line against the war, Bobby was silent on Vietnam.

Bobby's reticence on Vietnam has been ascribed to his awareness of the Kennedys' complicity in getting the United States embroiled there in the first place. Time and debate have produced a consensus that the Vietnam War was the product of overzealous experts who relied too much on flow charts, statistics, and systems analysis. It was Kennedy's "best and brightest" who dragged us into Vietnam, seeking to restore the global dominance America had enjoyed in the aftermath of World War II.[49] Christopher Lasch later attacked this meritocratic elite as an insular and blinkered group that saw itself as ruling by a kind of natural right. "It thinks of itself as a self-made elite owing its privileges to its own efforts," Lasch wrote. Lacking any sense of obligation to the past and freed from all petty human concerns, it applied a detached rational calculus to social problems of all kinds.[50]

The same deficiency afflicted the Johnson administration's War on Poverty. Bobby's idea of urban development contrasted sharply with the ham-fisted approach of the welfare state bureaucrats, whose preferred method was to knock down the slums and put up anonymous mass dwellings. The disastrous results are well known: the housing developments not only failed to become real communities, they actually wiped out the kinship networks that are the source of social order. (Lasch blames the destruction of poor neighborhoods partly on the welfare state's insistence on compulsory education and day care.) In contrast, Kennedy's idea of the community development corporation, modeled in Bedford-Stuyvesant, sought to regenerate blighted neighborhoods not from the top down but from the bottom up, by strengthening family bonds.

Bobby came out against the war in March 1967. A year later he had still not decided whether to challenge Johnson in November; but his presidential bid was widely anticipated. To many Americans it seemed inevitable and right that Bobby take his brother's place. Yet even as he professed to be a mere extension of and surrogate for Jack, Bobby had impressed those around him by his unusual capacity for growth. Many noted a newfound appreciation for complexity and depth that had not been seen before.

At last, on March 16, he announced his candidacy and campaigned across the country to enthusiastic crowds. Bobby's hesitation had cost him dearly, however, for it allowed Eugene McCarthy to become the leader of the Democratic opposition, attracting the antiwar youth who in the view of Bobby's advisers "belonged" to Kennedy. According to Garry Wills, it was Jack Kennedy who, "without a trace of radicalism himself," had launched the youth rebellion by "ignit[ing] the hopes of young people." One intended aspect of the new spirit of youthful activism was the Peace Corps; the unintended aspect was the Berkeley Free Speech Movement and the SDS. LBJ's unexpected withdrawal from the race on March 31 made it a contest between these two liberal Irish Catholics who both claimed Jack Kennedy's mantle—a contest that came down to the leadership of America's rebellious youth, whom Bobby could not attack without attacking his dead brother. "So far he's run with the ghost of his brother," McCarthy told a speechwriter. "Now we're going to make him run against it."

According to sociologist Lewis Feuer, the first student revolt in American history was staged at Harvard in 1766. Its leader was Asa Dunbar, the grandfather of Henry David Thoreau, and the cause was bad butter served at commons. The student slogan was not "Power to the People!" but "Behold our Butter stinketh!" Similar "bread and butter" revolts occurred at regular intervals at Harvard (Ralph Waldo

Emerson participated in one in 1818 and John Quincy Adams's son John was expelled for leading another in 1823). But on the whole they were a normal expression of generational ebullience and not a wholesale challenge to the authority of elders. Alexis de Tocqueville remarked on this harmonious feature of American society when he visited the country in the 1830s. Even the conflict over slavery failed to elicit condemnation of their elders by the young abolitionist firebrands; the Civil War generation earned the same respect as the Revolutionary one and gave renewed strength to American filiopietism.

The question is why the baby boom was different. One of the earliest chroniclers of the sixties student movement was Kirkpatrick Sale, who described it in his book *SDS* as a reaction to a far-reaching "crisis of belief" in the society's moral and intellectual values.[51] According to Sale, the young were particularly affected by this crisis: not only were there more of them than at any other time in American history and not only were they better educated than previous generations, they had also been provided with unprecedented material abundance and freedom of personal choice—advantages their parents, growing up at a time of Depression and war, had not enjoyed. This was certainly a tribute to the nepotistic ideal of making a better life for one's children, of giving them "the things we never had." But while this impulse was in many ways an expression of parental generosity, it did not engender gratitude on the part of the children—an attitude Sale traced to psychological tensions rooted in the permissive practices advocated by Dr. Benjamin Spock and other postwar child-rearing experts. The collapse of generational authority may also be related to the disappearance of male role models: not only was the typical working father absent much of the time, but with the loss of the extended kinship network, suburban teenagers were deprived of other sources of male guidance and restraint. Hence it is no great surprise that the unprecedented affluence and freedom of postwar society should have produced a generation of ingrates.[52]

Bobby Kennedy loved children, and his obvious rapport with them was part of his political appeal. Indeed his Christlike compassion for the children of the poor was at the core of his social activism. It therefore seemed natural for him to place himself on the side of radical youth against conservative old age, reprising his brother's role as the leader of an earlier (if much more respectful) youth revolt. Yet in order to accomplish this he had to complete the process of moving away from Joe's reactionary views. This would be harder for Bobby, since of all the brothers he was the one who had most closely modeled himself on his father, both in his political opinions and in his conduct as the head of his own family. Not only was he the only brother to match Joe's nepotistic feat as a progenitor, he also passed his father's emphasis on competition and toughness to his children. As one family friend observed, "He obviously felt that the method his father had used on him worked pretty well." Sometimes he would stop unexpectedly while playing a game and slap one of them in the face, then hug the weeping child, murmuring, "Kennedys don't cry," and, "Kennedys never give up." His sons' football games were "ultracompetitive," according to a neighbor, with frequent broken bones and bloody noses. He also indoctrinated the children in the family's creed of public service, which some might call indistinguishable from a sense of aristocratic entitlement.[53]

As Jack had campaigned on a presumed missile gap with the Soviets, Bobby pointed to a "generation gap" that was "suddenly widening." Without really endorsing their critique of American society, he expressed sympathy for the growing "alienation" of the young and said that it was "vital" for them to feel "that change is possible; that they will be heard; that the cruelties and follies and injustices of the world will yield, however grudgingly, to the sweat and sacrifice they are so ready to give." Yet in his own way Bobby too was a rebel against the Stimsonian orthodoxy of his elders, most notably in his critique of the welfare state and its effect on the American family.

The impact of the welfare state on families has been a focus of contention between left and right. But it is generally accepted that while filling an important need, welfare and similar programs also helped to undermine traditional family structures. Social security, for example, which reduced the dependence of the old on the young, helped to justify the increasing neglect of the old *by* the young. Likewise, AFDC relieved indigent fathers of guilt and indirectly encouraged them to abandon their families to the care of the state, and in some respects the welfare state has taken over the role of the father completely. Partly on the basis of such arguments, AFDC was abolished in 1996, and under George W. Bush the federal government actually began issuing arrest warrants for deadbeat dads.

Despite his reputation as an advocate of massive social spending, Bobby Kennedy was an early and perceptive critic of this process. Thus in 1967, at the same time that he advocated an enormous increase in the War on Poverty, Bobby attacked welfare as a source of crippling dependency and opposed it as a bureaucratic panacea for social ills requiring individual solutions. "Recent studies have shown," he said, "that higher welfare payments often encourage students to drop out of high school, that they often encourage families to disintegrate, and that they often lead to lifelong dependency."[54] Instead, he believed in giving people the training and tools they needed to rebuild their own neighborhoods and pull themselves out of poverty.

Bobby understood that both compassion and confidence are nurtured primarily by families. He understood this, Michael Beran argues, because he had experienced it in his own family. A weak, neglected junior growing up in the shadow of a powerful father and two accomplished older brothers, he nonetheless found his family a strongly supportive environment that nurtured his ambitions and gave him a sense of moral purpose. Joe Kennedy persuaded his children they could do anything they wanted, giving them the confidence to pursue the highest goals; the children of the poor required the same steady support and encouragement. Such reflections anticipated by decades the conservative critique of the welfare state and testified to Bobby's revolt against the enlightened bureaucratic paternalism of his Stimsonian elders.

Bobby's 1968 campaign, which sought to unite radical youth and working class ethnics, was somewhat schizophrenic. He wooed the young with talk of ending the war and fighting racism and appealed to the working class with talk of law and order. The strategy had mixed results. Bobby did well in Indiana and Nebraska, but McCarthy beat him in Oregon, and the race came down to California. A few days before the California primary, French writer Romain Gary predicted that Bobby would be killed: he was simply "too rich, too young, too attractive, too happy, too lucky, too successful."[55] Bobby himself was convinced that sooner or later he would share his brother's fate. It seemed to have the inevitability of Greek tragedy. On June 4, 1968, Robert Kennedy was shot dead in the kitchen of the Ambassador Hotel in Los Angeles, and Ted became the leader of the clan.

TED KENNEDY AND POSTMODERN NEPOTISM

The voters of Providence, Rhode Island, must have been greatly surprised on election day in 1988 when they opened their doors to find a grinning Sen. Ted Kennedy standing with his arm across the shoulders of his son Patrick, a twenty-year-old sophomore at Providence College. Patrick, whose interest in politics—like his residency in the state—was very recent, was running for state assembly against a popular Democratic incumbent. Once again, the family machine went into action, tapping its large fund-raising network and deploying an army of Kennedys across the state. Even John F. Kennedy Jr. came up from New York to lend his celebrity as "the sexiest man in America" to his cousin's campaign. But the biggest single factor was the presence of Patrick's father, parting the clouds and saying, in effect, "Behold, this is my son, in whom I am well pleased."

Ted himself was thirty when he ran his first race, in 1962, and he too drew heavily on the family's wealth and connections. But while Ted may have run on his brother's coattails in 1962, he was reelected in 1964 on the basis of his personal exertions. Like many young men advanced through nepotism, he evidently felt obliged to work twice as hard to prove his merit as anyone else. In contrast to his brothers, moreover, Ted was a good party man who devoted considerable time and energy to strengthening the state apparatus. As a result, his reelection margin was even larger than Jack's. The seat has remained his for these forty years.

Though he brashly pushed his way into the Senate, once there, he deferred to party leaders and waited his turn, patiently ascending the ladder of seniority. Even more than the House, the Senate is an exclusive club that operates on a basis of reciprocity. In effect, Teddy played the same role in the Senate that he had in his family: the cheerful and accommodating junior who agreed that "freshmen should be seen and not heard."[56] As a result, unlike his brothers, Teddy was liked and trusted by his colleagues.

Though JFK had promised to integrate federal housing, the White House did not press for civil rights through legislation but by legal activism and executive order. But the movement was growing increasingly radical, and in 1963, Bobby drafted a civil rights bill. After the assassination, President Johnson devoted his considerable energies to pushing it through Congress. Teddy played his part with a dramatic speech—his first after more than a year in the Senate—that touchingly invoked his brother's memory. When the Voting Rights Act came up in 1965, he and Bobby bucked the president's cautious lead, pushing hard for an amendment banning the poll tax. While the liberals narrowly lost, Ted earned respect for his courageous stand on the issue. His stewardship of the immigration reform debate was more successful. Immigration had been a family cause since 1898, when Representative Fitzgerald foiled an attempt by Henry Cabot Lodge to impose a literacy test on immigrants from southern and eastern Europe. (Fitz's Boston district included many Italians, Slavs, and Jews, so he was voting in his constituents' interest as well as standing up for principle.) The Immigration Act of 1965—promoted by Jack, drafted by Bobby, and pushed through the Senate by Ted—thus proceeded from a confluence of pragmatism, principle, and family tradition. The lifting of quota restrictions produced another massive wave of immigration, this time mainly from Asia and Latin America. Given that many of these new citizens could be expected to vote Democratic, the act has been called "the Kennedy family's greatest gift to the Democratic Party."[57] But in a larger sense, John F. Kennedy may be considered the father of the new multicultural American society that emerged in subsequent decades.

Even more important has been the legacy of that other great Kennedy project, the Civil Rights Act. This bill has been credited with transforming American society by dismantling the last vestiges of both the WASP establishment and the ethnic occupational monopolies. But it is not often recognized that much of this transformation came about through challenges to nepotism based on Title VII of the act, which forbade discrimination in employment based on race, religion, gender, or national origin. And indeed, it was during this period that the American war on nepotism entered its final, legalistic phase.

Nepotism has always been obnoxious to Americans, but for most of our history there was no legal remedy for it. Prior to the Civil Rights Act, most challenges to exclusionary employment practices were brought under the equal protection clause of the Fourteenth Amendment. Plaintiffs charged that blood-based favoritism infringed the rights of unrelated workers. But if employers could show that their discriminatory practices were justified by "business necessity," the state would not interfere. Such was the outcome in what may be the earliest such case, *Kotch v. Board of River Boat Pilot Commissioners*. In 1947, plaintiffs challenged the constitutionality of a Louisiana law that allowed the State Board of River Pilot Commissioners to monopolize the issuance of licenses. The board, composed of current and former pilots, had a history of issuing new licenses only to relatives, but the Supreme Court found that the practice, though exclusionary, met the crucial test of "rationality." Knowledge of local waterways was an important qualification for a pilot, and young men who grew up in an environment where this knowledge was transmitted naturally, along with other aspects of the craft, were more desirable from the point of view of safety and efficiency. Therefore the court found for the defendants.[58]

Although the Civil Rights Act gave new impetus to the American war against nepotism, these cases for the most part addressed the issue indirectly. By federal law, nepotism is objectionable only when the practice results in a pattern of discrimination based on race, gender, age, or national origin. This explains the truly amazing paucity of case law relating to nepotism. Indeed, in one case the court declared, "Nepotism of itself does not violate Title VII. To come within the Civil Rights Act, nepotism must somehow be related to a pattern of discrimination based on national origin or another protected class." However, given the natural desire of fathers to pass on assets and opportunities to their sons, de facto occupational monopolies were common, especially in trade unions, where membership could be controlled through apprenticeship programs that favored members' sons. Moreover, these monopolies were usually racial or ethnic in character.

Few of those charged with discrimination under the Civil Rights Act sought to defend their nepotistic practices on any positive ground. One exception was *Bonilla v. Oakland Scavenger Co.* The employer in this case gave open preference to families connected with the company's founders. The defense made a spirited argument that family members had a greater concern for the company and a greater interest in promoting its welfare. But since the founding families were all white, the court found that the company's nepotistic practices resulted in a pattern of racial exclusion and rejected the claim of rational discrimination based on business necessity.[59]

Title VII was remarkably effective as a means of breaking up racial or ethnic monopolies in blue-collar occupations. But it also opened the door to the first *attack* on nepotism rules in American history, brought by women intent on removing barriers to equal status in the workplace. Many public and private institutions had instituted nepotism rules during the Depression and the New Deal, when heightened sensitivity to the issue seemed to require a greater effort to eliminate family patronage. Most states passed nepotism laws in the following decades, and in 1967 a federal nepotism statute was passed. Though the bill's author has always denied it, the law was widely perceived as a response to Robert Kennedy's appointment as attorney general. (The law is still in force and is the main reason why Hillary Rodham Clinton could not be named to a cabinet position in her husband's administration.)[60] Beginning in the 1950s, private corporations had also begun to introduce nepotism rules. The rise in such rules was quite pronounced, going from 7 percent of American firms in 1955 to 28 percent in 1963 (an additional 36 percent had unwritten nepotism policies). Most of these rules were instituted not because of problems associated with nepotism but simply to avoid charges of favoritism. Further, while these policies were initially aimed at men and often did not even mention female relatives, as the numbers of women in the workplace increased many companies adopted explicit no-spouse rules. These barriers began to cause friction, particularly in universities, where women had made the most progress.[61]

Traditionally, female academics could not be employed in the same departments as their husbands or even at the same institution unless in secretarial and other minor positions or at a lower rate of pay. One feminist scholar has even argued that the wave of postwar antinepotism rules was a conscious effort to roll back female employment in order to make room for returning men.[62] As early as 1960 the American Association of University Women issued a report opposing these policies, and in 1971 the American Association of University Professors urged the rescinding of antinepotism rules as "unjust and unnecessary." Legal cases were brought, such as the 1969 class action suit against the Arizona Board of Regents, which was decided in favor of the plaintiffs. In a very short time, the offending policies were amended or repealed in universities across the country. Moreover, the trend continued in a wide range of settings, including newspapers, publishing companies, law firms, medical faculties, the sciences, and (as we have seen) the fields of politics, entertainment, and sports.[63]

The feminist attack on nepotism rules represented not only the first stirrings of a broader reaction against the postwar antinepotism régime but the emergence of a new meritocratic nepotism appropriate to the two-career family and its offspring. Legal scholar Elaine Shoben explicitly calls the partner preference programs adopted by many universities "a new form of nepotism," one that apparently seeks to harmonize merit and family interest. But its other main result is the return of the family name as an accepted form of social capital. In the old days, the greatest ambition of family entrepreneurs was to make a name that could be passed on to their descendants. This attitude of taking pride in a family name disappeared for the better part of a century. Now, with the advent of mass media and a glitzy celebrity culture that includes politicians, CEOs, and sports and entertainment figures, it is once again possible to make a name that can be passed on as family property.

It certainly seems ironic that while nepotism rules were being enforced in the cause of racial and class equity, they were simultaneously being challenged in the cause of gender equity—all the more so as these challenges were made on the same legal grounds and by appeal to the same principles of workplace morale and efficiency. This difference is usually explained as one of differing job contexts. But it can also be viewed from another angle: that of class warfare. In effect, a successful effort to break up incipient caste monopolies at the working class level was mirrored by an equally successful effort to eliminate barriers to caste formation at the middle or upper class level.

This could not have been evident at the time, but given the later tendencies to in-marriage and succession in many high-status professions, the outcome is becoming fairly clear. As early as 1982 Joan Wexler called attention to the dramatic rise in marriage among lawyers as women entered the legal profession, and their children often become lawyers as well. The children of doctors have long enjoyed a statistical advantage in admission to medical schools, and this trend is increasing with the number of medical marriages. Hollywood marriages have produced a large new group of second- and third-generation actors and producers. The same applies to singers and performers in the music industry, as well as journalists and writers. The admission of women to the armed forces has likewise resulted in a growing number of military marriages. Political marriages like that of Andrew Cuomo and Kerry Kennedy may lead to the formation of new dynastic blocs. Multigenerational families are also visible in sports, from baseball, football, and NASCAR racing to broadcasting and golf course design.

Rather than a unified class, like the Boston brahmins or the old Philadelphia and Knickerbocker elites, we seem to be witnessing the formation of a series of professional enclaves dominated by networks of established families. These families don't monopolize their field in the manner of medieval guilds, but they do employ dynastic strategies used by previous elites, and their offspring have advantages of access and opportunity that others don't enjoy. The fact that these processes are largely unconscious only indicates how deeply ingrained such strategies must be. Dynastic methods of caste formation don't have to be taught; they simply happen.

The Kennedys not only laid the legal foundation for the attack on antinepotism rules; they themselves supplied a model of the emerging meritocratic overclass and its postmodern form of dynastic nepotism. It was the Kennedys who pioneered the celebrity model of politics and the commercial branding strategy that goes with it. For those who fear that we are headed for an Indian-style caste hierarchy, however, the performance of the third generation illustrates the limits of dynastic succession in the new meritocratic arena.

To say that the present crop of Kennedys has not lived up to expectations is a massive understatement. The twenty-four grandchildren of Joseph P. Kennedy display the full range of post-sixties pathology: divorce, alcoholism, drug abuse, a predatory attitude toward women, and a palpable air of entitlement. In 1973 Joe Kennedy II drove a jeep off the road in Nantucket; the accident left a female passenger paralyzed for life. In 1983 Bobby Jr. was arrested for heroin possession; the next year his brother David died of a heroin overdose. Two years after that, Patrick Kennedy sought treatment for cocaine addiction while a student at Andover. In 1991 William Kennedy Smith was acquitted of rape after a sensational trial that exposed the equally debauched behavior of his uncle and cousin. In 1997 police investigated Michael Kennedy's sexual relationship with a fourteen-year-old baby-sitter; the bad publicity dissuaded his elder brother Joe from running for governor of Massachusetts. Later that year Michael was killed when he slammed into a tree while playing football on the ski slopes of Aspen. In 2002 the family hit bottom with the conviction of Kennedy cousin Michael Skakel for murder.

This is a grim record by any standards. Yet throughout this period, millions of families were silently going through the same crisis as the Kennedys. The signs of this crisis were everywhere: in rising rates of divorce, illegitimacy, and single parenthood; in drug and alcohol addiction, criminality, and widespread family dysfunction, including physical and sexual abuse. Related problems included growing crises in elder care, adoption, and foster care, teenage pregnancy, and rising rates of infanticide and child abandonment. All of this suggests a breakdown in the nepotistic system of mating, reproduction, and child rearing, one that has raised the question of whether a society that abandons all traditional arrangements can expect to replace its own population, let alone preserve its values and beliefs.

Ted Kennedy has presided over his large dysfunctional clan as best he could, but he has apparently been more inclined to participate as an equal in their revels than to act as a stern authority figure like Joe Sr.

As Ted's cousin Mary Lou McCarthy remarked: "No wonder the younger boys have all gotten in trouble at one time or another. With that as an example, my God."[64]

Politically, too, the family has fallen on hard times. Joe II, at one point the family's brightest light, gave up the family's Massachusetts congressional seat in 1998. John Jr. died in a plane crash. Andrew Cuomo ran a poor campaign for New York governor and pulled out two days before the primary. Bobby Jr. has worked hard to live down his early malfeasances, positioning himself as an environmental leader, but he remains trapped in his father's political mythology; as Michael Beran observed, his pilgrimage to visit anti-American protesters at Vieques in 2001 was a parodic echo of his father's famous visit to Cesar Chavez. One problem pointed out by Beran is the family's failure to follow the movement of people and power to the south and west. Unlike the Bushes, who have spread out across the country, the Kennedys have remained concentrated in the northeastern states of Massachusetts, Rhode Island, Maryland, and New York. The family seems to be resting on its laurels—a fatal error in a fluid and mobile society. These and other errors came home to roost decisively in 2002, when Mark Kennedy Shriver lost his primary bid for a Maryland congressional seat and Kathleen Kennedy Townsend lost the gubernatorial race to her Republican rival.

These unexpected defeats led some observers to proclaim "the end of the Kennedy dynasty." But as the success of the Bushes has shown, dynasticism not only has returned but has in a sense become a normal part of American politics. The Kennedy brand remains viable, and it is not inconceivable for a member of the fourth generation, untainted by the scandals of the second and the embarrassing failures of the third, to pick up the fallen torch.

CHAPTER 12

THE ART OF NEPOTISM

Summoning his daughters to the throne, an aging king announces his intention to divide his realm in thirds. But he will not divide it equally: the one who loves him best will get the most. The two elder daughters give insincere speeches that flatter the old king, but the youngest child refuses to cooperate. "I love your majesty according to my bond," she says with dry contractual precision, "no more nor less." The father flies into a rage and disinherits her, later declaring, "How sharper than a serpent's tooth it is to have a thankless child."

Most readers will recognize this as the opening scene of *King Lear,* Western literature's greatest dysfunctional-family epic. Though wreathed in smiles and sugared words, the scheming elder daughters hate their father and resent their younger sister, who has always been his favorite. Having nothing more to give them of material value, he is worthless in their eyes. They strip him of his retinue and cast him out on the heath with other beggars, fools, and madmen.

In premodern societies, a man without kin could be killed or enslaved with impunity. Indeed, a slave by definition is a person who has been ripped out of his sustaining kinship network. Since the essence of kinship is the obligation of mutual aid and support, people must be transported far from their native country in order to be exploited in this way, as Joseph was sold by his brothers to a caravan of traders on their way to Egypt. Lear therefore suffers the worst calamity that can befall a human being: not just the rupture of his family but the loss of every kinship tie that links him to society. Out on the blasted heath, naked to the elements, lashed by wind and rain, he returns to the condition of primal terror that exists in what is called the state of nature. Only the loyal Fool, who calls him "Nuncle," remains to remind him of what he has lost. Man, he understands, is nothing outside of this context of human relationships. "Is man no more than this?" he asks. "Thou art the thing itself: unaccommodated man is no more but such a poor bare, forked animal as thou art."

Lear's rapacious daughters are usually seen as unnatural ingrates and Lear their fond but foolish victim. And it is true that Goneril and Regan, as well as the bastard Edmund, are scheming Machiavels who recite the empty formulas of filial piety, manipulating kinship ties for personal advantage. Looked at from another angle, however, Lear gets pretty much what he deserves. For the gift that Lear bestows at the beginning of the play is really no gift at all, but an extortionary test in which he continues to hold all the cards. Lear intends to divide his kingdom but retain the title and prerogatives of king, including a retinue of a hundred knights, which will be an expensive charge upon the incomes of his daughters. Their ingratitude is terrible, but it is also the recompense of his false generosity—or what we might otherwise call his nepotistic malpractice.

Lear's example suggests that there is a right way and a wrong way to practice nepotism, and it is interesting to view this in terms of his failure to understand the gift relationship that governs generational transactions. Cordelia's answer to her father is a strict summation of the sources of filial duty:

You have begot me, bred me, lov'd me: I
Return those duties back as are right fit,
Obey you, love you, and most honour you.

This is what it means, for Cordelia, to be a "natural" child—loving, yes, but above all obedient and dutiful. Her response is an implied rebuke to Lear's assumption that *love* is the strongest moral bond. Instead, it is the reciprocal duties of parents and children that are the source of social order. If we relied on love alone for continuity, society would crumble and collapse.

Nepotism, properly understood, is an aspect of what anthropologists call the gift economy—the system of noncommercial exchanges that serves to regulate moral relations between individuals, families, and groups in a prestate society. This is the golden thread that links the narrow, reduced, and furtive nepotism of our time with the systematic nepotism of earlier societies going back to the first hunter-gatherers. As we have seen, America is not a country without nepotism; on the contrary, it is teeming with nepotism of every kind, at every level. But because our narrow conception of nepotism as favoritism for the undeserving is still at odds with our public creed of equality and merit, America lacks a positive statement of nepotism as an ethical activity. How can nepotism be practiced in a way that does not conflict with democratic values and ideals?

We have told the stories of a number of dynastic clans in order to show how they applied the nepotistic arts to the furtherance of their ambitions. (Although this has involved a somewhat anomalous use of the concept of nepotism, we have defined it to mean not just "undue preference for kin" but, more broadly, "doing things with kinship.") In each of these great families, success was a multigenerational project. The question is: how did they do it? How did they use nepotism and its cultural extensions in their rise to wealth and status? A brief review of these techniques should put us in a position to say which ones might be adapted to contemporary uses.

Each dynastic family has a founder, and while such founders may not always be the self-made men they would like us to think, they *are* unique in establishing a complex of habits, values, attitudes, traditions, and ideas that aid the family in its rise and become a living legacy to their descendants. The founder's personality is the main factor in forming this family culture—indeed, it is his personality writ large. The common characteristics of such founders are indomitable will, raw opportunism, and a keen sense of how to exploit events and people. Many are powerfully acquisitive (like Mayer Rothschild and the brahmin family founders) or seething with social resentment and prejudice (like Joe Kennedy), and these unattractive qualities can become an embarrassing legacy to later generations. Founders also display a strong grasp of the distinction between family and strangers and a willingness to treat outsiders as tools to family ends. These are the qualities possessed in abundance by the traditional mafia capo, who is admired for his talent in exploiting and manipulating others.

Another common feature of such founders is their intuitive grasp of dynastic techniques that no one appears to have taught them. These techniques are not learned in any formal way. Rather they are simply plucked out of the air by men who instinctively grasp how nepotism in its various forms may be harnessed to dynastic purposes.

Successful founders often start by braiding two families together in a single clan. Usually the paternal line dominates while the maternal family provides behind-the-scenes support; but there are many variations on this theme. This is what Augustus and Livia succeeded in doing, though in the end the Claudians usurped the Julians. It is how Arnulf of Metz and Pepin of Landen created the dynasty that produced Charlemagne. It is what Napoleon did with Josephine's family (Napoleon III was the child of a Bonaparte-Beauharnais marriage) and what George Washington hoped to do with the Custises. The Cabot-Lodges and other brahmin families also followed this strategy. The Rothschilds adhered to a much older practice of patrilinear marriage consistent with Hebraic tradition, combined with a pattern of strategic intermarriage with other wealthy Jewish families. In the twentieth century, the tactic has been used by ambitious familists like Carlo Gambino, who created a mafia dynasty through intermarriage with his Castellano cousins. Joe Kennedy married into the Fitzgeralds and forged the two families into a single clan, which he took over from within. Even the Bush dynasty represents the fruit of two lineages, the Walkers and the Bushes.

Successful founders also tend to have many children, and those who do not often seek to acquire them by other means, as Andrew Jackson did in surrounding himself with fatherless boys whom he raised up to be his loyal lieutenants. Founders establish high performance expectations for their sons and foster an intense atmosphere of sibling competition. Such competition hones the instincts necessary for family survival. It is also, from an evolutionary perspective, the best way to weed out the weaker vessels. Under the impetus of their demanding father, the Kennedy family became a roaring turbine of sibling competition, reflecting the sublimation of erotic and aggressive drives in the socially useful pursuit of power and status.

Founders also build an artificial clan around their family, using the time-honored methods of marriage, adoption, and patronage. Augustus spun a web of marriage and adoption so tangled and overlapping that his relatives must have been deeply confused by the tension between their dynastic roles and blood relationships. Christianity eliminated adoption and close marriage but added the useful instrument of godparenthood. Another dynastic technique is family apprenticeship. John Adams not only employed his sons as secretaries but encouraged his older sons to train the younger ones in the same way. This method produced several generations of outstanding American statesmen and diplomats.

Diversification and flexibility are key components of dynastic success. Times change, and successful families change with them. Unless the patriarch transmits his opportunistic instincts to the next generation, the family project may fail. This is difficult since the very success of great families may blunt the appetitive instincts and sense of social exclusion that fuel the ambition of founders, and the pattern of generational decline has been widely observed. Typically, the rapacity and acquisitive focus of the first generation gives way to the cautious, conservative ethos of the second and the spoiled and heedless frivolity of the third. This pattern continues in many business families today, giving rise to the familiar expression "Shirtsleeves to shirtsleeves in three generations." In order to avoid this fate, successful families must find ways to refresh or stimulate their creativity. One way of doing this is to bring in new blood, and many sons-in-law are chosen because they share the appetite and drive of the founder.

Not all the techniques of past dynastic families can still be used today. Arranged marriage has been left on the ash heap of history, and no one is proposing its return. So, thankfully, has indentured servitude. But dynastic marriage has not gone out of fashion altogether—it is still practiced in the political, business, and entertainment elites, although of course not by that name. And many other dynastic techniques continue to be useful, suggesting ways in which aspects of Ancient or Classical Nepotism might be applied in problem areas where the state has failed to make up for the destruction and collapse of kinship networks.

First, however, we must deal briefly with the case against nepotism as expressed by its contemporary critics. Those who express the strongest objections to nepotism see it as a means by which the upper class preserves its wealth and privileges. This is the concern that has been raised by those who see in the emergence of the New Nepotism troubling signs of an incipient caste system. Thus it is no surprise that policies governing the transmission of wealth have become controversial. George W. Bush campaigned for president partly on the promise of abolishing the "death tax." Critics warned that abolishing the estate tax would encourage the formation of dynastic families and give rise to an "aristocracy of wealth." Many also argued that it was counter to American principles of self-reliance and equality. But the issue was surprisingly popular with ordinary Americans—not just the richest 5 percent, who already know how to shield their wealth from taxation, but farmers, ranchers, and other small business owners who lack the means to do so. The popularity of estate tax repeal may be explained by the desire of ordinary Americans to pass on their wealth to their children. On the other hand, a case can be made that it is *more* nepotistic to do as Bill Gates plans to do, giving away most of his money and leaving his children a "mere" $10 million each. From a Darwinian perspective, it is a better reproductive strategy to leave your children just enough to give them a head start in life (or a competitive edge over their contemporaries), yet not so much that they are left with no impulse to strive.

But while Americans continue to argue about the transmission of material wealth, they have yet to grapple with the newest form of inheritance, namely the New Nepotism, in which not just wealth but social status may be passed on to one's heirs. In this context, the continuation of legacy quotas has also become controversial. If American society is indeed developing an overclass structure, its keystone is the system of academic and professional degree-granting institutions that control admission to many elite occupations.[1] In fact, the products of meritocracy seem quite willing to be coopted in this way. Many baby boomers facing the challenges of competitive prep school and college admissions (or even elite nursery schools) have decided it is perfectly okay to pull strings on their children's behalf. This is what some people have begun to call the "yuppie turnaround" on nepotism. Many Americans who publicly praise meritocracy and support affirmative action find it difficult to sacrifice their children's opportunities in the name of abstract principles of fairness.

Those who see in the New Nepotism a threat to equal opportunity have a point: there are indeed emergent caste tendencies in the American elite. Unchecked nepotism always leads to the formation of a caste system, and that is not something we should want. On the other hand, the market tends to punish any group or industry that closes itself off from new talent. Elites that fail to open their ranks to new blood doom themselves to irrelevancy and ultimate extinction. Moreover, while nepotism clearly plays a role in the formation of elites and upper classes, it has been equally useful in the creation of ethnic mutual aid associations, labor unions, and political machines. There is no inherent class bias in nepotism: all social classes practice it freely, and it is a fundamental fact of social organization that two hundred years of hostility have failed to uproot. Our uniquely American way of coming to terms with this inconvenient fact has been through a combination of meritocratic values and hypocrisy.

The other main objections are that nepotism rewards incompetence and fosters inefficiency, and that it violates American ideals of competition based on merit, not inherited advantage. But while nepotism may indeed shelter some incompetent family members from the consequences of their failures, the record of family contributions to the history of capitalism has been overwhelmingly positive. If this hadn't been true, the American economy would be a basket case instead of a thriving engine of prosperity. Nepotism can perhaps be blamed for being biased in favor of males. But women have done more to repeal antinepotism rules in recent decades than any other group, so it is hard to argue that such rules are necessary to level the playing field from the viewpoint of gender equality. (To the contrary, antinepotism rules were instituted after World War II partly to drive women out of the workplace.) Finally, while it may be true that nepotism offends against our democratic values, no single rule can be applied, since we do not in fact judge nepotism uniformly but on a case by case basis.

The reality is that while we condemn nepotism in general, we are quite willing to tolerate individual acts of nepotism so long as the beneficiary seems worthy or proves his or her worth after the fact. This is partly because as an ethical matter, our problem is not really with the nepotist, but with the nepotee. We are realists, after all, and we fully expect people to help their friends and relatives whenever they can. But we also expect the beneficiaries of such patronage to have enough self-respect not to accept that kind of help, especially when it is manifestly unfair to other people.

The real question, then, is not whether nepotism should continue, but how we can guarantee that it will be practiced in its place and not where it doesn't belong.

We might begin by acknowledging a distinction that is recognized by all of us, whether we realize it or not, between good nepotism and bad. Bad nepotism is something we all know when we see it. But what harm does it actually do? No one wants to be accused of nepotism; still less does anyone want to be regarded as its beneficiary, with all the stigma that implies. There is also the fact that nepotism, practiced badly, mainly ends up hurting those directly involved. Napoleon become the conqueror of Europe but was brought down (so historians say) by overreliance on his relatives. Carl Laemmle handed Universal Studios to his son on his twenty-first birthday; after Junior ran the company into the ground, father and son were both ousted by the shareholders. When Walt Disney died in 1966 he was succeeded first by his brother, then his son-in-law; the result was a string of failed movies and bad business decisions resulting in a hostile takeover. Edsel Ford nearly destroyed his father's auto company before it was rescued by outside management. In these cases, the fruits of nepotistic malpractice came home to roost on the heads of its practitioners. This leads to the conclusion that nepotism, practiced badly, is for the most part a self-punishing offense.

We also know *good* nepotism when we see it, but we tend not to call it nepotism, because it looks like something else. John Quincy Adams became ambassador to London through his father's manipulations but is still remembered as America's greatest secretary of state. The Dulles family also made great contributions to the nation's diplomatic service.[2] Theodore and Franklin Roosevelt both won their first elections purely on the strength of their family name, but are considered two of our greatest presidents. A succession of Cabots and Lowells founded the New England textile and banking industries and turned Boston into the commercial, intellectual, and cultural hub of the country. The Du Ponts built a family gunpowder business into a vast commercial empire; many of their scions were not only great businessmen but brilliant chemists and engineers. Tightly intermarried Jewish clans created a series of department store chains, a powerful group of legal and financial firms, and the Hollywood film industry. These great achievements are not considered part of the history of nepotism; rather they are viewed as cases in which able and dutiful sons carried on a proud family tradition. That doesn't mean the individuals in question didn't owe their opportunities to nepotism, only that we insist on clinging to our narrow and quite useless view of nepotism as preferential treatment for a relative who is grossly incompetent.

The problem, then, is not that nepotism continues to be practiced, but that it is often practiced badly or haphazardly. The solution is not to keep banging it with a hammer like a glob of mercury but to bring it out into the open and subject it to the highest possible standards. This means learning to recognize that nepotism is an art, and to observe the unwritten rules that have made it on balance a constructive and positive thing. These rules can be reduced to the following simple injunctions.

1. Don't embarrass me. Unlike kin selection, which implies no corresponding obligation, nepotism is a moral relationship. For the protégé, nepotism is a privilege, not a right; for the patron, it is a choice, not a compulsion. The patron shows generosity by conferring benefits on the protégé; respect and gratitude are owed in return. The relationship therefore involves reciprocal obligations. The first rule of patronage has always been that the protégé's actions and conduct reflect on the patron. By holding a sponsor responsible for his protégé's performance, the mandarins of the Chinese imperial bureaucracy introduced a powerful corrective to the potential for nepotistic abuses. This is also the protection built into the nepotistic equation. Nepotism is a two-way street.

2. *Don't embarrass yourself,* or, *You have to work harder than anyone else.* Democratic society is founded on a moral contract premised on equality, and those who enjoy advantages of birth must make an effort to counteract the natural resentment of those who do not. Because our culture insists on self-reliance as the standard of individual worth, this is as necessary to the protégé's self-respect as it is to blunt the edge of democratic envy. If the protégé is obliged to respect the patron, he is equally obliged to respect himself. You can't expect advantages to come to you unearned. This is what distinguishes the New Nepotism from the Old: other people must prove their merit before the fact, but nepotees must prove it after. John Quincy Adams is an example of this dutiful attitude. So was Bobby Kennedy. Both illustrate the peculiar burdens of heirship in a democratic society.

3. *Pass it on.* Although nepotism is considered selfish, it proceeds from a generous impulse to pass something on to one's children, and this we think of as entirely praiseworthy. After all, though we resent those who inherit too much wealth, we don't approve of wealthy parents who disinherit their children and leave everything to their pets. But if nepotism is in some respects a two-way street, it is also a one-way transaction; no immediate return can be expected beyond the normal obligation of children to care for their aged parents. To the extent that nepotism takes place in the context of a family enterprise, however, the spirit of it requires that its benefits be passed on to the next generation. We therefore express our gratitude to our parents in the form of generosity to our own children. This view of life as a multigenerational project was very apparent to our immigrant forebears. The motto of family founder P. J. Kennedy sums it up: "Be grateful and be loyal." This wholesome consciousness implies a certain humility and an acceptance of mortality. It also reflects an understanding of the conditions of remembrance—we forget those who give us nothing but revere and remember our benefactors. The more such generational transactions there are, the healthier for society as a whole.

Attentive readers will have noticed that these rules essentially recapitulate the principles of gift exchange articulated by Marcel Mauss: the obligation to give, the obligation to receive, and the obligation to repay. There is also an echo of the Hindu theory of *asrama,* or the three debts.

The parallel is not exact, of course. Nevertheless, nepotism at its best is still an aspect of the gift, and should be practiced in that spirit.

American history is often presented as a triumphal tale of expanding liberty and equality—an unfolding revolution whose end point has yet to be reached. A great part of this story involves the liberation of individuals from the bonds of their ethnic communities, kin groups, and nuclear families. The dominant tendency in American history—the great American innovation in kinship—has indeed been to liberate the element of reciprocal altruism from the bonds of the biological family and to put "chosen," or voluntary, ties on an equal and even superior footing with given, or "ascriptive," ones. Lincoln was the prophet of this expansive idea of American citizenship, and his defeat of the kin-based ethos of Southern nationalism opened the way for America to become a universal nation, in which we measure freedom by our distance from the blood-based solidarities of the tribe, the caste, and the clan.

Yet there is a continuing tension in American kinship with the principle of biological solidarity, and it is no accident that many of the sharpest controversies that divide us today bring society's interest in maintaining an orderly system of reproduction and succession (the essence of nepotism) into conflict with our commitment to individual freedom of choice.

For example, modern culture and technology have contrived to separate sex from reproduction and reproduction from marriage. The advent of birth control in the 1960s—hailed as a victory for culture over nature—sparked a sexual revolution that led (among other things) to skyrocketing rates of abortion, divorce, and single parenthood. According to current statistics, half of all marriages end in divorce, and the number of unmarried, or cohabiting, couples has dramatically increased. The enormous rise in illegitimacy and single parenthood means that many children are growing up poorer and that women have fewer resources to draw on. Moreover, young men who grow up without fathers are at higher risk for social pathologies like drug addiction, delinquency, and crime. The resulting fatherhood crisis has reached the point where the federal government has taken steps to track down and arrest divorced fathers who fail to make child support payments. Meanwhile the introduction of new reproductive technologies like in vitro fertilization, surrogacy, and cloning has begun to put enormous pressure on American legal conceptions regarding the family.[3] The status of adoption similarly reflects the tension between biology and culture. International adoptions reached new heights in recent years as thousands of American couples opened their arms to orphaned or unwanted children from all over the world. This would appear to be a testament to American inclusivity—the idea that anyone can be a member of the family.[4]

These trends have produced what many celebrate as an explosion of "new" family forms: stepfamilies and blended families, single parent families, foster and adoptive families, group families, surrogate families, gay families, and so on. Almost any combination of persons in any legal or social relationship can now be considered a family. The appearance of these pseudo-familial forms is yet another triumph for freedom of choice over nature. It substantiates our hopeful view—shared by the unfortunate Lear—that love is the highest social bond. Yet paradoxically, this explosion of new, voluntary families has been accompanied by a reversion to older forms and expressions of kinship and nepotism. Not only does the persistence of polygamy in Utah offer a scandalous rebuke to Christian monogamy, other "barbarous" practices seem to be making a comeback. In the nineteenth century, lonely sodbusters sent away for mail-order brides to share their work and keep them company. We have recently seen a spate of reality-based television shows like *The Bachelor* and *Who Wants to Marry a Millionaire?* in which single women have offered themselves as prospective brides to a man they have never met. Likewise, cousin marriage, long illegal in this country, has quietly experienced a renaissance.[5]

Interest in genealogy has also boomed, fueled by the ease of tracing family connections through the Internet. Genealogy was formerly the obsession of social climbers like Carlo Buonaparte, eager to insert their children into the system of European nobility. Yet according to the *New York Times,* "Executives of online ancestry services say that about 60 million people in the United States are involved in creating family histories, and that it is one of the most popular hobbies in the country."[6] A natural corollary has been the return of massive family reunions involving hundreds or even thousands of people. (One of the oldest and largest such events is the annual Neshoba County Fair in Philadelphia, Mississippi, which has been a favored spot for family reunions since 1889.) Books are published to help people plan such reunions, and a Family Reunion Institute has been founded to help the scattered branches of American families reconnect. In addition, ad hoc reunions for people with the same surname attract thousands of people, many of whom are not really related at all but come together with other members of their "clan" to search for common roots and interests.

Old-fashioned patriarchal fathers are routinely portrayed as unsympathetic figures, coldly insisting that their sons go to advantageous prep schools, dictating their career and life choices, and stifling their individuality. The ideal modern father is a gentle, supportive, noninterfering friend and benefactor. Yet while not everyone would embrace his abrasive and eccentric personality, most Americans acknowledge the singular accomplishment of Richard Williams, the father of international tennis sensations Venus and Serena Williams. One day Williams announced to his wife that they were going to have two more children (they already had three) and that he was going to turn them into tennis champions. Venus and Serena now routinely eliminate other competitors and face each other in championship matches that have spectators gripping their chairs. As a father, Williams represents what can only be called a throwback to Ancient Nepotism. His example is a testament to the nepotistic truth that where children are concerned, you get out what you put in. Though it may seem strange to modern eyes, this reversion is a natural outcome of subjecting the family and kinship to the principles of the free market.

In short, the United States today is a riot of old and new kinship forms, a nepotistic petri dish in which signs of a return to a premodern view of marriage and kinship coexist with the postmodern insistence on defining families as entirely voluntary. One sign of this new attitude is the apparent willingness to reexamine our legal view of kinship as based on genetic relationships. A recent California Supreme Court decision to award an unmarried boyfriend full paternal rights in a custody dispute with the child's biological mother represents a major victory for the American revolt against biology.[7]

This result may well be viewed as a further sign of our happy liberation from the constraints of biological kinship. Yet a sobering reminder of the limits to such freewheeling experimentation may be seen in the story of the devastating Oakland fires of 1991. In that catastrophic event, the largest urban fire in U.S. history, thousands of homes were incinerated in a matter of hours, reducing the inhabitants of this upscale Bay Area suburb to the naked and exposed condition of Lear on the heath. According to anthropologist Susanna Hoffman, whose home was one of those destroyed, "Though the community had long stood as a vanguard of cultural progressiveness, in the fury of the fire recent cultural innovations burned away like so much patina." Oakland (a neighbor of Berkeley) is one of the most progressive and egalitarian communities in America, peopled by individuals who "had marched well into the brave new world of social alliances." Most had migrated from elsewhere, embracing a definition of community based not on blood kinship but on friendship and spiritual affinity. Yet to their evident dismay, with the physical destruction of their community, many of these "higher" bonds collapsed. Numerous couples broke up, and so many friendships dissolved that the Alameda County Health Department brought in trauma specialists to help people cope with the loss. Meanwhile, hundreds of blood relatives appeared, many of whom had not been seen or heard from for years, bringing money, food, and clothing and providing the emotional and physical support that many friends did not.[8]

The lesson appears to be that while our voluntary ties may seem superior, it is only our *unchosen* ties that we can count on in a pinch. Despite (or maybe because of) the mobility and rootlessness of our society, many Americans agree with Robert Frost in defining home as the place where, when you have nowhere else to go, "they have to take you in." Indeed, notwithstanding the enthronement of altruism as the highest moral good, it can be argued that our primary obligation remains the support of our kin. We have a *duty* to be nepotistic, and if we fail to put our families first we may destroy the very sources of altruism on which society depends.

Subjecting kinship to the market has produced two countervailing tendencies: a tendency to emphasize freewheeling creativity in family relations, and an opposite tendency to return to ancient manifestations of nepotism in areas where they seem useful or necessary. This suggests that we have not so much been *liberated* from kinship as we have returned to a premodern *understanding* of kinship as something malleable and plastic, a means of extending nepotistic sentiments to persons not related by blood ties. Postmodern cultural conditions have allowed us to recover our aboriginal talent for assimilating strangers to existing kinship categories, and for creating new categories where old ones no longer suffice. This capability is not without its limits, but it also holds out the possibility of applying nepotistic forms and practices creatively to various problems of modern society.

The isolation of the modern individual reminds us of the pitiable condition of King Lear. Stripped of his sustaining kin connections, he stood naked to the elements in the same way that the citizen of a modern society, stripped of his extended family ties, stands naked to the power of the market and the envy and hostility of his fellows. This is the natural end point of the process, identified by the nineteenth-century legal historian Henry Maine, whereby "the Individual is steadily substituted for the Family, as the unit of which civil laws take account."[9] Gradually the functions of the family are assumed by the state until the family has no remaining purpose and becomes a strictly voluntary association. The result has been to break up not just the clan and extended family—an outcome favorable to capitalism and democracy—but the nuclear family itself. This process was beneficial to the cause of increasing individual freedom but it has now gone somewhat further than we wish and is in danger of reducing us to the primitive atom of kinship—the unit of mother and child. In this condition, the state is our only security. It is therefore no surprise that the father has been eclipsed in our society, to be replaced by the avuncular state. But as we are now finding out, the state is not an adequate replacement for the family.

The modern individual thus verges on the condition of a slave. For if a slave is a man without kin, what else is a man without kin but a potential or actual slave?

Must we yield to these pressures as though they were forces of nature? But they are not forces of nature. They are forces of culture, and culture is a human creation. Despite the modern tendency to posit a fundamental opposition between the state and the individual, the real constituents of human society are not individuals but families. The family has always been the default mode of social organization, and in periods of anarchy it is the family that emerges to preserve the social order. The alternative to the state is therefore not anarchic individualism but dynastic family rule. The state of nature is not the "war of all against all" envisioned by Hobbes but a return to the family enterprise of Vito Corleone.

Furthermore, despite our post-Freudian tendency to demonize the family as a setting of repression and anxiety, the family has always been the bulwark and defender of individual freedom. As Ferdinand Mount has wisely written, "The family is a subversive organisation. In fact, it is the ultimate and only consistently subversive organisation. Only the family has continued throughout history and still continues to undermine the State. The family is the enduring permanent enemy of all hierarchies, churches and ideologies."[10] We in our wealthy and powerful society have the luxury of indulging a drive for extreme individualism. But at some point in the future it is likely that our descendants will face the kind of economic or political challenges that may force them to fall back on their families, and when that time comes we can only hope that they have not become so dependent on the state that they have lost the primitive understanding of how to "do things" with kinship.

One prescription for the besetting anomie of modern individualism is to promote and encourage the formation of stable families. This has already been understood by many on both sides of the political divide. But there is no need to make a fetish out of the monogamous nuclear family, and where such families do not or cannot exist, we may rely on extended kin and kinlike surrogates. This is not to advocate a return to the system of Puritan patriarchy, in which people without families were assigned to live as servants in other people's homes; nor to the Cavalier vision of an extended patriarchal household. It is simply to note that in every era, people met the challenges of life partly through the creation of artificial families. We know from other contexts—the mafia, the military, the church, the labor movement—that it is possible to do this. People without families have an instinct for making them out of whatever materials they have at hand. We should therefore take steps to explore how this can be done as a matter of policy.

It is not my place to say exactly how. But it does seem to indicate returning certain governmental powers to the family and deemphasizing institutional answers to problems that can be managed more humanely by families and kin-based social networks. We should therefore strengthen the nuclear families that do exist, encourage people to live with and work with their kin, and stimulate the creation of extended kinship networks because they function as support groups, social insurance providers, and sources of labor and capital.[11] We should also promote the reconstruction of multigenerational households.[12] In addition, rather than simply enforcing nuclear family bonds by pursuing deadbeat dads, we should focus on strengthening the ties between single mothers and their kin. This would mean, among other things, defining a family as a group of relatives who live in nearby households rather than limiting this definition to those who dwell under one roof. We could also do more to promote informal adoption and recognize the nepotistic bonds of nonkin who assume responsibility for children not their own.

Another option would be to revive certain practices associated with family patronage. Apprenticeship programs have long been promoted as a means to bring young black men into the labor force. Mentoring programs should also be encouraged; the mentor often forms a kinlike bond with a young man or woman, and these bonds can become very close. (A large literature on mentoring exists, and national organizations like Big Brothers of America actively promote these surrogate, or pseudo-kinship, ties.) These bonds might be developed into real patron-client relationships, informed by the meritocratic rules of the New Nepotism.

Philanthropy is another area in which families can play a larger role. Every foundation in this country represents a decision by wealthy parents *not* to leave at least some of their money to their children, and that reflects a healthy check on nepotism—unless it is taken to extremes. In previous generations, large donors turned over their assets to professional managers, though family oversight continued at many large foundations. But the corporate model of philanthropy established by twentieth-century benefactors like Carnegie, Ford, and Rockefeller has increasingly been seen as unimaginative and bureaucratic by a new generation of wealth that seeks a more flexible, family-based approach. The recent crop of dot-com billionaires have made giving a family affair, as exemplified by Bill Gates, who put his father in charge of his multibillion-dollar foundation. Families of lesser wealth have also found great satisfaction in involving their children in giving. In order to be both more effective and more satisfying, philanthropy should be more nepotistic.[13]

Above all, it is high time for us to get over our ambivalence about the "return" of dynastic families. This country is now old enough to have accumulated a large number of great families. Though we have insisted for two hundred years on viewing ourselves as a society of striving individuals, the constructive contributions of these families are too obvious to deny any longer. Americans admire the Adamses, Roosevelts, and Kennedys, not just for their unity—a value that is becoming increasingly difficult to preserve in our mobile society—but for their sense of common purpose and the spirit of public service that they cultivate. There is much to be said for these "aristocratic" features of dynastic families, and as long as they observe the meritocratic rules of the New Nepotism, we really have no basis for complaint. Indeed we should not only respect these great families but imitate and try to be more like them, for this is precisely the kind of nepotism we need. Rather than seeking to shame or stamp out the *bad* kind of nepotism, we should reward and encourage the good.

The risks inherent in this kind of thing have been exaggerated and fail to reflect both the progress of meritocracy and the power of social envy in a democracy. Dynastic heirs walk on very thin ice in our society: we readily grant them the benefit of the doubt, but we subject them to extremely high standards, and at the first sign of failing to meet those expectations, the hammer comes down very hard.

Consider the contrast between the recent treatment of two juniors by the American press. John F. Kennedy Jr. was an immensely popular figure, America's crown prince. Though no high achiever intellectually (he failed the bar exam twice), he was a good-hearted, decent, and modest young man who bore the burdens of his legacy well. Though it was clear that should he choose to run for office, the heavens would rain money and endorsements on his head, he exuded no ambition other than to participate constructively in civic life. And while his Kennedy cousins were frequently linked to scandal, John Jr. distanced himself from their embarrassing excesses and pronounced them "poster boys for bad behavior." The whole world joined in grief when this American prince was killed along with his wife and sister-in-law in a plane crash in July 1999, a grief strongly tinged with regret for a son's lost opportunity to fulfill a great family legacy.

Edgar Bronfman Jr. was another young man who inherited a fortune and a legacy. The scion of his family's multibillion-dollar Seagram's Corporation, on becoming the company's chairman, Edgar traded in nearly $9 billion worth of stock in DuPont to buy controlling interest in Universal, PolyGram, and other entertainment companies, seeking to shift the family's interests from liquor to media in one fell swoop. He then engineered an ill-conceived merger with Vivendi, a French entertainment conglomerate that went into the tank soon after, taking with it billions in family assets. In December 2002 Vivendi began selling off the priceless modern art collection that the family had installed in their New York headquarters, eliciting howls of protest from aesthetically minded New Yorkers. As a result, Bronfman has become the favorite whipping boy of the international business press.

The differing treatment of these heirs shows how a democratic society regulates the ambitions of family scions. So long as you play the good son and behave responsibly with your patrimony, Americans are happy to acknowledge you. But when you overreach, the corrosive envy that drives so much of our egalitarian culture thrills to announce your destruction. The same ambivalence is seen in our reaction to the implosion of great families. We love to watch dynastic clans like the Binghams of Louisville and the Pritzkers of Chicago tear themselves apart in sibling squabbles over money. Yet at the same time, there is something in us that regrets the passing of these great families, which have held out for so long against the disintegrative tendencies of our fluid and mobile society. Nothing better illustrates our desire to have it both ways in this regard than our ambivalent addiction to the scandals of the British royal family.

Emulating dynastic families would be a good way to overcome some of the biggest problems and dissatisfactions of modern life. People who feel there's something missing in their family relationships are right: sons often complain they don't feel close enough to their fathers, and there's a reason—they're no longer out on the veldt learning to hunt and trap game or working together in a craft or business. Without such shared pursuits, fathers have less occasion to teach their children about life and get the satisfaction that goes with it. Richard Williams is an inspiring figure precisely because he shows that any father who really wants to play a major role in his children's lives, instilling that kind of drive and purpose in them, can do it, though it requires considerable efforts. It is also the best way of keeping your family close—an increasingly hopeless dream for American parents, who may invest twenty or thirty years and hundreds of thousands of dollars in their children, only to see them go off on their own, in many cases moving hundreds or thousands of miles away.

Nepotism has been judged harshly in light of our ideological view that we "ought" to love humanity more than our own family, that we "ought" to value efficiency and merit over personal loyalty, or that we "ought" to make it on our own instead of accepting help from relatives or friends. The truth is that very few people actually do this. Read the first ten pages of any distinguished person's memoir or biography and you are likely to find evidence of a significant debt to nepotism. Otto von Bismarck rose swiftly to a position of power by exploiting his mother's connections to the Prussian royal family. Albert Einstein, unable to obtain a university appointment, was taken on as an examiner in the Swiss Patent Office because the father of one of his classmates was director of the office; he used the next seven years to develop his special theory of relativity. The same thing often happens in America, and this has long been recognized even by the greatest proponents of merit.[14] Even Colin Powell, one of the most esteemed individuals in recent American history, owes his rise not to unaided merit but, in true Horatio Alger fashion, to a mixture of merit, luck, and the patronage of benevolent friends in the Republican Party.[15]

America has been called a universal nation, and it is now commonly argued that individualism is the highest good and that only by rising above our narrow and parochial connections to family, community, or ethnic group can we achieve the national unity we crave. Yet in truth, America does not invite the world to abandon the idea of kinship. Rather, America extends its inclusive vision of kinship to the world. America admits all nations but does not give up its claim to be a family. On the other hand, the American national family is far from being perfectly inclusive. Race remains the biggest problem in this country precisely because American blacks do not feel that this offer of universal kinship really extends to them, and they are correct in seeing their continued exclusion as the result of a narrow nepotistic preference of whites for other whites. The solution, however, is not to abandon the notion of national kinship but to begin to see blacks as members of the family.

The good news is that we are a lot closer to this goal than many realize. As journalist Brent Staples has pointed out, most American blacks are in fact of mixed-race descent. There is already a lot of genetic relatedness between American whites and blacks. For a long time this was considered a shameful secret, but it has recently surfaced in an undeniable way with the Jefferson-Hemings affair. For years, the descendants of Sally Hemings, a slave who was said to be Jefferson's concubine, had pressed for an acknowledgment of kinship on the part of the Jefferson family. In 1998, DNA analysis finally seemed to establish that at least one of Sally's children was a Jefferson (though it could not be proved that he was the offspring of Thomas himself), and the head of the Jefferson family association acknowledged as much. While the Hemings are still not allowed burial in the Monticello graveyard—the ultimate sign of inclusion—their recognition as family members is clearly a step in the right direction. Meanwhile, rising rates of interracial marriage have been hailed as an important breakthrough by everyone to the left of David Duke and to the right of Louis Farrakhan. According to the *New York Times*, mixed-race marriages "now number 1.5 million and are roughly doubling each decade."[16]

The ultimate solution to the American race problem is not to declare war on nepotism but to expand our definition of the national family. As we have seen, nepotism properly understood is not limited to the immediate family but can be extended to the band, the clan, the tribe, the caste, the ethnic group, and even to the nation. But for various reasons it has always stopped short of universal human kinship, and a fiction of common descent is therefore necessary, even for a universal nation. Lincoln made a start in this direction by shifting American citizenship onto a philosophical basis, but despite our tendency to view him as the founder of a new nationalism based entirely on allegiance to abstract principles, he drew the ethnic boundary at whites. Now we are a multiracial, polyglot society that needs new mythological parents. Anthropologists explain that when tribal groups amalgamate, they often invent a common ancestor to preserve the myth of common descent, and in our present circumstances such an exercise of the tribal imagination may also be in order. Just as Clovis founded the French nation by asserting that Franks and Gauls were both descended from Trojan heroes, future citizens of a multiracial America may wish to think of themselves as the "children" of Thomas Jefferson and Sally Hemings.

What does all this have to do with whether or not you should hire your nephew? Well, it may be objectively discriminatory, but since people are going to do it anyway, we may as well infuse nepotism with meritocratic principles so all of us may benefit. Moreover, if you can't be a brother to everyone, try being a better brother to the brothers you already have. Let families strive for public honors, since this has always been the soul of republican virtue and it is up to us in every generation to recover this tradition. The spirit of family enterprise gives dignity and meaning to our lives and is not only a spur to achievement but a check on excessive ambition. It also links the generations in a chain of generosity and gratitude. We would all be better off if we reflected more consistently and deeply not only on our debt to our ancestors, but also on what we owe to our descendants.

POSTSCRIPT

AMERICAN NEPOTISM TODAY

POLITICS

Political families are nothing new in American history. The Adamses of Boston are only the most famous members of a political elite that included the Livingstons of New York and Virginia, the Bentons of Missouri, and the Williams-Breckinridge-Clay family of the middle South and West. There have been Roosevelts in New York, Tafts in Ohio, Kennedys in Massachusetts, Stevensons in Illinois, Browns in California, DuPonts in Delaware, La Follettes in Wisconsin, Udalls in Arizona, and Bushes in Connecticut, Texas, and Florida. There are the patrician Rockefellers of New York, West Virginia, and Arkansas, and the populist Longs of Louisiana.[1]

Familial succession to political office appeared to decrease in the postwar period, but that trend has been dramatically reversed. In December 1998, Ronald Brownstein identified numerous political heirs running for office in both parties, including two-term Indiana governor (now Senator) Evan Bayh, Reps. Tom and Mark Udall, Janice Hahn, Charlie Gonzalez, Barbara Kennelly, Chet Culver, and George Wallace Jr. (who once toured with Hank Williams Jr. in a rock band). All were elected, including incumbent governors Jeb and George W. Bush and Ohio's Robert A. Taft III. (That year's dynastic losers included Don Bevill of Alabama, Pat Casey of Pennsylvania, Marjorie McKeithen of Louisiana, Gary King of New Mexico, Paul Hobby of Texas, and former representative James Longley Jr., running for the Maine governorship once held by his father. Meanwhile in Minnesota, after a "my three sons" gubernatorial primary that pitted the offspring of Hubert Humphrey, Walter Mondale, and Orville Freeman against one another, the election was won by Jesse Ventura.) Nor did Brownstein forget to mention successors already in office, such as Sens. Chris Dodd, Judd Gregg, Mary Landrieu, and Jay Rockefeller, Maryland lieutenant governor Kathleen Kennedy Townsend, Chicago mayor Richard M. Daley, then–HUD secretary Andrew Cuomo, and Reps. Jesse Jackson Jr., Harold Ford Jr., Patrick Kennedy, Joseph Kennedy II (since retired), Lucille Roybal-Allard, John E. Sununu, and John Dingell, whose family has represented their Detroit congressional district since the 1930s.[2] (A more recent crop of political successors is listed in the introduction.)

Many political successors are apprenticed to the calling from an early age. Brownstein observed that, since they were raised in an atmosphere of professional politics, "it's no coincidence that many of the second-generation politicians win their first elections at remarkably young ages." Marjorie McKeithen grew up in the Louisiana governor's mansion and ran her father's campaign for secretary of state when she was just out of college. George W. Bush worked at eighteen as an advance man for his father's Senate campaign in Texas. Evan Bayh campaigned in several states when his father ran for president in 1976, and managed his Senate race in 1980. These journeyman experiences make second-generation politicians much more at ease when they take their first turn in the ring.

Though successors are most visible in national politics, the phenomenon is really more common at the state and local levels. The Longs of Louisiana had a family member in public office from 1917 to 1987. The Bakers of Tennessee, the Fishes of New York, the Muhlenbergs of Pennsylvania, the Keans of New Jersey, and the Lodges of Massachusetts and Connecticut are all old political families that have had a member in office within the last decade or so. Though the heyday of machine politics is past, politically connected families like the Crottys of Buffalo, the Hamiltons of Philadelphia, and the Daleys of Chicago continue to exercise tremendous power both overtly and behind the scenes. In New York, there are Brunos in Albany, Espadas and Riveras in the Bronx, and

Molinaris in Staten Island. State senator Daniel R. Hevesi is the son of New York City comptroller Alan Hevesi. Meanwhile, in early 2001, half a dozen children of New York City Council members announced that they were running for their parents' seats. (The cause was New York's term limits law, which forbids anyone from holding more than two consecutive four-year terms.) Thus the son of Rep. José Serrano challenged an incumbent council member who was himself the son of state senator Pedro Espada Jr. Twenty-three-year-old Elizabeth Crowley announced her candidacy for the Queens council seat formerly held by both her parents. Candidate Peter Vallone Jr. announced that he would be running for his father's seat while the elder Vallone ran for mayor. Spouses were also involved, like the wives of Queens councilman Noach Dear and Brooklyn councilman Howard Lasher.[3]

The classic Chicago attitude toward nepotism was expressed by the late Mayor Richard J. Daley. Asked to explain why he had channeled city insurance contracts to his sons, the boss replied, "What would you think of a father who refused to help his own children?" Daley's son Richard Jr. is now mayor of Chicago, and nepotism is still the way the city does business. The family of former alderman Anthony Laurino is a good example: his son William Laurino is a former state assemblyman; his daughter Marie D'Amico, married to a retired deputy sanitation commissioner, recently pled guilty to collecting over $82,000 from three no-show government jobs. Another well-connected Chicago family are the Bradleys: the wife, mother, sister-in-law, and two brothers of assemblyman Richard T. Bradley have all held city jobs. Mayor Daley himself is the head of Chicago's most prominent political clan, and family patronage is a time-honored Daley practice. In 1955, Daley's father hired his cousin James as security chief. In 1980, after his election as state's attorney, Richard Jr. hired James's son as a top aide. According to the *Chicago Tribune*, "Despite reforms that have virtually outlawed political patronage, public payrolls in the Chicago area are seeded with dozens of relatives and in-laws of the mayor and his high-powered siblings." The *Trib* estimates that since the second Daley's election as mayor in 1989, at least sixty-eight relatives by blood or marriage have drawn city paychecks. In 1998 their combined salaries totaled over $3 million.[4]

Boston is another city where family matters. In 1989, *Boston* magazine reported that state Senate president William Bulger had hired several relatives at exaggerated salaries: his brother Jackie was a clerk at the juvenile court, and Bulger's sisters, niece, ex-wife, and children also had jobs "on the state." The story traced the dense web of family employment in state and local government. (Bulger, now president of the University of Massachusetts, has denied any knowledge of the whereabouts of his brother, reputed mobster James "Whitey" Bulger, a fugitive since 1995.) The same magazine later reported that Gov. Michael Dukakis had appointed campaign workers and their relatives to highly paid state jobs. Meanwhile, according to the *Boston Globe*, a new class of twenty-six police cadets included at least ten who were related to current or former Boston police officers. All were graduates of a special program apparently set up to circumvent affirmative action guidelines. One cadet was the son of Boston's mayor, Thomas Menino.

The incidence of political power couples is also increasing. So common has it been for political wives like Margaret Chase Smith, Jean Carnahan, and Mary Bono to follow their deceased husbands into office that one study of the phenomenon has been called "Over His Dead Body." But since the advent of the two-career couple, Washington has become more incestuous than ever before. Prominent examples include Bob and Elizabeth Dole, Richard and Lynne Cheney, and Bill and Hillary Clinton. But the phenomenon is extremely widespread. Many lobbyists are married to high-profile politicians or government officials, raising concerns about possible conflicts of interest.[5]

BUSINESS

The first trading and mercantile enterprises proudly proclaimed their family ownership, and some modern family businesses are very old. The owners of Japan's Hoshi Hotel have been in business since A.D. 718: this is its forty-ninth generation of family ownership. Venetian glassmakers Barovier and Toso were established in 1295. The Antinoris of Tuscany have been making wine since 1385. The Barettas have been making guns since 1526. Zildjian cymbals have been made by the same Turkish family since 1623, although now they are made not in Constantinople but in Norwell, Massachusetts.

Today nearly 95 percent of American businesses are family owned or controlled, including 40 percent of the Fortune 500. According to a study by the Institute for Family Enterprise at Bryant College, the nation's oldest family business is Tuttle Market Gardens of Dover, New Hampshire, a twelfth-generation business founded in 1640. Antoine's New Orleans restaurant has been in business since 1840 and is run today by fifth-generation family member Bernard Guste. The Minnesota furrier Albrechts was founded in St. Paul in 1855; Jesse James stole one of their handmade fur coats off a rack in 1876.

Craft and service professions are often family dominated. The Lairds of New Jersey have been making liquor since the turn of the eighteenth century, the Strohs of Michigan have been making beer since 1850, the Coors of Colorado since 1873. Anheuser-Busch of St. Louis has been in business for 150 years. Brown-Forman, makers of Jack Daniel's and Southern Comfort, has been a family business for over 130 years and ascribes its success to a policy of "planned nepotism." A radio ad for Molson's beer proclaims the family's tradition of fine brewing "since before there was a country called Canada." Seagram, another Canadian distiller, was owned and managed by the Bronfman family until quite recently.

Real estate is a long-term business conducive to family management. Multigenerational real estate clans include the Rudin, Rechler, Lefrak, and Rose families of New York, the Galbreaths of Cleveland, the Millers of Denver, the Whichards of Raleigh, the Crows of Dallas, and the Feinbergs, Ziffs, and Pritzkers of Chicago. There are many more in every large American city.

Funeral homes (like restaurants) are also conducive to family ownership. Kirk & Nice of Philadelphia was a family concern for nine generations; Rogers Funeral Home in Frankfort, Kentucky, has been burying people since 1802, Gardner & Son of Indiana since 1816. (The HBO series *Six Feet Under* dramatized the problems of a family of undertakers as they tried to cope with the loss of their patriarch and the attempts of a national chain to take them over.) Most funeral homes that cater to blacks are family owned.

Fireworks is another traditional family business. The Santoris, proprietors of fourth-generation Garden State Fireworks, were chosen to stage the bicentennial display over the Washington Monument. Another fireworks clan are the Gruccis of Long Island, whose family was struck by tragedy in 1983 when an explosion killed two family members. The Gruccis and their rivals the Zambellis of Pennsylvania are featured along with other fireworks families in George Plimpton's *Fireworks: A History and Celebration* (1984).

Many other specialized crafts are passed down from one generation to the next, such as glassblowing, candy making, and circus performing.[6]

In the past, most publishing companies were family owned. Today, a few holdouts remain, including McGraw-Hill, Walker Publishing, and John Wiley & Sons. According to president Tom Knudsen of Thomas Publishing, "At Thomas, we've succeeded because we've encouraged so many instances of nepotism. It leads to stability, longevity, and successful growth." The newspaper industry has also been a bastion of family ownership. The *Los Angeles Times* was founded and run for four generations by the fiercely independent Otis family. The Binghams of Louisville, a communications dynasty founded on the Flagler Standard Oil fortune and the ownership of the *Louisville Courier-Journal,* melted down spectacularly in a family feud in 1986. But others continue to thrive. Rupert Murdoch's News Corporation, founded by his father, Sir Keith Murdoch, has annual revenues of $13.8 billion; Murdoch's children all play major roles. The Knight-Ridder chain represents the merger of two family businesses that go back respectively to 1903 and 1892. Other family-based media empires include Cox Enterprises, founded in 1898 by James M. Cox, and Advance Publications, founded in 1922 by S. I. Newhouse Sr. Christie Hefner runs her father's *Playboy* publishing empire. There are also the Grahams of Washington, D.C., owners of the *Washington Post;* the Annenbergs, owners of a media conglomerate that included the *Philadelphia Inquirer, Seventeen,* and *TV Guide;* and the Ochs-Sulzberger clan, which still owns and runs the *New York Times.*

Most family businesses are small, but there is no necessary contradiction between corporate organization and family management. Examples of large family-run corporations, both public and private, include Occidental Petroleum, Carlson Cos., Levi-Strauss, McDonnell Douglas, Wang Laboratories, Ford Motor, Loews, Winn-Dixie, Weyerhauser, Marriott, W. R. Grace, Corning Glass, Koch Industries, Mars, Bechtel Group,

Publix Super Markets, Malone & Hyde, Milliken & Co., H Group Holdings, S. C. Johnson & Son, Reynolds Metals, and dozens more.[7]

Wall Street has a long tradition of family-based enterprises. The old-line WASP legal and financial firms were closely held family partnerships, and the Jewish families of Goldman, Sachs; Kuhn, Loeb; and Lehman Brothers imitated them by founding their own firms in the twenties and thirties. But while the world of finance and investing has become much more open and meritocratic, family traditions still have value in this area. Lebenthal & Co. is a third-generation Wall Street firm. Quick & Reilly, an aggressive family-run firm founded in 1974, pioneered the discount brokerage field. According to the *Wall Street Journal,* stockbrokers at Advest Group, Inc., in Hartford, Connecticut, traditionally bring sons and daughters into the firm. ("Good work ethics seem to run throughout families," said one corporate VP.) Moreover, many fast-track internship and training programs are filled with the sons and daughters of partners, associates, and clients.

Most press coverage of family succession in business is remarkably positive. Thus Brian Roberts, son of Comcast chairman Ralph Roberts, is credited with putting together the partnership that launched QVC. Brian, a Wharton graduate, worked his way up in various marketing and field positions before becoming the company's president in 1990. Asked about nepotism, Comcast executives said that it wasn't an issue because he had "paid his dues in lesser jobs." In 1993, James Cox Kennedy, chairman of Cox Enterprises, was praised as a dynamic business heir in the *Wall Street Journal.* ("He's always out to prove himself, over and over and over again," one colleague said.) In July 2001, *BusinessWeek* put Motorola's embattled CEO on its cover with the headline "Can Chris Galvin Save His Family's Legacy?" During the recent Internet boom, the *New York Times* noted a widespread tendency among youthful dot-com entrepreneurs to hire their parents, often retired businesspeople. According to the *Times,* "this curious form of reverse nepotism is up-ending traditional notions about family businesses, where the younger generations work their way up the ladder."[8]

Yet for every triumph, there is a tragedy. Reporting on the collapse of Joseph Brooks's reign as CEO of Lord & Taylor, the *Wall Street Journal* couldn't resist the headline "Family Misfortunes: A Father's Ambitions for His Son's Success Cripple Them Both." Brooks met his Waterloo in 1991 when he tried to force the success of his son Thomas, described as "a music major who dropped out of college and had a weight problem." In 1996, CNN founder Ted Turner fired his son Teddy after dissolving the small home video business he ran, though he retained Teddy's sister and wife in their jobs. Jessica Bibliowicz, the high-powered daughter of Citigroup chairman Sanford Weill, quit her father's company after being passed over for a coveted promotion and started her own business. (Her brother continues to work for their father.) And in 1999, ADM founder and chairman Dwayne Andreas had to be succeeded by his nephew G. Allen Andreas after his son and heir apparent, Michael Andreas, was implicated in a price-fixing scandal.

After a long period in which nepotism was viewed with disfavor, family succession has not only increased but has even become fashionable. As far back as 1988, *BusinessWeek* weighed the pros and cons of the trend in an article on "the New Nepotism," which maintained that "family rule" was making "a major comeback" at a broad array of companies established in the postwar boom, as their founders reached the end of their careers. According to the editor of *Family Business Review*, "More family businesses are being passed to new managers than at any time in U.S. history."[9]

Far from being embarrassed by their nepotistic practices, most family-owned companies call attention to them as a guarantee of stability and quality. According to Yale business professor Ivan Lansberg, family-run companies take a longer strategic view, are more humane employers, and display a strong work ethic; they also "worry a helluva lot more about quality because the boss's name is on the product." Not that there aren't many problems in family-owned businesses. Nepotism can harm efficiency, reduce flexibility, complicate succession, and create disincentives that may make it hard to attract top-quality managers. Yet family management is here to stay in large and small companies alike (the Wharton School offers a special course in dynastic management). One business journal has even noted that wise investors can profit from the frequently observed "nepotism effect," whereby a company's stock price arbitrarily drops when a family successor is announced, only to rebound shortly thereafter when market confidence is restored.

THE ARTS: LITERATURE

Family traditions exist among writers, as they do in other fields, but never before in such numbers.[10] Martin Amis started writing novels at an early age and has by now upstaged his father, Kingsley Amis. Author and editor Anne Fadiman is the daughter of writers Clifton Fadiman and Annalee Jacoby. Novelists Margaret Drabble and A. S. Byatt are sisters, and the Barthelme brothers—Donald, Frederick, and Steven—have all published multiple books. Bantam has published a trilogy of prequels to Frank Herbert's *Dune* by Brian Herbert. Christopher Tolkien, a professor of medieval English literature at Oxford like his father, has devoted much of his life to editing his father's unpublished papers and recently released a four-volume history of *The Lord of the Rings;* grandson Simon Tolkien has published a mystery novel. Jeff Shaara parlayed his father Michael's Pulitzer Prize–winning book on the Civil War, *The Killer Angels,* into a trilogy of historical novels. Novelist Molly Jong-Fast is the daughter of writers Erica Jong and Jonathan Fast, himself the son of Howard Fast. Susan Minot's sister Eliza Minot has published a well-received book based on the same family events depicted in Minot's own debut novel; their brother is said to be writing a book on a similar theme. The publisher of Rebecca Walker's memoir of growing up gay, black, and Jewish explains that Walker dropped her father's name and has "taken up the lineage of her mother, Alice." There has been a plethora of books by female relatives of John McPhee (two daughters and a niece). Nor should we omit Bliss Broyard, Christopher Buckley, Susan and Ben Cheever, Gautama Chopra, Carol Higgins Clark, Kiran Desai, Christopher Dickey, Cory Doctorow, Andre Dubus III, Ted Heller, Tama Janowitz, Malachy McCourt, Susan Merrell, Rebecca Miller, Shiva and V. S. Naipaul, Robin Pogrebin, Christopher Rice, David Rieff, Katie Roiphe, Margaret Salinger, Janna Malamud Smith, Paul and Ivan Solotaroff, Alexandra Styron, Marcel and Alexander Theroux, David Updike, Mark Vonnegut, Franz Wright, and many more (including myself, of course).

To an even greater extent, the small world of children's publishing is coming to resemble an incestuous family tree. Thacher Hurd is the son of Edith and Clement Hurd, who illustrated Margaret Wise Brown's *Goodnight Moon.* Jerry Pinkney has won three Caldecott Honor awards; his wife, Gloria, is the author of two children's books, both illustrated by her husband. Their son Brian has also won two Caldecotts, and his wife is children's author and editor Andrea Davis Pinkney. Lizzy Rockwell is the daughter of prolific authors Anne and Harlow Rockwell; she got her start when she was asked to complete her late father's last book. Ed Emberley's children Michael and Rebecca started out doing color overlays on dozens of his early children's books; the three of them recently did a book together *(Three)* showcasing their different styles. Javaka Steptoe, whose first book won the Coretta Scott King Award in 1998, also started out helping his father, the late John Steptoe. Young adult author Donna Jo Napoli has used her daughters Elena and Eva as illustrators. Many of these young people were steered to publication by their parents' own agents and editors.[11]

THE ARTS: MUSIC

Earlier we mentioned Sean and Julian Lennon, Jakob Dylan, the sons of Ringo Starr, and Enrique Iglesias. But there are numerous other musical successors. The Bee Gees were a brother act whose parents were both musical performers; younger brother Andy Gibb later launched his own solo career. Whitney Houston got her start at fourteen singing backup for her mother, Cissy Houston; her cousin is Dionne Warwick. Natalie Cole boosted her flagging career by recording a series of posthumous duets with her father, Nat King Cole. Monica Mancini got her start in her father's chorus at Lake Tahoe and launched her solo career with a collection of her father's songs. Vocal trio Wilson Phillips was formed in 1986 by sisters Carnie and Wendy Wilson (daughters of Beach Boy Brian Wilson) and Chynna Phillips (daughter of John Phillips from the Mamas and the Papas). Other musical offspring include Tal Bachman, Elijah Blue (son of Cher and guitarist Gregg Allman), Nick, Aaron, and Leslie Carter; Adam Cohen, Nona Gaye, Norah Jones (daughter of Ravi Shankar), Ziggy Marley, Joe Perry's son

Tony, Dee Snider's son Jesse, Chris Stills, Sting's son Jake, Emma Townshend, and Rufus Wainwright (son of Loudon Wainwright III and Kate McGarrigle). Sheryl Crow's father was a jazz musician, and vocalist Amy Helm is the daughter of the Band's Levon Helm. The first father-son duo in hip-hop are Master P and Lil' Romeo. There are also rapper Eazy-E's son Lil' E, and Beyoncé Knowles's sister Solange.

Motown was a family affair from the beginning. Recording impresario Berry Gordy was born in Detroit in 1929, the seventh of eight children. After a stint in the army, with family help he opened a record shop and started writing and producing songs. Friendship with Smokey Robinson led to the creation of two music labels and a publishing house. The "family atmosphere" of Motown—run literally out of the Gordy household—had much to do with its early success. Sisters Esther and Loucye had major roles, and Pops Gordy played surrogate father to a crew of teenage aspirants, including future Temptation David Ruffin, former Moonglow Harvey Fuqua, and Gordy's brother-in-law Marvin Gaye (married to Anna Gordy), who worked as a session musician before launching a solo career. Gordy's daughter (with Diana Ross) Rhonda Ross Kendrick is an actress, as is her half sister Tracee Ellis Ross. Gordy's brother Robert and sons Stefan and Rockwell also have singing and acting credentials. The Jacksons are another Motown family that have become an entertainment dynasty. Building on the success of the Jackson 5—the family act created by their father, musician Joseph Gordy—Michael and Janet Jackson both have lucrative solo careers. Brother Jermaine, once married to Hazel Gordy, is the father of actor Jermaine Jackson II and the uncle of actress Lark Voorhies.

A whole book could be written on family ties in the country-western industry—the Carter-Cash dynasty is the leading example. Ezra and Maybelle Carter drove down out of the mountains of Virginia in 1927 with their daughters to become the "first family" of country music. The group included June and Anita Carter, their cousin Sara, and Sara's husband, A. P. Carter, who was also Ezra's brother. Anita made her radio debut at age four. June Carter married Johnny Cash; their daughter Rosanne Cash now has her own career. Other well-known family acts (to name just a few) include the Baileys, Dillards, Forbeses, Lewises, Kendalls, Wilkinsons, Osbornes, and Stanleys. Contemporary successors include Pam Tillis, Hank Williams Jr., Wynonna Judd, Lisa Marie Presley, and Patsy and Peggy Lynn.

Jazz also has its share of family acts and traditions, including Duke and Mercer Ellington; Ellis Marsalis and his sons Wynton, Branford, Jason, and Delfeayo; jazz family Thad, Hank, and Alvin Jones; Dave Brubeck and his four sons, trombonist Ray Westray, the Heath brothers, the Brecker brothers, Thelonius Monk Jr., Alice and Ravi Coltrane, and jazz matriarch Jeanne Arland Peterson and her five musical children.[12] Quincy Jones has a growing brood of entertainer children, including actresses Kidada and Rashida Jones and composer-actor Quincy Jones III. There are also Irving Basie, Walter Bishop Jr., Art Blakey Jr., Neneh and Eagle-Eye Cherry (offspring of Don Cherry), Denardo Coleman, Lydia DeJohnette, Kenny Drew Jr., Miles Evans, Matthew Garrison, Robert Irving III (Miles Davis's cousin), Karen Mantler, René McLean, Sue Graham Mingus, Charnett Moffett, Joshua Redman, Orrin Evans, Eric Mingus, Maxine Roach, John Sanborn, Vince Tatum, Nasheet Waits, Marvin Zawinul, and Ben Zwerin.

THE ARTS: HOLLYWOOD

According to historian Neal Gabler, the founders of the great Hollywood studios were all flamboyant nepotists, and there is a well-established tradition of family succession in the movie business. In their now somewhat dated *Hollywood Dynasties* (1984), Stephen Farber and Marc Green provided a list of Oscar winners with a famous family member between 1970 and 1984, including Jane Fonda, Liza Minnelli, Tatum O'Neal, Richard Zanuck, Michael Douglas, and Vanessa Redgrave. Other prominent successors of that era included Douglas Fairbanks Jr., Peter Fonda, John Huston, screenwriters Budd Schulberg and Ring Lardner Jr., James MacArthur (son of Helen Hayes), Sally Field (stepdaughter of former Tarzan Jock Mahoney), Lainie Kazan, Lena Horne, Sissy Spacek (cousin of Rip Torn), Warren Beatty (brother of Shirley MacLaine), and Juliet and Hayley Mills (daughters of John Mills).

Today, the number of Hollywood offspring and siblings has increased exponentially. A by no means exhaustive list includes Casey Affleck, Danny Aiello II, Edward Albert, Eva Amurri (daughter of Susan Sarandon), David and Michael Anderson, Jennifer Aniston; the late Matthew Ansara (son of Barbara Eden), David, Alexis, and Patricia Arquette; Peter Aykroyd, Adam Arkin, Desi Jr. and Lucie Arnaz, Sean Astin; Stephen, Daniel, Alec, William, and Joseph Baldwin; Drew Barrymore, Jim Belushi, Shari Belafonte, Corbin and Collin Bernsen, Lorraine and Elizaeth Bracco, Jeff and Beau Bridges, Matthew Broderick, Josh Brolin, Kate Burton, Jake Busey, Ronnie and Scott Caan, Nicolas Cage, Frank Capra Jr. and Frank Capra III; David, Keith, Robert, and Bruce Carradine (the family includes half brother Michael Bowen, David's daughter Kansas, and nieces Ever Carradine and Martha Plimpton); George Clooney, the children of actor Kit Culkin (Shane, Macaulay, Kieran, Quinn, Christian, and Rory), Jamie Lee Curtis, and John, Joan, Bill, Susie, and Ann Cusack; Mike, Maryam, and Olivia d'Abo; Charlotte and Christopher D'Amboise, Michael and Peter DeLuise, Elizabeth and Kathleen Dennehy, Guillaume and Julie Depardieu, Laura Dern, Kevin Dillon, Cameron Douglas, Eric Douglas, Robert Downey Jr., Richard and Lorin Dreyfuss, Alison Eastwood, Miguel Ferrer (also George Clooney's cousin), Sean Ferrer; Martha, Joseph, Ralph, and Magnus Fiennes; Carrie Fisher, Bridget Fonda, Hallie Foote, John Clark Gable, Donal Gibson, screenwriter Tony Gilroy, Tony Goldwyn, Omar Gooding, Melanie Griffith, Michael Gwynne, Ashley Hamilton, Jim Hanks, Fraser Heston, Laurie Holden, Scott Holden, Clint Howard, Kate Hudson, Helen Hunt, Anjelica and Danny Huston, Timothy Hutton, Angelina Jolie, Ashley Judd, Nastassja Kinski, Lorenzo and A. J. Lamas, Jonathan LaPaglia, Chris Larkin, Brandon Lee; Malcolm, Joie, Cinqué, David, and Bill Lee (Spike Lee's cousin, sisters, brother, and father); Chris Lemmon; Juliette, Dierdre, and Lightfield Lewis; Chad Lowe, Jett Lucas, Jenny Lumet, Lee Majors II, Charlie Matthau (and his cousin Juliette Gruber), Chad McQueen, Christopher Mitchum, Paul Newman's daughters Susan and Lissy Newman and Nell Potts, Aaron and Mike Norris, Hugh O'Connor; Tarquin, Tamsin, Julie Kate, and Richard Olivier, Gwyneth Paltrow, Chris Penn, Dedee Pfeiffer; Chynna, Mackenzie, and Bijou Phillips; Amanda Plummer; River, Summer, Rain, and Joaquin Phoenix; Sidney Poitier, Freddie Prinze Jr., Dennis and Randy Quaid, Aidan, Paul and Declan Quinn, Rob Reiner,

Natasha and Joely Richardson, Craig Rivera, Melissa Rivers, Julia and Eric Roberts, Campbell Scott, brothers Charlie Sheen and Ramon and Emilio Estevez (and their uncle Joe Estevez), Christian and Ryan Slater, Mira Sorvino, Frank Stallone, Ben Stiller, Kiefer Sutherland, Don and Patsy Swayze, Joey Travolta, David Tuchman (son of Juliet Mills); John, Nicholas, and Aida Turturro; Ron Van Cleef, Barry Van Dyke, the Wayans family (Keenen Ivory and siblings Damon, Kim, Marlon, and Shawn Wayans, nephews Michael and Damon Wayans Jr., and nieces Nadia and Cara Mia Wayans), Natasha Gregson Wagner, Ethan Wayne, and Tahnee Welch. The Hollywood Foreign Press always selects a second- or third-generation actor to honor at the Golden Globe Awards.[13]

The Coppolas deserve their own paragraph. Francis Ford Coppola and his composer father, Carmine, both won Oscars for *The Godfather Part II.* Coppola has cast his uncle Anton, his sister Talia Shire, and his children Sofia and Roman in his *Godfather* movies. Sofia has produced or directed several movies and is married to director Spike Jonze. Roman has also launched a career as a producer and director. Coppola's nephew Nicolas changed his name to Cage (though that didn't fool anyone in Hollywood), but his brother Christopher Coppola has directorial ambitions. Talia's son Jason Schwartzman has also gone into the family business; his brother Robert, "inspired" by the example of their cousin, changed his name to Schwartzman-Cage.

Nor has the phenomenon been limited to actors. Producer Bert Schneider is the son of Columbia Pictures chairman Abe Schneider. Alan Ladd Jr. was also the son of a legendary producer. Director Peter Davis is the son-in-law of Herman Mankiewicz. Sibling directing teams include the Coens, Hugheses, Wachowskis, and Farrellys. In the 1980s, Paul Bludhorn was VP for acquisitions at Paramount while his father, Charles, was chairman of parent company Gulf + Western. Hollywood has so many Jaffes in top management that it is hard to keep their relationships straight. Family traditions have also loomed large in Hollywood's craft guilds and unions. Mason Cardiff is the son of cinematographer Jack Cardiff. George Westmore created the first Hollywood makeup department, and five or six other Westmores went into the business. Butlers and Stradlings are well represented in cinematography, and the Steinkamps are a dynasty of film editors. Michael Minkler, who won an Oscar in 2003 for his work on the movie *Chicago*, is a third-generation sound man. The late composer Alfred "Pappy" Newman, who won nine Oscars, was the brother of composers Emil and Lionel Newman, the father of composers Thomas, Maria, and David Newman, the great-uncle of composer Joey Newman, and the uncle of composers Carroll and Randy Newman.

The multiple couplings, marriages, and remarriages within this privileged class, resulting in a web of children, stepchildren, half siblings, uncles and aunts, nieces, nephews, and cousins, have made the Hollywood community increasingly resemble an inbred occupational caste.

THE ARTS: TELEVISION

Television has long been a family business. Alan and Antony Alda are the sons of vaudevillian Robert Alda; Alan's daughters Elizabeth and Beatrice also have extensive TV credits. Rob Reiner got his start when his father's friend Norman Lear cast him in *All in the Family;* Rob's brother Lucas and stepdaughter Tracy also work in television. *Dallas* star Larry Hagman was the son of Mary Martin; his daughter, Heidi, works in television; he is also the godfather of Bridget Fonda. John Ritter is the son of Tex Ritter and the father of Jason Ritter. The Carradines (above) have starred in many TV productions. Charles W. Fries, considered the "godfather" of the television movie, was the father of editor Thomas Fries (father of actress Brooke Fries) and producers Butch, Christopher, and Jon Fries. Dick Van Patten is the brother of actress Joyce Van Patten, the half brother of Timothy Van Patten, and the father of James, Vincent, and Nels Van Patten. Grant Tinker cofounded MTM with his former wife Mary Tyler Moore and is the father of director Mark and writer John Tinker. Aaron Spelling cast his daughter Tori in *Beverly Hills, 90210;* son Randy Spelling is also an aspiring actor. Telly Savalas cast his brother George on *Kojak;* his son Nick is also an actor. (Telly is also the godfather of Jennifer Aniston.) Steven Bochco has cast his wife, sister, and brother-in-law in many of his shows: "'Bochco,'" he says good-naturedly, "is Polish for 'nepotism.'" His son Jesse now co-produces *NYPD Blue*. Famous husband-

and-wife creative teams include Carol Burnett and producer Joe Hamilton, Elizabeth Montgomery and *Bewitched* director William Asher, Mary Tyler Moore and Grant Tinker, Lucille Ball and actor-producer Desi Arnaz, Roseanne Barr and producers Bill Pentland and Tom Arnold. Producer Garry Marshall and director Penny Marshall and their sister Ronny Hallin are the children of *Mork & Mindy* producer Anthony Marshall. Garry hired Penny for *The Odd Couple* and *Laverne & Shirley*, and also hired Ronny as a coproducer. His children Lori, Scott, and Kathleen have all been cast in his productions, and niece Tracy is the stepdaughter of Rob Reiner. Ronny's daughters Penny Lee, Judy, and Wendy also work in film and television.

According to a 1993 industry survey, nepotism remains rife in the television business, causing bitter grumbling in the ranks.[14] But the practice does have partisans. Comedian Joan Rivers defended her daughter, who now has her own television career, against a charge of nepotism. "I feel very sorry for Melissa because she's very good at what she does . . . and somebody said to her the other day, 'You're just there because of your mother.' It's so mean." Asked, "Do you believe in nepotism?" Rivers replied, "Yes, I believe totally in nepotism. I believe charity begins at home. I believe you take care of your own first. I believe that blood is thicker than water. I believe that when you're down and out, who takes you in? It's all cliches—and it's all true."[15] In like spirit, comedian Eddie Murphy explained why he had signed his stepfather as a tour promoter and put his brothers in charge of his merchandising companies: "The people that are related to me are as competent or more competent than anybody else that I'm going to work with and I know my best interests are at heart." Murphy added, "I've always wanted to get my family more involved in the business side of my career, because nepotism isn't a thing that's practiced enough among blacks."

SPORTS

Family ties increasingly permeate sports and sports-related professions. In baseball, the number of father-son combinations has grown exponentially, from one in 1903 to thirty-six in 1945, sixty-six in 1965, and 134 in 1994.

According to *Psychology Today* (August 1985), the sons of former major-league players are fifty times more likely than nonfollowers to reach the major leagues, though their performance is no better than average.

The brother act is a major-league tradition—the Delahantys of Philadelphia, the Waners of Pittsburgh, pitchers Dizzy and Paul "Daffy" Dean, Rick and Gaylord Perry, Greg and Mike Maddux. Three Alou brothers played on the 1963 San Francisco Giants, and at one point it was an all-Alou outfield. Red Sox fans used to chant: "He's better than his brother Joe, Dominic DiMaggio!" (A third DiMaggio brother, Vince, played center field for the Pittsburgh Pirates.) This is to say nothing of the brother acts in which one brother predominated, including Henry and Tommie Aaron, Jason and Jeremy Giambi, Christy and Henry Matthewson, Cal and Billy Ripkin, Barry and Steve Larkin.

Better-known baseball families include the Alomars, the Armases (father Tony and sons Tony Jr. and Marcos), the Bells (Gus, his son Buddy, and his grandsons David and Mike), the Boones (Ray Boone, his son Bob, and Bob's sons Bret and Aaron), Yogi Berra and his son Dale, Dolph and Doug Camilli, Randy Hundley and his son Todd (both catchers), Julian Javier and his son Stan, the Macks (Connie and Earle), Hal and Brian McRae, Manny Mota and his sons Andy and Jose, Dick and Robb Nen, Tim Raines Sr. and Jr., Pete Rose Sr. and Jr., Diego Segui and his son David, George Sisler and his sons Dick and Dave. Yankee pitcher Mel Stottlemyre has coached one of his sons at the major-league level. Left fielder Barry Bonds is the son of Bobby Bonds and the godson of Willie Mays. Then there are the Tanners, Chuck and Bruce; Jose and Danny Tartabull, Mike and Tom Tresh, Dixie Walker and his sons Dixie Jr. and Harry, and Maury and Bump Wills.

No other sport shows this degree of father-son tradition, unless it is hockey. The legendary Gordie Howe (known as Mr. Hockey) is the father of players Mark and Marty Howe. In Canada, brothers Maurice and Henri Richard played for the Canadiens, Tony and Phil Esposito dominated the NHL at their respective positions, and Brett Hull followed in the footsteps of his father, Bobby, and uncle Dennis, both of whom played for the Chicago Blackhawks. Now there is Eric Lindros and his brother Brett, Keith and Wayne Primeau, and Claude and Jocelyn Lemieux.

In football, NFL quarterback Peyton Manning is the son of longtime

New Orleans Saints quarterback Archie Manning; his younger brother Eli quarterbacked for Ole Miss. Much attention was paid to the career of Walter Payton's son Jarrett Payton. Now the focus is on Kellen Winslow Jr., the son of San Diego Chargers' Kellen Winslow. There are also twins Ronde and Tiki Barber and father-son quarterbacks Bob and Brian Griese.

Basketball's Kobe Bryant, the son of former NBA player Joe "Jellybean" Bryant, jumped directly from high school to the Los Angeles Lakers. Orlando Magic's Grant Hill is the son of Calvin Hill, a star receiver for football's Dallas Cowboys. Hall of Famer Rick Barry saw three of his sons, Drew, Jon, and Brent, follow him to the NBA. Arizona's Luke Walton, Princeton's Nate Walton, and San Diego's Chris Walton are all the sons of Bruins great Bill Walton. Natalie Williams, who plays for the Utah Starzz of the Women's NBA, is a daughter of NBA journeyman Nate Williams. And when it comes to coaching, an essentially intellectual exercise that can be taught, father-and-son acts are common, especially in college basketball. Tom Penders and his son Tom Jr. coached together at both Rhode Island and George Washington Universities. Bobby Knight hired his son Pat—who played guard for Indiana from 1991 to 1995—as an assistant coach for IU in 1998. Rhode Island University's Jim Harrick brought his son Jim Jr. on board as an assistant in 1998. Harrick had previously played under his father at Pepperdine from 1984 to 1987. Valparaiso's Homer Drew also coached his son, star player Bryce Drew.

Boxing seems relatively immune to dynastic succession, but this has not stopped promoters from staging fights for the daughters of famous heavyweights. In February 1999 Laila Ali, the twenty-one-year-old daughter of former heavyweight champion Muhammad Ali, announced her intention to enter the world of women's professional boxing. A few months later, Jacqui Frazier-Lyde, the thirty-eight-year-old daughter of Muhammad Ali's old rival Joe Frazier, declared her intention to carry that rivalry into a new generation by becoming a boxer herself.[16]

In auto racing, an equipment-intensive sport with a high financial barrier to entry, it pays to have family connections. The most famous racing family are the Andrettis: Mario, his sons Jeff and Michael, and nephew John. The Earnhardts are the first family to have three generations win NASCAR racing championships. The Pettys are a four-generation racing dynasty. Other prominent NASCAR families include the Allisons, Bakers, Jarretts, and Burtons. (NASCAR itself is a family enterprise: chairman Bill France Jr. inherited the business from his father and will soon pass the reins to his children Brian and Lesa France Kennedy.) Father-son traditions also appear among race car machinists.

The insular world of sports broadcasting has two main dynasties: the Carays (Harry Caray, his son Skip, and grandson Chip) and the Alberts (brothers Marv, Al, and Steve, and Marv's son Kenny). According to *Sports Illustrated,* the Carays and Alberts "have made nepotism so cool that there are, at last count, 13 different father-and-son combinations in the business, not to mention a few brother acts." Other broadcasting families include Marty and Thom Brennaman, Jay Randolph Sr. and Jr., Gary and Trey Bender, Bob and Dave Neal, Ernie Johnson Sr. and Jr., Al and Wally Shaver, Joe and Steve Garagiola, Will and Sean McDonough, Harry and Todd Kalas, and Joe and the late Jack Buck. Reporter Steve Wulf advances several reasons for the boom, the most obvious being nepotism: "In many cases, fathers did open doors for their kids." But as he is quick to point out, this favoritism was not bestowed unworthily: "the quality of the second generation is almost as impressive as the quantity." Besides, in the words of Skip Caray, nepotism "gets you only so far in this business."[17]

THE PROFESSIONS

Access to professional life in this country used to be exclusively through family ties or the patronage of established figures. (John Adams himself advised an ambitious young lawyer to cultivate the patronage of the leading lawyers in Massachusetts.) Since World War II, such access has been increasingly meritocratic and based on professional degrees. Yet here, too, family traditions appear to be making a comeback.

Banking, once dominated by family-owned institutions, has for the most part yielded to rational bureaucratic reform. But a handful of family-owned banks continue to thrive, like Boston Bancorp and its subsidiary South Boston Savings, which openly practice nepotism. Medicine and law have also been careers in which children tend to follow their parents. In the eighteenth and nineteenth centuries, American medicine was dominated by Cushings and Sturgises in Boston and the family of Benjamin Rush in Philadelphia, and many law firms were family partnerships that passed from father to son. Though both professions have become more meritocratic, the rising number of women in both fields has led to a surge in professional marriages. The offspring of these marriages will undoubtedly enjoy advantages in competing for access and resources. (In 1988, a study found that children of doctors are 14 percent more likely to be admitted to medical school than nonsuccessors, though they performed no better on average.)[18]

The military in every country is known for its familial traditions. Douglas MacArthur's father was also a general, who arranged for his son to serve as an aide to President Theodore Roosevelt. George S. Patton descended from a distinguished military family—Pattons had fought in every American war since the Revolution—and his son George S. Patton IV also went to West Point and became a general in turn. There are many more examples, too numerous to list.[19] Since the admission of women in large numbers, the rising number of military marriages suggests a likely increase in successors in the next generation. Coverage of the 2003 war in Iraq reflected this new reality with profiles of various multigenerational families serving together in the Gulf.

Religious pulpits have often been handed from father to son. The Mathers of Boston and the Muhlenbergs of Pennsylvania (who founded the Lutheran Church in America) were two of this country's most important religious dynasties. This tradition continues today, especially in the nation's black churches, where the most famous example was the Reverend Martin Luther King Jr., son of an influential Baptist preacher. More recently, both the children of Billy Graham have entered the family business: Franklin Graham officiated at the inauguration of George W. Bush, and Anne Graham Lotz has her own ministry.

Architecture is not notably a family business, but the sons of Chinese architect I. M. Pei work for their father and continue his tradition. According to the *Wall Street Journal*, "The Pei name has helped the brothers land world-class commissions in China, Indonesia, and Singapore."

Fashion is another business where an established brand name is a vital asset, and most of the great European houses—particularly the Italian ones like Gucci and Prada—are long-established family businesses. Even in this country, a new generation of designers is using the family name to launch careers, including Gaby Karan, Lulu Johnson, Andy Spade, Jade Jagger, Alexandra Von Furstenberg and Stella McCartney—who has cleverly parlayed her father's fame into a blizzard of publicity for the launch of her own line of clothes and retail outlets. Ralph Lauren is also a closely held family business. Meanwhile, thirteen-year-old model Anna Cleveland, who is the daughter of '70s legend Pat Cleveland, recently signed with Donald Trump's T Management agency.

Particularly hard to break into is the small, exclusive world of golf course design. The leading designer today is Tom Fazio, who apprenticed under his uncle George Fazio, a top designer of the 1960s and 1970s. Other leading figures include Robert Trent Jones Jr. and Rees Jones, sons of Robert Trent Jones Sr., the dominant designer of the fifties and sixties. Pete Dye is a self-made man, but his brother Roy, wife Alice, son Perry, and other Dyes now have golf course designs to their credit. Retired pro Jack Nicklaus is now a prominent and highly paid golf course designer who has gone into business with his son Jack Nicklaus II. There are also numerous regional family dynasties, here and abroad, including the Bells of Louisiana, the Gordons on the East Coast, the Hawtrees of England, the Mapleses of North Carolina, the Maxwells of the Midwest, the Packards of Chicago, and the (abroad) Parks of Scotland.[20]

Journalism also has its share of high-profile successors, including Chris Wallace, Andrew Rosenthal, James Reston Jr., Chris Buckley, Joel Brinkley, Steve and Tim Forbes, and Andrea Koppel. John Moyers is the director of the "public interest" website TomPaine.com, which is supported by a foundation chaired by his father, Bill Moyers. Many successors are admired figures in their own right, like Mark Abel at the *San Francisco Chronicle*, or the late Michael Kelly, son of a *Washington Daily News* reporter. In broadcast news, there are weathermen Frank and Storm Field. A special subset are the offspring of neoconservative writers and intellectuals, including John Podhoretz, Bill Kristol, Daniel Wattenberg, Jonah Goldberg, and Joshua Gilder.

But this is merely the tip of the iceberg: as any working journalist will tell you, daily newspapers all over the country are rife with nepotism. Not only that, the inbreeding tendencies common to most other professions are proceeding at a rapid rate. (ABC News correspondent Cokie Roberts, the ultimate Washington insider, is the daughter of Rep. Hale Boggs of Louisiana, sister of superlobbyist Thomas Boggs, and wife of *Times* reporter Steven V. Roberts.) According to *Editor & Publisher*, given the intensity and social isolation of newsroom life, dating and marriage are common among journalists. For every journalistic power couple, like Ben Bradlee and Sally Quinn of the *Washington Post* or Nicholas Kristof and Sheryl WuDunn of the *New York Times*, there are dozens of others that no one has heard of. The result has been a widespread modification of nepotism rules to accommodate the two-career family.[21]

Intellectual traditions have also been known to run in families, as a famous nineteenth-century study of "hereditary genius" by Francis Galton sought to demonstrate (Galton himself was the cousin of Charles Darwin). In the United States such traditions have been rarer, although in the eighteenth and nineteenth centuries—and well into the twentieth—they were common enough. The best-known cases are those of the Cabots and Lowells (and Jameses and Holmeses), who founded Harvard and other great cultural institutions of Boston. Since the grip of the WASP ascendancy was broken after World War II, college faculties have remained fairly meritocratic. Yet academic traditions do exist—think of the two Arthur Schlesingers, Sovietologist Richard Pipes and Middle East scholar Daniel Pipes, historians Christopher Lasch and Elisabeth Lasch-Quinn, David Rieff, son of Susan Sontag and Phillip Rieff, linguists William and Noam Chomsky, historians Philip and Eric Foner, sociologist Robert K. Merton and economist Robert C. Merton, critic Alfred Kazin and historian Michael Kazin, or historian Donald Kagan and historians Robert and Frederick Kagan. There are also Sean and Amy Wilentz (children of anthologist Elias Wilentz), American historians Robert and Matthew Dallek, Russia expert and author Matthew Brzezinski (nephew of Zbigniew Brzezinski), economists John Kenneth Galbraith and Jamie Galbraith, Alger and Tony Hiss, and black history scholars Herbert and Bettina Aptheker. The big development, however, is once again the massive increase in the number of academic couples over the last thirty years. Due to rising female employment, a series of legal challenges to nepotism rules were brought in the sixties and seventies, and in a remarkably short time they had been repealed in private colleges across the country. Many universities now actively recruit married couples with elaborate "partner preference" programs. By the early 1990s, nearly one-third of all full-time faculty members had spouses or partners who were also academics. In time, this may result in an increased proportion of successors in academic careers. Thus caste tendencies are at work even in this meritocratic sector.[22]

Nor are such tendencies confined to elite professions. The father-son tradition in labor unions continues, and in many cases it is impossible to get into a union unless you have a family connection. This may explain why the occasional scandals involving nepotism on the part of union leaders do not evoke much outrage from the rank and file. Frederick W. Devine, head of the Carpenters and Joiners of America, survived multiple federal investigations of nepotism and fiscal abuse; in 1996 he was finally dismissed on charges of corruption and favoritism to mobsters. Chicago Teamsters Local 714—with a peak membership of about eleven thousand—was run for decades by the family of William Hogan Sr., who founded the local in 1934 and left it to his son William Jr., who passed it to his own son Robert in 1999. Robert in turn appointed his uncle to a newly created position as the union's administrative director. (Defending the appointment, Hogan said, "the history of the union movement in the U.S. is that people take care of their children and their relatives.") According to the *Chicago Tribune*, "Hogan brothers, sons, nephews and cousins hold a variety of positions with the union." Meanwhile, in August 1996, James P. Hoffa Jr. ran for president of the International Brotherhood of Teamsters, the union his father led until his disappearance in 1975. The election was marked by bitter charges and countercharges of nepotism between Hoffa and incumbent president Ron Carey, who was said to have obtained jobs for many of his relatives, especially in Hollywood locals that serve the movie industry. (The results of that contested election were thrown out and a new one held in 1998, which Hoffa won.)

The prevalence of family ties in municipal police and fire departments is also well established. According to the *St. Louis Post-Dispatch*, four generations of Walshes have served as policemen since 1884, and three generations of Nienhauses have been firemen. (The Neinhauses are one of several firefighting clans—there are also Donovans and Pollihans—but they are the most numerous, with four brothers and a cousin currently active, and a sister married to another firefighter.) This pattern is widespread throughout the country. According to the *Detroit News*, "nepotism is common at police agencies throughout Metro Detroit." Thus, in Mount Clemens, police chief Donald Geary had hired three sons and a nephew; other departmental families included Sullivans, Browns, Kelloggs, Lemkes, and Lennons. Maj. Thomas Quisenberry, who has two brothers in the Warren police department, is descended from a family of police officers in County Cork, Ireland. Even in big-city departments the continuity of these traditions was brought home viscerally in the lists of dead firemen after the World Trade Center disaster.[23]

How did all these children and spouses and siblings get their jobs? Nepotism in the traditional sense cannot have been involved in more than a handful of cases. Yet at the same time, it obviously didn't happen by accident, and in all these areas there is a remarkable sameness in the accounts successors give about the process of succession: they grew up around the business and developed an early interest in it; their parents never pressured them, and encouraged them to pursue their own ambitions; doors were sometimes opened, and people often proved happy to do favors for the children of important and powerful colleagues; but once in the door, the successors had to prove themselves to a skeptical public. Moreover, psychologically, they often feel the need to go on proving themselves and are haunted by the fear that nothing they do will ever be good enough. For them, success is a question not just of meeting expectations but of exceeding them, and not once but again and again.

As long as the successors fulfill this prescription—instinctively following the three rules of meritocratic nepotism—they are forgiven for their advantages. But when they fail to meet those expectations, they are mercilessly hounded from the stage. The knowledge of this inevitability acts as a sobering influence. It tends to make them appraise their own talents more modestly, and work harder to ensure their acceptance. They bend over backwards not to seem spoiled or entitled. It also suggests that the open, meritocratic American system is not in any grave or serious danger from this phenomenon. While the castelike tendencies seen in earlier times and places are proceeding apace in our society, meritocratic values are too deeply ingrained to allow the formation of true occupational castes.

ACKNOWLEDGMENTS

Having been an editor for most of my professional life, I've been thanked many times for my role in the bookmaking process. Now it is my turn to do the thanking.

Betsy Lerner signed this book for Doubleday and encouraged me to make the transition from editor to author. My foremost debt of gratitude goes to her.

I owe an equal debt to Robert Levine: much more than a lawyer and agent, he is my very dear friend and trusted consigliere.

Time is the greatest luxury for any author to have, and I owe this gift of time to the indulgence of Doubleday's publisher, Steve Rubin, and editorial director, Bill Thomas, who not only extended my deadline but gave me a home as an editor. I also wish to thank my Doubleday colleagues Michael Palgon, Suzanne Herz, Jackie Everly-Warren, John Fontana, Kendra Harpster, Miriam Abramowitz, Rakesh Satyal, Claire Roberts, Louise Quayle, Bette Alexander, and Carol Lazare.

In particular, I have been privileged to come under the wing of Gerry Howard, my editor, colleague, and friend. His firm hand and steady guidance, deep intellectual seriousness, and sound commercial sense saved me from several near-derailments. Now it can truly be said that he is an editor's editor.

After I had sailed far enough out to sea to get thoroughly lost, Didi Goldenhar came to my rescue. She kept my eyes on the horizon and helped keep my chin above water. I can't possibly thank her enough. I am also indebted to Mark Oppenheimer, who provided valuable research assistance, as did Sonja Starr and Nicholas Reith. My brother Daniel Oscar Bellow made heroic contributions to this effort and in the process helped me to understand the real meaning of family enterprise. I hope to repay him in kind. Thanks also to those who read and commented on the proposal and earlier drafts, including Ruth and Roger Newton, Cynthia Stuart, Peter Dougherty, Norah Vincent, Peter Meyer, Jim Gollin, John Ekizian, Michael Lind, Steve Sailer, Jack Diggins, Robin Fox, Steven Pinker, Van Gosse, and John Gartner. I am grateful for the interest and advice of Daniel Yankelovich, Harriet Zuckerman, William Bowen, Allan Carlson, Robert Kaplan, Arthur Herman, Stephen Schwartz, and Francis Fukuyama. I would also like to mention Peter Edidin, Ben Cheever, Richard Pine, Rafe Sagalyn, Adam Hanft, Nelson Aldrich, Lewis Lapham, David Gordon, Gara LaMarche, Richard Brookhiser, Les Lenkowski, Susanna Hoffman, Tom Schactman and the staff at the Writers Room, Cris Rapp, Elly Davis, Paula Marsili, Dennis Kardon and Shelley Lewis, Carol Irving, Ronna Cook and Robert Patchen, and Julie and Paolo Cucchi.

I dedicated this book "to all my fathers," and some readers may be wondering what that means. Americans as a rule get only one father, but people in traditional societies have many: a genitor or biological father and a variety of "social" fathers including uncles, teachers, godfathers, masters, and mentors. I too have had many fathers, but three merit special acknowledgment: Saul Bellow, who gave me his name, his genes, and a legacy to live up to; Joseph Bedics, my stepfather, whose gentle instruction helped me to become a better husband, son, and father; and the late Erwin Glikes, who taught me my trade and showed by his example what it means to be an editor and publisher. I also wish to thank my mother, Sondra Bellow, who encouraged me from an early age to make a vocation of reading and writing.

The idea for this book was first suggested to me by my wife, Rachel Bellow. Although it took me twice as long as we both expected, at the moment of truth she came through for me, as always. Throughout this difficult process, she has been the first person I turned to, the one whose insights and advice I trusted most, and she is still the only woman in the world I've ever wanted to impress.

I began this history of nepotism with the perspective of a son, and finished with that of a father. To my daughters, Lily and Eden Bellow, I wish to say that your contributions to the writing of this book have been as real and important as anyone's, and that more than anyone else, this book has been written for you. It is my hope to make you proud and to transmit to you the passion for books and ideas that runs in both sides of your family. Here is one-half of your legacy: do with it whatever you choose.

NOTES

INTRODUCTION: THE NEW NEPOTISM—AND THE OLD

1. George W. Bush's victory over Texas governor Ann Richards, another old foe of his father's, had been seen in a similar light.

2. Andrew Sullivan, "All in the Family," *New York Times Magazine,* Sept. 3, 2000; Lars-Erik Nelson, "Legacy," *New York Review of Books,* Feb. 24, 2000; Hendrik Hertzberg, "Someday, All This Will Be Yours," *New Yorker,* June 14, 1999.

3. Assistant Attorney General Deborah Daniels is the sister of OMB director Mitchell E. Daniels Jr. Chuck James, also at Justice, is the son of the director of the Office of Personnel Management and a Labor Department official. White House political director Ken Mehlman is the brother of Assistant Commerce Secretary Bruce Mehlman. Deputy White House press secretary Scott McClellan is the brother of Mark McClellan, a member of the president's Council of Economic Advisers. The director of the Federal Trade Commission's Office of Policy Planning is married to a senior official in the U.S. trade representative's office. FCC commissioner Kevin Martin is married to Cathie Martin, an aide to Vice President Cheney. Justice William Rehnquist's daughter works at the Department of Health and Human Services. Dana Milbank, "In Appointments, Administration Leaves No Family Behind," *Washington Post,* Mar. 12, 2002.

4. Helen Thomas, "Bush Keeps It All in the Family," *Seattle Post Intelligencer,* Aug. 17, 2001; Andrew Sullivan, "Hot Heir," *New Republic,* Feb. 5, 2001.

5. Pelosi's brother Thomas D'Alessandro III also became mayor of Baltimore, and she married Paul F. Pelosi, the scion of another Catholic political family from San Francisco.

6. According to one scholar, twenty-one of our first thirty-six presidents can be linked by blood or marriage. In addition, of the ninety-one Supreme Court justices appointed from 1789 to 1957, almost 60 percent came from judicial or political families. All told, the American office-holding class prior to World War II comprised 165 families linked by forty-five identifiable kinship networks. Don M. Kurtz III, ed., *The American Political Family,* University Press of America (Lanham, Md.), 1993, 4–6, 99.

7. In a 1998 survey article, journalist Ronald Brownstein cited a surprisingly long list of successors in contemporary politics. "The Successor Generation: American Politics As a Family Business," *American Prospect,* Dec. 1998. See Postscript for more details.

8. ". . . If you must hire the sons, daughters, cousins etc. make sure they *do* learn their 'jobs'"; "be wary of prima donnas who arrive via nepotism"; "stop hiring relatives and friends, hire people who know what they're doing"; "it would be lovely if the influential people in our industry would hire the brightest and most hard-working young people, rather than just hire their own nephews and kids"; "this is truly a business of who you know, not what you know"; "stop hiring the children of friends"; "fewer relatives, less bullshit." Lane Michael Bloenbaum, "The Relationship Between the Permeability of the

Television Industry in Southern California and Academic Preparation for Careers in Television," Ph.D. dissertation, University of California, Los Angeles, 1993, 211–12.

9. Deborah Cooksey and Marilyn Easter, "*Q:* What Do You Call White Affirmative Action? *A:* Nepotism," *On the Issues,* summer 1996.

10. Matthew S. Goldberg, "Discrimination, Nepotism, and Long-Run Wage Differentials," *Quarterly Journal of Economics* 97 (1982): 307. Italics added. Derrick Bell, *Faces at the Bottom of the Well: The Permanence of Racism*, Basic Books (New York), 1992, 56. On racial and ethnic nepotism, see Pierre L. Van den Berghe, *The Ethnic Phenomenon*, Elsevier (New York), 1991; Tatu Vanhanen, *The Politics of Ethnic Nepotism: India As an Example,* Sterling Publishers (New Delhi), 1991; and Tatu Vanhanen, ed., *Ethnic Conflicts Explained by Ethnic Nepotism,* JAI Press (Stamford, Conn.), 1999.

11. See Michael Lind, *The Next American Nation: The New Nationalism and the Fourth American Revolution,* Free Press (New York), 1995; Charles Murray and Richard D. Herrnstein, *The Bell Curve: Intelligence and Class Structure in American Life,* Free Press (New York), 1994; Christopher Lasch, *The Revolt of the Elites and the Betrayal of Democracy,* Norton (New York), 1995; Mickey Kaus, *The End of Equality,* Basic Books (New York), 1992; Nicholas Lemann, *The Big Test: The Secret History of the American Meritocracy,* Farrar Straus and Giroux (New York), 1999. As Lasch explains, "Doctors used to marry nurses, lawyers and executives their secretaries. Now upper-middle-class men tend to marry women of their own class, business or professional associates with lucrative careers of their own." Lasch, *Revolt of the Elites,* 33.

1. WE'RE ALL GOODFELLAS NOW

1. Francis A. J. Ianni with Elizabeth Reuss-Ianni, *A Family Business: Kinship and Social Control in Organized Crime,* Russell Sage Foundation (New York), 1972, 16.

2. The capo's violence has a dual purpose: it creates fear and respect outside the family, and trust and loyalty within it. Many mafiosi began their careers with acts of conspicuous violence and subsequently relied upon their reputation as a man of strength and will. *"Basta la fama"* wrote one nineteenth-century observer—"Reputation is enough."

3. A child may have as many godparents as the parents can arrange. In Moche, a coastal Peruvian town studied by anthropologist Robert Brain, a man may have sixty or seventy *compadres,* any one of whom he can call on for aid in a crisis.

4. Judith Chubb, *The Mafia and Politics: The Italian State Under Siege,* Center for International Studies, Cornell University (Ithaca), 1989, 19–20.

5. Castellano set up his sons Paul Jr. and Joseph in the meat and poultry business and placed his son Philip in a Staten Island construction company with an uncanny ability to land big contracts in New York. He liked to boast that he had made all of his sons millionaires.

6. Gotti died of cancer, alone in his cell, in June 2002.

7. Ianni, *A Family Business,* 133. E. Digby Baltzell, *Puritan Boston and Quaker Philadelphia,* Free Press (New York), 1979, 46.

8. "If the real function of kinship is to affiliate individuals into a system of reciprocity and exchange, there seems to be no reason why the kinship relationship cannot be artificially produced . . . and why a nonbiological, extra-genealogical family unit and spirit cannot be engendered." Ianni, *A Family Business,* 165.

9. Maureen Dowd, "Beware Guys Named Junior," *New York Times*, Jan. 26, 2000.

10. John H. Davis, *Mafia Dynasty: The Rise and Fall of the Gambino Crime Family*, Harper Paperback (New York), 1994, 240.

2. FROM BIOLOGY TO CULTURE

1. Mary Maxwell, ed., *The Sociobiological Imagination*, SUNY Press (Albany), 1991, 18.

2. As Matt Ridley points out, everything alive is essentially a society of cooperating individuals. All living organisms are composed of millions or billions of cells whose very existence is impossible without all the others. The human body is a massive colony comprising millions of highly specialized cells united in a cooperating whole by intercellular nepotism. Each cell contains the whole genetic pattern, yet only sperm and egg cells get to reproduce.

3. Bert Holldobler and Edward O. Wilson, *The Ants*, Harvard University Press (Cambridge), 1990, 179.

4. P. W. Sherman, "Nepotism and the Evolution of Alarm Calls," *Science* 197 (1977): 1246–53; see also Raghavendra Gadagkar, *Survival Strategies: Cooperation and Conflict in Animal Societies*, Harvard University Press (Cambridge), 1997, 87–88, and Robert Wright, *The Moral Animal: The New Science of Evolutionary Psychology*, Pantheon (New York), 1994, 158.

5. Gadagkar, *Survival Strategies*, 107.

6. Sarah Blaffer Hrdy, *Mother Nature: A History of Mothers, Infants, and Natural Selection*, Pantheon (New York), 1999, xviii. Helen Fisher, " 'Wilson,' They said, 'You're All Wet!' " *New York Times*, Oct. 16, 1994.

7. Matt Ridley, *The Origins of Virtue; Human Instincts and the Evolution of Cooperation*, Viking (New York), 1997, 28.

8. In Williams's view, there was no need for altruism toward nonrelatives to result from a conscious intention: it could simply have emerged from ordinary competition among individuals who "decide" that by cooperating with others they may increase their own chances of genetic survival.

9. Other altruistic behaviors include adoption and surrogate parenting. Yet the overwhelming majority of such cases involve older siblings and other close relatives, including the probable father.

10. Hrdy, *Mother Nature*, 51.

11. Ibid., Some mammals cull their litters or may abandon them altogether to maximize reproductive efficiency; hamster mothers eat their rejected pups.

12. James Q. Wilson, *The Moral Sense*, Free Press (New York), 1993, 45, 23.

13. Robert Wright and Randy Cohen give a clear account of biochemical bonding in "The Absurdity of Family Love," *Slate*, Jan. 31, 1997.

14. Wright, *The Moral Animal*, 190. "Animals, including people, often execute evolutionary logic not via conscious calculation, but by following their feelings, which were designed as logic executers." These primitive "feelings" are rooted in the limbic region of the brain—the oldest portion and the one that humans share with other animals.

15. Ibid., 202.

16. Maxwell, *Sociobiological Imagination*, 18.

17. I am aware that the subject of incest and marriage is a vast and controversial af-

fair. I have no wish to take sides in the great debate between functionalists and structuralists. Whether incest represents (as Lévi-Strauss suggests) the human act of saying "no" to nature or (as Robin Fox contends) a way of saying "yes" does not affect our argument one way or the other.

18. Exceptions have been made for political reasons, as in Peru and ancient Egypt, which both practiced a dynastic form of brother-sister marriage. Many cultures also sanction borderline cases of incest. In some African societies a man may marry a woman and several of her nieces. Likewise in Tibet a man may marry a mother and her daughter, though the practice is forbidden in most other societies.

19. Claude Lévi-Strauss, *The Elementary Structures of Kinship*, rev. ed., Beacon Press (Boston), 1969, 39.

20. Carleton S. Coon, *The Hunting Peoples*, Little, Brown (Boston), 1971, 218.

21. One of the first anthropologists to notice this widespread peculiarity of primitive societies was Bronislaw Malinowski, who described the symbolic commerce in arm shells and necklaces that links the islands of the Trobriand archipelago in a system of ritualized exchanges. The gifts never stopped with one person for long but were kept in continual motion, and as with a chain letter, it was considered bad luck to break the cycle.

22. Marcel Mauss, *The Gift: Forms and Functions of Exchange in Archaic Societies*, trans. Ian Cunnison, W. W. Norton (New York), 1967.

3. CLAN, CASTE, AND TRIBE

1. Katheryn Gallant, "The Art of Stealing," *Brazzil*, Mar. 31, 1997, 10; John McBeth, "Family Firm: Muslim Governor Accused of 'Unparalleled' Nepotism," *Far Eastern Economic Review*, Sept. 2, 1993; Jenny Parris, "Greece's Papandreou Copies Predecessor: Gives Kin Top Jobs," *Wall Street Journal*, Oct. 15, 1993.

2. Ronald Wraith and Edgar Simpkins, "Nepotism and Bribery in West Africa," in Arnold J. Heidenheimer and Michael Johnston, eds., *Political Corruption: Concepts and Contexts Handbook*, Transaction (New Brunswick), 2002, 332, 346.

3. José Veloso Abueva, "The Contribution of Nepotism, Spoils, and Graft to Political Development," in Heidenheimer and Johnston, *Political Corruption*, 534. Stanislav Andreski, "Kleptocracy as a System of Government in Africa," in ibid., 352.

4. Human societies do not evolve or progress in any natural or necessary way. Societies adapt their kinship patterns "up" or "down" according to their needs, and the same society may pass through different types of kinship structure over time.

5. To reinforce the fiction that they are large families, people are forbidden to marry within their lineage or clan. The different clans that constitute the tribe therefore continue to exchange wives on the model of the simpler moiety system. While this pattern can become extremely complicated (as in the eight-class marriage system of Australian Aborigines), it also has considerable elegance. For while a unilineal system necessarily excludes a large number of genetic kin, these relatives may later be "recaptured" as spouses and in-laws.

6. There is a large matrilineal belt in Central and West Africa. Matrilineal societies are also found in southern India and among the Indian tribes of the southwestern United States. Matrilineal does not mean matriarchal: while women own property in these societies, it is men who inherit and manage it. Nevertheless, women in matrilineal societies have a good deal of personal freedom. Marital relationships are brittle and un-

stable; infidelity is frequent, and a woman may divorce her husband simply by putting his belongings outside the door. Given the resulting paternal uncertainty, nepotism tends to be directed more at nephews, whose biological relatedness to their maternal uncle is not in doubt. A man's nepotistic impulses are therefore divided between his own sons and the nephews who will inherit his property. Hence the traditional saying among the matrilineal Ashanti: "Your nephew is your enemy."

7. Henri Konan Bedie, Houphouët-Boigny's handpicked heir apparent, was from the president's Bauole tribe. Other African leaders who have surrounded themselves with fellow tribesmen include the late Samuel K. Doe of Liberia (Krahn), Mobutu Sese Seko of Zaire (Gbande), Daniel arap Moi of Kenya (Kalenjin), Paul Biya of Cameroon (the Beti, Barre, and Marehan clans), Hastings Kamuzu Banda of Matawi (Chiwe), Ibrahim Babangida of Nigeria (Muslims), and Jerry Rawlings of Ghana (Ewe). About 70 percent of Gen. Gnassinghe Eyadama's army in Togo were drawn from his Kabye tribe. George B. N. Ayittey, *Africa Betrayed,* St. Martin's Press (New York), 1992, 196.

8. Stanislav Andreski, "Kleptocracy as a System of Government in Africa," in Heidenheimer and Johnston, eds., *Political Corruption,* 353.

9. Eunuchs were considered prone to "female" vices such as jealousy and spite, and were also addicted to gambling. Confucius is supposed to have said: "These two can neither be taught nor controlled—palace wives and eunuchs."

10. Matt Ridley, *The Origins of Virtue: Human Instincts and the Evolution of Cooperation,* Viking (New York), 1997, 258–59.

11. One son of Deng's chaired the Chinese Federation for the Disabled and was previously involved in a failed state-owned company; another headed a Hong Kong–based construction company that has been implicated in corruption. One daughter was vice minister in charge of the State Science and Technology Commission; another was Deng's private secretary and has written a best-selling biography of her father. One son-in-law was director of the Armament Department, in charge of the enormous budgets used to buy weapons and equipment for the world's largest army; another ran a state corporation dealing in precious metals and chairs two Hong Kong property companies.

12. The *Mahabharata* is the story of a family feud between two groups of cousins, the Kauravas and Pandavas; the *Ramayana* centers on a woman's intrigues to secure succession for her son by displacing the son of an elder co-wife.

13. Irawati Karve, *Kinship Organization in India*, Asia Publishing House (New York), 1968, 138.

14. The caste system probably originated in the domination of indigenous Dravidian peoples by Aryans who invaded northern India in the second millennium B.C. In addition to a more technically advanced civilization, the Sanskrit-speaking Aryans brought with them the Vedic religion that became the basis of Hinduism, and their priestly class is the probable antecedent of the Hindu Brahmin caste. The ultimate origin of caste in a system of ethnic overlordship is reflected in the observation of one scholar that, even today, "a man's social status varies in inverse ratio to the width of his nose."

15. According to Irawati Karve, caste and tribe in India are almost interchangeable: "A caste of today . . . may have been a former tribal group. A group of tribes . . . may function like a caste." Even the self-governing nature of castes may be "a vestige of tribal organization." Karve, *Kinship Organization in India,* 15.

16. Despite the rigidity of the caste system, *jatis* were not necessarily fixed or lim-

ited in number. New *jatis* arose all the time. In ancient India, for example, as trade increased and towns and urban settlements arose, specialized crafts were monopolized by groups of families who intermarried and inhabited the same district; these guilds became new castes. Migrating peoples from elsewhere in Asia were integrated into the Hindu social structure by according them an occupational niche and a corresponding place in the ritual hierarchy. In addition, many castes are really occupational "clusters" that monopolize a range of skills, affording greater flexibility. By gradually substituting "higher" vocations for "lower" ones, a *jati* could improve its ritual status.

17. The ancient Hindu codes and epics are obsessively concerned with the threefold obligation Mauss identified as central to the gift economy: the obligation to give, the obligation to receive, and the obligation to repay. The *Mahabharata* itself is the story of "a tremendous potlatch" in which land, food, cattle, and other goods actually speak and express their desire to be given away, promising ample return. "Such economic theology is developed at great length in the rolling periods of the innumerable cantos," Mauss observes, "and neither the codes nor the epics ever tire of the subject." Marcel Mauss, *The Gift: Forms and Functions of Exchange in Archaic Societies,* trans. Ian Cunnison, W. W. Norton (New York), 1967, 55.

18. Nehru's sister Vijaya Lakshmi Pandit became the leading figure in India's foreign diplomacy and was later the first woman president of the UN General Assembly.

19. Sanjay was allowed to handpick at least a hundred of the party's three-hundred-odd nominees, increasing his parliamentary faction. Many noted the government's tendency to award lucrative contracts to Sanjay's friends while prosecuting his political enemies, and he was referred to in the press as Raj Kumar—Crown Prince.

20. Tatu Vanhanen has argued that ethnic solidarity is really a form of nepotism, since an ethnic group is really just "a very large extended family that inbreeds to some extent." "Communalism, casteism, nationalism, patriotism, racism, and regional solidarity are forms of nepotism adapted to large societies.... The term 'ethnic nepotism' can be used to cover this kind of nepotism at the level of extended kin groups." Tatu Vanhanen, *The Politics of Ethnic Nepotism: India as an Example,* Sterling Publishers (New Delhi), 1991, 11–12.

21. Most Indian parties are regional, and while many voters support the larger, national or seminational parties, these dominate the core of northern India—the relatively homogeneous Hindi heartland. Opposition parties are stronger at the periphery (the "three corners" of India) and represent minority group interests. In other words, support for regional parties corresponds to ethnic cleavages, and all significant separatist movements have been concentrated in these areas.

22. "The earthquake has shown how a nation weak in some things... has other strengths that will help surmount these grim days." Joseph Coleman, "Quake Can't Shake Caste System," Associated Press, Feb. 7, 2001. John F. Burns, "India's Extended Families Help Orphans of the Quake: A Source of Strength Amid Revealed Weakness," *New York Times,* Feb. 5, 2001.

23. Ved Mehta, *A Family Affair: India Under Three Prime Ministers,* Oxford University Press (New York), 1982, 144–45.

24. *News India and Times,* Dec. 27, 1996.

25. Barry Bearak, "Katni Journal: A Pox on Politicians, a Eunuch You Can Trust," *New York Times,* Jan. 19, 2001.

26. See especially Jack Goody, *The Development of the Family and Marriage in Europe,* Cambridge University Press (New York), 1983; *The East in the West,* Cambridge University Press (New York), 1996; *The European Family: An Historico-Anthropological Essay,* Blackwell Publishers (Oxford), 2000.

4. CLASSICAL NEPOTISM

1. The one instance where father-son succession occurs—the case of Gideon's son Abimelech—ends badly. Abimelech butchers seventy of his brothers and makes himself ruler of Israel, but is killed after an abortive reign characterized by rebellion and mass murder.

2. Most societies that still permit cousin marriage prefer the marriage of cross cousins (the children of a brother and a sister). Marriage between first cousins and also between uncles and nieces has long been a Jewish ideal. While such unions are illegal in most Western societies, the law of Rhode Island still exempts Jews from the prohibition against uncle-niece marriage.

3. God does make a compensating promise to Abraham: "But the slave-girl's son I will also make into a great nation, for he is your child too." Ishmael goes on to have twelve sons and through them becomes the father of the Arabs, who still regard Abraham as their ultimate ancestor.

4. Just as Abraham receives God's blessing as the father of a mighty nation, Sarah is recognized as the ultimate Jewish mother: "I will bless her, and she shall be a mother of nations; kings of people shall come from her" (Genesis 17:16b).

5. Later on, Esau tries to make up for his error by marrying one of Ishmael's daughters, but this is not an adequate solution, since Ishmael himself is not a product of patrilineal, or agnatic, endogamy, descended on both sides from Abraham's father.

6. As a result of Laban's deception, Jewish custom has the father-in-law lift the bride's veil to demonstrate to the groom that he is not being cheated.

7. Given the degree of paternal uncertainty in the earliest human societies, the offspring's bond with its mother's brother was probably stronger and more secure than its bond with the putative father. According to Robin Fox, uncles *precede* fathers in evolutionary time. Thus, Fox speculates, it is the avunculate, not (as Lévi-Strauss believed) the incest taboo, that is "the defining principle of humanity and culture." Robin Fox, *Reproduction and Succession: Studies in Anthropology, Law, and Society,* Transaction (New Brunswick), 1993, 229.

8. Joseph is one of several younger sons (including Abel, Isaac, Jacob, Moses, David, and Solomon) whom, as Paul Johnson has observed, "it seems the peculiar purpose of the Bible to exalt." Paul Johnson, *A History of the Jews,* Harper (New York), 1987, 24. Joseph is also the first in a long line of "court Jews" who used their position to benefit their kin and coreligionists. While Joseph used his ingenuity to help Pharoah enslave his own subjects, he "settled his father and his brothers, and gave them a possession in the land of Egypt, in the best of the land" (Genesis 47:11).

9. See Deuteronomy 28:62–63.

10. Salo Baron noted the rabbis' "vigorous insistence upon procreation . . . and their vehement injunctions against any waste of semen." Kevin MacDonald, *A People That Shall Dwell Alone: Judaism As a Group Evolutionary Strategy,* Praeger (Westport, Conn.), 1994, 36.

11. Moses also ended the practice of vicarious punishment—the sins of the father

were no longer to be visited upon the children: "Fathers may not be put to death for their sons, nor sons for fathers."

12. Deuteronomy 23:20 states, "Thou shalt not lend upon interest to thy brother."

13. MacDonald, *A People That Shall Dwell Alone,* 45.

14. Most scholars agree that the version of David's story in the book of Samuel was largely propaganda justifying his displacement of Saul.

15. Saul's clan remains active, however, and David later executes all of Saul's surviving sons. He spares only Jonathan's son Mephibosheth, a cringing cripple-footed boy whom he keeps in the palace, possibly as a hostage—presumably also so that no one can accuse him of expunging Saul's line.

16. Johnson, *A History of the Jews,* 57.

17. The following discussion is largely derived from Barry Strauss, *Fathers and Sons in Athens: Ideology and Society in the Era of the Peloponnesian War,* Princeton University Press (Princeton), 1993.

18. The toughness and integrity of Greek fighting units were due to their being based largely on kinship; a man is less likely to run from danger if it means leaving his father and brothers to face death alone.

19. Plato also warned in the *Republic* that in a democracy, young people lose respect for their elders, and fathers fear their sons.

20. Strauss, *Fathers and Sons in Athens,* 16.

21. Our modern word "tribe" derives from the Latin *tribus,* meaning a third part of the people. Each tribe contained ten *curiae,* and each *curia* contained ten *gentes.* The Roman *curia* was analogous to the Greek phratry, a military brotherhood composed of men from related families, inhabiting a common district, and probably bound by ties of intermarriage.

22. *Virtus* is the generative quality that a father passes on to his son, and it begets a natural ambition to equal his achievements.

23. Adoption was extremely common as a means of securing an heir or cementing an alliance among the Roman upper classes. Any scion of a noble house would do, but most families preferred a patrilineal relative.

24. Gaston Boissier, *Cicero and His Friends: A Study of Roman Society in the Time of Caesar,* G. P. Putnam's Sons (New York), 1925, 114.

25. The will was the keystone of the Roman system of private ownership and was intended to keep property in the lineage rather than reverting to the *gens.* The state monopoly on justice was another blow to the old clan-based system of private vengeance.

26. Ronald Syme, *The Roman Revolution,* Oxford University Press (London), 1960, 12. Caesar first married the daughter of Cinna, a close associate of Marius. When the Marians were overthrown by Sulla, he went into hiding; only the intercession of his mother's well-connected kinsmen saved his life. Caesar then married Sulla's granddaughter. After his mother caught the frivolous Pompeia in an adulterous intrigue, he divorced her and married Calpurnia, the daughter of the leading man in Rome. The family connections between the mothers of Calpurnia and Caesar suggest that the two women contrived this mutually advantageous match.

27. Ibid., 23.

28. The faction of Cato and Pompey was composed of four great families united by *amicitia* and marriage against Caesar and Crassus, who represented the interests of the

plebeians and the new monied class. Servilia was displeased by her son's adherence to Pompey and disapproved of his marriage to Porcia. Yet she ended up presiding as a kind of materfamilias over the anti-Caesarean faction, which included her stepbrother Cato, her sons Marcus and Decimus, her son-in-law Cassius, and other close relatives.

29. In addition to the Claudian alliance obtained through Livia, other matches linked Augustus to (Syme says "ensnared") the patrician houses of the Cornelii Scipiones, the Aemilii Lepidi, the Valerii, and the Fabii. Syme, *Roman Revolution,* 378–79.

30. Unmarried men and women were also forbidden to attend public entertainments and were limited in the amount of money they could receive as a legacy.

5. THE SON MADE PERFECT

1. For this and other details of the succeeding account, see Robert H. Eisenman, *James the Brother of Jesus: The Key to Unlocking the Secrets of Early Christianity and the Dead Sea Scrolls,* Viking (New York), 1997.

2. Henry Chadwick, *The Early Church,* Penguin (Harmondsworth), 1968, 17–23.

3. Jack Goody, *The Development of the Family and Marriage in Europe,* Cambridge University Press (New York), 1983, 93.

4. Jack Goody, *The European Family: An Historico-Anthropological Essay,* Blackwell (Malden, Mass.), 2000, 36.

5. According to Marcel Mauss, "Germanic civilization . . . remained esentially feudal and peasant. . . . In earlier times it had developed the potlatch and more particularly the system of gift exchange to an extreme degree." Marcel Mauss, *The Gift: Forms and Functions of Exchange in Archaic Societies*, trans. Ian Cunnison, W. W. Norton (New York), 1967, 59.

6. Arius (c. 318) taught that Jesus was a supernatural creature not quite human and not quite divine. Arianism was declared heretical by the church and disappeared in the seventh century.

7. Whether these royal wards should be considered foster sons or hostages is a matter of perspective. According to Marcel Mauss, the giving of hostages as the basis for an alliance is a survival of the tribal gift economy in the early medieval monarchy: "links, alliances and mutual assistance came into being by means of the pledge, the hostage and the feast or other acts of generosity." Mauss, *The Gift*, 59.

8. "A veritable stream of noblemen poured out from Austrasia, the core of Carolingian power, into the other parts of the Frankish west. These newcomers fused with the local families into a new aristocracy; and this in its turn moved into Bavaria and Italy and all the other newly-conquered territories." Heinrich Fichtenau, *The Carolingian Empire,* trans. Peter Munz, Blackwell (Oxford), 1957, 110.

9. The negative reciprocity of the feud is a corollary to the positive reciprocity of gift exchange, and it strongly marked the Germanic tribes. According to Peter Munz, "Many tribes are groups of clans who keep together in a larger unit because they habitually feud with one another." Charles's attempt to create a unified legal system was the first great step toward the achievement of a monopoly of justice by the state. After his death, however, the suppression of the feud tended to increase rather then lessen instability. "Rivalry and competition for the highest prize being thus impossible, the inhabitants of the kingdom were no longer kept together by the desire of some local magnates to win it. The consequent absence of civil war, paradoxical though this may seem, weak-

ened rather than strengthened the bonds of society." Peter Munz, *Life in the Age of Charlemagne*, Putnam (New York), 1969, 144–45.

10. "The best-served hero was he whose warriors were all joined to him either by the new, feudal relation of vassalage, or by the ancient tie of kinship—two equally binding ties which were ordinarily put on the same plane.... Devotion reached its highest fervor when the two solidarities were mingled, as happened... to Duke Begue whose thousand vassals were *trestous d'une parente*—'everyone of the same kin.'" Bloch, *Feudal Society*, 124.

11. Shakespeare is, as always, our best guide to this phenomenon. In *King Lear* he has the bastard son of Gloucester make the case:

Wherefore should I
Stand in the plague of custom, and permit
The curiosity of nations to deprive me,
For that I am some twelve or fourteen moon-shines
Lag of a brother? Why bastard? Wherefore base?
When my dimensions are as well compact,
My mind as generous, and my shape as true,
As honest madam's issue?

12. Georges Duby, *The Chivalrous Society*, trans. Cynthia Postan, University of California Press (Berkeley), 1977, 122.

13. W. O. Farnsworth, *Uncle and Nephew in the Old French Chansons de Geste*, Columbia University Press (New York), 1913, 61.

14. Even more revealing is the subplot involving Roland's feud with his stepfather Ganelon. As the poem begins, Charles has called a council to discuss sending an envoy to the Saracens. Roland mischievously nominates Ganelon to undertake the dangerous assignment. Ganelon swears vengeance, and uses his embassy with the Saracen king to plot the ambush of the Franks. For this he is later charged with treason, and the poem closes with his trial. There, Ganelon appears with thirty kinsmen: these "oath helpers" have come to make a show of solidarity, although they risk sharing Ganelon's punishment. Ganelon argues that he cannot be charged with treason, since he was following the dictates of a private feud. Therefore (per tribal custom) the outcome must be decided by judicial combat. Two men are chosen for a test of strength. When his champion is defeated, Ganelon is torn apart by horses and his kinsmen are hanged.

15. Robert H. Bates, *Prosperity and Violence: The Political Economy of Development*, Norton (New York), 2002, 62.

6. THE GOLDEN AGE OF NEPOTISM

1. So common was the fathering of children by Catholic priests that its survival is reflected in English usage well into the nineteenth century, to wit: "The only ones who did not call a priest 'Father' were his own children; they called him Uncle" (*Oxford English Dictionary*). *Merriam-Webster's Collegiate Dictionary* still lists, as a subordinate definition of "nephew," "illegitimate son of an ecclesiastic."

2. Innocent III (1198–1216), the second Conti pope, was made a cardinal by his uncle Clement III. Innocent expunged members of the rival Savelli family from various church offices and installed his own relatives. He was succeeded by the Savelli pope

Honorius IV, who restored his clan to power. His successor, Innocent's nephew Gregory IX, reinstated his Conti relatives.

3. Clement VI (1342–52) was a shameless nepotist who also pioneered the sale of indulgences. Boniface IX (1389–1404), an outstanding administrator, was also infamous for nepotism. Desperately in need of money, he openly sold offices to the highest bidder.

4. Richard B. Hilary, "The Nepotism of Pope Pius II, 1458–1464," *Catholic Historical Review* LXIV, no. 1 (Jan. 1978): 33–35.

5. When Vanozza grew too old for him, Borgia, then a fifty-eight-year-old cardinal, took up with sixteen-year-old Giulia Farnese. Forty years his junior, she was already married to the son of Borgia's cousin. His first act as pope would be to elevate Giulia's brother Alessandro. Called "the petticoat cardinal," he later became Paul III.

6. Michael Mallett, *The Borgias: The Rise and Fall of a Renaissance Dynasty,* Barnes & Noble (New York), 1969, 169.

7. In *Against the Current: Essays in the History of Ideas,* Viking (New York), 1980, Isaiah Berlin observed that many of the most successful nationalist leaders in history came "from outside the society they led, or at any rate from its edges, the outer marches." This outsider status helps explain their "fiery vision" and their exaggerated contempt—or admiration—for the societies they ultimately transformed. Berlin cited Napoleon, Stalin, Hitler, and Theodor Herzl as examples, and we might add to the list a figure like Alexander Hamilton. This notion (which also receives mention in Ron Rosenbaum's *Explaining Hitler: The Search for the Origins of His Evil,* HarperCollins [New York], 1992). sheds interesting light on their careers. The point we are making here is somewhat different: families that originate in marginal or backward areas where the church and state have not succeeded in breaking up the older clan-based solidarities have a distinct advantage in their host societies.

8. Theo Aronson, *The Golden Bees: The Story of the Bonapartes,* New York Graphic Society (Greenwich, Conn.), 1964, 3.

9. The genealogy on which Carlo's patent of nobility was based was crude and highly questionable. Carlo would invest a great deal of time and energy over the years refining and improving it.

10. Among the school's attractions was the promise of a dowry of three thousand francs for poor girls. Elisa spent eight years at the school until it was closed by the revolution, an event that helped to turn her brother into a reactionary. She never received the promised dowry.

11. Dorothy Carrington, *Napoleon and His Parents: On the Threshold of History,* Dutton (New York), 1990, 168.

12. R. F. Delderfield, *The Golden Millstones: Napoleon's Brothers and Sisters,* Harper & Row (New York), 1964, 5.

13. As Robespierre declared, "The country has the right to raise its children; it should not entrust this to the pride of families or to the prejudices of particular individuals, which always nourish aristocracy and domestic federalism." Love of country was higher than filial love; indeed "the family of French legislators is the country." Lynn Hunt, *The Family Romance of the French Revolution,* University of California Press (Berkeley), 1992, 67, 79.

14. Natalie Zemon Davis, *The Gift in Sixteenth Century France,* University of Wisconsin Press (Madison), 2000, 15. In Rabelais's *Gargantua,* Panurge delivers a long en-

comium to the gift economy, including a comic attack on the justice of canceling debts: "For Nature has created man for no other purpose but to lend and borrow."

15. In 1802, Napoleon sent Leclerc to put down a slave revolt on Santo Domingo, where he died of yellow fever. Pauline returned a widow and within a year had married the Italian prince Camillo Borghese.

16. Carrington, *Napoleon and His Parents,* 130, 190.

17. "During the early period of Mongol domination in Iraq, the Jew Sa'd ad-Daula filled his administration with 'his brothers, kinsmen, and coreligionists.'... His fall resulted in violence directed at the entire Jewish community... [W]hen Samuel Oppenheimer (1630–1703) obtained the right to settle in Vienna, he brought with him around 100 other Jewish families who were directly dependent on him." Kevin MacDonald, *A People That Shall Dwell Alone: Judaism As a Group Evolutionary Strategy,* Praeger (Westport, Conn.), 1994, 144.

18. "Parental investment is the cost of reproduction in terms of time, food, defense of offspring, teaching of offspring; et cetera.... Competition for resources tends to result in animals having fewer and more widely spaced offspring, prolonged parental care, longer life span, and lower mortality rates at all stages of the life span. In humans, the prototypical high-investment pattern is also associated with high intelligence, delay of sexual maturation, stable pair bonding, and high levels of parental involvement with children." Ibid., 199–200.

19. Amos Elon, *Founder: A Portrait of the First Rothschild and His Time,* Viking (New York), 1996, 98.

20. Ibid., 103.

21. Ibid., 110.

22. Chaim Bermant, *The Cousinhood,* Macmillan (New York), 1971, 1.

23. Wellington's army in Portugal had run out of money and the British seemed unable to supply it. Nathan not only sold the needed bullion to the government but used his family network to deliver it by way of France itself. He arranged for a fleet of ships to run the French blockade and deliver the gold to Jacob, who brought it to Paris, dressed as a woman to deceive the police. Jacob converted the English guineas into bills on Spanish and Portugese banks. These in turn were smuggled to Wellington. It is said that between 1811 and 1815, the Rothschilds transferred over 20 million pounds to Wellington and other English allies.

24. Niall Ferguson, *The World's Banker: The History of the House of Rothschild,* Weidenfeld & Nicholson (London), 1998, 137.

25. European financial markets plunged on the news of Nathan's death. Nathan may have felt that being regarded as a dark financial wizard was good for business, but this reputation would in time fuel popular fears of an international Jewish conspiracy.

26. Ferguson, *The World's Banker,* 328.

7. COLONIAL NEPOTISM

1. The marriage of stepsiblings Maria Cotton and Increase Mather produced the eminent preacher Cotton Mather, who shared a Boston pulpit with his father for forty years. A series of strategic marriages joined the Mather-Cotton dynasty to other leading families, including the Dudleys, Bradstreets, Winthrops, and Sewalls. The Mather dy-

nasty died out in Boston at the time of the Revolution but the family moved on to other states. The leading role played by the Mathers over the next three hundred years in religion, education, business, and government is unsurpassed by that of any other American family. E. Digby Baltzell, *Puritan Boston and Quaker Philadelphia,* Free Press (New York), 1979, Appendix III, 508–509.

2. Since families had been ordained by God as the basis of society, no one in the colony could be without one. Single persons were viewed as prone to moral turpitude, and laws were passed requiring them either to establish their own artificial families by taking on servants and boarders or to enter service in someone else's household.

3. In a sermon called "A Father's Resolutions," Cotton Mather waxed lyrical on the duties of parents toward children: "Parents, Oh! how much ought you to be continually devising for the good of your *children*! Often devise how to make them 'wise children'; how to give them a desirable education, an education that may render them desirable; how to render them lovely and polite, and serviceable in their generation. . . . There is a world of good that you have to do for them. You are without the natural feelings of humanity if you are not in a continual agony to do for them all the good that ever you can."

4. Edmund S. Morgan, *The Puritan Family: Religion and Domestic Relations in Seventeenth-Century New England,* Harper & Row (New York), 1966, 168–69.

5. Since the Puritans also adhered to the Christian injunction against the marriage of cousins, the prospect of remarriage could be difficult. Thus for Puritans (unlike the biblical patriarchs) marriage with a deceased wife's sister or cousin would be incest.

6. Morgan, *The Puritan Family,* 174.

7. Ibid., 185, 186.

8. "Surprising though it may seem," Philip Greven concludes, "political independence in 1776 might have been rooted in the very character of many . . . American families." Philip J. Greven Jr., *Four Generations: Population, Land, and Family in Colonial Andover, Massachusetts,* Cornell University Press (Ithaca), 1970, 282.

9. Randolph's rise to fortune was "spectacular," writes Nathan Schachner. "Whatever he touched turned literally to gold. . . . Nor was he less successful in his family, nine of whom survived the fevers and the accidents of childhood to produce in turn the most bewilderingly abundant progeny that even Virginia, notable in such matters, has ever seen." Nathan Schachner, *Thomas Jefferson: A Biography,* T. Yoseloff (New York), 1957, 7.

10. It was Richard Henry Lee—whose maiden speech in the House of Burgesses in 1759 had called for the emancipation of the slaves—who introduced a resolution in Congress on July 2, 1776, that the colonies should declare their independence. Later he proposed a series of constitutional safeguards that became the Bill of Rights. His cousin Lighthorse Harry Lee was one of Washington's greatest generals. Harry's son Robert E. Lee, the flower of the Virginia aristocracy, is one of the most admired men in American history.

11. David Hackett Fischer, *Albion's Seed: Four British Folkways in America,* Oxford University Press (New York), 1989, 222. John Randolph's advice, recorded in the diary of George Fisher, is cited in Rhys Isaac, *The Transformation of Virginia, 1740–1790,* University of North Carolina Press (Chapel Hill), 1982, 145. Isaac gives a thorough description of the structure of patriarchal authority in colonial Virginia.

12. "As early as 1660, every seat on the Council was filled by members of five related connections. As late as 1775, every member of that august body was descended from a councilor who had served in 1660." Ibid., 222.

13. Ibid., 318.

14. "The only safe way of perpetuating pure slavery is systematically to split up all kin groups among slaves and to prevent their reproduction." Pierre L. Van den Berghe, *The Ethnic Phenomenon,* Elsevier (New York), 1981, 122.

15. Gordon Wood, *The Radicalism of the American Revolution,* Alfred A. Knopf (New York), 1991, 88.

16. Fischer, *Albion's Seed,* p. 325

17. Stephen Hess, *America's Political Dynasties,* Transaction (New Brunswick), 1997, 58–59.

18. Fischer, *Albion's Seed,* 430.

19. Franklin and his brother eventually reconciled, and on James's death, in 1735, he asked Ben to raise his son Jemmy and teach him the printer's trade. Franklin took his nephew on as an apprentice, but their relationship turned out to be nearly a repeat of Franklin's with James.

20. Franklin was extremely bitter when the British removed him from this post in 1774. The Continental Congress promptly reappointed him to the position, which he held until he sailed for France in 1776.

21. Paul Leicester Ford, *The Many-Sided Franklin,* Century Co. (New York), 1899, 36.

22. "All the landed gentry of western Massachusetts were bound together by blood or marriage. The members of six families of Hampshire County held two-thirds of all county offices—creating what has been called 'a county-wide family magistracy.' The half dozen families that dominated the eighteenth-century South Carolina council were linked in a similar way.... In Virginia seats on the grand juries as well as on the vestries and county courts fell to the same families year after year." Wood, *Radicalism,* 44–48.

23. "The colonists are yet but Babes that cannot subsist but on the Breasts, and thro' the Protection of their Mother Country," one colonist had written in 1741, echoing a pervasive contemporary theme. The British used the same vocabulary, calling the colonists "children planted by our Care, nourished up by our Indulgence... [and] protected by our Arms." Michael Paul Rogin, *Fathers and Children: Andrew Jackson and the Subjugation of the American Indian,* Alfred A. Knopf (New York) 1975, 22–23; Harlow Giles Unger, *John Hancock: Merchant King and American Patriot,* John Wiley & Sons (New York), 2000, 81; Wood, *Radicalism,* 165. See also Jay Fliegelman, *Prodigals and Pilgrims: The American Revolution Against Patriarchal Authority, 1750–1800,* Cambridge University Press (New York), 1982.

24. Rogin, *Fathers and Children,* 25.

25. Hutchinson's brother was justice of the Common Pleas, his son was judge of Probate, his wife's brother-in-law Andrew Oliver was lieutenant governor, and Chief Justice Peter Oliver was the father of his daughter's husband.

26. Sam Adams—a prodigal son who bankrupted the brewery his father had left him and embezzled public funds after his father's friends got him appointed tax collector—left his son nothing, declaring that no one should expect any "advantage in point of Promotion from his Connections with men." Wood, *Radicalism,* 205.

27. Ibid., 200–201.

28. Highly influential in spreading this gospel of enlightened universalism was the institution of freemasonry. The masons were a secret fraternal organization to which

many of the American founders belonged. Gordon Wood calls masonry "a surrogate religion" that promoted the ideals of Christian brotherhood without sectarianism. According to DeWitt Clinton, masonry created an "artificial consanguinity" that had "as much force and effect, as the natural relationship of blood."

29. Wood, *Radicalism*, 147.

8. THE CITY OF BROTHERLY LOVE

1. Gordon Wood, *The Radicalism of the American Revolution,* Alfred A. Knopf (New York), 1991, 290.

2. Washington used the phrase most famously in his emotional farewell to his troops: "Who, that was not a witness, could imagine that the most violent local prejudices would cease so soon; and that men, who came from different parts of the continent, strongly disposed by the habits of education to despise and quarrel with one another, would instantly become but one patriotic band of brothers?"

3. Other Washington friends and neighbors included the Monroe and Marshall families; both would contribute great figures to American history. Farther neighbors included the Masons, Harrisons, Randolphs, Calverts, Lees, and other families, all part of the dense web of kinship, social life, and business interests uniting the Virginia gentry.

4. Mark J. Rozell, William D. Pederson, and Frank J. Williams, eds., *George Washington and the Origins of the American Presidency,* Praeger (Westport), 2000, 88.

5. "Few have experienced such care and attention from real parents as I have done," he wrote from college in New York. Miriam Anne Bourne, *First Family: George Washington and His Intimate Relations,* W. W. Norton (New York), 1982, 67.

6. John C. Fitzpatrick, ed., *The Writings of George Washington from the Original Manuscript Sources 1745–1799,* Government Printing Office (Washington, D.C.), 1939, 30:366.

7. J. J. Perling, *Presidents' Sons: The Prestige of Name in a Democracy,* Odyssey Press (New York), 1947, 449.

8. Ibid., 355.

9. Mark J. Rozell, et al., eds., *George Washington,* 89.

10. Fitzpatrick, ed., *Writings of George Washington,* 30:238.

11. A nineteenth-century historian said that New York, like Gaul, was divided in three parts—the Clintons, the Livingstons, and the Schuylers. "The Clintons had *power,* the Livingstons had *numbers,* the Schuylers had *Hamilton.*"

12. George Clinton had become governor in 1777 during the Revolution and retained the post for twenty-seven years. His nephew DeWitt Clinton started as his secretary, became a U.S. senator, then mayor of New York.

13. Hypergamy means "marrying up" above one's class. Gore Vidal, "The Four Generations of the Adams Family," *United States,* Random House (New York), 1993, 645.

14. Ibid., 649.

15. Perling, *Presidents' Sons,* 4.

16. Ibid., 5.

17. In a famous letter to his oldest son, Adams wrote: "You come into the world with advantages which will disgrace you if your success is mediocre. And if you do not rise to the head not only of your Profession, but of your Country, it will be owing to

your own Laziness, Slovenliness, and Obstinacy." Paul C. Nagel, *Descent from Glory: Four Generations of the John Adams Family,* Oxford University Press (New York), 1983, 53.

18. Stephen Hess, *America's Political Families,* Transaction (New Brunswick), 1987, 24.

19. Sidney Aronson, *Status and Kinship in the Higher Civil Service: Standards of Selection in the Administrations of John Adams, Thomas Jefferson, and Andrew Jackson,* Harvard University Press (Cambridge), 1964, 4, 5.

20. Perling, *Presidents' Sons,* 13.

21. Pickering himself was one of the greatest nepotists in the federal government. In 1797, as secretary of state, he sent his son as secretary to the American ambassador in Lisbon, and in 1799 he persuaded the ambassador to London to give his son the same position. For another son, he obtained a naval commission. He appointed a nephew consul at Hamburg, then London, gave his brother and nephew government shipping business, and obtained a naval command for another nephew. Other leading federalists—including Knox, Wolcott, McHenry, Rush, and Boudinot—all did as much for their relatives. White, *The Federalists,* 281–84.

22. Nagel, *Descent from Glory,* 120.

23. Ibid., 79.

24. Ibid., 77.

25. David F. Musto, "The Adams Family Myth," in Don M. Kurtz II, ed., *The American Political Family,* University Press of America (Lanham, Md.), 1993, 23.

26. Marie Kimball, *Jefferson: The Scene of Europe, 1784–1789,* Coward-McCann (New York), 1950, 254.

27. Aronson, *Status and Kinship,* 227. "From Paris, Lyon, and then Geneva, Jefferson sent his alter ego across the Alps to Turin, Milan, and Venice, then through the ancient cities of Verona, Padua, Bologna, and on to Rome, where he remained for more than three months. From all these places Short delighted the heart of his patron by sending long accounts of everything that would interest him, from the making of wine and macaroni, to the glories of Rome, of which he had so long dreamed but which he was never to see. Now he viewed it all through the eyes of this young man, whom he had taught to see and think as he did, and who was more satisfactory than a son." Kimball, *Jefferson,* 280.

28. Nathan Schachner, *Thomas Jefferson: A Biography,* Thomas Yoseloff (New York), 1957, 388.

29. During the election of 1800 a pamphlet called *The Family Compact of Connecticut* exposed the intimate connections between the state's political, commercial, and religious leaders. The pamphlet named Timothy Dwight (president of Yale), "generally known as the Pope"; Dwight's brother-in-law Senator James Hillhouse; his brother Theodore Dwight, a candidate for Congress; Representative Morris, married to Dwight's sister; Rep. Hosmer, related by marriage to Hillhouse; Treasury secretary Oliver Wolcott; Rep. Chauncy Goodrich, married to Wolcott's sister; Chauncy's brother Elizur Goodrich; Hillhouse's cousin Rep. Roger Griswold, and several others.

30. Aronson, *Status and Kinship,* 141.

31. William Nisbet Chambers, *Political Parties in a New Nation: The American Experience, 1776–1809,* Oxford University Press (New York), 1963, 170.

32. Quoted in Adrienne Koch, *Jefferson and Madison: The Great Collaboration*, Alfred A. Knopf (New York), 1950, 223–24.

33. Adams's kinship cluster included J. Q. Adams, in-laws Joshua and Thomas Johnson, and William Cranch. Cranch was related to Attorney General Theophilus Parsons and ambassador to France Elbridge Gerry—all of whom married members of the Greenleaf family. Boudinot, director of the mint, brought in his niece's husband, Benjamin Rush; his nephew Lucius Horatio Stockton; and William Griffith, who had married Boudinot's niece. Rush was appointed over forty other applicants. Chief Justice John Marshall's brother James was made a judge, as were his brothers-in-law George Keith Taylor and William McClung. Secretary of War Roger Griswold and Treasury secretary Oliver Wolcott were first cousins and relatives of Chief Justice Oliver Ellsworth, later minister to France. Jefferson's cluster was based mainly on the Randolphs, including Edmund Randolph, John Randolph, and his uncle Thomas Tudor Tucker. Aronson, *Status and Kinship*, 148–51.

34. Hess, *America's Political Dynasties*, 110–11. The Livingstons were disciplined dynasts: according to Hess, five Livingston daughters were married to congressmen in one generation. Jefferson's party also drew on the support of the dynastic Clinton family, which controlled virtually all of New York's patronage appointments. In 1803 DeWitt Clinton, then a U.S. senator and a solid supporter of Jefferson, proposed himself for mayor of New York, which was then an appointive position; his petition was successful.

35. Leonard D. White, *The Jeffersonians: A Study in Administrative History, 1801–1829*, Macmillan (New York), 1951, 366–67.

36. Nourse, a Virginian, was appointed to the Treasury Department in 1789 and remained there until removed by Jackson, in 1829. His son Maj. Charles J. Nourse became chief clerk of the War Department. His other sons Joseph, Michael, and John were all employed as clerks in their father's office.

37. "[M]ake up your mind . . . to come & enter sturdily on the public stage. I now know the characters on it, and assure you candidly you may be anything you please at home or abroad as soon as you shall make yourself known and possess yourself of American affairs." Schachner, *Thomas Jefferson*, 404.

38. Ibid., 880.

9. THE NINETEENTH CENTURY

1. Frederic Cople Jaher, *The Urban Establishment: Upper Strata in Boston, New York, Charleston, Chicago, and Los Angeles*, University of Illinois Press (Urbana), 1982, 39. "Her success in this legalized piracy was probably the greatest contribution of seaboard Massachusetts to the common cause." Samuel Eliot Morison, *The Maritime History of Massachusetts, 1783–1860*, Northeastern University Press (Boston), 1921, 29.

2. The position of supercargo seems to have been specially reserved for relatives in need of employment or business experience, probably because large sums of money were involved. See also Kenneth W. Porter, *The Jacksons and the Lees: Two Generations of Massachusetts Merchants, 1765–1844*, Harvard University Press (Cambridge), 1937.

3. Farmers and artisans favored cousin marriage, since it tied nephews and cousins to the family enterprise. Merchants preferred the capital-intensive strategy of sibling exchange. While this pattern had a tendency to dilute patriarchal authority, the children of

such marriages enjoyed greater freedom in career and marriage choices. This in turn enhanced the family's flexibility and its ability to exploit new opportunities.

4. Morison, *Maritime History*, 24. Higginson wrote, "To the Essex Junto, Jefferson himself seemed but a mutineering first mate, and his 'rights of man' but the black flag of a rebellious crew. They paid the penalty of their own aristocratic habits." Charles Warren, *Jacobin and Junto: Or, Early American Politics As Viewed in the Diary of Dr. Nathaniel Ames, 1758–1822*, Harvard University Press (Cambridge), 1931, 163–64 n. 3.

5. The first such charter was granted in 1784 for the Massachusetts Bank. By 1835, there were over sixty private banks in Rhode Island alone. Naomi Lamoreaux, "Banks, Kinship, and Economic Development: The New England Case," *Journal of Economic History* 46, no. 3 (Sept. 1986): 647–67.

6. Tamara K. Hareven, ed., *Family and Kin in Urban Communities, 1700–1930*, New Viewpoints/Franklin Watts (New York), 1977, 47.

7. Betty G. Farrell, *Elite Families: Class and Power in Nineteenth-Century Boston*, State University of New York Press (Albany), 1993, 30.

8. R. W. B. Lewis, *The Jameses: A Family Narrative*, Farrar, Straus and Giroux (New York), 1991, 200. Thanks to Ruth Newton for pointing this out.

9. The Higginson-Amory branch, descended from John the Rebel, were noted for their achievements in administration, law, and education. The Cabot-Jackson branch, founded by Francis Cabot Lowell, led the way in manufacturing and finance. Charles Lowell, the youngest son of the Old Judge, produced six children whose marriages further ramified the Lowell kinship network. The line he founded distinguished itself in the ministry, culture, and the arts.

10. According to Betty Farrell, the continuing importance of the brahmins in an era of corporate capitalism may be seen from their involvement in such twentieth-century industrial ventures as Bell Telephone, General Electric, U.S. Mining Co., and United Fruit. Brahmins and their relatives held over 50 percent of the stock in the monopoly telephone business, and various sons-in-law, cousins, and nephews held fully half the company's directorships even after it was reorganized under professional management as AT&T in the early twentieth century. Nor were the brahmins excluded from the new investment banking firms that took the place of the old family banks. While the 1905 Boston *Directory of Directors* lists only eighteen individuals by the name of Lowell, Jackson, Appleton, or Lawrence, there are at least 110 individuals of other names with connections to the Lawrence kin network alone.

11. When asked why he had killed so many McCoys, Devil Anse Hatfield replied, "A man has a right to defend his family."

12. Alexanders settled thickly in Catawba County, North Carolina: the census of 1790 listed three hundred nuclear families of the name. Other large clans—the Polks of Mecklenburg, the Calhouns of Long Cane, the Grahams of Yadkin, and the Crawfords of upper Georgia—settled in similar patterns.

13. Frederic Austin Ogg, *The Reign of Andrew Jackson: A Chronicle of the Frontier in Politics*, Yale University Press (New Haven), 1919, 6.

14. David Hackett Fischer, *Albion's Seed: Four British Folkways in America*, Oxford University Press (New York), 1989, 687, 690.

15. Much ink has been expended to justify Jackson's behavior in this matter, but Fischer views it as an instance of traditional bride capture. According to Fischer, two

types of abduction were then recognized: voluntary abduction, in which the bride consented, and involuntary abduction, in which she did not. The fact that Jackson's behavior did not outrage the local community suggests that he was acting out a familiar scenario.

16. Other controversies surrounding Jackson included his execution of "deserters," his unauthorized invasion and seizure of Florida, his putative ties with the conspirator Aaron Burr, and the killing of Indian women by his troops.

17. Lorman Ratner, *Andrew Jackson and His Tennessee Lieutenants: A Study in Political Culture,* Greenwood Press (Westport), 1997, 22–23.

18. Adams, also like his father, abhorred nepotism and refused to help his wife's relatives, who seemed "like locusts besieging the White House." Paul C. Nagel, *Descent from Glory: Four Generations of the John Adams Family,* Oxford University Press (New York), 1983, 153.

19. Michael Paul Rogin, *Fathers and Children: Andrew Jackson and the Subjugation of the American Indian,* Alfred A. Knopf (New York), 1975, 50.

20. In J. Q. Adams, the Puritan conscience mutated into the tradition of upper class reform that has produced some of our nation's greatest figures. In retirement he also began the herculean task of compiling and editing his father's papers, published a biography of his father, and in other ways displayed that tendency to ancestor worship which sooner or later besets all dynastic families.

21. Claude G. Bowers, *The Party Battles of the Jackson Period,* Houghton Mifflin (New York), 1922, 71. Jefferson appointed Robert Patterson to the mint in 1805; Jackson continued his son-in-law in the post and on his retirement appointed Patterson's son.

22. James Truslow Adams, *The Adams Family,* Little, Brown (Boston), 1930, 190.

23. Rogin, *Fathers and Children,* 263.

24. Jackson's Tennessee friends the Gwin brothers controlled Mississippi patronage; a group of Jackson cronies called "the nucleus" distributed patronage through the Florida land office; and patronage in Arkansas flowed to the "hungry kinfolk" of frontier nabob John Sevier. Aronson, *Kinship and Status,* 141; Rogin, *Fathers and Children,* 264.

25. William Hesseltine writes that Grant filled his Cabinet with so many old army friends that his opponents muttered darkly of a military coup. He gave out numerous appointments to repay personal debts, especially to those who had helped him and his family before the war, and made others at the behest of his father and wife. (Julia Grant's brother became collector at New Orleans and later embarrassed Grant with his corruption.) But Grant's nepotism had begun years earlier, with the appointment of his son to West Point by President Johnson. Fred Grant graduated last in his class and was attached to the staff of Grant's friend General Sherman. Ulysses Grant Jr. launched his career as a banker by exploiting his father's connections. One published list identified forty-two federal employees supposed to be Grant's relatives. Opposition journalists made much of these appointments, editorializing that "the first requirement for an office was relationship with the Grants." One remarked, "No President was ever 'got in the family way' so soon after inauguration." When he ran for reelection in 1872, Senator Sumner alleged that Grant had used his office "to advance his own family on a scale of nepotism dwarfing everything of the kind in our history." He colorfully called it "a dropsical nepotism swollen to elephantiasis." William B. Hesseltine, *Ulysses S. Grant, Politician,* Dodd, Mead (New York), 1935, 154–55.

26. Aronson, *Kinship and Status*, 18.

27. Albert J. Beveridge, *Abraham Lincoln, 1809–1858,* vol. 1, Houghton Mifflin (Boston), 1928, 110.

28. Benjamin Thomas observes that his ability to pay 118 pounds in cash for his first farm at Mill Creek shows "evidence of thrift and enterprise," and concludes, "the picture of Thomas Lincoln as a lazy ne'er-do-well has been unfairly overdrawn." Benjamin Thomas, *Abraham Lincoln: A Biography,* Alfred A. Knopf (New York), 1952, 5.

29. Hananiah's son Davis Lincoln had moved to Indiana with his father and became justice of the peace in Spencer County. The sons of Uncle Mordecai were also established in Illinois. James Bradford Lincoln served as a justice on the Hancock County Court and was later county commissioner and U.S. land commissioner. Another cousin, also named Abraham Lincoln, owned nearly a thousand acres and became justice of the peace in Grayson County. In addition, though Lincoln probably did not know about them, his Salter ancestors had included an assemblyman, a speaker of the New Jersey assembly, and an acting governor and royal councillor; a distant cousin, Levi Lincoln, had been a Revolutionary officer and Thomas Jefferson's attorney general.

30. Thomas L. Purvis, "The Making of a Myth: Abraham Lincoln's Family Background in the Perspective of Jacksonian Politics," in Don M. Kurtz II, ed., *The American Political Family,* University Press of America (Lanham, Md.), 1993, 37.

31. Nathaniel Wright Stephenson, *Lincoln: An Account of His Personal Life, Especially of Its Springs of Action As Revealed and Deepened by the Ordeal of War,* Bobbs-Merrill (Indianapolis), 1922, 31.

32. William E. Barringer, *Lincoln's Vandalia: A Pioneer Portrait,* Rutgers University Press (New Brunswick), 1949, 114, 126.

33. David Herbert Donald, *Lincoln,* Simon & Schuster (New York), 1995, 101.

34. "If two friends aspire to the same office, it is certain both cannot succeed. Would it not, then, be much less painful to have the question decided by mutual friends some time before, than to snarl and quarrel till the day of election and then both be beaten by the common enemy?" "Address to the People of Illinois," March 4, 1843, in Ray P. Basler, ed., *Collected Works of Abraham Lincoln,* Rutgers University Press (New Brunswick), 1959, I:315–16.

35. In contrast, Luigi Barzini has written that in Italy, with its long history of factional strife and disunion, such division is a matter of policy: "A well-run family must split in all civil wars." See Luigi Barzini, *The Italians,* Atheneum (New York), 1964, 193.

36. Grady McWhiney, *Cracker Culture: Celtic Ways in the Old South,* University of Alabama Press (Tuscaloosa), 1989, xvii.

37. Daniel W. Crofts, *Reluctant Confederates: Upper South Unionists in the Secession Crisis,* University of North Carolina Press (Chapel Hill), 1989, 47.

38. "The right of self-determination . . . helped many Southerners broaden their affection for kin and local community into a powerful sense of loyalty to a cause that would eclipse differences of class and even of political ideology." George C. Rable, *The Confederate Republic: A Revolution Against Politics,* University of North Carolina Press (Chapel Hill), 1994, 47.

39. William H. Townsend, *Lincoln and the Bluegrass: Slavery and Civil War in Kentucky,* University of Kentucky Press (Lexington), 1955, viii; Stephen Hess, *America's Political Dynasties,* Transaction (New Brunswick), 1987, 254.

40. Thomas, *Abraham Lincoln,* 231.

41. Harry J. Carman and Reinhard H. Luthin, *Lincoln and the Patronage,* Columbia University Press (New York), 1943, 10.

42. Chase's brother became marshal for the Northern District of New York, Cameron's son was made a military paymaster, and Welles secured a promotion for his son. Bates placed one son in his office, secured the appointment of a second to West Point, and got a third promoted in the army. Smith made his son librarian of the Interior Department. Vice President Hamlin had his brother appointed trade commissioner to Canada.

43. Two of Thurlow Weed's friends were posted to Belgium and Denmark. A friend of Cameron's became minister to Norway and Sweden. The low-status Latin postings served as a dumping ground for minor Republican leaders disappointed in their quest for better places. Carman and Luthin, *Lincoln and the Patronage,* 95.

44. Carman and Luthin, *Lincoln and the Patronage,* 17. See also William Ernest Smith, *The Francis Preston Blair Family in Politics,* Macmillan (New York), 1933.

45. Responding to Lincoln's offer, Lee said: "Mr. Blair, I look upon secession as anarchy. If I owned the four millions of slaves I would cheerfully sacrifice them to the preservation of the Union, but to lift my hand against my own State and people is impossible." The next day Virginia seceded, and Lee returned to head its army. Stephen Hess, *America's Political Dynasties,* Transaction (New Brunswick), 1987, 73.

46. Of Lincoln's friends, Judge Davis became a Supreme Court justice; Norman Judd became minister to Prussia; Gustave Koerner, minister to Spain; Jackson Grimshaw, a collector of internal revenue; Archibald Williams, district judge for Kansas; Ward H. Lamon, U.S. marshal for the District of Columbia; and Anson G. Henry, surveyor general for Washington Territory. Mark Delahay became surveyor general for Kansas and Nebraska, and in 1863 Lincoln simultaneously raised him to judge of the District Court for Kansas and nominated him to the Senate. Angry protests were immediately heard. Lincoln rammed the appointment through, but Delahay's judicial misconduct was so flagrant that impeachment proceedings were instituted and he resigned. Carman and Luthin, *Lincoln and the Patronage,* 117–18.

47. Ibid., 140–41.

48. Ibid., 112.

49. Ibid., 59, 67–68. One inveterate office seeker who did *not* receive an appointment from Lincoln was Herman Melville, who earlier had tried to get Franklin Pierce to give him the American consulate in Florence. In 1846 he had presented political boss Thurlow Weed with a copy of his novel *Typee,* in hopes of getting a job at the Treasury. After Lincoln's election Melville asked his uncle, who had influence in Republican circles, to intervene on his behalf, and also had his friend Richard Henry Dana write on his behalf to Senator Sumner. He even went to Washington to meet the vice president, to no avail. Finally in 1866 he obtained a job as an inspector at the New York Custom House, which he held for nineteen years.

50. Sensitive to the need to bring the large midwestern German population into the fold, Lincoln made sure to include a plank in the Republican platform endorsing open immigration.

51. Speech at Chicago, Illinois, July 10, 1858, quoted in Richard Nelson Current,

What Is An American? Abraham Lincoln and "Multiculturalism," Marquette University Press (Milwaukee), 1993, 11.

52. The Chinese had already become the fastest-growing group in American society. With the discovery of gold in the 1840s, thousands of Chinese came to California, and by 1852 there were over 24,000 at work in the mines of the West. Ethnic prejudice and agitation by white workers led to the imposition of punitive taxes intended to discourage further migration. Nevertheless, by the 1870s Chinese represented a quarter of all American miners, and many of them branched into fishing and sharecropping or were recruited for lumber and railroad work. Thousands more came in via Cuba, and in a very short time Chinese workers were being used as strikebreakers in factories and mills in Pennsylvania and other eastern states. Urban colonies sprang up in all the seaboard cities, and these Chinatowns became the center of a thriving ethnic economy. Yet the Chinese were considered an alien race too different to be assimilated into the majority white American society, and fears of an "Oriental invasion" led to the passage of numerous anti-Chinese ordinances and laws, culminating in the Chinese Exclusion Act of 1882.

53. A separate diaspora of families fleeing the destruction of the Confederacy spread west and south: one such group ended up in Brazil, where they retained many aspects of their heritage. See Cyrus B. Dawsey, *The Confederados: Old South Immigrants in Brazil,* University of Alabama Press (Tuscaloosa), 1995.

54. These settlements became the staging areas for a second wave of migration; moreover, the new colonies remained closely connected to the mother settlements by kin and marriage ties. Jon Gjerde, *The Minds of the West: Ethnocultural Evolution in the Rural Middle West, 1830–1917,* University of North Carolina Press (Chapel Hill), 1997, 96.

55. At Oneida, though "special love" was banned—whether between a man and a woman or between parents and children—the bonds of nature could not be abolished. Sexual jealousy inevitably divided the group, and Noyes's proclivity for reserving the choicest females to himself and his son eventually turned the other males against him.

56. The settlement of Utah has been called "the most impressive colonizing program in the history of the American West." Between 1847 and the death of Brigham Young, in 1877, more than three hundred Mormon communities were established in what are now the states of Utah, Idaho, Wyoming, Arizona, Nevada, California, and Hawaii. Richard D. Poll et al., eds., *Utah's History,* Utah State University Press (Logan), 1989, 133.

57. Lawrence Foster, *Women, Family, and Utopia: Communal Experiments of the Shakers, the Oneida Community, and the Mormons*, Syracuse University Press (Syracuse), 1991, 128.

58. Lionel Tiger explains that polygamy is a survival of primate politics, where dominance is expressed through the sexual control of females. It is also why, in Western societies, de facto polygamy is often practiced by men at the top of the social pyramid. "Even our latter-day bureaucratic polygamists can do this by the (theoretically) asexual method of controlling bevies of typists, research assistants, secretaries, nurses, receptionists, and other more or less skilled females." Lionel Tiger and Robin Fox, *The Imperial Animal,* Holt, Rinehart and Winston (New York), 1971, 83.

59. Though Mormons nominally disavowed polygamy in 1890, the practice has continued to this day, as does marriage between kin: one recent case involved a young Mormon bride who ran home to her father and was promptly returned to her husband—who was also her uncle.

60. Martin Ottenheimer, *Forbidden Relatives: The American Myth of Cousin Marriage,* University of Illinois Press (Urbana), 1996, 113.

61. This theory is expounded in Morgan's classic *Ancient Society,* published in 1877. His evolutionary scheme was adopted by Karl Marx, whose extensive notes on Morgan were eventually turned into a book by Friedrich Engels, *The Origin of the Family, Private Property and the State.*

62. Ottenheimer, *Forbidden Relatives,* 110.

63. Cousin marriage had been common in America before the Civil War. Even in New England, the practice was adopted by rich families who sought to consolidate their wealth. Morgan also married his first cousin, but changed his mind under the influence of vulgar Darwinism and inveighed against it as counter to the "civilizing" trend.

64. One of the most colorful figures in this bloody campaign was George Armstrong Custer, a hero of the Civil War who was also a flamboyant nepotist. Two brothers, a brother-in-law, and a nephew were all killed with him at Little Big Horn.

65. After the last outburst of violent resistance in the 1880s and 1890s, the 250,000 remaining Indians became wards of the U.S. government, and in many cases their children were transported thousands of miles away to government-funded boarding schools, where they were trained for manual vocations. The removal of these children stripped them of their cultural heritage and completed the despoliation of the Indian tribes.

66. "Clannishness was inherent in the family, and they naturally sided with their outlaw relatives, exulted in their deeds, perhaps boasted of their relationship, and regretted their deaths and imprisonments." Paul I. Wellman and Richard Maxwell Brown, *A Dynasty of Western Outlaws,* University of Nebraska Press (Lincoln), 1986, 159.

67. In New Mexico, local political dynasties were founded by marshals named Martinez, Chavez, and Romero. The last of these came to power in 1912 through his ability to deliver Republican delegates to William Howard Taft. Larry D. Ball, *The United States Marshals of New Mexico and Arizona Territories, 1846–1912,* University of New Mexico Press (Albuquerque), 1999, 157; *Desert Lawmen: The High Sheriffs of New Mexico and Arizona, 1846–1912,* University of New Mexico Press (Albuquerque), 1992, 34.

10. THE ROOSEVELTS

1. The Pendleton Act doesn't outlaw nepotism so much as it establishes a limit on family employment in government service. Section 9 reads: "That whenever there are already two or more members of a family in the public service in the grades covered by this act, no other member of such family shall be eligible to appointment to any of said grades."

2. James Brady, who later became governor of the Alaska Territory, was one of those whom Roosevelt "picked up off the streets of New York" and sent west for a fresh start in life. Roosevelt also kept up with the boy, continuing to write him letters of encouragement. Brady never forgot his debt to Teddy's father. Stephen Hess, *America's Political Dynasties*, Transaction (New Brunswick), 1987, 178.

3. Gould and Vanderbilt once paid the same legislator, respectively, $75,000 and

$100,000 for his vote (he voted for one but kept the other's money). Tammany's William Tweed took a kickback of 65 percent from contractors hired to construct the New York County Courthouse; after thirteen years and $13 million, the courthouse was still unfinished when a muckraking campaign by the *New York Times* sent Tweed to jail. Samuel P. Orth, *The Boss and the Machine: A Chronicle of the Politicians and Party Organization,* Yale University Press (New Haven), 1919, 48.

4. The Perrys had been heroes in the Revolution and the War of 1812 and always performed brilliantly in the nation's service. They were also very clannish and never missed on opportunity to advance a family member. This practice reached its peak when Commodore Matthew Perry—a third-generation naval officer and one of the most admired men of his day—commissioned a new vessel on which his "advanced" training ideas would be tested. Seventy-two apprentices were to be taken on board for this prestigious cruise, and applications flooded in. When the ship sailed it was manned by fresh-faced scions of the American naval establishment, many of them related to Perry. Edward M. Barrows, *The Great Commodore: The Exploits of Matthew Calbraith Perry,* Bobbs-Merrill (Indianapolis), 1935, 140–42.

5. The cultural dominance of the WASP elite was maintained through their purchase on the faculties of major universities, in the publishing houses of Boston and New York, and in the person of such writers as Henry Adams, Henry James, Edith Wharton, and William Dean Howells. The leading American painters of this period, Winslow Homer, Mary Cassatt, and John Singer Sargent, were also members of elite families who had studied abroad.

6. Thomas Sowell, *Ethnic America: A History,* Basic Books (New York), 1981, 32.

7. In New York, the Bowery's Big Tim Sullivan installed his cousins in important posts; Brooklyn's Hugh McLaughlin depended on an older sister and a nephew; Tweed relied on his two sons; Richard Croker got public jobs for his father, brother, and nephews; and Charles F. Murphy was brought in by his two older brothers. Big Tim Sullivan was "a warmhearted giant" who collected graft like Robin Hood and distributed it to the poor in the form of food and clothing. At his death, in 1913, twenty-five thousand people attended his funeral. Kansas City boss Jim Pendergast was praised in similar terms: "He will go down in his pockets for his last cent to help a friend." Harold B. Zink, *City Bosses in the United States: A Study of Twenty Municipal Bosses,* Duke University Press (Durham), 1930, 27.

8. William L. Riordan, *Plunkitt of Tammany Hall: A Series of Very Plain Talks on Very Practical Politics,* Bedord Books (Boston), 1994, 64.

9. Ibid., 119–20.

10. Alice was Saltonstall's cousin and the daughter of George Cabot Lee of Boston's venerable Lee, Higginson & Co. The families had adjoining estates.

11. Years later he told Jacob Riis, "I tried faithfully to do what Father had done, but I did it poorly... in the end I found that we have each to work in his own way to do our best; and when I struck mine, though it differed from his, yet I was able to follow the same lines and do what he would have had me do."

12. David G. McCullough, *Mornings on Horseback,* Simon & Schuster (New York), 1981, 311.

13. Hess, *America's Political Dynasties,* 181.

14. McCullough, *Mornings on Horseback*, 355, 360.

15. In 1895 Bamie married Adm. William S. Cowles and had a son at forty-three. Yet her husband and son never replaced Teddy as the center of her world.

16. "Appointments and promotions were made almost solely for money: there was a well-recognized tariff of charges ranging from $200 to $300 for an appointment as patrolman, to $12,000 or $15,000 for promotion to the position of captain, and the money was reimbursed to those who paid it by an elaborate system of blackmail from gamblers, liquor dealers and keepers of disorderly houses." William Dudley Foulke, *Roosevelt and the Spoilsmen*, National Civil Service Reform League (New York), 1925, 44.

17. The navy job had been an Adams family fief for many years. Now it became a Roosevelt family fief. FDR served in the same position under Wilson. Theodore Jr. held the post under Harding and Coolidge, and was succeeded by Theodore Douglas Robinson. Under FDR, the job was held in succession by Henry L. Roosevelt and Nicholas Roosevelt.

18. Harold F. Gosnell, *Boss Platt and His New York Machine: A Study of the Political Leadership of Thomas C. Platt, Theodore Roosevelt, and Others*, University of Chicago Press (Chicago), 1924, 148.

19. "It would be an entire mistake to suppose that Mr. Platt's lieutenants were either all bad men or all influenced by unworthy motives. He was constantly doing favors for men. He had won the gratitude of many good men.... Some of his strongest and most efficient lieutenants were disinterested men of high character." Ibid., 66.

20. "In fact, all the moneyed interests that make campaign contributions of large size and feel that they should have favors in return, are extremely anxious to get me out of the state," Roosevelt wrote. Ibid., 118.

21. James MacGregor Burns and Susan Dunn, *The Three Roosevelts: Patrician Leaders Who Transformed America*, Atlantic Monthly Press (New York), 2001, 95. From the sociobiological perspective, this emphasis on the vitality of children really involves a concern with the transmission of our genes. It is not an altruistic concern for the poor but biological nepotism that leads us to devise ways to limit our children's wealth, lest it leave them weak and enervated. It is a better reproductive strategy to leave your children just enough to give them a head start in life, yet not so much that they have no incentive to strive and achieve on their own.

22. "Most of the desirable jobs throughout the biggest corporations and banks are filled to an astonishing extent by men who are either collateral descendants of the wealthy families, married to direct or collateral descendants, or connected by blood relationships with persons directly or indirectly related." "The Rockefeller sons, nephews, and cousins... are strewn throughout the Rockefeller enterprises in positions which they could never have hoped to attain... without family sponsorship." When Henry Ford appointed his son Edsel to the presidency of the Ford Motor Company, he was mystified by cries of nepotism. Ford "naively exclaimed that he thought the 'real story' lay in the fact that a youngster just out of his teens should show such ability that he was placed in charge of a billion-dollar enterprise!" Ferdinand Lundberg, *America's Sixty Families*, Vanguard Press (New York), 1937, 18–22.

23. Geoffrey C. Ward, *Before the Trumpet: Young Franklin Roosevelt 1882–1905*, Harper and Row (New York), 1985, 314.

24. Ibid., 314–15.

25. Hess, *America's Political Dynasties,* 188.

26. FDR was not very adept at securing patronage for his constituents. For one thing, civil service had cut into the supply of available jobs. "Often, as a last resort, he urged his friends to take merit examinations. The protests were raucous." Alfred B. Rollins, *Roosevelt and Howe,* Alfred A. Knopf (New York), 1962, 47.

27. Ibid., 61.

28. Hess, *America's Political Dynasties,* 189.

29. Though Franklin had few ties to the New York business community, he did have connections through his Delano relatives with the Baltimore-based Fidelity and Deposit Co. of Maryland. His uncle Frederic A. Delano was deputy chairman of the Federal Reserve Bank of Richmond, and his cousin Lyman Delano was heavily involved in Southern railroad interests and was linked to Baltimore's wealthy Walters family. The family also had a double link to the Astors through the marriages of Franklin's half brother James and uncle Franklin Delano to Astor heiresses. In 1932, Vincent Astor was a member of the Democratic National Finance Committee.

30. Smith was a product of the Tammany machine who had started as an errand boy and protégé of district boss Tom Foley. Famed for his integrity, Smith represented the best of the immigrant political tradition. The nation wasn't ready for a Catholic president, however, and Smith was defeated.

31. "Joseph Seligman and his wife were first cousins, and in the next generation Joseph's brother's daughter married Joseph's sister's son. Meyer Guggenheim married his stepsister, and a Lewisohn married his own niece.... Three Seligman brothers married three sisters named Levi; several other Seligmans married Walters, and several married Beers. The Seligmans also followed the Jewish practice of offering widows in the family to the next unmarried son.... Kuhn, Loeb & Company was originally composed of a particularly tight network of love—with Kuhn and Loeb (who were brothers in law) both related to Abraham Wolff, another K-L partner whose daughter married yet another partner, Otto Kahn. A Loeb son married a Kuhn daughter, and another Loeb daughter married another partner, Paul Warburg, while Jacob Schiff's daughter Frieda married Paul Warburg's brother Felix (a partner too)." Stephen Birmingham, *"Our Crowd": The Great Jewish Families of New York,* Harper & Row (New York), 1976, 8–9.

32. "While poverty has been blamed for the large number of break-ups of Irish families in the nineteenth century, similar poverty among Italian immigrants at the turn of the century did not lead to any such result, nor did the Italians accept charity or resort to prostitution nearly as often as the Irish or other groups in such circumstances." Sowell, *Ethnic America,* 281.

33. David Brody, *In Labor's Cause: Main Themes in the History of the American Worker,* Oxford University Press (New York), 1993, 112. Kevin Kelly, *Making Sense of the Molly Maguires,* Oxford University Press (New York), 1998.

34. James M. Motley, "Apprenticeship in the Building Trades," in Jacob H. Hollander and George E. Barnett, eds., *Studies in American Trade Unionism,* Henry Holt (New York), 1912, 269.

35. Gompers himself led the charge against continued immigration—based mainly on racial hostility to Asian and east European workers—that resulted in a series of exclusion acts in the 1920s. Agitation against Asians had already resulted in a Chinese Exclusion Act in 1882.

36. Sylvia Kopald Selekman, *Rebellion in Labor Unions,* Boni & Liveright (New York), 1924, 264.

37. To the extent that class consciousness existed before, one historian observes, it came more easily to the foreign born because they had "no brothers, or uncles or cousins . . . in the ranks of American capitalists." Eli Ginzberg, *The Labor Leader: An Exploratory Study,* Macmillan (New York), 1948, 49.

38. Ibid., 46.

39. In 1996 a hotly contested election pitted IBT president Ron Carey against James Hoffa Jr. and William Hogan Jr. Hoffa was the son of longtime teamster president Jimmy Hoffa; Hogan's father had founded IBT Local 714 in 1934 and headed it until his retirement in 1990. Both sides engaged in charges of nepotism.

40. Lizabeth Cohen, *Making a New Deal: Industrial Workers in Chicago, 1919–1939,* Cambridge University Press (Cambridge), 1990, 247. The role of tribal nepotism in helping Jews come through the Depression ahead of other groups deserves particular attention. Jews experienced the same collapse of ethnic institutions: in 1930, the Jewish-owned Bank of the United States failed, taking with it the savings of 400,000 depositors. In New York City alone, nearly 10,000 Jewish businesses went under. Yet Jewish communal integrity and in-group nepotism kicked in immediately, with strong positive results. Jewish wives went to work or started home-based sidelines that earned extra income. Children worked part-time and contributed to the family budget. Older children often sacrificed opportunities for higher education and went to work so younger siblings could stay in school. Despite these constraints, the overall level of Jewish education was higher than in the previous immigrant period. Nor were daughters penalized when family resources allowed: Jewish girls went to college more frequently than did other American women.

41. Paramount was initially funded by the Jewish firm of Kuhn, Loeb with a loan of $10 million, courtesy of Otto Kahn, brother of Zukor's partner Felix Kahn.

42. According to Stephen Farber and Marc Green, "Columbia was dubbed the Pine Tree Studio because of its numerous "Cohns." And the initials MGM were said to stand for "Mayer's-Ganz-Mishpochen" (Yiddish for "Mayer's whole family") because Louis B. Mayer loaded the payroll with so many of his relatives, including his brother, his nephew, and his son-in-law, David Selznick." Stephen Farber and Marc Green, *Hollywood Dynasties,* Delilah Communications (New York), 1984, 17.

43. The price for these favors was high. Displaying the typical psychology of the self-made man, the moguls were often coarse and domineering, and if they gave out jobs to relatives it was the relatives who were being exploited. The moguls quarreled with their brothers, suffocated their daughters, and drove their sons relentlessly. Neal Gabler, *An Empire of Their Own: How the Jews Invented Hollywood,* Crown (New York), 1988, 70.

44. The number of non-civil-service jobs grew to four hundred thousand by 1936. Patricia Wallace Ingraham, *The Foundation of Merit: Public Service in American Democracy,* Johns Hopkins University Press (Baltimore), 1995, 46.

45. Martin and Susan Tolchin, *To the Victor . . . : Political Patronage from the Clubhouse to the White House,* Random House (New York), 1971, 257.

46. Beth S. Wenger, *New York Jews and the Great Depression: Uncertain Promise,* Yale University Press (New Haven), 1996, 127.

47. Burns and Dunn, *The Three Roosevelts,* 96.

48. "One's own children were no longer needed as an investment towards security in later life. Indeed, the 'value' of children had been precisely reversed. In the welfare state . . . one could improve one's immediate standard of living . . . by having only one—or even better—no children at all." Jon Davies, ed., *The Family: Is It Just Another Lifestyle Choice?* Choice in Welfare No. 15, IEA Health and Welfare Unit (London), 1993, 37.

49. Allan Carlson, "Sanctifying the Traditional Family: The New Deal and National Solidarity," *The Family in America*, May 2002.

50. Raymond Clapper, *Racketeering in Washington: Being an Account from Authoritative Records of the Grafting in Small and Great Things by Our Senators and Members of the House of Representatives and Executives in Public Departments*, L. C. Page (Boston), 1933, 58 ff.

51. The closest blood relatives, in direct line, are a person's parent and child (first degree). Next are a person's grandparent and grandchild or—laterally—brother and sister (second degree). A person's great-grandparent, in direct line, and—laterally—aunt, uncle, nephew, and niece are in the third degree. Great-great-grandparent, first cousin, and great-aunt and great-uncle are next in line.

52. Hess, *America's Political Dynasties*, 201.

11. HEIRS APPARENT

1. Kennedy reappointed J. Edgar Hoover and Allen Dulles at FBI and CIA, put in Dean Rusk at State and C. Douglas Dillon at Treasury, appointed Robert McNamara to Defense, and named McGeorge Bundy to head the National Security Council.

2. Victor Lasky, *Robert F. Kennedy: The Myth and the Man*, Trident Press/Simon & Schuster (New York), 1968, 163.

3. Kennedy first offered the job to Connecticut governor Abraham Ribicoff, then to Adlai Stevenson, but both turned it down.

4. Richard C. Whalen, *The Founding Father: The Story of Joseph P. Kennedy*, Regnery Gateway (Washington), 1993, 468.

5. "I thought it was an appalling idea," said Harris Wofford, who was working on the transition. "I couldn't believe they were actually considering it." C. David Heymann, *RFK: A Candid Biography of Robert F. Kennedy*, Dutton (New York), 1998, 188–90.

6. O'Connor calls this "an observable pattern in immigrant life so striking that it is impossible to dismiss as mere coincidence." Thomas O'Connor, *The Boston Irish: A Political History*, Little, Brown (Boston), 1995, 99–101.

7. Fitzgerald's only notable achievement during his three terms in Congress was his opposition to a literacy bill, sponsored by Sen. Henry Cabot Lodge, aimed at restricting the flow of immigration from southern and eastern Europe.

8. James Fitzgerald was a successful tavern and hotel keeper who was said to have contributed $50,000 to his brother's campaigns. Henry, whom Fitz employed as a clerk in his insurance business and later got elected to the assembly, was put in charge of patronage. Michael became the city's health inspector, and a minor place was found for Joe, a brain-addled veteran of the Spanish-American War whose job was to hand deliver the morning traffic report to city hall, which earned him the title of "the human postage stamp."

9. According to Ronald Kessler, Joe's grades could not have won him acceptance at Harvard without pull, and he suggests that Mayor Fitzgerald "made a call to the college

at P.J.'s request." Ronald Kessler, *The Sins of the Father: Joseph P. Kennedy and the Dynasty He Founded,* Warner Books (New York), 1996, 17.

10. Doris Kearns Goodwin, *The Fitzgeralds and the Kennedys,* St. Martin's Press (New York), 1987, 216.

11. "For friends and their family members there were job recommendations, thank-you notes for suggesting pay raises to a number of employers, appointments or promotions resulting from the right words whispered in the right ears, travel reservations secured through hotel managers whose investments he oversaw. He offered investment opportunities to uncles and cousins." Amanda Smith, ed., *Hostage to Fortune: The Letters of Joseph P. Kennedy,* Viking (New York), 2001, 7.

12. Foremost among Joe's inner circle was Eddie Moore—amanuensis, bagman, and procurer. Moore became a virtual member of the family, standing godfather to Rosemary Kennedy; Joe's youngest child would be named for this loyal retainer.

13. Joe told Bernard Baruch that he had established these trusts to ensure his children's independence, so they could "spit in my eye" if they wanted, but Ronald Kessler writes, "This was self-serving hokum. The truth was that it was a way of tying the children to him." Kessler, *Sins of the Father,* 48. Doris Goodwin writes, "the trust was a mechanism for binding his children permanently to his own dreams for the Kennedy family." Goodwin, *The Fitzgeralds and the Kennedys,* 602.

14. According to Michael Knox Beran, "the Kennedys invented their own system of confidence-building, created their own inventory of tools and techniques. . . . Whenever he greeted his father, Jack Kennedy would make a fist, and the older man would wrap his hands around it, as if to affirm the son's strength." Michael Knox Beran, *The Last Patrician: Bobby Kennedy and the End of American Aristocracy,* St. Martin's Press (New York), 1998, 147–48.

15. Bobby recalled lying in bed at night listening to the sound of Joe Jr. "banging Jack's head against the wall." Edward J. Renehan, *The Kennedys at War, 1937–1945,* Doubleday (New York), 2002, 7.

16. Whalen, *Founding Father,* 91. The same rules applied to visitors. Many a young schoolmate was cruelly shown up in family games of touch football.

17. Renehan, *The Kennedys at War,* 3. Unlike his father, whose motto was "Be grateful and be loyal," Kennedy "was known both for discarding friends when they had served their purpose and for knifing in the back those who had helped him." Kessler, *Sins of the Father,* 90.

18. Joe professed great fondness for Jimmy, saying that he regarded himself as the young man's "foster father," but the relationship was based largely on Joe's ability to exploit his political ambition and his weakness for liquor and women. Jimmy had set himself up in the insurance business and Joe allowed him to underwrite his overseas liquor shipments and helped him become president of the National Grain Yeast Corporation, which became a big business when beer went back into production.

19. Kennedy had published a book in 1936 (ghostwritten by Arthur Krock) called *I'm for Roosevelt.* In chapter one, "In Which the Father of Nine Children Explains What He Thinks this Election Means to Them," Kennedy expressed his commitment to the New Deal in nepotistic terms: "I put down these few thoughts about our President, conscious only of my concern as a father for the future of his family." Joseph P. Kennedy,

I'm for Roosevelt, Reynal & Hitchcock (New York), 1936, 3. Later he expressed his opposition to war in similar terms: "I should like to ask you all if you know of any dispute or controversy existing in the world which is worth the life of your son, or of anyone else's son?" Renehan, *The Kennedys at War,* 62.

20. Renehan, *The Kennedys at War,* 161; Seymour Hersh, *The Dark Side of Camelot,* Little, Brown (Boston), 1997, 24. Joe sent copies of the book to Winston Churchill and the queen.

21. Renehan, *The Kennedys at War,* 173.

22. "Jack was wary of upsetting what observers outside the family often referred to as the Kennedys' 'hierarchical' family structure." Ibid., 191.

23. In Washington, Jack began an affair with Inga Arvad, a Danish journalist suspected of being a Nazi agent. The liaison came to the attention of J. Edgar Hoover, who shot the father a warning. Joe took steps to get Jack out of Washington, transferring him to a PT training unit in Norfolk.

24. Renehan, *The Kennedys at War,* 273.

25. Rose would not countenance her daughter's marriage to a Protestant, but Joe was pleased and signaled that she could "do no wrong" as far as he was concerned.

26. Reportedly Joe paid the incumbent, James Michael Curley, $12,000 to get out of the way. Kessler, *Sins of the Father,* 291–92.

27. Among other tricks, Joe paid a plumber with the same name as a legitimate candidate to enter the race and split his votes.

28. Whalen, *Founding Father,* 432; Laurence Leamer, *The Kennedy Men 1901–1963: The Laws of the Father,* William Morrow (New York), 2001, 298–99.

29. Hess, *America's Political Dynasties,* 511.

30. Lawford was the partner of record for Joe's investment in the mafia-financed Cal-Neva Lodge outside of Reno. Richard D. Mahoney, *Sons and Brothers: The Days of Jack and Bobby Kennedy,* Arcade Publishing (New York), 1999, 43.

31. Joe appears not only to have upgraded his view of Bobby, but increasingly to have identified with him as well. "Bobby hates the way I do," he said approvingly. "When Bobby hates you, you stay hated."

32. As usual, Jack delegated the unpleasant task of calling Joe to Bobby. Mahoney, *Sons and Brothers,* 19.

33. Joe Kennedy is supposed to have called a meeting of mafia bosses in early 1960 to solicit their support for Jack. If so, however, he was not unique. Lyndon Johnson and Richard Nixon reportedly also had mob ties. Ibid., 43–44.

34. Asked how much he would need to place Jack's name at the top of the slate, one county chairman said, "Thirty-five," meaning $3,500; he was given $35,000. Joe Kennedy's partner Eddie Ford drove through the state with a suitcase full of money. Cardinal Cushing later told Humphrey that Bobby had paid black ministers to get out the vote. Ibid., 52–53.

35. Whalen, *Founding Father,* 454–55. Descended on both sides from leading Texas families, LBJ grew up poor but believing that he had "a birthright to prominence and influence over other men," according to Robert Dallek. His father had been a two-term state legislator, and his mother was a Baines, from an illustrious family of ministers, physicians, and legislators. Lyndon rose through the patronage of a long series of surro-

gate fathers, the most important of whom was Sam Rayburn, the powerful Texas congressman and Speaker of the House, who had served with his father in Austin. Rayburn helped him obtain a position as Texas director of the National Youth Administration and then a congressional seat. Lyndon's father-in-law, Thomas Jefferson Taylor, the richest man in his part of Texas, also aided his son-in-law's rise. See Robert Dallek, *Lone Star Rising: Lyndon Johnson and His Times,* Oxford University Press (New York), 1991.

36. Whalen, *Founding Father,* 457.

37. In Illinois more votes were reported than had actually been cast, while in Texas, as many as 150,000 votes that were cast were never reported. Since Kennedy won Texas by fifty thousand votes and Illinois by only ten thousand, these narrow margins could have made the crucial difference.

38. Chauncey, who became the first head of the Educational Testing Service, was a descendant of New England ministers and heir to the Puritan tradition that grace was "individual and irrespective of social rank." Nicholas Lemann, *The Big Test: The Secret History of the American Meritocracy,* Farrar Straus & Giroux (New York), 1999, 10.

39. Ibid., 47.

40. Beran, *The Last Patrician,* 26, 76.

41. According to Patrick Anderson, Dave Powers was "put on the payroll primarily because he amused the President." Jack's *PT-109* buddy Red Fay became undersecretary of the navy. Ted Reardon, Jack's old congressional assistant, was also given a job, and Muggsy O'Leary, Kennedy's "chauffeur and errand runner" in the Senate, was put on the Secret Service payroll. Patrick Anderson, *Presidents' Men: White House Assistants of Franklin D. Roosevelt, Harry S Truman, Dwight D. Eisenhower, John F. Kennedy, and Lyndon B. Johnson,* Doubleday (Garden City), 1968, 197.

42. Garry Wills, *The Kennedy Imprisonment: A Meditation on Power,* Little, Brown (Boston), 1994, 174.

43. Michael Walzer, *Spheres of Justice: A Defense of Pluralism and Equality,* Basic Books (New York), 1983, 147.

44. Heymann, *RFK,* 258, 262.

45. A good example of Bobby's high-handed attitude is his use of what were called "police state tactics" in resolving a crisis over steel prices in 1962. Mahoney, *Sons and Brothers,* 141, 153.

46. Goodwin, *The Fitzgeralds and the Kennedys,* 807.

47. The Kennedy brand was so well established that when a stockroom foreman from South Boston who happened to be named John F. Kennedy ran for state treasurer, he was elected without campaigning. Hess, *America's Political Dynasties,* 519.

48. Whalen, *Founding Father,* 478.

49. Robert McNamara is considered the virtual embodiment of this meritocratic elite, reflecting both its brilliance and its arrogance. Years later he would confess to this blind arrogance in a breast-baring memoir that lamented his own role in escalating American involvement in Indochina. Another key figure was McGeorge Bundy, described in Walter Isaacson's obituary in *Time* as personifying "the hubris of an intellectual elite that marched America with a cool and confident brilliance into the quagmire of Vietnam."

50. Christopher Lasch, *The Revolt of the Elites and the Betrayal of Democracy,* W. W. Norton (New York), 1995, 39.

51. Though economic and political causes were not wanting, Sale gave special em-

phasis to social problems centered on the family. "The *social* fabric of the nation was clearly tattered: families were no longer the places where the young learned their values or the old sought their solace; marriages collapsed at a greater and greater rate, or were artificially sustained after the life had left them; sexuality was seen, and used, as a commodity." This analysis (coming in the context of a much more radical critique of American power and business) sounds very conservative today, especially the focus on divorce and illegitimacy and the impact of the sexual revolution. Kirkpatrick Sale, *SDS,* Random House (New York), 1973, 18.

52. One problem with the Vietnam War is that it was fought by a draft army that did not include the country's elites, who chose not to send their sons to Southeast Asia. As columnist James Reston wrote, Selective Service was "a system whereby poor boys are selected to go to Vietnam and rich boys are selected to go to college." Terry Anderson, *The Movement and the Sixties,* Oxford University Press (New York), 1996, 159. It is perhaps not accidental that elite students who enjoyed college deferments obtained by their parents were among the war's most vocal opponents. Thus, for example, McNamara's son Craig was one of the leaders of the Berkeley student movement.

53. Writing to his son Michael about George Wallace's notorious stand in the schoolhouse door, he said, "By the time you become attorney general, perhaps behavior like Wallace's will no longer be possible."

54. Beran, *The Last Patrician,* 106.

55. Heymann, *RFK,* 486.

56. The link between Teddy's upbringing and his behavior in the Senate did not go unnoticed. Meg Greenfield described him as showing "all the attributes in public life of the ninth child." James MacGregor Burns, *Edward Kennedy and the Camelot Legacy,* W. W. Norton (New York), 1976, 99.

57. The reform act was also the repayment of a political debt: ethnic minorities had tilted the election to Kennedy in New York, Hawaii, Texas, Illinois, New Jersey, and New Mexico. Patrick Reddy, "JFK's Immigration Legacy," UPI, Dec. 4, 2001.

58. The court cited "the advantages of early experience under friendly supervision" as well as "the benefits to morale and esprit de corps which family and neighborly tradition might contribute." *Kotch* is no longer considered "good law" and it would probably be decided differently today, after four decades of antidiscrimination decisions based on Title VII, particularly the Court's 1971 "disparate impact" finding in *Griggs v. Duke Power Co.* But while a minority opinion in *Kotch* objected that nepotism—discrimination based on blood—violated the constitutional right of each person to be treated as an individual and not as a member of a group, even the dissenting justices acknowledged that something of real value had been lost with the shift from a traditional, family-based mode of economic life to a modern industrial one. "Indeed, something very worth while disappeared from our national life when the once prevalent familial system of conducting manufacturing and mercantile enterprises went out and was replaced by the highly impersonal corporate system for doing business." John David Skrentny, *The Ironies of Affirmative Action: Politics, Culture, and Justice in America,* University of Chicago Press (Chicago), 1996, 54. The rationality defense began to give way even before the Civil Rights Act, with *State Commission of Human Rights v. Farrell* (1964), which held that a union apprenticeship program giving preference to sons and sons-in-law was racially discriminatory, even though such preferences were historically typical of guilds.

59. Such cases multiplied in the 1980s and were overwhelmingly successful. Once a disparate impact has been established, the burden of demonstrating "business necessity" falls to the defendant, and defendants have rarely been able to do so. (In *E.E.O.C. v. Steamship Clerks' Union* a group of black and Hispanic plaintiffs challenged the union's nepotistic hiring practices: the union's defense that nepotism maintains "family traditions" was not persuasive.) A controversial ruling in *Wards Cove Packing v. Atonio* (1989), a nepotism case in which the court raised the standards for proving disparate impact, led to the Civil Rights Act of 1991, which amended Title VII to make it easier to prove statistical disparities.

60. Passed as part of the Postal Rates and Federal Salaries Act, the 1967 nepotism law does not prohibit the employment of relatives or spouses in the same federal agency; rather it prevents officials from influencing decisions affecting the employment of such relatives. Other federal statutes authorize specific agencies to establish their own nepotism rules. It is also noteworthy that most federal and state statutes endorse the civil law method of determining degrees of consanguinity, a standard that is more lenient and encompasses fewer relatives than the alternative common law and canon law methods.

61. There was in fact a tremendous variation and lack of consistency in antinepotism policies in both business and academic institutions. Most rules barred relatives from working in the same department or supervising one another's work. But according to legal scholar Joan Wexler, "Dramatic differences in policy exist even within the same company. Two corporations reported that certain departments or divisions have different rules, some banning and others encouraging the hiring of relatives. Ten other corporations draw distinctions among management levels, with restrictions on the hiring of relatives becoming more stringent as the management level rises." In cases where employees married, most rules required the partner with less seniority to transfer or resign. Since women were relative latecomers to both the corporate and academic marketplace, this requirement penalized them unfairly. Joan G. Wexler, "Husbands and Wives: The Uneasy Case for Nepotism Rules," *Boston University Law Review* 62 (1982): 82.

62. Margaret W. Rossiter, *Women Scientists in America: Before Affirmative Action, 1940–1972,* Johns Hopkins Press (Baltimore), 1995.

63. One index of how far we have come is the practice, now routine, of offering tenure-track positions to married couples, even though it often appears that only one is really wanted. It is now commonplace for colleges to offer special deals to academic couples and to advertise their "partner preference" programs. When Columbia University dropped its nepotism rules, provost Stephen Rittenberg remarked: "We're anti-antinepotism."

64. Kessler, *Sins of the Father,* 425.

12. THE ART OF NEPOTISM

1. There is no question that the children of doctors and lawyers enjoy a statistical advantage in admission to medical and law school. No one can explain how this occurs; it simply "happens."

2. Secretary of State John Foster Dulles was the grandson of John W. Foster, secretary of state under President Benjamin Harrison (himself the grandson of a former president), and the nephew of Robert M. Lansing, secretary of state under Woodrow

Wilson. His brother Allen became the founding director of the OSS and CIA, and their sister Eleanor ran the German desk at the State Department during the Berlin Crisis. In all, an unparalleled record of family service. Leonard Mosley, *Dulles: A Biography of Eleanor, Allen, and John Foster Dulles and their Family Network,* Dial Press (New York), 1978.

3. In 1986, a surrogate mother named Mary Beth Whitehead asserted her claim to the child known to legal history as "Baby M," despite not being its genetic parent. Whitehead's custody suit was rejected, but the issues were so threatening to normal notions of motherhood that several countries have taken steps to control or outlaw such contracts.

4. In 2001, over twenty thousand foreign children, mostly from China and Russia, were adopted by American families.

5. Despite the widespread popular belief that cousin marriage leads to genetic deformities, a recent study by the National Society of Genetic Counselors has announced that cousin marriage does not appreciably increase the chance of birth defects. Encouraged by this news, married cousins are coming out of the closet, establishing a national membership organization and an informational website, called Cousin Couples.

6. Bob Tedeschi, "E-Commerce Report," *New York Times,* Sept. 23, 2002.

7. "The unanimous ruling… followed similar recent rulings in other states, adding weight to what seems to be an expansion of the criteria for being a parent. The California court effectively ruled that biology does not necessarily establish the only claim to parenthood and that, in some cases, parenthood can also be achieved through love and responsible conduct." Michael Janofsky, "Custody Case in California Paves Way for 'Fathers,' " *New York Times,* June 8, 2002.

8. "Like clans gathering, mothers, sisters, fathers, brothers, cousins arrived. Relatives sent family heirlooms.… Siblings returned borrowed property, sent money, and took in children.… Extended families, such as they were, stood up and were counted in both presence and presents." Susanna M. Hoffman, "The Regenesis of Traditional Gender Patterns in the Wake of Disaster," in Anthony Oliver-Smith and Susanna M. Hoffman, eds., *The Angry Earth: Disaster in Anthropological Perspective,* Routledge (New York), 1999, 181.

9. "The state, despite its persecution of the individual from time to time, is much happier with individuals as units than with kinship groups for the simple reason that they are easier to control.… Thus, it comes easily to the nation-state to promote the values of individualism while remaining totally suspicious of the claims of kinship." Robin Fox, *Reproduction and Succession: Studies in Anthropology, Law and Society,* Transaction (Rutgers), 1993, 184.

10. Ferdinand Mount, *The Subversive Family: An Alternative History of Love and Marriage,* Free Press (New York), 1992, 1. Alexis de Tocqueville said much the same thing: "As long as family feeling was kept alive, the opponent of oppression was never alone; he looked about him and found his clients, his hereditary friends, and his kinfolk.… But when patrimonial estates are divided, and when a few years suffice to confound the distinctions of race, where can family feeling be found?"

11. A movement for "restorative justice" brings the families of criminals and their victims together to effect a reconciliation, and has experimented successfully with the creation of artificial families to help youthful offenders transition back to normal social

life. For more than thirty years, a Philadelphia organization called the House of Umoja has been a surrogate family for young gang members seeking an escape from the violent life of the streets. Likewise, a welfare-to-work organization called "America Works" has used family-based networks to recruit, train, place, and oversee thousands of people in well-paid entry-level jobs.

12. Grandmothers have lately been recognized as crucial figures in the lives of young children. As the *New York Times* reports, "The presence or absence of a grandmother often spelled the difference in traditional subsistence cultures between life or death for the grandchildren." (Natalie Angier, "The Importance of Grandma," *New York Times,* November 5, 2002.) Instead of warehousing grandmothers in suburban retirement villages, we might put that untapped nepotistic energy to use by offering tax incentives to people with elderly parents at home. Not only would this reduce the cost of day care, it might also reduce the costs of social insurance and health care for seniors.

13. If we are really interested in the regeneration of social bonds, we might take a cue from an unlikely source: the satirical novels of Kurt Vonnegut. In *Cat's Cradle,* his bogus holy man, Bokonon, invents a religion that posits the idea of a "karass," a word that describes true kinship, whether by blood or by circumstance, "a team [of people] that do[es] God's Will without ever discovering what they are doing." Vonnegut returns to this theme in *Slapstick,* when Wilbur Swain, the newly elected president of the United States, decides to establish ten thousand artificial clans with names like Daffodil and Chipmunk, to which Americans are randomly assigned, taking the totem as their middle name and accepting the obligation to treat other "clan" members as family. The president's program, called "Lonesome No More," is a tremendous success. Though presented ironically, President Daffodil-Swain's scheme only seems absurd in the American context. In fact it is quite similar to the approach taken by the neo-Confucian officials of the Sung dynasty, who encouraged the regeneration of clans as a means of restoring social order in chaotic times.

14. Here, for example, is General Alexander Haig on how he got his start in the military: "Then, in the first semester of my sophomore year at South Bend, Uncle John Neeson stepped forward, as he had done so many times before, to make my chosen future possible. Through his connections, I was awarded a congressional appointment to the West Point class of 1947, and this time, thanks to my intellectual awakening at Notre Dame and the string of A's that were its result, I was good enough to be accepted." Alexander M. Haig Jr., with Charles McCarry, *Inner Circles: How America Changed the World,* Warner Books (New York), 1992, 12. Note that Haig's self-confidence and pride in his accomplishments are so secure that he thinks nothing of admitting that he got his start through nepotism. The general's son Brian Haig has followed in his footsteps, attending West Point and then becoming a special assistant to the Joint Chiefs of Staff.

15. According to the *New Republic,* Powell's career supports both points of view in the affirmative action debate: it demonstrates "that a strong family, hard work, and education—not government help—are the keys to overcoming discrimination," and also that success (especially in Washington) is very much a matter of having the right connections (in Powell's case, the Nixon hands whom he first met as a White House fellow in the 1970s). TRB concludes, "Powell's life story, like those of many if not most Amer-

icans of all races, supports the view that neither talent, hard work, personal connections, nor race alone can guarantee success. They all play a part."

16. Nicholas Kristof, "Love and Race," *New York Times,* Dec. 6, 2002. Golf champion Tiger Woods has contributed to this blurring of racial distinctions by disavowing any description of himself as black and inventing a new term—"Cablinasian"—to describe his ethnic background. In early 2003, Harvard Law School professor Randall Kennedy published a book, *Interracial Intimacies,* which celebrated the rise in black-white intermarriage.

POSTSCRIPT: AMERICAN NEPOTISM TODAY

1. See Stephen Hess, *America's Political Dynasties,* Transaction (New Brunswick), 1966. Hess listed eighteen dynastically connected members of the then–U.S. Senate and, in Congress, twelve sons of congressmen, two sons of senators, four representatives with a brother in Congress, three whose husbands were in Congress, and at least six others with more distant blood relations.

2. Ronald Brownstein, "The Successor Generation: American Politics As a Family Business," *American Prospect,* Dec. 1998.

3. Reacting to suggestions that his mother's nineteen-year incumbency would give him an unfair advantage in pursuing her seat, candidate Donald Wooten declared, "Nothing is being handed to me. I didn't grow up with some silver spoon in my mouth." Asked whether his daughter's upcoming bid for his Bronx council seat smacked of nepotism, Rev. Wendell Foster responded: "Jesus is the son of God. Do you call that nepotism?"

4. Daleys and their in-laws may be found at the city's Departments of Transportation, General Services, Parks, Aging, Water, Education, Police, Fire, Aviation, Streets and Sanitation, and Sewers, and in the sheriff's and state's attorney's offices. Bob Secter and William Gaines, "Daley Inc.: Patronage Blooms on Family Tree," *Chicago Tribune,* June 13, 1999.

5. For a survey of the power couple phenomenon during the Clinton administration, see Burt Solomon, "In a Well-Connected Administration Political Power Often Comes in Pairs," *National Journal,* July 3, 1993; also Rebecca Borders, "Democrat Power Couples," *American Spectator,* Sept. 1995.

6. Ringling Brothers' animal trainer Sara Houcke is a seventh-generation circus performer whose family goes back to the eighteenth century. Glenn Collins, "Tiger Tiger Burning Bright," *New York Times,* Feb. 24, 2000. See also Donnalee Frega, *Women of Illusion: A Circus Family's History,* St. Martin's Press (New York), 2001, and Ernest Albrecht, *The New American Circus,* University Press of Florida (Tallahassee), 1995, for an account of family traditions in the circus, including the world-famous Pickle Family.

7. *BusinessWeek,* Apr. 4, 1988, 106–9.

8. Katie Hafner, "Mother, I'm the Boss Now," *New York Times,* July 2, 2000.

9. "The New Nepotism: Why Dynasties Are Making a Comeback," *BusinessWeek,* Apr. 4, 1988.

10. Aristophanes' son became a successful comic poet, and Aeschylus, Sophocles, and Euripides all had sons who wrote tragedies. More recent examples include the Dumas, Trollope, James, Lowell, Sitwell, Waugh, Brontë, and Mann families.

11. Diane Patrick, "A Living Legacy," *Publisher's Weekly,* Feb. 8, 1999, 120.

12. Jeanne Peterson's recent album, *My Calendar,* was produced by her son Paul,

who says, "I believe that this is Mom at her best. Her talent never ceases to amaze me, and she truly gets better with time. I'm proud to be her son!"

13. The source for most of this material, and for the television industry below, is the cross-referenced biographical index of the Internet Movie Database.

14. Lane Michael Bloenbaum, "The Relationship Between the Permeability of the Television Industry in Southern California and Academic Preparation for Careers in Television," Ph.D. dissertation, University of California, Los Angeles, 1993. See Introduction (above) for further details.

15. Gia Kourias, "Cry Me a Rivers," *TimeOut New York,* Aug. 20, 1998.

16. In a story about another boxing-connected family, the *Times* profiled referee Arthur Mercante Jr., whose father refereed the first Ali-Frazier fight and was inducted into the Boxing Hall of Fame in 1995, while his uncle Joe Monte was a boxer who once went eight rounds with Max Schmeling. *New York Times,* Mar. 23, 1999.

17. Steve Wulf, *Sports Illustrated,* Nov. 2, 1992.

18. Bernard F. Lentz and David N. Laband, "Why So Many Children of Doctors Become Doctors: Nepotism vs. Human Capital Transfers," *Journal of Human Resources* 24, no. 3.

19. See, for example, Mary Edwards Wertsch, *Military Brats: Legacies of Childhood Inside the Fortress,* Fawcett Columbine (New York), 1991.

20. Thanks to UPI's Steve Sailer for this information.

21. Lawrence Muhammad, "Newspaper Nepotism Rules: No Spouses Need Apply," *Editor & Publisher,* July 18, 1987.

22. The hiring of academic couples was common in black colleges going back to the nineteenth century. Many black colleges were founded and run by members of one family for several generations, and their familistic ethos usually extended to the community at large. Though nepotism rules were instituted at many black colleges during the Depression, ways were often found to get around them. The number of black academic couples decreased as mainstream opportunities expanded in the seventies and eighties, but nepotism played a major role in sustaining the careers of black female academics for most of the twentieth century. Linda M. Perkins, "For the Good of the Race: Married African-American Academics—A Historical Perspective," in Marianne A. Ferber and Jane W. Loeb, eds., *Academic Couples: Problems and Promises,* University of Illinois Press (Urbana), 1997, 92–96.

23. Joe Holleman, "Bloodlines on the Blue Line," *St. Louis Post-Dispatch,* Dec. 1, 2002. See also Brian McDonald, *My Father's Gun: One Family, Three Badges, One Hundred Years in the NYPD,* Dutton (New York), 1999.

INDEX

Aaron, 122
Abel, 117
Abimelech, 518*n*
Abishag, 113, 114
Abraham, 116, 117–19, 120, 121, 164–65, 245, 518*n*
Absalom, 126, 300–301, 356
academic appointments, 506–7, 544*n*, 548*n*
Adams, Abigail Smith, 294, 295, 296, 298–99, 305, 426
Adams, Charles, 300–301
Adams, Charles Francis, 301, 357
Adams, John, 12, 251, 259, 260, 272, 273, 278, 284, 288, 292–302, 305, 306, 307, 308, 312, 314, 316, 426, 503, 526*n*–27*n*, 528*n*
Adams, John Quincy, 294, 295–98, 300, 301–2, 305, 328, 335–37, 340, 470, 472, 526*n*, 530*n*
Adams, Samuel, 251, 260, 273, 525*n*
Adams, Thomas Boylston, 301
Adams family, 251, 260, 292–302, 312–13, 536*n*
Addams, Jane, 377
Adonijah, 113–14, 126
adoption, 67, 75, 147, 152–53, 156–57, 168, 173, 182, 215–16, 237, 333, 338, 467, 474, 479, 519*n*, 545*n*
adultery, 94, 122, 156, 255, 333
Aegeus, 133–34
Aeneas, 142, 145
Aeschylus, 134, 135
Aesop, 344–45, 346, 350
Africa, 81–89, 94, 100, 101, 103, 110, 115, 116, 158
African Americans, 13–14, 368, 402–3, 408, 443, 449–51, 479, 483–84, 547*n*, 548*n*
  affirmative action and, 13, 547*n*
  see also racism; slavery
agriculture, 84, 85, 100, 106, 111, 186, 342, 353–54, 394
Agrippa, Marcus, 155, 156
Albion's Seed (Fischer), 243
Alcibiades, 128–29, 137–39, 157, 391, 415–16
Alexander the Great, 99–100, 158
Alexander VI, Pope, 190, 191, 195–200, 201
altruism, 16, 53–61, 63–64, 68–69
  see also reciprocal altruism
ambition, 393, 396, 416–17, 419, 428, 447
American Federation of Labor (AFL), 402
American Revolution, *see* War of Independence, U.S.
amicitiae, 146, 150, 519*n*–20*n*
Amnon, 126
Analects (Confucius), 92
Anastasia, Albert, 40, 42
Anastasio, Tough Tony, 40
ancestral cults, 70, 86, 91, 94, 95–96, 103, 111, 115, 143, 167, 530*n*
Andreski, Stanislav, 83, 88
Antigone (Sophocles), 140
Antony, 151–55, 449
ants, 50–51, 53–54, 55, 57–58
apprenticeships, 401–2, 479
Ariadne, 134
aristocracy:
  Athenian, 137–39
  European, 181–83, 185–87, 203, 204–5, 209, 233–34, 271, 378, 482
  "natural," 12–13, 440–41
  non-Western, 87, 92–94
  Roman, 141–42, 148, 151, 155–58
  in U.S., 256–57, 260–62, 302–3, 306, 307, 316–28, 369–70, 372, 373–74, 378–79, 385, 391–92, 432–33, 441, 480
Aristophanes, 138–39

Arius, 520*n*
Arnulf of Metz, 172–73, 175, 466
Aronson, Sidney, 307
Aronson, Theo, 203–4
Arthur, Chester A., 370
Arthurian legends, 184–85, 342
arts, 493–500
Arvad, Inga, 435, 448, 541*n*
asrama, 102–3, 472
Athens, 128–41, 390–91, 519*n*
auctoritas, 145, 146, 156
Augustine, Saint, 168, 177
Augustus, Emperor of Rome, 96, 142, 152–58, 174, 215, 449, 466, 520*n*
Autocrat at the Breakfast Table, The (Holmes), 320
avunculate relationships, 121, 161–62, 183–84, 217, 222, 234, 516*n*, 518*n*
Axelrod, Robert, 60
Ayittey, George, 87

Bache, Benjamin Franklin, 269–70
Bache, Richard, 270
bachelors, 73, 94, 103, 520*n*
Baker, Edward, 349–50, 351
Baltzell, Digby, 44, 245, 266, 378, 441
Balzac, Honoré de, 233
"band of brothers," 279, 281, 285, 442
Banfield, Edward, 34
banking, 186–87, 221–38, 321–22, 399, 422–23, 503
Barbour, Henry, 5
Baron, Salo, 518*n*
Barras, Paul, 212, 214
Barzini, Luigi, 531*n*
Bates, Edward, 356
Bathsheba, 113–14
Beauharnais, Eugène de, 215
Beauharnais, Hortense de, 215–16
Beck, Dave, 436
Bell, Derrick, 13–14
Bellow, Saul, 23
Beowulf, 162, 184, 185, 188
Beran, Michael Knox, 441, 454, 462
Berkeley, William, 251–52, 254
Berlin, Isaiah, 522*n*
Bible, 113–28, 165–66, 176, 245–46, 249, 345, 346, 426, 518*n*–19*n*
Bickel, Alexander M., 419
bilateral descent, 84–85, 148, 181, 264
Bill of Rights, 15, 524*n*
Bilotti, Tommy, 42
Birmingham, Stephen, 399
Bismarck, Otto von, 482
Black, Van Lear, 396
Blaine, James G., 380–81, 382
Blair, Elizabeth, 358
Blair, Francis Preston, 358
Blair, Francis Preston Jr., 358
Blair, Montgomery, 358
Blair family, 358
Bloch, Marc, 162
Bonanno, Bill, 43
Bonanno, Joseph, 41
Bonaparte, Caroline, 125, 208, 214, 215, 216, 217, 218, 219
Bonaparte, Elisa, 206, 207, 208, 212, 217, 219–20, 522*n*
Bonaparte, Hortense, 215–16, 217
Bonaparte, Jérôme, 208, 212, 215, 216, 217, 218, 219
Bonaparte, Joseph, 205, 206, 207, 208, 211, 212, 214, 216, 217, 218, 219
Bonaparte, Josephine de Beauharnais, 212, 214, 215–16, 217, 466
Bonaparte, Louis, 205, 208, 212, 215–16, 218, 219
Bonaparte, Lucien, 207, 208, 210–11, 212, 213, 214, 215, 216, 217, 218, 219, 220
Bonaparte, Pauline, 208, 212, 214, 216, 218
Bonaparte family, 204–8, 219–20, 236, 435
  see also Napoleon I, Emperor of the French; Napoleon III, Emperor of the French
Bonds, Barry, 9
Boniface, Saint, 175, 176
Boniface IX, Pope, 522*n*
Bonilla v. Oakland Scavenger Co., 458
Borgia, Cesare, 190–202, 312, 522*n*
Borgia, Juan, 196–98, 201
Borgia, Lucrezia, 190–91, 198
Borgia family, 203, 236, 435
Bossier, Gaston, 147
Boston, Mass., 324–25, 327, 353, 488
Boston Associates, 316–17, 320, 325
Boston brahmins, 316–28, 422, 425, 444, 465, 466, 529*n*
Bowles, Erskine, 5
Boylston, Susanna, 293
Braddock, William, 282
Bradley, Bill, 46

Brady, James, 534*n*
Brahmins, 104, 105, 106, 516*n*
Brain, Robert, 76
bride abductions, 144, 330, 529*n*–30*n*
Bronfman, Edgar Jr., 481
Brookhart, Smith W., 411
Brownstein, Ronald, 485, 486, 512*n*
Brutus, Lucius Junius, 144, 145
Brutus, Marcus, 141, 150–51
Bryant, Kobe, 9
Buchanan, James, 352
Buderus (Rothschild agent), 226, 227, 229–30
Bundy, McGeorge, 441, 542*n*
Buonaparte, Carlo, 203, 204–8, 219–20, 227, 344, 474, 522*n*
Buonaparte, Letizia Ramolino, 202, 203, 204, 205, 206, 208, 211, 212, 217, 218, 219
bureaucracies, 82, 88, 89, 92, 94–95, 100, 106, 110, 126, 155–56, 174, 179, 191, 192
Burns, Max, 5
Burr, Aaron, 306–7, 309–10
Bush, George H. W., 2, 6
Bush, George W., 1–4, 5–6, 7, 454, 468
Bush, Jeb, 2, 4
Bush family, 1–3, 313, 447, 462, 466
business, 7–12, 109–10, 221–38, 251, 255, 316–28, 373–74, 457–58, 467, 469, 470, 488–92, 543*n*–44*n*
Butler, Edward, 375–76
Byrd, Mary Horsmanden Filmer, 253
Byrd, William, 253
Byrd, William, II, 261
Byzantium, 167, 169, 191–92

Cabot, George, 318
Cabot family, 215, 318, 466, 471, 529*n*
Caesar, Julius, 141–42, 143, 149–54, 449, 519*n*–20*n*
Cain, 117
Caldwell, John, 409
Calhoun, John C., 335, 340, 348
Calixtus III, Pope, 193–95, 201
Cameron, Simon, 356
Canaan, 116, 119, 124
capitalism, 14, 17, 25, 80, 97, 110, 111, 186–87, 224, 251, 318–19, 321–22, 338, 373, 389, 392, 422, 429, 477, 529*n*
Carloman, King of the Franks, 175, 176
Carlson, Allan, 409, 410
Carman, Harry, 358, 359
Carnahan, Jean, 5
Carolingian Empire, 172–85, 520*n*–21*n*
Carr, Peter, 304
Carrington, Dorothy, 219–20
Carter, Robert, 253
Carter, Robert Wormley, 261
Carthage, 147–48
Cassidy, Butch, 367
Cassius, 151, 152, 153
Castellamarese War (1930), 39, 40
Castellano, Paul, 40, 42, 43, 46
caste system, 81, 101–5, 109–10, 469, 508, 516*n*–17*n*
Castro, Fidel, 444, 445
Catholic Church, 11, 20, 96, 158–79, 184, 189, 191–201, 374, 398, 433, 436–39, 461–62, 521*n*–22*n*
Cato, 150–51, 519*n*–20*n*
Cat's Cradle (Vonnegut), 546*n*
Cavalier migration, 243, 252–53, 260–61, 262, 263, 280, 478
Ceauşescu, Nicolae, 98
celibacy, voluntary, 53–54
"chain migration," 244–45, 363–64
Chao, Elaine, 3
charitable endowment, 321, 322, 479–80
Charlemagne, 160–61, 175, 176–79, 180, 181, 183, 184, 466, 520*n*–21*n*
Charles the Bald, King of the Franks, 179
Chase, Salmon P., 356
Chauncey, Henry, 440, 542*n*
Cheney, Elizabeth, 3
Cheney, Lynne, 7
chieftains, 87, 173, 175, 180, 334, 339
children:
  as assets, 75, 77, 158, 338
  development of, 63–66, 69, 73
  education of, 246–47, 271–72, 346, 373–74, 400, 409, 424, 425–26, 452, 538*n*
  legal rights of, 337, 338
  obligation felt by, 67, 404–5, 409–10, 452–53, 539*n*
Chinese civilization, 71, 89–99, 100, 101, 103, 106, 110, 115, 116, 158, 191–92, 461, 471, 516*n*
Chinese Exclusion Act (1882), 533*n*, 537*n*

chivalry, 161–62, 180, 184–85
Choate, Joseph, 385
Chou En-lai, 99
Christianity, 11, 17, 20, 96, 112, 158–79, 184, 189, 191–201, 245–46, 251, 262–67, 346, 352, 365, 374, 398, 433, 436–39, 461–62, 467, 521*n*–22*n*
Cimon, 135–36
Cincinnatus, 145, 329
City of God (St. Augustine), 177
Civil Rights Act (1964), 449–50, 456–58
civil rights movement, 10, 18, 443, 446–47, 449–50, 456–58
civil service, 94–95, 370, 376–77, 380, 410–13, 537*n*
Civil War, American, 243, 260, 263, 342, 352–56, 365, 386, 452
clans, 81, 83, 85–87, 89–99, 100, 103, 111, 115, 116, 124, 130, 143, 149, 154, 155, 173, 186, 187, 189, 201, 203–4, 237, 253–55, 330–35, 467, 521*n*–22*n*
Clapper, Raymond, 411, 412
Clary's Grove boys, 341, 346
Classic of Filial Piety (Confucius), 92
class system, 12, 14, 19, 24, 181–83, 185–87, 353–54, 404, 434, 468–69, 538*n*
Clay, Henry, 328, 329, 348
Cleinias, 137
Cleisthenes, 130, 135
Clement V, Pope, 193, 521*n*–22*n*
Cleopatra, 154, 155
Cleveland, Grover, 381, 384
clientele, 149, 151, 153
Clifford, Clark, 419
Clinton, Bill, 2
Clinton, DeWitt, 526*n*
Clinton, Hillary Rodham, 7, 458
Clinton family, 306, 526*n*
Clotaire I, King of the Franks, 174
Clotaire II, King of the Franks, 175
Clouds (Aristophanes), 139
Clovis, King of the Franks, 173–75, 178, 179, 181, 484
coercion, 59, 62, 75, 128, 342, 356
Coffee, John, 334–35
Cohen, Lizabeth, 404–5
Colombo, Joe, 41
Colonna family, 193, 194, 197, 199, 200
Common Sense (Paine), 272
communism, 97–99, 434
compareggio, 35–36, 44
compari, 35, 36, 38
compassion, 69
Conant, James B., 440
Confucius, 89, 90–92, 95–97, 122, 130, 254, 516*n*
Conkling, Roscoe, 370, 371, 372, 383
connubium, 74–75, 215
Constitution, U.S., 15, 274, 290, 292, 303, 315–16, 362, 457
Cooksey, Deborah, 13
Coon, Carleton, 74
Coppola, Francis Ford, 29
Corkran, Francis S., 360–61
corruption, political, 79–83, 88, 110–11, 142–43, 340, 370, 372, 375, 376–77, 384, 410–13, 530*n*, 535*n*
Corsica, 203–7, 209, 210–11
Cotton, John, 245
Cousinhood, 228–29
Cox, James M., 395
Crassus, 149, 150, 519*n*–20*n*
Crédit Mobilier, 234–35
Creon, 140
crime, organized, 39–40, 44–45, 367, 400, 436
Crofts, Daniel, 354
Culpeper, Frances, 254
Cuomo, Andrew, 5
Curley, James Michael, 413
Custer, George Armstrong, 534*n*
Custis, George Washington Parke, 284–85
Custis, Jacky, 283

Dalai Lama, 14
Dallek, Robert, 541*n*–42*n*
Darwin, Charles, 55, 58
David, 113–14, 124–27, 138, 176, 300–301, 355, 519*n*
Davis, Jefferson, 353
Davis, John H., 42
Dawkins, Richard, 55
Declaration of Independence, 15, 302, 368
Delahay, Mark, 532*n*
Delderfield, R. F., 209
Dellacroce, Neal, 42

democracy:
Athenian, 129, 130, 133, 135–41, 143, 390–91, 415–16, 519*n*
in U.S., 6, 12, 15, 18–19, 46–47, 272–76, 302, 314, 320, 329–30, 339, 342–43, 370, 390–91, 415–16, 465, 469–70, 471, 477
Democratic Party, U.S., 335, 352, 358, 369, 393–96, 403, 406–7, 437–39, 451, 456
Deng Xiaoping, 98, 99, 516*n*
descent rule, 84–85
Deuteronomy, Book of, 123, 249
Dever, Paul, 432
Disney, Walt, 470
Disraeli, Benjamin, 235
divorce, 148, 155, 168, 173, 177, 180, 209, 216, 217, 271, 275, 338, 365, 414, 473, 516*n*
Dixon, James, 360
Dole, Elizabeth, 5, 7
Donald, David, 344, 349
Donelson, Andrew Jackson, 334, 340
Donelson, John, 332
Douglas, William O., 436
Dowd, Maureen, 2, 45–46
dowries, 148, 182, 522*n*
Duby, Georges, 162, 181, 183
Dulles family, 470–71, 544*n*–45*n*
Dunbar, Asa, 451
Du Pont family, 471
Dylan, Jakob, 8–9

Earp, Wyatt, 367
Easter, Marilyn, 13
Eaton, John Henry, 339
Eaton, Peggy Timberlake, 339–40
Edwards, Cyrus, 348
Edwards, Ninian Wirt, 348, 349
Einstein, Albert, 482
Eisenhower, Dwight D., 442
elders, 87, 123, 409–10, 519*n*
elephants, 50, 51, 66
Elizabeth I, Queen of England, 186
Elon, Amos, 228
Enemy Within, The (R. F. Kennedy), 440
"enlightened paternalism," 271, 312
entail, 17–18
entrepreneurship, 17, 189, 224–25, 230, 237, 327, 332
Esau, 119–20, 518*n*
Essex Junto, 306, 318, 319–20, 326
Ethics for the New Millennium (Dalai Lama), 14
Etruscans, 143, 144
eunuchs, 95–96, 110–11, 191–92, 461, 516*n*
Euripides, 134
Europe:
aristocracy of, 181–83, 185–87, 203, 204–5, 209, 233–34, 271, 378, 482
civilization of, 100, 128, 136, 158–59, 162–63, 168, 179, 202
class system of, 181–83, 185–87
Evans, F. S., 360–61
Evans-Pritchard, E. E., 86
evolution, 52, 55, 58, 63, 67, 69–70, 72–73, 77–78, 514*n*
Exodus, Book of, 121

Fables (Aesop), 345–46
Faces at the Bottom of the Well (Bell), 13
Fairfax, Thomas, 281, 282
familia, 180–82, 194
families:
authority of, 91–92, 103, 145, 171, 177, 271, 276, 285–86, 369, 404–5, 409–10, 452
"brands" of, 425, 437
in caste systems, 101–5, 109–10
close associates of, 424–25, 435–36, 442, 443, 448
compound, 69–70, 100–103, 303
corporate, 425–26
crime, 29–49
disintegration of, 353–56, 453–54, 463–65, 481–82
dynastic, 7, 19, 86, 100, 107–8, 114, 116, 124–25, 141–42, 146–51, 155–58, 172–75, 181, 185–87, 189–91, 201–2, 219–22, 228–29, 233, 236–37, 245, 261–62, 271–72, 292, 300, 304, 316–26, 415–16, 420–21, 422, 430, 431, 449, 454, 455, 460, 465–71, 480–82, 530*n*
extended, 17, 34, 84, 89–99, 162, 163, 173, 246–47, 256, 264, 266, 338, 364, 367, 474–75, 479, 545*n*, 546*n*

fraternal harmony and, 101–2, 123, 182, 230–31, 276, 279, 285–86, 291–92, 355, 420, 437, 440, 442,467
honor of, 34–35, 183–84, 252, 255, 256, 286, 334, 339–40, 353, 386
kinship ties of, 62–63, 66, 67, 68–69, 71, 73–76, 100, 101–2, 111–12, 159, 170–71, 179–80, 228–29, 247–48, 250, 287–88, 324–25, 338, 354–55, 364–65, 400, 452, 463–65, 473–79, 545*n*
legal status of, 112, 142, 144, 148, 156, 474
nuclear, 17, 34, 64–65, 71, 72, 85, 189, 246–47, 256, 271, 338, 478, 479, 529*n*
political influence of, 145–46, 339, 341, 351–52, 432–40, 442–43, 448–49, 455
size of, 418, 423, 466–67, 515*n*
society and, 254, 272–73, 477–79, 483–84, 522*n*, 543*n*, 545*n*
surrogate, 285–86, 541*n*–42*n*
survival of, 63, 67, 69–74, 364–65
traditional, 96–97, 365, 404–5, 409–10, 473–74
values of, 22, 44–45, 58, 67–69, 130, 263–65, 320, 424–25
see also children; fathers; mothers; parents

familism, 34, 421, 422, 427–28, 447
Family Compact of Connecticut, The, 527*n*
Farnsworth, William, 183–84
Farrell, Betty G., 323, 325, 327, 529*n*
fathers:
authority of, 101–2, 103, 124, 129–35, 140–41, 144–45, 148, 166–67, 185, 276, 278–79, 313, 338, 475
corporate, 416–17
"political," 268–69, 278–80, 285–86, 295, 312, 356
sons and, 91–94, 116–17, 123, 131–35, 138–41, 145, 148, 153, 162, 168, 185–86, 230–31, 248, 258, 261, 276, 325–26, 327, 338, 346, 372, 381, 390–91, 401–2, 416–17, 418, 439, 452, 464–65, 482
surrogate, 133, 278–82

"Father's Resolutions, A" (Mather), 523*n*–24*n*
Fatico, Carmine "Charlie Wagons," 41
Federalist, 279
Federalist Party, 309, 316, 319–20, 333, 336
feminism, 10, 13, 446–47, 459–60
Ferguson, Niall, 233, 234
Fess, Simeon D., 411
feudalism, 17, 88, 89–92, 126, 161–63, 177–87, 192, 259, 391, 521*n*
feuds, 77, 86–87, 172, 175, 179, 180, 185, 188–89, 285–86, 330, 353, 391, 443, 444, 521*n*
Feuer, Lewis, 451
filial piety, 91–94, 116–17, 123, 132–33, 134, 135, 139–40, 145, 153, 168, 230–31, 248, 372, 381, 390, 418, 452, 464–65
Fischer, David Hackett, 243, 245, 246, 254, 256, 258, 260, 261, 330, 331, 352, 529*n*
Fisher, Helen, 58
Fitzgerald, John Francis, 421–22, 423, 424, 429, 431, 434, 448, 456, 539*n*–40*n*
Flo (chimpanzee), 61–62
Ford, Edsel, 470, 536*n*
Ford, Harold, Jr., 5
Ford, William, 8
Forrestal, James, 431
Fourteenth Amendment, 457
Fox, Robin, 71, 121, 518*n*
Franklin, Benjamin, 262–70, 525*n*
Franklin, James, 267, 525*n*
Franklin, John, 267, 268, 269
Franklin, Peter, 268, 269
Franklin, Temple, 269
Franklin, William, 268, 269
fraternal harmony, 101–2, 123, 182, 230–31, 276, 279, 285–86, 291–92, 356, 420, 437, 440, 442, 467
Frazier, James, 86
Frelinghuysen, Rodney, 6
French Revolution, 209–14, 221, 227, 232, 290, 378, 522*n*
Freneau, Philip, 291
Freud, Sigmund, 22, 48, 70, 72
Frick, Henry Clay, 389
friendship, 35, 37, 57, 67, 146–47, 342, 346–52, 353, 354, 377, 475–76, 531*n*
Frost, Robert, 476
Gadagkar, Raghavendra, 52, 57–58

Galante, Carmine, 41
Gallatin, Albert, 307
Galton, Francis, 506
Gambino, Carlo, 38, 40–42, 43, 466
Gambino, Tommy, 40, 43
Gandhi, Feroze, 107
Gandhi, Indira, 107–8
Gandhi, Mohandas K., 102, 106, 108
Gandhi, Priyanka, 111
Gandhi, Rajiv, 107, 108
Gandhi, Sanjay, 107, 108, 517*n*
Gandhi, Sonia, 111
Ganelon, 521*n*
Garfield, James A., 370, 383
Gargantua (Rabelais), 522*n*–23*n*
Gary, Romain, 454
Gates, Bill, 468, 480
genealogy, 84–87, 89, 92–94, 181, 249, 253–54, 273, 325, 474, 522*n*
Genovese, Vito, 40
gens, 143, 144, 519*n*
George, Henry, 382
German Americans, 361, 398–99, 400, 401
Giancana, Sam, 443
Gibbon, Edward, 167
Gift, The (Mauss), 76–77
gift economy, 76–77, 86, 105, 173, 175, 185, 210, 259, 359–60, 377, 423, 464, 465, 472–73, 515*n*, 517*n*, 520*n*, 523*n*
God, 116–17, 123–24, 128, 164–65, 248
Godfather movies, 29–33, 36, 44, 46, 47
godparents, 33, 35–36, 93, 171, 467, 513*n*
Goering, Hermann, 236
Goldberg, Matthew S., 13
Golden Rule, 262, 265, 345
Gompers, Samuel, 402
Goodall, Jane, 61
Goodwin, Doris, 422, 432
Gore, Albert Jr., 1–3, 6, 45–46
Gore, Albert Sr., 2
Gosnell, Harold, 387
Gotti, John, 41, 42–43
government appointments, 91–92, 107–8, 130, 141–42, 177–79, 285–86, 289–92, 406–10
Grant, Ulysses S., 340, 341, 370, 530*n*
Gravano, Salvatore "Sammy the Bull," 43
Graves, Robert, 154
Great Britain, 100, 105, 270–76, 278, 280, 290, 428–29, 482, 525*n*
Great Depression, 391–92, 397, 404–7, 428, 458, 538*n*
Greece, ancient, 112, 128–41, 390–91, 446, 519*n*
Greek Way, The (Hamilton), 446
green-fronted bee-eater, 54, 58, 59
Greven, Philip, 249–50, 524*n*
Guinevere, 184–85
Guiteau, Charles, 370

Hagar, 118
Haig, Alexander, 546*n*–47*n*
Haimon, 140
Hamilcar Barca, 147
Hamilton, Alexander, 286–91, 299–300, 302, 306, 310, 312, 335–36, 388, 522*n*
Hamilton, Edith, 446
Hamilton, Nigel, 433
Hamilton, William D., 55–56, 57, 58
Hamilton's Rule, 56, 58, 64
Hamlet (Shakespeare), 189
Hancock, John, 259–60
Hanna, Mark, 385, 388
Hannibal, 147–48
Hardin, John, 349–51
harems, 94, 95–96, 114, 126, 127
Harilelas, 110
Harrison, Benjamin, 311, 384
Harvard University, 323–24, 379, 392–93, 422, 429, 433–34, 440, 451–52, 539*n*
Hawthorne, Nathaniel, 241–42, 275
Hayes, Rutherford B., 370, 372
Hearst, William Randolph, 414, 428
Heine, Heinrich, 233
Helm, Ben Hardin, 355–56
Hemings, Sally, 483, 484
Henry, William A., 20
Henry V (Shakespeare), 279
Hera, 132
Herndon, William, 343–44, 350
Hersey, John, 431
Hertzberg, Hendrik, 3, 19
Hess, Stephen, 382, 395, 414, 415, 547*n*
Hesseltine, William, 530*n*
Hewitt, Abram, 382
"hierarchical communalism," 245
Higginson, Thomas Wentworth, 320
Hightower, Jim, 2

Hinduism, 100–105, 109–10, 111, 516*n*–17*n*
Hitler, Adolf, 202–3, 428, 432
Hobbes, Thomas, 478
Hoffa, James, 436, 443, 445
Hoffa, James Jr., 403, 507
Hoffman, Susanna, 476
Hollywood, 9, 405–6, 425, 436, 496–99, 538*n*
Holmes, Oliver Wendell, 320, 323
Homestead Act (1862), 363
Hoover, J. Edgar, 434, 541*n*
Horatius, 145
Hosea, 124
Houphouët-Boigny, Félix, 88, 516*n*
Houston, Sam, 335
Howe, Louis, 394–95, 396, 397, 407
Hrdy, Sarah Blaffer, 58, 62, 63–64
Hughes, H. Stuart, 449
Hugo, Victor, 201
Hull, John, 248
Humphrey, Hubert, 415, 438
hunter-gatherers, 72, 76, 84–85
Hussein, Saddam, 6
Hutcheson, William L., 403
Hutchinson, Tim, 4–5
hymenopterans, 53–54, 57, 96, 118
hypergamy, 293, 294

I, Claudius (Graves), 154
Ianni, Francis, 43–44
Icarus syndrome, 430
Iglesias, Enrique, 9
illegitimacy, 173, 177, 182, 209, 255, 338, 344, 473, 521*n*
I'm for Roosevelt (J. P. Kennedy), 540*n*–41*n*
immigrants, 30, 38–39, 75, 108, 244–45, 249–50, 257–58, 271, 278, 324, 330–34, 354, 361–64, 374–75, 377, 385, 397–404, 405, 420, 421, 432, 456, 532*n*, 537*n*, 539*n*
Immigration Act (1965), 456
inbreeding, 59, 64, 366
incest, 58, 62, 70, 71, 75, 121, 171, 180, 435, 515*n*, 518*n*
"inclusive fitness," 56
In Defense of Elitism (Henry), 20
indentured servitude, 256–58, 260, 262, 267, 275, 467
India, 99–111, 115, 116, 158, 516*n*–17*n*
Indians, American, 71, 74, 248, 366–67, 534*n*
individualism, 18–19, 48, 78, 84, 99, 111, 159, 168, 186, 189, 202, 242, 331, 345–46, 363, 367, 382, 477–78, 482–83
Industrial Revolution, 232, 316, 405
infanticide, 65
infant mortality, 182
Innocent III, Pope, 521*n*
Innocent VIII, Pope, 196
insects, 53–54, 57, 58, 96, 118
International Longshoremen's Association (ILA), 40
Ion, 130
Irish Americans, 361, 375, 398–99, 400, 401, 420, 421, 424–25, 448, 537*n*
Isaac, 118, 119–20, 165
Ishmael, 118, 518*n*
Islam, 106, 108–9, 160–61, 518*n*
Ismailis, 109–10
Italian Americans, 33–35, 398, 400, 401, 537*n*

Jaan, Kamla, 110–11
Jackson, Andrew, 310, 328–41, 346, 347, 358, 363, 370, 407, 529*n*
Jackson, Patrick Tracy, 316, 326
Jackson, Rachel, 332–34, 338, 339
Jacob, 120–21
Jacobins, 209–10, 213
Jains, 109
James, William, 323
James (brother of Jesus), 163
James gang, 367
jatis, 104, 516*n*–17*n*
Jay, Nancy, 119
Jefferson, George, 308
Jefferson, Jane Randolph, 303
Jefferson, Martha Washington, 304
Jefferson, Martha Wayles Skelton, 304
Jefferson, Peter, 303
Jefferson, Thomas, 12, 18, 253, 289–92, 297, 300, 302–11, 314, 316, 319, 443, 483, 484, 527*n*, 528*n*
Jerome, Saint, 168
Jesse, 125
Jesus Christ, 163–66, 171, 345, 520*n*
Jews, 112, 113–28, 163, 164–65, 166, 222–24, 227–28, 230–34, 244, 245,

375, 390, 399–400, 401, 405, 408, 425, 466, 471, 518*n*–19*n*, 523*n*, 538*n*
Jiang Zhumin, 99
Joab, 126
Johnson, Benjamin, 365
Johnson, Lyndon B., 415, 439, 446, 447, 449–50, 451, 456, 541*n*–42*n*
Johnson, Paul, 125–26, 518*n*
Jonathan, 125
Joseph (father of Jesus), 164
Joseph (son of Jacob), 121, 463, 518*n*
Joshua, 124
journalism, 8, 505–6
Judah, 124, 125–26, 127
Judd, Norman, 352
Julia (daughter of Augustus), 154, 156
Julia (daughter of Caesar), 150–51
Julio-Claudian clan, 154, 155–58, 215, 466
Julius II, Pope, 200
Jung Chang, 98

Kabila, Laurent, 82
Karve, Irawati, 101–3, 516*n*
Keating, Kenneth, 447
Kempton, Murray, 435
Kennedy, Edward M., 445–46, 448–49, 455–56, 461–62, 543*n*
Kennedy, Jacqueline Bouvier, 436, 442, 446
Kennedy, John F., 407, 415, 418–20, 424, 425, 427, 429, 430–46, 447, 449–50, 451, 453, 454–55, 456, 540*n*, 541*n*–42*n*
Kennedy, John F. Jr., 455, 480–81
Kennedy, Joseph P. Jr., 423, 426–31, 432, 437, 440, 445, 539*n*
Kennedy, Joseph P. Sr., 375, 419–40, 444–45, 447, 448, 453, 461, 465–66, 540*n*–41*n*
Kennedy, Mike, 407
Kennedy, Patrick, 455
Kennedy, P. J., 421, 422, 472
Kennedy, Randall, 547*n*
Kennedy, Robert F., 418–20, 433–35, 436, 437, 442–55, 456, 472, 540*n*, 541*n*, 542*n*
Kennedy, Rose Fitzgerald, 423, 426, 433
Kennedy family, 5, 313, 418–62, 467
Kenny, Kevin, 401
Kessler, Ronald, 424, 539*n*
Kim Jong Il, 98
King Lear (Shakespeare), 463–65, 474, 477, 521*n*
kinship:
  artificial, 35, 78, 513*n*–14*n*
  family connections in, 62–63, 66, 67, 68–69, 71, 73–76, 100, 101–2, 111–12, 159, 170–71, 179–80, 228–29, 247–48, 250, 287–88, 324–25, 338, 354–55, 365, 400, 452, 463–65, 473–79, 545*n*
  feudal, 180–85
  nepotism and, 16–17, 23–24, 44, 55–58, 59, 62–63, 81, 84–86, 111–12, 129–31, 144, 237, 278, 313, 325–27, 349, 473–79, 515*n*
  selection in, 55–58, 59, 60–63, 68–69, 127–28, 341, 471
  universal, 165, 180, 362–63, 368, 406–7, 482, 483–84, 525*n*–26*n*
  see also families
Kirk, Alan, 430
knighthood, 160–62, 180, 182–85
Kotch v. Board of River Boat Pilot Commissioners, 457, 543*n*
Kotkin, Joel, 109, 115, 230
Krock, Arthur, 425, 429, 432
Kronos, 72, 132, 421
Kufuor, John Agyekum, 82

Laban, 120–21, 518*n*
labor, division of, 54, 60, 69
labor movement, 389, 397–403, 436, 507
Laemmle, Carl, 405–6, 470
La Guardia, Fiorello, 408
Lamoreaux, Naomi, 321
Lancelot, 184–85, 342
land distribution, 97, 254, 265
Landrieu, Mary, 5
Lansberg, Ivan, 492
Lasch, Christopher, 19, 450–51, 513*n*
Laurens, John, 286
Lawford, Patricia Kennedy, 436
Lawrence family, 325, 326, 529*n*
leadership, 334–35, 336–37, 342, 346, 348, 378, 431, 432–33
Leah, 120
Leamer, Laurence, 435
Leclerc, Victor-Emmanuel, 212, 213, 214, 523*n*

Lee, Anne Constable, 253
Lee, Philip, 261
Lee, Richard, 253
Lee, Richard Henry, 524*n*
Lee, Robert E., 285, 532*n*
Lee, Samuel Phillips, 359
Lee family, 251–53, 261, 285
Lemann, Nicholas, 441
Lennon, Julian, 8–9
Lennon, Sean, 8–9
Lepidus, Marcus, 153, 154
Lévi-Strauss, Claude, 73
Lewis, R. W. B., 323
Lewis, William B., 335
Lewis, W. T., 333
liberty, 251, 263, 265, 345, 473
Life of St. Arnulf, 176
Lincoln, Abraham, 341–63, 365, 368, 406, 407, 473, 484, 531*n*, 532*n*
Lincoln, Isaac, 347
Lincoln, Mary Todd, 349, 355
Lincoln, Mordecai, 343, 347
Lincoln, Nancy Hanks, 343, 344
Lincoln, Robert Todd, 359
Lincoln, Samuel, 343
Lincoln, Sarah Johnston, 344
Lincoln, Thomas, 343–44, 346, 347, 531*n*
Li Peng, 99
Lippmann, Walter, 406
literature, 493–94
Livia Drusilla, 154, 155, 157, 215, 466, 520*n*
Livingston, Edward, 309
Livingston, Robert, 6–7
Livingston family, 306, 309, 528*n*
Livy, 143, 146
Locascio, Frank, 43
Locke, John, 271
Lodge, George, 448–49
Lodge, Henry Cabot, 382, 384, 385, 387, 388, 456
Lodge, Henry Cabot Jr., 434–35
Lodge family, 215, 318, 466
Logan, Stephen T., 349
Lomasney, Martin, 376
Longworth, Alice Roosevelt, 395–96
Lowell, Francis Cabot, 316, 318
Lowell, John, 318
Lowell, John Amory, 326
Lowell family, 317, 318–19, 327, 471, 529*n*
loyalty, 88–89, 177–78, 180–81, 183–85, 331–32, 335–36, 340–41, 375–76, 443, 531*n*
Lucchese, Tommy, 38, 41, 43
Luce, Henry R., 429
Luciano, Lucky, 39–40
Lucrezia Borgia (Hugo), 201
Lundberg, Ferdinand, 391

McBeth, John, 79
McCarthy, Eugene, 451, 454
McCarthy, Joseph, 434, 435, 436
McCarthy, Mary Lou, 462
McCarty, Bill, 367
McClellan, John, 436–37
McCormack, Edward J., 448–49
McCullough, David, 384
MacDonald, Kevin, 123–24
McGraw, Harold, III, 8
Machiavelli, Niccolò, 190, 200
machines, political, 369–70, 372, 374–78, 383, 386–87, 395, 397–98, 400, 406, 422
McIlvane, Joshua H., 366
Mack, John, 393, 395
McKellar, Kenneth, 407
McKinley, William, 385, 388
McNairy, James, 332
McNamara, Robert, 441, 542*n*
Madison, James, 279, 302, 311
Maecenas, 155
mafia, 3, 29–49, 186, 232, 419, 424, 425, 436, 437, 443–44, 466, 513*n*, 541*n*
Magee, Chris, 375
Magoffin, Beriah, 355
Mahabharata, 100, 101, 103, 516*n*, 517*n*
Mahoney, Richard, 445
Maine, Henry, 21, 477
Malinowski, Bronislaw, 515*n*
Mangano, Vince, 40, 42
Mann, Horace, 338
Manning, Peyton, 9
Mao Zedong, 97, 98–99
Maranzano, Salvatore, 39
Marathon, Battle of, 135, 136, 138
Marawaris, 109
Marbeuf, comte de, 205, 206–7
Marie Louise, Empress of the French, 217–18
Marius, 149

marriages:
advantageous, 293, 294, 350, 435–36
arranged, 75, 78, 102, 188–89, 223, 234, 325, 467
consanguineous, 117, 222, 365–66, 515*n*
of cousins, 18, 71, 117, 170, 222, 250, 253–55, 319, 325, 365–66, 369, 392, 393, 474, 518*n*, 529*n*, 534*n*, 545*n*
dynastic, 149, 150–51, 154, 155–58, 211, 212, 237, 293, 294, 466
endogamous, 123, 127–28, 320, 366, 518*n*
exogamous, 71, 118, 127, 366, 435
interracial, 483–84, 547*n*
kinship ties of, 62, 84–86, 144, 325–27, 349, 515*n*
levirate, 122–23, 173
occupational, 460, 513*n*, 544*n*
as religious duty, 103, 122–23
sibling exchange, 71, 529*n*
as survival strategy, 72–74, 94
tribal alliances and, 73–76, 87, 117
Martin V, Pope, 193
Mary, 163, 171, 184–85
Masseria, Joe, 38, 39
"maternalists," 410
Mather, Cotton, 247, 524*n*
Mather, Eleazar, 249
Mather, Increase, 246
Mather, Richard, 245
matrilineal descent, 85, 119, 120, 150, 162, 181, 515*n*–16*n*
Matthew, Gospel of, 166
Mauss, Marcel, 76–77, 105, 472, 517*n*, 520*n*
Maxwell, Mary, 52, 69
Mayer, Louis B., 538*n*
media, mass, 420, 439–40, 474, 499–500
Medici family, 186–87, 224
Mehta, Ved, 110
Melville, Herman, 315, 320, 532*n*
mentors, 304–5, 313, 479
Mephibosheth, 519*n*
mercantilism, 159, 173, 186–87, 189, 245, 273, 316–28, 529*n*, 544*n*
Merovingian Empire, 173–76
Michal, 125
middle class, 186, 209, 238, 365, 367–68, 369, 377–78, 388, 389–90, 393, 397, 416, 418
military service, 131, 147–48, 189, 503
Miltiades, 136
Minos, 134
Mitchell, J. R., 410, 411, 412
Moi, Daniel arap, 82
mole rats, 54, 58
Molly Maguires, 401
monarchy, 12, 77, 87, 89–90, 92, 94, 95–96, 113–14, 116, 124–27, 143, 144, 175–79, 181, 209, 259, 273, 278, 280, 290, 443
monogamy, 64–65, 177, 363–66, 474, 478
monotheism, 112, 114, 116–18, 122, 165
Monroe, James, 304, 305, 328, 329
Moore, Eddie, 540*n*
Mordred, 185
Morgan, Edmund S., 248, 249
Morgan, J. P., 386, 389
Morgan, Lewis Henry, 21, 366, 534*n*
Morison, Samuel Eliot, 319–20
Mormons, 363–66, 412, 533*n*, 534*n*
Morrill Anti-Bigamy Act (1862), 363, 365
Morton, Frederic, 234
Moses, 96, 121–24, 127, 130, 163, 227, 519*n*
Mother Nature (Hrdy), 63
mothers, 50, 61–66, 68, 171, 477, 534*n*
surrogate, 50, 68, 545*n*
Mount, Ferdinand, 478
Mouser, Grant E., 411
Mugabe, Robert, 82
Muhlenberg, Frederick, 309
Muhlenberg, Peter, 309
Munz, Peter, 520*n*
Murat, Joachim, 125, 213, 214, 215, 217, 218
Murdoch, Lachlan, 8
music, 494–96
Musto, David F., 301–2
Mwanawasa, Levy, 82
"My Kinsman, Major Molineux" (Hawthorne), 241–42, 275

Nagel, Paul, 298, 300, 301
Napoleon I, Emperor of the French, 96, 125, 174, 202–21, 229, 230, 287, 312, 331, 466, 470
Napoleon III, Emperor of the French, 217, 219, 234–35, 466, 522*n*, 523*n*
Nast, Thomas, 383
Nathan, 113–14

nation-states, 87–88, 124, 125–26, 130, 186
naturalistic fallacy, 52
natural selection, 55–56, 57, 66
Navasky, Victor, 443
negative reciprocity, 60, 351, 353, 520*n*
Nehru, Jawaharlal, 100, 106–7
Nelson, Lars-Erik, 3
Nelson, Thomas Jr., 286
nepotism:
  Ancient, 17, 18, 81, 83, 88, 89, 100, 104, 158, 468, 475, 476–77
  art of, 463–84
  bad vs. good, 15–16, 22, 470–73, 480
  biological, 16–17, 19, 22–23, 44, 50–69, 70, 78, 111, 168, 466–67, 473, 475–76, 514*n*, 534–36*n*
  Classical, 17, 18, 112, 143–44, 156, 158, 209, 221, 237, 261, 338–39, 374, 420, 468
  criticism of, 4, 11–16, 17–19, 30–31, 237–38, 243–44, 272–79, 307–14, 328–41, 363, 410–13, 420, 442–43, 468–70
  cultural influence of, 52–53, 77–78, 322–24, 352–56
  definition of, 11, 23–24, 191, 521n
  ecclesiastical, 11, 20, 461–62, 521*n*
  egalitarianism vs., 16–17, 114, 129–30, 133, 144, 145–46, 249–50, 251, 256, 263–66, 274–75, 278, 307–8, 342, 420, 481
  elitism and, 12, 18–19, 328, 373–74, 378, 391–92, 416, 469
  erotic element in, 52, 62–63, 69–72, 75, 121, 134, 140, 171, 180, 515*n*, 518*n*
  ethnic, 108, 109–10, 368, 369, 374–78, 397–403, 408, 418, 473, 517*n*
  evolution of, 52, 55, 58, 77–78, 514*n*
  generational transition and, 132–33, 138–41, 145–46, 418, 460–62, 465, 467, 479, 484
  legal status of, 369, 370, 410–12, 420, 449–50, 456–60, 469–70, 534*n*, 543–44*n*
  meritocracy vs., 3, 10, 12–13, 15, 17–18, 19, 80–81, 106, 115, 182, 207, 273, 292–93, 307–8, 319, 320, 329, 339, 342, 347, 370, 377–78, 389–90, 420, 427, 440–45, 459, 468–69, 503, 506–8, 542*n*–43*n*
  morality of, 25, 56–57, 67–69, 80–81, 88, 139–40, 251
  natural history of, 50–78
  New, 7–11, 14–16, 19–20, 468–69, 472, 479, 480
  Old, 10–11, 14–18, 47–48, 449, 472
  patronage and, 12–13, 36–37, 82–83, 105, 111, 145–47, 149, 151, 152, 155–56, 192, 202–3, 212, 214–21, 256, 259–60, 268–70, 273, 278, 281–83, 296–98, 309–14, 329, 332–33, 336–37, 339, 356–61, 370, 406–8, 418–20, 458, 471
  political, *see* politics, political influence
  postmodern, 460–62
  psychology of, 2, 22, 48, 68, 69, 70, 426, 432, 445
  symbolic, 351–52, 354
  values transmitted by, 16, 44–45, 77–78, 92–94, 134–35
nepotismo, 11, 20, 191
New Deal, 18, 369, 397, 406–10, 420, 458
New England, 243, 244–51, 255, 256, 275, 315–16, 326, 329, 409, 534*n*
New Testament, 165–66
New York Customs House, 371–72, 383, 384
New York Police Department, 384–85
Nicholas III, Pope, 193
Nicias, 128
Nipotismo di Roma, Il, 20
Nixon, Richard M., 439
Noah, 122
nobility, feudal, 162, 177–87, 192–93, 259
nomadic pastoralism, 100, 115–16
Nourse, Joseph, 310, 336, 528*n*
Noyes, Joseph, 364, 533*n*
Numbers, Book of, 121–22

O'Connor, Thomas, 421, 539*n*
Octavia, 154
O'Donnell, Ken, 434
Oedipus, 134, 140
Offut, Denton, 341, 347
Old Testament, 113–28, 165, 176, 345, 364, 426, 518*n*–19*n*
oligarchy, 12, 48–49, 142, 155, 378
Olivier, 160, 184
Onan, 123

Oneida community, 364, 533*n*
Operation Anvil, 431
Oppenheim, Wolf Jakob, 225
Oppenheimer, Samuel, 523*n*
organized crime, 39–40, 44–45, 367, 400, 436
Orsini family, 193, 194, 195, 197, 200
Ottenheimer, Martin, 366
Ouranos, 132
Overton, John, 334
Owsley, Frank L., 354

Page, John, 311
Paine, Thomas, 272
Pangandaman, Lininding, 79
Paoli, Pascal, 204, 210–11
papacy, 174, 176, 178–79, 190, 191–201, 215, 522*n*
Papandreou, Andreas, 79–80
parents, 54, 58, 61–66, 223, 364, 413–15, 464–65, 477, 522*n*–23*n*, 545*n*
Parker, John, 275
paterfamilias, 144–45, 156, 307
patriarchy, 13, 47–48, 86, 89–90, 92, 101–2, 112, 115, 129–35, 140–41, 148, 158, 165–66, 171, 209, 210, 230, 246, 248, 257, 260–61, 271–72, 273, 275, 312, 338, 369, 410, 425–26, 475, 478, 529*n*
patrilineal descent, 85–86, 117–19, 120, 121, 143, 162, 181, 183, 519*n*
Paul, Saint, 163–66, 345
Pelosi, Nancy, 5
Pendergast, Jim, 375, 535*n*
Pendleton Act (1883), 370, 534*n*
Penn, William, 263, 264–65
Pennsylvania, 243, 262–70, 345
Pepin III, King of the Franks, 175–76
Pepin of Landen, 173, 175
Percy family, 186
Pericles, 129, 135–37, 138, 139, 140, 390–91, 415, 416
Perkins and Co., 317
Perry, Matthew, 535*n*
Persians, The (Aeschylus), 135
Philadelphia, Pa., 262–70
Philippi, Battle of, 153–54
phratries, 130, 143, 519*n*
Pickering, Charles W., 5
Pickering, Chip, 5
Pickering, Thomas, 299, 527*n*
Pinker, Steven, 52
Pitt-Rivers, Julian, 37
Pius II, Pope, 195–96
plantation system, 255, 258–59, 260–61, 304–5
Plato, 136–37, 139–40, 519*n*
Platt, Thomas, 382, 383, 384, 385, 386–88, 536*n*
Plunkitt, George Washington, 376–77
Po Ch'in, 90
politics, political influence, 1–7, 12, 24, 36–37, 89–90, 132, 135–36, 142–47, 155–56, 202–3, 209–21, 253–54, 255, 261–62, 309–14, 328–41, 356–61, 393, 406, 418–20, 432–33, 438–39, 485–88
  corruption in, 79–83, 88, 110–11, 142–43, 340, 370, 372, 375, 376–77, 384, 410–13, 530*n*, 535*n*
  factions in, 109, 146–47, 192, 195–96, 268, 277–79, 288, 289, 299–300, 305–6, 329, 335, 339–40, 349, 368, 374–78, 517*n*
  of families, 145–46, 339–40, 341, 351–52, 432–40, 442–43, 448–49, 455
  "fathers" in, 268–69, 278–80, 285–86, 295, 312, 356
  machines in, 369–70, 372, 374–78, 383, 386–87, 395, 398, 400, 407, 422
  wealth and, 322–23, 410–13, 437, 438, 440, 455, 479–80
  women and, 384, 396, 433, 435, 449
Polk, James K., 335
Pollock, James, 360
Polo, Marco, 187
polygamy, 18, 65, 74, 87, 94, 95–96, 119, 126, 168, 363–66, 369, 474, 533*n*
Polynices, 140
Pompey, 149–51, 154, 519*n*–20*n*
populism, 389, 391–92
Porus, 99–100
potlatch ceremony, 76, 77
poverty, 33–35, 407, 450–51, 453–54, 537*n*
Powell, Colin, 482–83, 547*n*
Powell, Michael, 3, 4
priests, 122, 124, 126, 162, 191–92, 222
primates, 61, 64–65, 67, 71
primogeniture, 17–18, 113–14, 181, 209,

249, 250, 255, 260, 261, 271, 319, 321, 446
Prince, The (Machiavelli), 190
Pringle, Henry, 390
Profaci, Rosalie, 43
Prohibition, 38–39, 424
Protestant Ethic, The (Weber), 251
Pryor, Mark, 5
Puritans, 243, 244–52, 253, 256, 262, 263, 264, 266, 293, 317, 320, 331, 336, 352, 365, 478, 524*n*
Puzo, Mario, 29, 33

Quakers, 243, 262–67, 345, 352, 365

Rabelais, François, 523*n*
Rachel, 120
racism, 13–14, 18, 84, 103–4, 390, 402–3, 456–58, 459
Raleigh, Walter, 252
Ramayana, 100, 516*n*
Randolph, A. Phillip, 402
Randolph, Edmund, 304
Randolph, John, 254, 308, 524*n*
Randolph, Thomas Mann Jr., 304
Randolph, William, 253
Randolph family, 215
Rayburn, Sam, 542*n*
Rebekah, 117, 119
reciprocal altruism, 59–61, 62, 68–69, 76–77, 78, 86, 91, 123–24, 128, 262–63, 265–66, 341, 349–51, 356, 361, 368, 375, 423, 455–56, 473, 476, 514*n*
Reformation, 192, 251
Rehoboam, 127
religion, 86, 103, 111, 112, 116–17, 122–23, 131, 163–66, 167, 504
Renaissance, 190–202
Renehan, William, 427
Republican Party, U.S., 305–6, 349, 351–53, 358–60, 365, 369, 370, 379–83, 386–87, 393, 395–96
Republic (Plato), 140, 519*n*
Reston, James, 543*n*
revenge, 86–87, 189
Richmond Junto, 335
Ridley, Matt, 52, 59, 69, 98, 514*n*
Riis, Jacob, 385
Robertson, Thomas Bolling, 310
Robespierre, Augustin, 211
Robespierre, Maximilien-François-Marie-Isidore de, 210, 522*n*
Rockefeller family, 536*n*
Rogin, Michael, 329–30, 338
Roland, 160–62, 180, 183, 184, 185, 334, 521*n*
Roman civilization, 112, 131, 141–58, 167, 168–71, 174, 179, 222, 378, 519*n*–20*n*
Romeo and Juliet (Shakespeare), 188–89
Romney, Mitt, 4
Romulus and Remus, 142
Roosevelt, Bamie, 384
Roosevelt, Corrine, 384, 395
Roosevelt, C. V. S., 371
Roosevelt, Edith Carow, 383
Roosevelt, Eleanor, 384, 392, 393, 396, 410, 414, 416
Roosevelt, Franklin D., 329, 369–70, 378, 380, 391–417, 428, 429–30, 471, 536*n*, 537*n*
Roosevelt, Franklin D. Jr., 414–15, 437
Roosevelt, Henry Latrobe, 412–13
Roosevelt, Jimmy, 413, 414, 415, 428, 540*n*
Roosevelt, Quentin, 413
Roosevelt, Robert Barnwell, 379, 380
Roosevelt, Sara Delano, 392, 396
Roosevelt, Theodore Jr., 396, 413–14
Roosevelt, Theodore Sr., 371–72, 379, 380, 384, 385, 387, 390–91, 535*n*
Roosevelt, Theodore "Teddy," 369–93, 394, 395, 396, 408, 413, 415, 416, 417, 425, 471, 535*n*–36*n*
Roosevelt family, 313, 369–417, 536*n*
rotation, office, 337, 349–51
Rothschild, Amschel, 228, 229, 231, 232, 235
Rothschild, Carl, 229, 231, 234, 235
Rothschild, Hannah Levi, 228–29
Rothschild, Jacob, 523*n*
Rothschild, James, 229, 230, 232, 233, 234, 235
Rothschild, Lionel, 233–34, 235
Rothschild, Mayer Amschel, 221, 224–31, 236–37, 465
Rothschild, Nathan, 228, 232, 233, 234, 523*n*
Rothschild, Salomon, 228, 230, 231, 232, 234, 235
Rothschild family, 127, 221–38, 435, 466

Rowe, James L., 407
Roybal-Allard, Lucille, 5
Rusk, Dean, 441
Russo, Giuseppe Genco, 37
Ryder, Norman, 409

Sa'd ad-Daula, 523*n*
Sahlins, Marshall, 60
Sale, Kirkpatrick, 452, 543*n*
Samuel, 114, 176
Sarah, 117, 118, 518*n*
Saul, 114, 124–25, 126, 519*n*
Scalia, Eugene, 3
Schachner, Nathan, 305, 310, 311, 524*n*
Schlesinger, Arthur, M. Jr., 6
Scholastic Aptitude Test (SAT), 440–41
Schulberg, Budd, 9
Schuyler, Philip, 288
Scipio, Lucius Cornelius, 147
Scipio, Publius, 147–48
Scots Irish migration, 243, 330–34, 363
Scotto, Young Tony, 40
Scribonia, 154
SDS (Sale), 452
Selfish Gene, The (Dawkins), 55
"self-made men," 202, 204, 242, 266–68, 292–93, 342–43, 381, 421, 538*n*
Servilia, 150, 520*n*
Sewall, Samuel, 248
Seward, William, 356–57
sexuality, 53–54, 56, 57–58, 64, 66, 69–72, 119, 122–23, 435, 473
Shakespeare, William, 188–89, 279, 463–65, 474, 477, 521*n*
Shang dynasty, 89–90
Shang-Ti, 90
Shastri, Lal Bahadur, 107
Shoben, Elaine, 459
Short, William, 305, 310–11, 527*n*
Shriver, Eunice Kennedy, 427, 435
Shriver, Mark Kennedy, 5, 462
Sicilian Expedition (415 B.C.), 128–29
Sieyès, Emmanuel-Joseph, 213–14
Sikhs, 108, 109
Simon, Bill Jr., 5
Simpkins, Edgar, 82
Sindhis, 109
Sixtus IV, Pope, 196
Slapstick (Vonnegut), 546*n*
slavery, 256–57, 258–59, 260–61, 302, 303, 311, 336, 345, 351, 353, 354, 365, 452, 463, 477, 483, 484, 524*n*, 525*n*, 532*n*
Smathers, George, 419
Smith, Alfred E., 537*n*
Smith, Caleb B., 356
Smith, Jean Kennedy, 435
Smith, Joseph, 364
Smith, Stephen, 435–36
Smith, William Stephens, 298–99
Smoot, Reed, 411–12
Social Security Act (1935), 408–10, 453–54
society:
- assimilation in, 117, 131, 233–34, 259
- authoritarian, 97–99
- class system in, 12, 14, 19, 24, 181–83, 185–87, 353–54, 404, 434, 459, 468–69, 538*n*
- competitive, 50–51, 55, 72–73, 514*n*
- cooperative, 50, 51–53, 55, 58, 59–61, 69
- families and, 254, 272–73, 477–79, 483–84, 522*n*, 543*n*, 545*n*
- generational change in, 446–48, 451–53, 543*n*
- hierarchical, 70, 111, 129–30, 256, 264, 270–72
- industrial, 232, 253, 314, 316, 322, 327, 342, 351, 352, 353, 373, 405
- modern, 78, 82, 85, 100, 105–8
- multiethnic, 144, 456, 483–84
- non-Western, 78, 79–112
- pluralistic, 108, 265, 342, 361–63, 406–7, 408, 447
- private vs. public spheres of, 139–40, 158, 237
- reform of, 96–99, 169–72, 272–76, 522*n*
- upward mobility in, 312, 378, 462, 481–82
- Western, 111–49

Sociobiology (Wilson), 51–52
Socrates, 137, 138, 139
Solomon, 113–14, 126–27
Solon, 130
Song of Roland, 160–62, 183, 184, 188
Sophocles, 134, 140
Sowell, Thomas, 375
Spanish-American War, 385–86, 387
Speed, Joshua, 348–49
Spheres of Justice (Walzer), 443

Spock, Benjamin, 452
spoils system, 337
sports, 501–3
Staples, Brent, 483
Starr, Ringo, 9
Starkey, Zak, 9
Stevenson, Adlai, 436
Stimson, Henry, 441
Stimsonians, 441, 453, 454
Stone, Galen, 423
Stone, Ulysses S., 410–11
Story, Sarah, 245
Stoughton, William, 249
Straus, Oscar, 390
Strauss, Barry, 133, 134, 139, 140
Stuart, David, 283
Stuart, John Todd, 348, 349, 352
Suetonius, 154
Suharto, Mohamed, 80
Sullivan, Andrew, 3, 4, 19
Sung dynasty, 95, 546*n*
Sununu, John E., 4–5
Supreme Court, U.S., 3, 389, 457, 512*n*
survival, struggle for, 55, 63, 67, 69–70, 72–73
Syme, Ronald, 48–49, 142, 149, 150

Tacitus, 154, 157
Talmud, 122, 222
Tamar, 126
Tammany Hall, 383, 407, 537*n*
Tatum, Elinor Ruth, 7–8
Tatum, Wilbert, 8
taxation, 179, 387, 389–90, 408, 416, 468
Taylor, Thomas, 311
Taylor, Zachary, 351
television, 499–500
Terah, 117–18
territoriality, 58, 69–70, 72
Thalberg, Irving, 9, 405
Theseus, 130, 133–35, 141, 390
Thomas, Benjamin, 531*n*
Thomas, Helen, 4
Thoughts on Education (Locke), 271
"three debts," 103
Thucydides, 137
Thurmond, Strom Jr., 4
Tiberius, 154, 156, 157
Tieri, Funzi, 41
Tiger, Lionel, 533*n*
Tit for Tat, 60, 68, 351
Tlingit Indians, 74
Tocqueville, Alexis de, 338, 452, 545*n*
Totem and Taboo (Freud), 70
Townsend, Kathleen Kennedy, 5, 462
tribalism, 73–76, 81, 83–89, 100, 112, 113–28, 142–43, 162–63, 177, 179, 180, 184–87, 366–67, 519*n*
Trivers, Robert, 60, 64
Truman, Harry S, 376
trust, personal, 60, 67, 69
trusts:
  business, 387, 389
  testamentary, 321, 327
Tudor, Thomas Tucker, 308
Tweed, William, 383, 535*n*
Two Treatises on Government (Locke), 271

United States:
  aristocracy in, 256–57, 261–62, 302–3, 306, 307, 316–28, 369–70, 372, 373–74, 378–79, 385, 391–92, 432–33, 441, 480
  colonial period of, 251–72, 524*n*–25*n*
  democracy in, 6, 12, 15, 18–19, 46–47, 272–76, 302, 314, 320, 329, 338, 342, 370, 390–91, 415–16, 465, 469–70, 471, 477
  frontier of, 330–32, 345–46, 363–64, 366, 367–68, 381–82
  national identity of, 270–79, 342, 351–52, 354, 361–64, 390, 483–84, 525*n*
  nepotism in, 4, 6–7, 12–20, 158, 237–38, 243–44, 270–76, 372, 410–13, 420, 442–43, 465, 468–69, 485–508
  nineteenth-century society in, 315–53, 368, 369
  post-Revolutionary period of, 277–314
  Southern states of, 251–62, 315–16, 337–38, 353–56, 363, 473, 531*n*–32*n*
  utopian communities, 364, 533*n*

Valachi, Joseph, 444
Van Buren, Martin, 329, 335, 340
van den Berghe, Pierre, 13, 258
Vanhanen, Tatu, 517*n*
vassalage, 177–78, 180–81
Vidal, Gore, 293
Vietnam War, 2, 446, 450, 451, 542*n*–43*n*
villages, 85–86, 87, 100, 103

Virgil, 145
Virginia, 243, 251–62, 273, 280–81
virtus, 145, 519*n*
Vonnegut, Kurt, 546*n*
Voting Rights Act (1965), 456

Walker, Charles Jr., 5
Wallace, Edward, 359
Wallace, Henry, 407
Walzer, Michael, 443
Wang Shou-yu, 98
Ward, Geoffrey C., 392, 393
War of 1812, 320, 328, 333
War of Independence, U.S., 257, 270–79, 286–87, 294–95, 315–16, 317, 318–19, 329, 331, 362, 452
War on Poverty program, 449–51, 454
Warren, John, 324
Washington, Augustine, 280–81
Washington, Booker T., 390
Washington, Bushrod, 283, 284
Washington, George, 145, 256, 269, 270, 274, 278–92, 296–99, 302, 305, 307, 310, 312, 442, 466, 526*n*
Washington, Lawrence, 281–82
Washington, Martha Custis, 282–83, 284
WASP establishment, 6–7, 369, 373–74, 392, 400, 403, 406, 422, 425, 428, 432–33, 434, 440, 441, 456, 535*n*
wealth:
  accumulation of, 147, 148, 195, 227, 232, 255, 377–78, 424, 425
  inheritance of, 16, 18, 19, 85, 86, 93–94, 101–2, 106, 113–18, 129, 131–32, 133, 141, 145, 148, 167–68, 173, 174–75, 179, 180, 181, 209, 246–50, 251, 255, 260, 261, 271, 274–75, 317, 319, 321, 327, 332, 338, 387–90, 408, 416, 446, 468–69, 472, 519*n*, 534*n*
  political influence of, 322–23, 410–13, 437, 438, 440, 455, 479–80
  transfer of, to the church, 167–68, 170
Weber, Max, 251
welfare state, 409–10, 441, 447, 450–51, 453–54, 539*n*
Welles, Gideon, 356
Wen the Civilized, 90
wergild, 185
West Indian guppy, 60
Wexler, Joan, 460
Whalen, Richard, 421, 437, 438
whales, 51
Whig Party, 346–47, 349–51, 353
White, Theodore, 438
Whitehead, Mary Beth, 545*n*
Why England Slept (J. F. Kennedy), 429
"Why the Ward Boss Rules" (Addams), 377
Wild Swans (Chang), 98
Wilhelm of Hanau, 226, 227, 229
Williams, George C., 59–60, 514*n*
Williams, Richard, 475, 482
Williams, Serena, 475
Williams, Venus, 475
wills, 152–53, 167, 519*n*
Wills, Garry, 442, 451
Wilson, E. O., 51, 54, 55
Wilson, James Q., 67–68
Wilson, Woodrow, 394, 395
women:
  domestic role of, 338, 383–84, 404–5 410, 426
  equality of, 168, 264, 365, 410, 458–60
  in labor force, 469, 544*n*
  legal rights of, 338, 458–60
  as mothers, 50, 61–66, 68, 171, 477, 545*n*
  nepotism by, 61–66, 94, 101–2, 325
  political influence of, 384; 396, 433, 435, 449
Wood, Gordon, 260, 272, 273, 526*n*
Wood, Leonard, 386, 395
Woods, Tiger, 547*n*
Wooten, Daniel, 547*n*
work ethic, 224, 317
working class, 374–75, 404
World War I, 235, 413, 423
World War II, 414, 423, 428–32, 433
Wraith, Ronald, 82
Wright, Robert, 55, 60, 67, 69
Wrigley, William Jr., 8
Wyler, William, 9

Xanthippos, 135

Young, Brigham, 364, 365
"yuppie turnaround," 468–69

Zeus, 132, 137, 165
Zoroastrianism, 110